TEEN Health

COURSE 3

TEEN Health

COURSE 3

Mary Bronson Merki, Ph.D.

Glencoe McGraw-Hill

New York, New York
Columbus, Ohio
Woodland Hills, California
Peoria, Illinois

Meet the Author

Mary Bronson Merki has taught health education in grades K–12, as well as health education methods classes at the undergraduate and graduate levels. As Health Education Specialist for the Dallas School District, Dr. Merki developed and implemented a district-wide health education program, *Skills for Living,* which was used as a model by the state education agency. She also helped develop and implement the district's Human Growth, Development and Sexuality program, which won the National PTA's Excellence in Education Award and earned her an honorary lifetime membership in the state PTA. Dr. Merki has assisted school districts throughout the country in developing local health education programs. In 1988, she was named the Texas Health Educator of the Year by the Texas Association for Health, Physical Education, Recreation, and Dance. Dr. Merki is also the author of *Glencoe Health,* a high school textbook adopted in school districts throughout the country. She currently teaches in a Texas public school where she was recently honored as Teacher of the Year. Dr. Merki completed her undergraduate work at Colorado State University in Fort Collins, Colorado. She earned her masters and doctoral degrees in health education at Texas Woman's University in Denton, Texas.

Editorial and production services
provided by Visual Education Corporation, Princeton, NJ.

Design by Bill Smith Studio, New York, NY.

Glencoe/McGraw-Hill
A Division of The ***McGraw-Hill*** *Companies*

Send all inquiries to:
Glencoe/McGraw-Hill
21600 Oxnard Street, Suite 500
Woodland Hills, California 91367

ISBN 0-02-653205-0 (Course 3 Student Text)
ISBN 0-02-653206-9 (Course 3 Teacher's Wraparound Edition)

Printed in the United States of America.

1 2 3 4 5 6 7 8 9 003 06 05 04 03 02 01 00 99 98

Health Consultants

Unit 1
Your Total Health

E. Laurette Taylor, Ph.D.
Associate Professor
Department of Health and Sport Sciences
The University of Oklahoma
Norman, Oklahoma

Howard Steven Shapiro, M.D.
Assistant Professor of Psychiatry
School of Medicine
University of Southern California
Senior Attending Physician
Cedars Sinai Medical Center
Los Angeles, California

Unit 2
Social and Consumer Health

Richard Papenfuss, Ph.D.
Associate Professor of Health Education
Arizona Health Sciences Center
University of Arizona
Tucson, Arizona

David Sleet, Ph.D.
Associate Director for Science
Unintentional Injury Prevention
Centers for Disease Control and Prevention (CDC)
Atlanta, Georgia

Unit 3
Fitness and Nutrition

Kathleen Morgan Speer, Ph.D.; R.N.
Children's Medical Center of Dallas
Dallas, Texas

Peter Wood, D.Sc.; Ph.D.
Center for Research in Disease Prevention
Stanford University
Palo Alto, California

Unit 4
Your Physical Health

David Allen, M.D.
Infectious Disease Associates
Dallas, Texas

Mark Dignan, Ph.D., M.P.H.
Chair, Center for Community Studies
AMC Cancer Research Center
Denver, Colorado

Unit 5
Avoiding Substance Abuse

Pamela Luna, Dr.P.H.
RIMS–Healthy Kids Regional Center
California Department of Education
Riverside, California

Prevention Materials Review Unit
National Clearinghouse for Alcohol and Drug Information
Rockville, Maryland

Unit 6
Safety and the Environment

Sharon Gonzales, M.A.; R.N.
West Windsor–Plainsboro Middle School
Plainsboro, New Jersey

Diane Imhulse
National Safety Council
Itasca, Illinois

Teacher Reviewers

Unit 1
Your Total Health

Pamela R. Connolly
Subject Area Coordinator for Health Education
Pittsburgh Catholic Schools
Oakland Catholic High School
Diocese of Pittsburgh
Pittsburgh, Pennsylvania

Essie E. Lee, Ed. D. Professor Emerita
Hunter College New York City
Professor Community Health Sciences

Lynn Westberg
Health Education Department Head
Kearns High School
Salt Lake City, Utah

Laura Williams
Health and Science Teacher
Memphis City Schools
Memphis, Tennessee

Unit 2
Social and Consumer Health

Martha R. Roper
Health Teacher
Parkway South High School
Manchester, Missouri

Deborah L. Tackman, B.S., M.E.P.D.
Health Education Instructor
North High School
Eau Claire, Wisconsin

Brenda C. Wilson
Director of Health Education
Iredell Statesville Schools
Statesville, North Carolina

Unit 3
Fitness and Nutrition

Raynette Evans
Director of Health, Physical Education, and Athletics
Bibb County Public Schools
Macon, Georgia

Robin Gray Ballard
Health Educator
Suva Intermediate School
Montebello Unified School District
Montebello, California

Ed Larios
Department Chair
Health and Physical Education Department
Burlingame High School
Burlingame, California

Unit 4
Your Physical Health

Randall F. Nitchie
Health Specialist
Osseo Public Schools, District #279
Maple Grove, Minnesota

Ann Orman
Science/Health Teacher
West End Middle School
Nashville, Tennessee

Unit 5
Avoiding Substance Abuse

Beverly J. Berkin, CHES
Health Education Consultant
Bedford Corners, New York

Dona Carmack
Health Educator
Burlingame High School
Burlingame, California

Claudia Thorn
Coordinator, Staff Development
Prevention Education Center K–12
Sacramento County Office of Education
Sacramento, California

Unit 6
Safety and the Environment

Ed Hedges
Health Education Teacher
Central High School
Phoenix, Arizona

JoCyel Rodgers
Health Teacher
Glencrest Middle School
Fort Worth, Texas

Liz Clark, M.S.
Connections Consulting
Three Rivers, California

Contents

Unit 1
Your Total Health

Unit 2
Social and Public Health

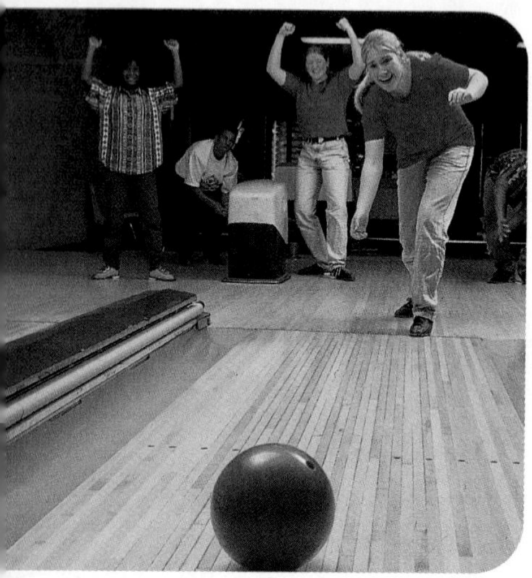

Unit 3
Fitness and Nutrition

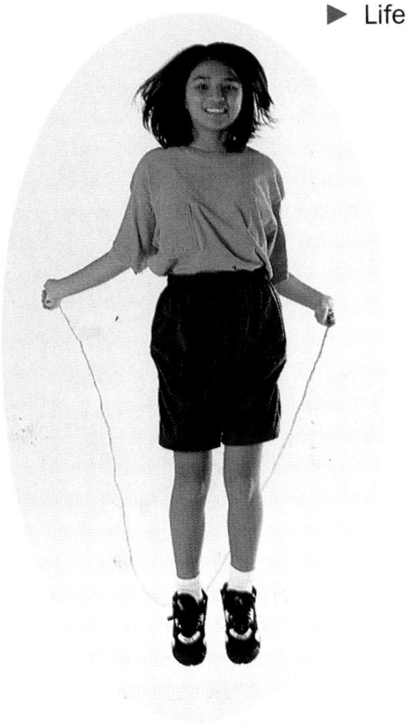

Unit 4
Your Physical Health

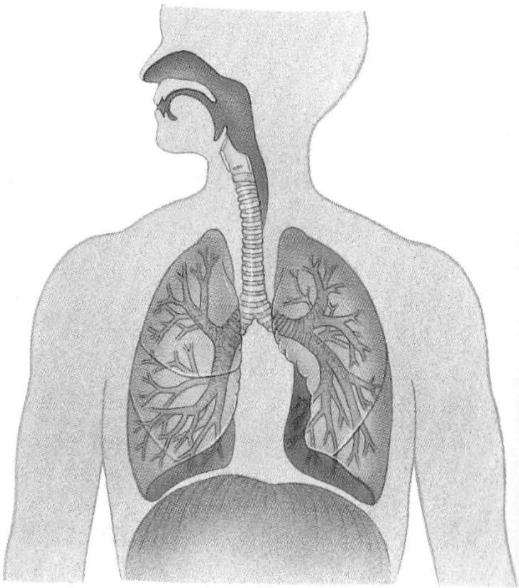

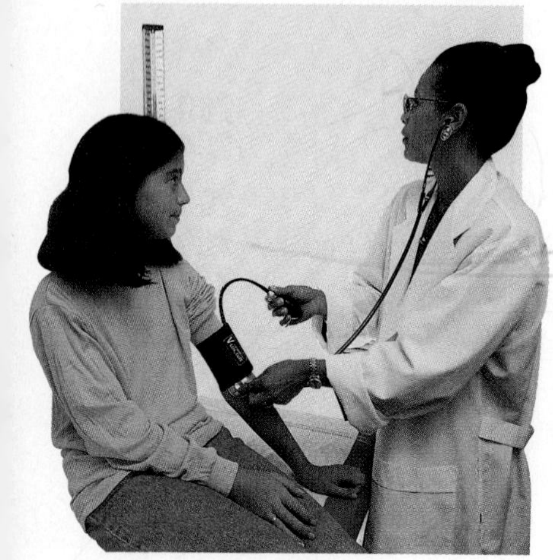

Unit 5
Avoiding Substance Abuse

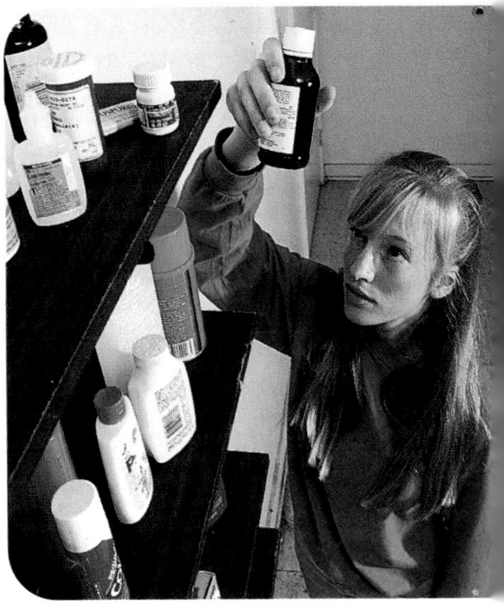

Unit 6
Safety and the Environment

Features

Health Lab

Life Skills

Making Healthy Decisions

Personal Inventory

TEEN HEALTH DIGEST

People at Work

Teens Making a Difference

CON$UMER FOCU$

HEALTH UPDATE

Sports and Recreation

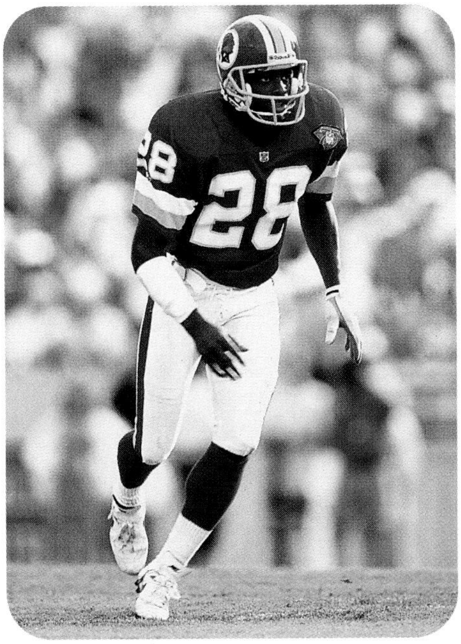

Myths and Realities

Personal Trainer

Unit 1
Your Total Health

Chapter 1

Wellness and Your Total Health

Chapter 2

Looking and Feeling Good

Chapter 3

Being Mentally and Emotionally Healthy

Chapter 1

Wellness and Your Total Health

Student Expectations

After reading this chapter, you should be able to:

1. Explain the concept of wellness.
2. Recognize how your attitudes and behavior affect your level of health.
3. Explain how to make responsible health decisions.
4. Recognize how setting goals and taking action affect self-esteem.

Teen Chat Group

Margaret: This year is off to a great start. I've been chosen for the All-Star soccer team, I like all my classes, and I'm making a lot of great friends.

Ben: Maybe it's starting out great for you, but I have a lot more homework in my classes. Plus, I have band practice, and I wanted to try out for basketball. With all this homework, I barely have time to see my friends these days.

Sarah: When classes first started, I wasn't sure how I was going to manage it all either. It helps to work out a schedule of all your activities; otherwise it could all get really overwhelming. You need to have time with your friends, as well as for school and sport activities.

Margaret: If you'd like Ben, Sarah and I could help you make out a schedule.

Ben: Sure, that would be really great!

in your journal

In each chapter, you will be asked to write entries in your journal. These are your private reflections and thoughts and are for your use only. Read the dialogue on this page. How do you balance the different responsibilities in your life? Do you make choices that help you stay healthy? Start your private journal entries on wellness and total health by answering these questions:

- What advice would you give to anyone who wishes to stay healthy?
- Do you consider yourself healthy?
- Do you have any behavior, related to health, that you would like to change?

When you reach the end of each chapter, you will use your journal entries to make an action plan.

Lesson 1

Wellness and the Health Triangle

This lesson will help you find answers to questions that teens often ask about being healthy. For example:

- **What does being healthy really mean?**
- **What do I need to know to be healthy?**
- **What is the difference between health and wellness?**

Words to Know

health
wellness

What Is Health?

What is your definition of health? Many people think that being healthy is not being sick. Others think that if a person is in good physical shape, that person is healthy.

Take a closer look and you may see that being healthy involves more than physical well-being. Do you know students who are always getting into fights? Would you call these people healthy? What about a person who seems unhappy no matter what he or she does? Being in good physical shape is important. Yet there is much more than that to good health.

You make choices every day that affect your health. You decide what to eat, who will be your friends, and how to spend your time. Do you know which choices lead to good health and which do not? This book will help you learn to recognize the choices that are best for you. It will also give you the chance to look at your health habits now. Then you can decide whether you need to change any of your behavior to become a healthier person.

Exercising is one choice you make that affects your health.

The Foundations of Health

Besides physical health, your total health picture includes your mental/emotional health and your social health. In other words, being healthy also means feeling good about yourself and getting along with others. **Health** is *a combination of physical, mental/emotional, and social well-being.* **Figure 1.1** explains more about these three sides of health.

The Health Triangle

The three sides of your health are connected, like the sides of a triangle. Each side affects the other two sides. For example, being physically tired or being hungry can make you grouchy. Being depressed for a long time can make you feel physically weak and run-down. Experiencing problems in getting along with others can make you feel bad about yourself.

Being healthy means having a balanced health triangle. It is not hard to have a balanced health triangle. All you have to do is decide to take action to keep each side of your triangle healthy.

in Your journal

What choices have you made today that may affect your physical, mental/emotional, and/or social health? Do you feel good about these choices? Why or why not? If you could change one of these choices, which would it be? Why? Do you feel that you are generally healthy or unhealthy? Write your answers in your private journal.

interNET CONNECTION

Explore further the three aspects of your total health and what you can do to keep each side in balance.

http://www.glencoe.com/sec/health

Figure 1.1

The Health Triangle

The three sides of health combine to form the health triangle.

Physical health includes total care of your body. This involves keeping your body fit, practicing cleanliness and good grooming habits, and eating a well-balanced diet.

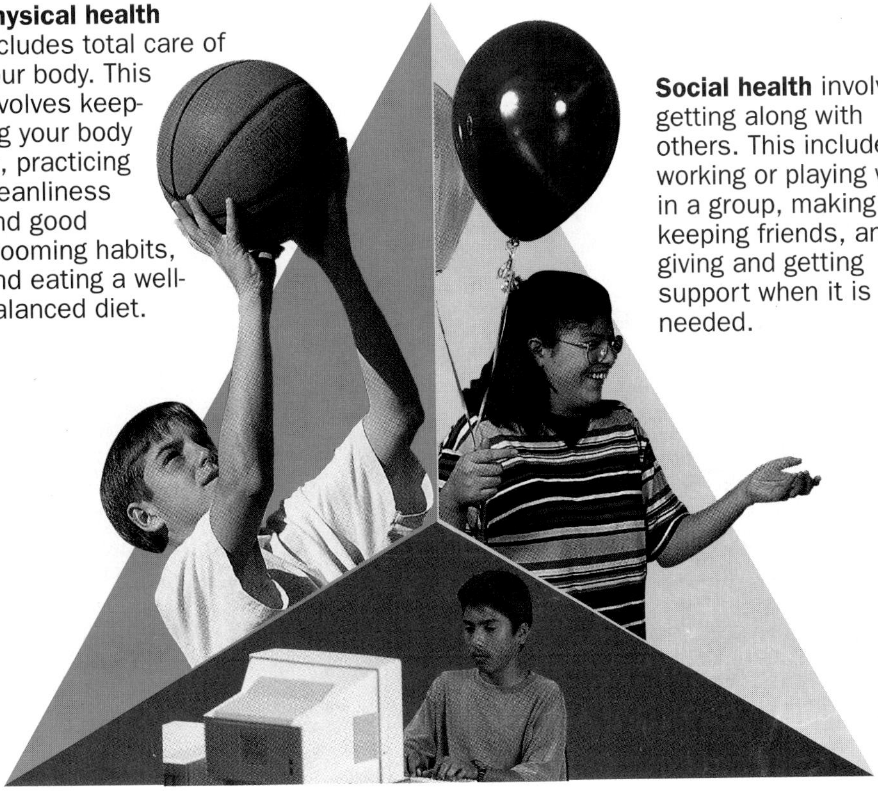

Social health involves getting along with others. This includes working or playing well in a group, making and keeping friends, and giving and getting support when it is needed.

Mental and emotional health includes liking who you are and accepting yourself. This involves expressing emotions in a healthy way, facing life's problems, and dealing with its pressures or stresses in a positive way.

Q&A

This Is Health?

Q: Roland, who's 14, brags that he's never been sick a day in his life. He spends hours in front of the TV. He loves junk food, hates fruits and vegetables, and laughs at people who exercise. I say he's not as healthy as he claims. Am I right?

A: Yes, you are right! Roland's health triangle is not balanced. He may find, in the future, that his choices start to affect his health.

Language Arts Connection

What Is in a Word?

The word health comes from an Old English word meaning "to make sound, whole, or well." The word comes from the same root as the word heal.

Each side of your triangle is equally important to good health. By working to keep the sides balanced, you will be on your way toward becoming a healthy person. **Figure 1.2** shows what can happen if your health triangle is not in balance. When one side becomes more important than the others, the other sides suffer.

The following scenarios describe the health triangles of three teens. Do any of them sound like yours?

- Jordan has lots of friends. He spends most of his time getting together with them. They play video games, go to the beach, or watch movies. Jordan has never been very good at sports or school, and he does not try to change that.
- Tamara has a few close friends and sees them primarily on weekends. She is busy most weeknights with basketball practice and homework. Geography is her favorite subject.
- Aaron does not spend much time with friends or family because he has soccer practice on weeknights and baseball games on weekends. His grades, which used to be good, are slipping and his parents are annoyed because he's not doing his chores.

Practicing *good* health habits helps you balance your health triangle. It also lessens your chances of illness and helps you stay well. Good health habits include:

- choosing the right foods.
- avoiding tobacco, alcohol, and other drugs.
- taking part in a regular exercise program.
- learning ways to handle stress.
- getting along well with others.

HEALTH LAB

Wellness Survey

Introduction: Why should teens be concerned about staying healthy or becoming healthier than they are now? The answer is easy. Prevention is easier than cure. It takes much more time and effort to cure an illness than to keep the body well. Also, more serious health problems can occur as a result of poor health choices.

Objective: With one or more classmates, develop a health survey to give to a sample of

Figure 1.2

Three Health Triangles

Match these triangles with the scenarios on page 6. Which of these triangles are unbalanced? What needs to happen to make them balanced again?

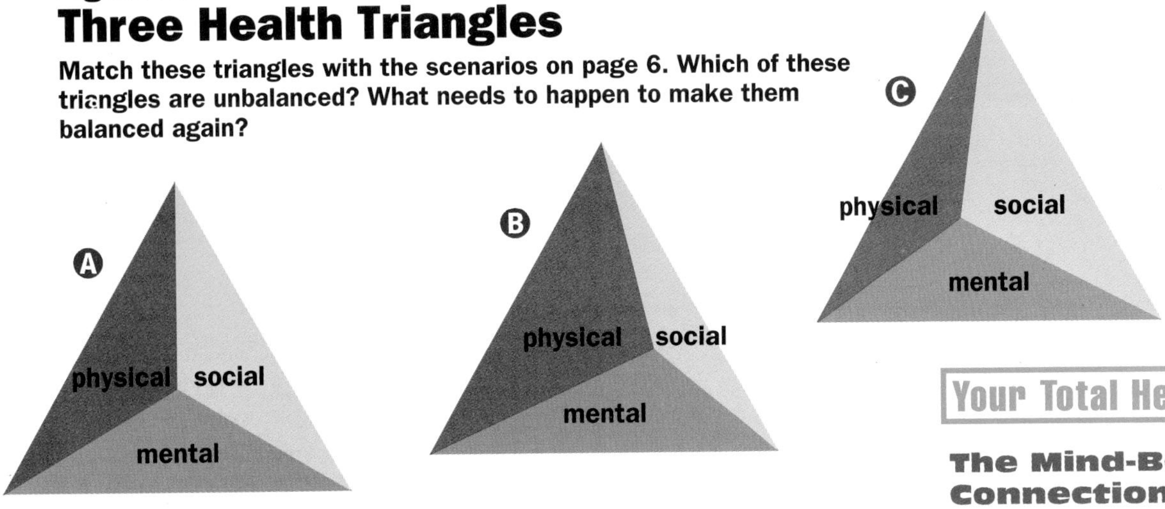

What Is Wellness?

Wellness is *an overall state of well-being, or total health.* It is a way of life. It involves making choices and decisions each day that promote good health.

Decision Making for Wellness

What kinds of decisions do you make every day that affect your health? The way you spend your time and the foods you choose to eat are two decisions. After school, do you practice a musical instrument, review your Spanish vocabulary, ride your bike, or do you just watch television? Do you eat fruit or yogurt for an after-school snack, or do you eat potato chips, cake, or candy?

The everyday decisions you make will affect your health for years to come. Of course, watching television one day a week after school or having candy for one afternoon snack will not harm your health. Daily habits have a long-term effect on you.

Your Total Health

The Mind-Body Connection

The three sides of total health affect one another to such a large degree that some physicians have begun to give the following advice to people who are scheduled for major surgery:

- Think one happy thought every hour, or as needed, for each of the three days leading up to the surgery.
- Take an extra-large dose of visits from family and close friends the day before the surgery is scheduled.

students in your school. Use the survey to find out how aware students are about the following:

- their physical, mental and emotional, and social health
- the choices affecting their health triangle

Materials and Method: On a sheet of paper, list questions to see how much students know about their physical, mental/emotional, and social health and the choices they make that affect their health triangle. A few sample questions are: Is getting plenty of sleep essential to good health? Are there good ways and bad ways to express your anger? Do you need to know how to communicate with others to be healthy?

With the help of your teacher, make copies of the survey and distribute them to your classmates. Ask the students to return the survey to your teacher.

Observation and Analysis: Tally the responses in the surveys. Write an article about the results of the survey for the school newspaper.

The Wellness Continuum

The wellness continuum shown in **Figure 1.3** is a scale that shows a person's level of wellness, from a low level to a high level. People on the left side of the continuum, the low level, usually rely on someone else to help them maintain their health. People on the right side of the continuum, the high level, are usually responsible, have a high level of self-discipline, and have personal goals.

in your journal

Make a list of all the people you know who are at least partly responsible for good health choices you have made. For example, who helped you decide to have regular dental checkups? Then make a list of your own behaviors that may have led to good health habits in others. Write the lists in your journal.

Maintaining Your Wellness

The people on the right side of the continuum accept responsibility for maintaining their own health. However, the level of wellness for most people is not high. The levels usually cluster around the midpoint on the continuum. Why do you think this is so? On what point of the continuum do you fall? What steps can you take to improve your position on the health continuum?

The choices you make regarding your health will influence your level of wellness for the rest of your life. Can you think of choices you make that help you to maintain your wellness? Can you think of areas that need improvement? What can you do to work toward maintaining a high level of wellness for yourself?

Figure 1.3
The Wellness Continuum
This illustration shows examples of physical, mental/emotional, and social conditions and where they are placed in relation to a person's level of wellness.

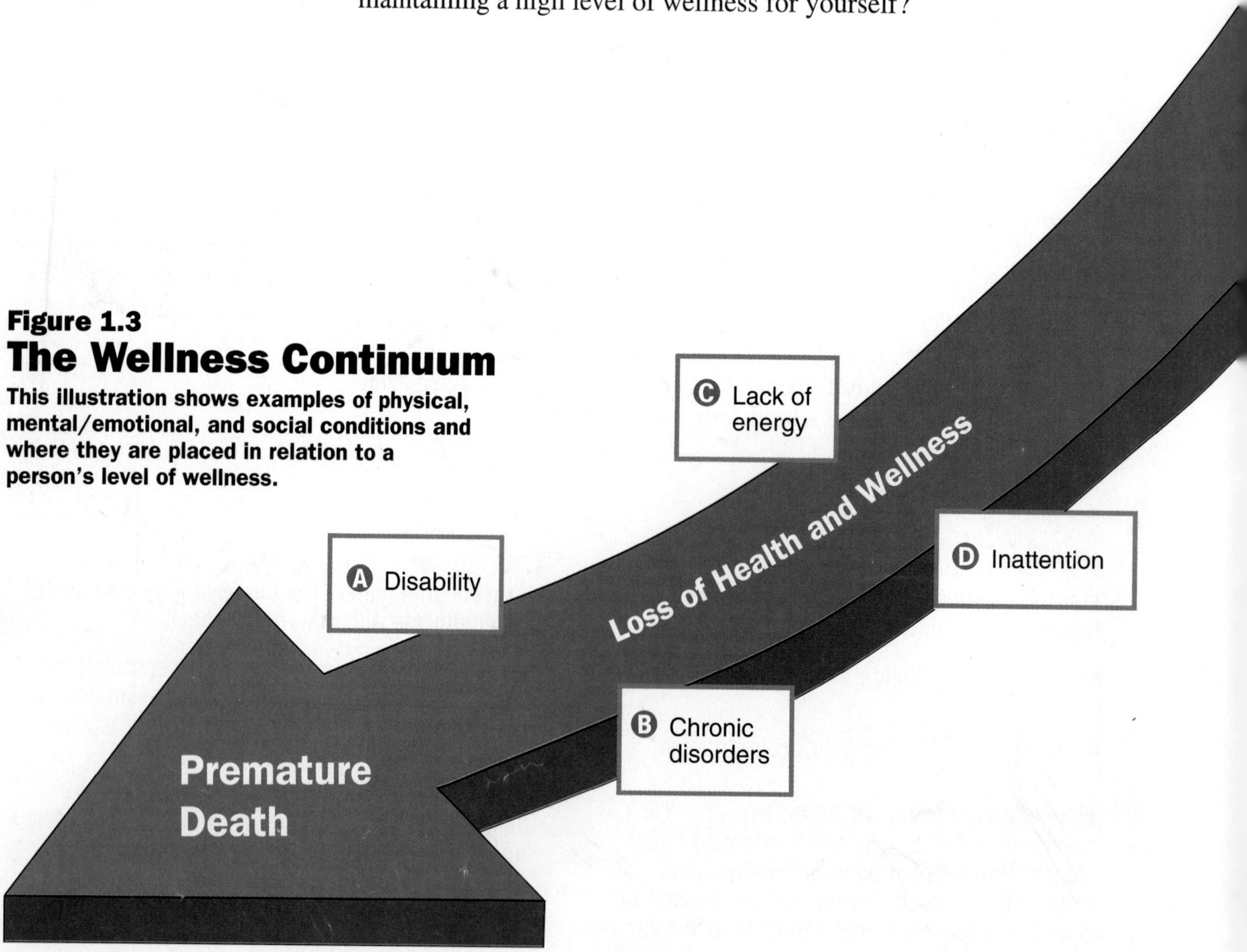

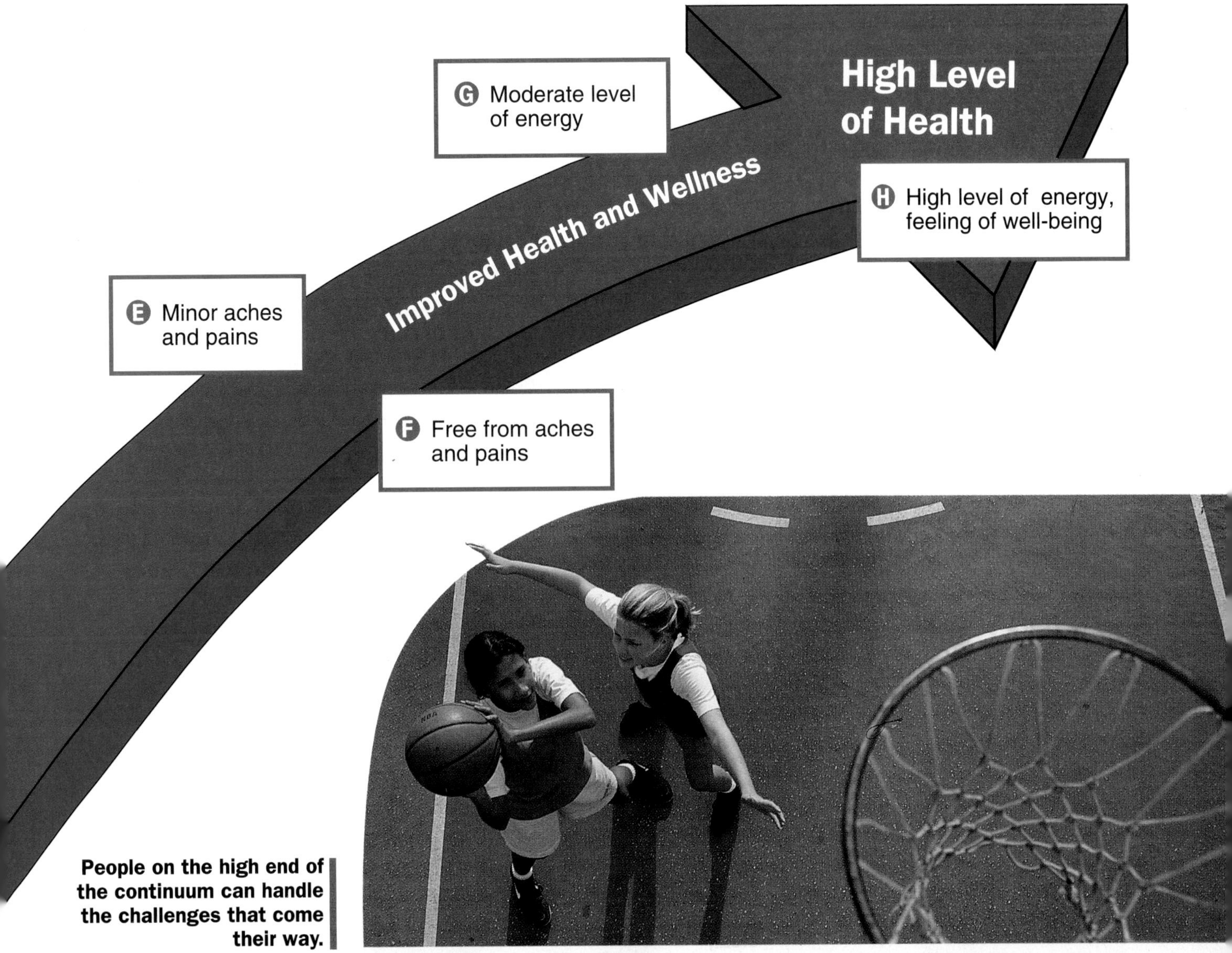

People on the high end of the continuum can handle the challenges that come their way.

Review
Lesson 1

Using complete sentences, answer the following questions on a separate sheet of paper.

Reviewing Terms and Facts

1. **Vocabulary** Define the term *health.* Use it in an original sentence.
2. **Compare and Contrast** Use your own words to explain the difference between health and wellness.

Thinking Critically

3. **Describe** List three signs of a person whose health triangle is not balanced.
4. **Suggest** What are some ways that you can improve your position on the wellness continuum?

Applying Health Concepts

5. **Personal Health** Draw your own health triangle. If your triangle is balanced, make a list of recent choices and decisions you have made to keep the three sides equal. If the triangle is unbalanced, list specific ways you can help balance it.

Lesson 2

Taking Responsibility for Your Health

This lesson will help you find answers to questions that teens often ask about taking responsibility for their health. For example:

- **How do heredity, environment, and available health care affect my health?**
- **Is my environment healthy?**
- **How do behavior and attitudes affect my health?**
- **How can I develop habits to improve my health?**

Words to Know

heredity
environment
behavior
attitudes
lifestyle factors
health education

Factors That Affect Your Health

The health choices you make every day are a major factor in your total health. In addition to your choices, other factors affect your health. They are heredity, environment, and available health care (see **Figure 1.4**).

Figure 1.4
Influences on Your Health
The three factors that affect your health are heredity, environment, and available health care.

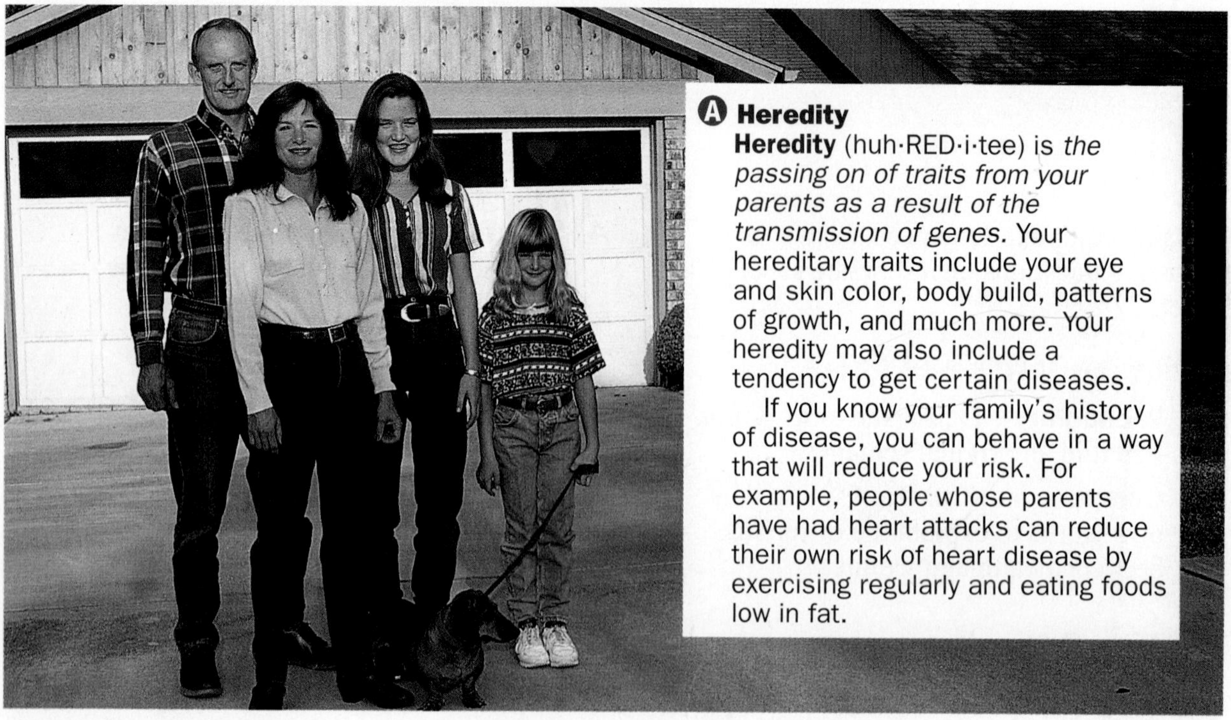

A Heredity
Heredity (huh·RED·i·tee) is *the passing on of traits from your parents as a result of the transmission of genes.* Your hereditary traits include your eye and skin color, body build, patterns of growth, and much more. Your heredity may also include a tendency to get certain diseases.

If you know your family's history of disease, you can behave in a way that will reduce your risk. For example, people whose parents have had heart attacks can reduce their own risk of heart disease by exercising regularly and eating foods low in fat.

B Environment

Environment (en·VY·ruhn·ment) is *the sum total of your surroundings.* It includes the place where you live, the school you attend, and the people you see often.

Where you live can be very important. If you live in a warm climate, for example, your skin may be exposed to more hours of sunlight. You can, however, behave in ways that minimize your risk of overexposure to the sun. You can learn how to protect your skin and eyes from the sun's damaging rays.

The people in your environment can affect your health choices, both positively and negatively. For example, if you see many of your friends trying out for sports teams at school, you may become interested in trying out as well.

C Available Health Care

Available health care, the third factor, is determined by where you live. A person living in a major city will probably have more doctors and clinics to choose from than a person in a small town.

To get the most out of available health care, you need to have regular health maintenance such as immunizations, dental checkups, and physical examinations. Keeping up on current health care information can also help you choose the best ways to promote and protect your health.

Although you have little or no control over these factors, the way you behave has an effect on them. Your **behavior** is *the way you act in many different situations and events in life.* Your behavior can have a positive or negative impact on any or all of the factors. Since you can control your behavior, you need to do everything you can to make health choices that are best for you. **Figure 1.4** shows how behavior is linked with the factors that affect your health.

Taking Control

Taking control of your health depends on more than just recognizing healthy choices. Your personal **attitudes** (AT·i·toodz)—your *feelings and beliefs*—also play a role in how well you take care of yourself. You need to believe that making good choices and developing good health habits can affect your health.

Your attitude also includes the way you feel about yourself. If you like who you are and feel that other people like you, you will want to take care of yourself. You will want to be at your best in all areas. To ensure that you are at your best, you will make choices that protect and promote your health.

Your parents are a good source of information and advice on staying healthy, but only you can take the necessary action to be healthy.

LIFE SKILLS

Making Health a Habit

A first step toward improving yourself and your total health is to know yourself. Take an honest look at your behavior. Do you see yourself as a responsible person? Do you feel that adults should give you more responsibility? Do you show that you are ready for it? There are ways that you can demonstrate your readiness. For example:

- If you see something that needs doing, do it without waiting to be told.
- Do your schoolwork and turn it in on time.
- Do your household chores without having to be reminded.
- Follow through on your promises.
- Show up on time.
- Finish tasks that you start, and clean up after yourself.

You can also improve yourself by practicing the lifestyle factors listed in **Figure 1.5** on page 14. Are all of those factors part of your present daily routine? If not, try the following:

- Identify a habit you want to start. On a piece of paper, write it down four times. Next to the habit, write at least two benefits you could gain from making it part of your routine.
- Practice the habit at least four times in the next week. Each time, circle one of the times you wrote it on your list. Also circle the benefits you got from practicing the habit.

Steps to Responsible Health

Taking care of your health is mainly your own responsibility. The list that follows shows the three basic steps you should take in accepting responsibility for your health.

- **Find out how much you know about your health.** This means knowing at any time your health level on each of the three sides of your health triangle. You can determine this by taking a self-health inventory such as the one on page 25.
- **Get good, reliable information on how to stay healthy or improve your health.** Breakthroughs in health are happening all the time. By reading magazines or newspapers, you can keep up-to-date on events that could affect your health.
- **Take action.** This means setting realistic goals for yourself. If you decide you want to lose weight, do it gradually, following a sensible, safe eating plan. Taking action also means becoming actively involved in your total health. Eating a bowl of high-fiber cereal and fruit each morning is not enough if you are going to snack on sweets the rest of the day. Working to maintain a high level of wellness is a full-time job.

Science Connection

Choosing with Care ACTIVITY!

Some athletes believe that products such as bee pollen and ginseng root will give them extra strength and power. However, beliefs such as these have been challenged by scientists in the fields of medicine and nutrition. Look through current magazines for advertisements of "health" products. List the ones that may not stand up to scientific scrutiny.

Shaping Your Future

What habits affect your health? After studying many different types of people over the years, health experts have identified certain habits that can make a difference in people's lives. Those who practice these *life-related habits,* or **lifestyle factors,** appear to live longer and be happier. **Figure 1.5** on page 14 illustrates these habits. How many of them do you practice regularly?

Follow-up Activity

Think about the times you demonstrated responsibility in the past week. If responsibility is still lacking, choose one of the suggested ways for showing you are responsible. Record the number of times you perform that particular action during the next week.

Then select a healthy behavior you would like to make part of your life. Practice making it a part of your daily routine. Evaluate your progress at the end of a week.

Figure 1.5
Lifestyle Factors

Positive lifestyle factors like these can affect your health now and for years to come.

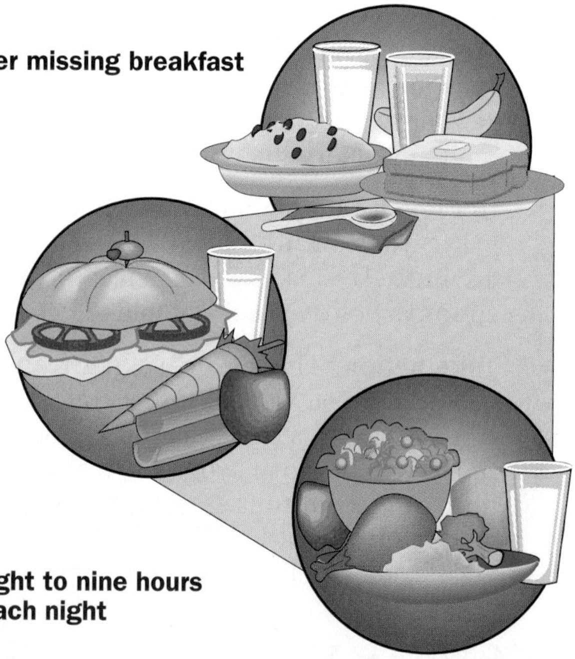

Never missing breakfast

Eating three meals a day, each at a regular time

Getting eight to nine hours of sleep each night

Social Studies Connection

Where in the World? ACTIVITY!

Many diseases in the United States are referred to as "lifestyle diseases." Heart disease, diabetes, arteriosclerosis, high blood pressure, and some types of cancer have been linked to poor eating habits, sedentary living, and unhealthy work environments. Select two countries in different parts of the world and research the presence or absence of similar lifestyle diseases in those locations. Also identify the factors that contribute to the presence or absence of the diseases.

Staying Informed

Because good health is part of a happy, satisfying life, learning how to get and stay healthy should be an important part of your life. That is why health education is so important. **Health education** means *providing health information in such a way that it influences people to change their attitudes and take positive actions regarding their health.* The goal of health education is to help people live long and productive lives.

Health education is more than just learning health facts. It can help you gain the tools you need to maintain and improve your total health and wellness. You can use health facts you learn in all areas of your life.

Staying at a recommended level of weight

in Your Journal

What types of health education are you exposed to? How has this education influenced you to take positive actions toward your health? In your private journal, write a paragraph that answers these questions.

Doing vigorous exercise for 20 to 30 minutes at least three to four times each week

Avoiding tobacco, alcohol, and other drugs

Review

Lesson 2

Using complete sentences, answer the following questions on a separate sheet of paper.

Reviewing Terms and Facts

1. **Vocabulary** Which of the following terms are factors affecting your health that you *can* change: *heredity, behavior, environment, attitudes, lifestyle factors?*
2. **Give Examples** What are three steps you can take toward more responsible health habits?

Thinking Critically

3. **Synthesize** Imagine you live in a town that has many hills. Give an example of two health habits—one good, one bad—that you might develop on the basis of this environment.
4. **Analyze** Look at the list of lifestyle factors in **Figure 1.5.** Choose one and think of ways you could help someone develop it as a personal health habit.

Applying Health Concepts

5. **Personal Health** Find out what kinds of diseases can be passed down through generations of a family. Choose one of the diseases, and read current information about the medical advances being made to combat the disease. Report your findings to the class.
6. **Consumer Health** Prepare a survey of the available health care in your community. Report your findings in the form of a pamphlet.

TEEN HEALTH DIGEST

Teens Making a Difference

Face-to-Face with Volunteens

Sixty-four concerned teens are making a difference in Tulsa, Oklahoma.

These teens, from Nathan Hale High School, form the Youth Volunteer Corps—also known as the "Volunteens." In four years, Volunteens have given more than 1,000 hours of service to the community, working on projects such as

- giving holiday gifts to the needy.
- tutoring younger children.
- visiting senior citizens.
- working in drug awareness programs.

The Volunteens prefer working face-to-face with people, according to group leader Lam Le. "We get to see how we affect their lives and how much our work is appreciated," Lam says.

People at Work

Community Health Worker

Name: Laura Watson

Job: Community Health Director, Somerset County Medical Center

Education: Studied public health in a four-year college

Professional Goals: To teach people of all ages how to promote health and prevent illness

Favorite Part of Job: "Talk-Ins for Teens," discussions which cover topics such as nutrition and first aid

Quote: "The teens' curiosity and enthusiasm are catching!"

Try This:

Find out if your local hospital has a community health program. If so, see which courses are offered and try one out.

Myths and Realities

High-Risk Behavior

BEWARE

Sure, you may get injured riding a bike without a helmet, but it won't kill you, right?

Wrong!

The fact is, hundreds of bike riders under the age of 15 are killed each year. Your risk of dying or being seriously injured in a bike accident is much higher if your head is unprotected. A helmet can reduce the risk of head injury by as much as 85 percent!

Here are some other high-risk behaviors, each of which can harm—or even kill—you *instantly:*

- **Not buckling up.** Wearing a safety belt greatly increases your chances of surviving a car crash.
- **Skating unprotected.** Helmets, wrist guards, and knee and elbow pads make in-line skating much safer.
- **Swimming without supervision.** Drownings can often be prevented by a lifeguard's supervision.

Try This:

List high-risk behaviors that anyone can avoid. Keep the list where you will see it every day.

HEALTH UPDATE

Mapping the Human Genome

Fact: More than 4,000 diseases are caused by genetic defects. Soon we may know exactly which human genes cause each of those diseases.

Since 1990 the U.S. Department of Energy has sponsored the Human Genome Project. A human genome is all of the genetic material in a human cell. (The differences from one person to another are extremely small—so scientists talk about *the* human genome, as if there were only one.) The Human Genome Project's goals are to:

- complete a map of the human genome.
- develop ways to identify and locate the genes responsible for diseases and those crucial to healthy development.
- explore the ethical, legal, and social implications of genome research. This includes issues of privacy and the fair use of genetic information.

Making Decisions About Health

This lesson will help you find answers to questions that teens often ask about decisions. For example:

▶ **Are all risks bad?**
▶ **How can I learn to make better decisions?**
▶ **How do my decisions affect my health?**
▶ **How do my decisions affect other people?**

Words to Know

risk behavior
precaution
decision making
values

Cultural Connections

Opposites Attract ACTIVITY!

The ancient Chinese principles called yin and yang say that conflicting forces are part of the natural order. For example, opposites, such as hot and cold, are necessary in order to appreciate each one.

Yin and yang can be compared to differences of opinion or opposing points of view. These differences often help people arrive at balanced decisions that are mutually agreeable.

List some differences of opinion that you had to weigh to arrive at a decision about a situation.

Decisions Come in All Sizes

An important part of good mental health is being able to face problems and work on finding solutions to them. We all have problems, some of them major, some of them minor. Decision making can be used to solve many of these problems. Knowing how to make decisions is an important skill to develop. **Figure 1.6** illustrates some of the major decisions that teens face.

Figure 1.6
Major Decisions

A teen might ask himself or herself questions similar to these when facing major decisions.

Should I get a part-time job? What type would I like?

Should I get training after high school? What kind of training should it be?

Should I go to a party where there will be alcohol and drugs?

Should I participate in a sports program? Which one?

Examining the Risks

Many actions you take involve risks. A **risk behavior** is *the possibility that an action may cause injury or harm to you or others.* When you take a risk, you expose yourself and others to possible danger. For example, if you decide not to wear a helmet when you ride your bike, this would be considered a risk behavior.

You cannot avoid all risks. You take a risk whenever you cross the street or climb the stairs. However, reasonable risks such as these are not likely to injure you or someone else.

in Your Journal

Write an example of one situation you were involved in during the past week that involved a risk behavior. In your journal, write a paragraph about how and why you decided to take the risk.

Risky Situations

Unreasonable risks carry with them the likelihood that someone will get hurt now or in the future. The best way to lower the risk is to avoid risky situations. For instance, do not pick a fight with someone you disagree with. Instead, express your feelings in a calm manner and walk away before the conflict turns violent.

Taking Precautions

You can cut down on the risks you take by planning ahead and taking precautions. A **precaution** is *a planned action taken before an event to increase the chances of a safe outcome.* For example, learning to ski can be a high-risk activity. However, you can make it less risky by using safe equipment and by taking ski lessons.

Before making any major decisions, think about the risks involved. Then ask yourself these questions:

- Are they necessary risks?
- If the risks are reasonable, what precautions can I take to increase my chances of a safe outcome?
- If I am taking risks to show off or to feel important, what could I do instead to feel better about myself?

This teen's mountain climbing is a risk behavior because she could injure herself while doing it.

Six Steps of Decision Making

Whenever you must make a major decision, it helps to know as much as you can about the decision-making process. **Decision making** is *the process of making a choice or finding a solution.* It involves a series of steps you can follow. **Figure 1.7** illustrates these steps. Which of these steps do you use in making decisions?

Figure 1.7

The Decision-Making Process

Making a major decision will be easier if you use this six-step process.

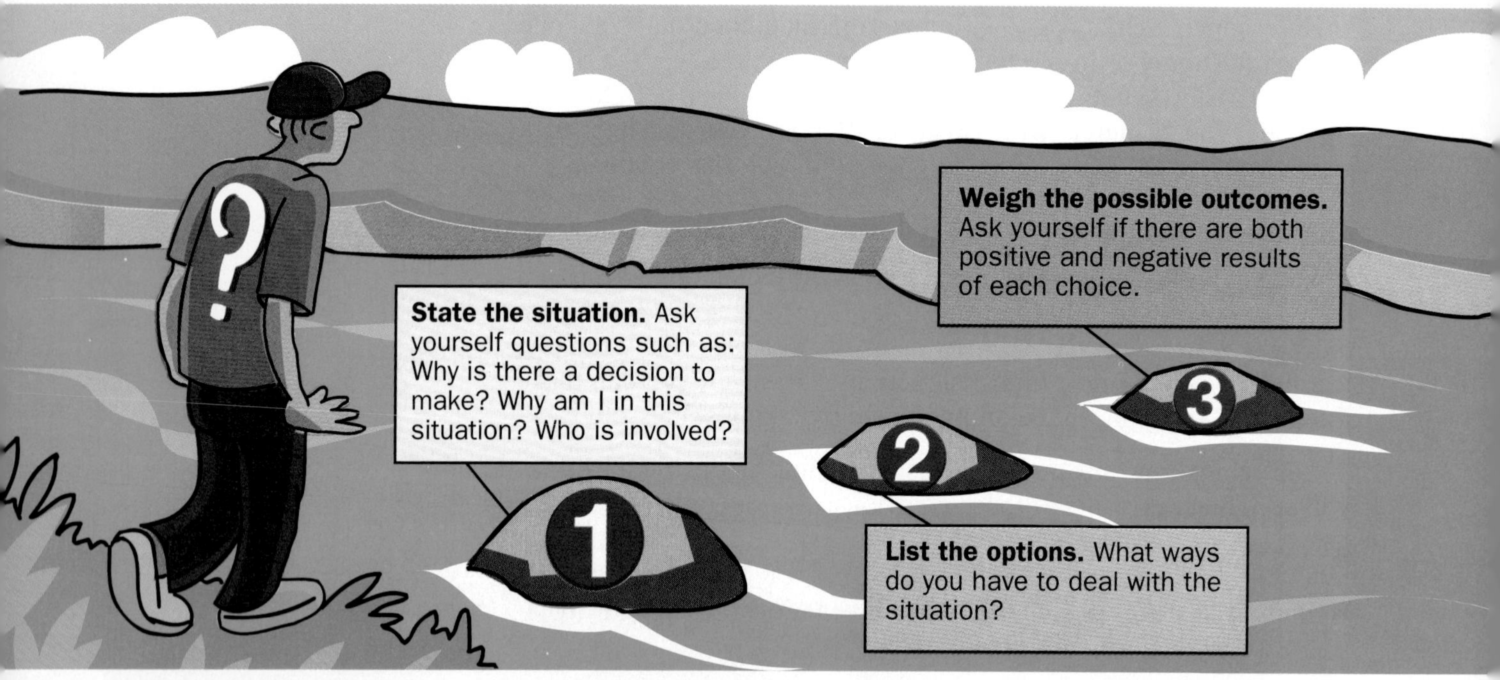

State the situation. Ask yourself questions such as: Why is there a decision to make? Why am I in this situation? Who is involved?
List the options. What ways do you have to deal with the situation?
Weigh the possible outcomes. Ask yourself if there are both positive and negative results of each choice.
1
2
3
?

MAKING HEALTHY DECISIONS

Cooperative Decisions

Kim has been chosen to be in the school play. If she accepts the part, she will have to attend practice for one hour every day after school for three weeks. Kim is very happy about being chosen. She loves drama and hopes to be an actress.

Kim's mother also is happy about the good news. However, she has a problem with Kim's required practice time. She is a nurse and works a twelve-hour shift on Mondays, Wednesdays, and Fridays. She counts on Kim to pick up her five-year-old daughter, Lee, from kindergarten after school on the days that she works. On those days, Kim looks after Lee and prepares part of the evening meal. Their mother returns home from work about 7:15 p.m.

Kim really wants to be in the play, but her mother depends on her to look after Lee. Should Kim tell the drama teacher she cannot be in the play? If she accepts the part, who will pick up Lee from kindergarten and look after her? Kim and her mother decide to use the steps in decision making to help them solve their problem:

1. **State the situation**
2. **List the options**
3. **Weigh the possible outcomes**
4. **Consider your values**
5. **Make a decision and act**
6. **Evaluate the decision**

Evaluating Your Decision

After you have made the decision and taken action, reflect on what happened. You might ask yourself the following questions:

- What was the outcome? Was it what I expected?
- How did my decision affect each part of my health triangle?
- How did my decision affect the way I feel about myself?
- What effect did my decision have on others?
- What did I learn? Would I take the same action again?

in your journal

How can you apply what you have learned about decision making to your own life? Think about some of the situations you face at home and with your friends. In your journal, apply the six steps to your decision making.

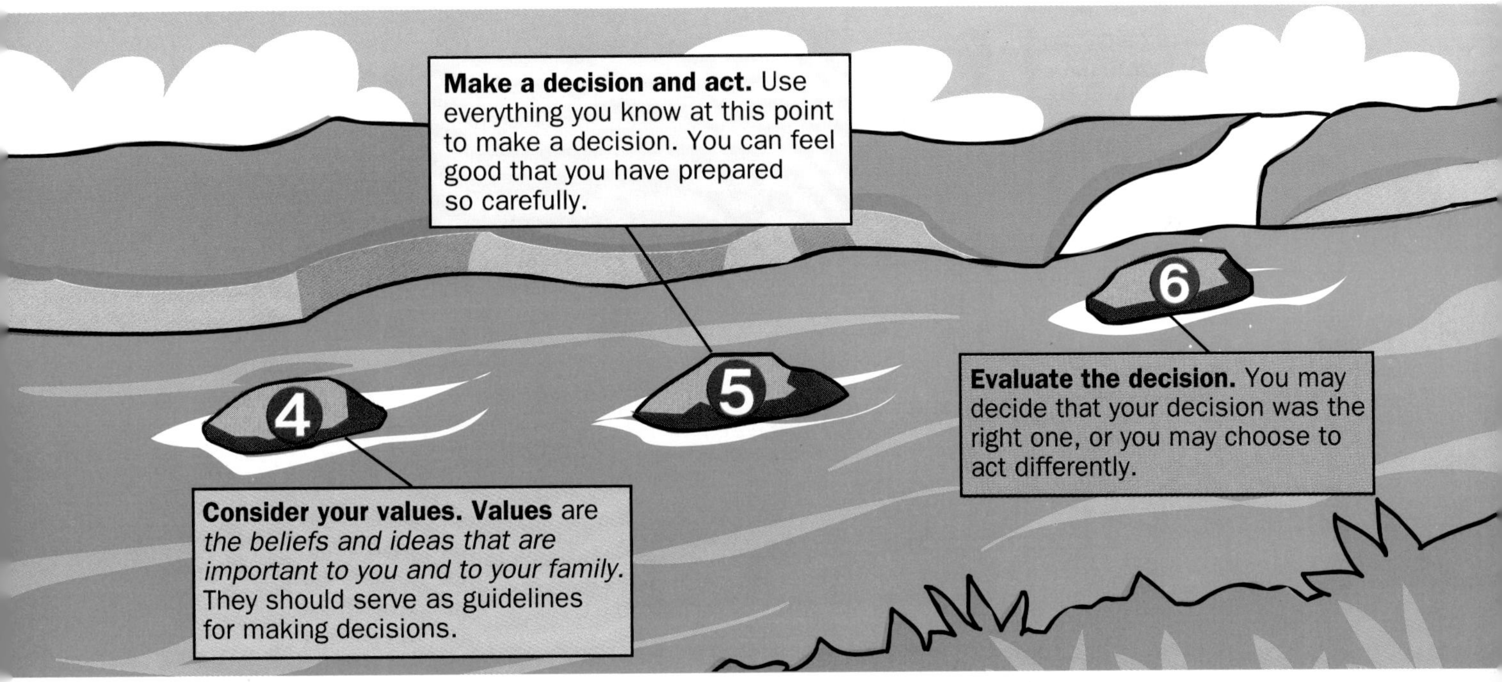

Make a decision and act. Use everything you know at this point to make a decision. You can feel good that you have prepared so carefully.

Evaluate the decision. You may decide that your decision was the right one, or you may choose to act differently.

Consider your values. Values are *the beliefs and ideas that are important to you and to your family.* They should serve as guidelines for making decisions.

Follow-up Activities

1. Apply the six steps of the decision-making process to Kim's story.
2. Along with a partner, role-play a scene in which Kim turns down the offer to be in the play. Have her share her feelings in a dialogue with the audience.
3. Role-play a scene in which Kim and her mother work together to create a course of action that satisfies both of them.

Practice Makes It Easier

It helps to practice decision making ahead of time. For instance, think about some of the problems that you or your family face. Go through all six steps to come up with a healthy solution for each problem. This can help you prepare for times when major decisions come your way.

The more you practice the steps of the decision-making process, the easier decision making becomes. Do not hesitate to ask your parents and other people whose judgment you respect for their suggestions. In time, the practice will prepare you so you will be able to make wise decisions on your own.

If you practice using the decision-making process, you will be prepared to make healthy decisions that are right for you.

Lesson 3 Review

Using complete sentences, answer the following questions on a separate sheet of paper.

Reviewing Terms and Facts

1. **Vocabulary** What is the difference between a *risk behavior* and a *precaution?*
2. **Give Examples** What are four real-life examples of major decisions that teens often make?

Thinking Critically

3. **Suggest** Identify a major decision teens might have to make. Suggest some precautions that they could take to reduce the risks involved in the decision.
4. **Analyze** Think of a decision you have made in the past year. Compare your process with the steps given in this lesson. Which of these steps did you use? Which did you not use? How might the outcome have been different if you had used all six steps?

Applying Health Concepts

5. **Growth and Development** Write a conversation a teen might have with himself or herself in which the teen decides whether or not to smoke a cigarette. Use the steps in the decision-making model. You might tape the conversation to share with the class.

Lesson 4

Setting Goals and Making Action Plans

This lesson will help you find answers to questions that teens often ask about goals. For example:

- **What is a goal?**
- **How does setting goals affect my self-esteem?**
- **Why do I need to set goals?**
- **How can I achieve my goals?**

Words to Know

goal
self-esteem

Why Set Goals?

How do you feel about your life? Do you believe that life is something that happens to you, or do you believe that life is something over which you have some control?

You can help give your life direction by setting goals. A **goal** is *something you aim for.* Reaching any goal takes planning and effort. Goals are important to your **self-esteem,** or *the way you feel about yourself.* People who set goals and achieve them feel better about themselves and about their lives.

If you do not have any goals, ask yourself why. Are you afraid of failing or afraid of being made fun of? Then ask yourself how you can remove the obstacles that keep you from setting goals and working to achieve them.

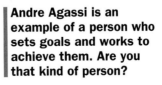

Andre Agassi is an example of a person who sets goals and works to achieve them. Are you that kind of person?

Your Total Health

The Whole Picture

Goals that you set for one area of your life often lead to the achievement of goals in other areas. For example, if you work to reach a goal to be on the swim team, you probably will achieve some fitness goals, too. If you make the team, you may reach goals such as increasing your circle of friends and managing stress better.

The Importance of Goals

Your goals are important because they keep you focused and on track. They help you identify what you want out of life. They also help you use your time, energy, and other resources wisely.

Some goals, such as completing a homework assignment, are short term. Others take longer to achieve. Earning enough money to buy a new bike is a long-term goal. Finishing school and learning to play a musical instrument are also long-term goals.

Both long-term and short-term goals are important. For instance, suppose you wanted to run 5 miles in a race sponsored by your community's park district. The race is two months away. To attain this long-term goal, you need to set some short-term goals. These are like stepping-stones that you could manage one at a time.

Figure 1.8 shows all the short-term goals you could set to help you reach your long-term goal. You might set short-term goals of exercising fifteen to thirty minutes every day and of changing your diet to prepare yourself to run the race. By running the race, you will achieve your long-term goal and boost your self-esteem.

in your journal

Choose two long-term goals you would like to achieve. For each long-term goal, set a few short-term goals that will help you achieve the long-term goal. Write your goals in your private journal.

Figure 1.8
Short-Term and Long-Term Goals
This teen set a series of short-term goals that helped him achieve his long-term goal. Have you ever used a process like this to set and achieve goals?

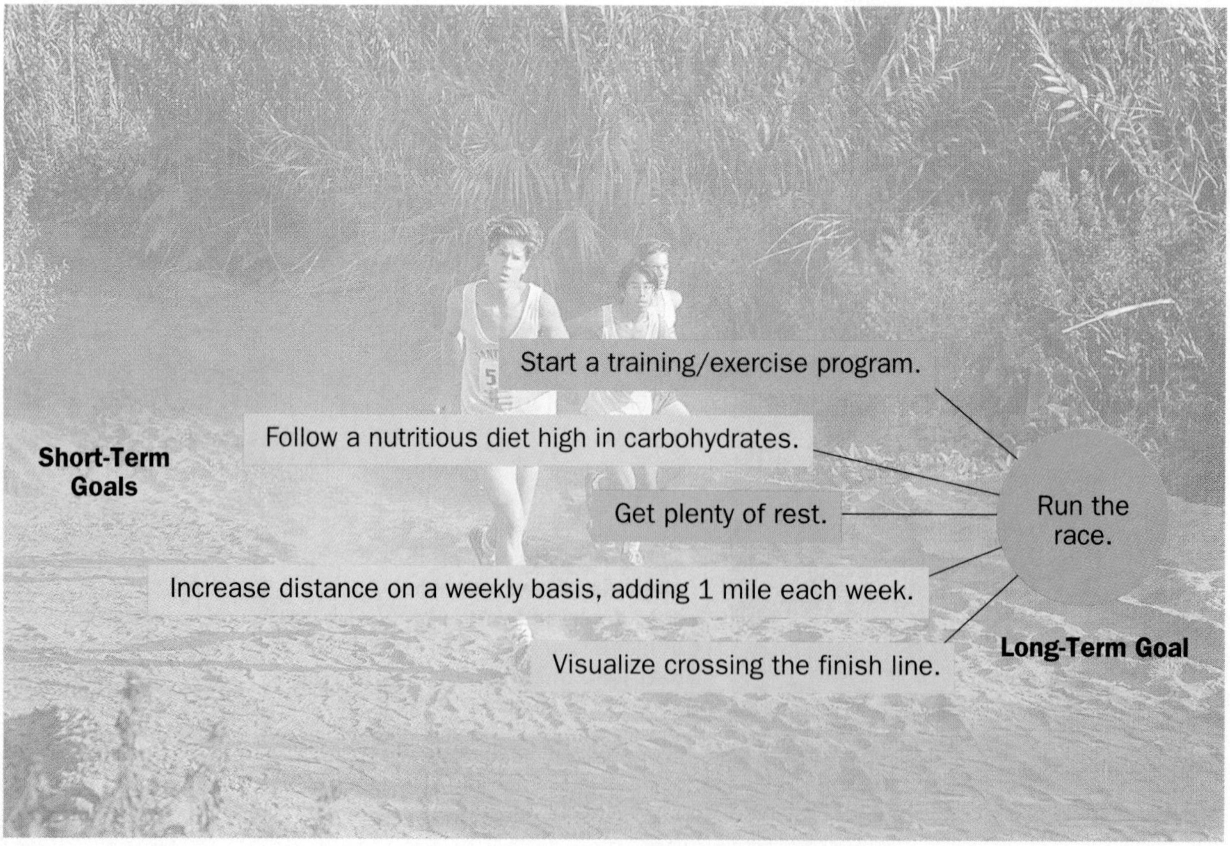
Start a training/exercise program.
Follow a nutritious diet high in carbohydrates.
Short-Term Goals
Get plenty of rest.
Run the race.
Increase distance on a weekly basis, adding 1 mile each week.
Visualize crossing the finish line.
Long-Term Goal

Personal Inventory

WHAT IS YOUR WELLNESS SCORE?

Although some factors may be out of your control, your level of wellness is mainly up to you. This is because you are in charge of your attitudes, goals, and decisions.

On a separate sheet of paper, write yes or no for each statement below. Your answers can help identify goals you need to set to improve your level of wellness. Total your number of yes responses. Compare your score with the ranking at the end of the survey.

1. I generally like and accept who I am.
2. I deal with stress in positive ways.
3. I eat a healthy breakfast every day.
4. If I have a problem with someone, I try to work it out.
5. I do at least 20 minutes of aerobic exercise at least three times each week.
6. I express my emotions in healthy ways.
7. I share my thoughts and feelings with others.
8. I stay within 5 pounds of my weight range.
9. I can accept constructive criticism.
10. I use a seat belt whenever I ride in a car.
11. I get at least 8 hours of sleep at night.
12. I enjoy being alone at times.
13. I do not use alcohol or illegal drugs.
14. I feel that I communicate well with others.
15. I refuse to ride with drivers who have been using alcohol or other drugs.
16. I have at least one hobby that I enjoy.
17. I do not use tobacco.
18. I work well in a group.
19. I have at least one or two close friends.
20. I say no when people ask me to do things that might threaten my health or safety.

Check out your score. Give yourself 1 point for each yes. A score of 16–20 is very good. A score of 11–15 is good. A score of 6–10 is fair. If you score below 5, you need to look seriously at the choices and decisions you make each day.

Making an Action Plan

Setting goals is a skill that you can use in all areas of life. It is a process that gives you direction, a framework within which to work, and a timetable for completing the work. **Figure 1.9** shows the steps one teen used to improve her goal-setting skills and, as a result, her self-esteem. Following these steps can be a big help to you when you set your own goals.

in your journal

Think of two short-term goals you want to reach this week. Use the steps for goal setting to plan how you will reach one of these goals. Write your plan in your journal.

Figure 1.9

The Action Plan Process

The process of setting goals is easier if you follow the six steps this teen did.

Step 1. Identify your goal and put it in writing.
Getting a solo in the school choir concert.

Step 2. List what you will do to reach your goal.
Do voice exercises every day.
Choose a song to sing for tryouts.
Practice singing the song every day.

Step 3. Identify sources of help and support.
Ask a friend to help me pick a song.
Have my voice teacher help me practice the song.
Talk to my parents about my goal to get their support and advice.

Step 4. Give yourself a certain period of time to reach your goal.
I have 2 weeks to prepare because that is when tryouts take place.

Step 5. Set up checkpoints to check on how well you are doing.
After 1 week of practicing, sing for my sister (the music major) at college.
The day before tryouts, sing the song a cappella for my voice teacher.

Step 6. Give yourself a reward once you have achieved your goal.
If I get the solo, my friends and I will celebrate at our favorite restaurant.

This teen's voice teacher is helping her work toward her goal.

Whether you achieve your goal or not, you deserve a treat for working hard toward reaching it.

Making a Difference

Having goals can make a difference. Goals can help you get control of your life. Goals can prepare you to face whatever comes along in your life, and they help boost your self-esteem.

Having goals can also make a difference to the people around you. By having a focus in your life, you raise your self-esteem. In turn, you enhance your relationships with family and friends and widen the circle of people you know. In this way, you make a difference in the lives of others as well as in your own.

Review Lesson 4

Using complete sentences, answer the following questions on a separate sheet of paper.

Reviewing Terms and Facts

1. **Vocabulary** Define the term *self-esteem.* Use it in an original sentence.
2. **Give Examples** List short-term and long-term goals that people you know set and achieve.

Thinking Critically

3. **Suggest** What are some goals that you could set to improve your level of health?
4. **Analyze** List the different groups to which you belong. Choose one group and list the goals, formal or informal, of the group.

Applying Health Concepts

5. **Growth and Development** With a classmate, create a mural depicting some of the community's or school's goals. Display and discuss the completed mural.
6. **Health of Others** Find examples in newspapers, magazines, and books about people who achieved goals that made a difference to themselves and to others. Share your examples with the class.

Chapter 1 Review

Chapter Summary

- **Lesson 1** Health is a combination of physical, mental/emotional, and social well-being. A person's level of wellness is determined in part by choices and decisions made throughout life.
- **Lesson 2** Heredity, environment, available health care, and your behavior—which includes the health choices you make—are factors that affect your health. Lifestyle factors, or habits, affect your future health.
- **Lesson 3** You can avoid risky situations by planning ahead and taking precautions. The six steps of decision making can help you evaluate risks and make healthy decisions.
- **Lesson 4** A goal is something you aim for that takes planning and effort. Goals are important for healthy self-esteem. An action plan can help you reach your goals.

Reviewing Key Terms and Concepts

Using complete sentences, answer the following questions on a separate sheet of paper.

Lesson 1

1. What are the three sides of health?
2. Describe a low level of wellness.

Lesson 2

3. Name three factors that affect your health over which you have little control.
4. What is *health education?*

Lesson 3

5. Define *decision making.*
6. What are *values?*

Lesson 4

7. Why is it important to set goals?
8. What are the six steps of an action plan?

Thinking Critically

Using complete sentences, answer the following questions on a separate sheet of paper.

9. **Hypothesize** How might a person on the midpoint of the wellness continuum move along the continuum after adding a regular exercise program several times a week?
10. **Analyze** How might your personal attitudes influence your lifestyle?
11. **Give Examples** What are some precautions you can take in your daily activities to cut down on risks?
12. **Explain** How does an action plan help you to accomplish your goals?

Your Action Plan

To balance your health triangle, you need to set a goal. Look back through your private journal entries for this chapter. What health choices or changes do you want to make?

Step 1 Decide on a long-term goal and write it down. Make sure that your goal is achievable.

Step 2 Think of a series of short-term goals that will help you achieve your long-term goal. Write these down.

Step 3 Plan a timetable for reaching your short-term goals. Check your schedule to keep yourself on track.

When you reach your long-term goal, reward yourself and celebrate.

In Your Home and Community

1. **Health of Others** Create a "Teen Help" bulletin board in your classroom. The board should include names, addresses, and phone numbers of people and places teens could turn to whenever they need help with their physical, mental/emotional, and social well-being. You might look in the telephone directory under the words *mental, emotional, youth,* and *crisis.* Your school librarian or teacher may also be able to help you locate names of sources.
2. **Growth and Development** Ask a parent or other adult at home to tell you about an important decision he or she had to make as a teen. Find out how the decision was made and if he or she believes that it was the right choice.

Building Your Portfolio

1. **Role Model** Read a magazine article or book about a person you admire. List the lifestyle factors that are a part of this person's life. List examples of how the individual's attitudes influenced his or her life. Include the lists in your portfolio.
2. **Promoting Health** Create a full-page, full-color magazine advertisement for teen readers. Feature one or more ways that teens can make a difference by setting and carrying out their health goals. Include your advertisement in your portfolio.
3. **Personal Assessment** Look through all the activities and projects you did for this chapter. Choose one or two that you would like to include in your portfolio.

Chapter 2

Looking and Feeling Good

Student Expectations

After reading this chapter, you should be able to:

1. **Explain how to have healthy skin, hair, and nails.**
2. **Describe how to take care of your mouth and teeth.**
3. **List ways to care for your eyes and ears.**
4. **Discuss the importance of good foot care and good posture.**

Teen Chat Group

Kiame: Hey, Jeremy, you haven't said a word all day. What's wrong?

Jeremy: I just got braces and I don't want anyone to see them.

Susan: Why? It's not like you're the only one at our school wearing braces. Greg wears them too.

Jeremy: Yes, but he'll be getting his braces off soon.

Nathan: How long do you have to wear yours?

Jeremy: I'm not sure. I guess until my teeth are straight.

Kiame: Well, you can't give up talking forever. You'll go crazy.

Susan: Besides, your real friends won't care that you wear braces.

Jeremy: I guess you're right. If I'm lucky and ever get these things off, I should have pretty good high school senior pictures.

in your journal

Read the dialogue on this page. Does it sound familiar? Have you ever felt insecure about your appearance? This chapter will discuss how to feel better about your looks. Start your private journal entries on looking and feeling good by answering these questions:

- **In general, how do you feel about your appearance? Do you like the way you look?**
- **How do you think others see you?**
- **How can your personal habits improve the way you look and feel?**
- **Are good health and appearance related?**

When you reach the end of the chapter, you will use your journal entries to make an action plan.

Lesson 1

Healthy Skin, Hair, and Nails

This lesson will help you find answers to questions that teens often ask about their skin, hair, and nails. For example:

- **How can I make sure I don't have body odor?**
- **Why does my face break out?**
- **Why do some people have naturally curly hair?**
- **How can I have better-looking fingernails?**

Words to Know

epidermis
dermis
subcutaneous layer
melanin
pores
sebum
dermatologist
follicle
dandruff
head lice
cuticle
keratin

Your Skin

Your skin is a body organ like your heart or brain. In fact, it is the largest organ of all. Your skin is on view to everyone you meet. That is why it plays such an important role in your appearance.

Your skin performs several important functions for your body. **Figure 2.1** describes these functions.

Figure 2.1

The Skin's Functions

Besides having a great effect on your overall appearance, your skin performs many important functions.

Ⓐ The skin is a shield against water. Like a formfitting raincoat, your skin keeps out water when you swim or take a bath.

Ⓑ The skin is a defense against germs. That is why people badly burned in fires have such a high risk of infection. That is also why you need to administer first aid for open cuts.

Ⓒ The skin helps control body temperature. Blood circulation beneath the surface of the skin increases or slows down depending on your internal temperature. If it increases, perspiration is released through your pores, and your skin cools. If it slows down, sweating stops and body heat is conserved.

Ⓓ The skin works as a sense organ. Nerve endings in the skin let you know when something touches your body. They let you feel different textures. They also allow you to tell the difference between hot and cold and to feel pain as a way of protecting you.

The Parts of the Skin

Your skin has two main layers, an outer layer and an inner layer. The *outermost layer of skin* is called the **epidermis** (e·puh·DER·mis). The *thick inner layer of skin* is called the **dermis** (DER·mis). Below the dermis is *a layer of fat tissue* called the **subcutaneous** (suhb·kyoo·TAY·nee·uhs) **layer. Figure 2.2** describes the parts of the skin.

Many layers of cells make up the epidermis. As new cells are manufactured deep down, old ones at the surface are shed. This process of making and replacing cells is continuous. Through shedding, you replace your outer skin about once a month. If you live to be 70, you will wear more than 800 new coats of skin!

interNET CONNECTION

Visit cyberspace for good health habits that will help you feel and look your best.

http://www.glencoe.com/sec/health

Figure 2.2

The Skin

The skin is made up of an outer layer, a thick inner layer, and a layer of fat tissue.

A Epidermis
The cells in the deepest part of the epidermis produce **melanin** (MEL·uh·nin), *the substance that gives the skin most of its color.*

B Dermis
The dermis contains blood vessels, nerve endings, hair follicles, and two types of glands. Oil glands produce oils that keep the skin soft and waterproof. Sweat glands secrete perspiration, which is released through **pores,** or *tiny holes in the skin.*

C Subcutaneous Layer
The subcutaneous layer has fat cells and connects the skin to bone and muscle.

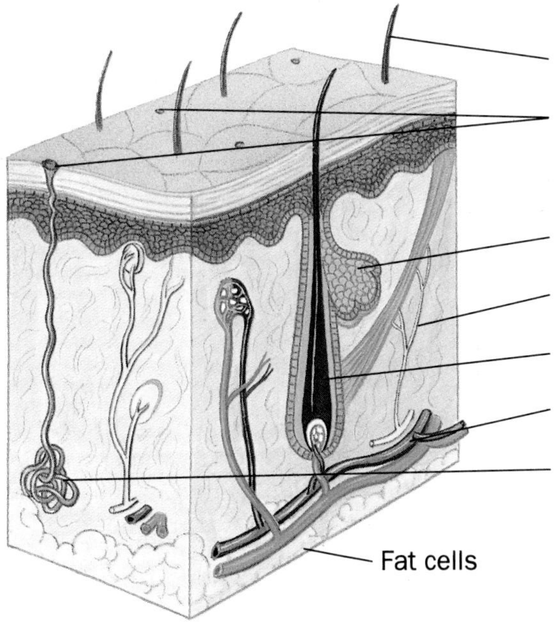

Taking Care of Your Skin

Your skin is a vital organ of your body. Good health habits, along with good grooming, promote healthy skin. Proper skin care should be part of your daily routine.

- Take a bath or shower every day. During the early teen years, the sweat glands become more active. The best way to care for your skin is to keep it clean. Daily bathing or showering with soap will rid your skin of bacteria and excess oils.
- Apply deodorant or antiperspirant daily. Sweat glands are numerous under the arms. Any bacteria there may act on perspiration and cause an unpleasant odor. Deodorants and antiperspirants cover up the odor, and antiperspirants help the area remain dry.

Q&A ?

"Pruny" Skin

Q: Why do my hands and feet get all wrinkled and pruny after I've been in the water for a while?

A: Because the skin on the palms of your hands and the soles of your feet contains no oil glands to keep water out.

Acne

A skin problem common to teens is acne, in which oil glands produce great quantities of *a whitish, oily substance* called **sebum** (SEE·buhm). Eventually sebum clogs the pores, causing the problems shown in **Figure 2.3.** If the condition is serious, you may want to see a **dermatologist** (DER·muh·TAHL·uh·jist), *a doctor who treats skin disorders*. You can also practice the do's and don'ts in the list below.

Diet does not *cause* acne, but certain foods may contribute to it. If the condition worsens after a person eats a certain food, it would be wise not to eat that food for a while.

Figure 2.3

Types of Acne

Whiteheads, blackheads, and pimples are three common types of acne.

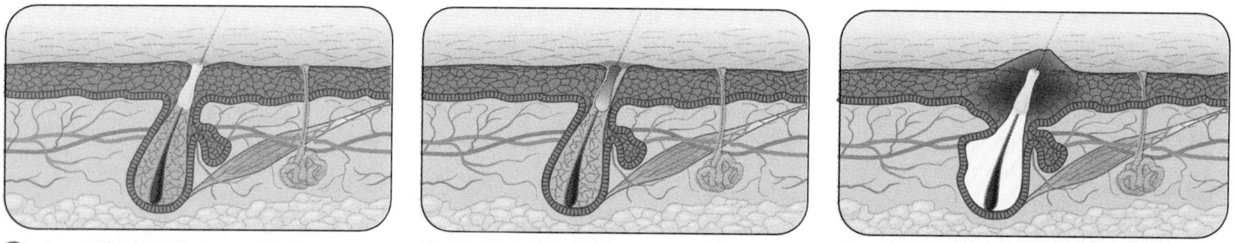

A A *whitehead* is a pore that is plugged with sebum.

B A *blackhead* is a pore that is plugged with sebum and darkens because it becomes exposed to the air.

C A *pimple* is a clogged pore that has become infected and filled with pus. The skin becomes red and inflamed at the site of the pimple.

in your journal

You have just read some ways of taking care of your skin. Now use your journal to help you evaluate your skin. For a period of one week, keep a record of how often you bathe, wash your face, use deodorant, and protect your skin from the sun.

DO'S

- Wash the infected area at least twice a day, morning and night, with a mild soap and warm water.
- Use acne-fighting preparations recommended or prescribed by your doctor.
- Get lots of exercise and rest.
- Eat a well-balanced diet.

DON'TS

- Avoid using heavy or greasy creams or makeup.
- Avoid rubbing areas affected by acne.
- Avoid picking or squeezing pimples, which can spread the infection and result in a scar.
- Avoid touching the infected areas with your fingers.

Other Skin Problems

Other skin problems are caused by different types of germs:

- **Warts** are small growths on the skin caused by a virus. Report any changes in the color or size of a wart to your doctor.
- **Boils** are skin infections accompanied by swelling, redness, and a buildup of pus. Boils are caused by bacteria.
- **Cold sores** are caused by a virus called herpes simplex I. The blisters appear as small sores on or near the lips and usually go away in 10 to 14 days. They can spread if scratched or broken.

What Causes Sunburn?

If you have ever spent much time in the sun, you know that it affects people differently. Some people tan easily. Others burn when they are in the sun without proper protection.

Sunburn is caused by ultraviolet (UV) rays, or the light rays that come from the sun. Concern about exposure to UV rays has grown in recent years. In addition to causing sunburn, UV rays make the skin age and wrinkle faster, may lead to skin cancer, and an eye condition called *cataracts* (KA·tuh·rakts).

Even on overcast days, the UV rays of the sun can damage your skin.

To help people protect themselves from dangerous UV rays, the National Weather Service now predicts the next day's *solar-hazard rating* in its daily weather reports. Officially called the Ultraviolet (UV) Index Forecast, this rating is given for 58 cities. The rating ranges from 0 to about 15 with *0* being a minimal health risk and *10 and over* being a very high health risk. **Figure 2.4** lists the ranges, risk of harm from sun exposure, and warnings that comprise the UV Index.

Figure 2.4

The Ultraviolet Index

Pay attention to the solar-hazard rating for days when you will be out in the sun, and follow the appropriate warning on the index.

Solar-Hazard Rating	Health Risk and Warnings
0 to 2	**Minimal risk** Most people can stay in the noon sun up to 1 hour without burning.
3 to 4	**Low risk** Fair-skinned people may burn in less than 20 minutes during the middle of the day. Wear a sunscreen, hat, and sunglasses.
5 to 6	**Moderate risk** Fair-skinned people may burn in less than 15 minutes. Use a sunscreen with a sun protection factor (SPF) value of at least 15, a hat, and sunglasses.
7 to 9	**High risk** Fair-skinned people may burn in less than 10 minutes. Use a sunscreen with an SPF value of at least 15, a hat, and sunglasses. Limit time spent in the midday sun.
10 and over	**Very high risk** Fair-skinned people may burn in less than 5 minutes. Avoid sun exposure between 10:30 A.M. and 3:30 P.M. Use sunscreen with an SPF value of 20 to 30, and wear sunglasses and protective clothing.

Your Hair

The hair that you see is made of dead cells. **Figure 2.5** shows that its roots are in the dermis, housed in *small pockets* called **follicles** (FAHL·i·kuhlz). As new hair cells are formed, old ones are forced outward through the surface of the skin and die.

Figure 2.5
The Hair

The part of the hair that you can see is the hair shaft. The hair follicle and root are imbedded in the skin.

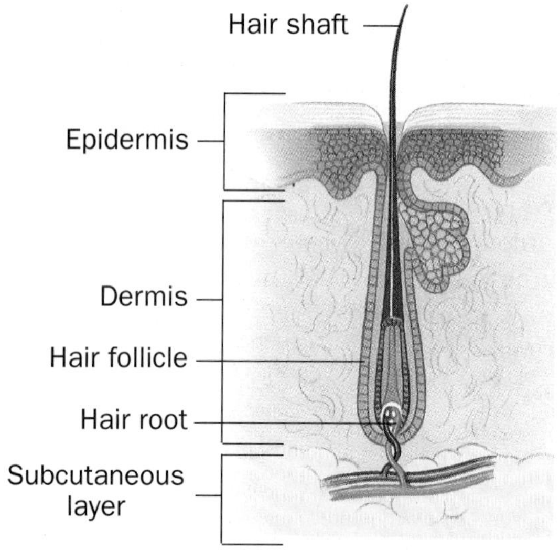

Hair takes its color from melanin. Hair color is inherited, or passed on to you by your parents. The shape of the hair shaft determines whether your hair is wavy, curly, or straight.

Taking Care of Your Hair

For healthy hair, your daily routine should include the following:

- Brush your hair once a day to remove dirt and to move oils down the hair shaft. The oils make hair shiny and attractive.
- Wash your hair frequently with a gentle soap or shampoo. Let your hair dry by itself. The heat from electric blow dryers can rob your hair of oils, making hair ends rough and dry. Dyes, permanents, and hairspray can damage hair as well.

LIFE SKILLS

Protecting Yourself from the Sun

Many people used to think that sunshine was good for you. People with deep tans were thought to be "the picture of health." Research has shown otherwise. Medical authorities now know that prolonged exposure to the sun is harmful.

Protecting your skin during the first 18 years can reduce the risk of some types of skin cancer by up to 78 percent. This means that warnings of prolonged sun exposure have special urgency for teens. What's more, as the earth's ozone layer continues to shrink, sunlight will become even more dangerous. The ozone layer helps prevent the sun's harmful ultraviolet (UV) rays from reaching the earth.

If you are planning to spend time outdoors, play it safe. It can make a dramatic difference in your skin appearance for years to come. You can take several actions to protect your skin from the sun.

- Avoid being in direct sunlight between 10:00 a.m. and 2:00 p.m. This is when the sun's rays are most intense.
- Apply sunscreen generously to all exposed skin. Sunscreens are oils, lotions, and creams that filter out the sun's UV rays. Choose a waterproof sunscreen with a sun protection factor (SPF) of 15 or higher.

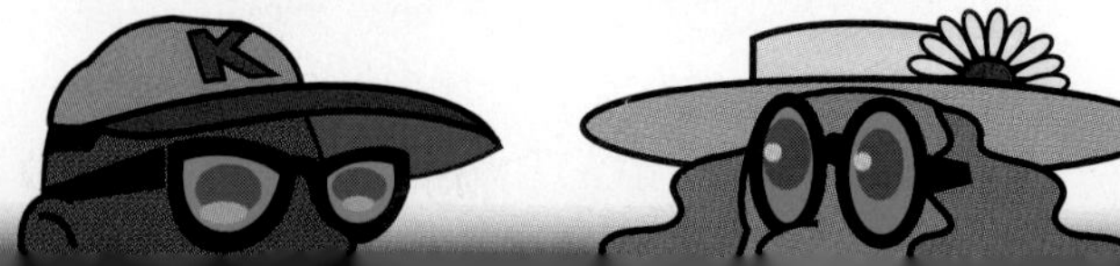

Hair and Scalp Problems

Dandruff (DAN·druhf), a common scalp problem, is a *flaking of the outer layer of dead skin cells:* It is usually caused by a dry scalp. Often, a person can control dandruff by washing. Sometimes a special dandruff shampoo is needed. If the problem persists, see a doctor. You may have a skin infection.

At times, an itchy scalp is caused by **head lice,** *parasitic insects that live in the hair.* Head lice are very common and very easy to catch from someone else. That is why you should avoid sharing brushes and combs with other people. You can control head lice by using a medicated shampoo. Also be sure to wash all bedding, towels, and clothing that have come into contact with the scalp. Others in the family also may need to be treated at the same time. If left untreated, head lice can lead to infection.

Cultural Connections

Hairstyles ACTIVITY!

In many cultures, hair is more than a covering for the head. People use their hair to express their religious and political beliefs as well as their social status. A hairstyle can identify a person as belonging to a certain group. Find examples of cultural influences on hairstyles, and share them with your classmates.

Your Nails

How do your fingernails look? Are they usually dirty or clean? Do you bite your nails, or are you careful about trimming them? Good nail care is important for your appearance and total health.

Fingernails and toenails, like hair, are dead cells that grow out of living tissue located in the dermis. Around the nails is *a nonliving band of epidermis* called the **cuticle** (KYOO·ti·kuhl).

Taking Care of Your Nails

Caring for your nails means trimming them and using plenty of soap when you wash to clean underneath the nails. If your hands are very dirty, use a gentle brush under the nails and around the cuticles. **Figure 2.6** on page 38 shows additional ways to keep your nails healthy and looking their best.

- Wear sunglasses that filter UV rays and protective clothing. Wear a hat with a wide brim that shades your face and neck. If you are working outdoors, wear long pants and a long-sleeved shirt.
- Beware of reflected light. Surfaces such as water, sand, cement, and snow (light-colored surfaces) can reflect harmful radiation.
- Bring a big umbrella to the beach, or seek a shady area. Realize, however, that the umbrella by itself will not guarantee protection.
- If you wear makeup, use moisturizers, lipbalms, and creams that contain sunscreen ingredients.
- Be careful even when the sun is not shining. On cloudy days, up to 80 percent of the sun's rays still penetrate the clouds.

You might think you can get a safe tan by using a sunlamp or by going to a tanning salon. Sunlamps and tanning salons, however, will expose you to dangerous long-wave UV rays and should never be used. You could use a self-tanning lotion to give yourself the appearance of a tan for a few days, but beware that self-tanners do not take the place of sunscreen.

Follow-up Activity

Young children tend to spend even more time outdoors than teens. Plan a way to teach young children about protecting themselves from the sun. You might prepare a picture book or present a puppet show. Be a role model for younger brothers or sisters by protecting your own skin from exposure to the sun.

Nail Problems

The nails on your fingers and toes contain **keratin** (KEHR·uh·tin), *a substance that makes nails hard.* Sometimes minor problems can affect nails. *Hangnails* are splits in the cuticle along the edge of the nail. Once you have carefully cut away the splintered edge, the cuticle will grow back in several days. An *ingrown toenail* occurs when the nail pushes into the skin on the side of the toe. This can happen when toenails are cut too short. If the toe becomes red and inflamed, infection may have set in. This sign is your cue to see your doctor.

Figure 2.6

Caring for Your Nails

The basic tools to use when caring for your nails are a cuticle stick, nail clippers, and an emery board.

Ⓐ Use a cuticle stick to push back the cuticle. First soften the cuticle with warm water. This makes it easier to push back the cuticle. You can also apply a cuticle remover.

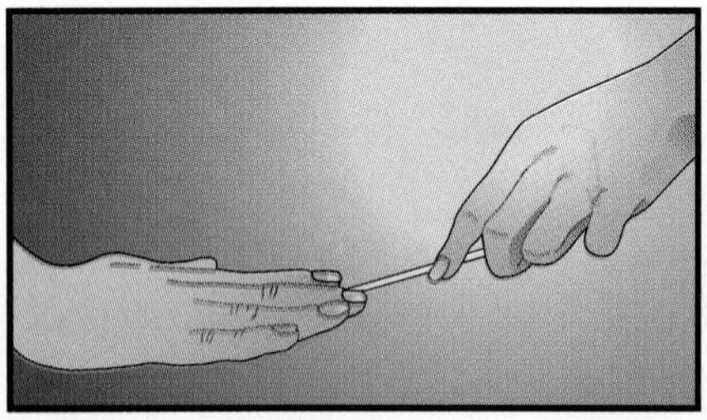

Ⓑ Use a nail clipper or small scissors to trim your nails. Fingernails should be slightly rounded at the ends. Cut toenails straight across, with the nail at or slightly beyond skin level. If you cut the nail any shorter you risk infection.

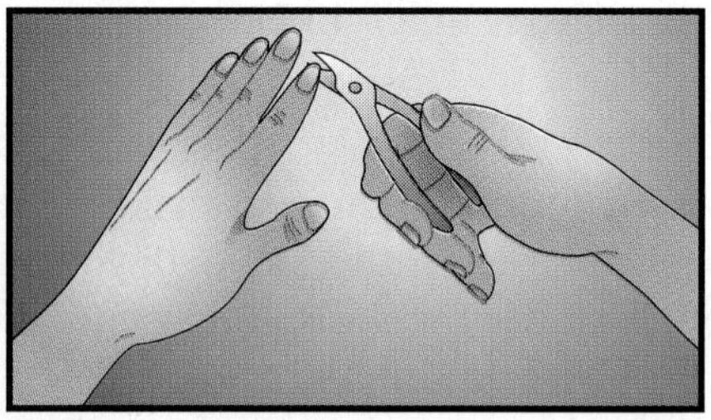

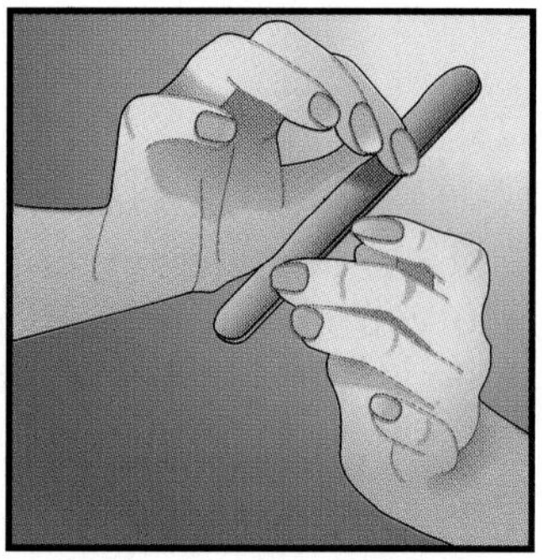

Ⓒ Use an emery board or nail file to help round out the ends of your fingernails. An emery board also smooths out rough edges.

Lesson 1 Review

Using complete sentences, answer the following questions on a separate sheet of paper.

Reviewing Terms and Facts

1. **Recall** What is a *dermatologist?*
2. **Vocabulary** Which of the following terms does not refer to part of your nails: *keratin, cuticle, follicle?*

Thinking Critically

3. **Analyze** Your classmate Ted starts sunbathing as soon as it gets warm. It seems he has a tan most of the year. He says that "a little sun" is good for you. What do you think?
4. **Hypothesize** What are some ways teens treat their hair that might not be "sensible"? Explain your answer.

Applying Health Concepts

5. **Consumer Health** Check the labels of several acne medications. Note the ingredients they have in common. Write an advertisement about a "new" product. Identify the ingredients in the product that will make it effective in controlling acne.
6. **Personal Health** Prepare a video on how to give yourself a manicure and a pedicure. Follow the directions for nail care in this lesson. Present the video to the class.

Lesson 2

Healthy Mouth and Teeth

This lesson will help you find answers to questions that teens often ask about their mouth and teeth. For example:

- **Why do I get cavities?**
- **What is the right way to brush and floss my teeth?**
- **How can I keep from having bad breath?**

Words to Know

tissue
periodontium
crown
neck
root
plaque
tartar
abscess
gingivitis
malocclusion

Your Mouth and Teeth

When you smile, you make yourself and others feel good. Clean teeth and gums and a fresh breath enhance your smile. Make tooth care a part of your daily grooming. This lesson will tell you how.

The Jobs of the Mouth

Your mouth, teeth, and tongue are responsible for some actions that are very important to your health. These include tasting, digestion, and speech. The list below explains these actions.

- **Tasting.** You taste by means of sensitive areas of the tongue called taste buds. When food touches the taste buds, a signal goes to the brain. The brain identifies the food as either sweet, sour, salty, or bitter.
- **Digestion.** Digestion starts in your mouth. Your teeth tear and crush the food. Saliva in your mouth moistens the food and starts to change it chemically before you swallow it.
- **Speech.** All the consonant and vowel sounds you make are determined by precise placements of the tongue, lips, teeth, and other parts of your mouth.

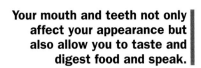

Your mouth and teeth not only affect your appearance but also allow you to taste and digest food and speak.

in your journal

As long as they are healthy, teeth that have spaces between them or that slightly overlap are part of a person's uniqueness. In your journal, describe how your teeth and a friend or family member's teeth affect that person's smile.

The Teeth

In addition to helping you chew food, your teeth help shape and structure your mouth. They also contribute to your appearance.

Parts of the Tooth

A tooth is a living structure. **Figure 2.7** shows the three main parts of the tooth: the crown, the neck, and the root. Each tooth also contains the following types of **tissue,** or *groups of cells:* enamel, dentin, pulp, and cementum.

The area around the tooth is the **periodontium** (pehr·ee·oh·DAHN·shee·um). This is *a structure made up of the jawbone, the gums, and connectors called ligaments.* It supports the teeth.

Types of Teeth

Usually the mouth has room for a total of 32 teeth. Each tooth has a specific name and function (see **Figure 2.8**).

Figure 2.7

The Tooth

The tooth is made up of many parts.

Ⓐ The **crown** is *the part of the tooth visible to the eye.*

Ⓑ The **neck** is *the part of the tooth between the crown and the root.*

Ⓒ The **root** is *the part of the tooth inside the gum.*

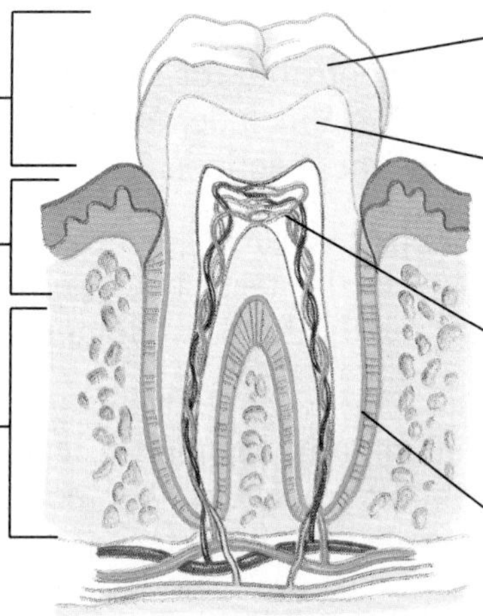

Ⓓ **Enamel** (ee·NA·muhl) is *the hard material that covers the crown of a tooth.*

Ⓔ **Dentin** (DEN·tin) is *bonelike material surrounding the pulp of a tooth.*

Ⓕ **Pulp** is *soft, sensitive tissue containing nerves and blood vessels deep within the root of a tooth.*

Ⓖ **Cementum** (se·MEN·tuhm) is *thin, bonelike material covering the root of a tooth.*

Figure 2.8

The Types of Teeth

Each type of tooth has a specific function.

Ⓐ **Incisors** (in·SY·serz), the eight center teeth, cut into and tear food.

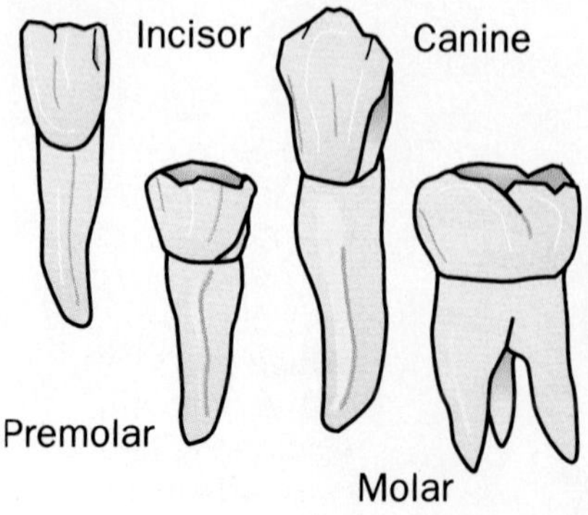

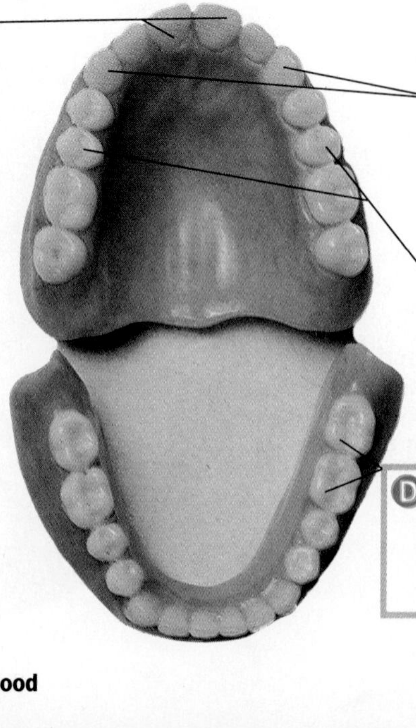

Ⓑ **Canines** (KAY·nynz), four pointed teeth next to the incisors, grasp and tear food.

Ⓒ **Premolars** (PREE·moh·lerz) are the eight short teeth between canines and molars.

Ⓓ **Molars** (MOH·lerz), the twelve stubby teeth in the back of the mouth, do the major work of chewing.

What Causes Tooth Decay?

Good, regular oral care is necessary for healthy, clean teeth. Regular brushing after eating and before bedtime is essential. Flossing is also important because you often miss hard-to-reach spots with your toothbrush.

If teeth and gums are not cared for properly, problems can result. One of the most common problems is tooth decay. In fact, 96 percent of all Americans have at least one cavity. Yet tooth decay is also one of the most preventable diseases in the United States.

Figure 2.9 shows how healthy teeth develop cavities. If left untreated, cavities grow larger and larger. A tooth may eventually become so decayed that it needs to be removed.

Cultural Connections

Diet and Decay

Every cultural group has traditional foods and ways of eating. The dietary customs of some groups are more healthful than those of other groups. The Inuit people of Alaska once had almost no tooth decay. Then they began eating the sugar-enhanced diet that most Americans eat. Now Inuits have the same rate of tooth decay as other Americans.

Figure 2.9

The Process of Tooth Decay

When teeth are not cared for properly, tooth decay follows this process.

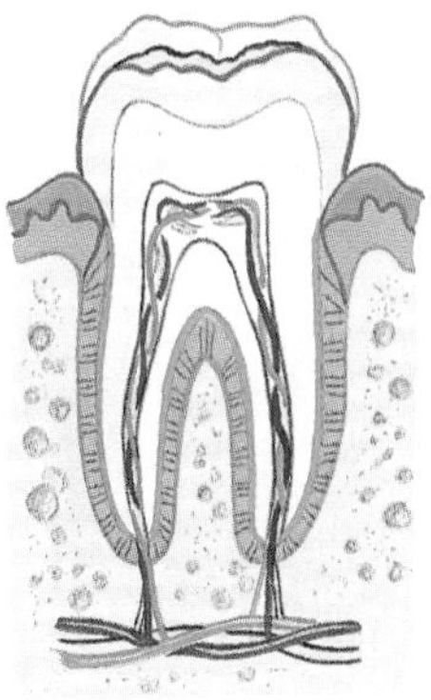

A. Air, food, and bacteria in your mouth form a sticky film called **plaque** (PLAK) on your teeth. Plaque combines with sugar to form acid. If not removed, plaque hardens into **tartar** (TAR·ter).

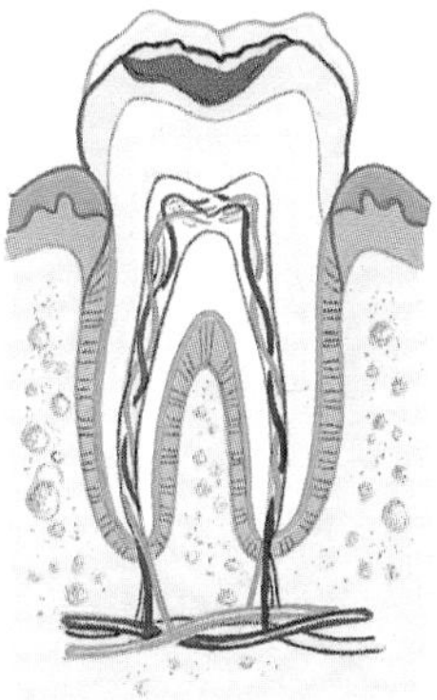

B. Acid under the plaque or tartar eats a hole, or cavity, in tooth enamel.

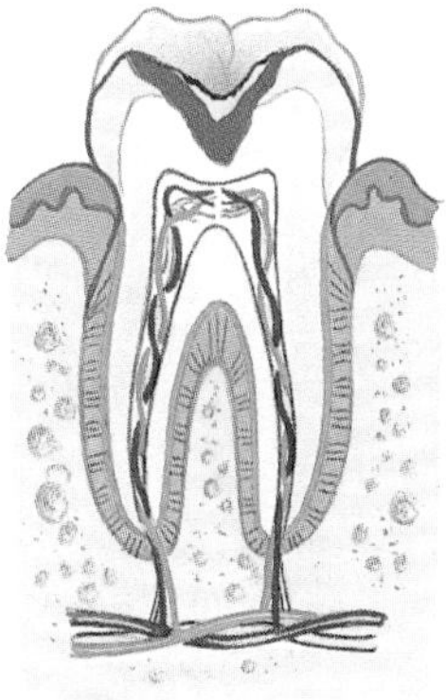

C. The decay spreads to the dentin.

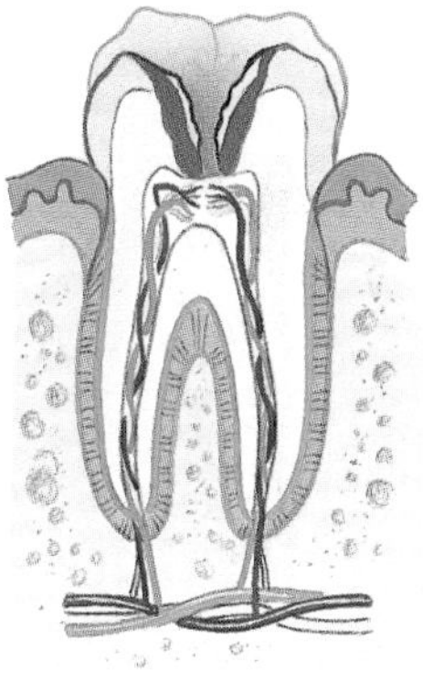

D. The decay then spreads to the pulp, where it exposes a nerve. Air hitting the exposed nerve causes your tooth to ache.

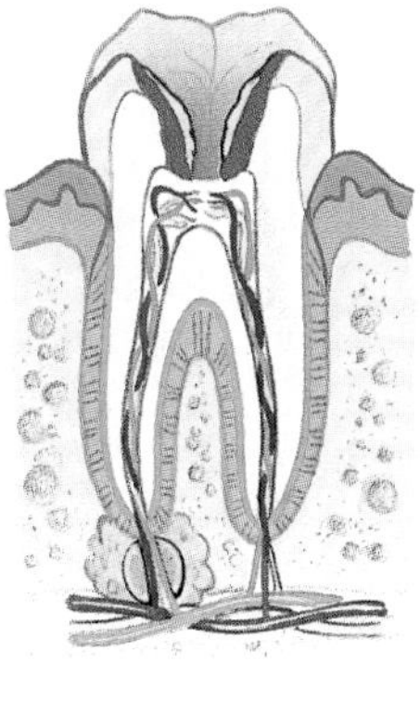

E. If the decay is not stopped, it moves into the roots and *pus collects in the bone sockets around the tooth.* This very painful condition is known as an **abscess** (AB·sess).

Proper Brushing Technique

Figure 2.10 shows you how to brush your teeth properly.

Figure 2.10

How to Brush Your Teeth

If you brush your teeth properly, you can prevent tooth decay.

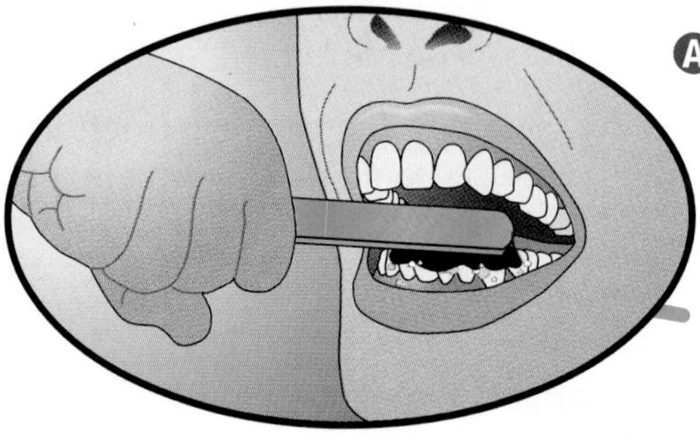

Ⓐ Brush the outer surfaces of both your upper and lower teeth. Using small strokes, gently scrub across each tooth.

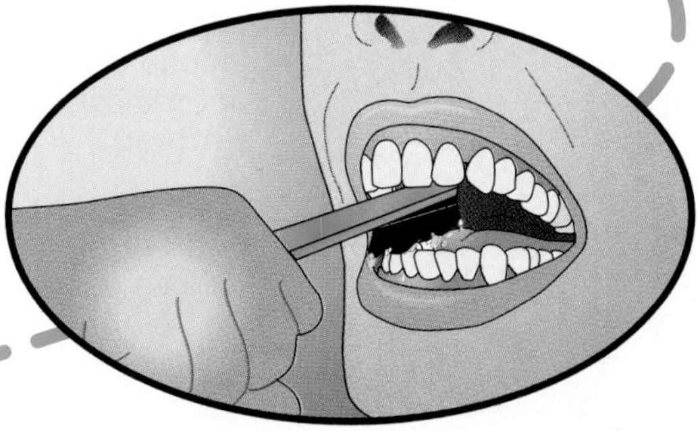

Ⓑ Brush the chewing surfaces of your molars and premolars.

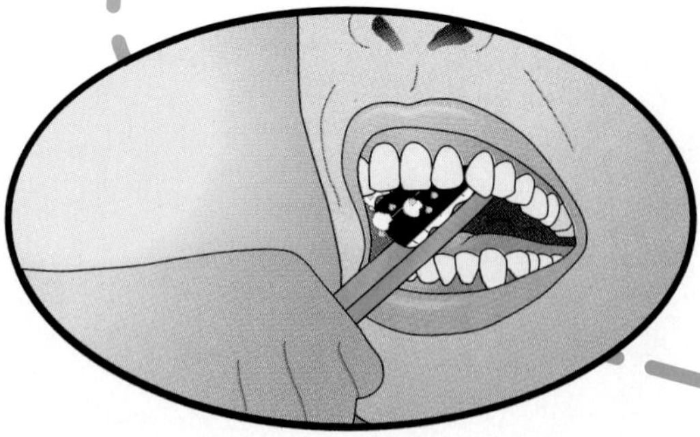

Ⓒ Use an up-and-down motion to brush the inside surfaces of your incisors.

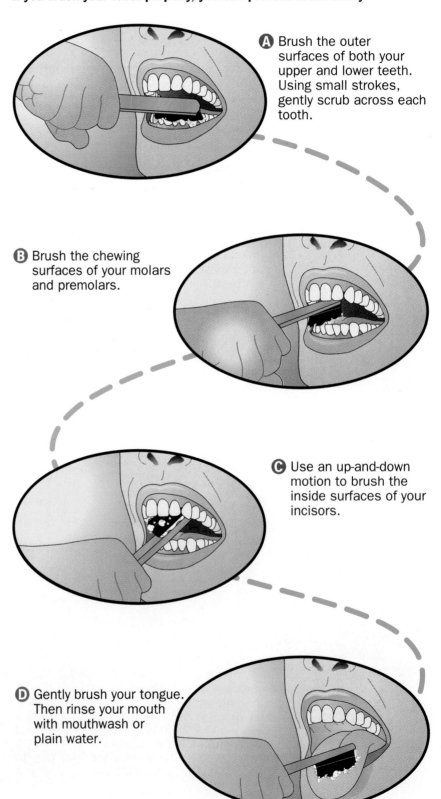

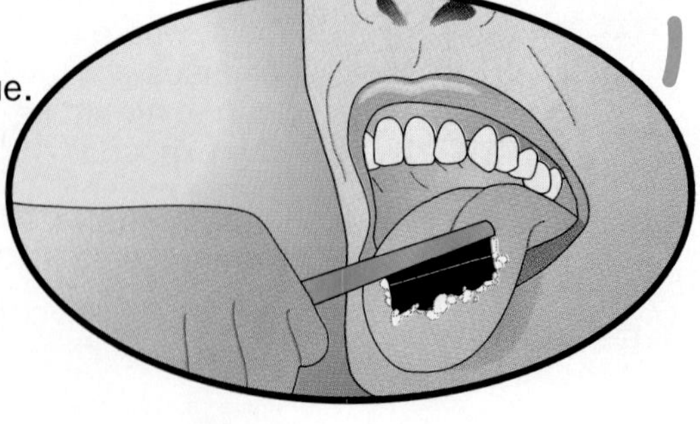

Ⓓ Gently brush your tongue. Then rinse your mouth with mouthwash or plain water.

? Q&A

Buying a Toothbrush

Q: I never know what kind of toothbrush to buy. Can you help me?

A: Buy a soft or medium-soft toothbrush. A brush that's too stiff may not get into crevices. It also may cause your gums to bleed. Buy a toothbrush with a small head so you can get at every tooth. Be sure to change toothbrushes regularly. Bent or frayed brushes are ineffective.

Proper Flossing Technique

Figure 2.11 shows you how to floss your teeth properly.

Figure 2.11

How to Floss Your Teeth

If you floss your teeth properly, you can prevent tooth decay as well as gum disease in hard-to-reach spots.

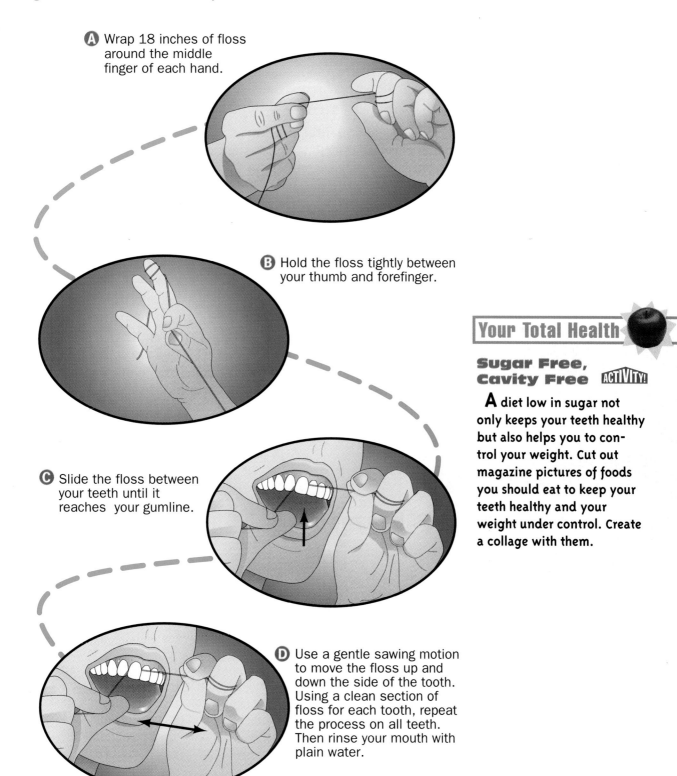

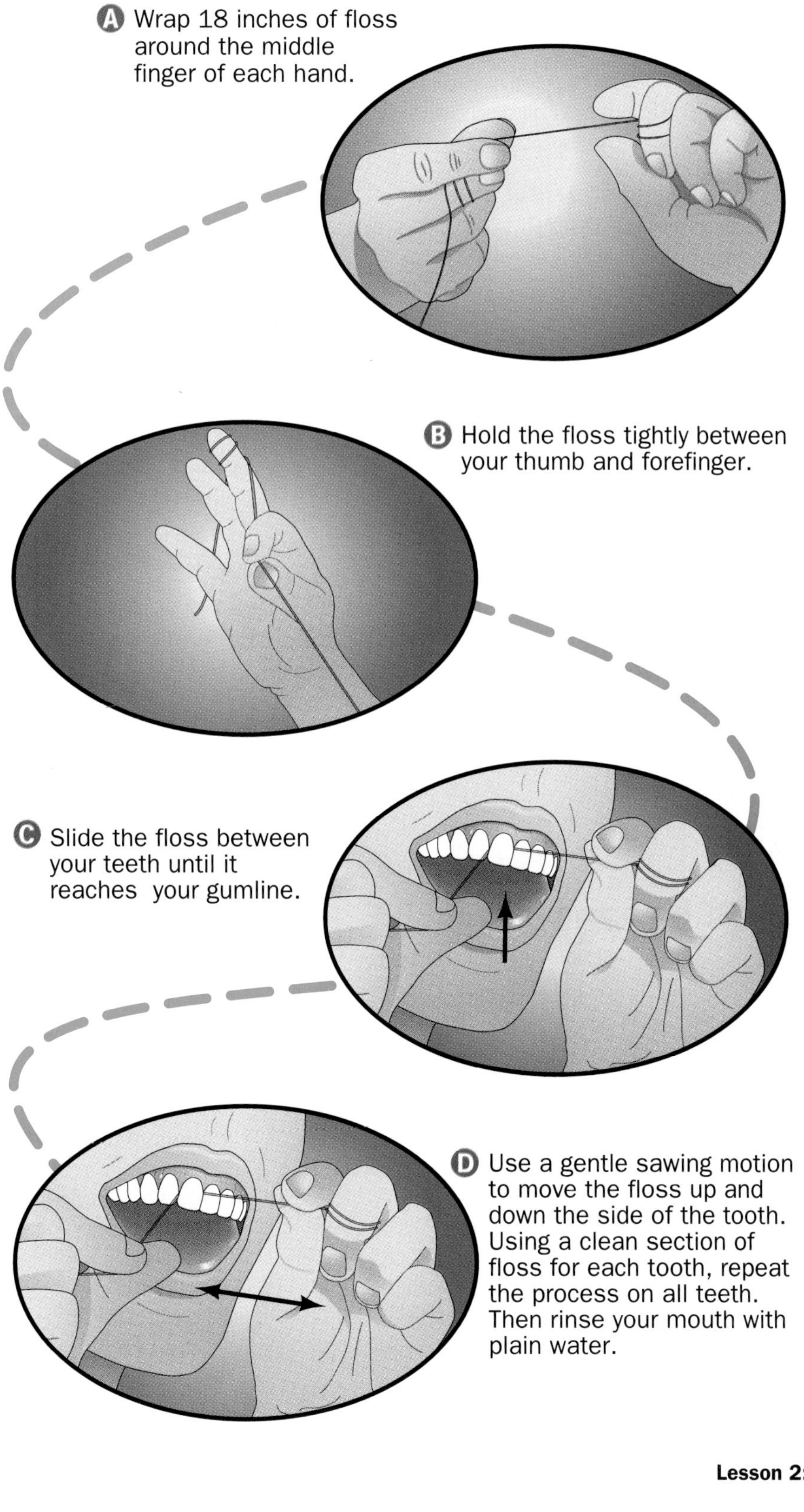

A Wrap 18 inches of floss around the middle finger of each hand.
B Hold the floss tightly between your thumb and forefinger.
C Slide the floss between your teeth until it reaches your gumline.
D Use a gentle sawing motion to move the floss up and down the side of the tooth. Using a clean section of floss for each tooth, repeat the process on all teeth. Then rinse your mouth with plain water.

Your Total Health

Sugar Free, Cavity Free ACTIVITY!

A diet low in sugar not only keeps your teeth healthy but also helps you to control your weight. Cut out magazine pictures of foods you should eat to keep your teeth healthy and your weight under control. Create a collage with them.

Taking Care of Your Teeth

A study by the National Institute of Dental Research recently reported that the number of school-age children without cavities in their permanent teeth has doubled in the past two decades. You can be part of this trend by practicing sensible dental care.

- **Brush your teeth after eating.** Bacteria work rapidly, so you must remove food particles within minutes after eating.
- **Floss between your teeth.** Dental floss can reach food particles and plaque that cannot be reached with a toothbrush.
- **Reserve starchy foods and foods high in sugar for mealtimes.** Mealtime beverages and saliva production help rinse the mouth of acid-producing sugar.
- **Have regular dental checkups.** A dentist and dental hygienist can clean your teeth and spot signs of tooth decay and gum disease before they become serious problems.

in your journal

You have just read about ways to keep your mouth, teeth, and gums healthy. Use your journal for a week to write down everything you eat, the times you eat, and the times you brush your teeth. At the end of a week, write a paragraph evaluating your dental habits. Do you brush and floss after eating? Do you eat a healthful diet?

Other Problems

Other problems of the mouth and teeth can result from poor oral health or heredity. **Gingivitis** (jin·juh·VY·tis) is a common disorder in which *gums become red and swollen and bleed easily.* It is caused by improper dental care, plaque, or misaligned teeth. If gingivitis is untreated, it can lead to a more serious gum disease called *periodontitis* (pehr·ee·oh·dahn·TY·tis).

Another problem called **malocclusion** (ma·luh·KLOO·zhuhn) is *a condition in which the teeth of the upper and lower jaws do not align properly.* It may be caused by heredity, thumb sucking, or tooth loss. Orthodontists treat malocclusion by recommending braces or other appliances to help align teeth.

HEALTH LAB

Attacking Plaque

Introduction: Bacteria-forming plaque constantly lurks in your mouth. It waits for a chance to build up on your teeth and harden. If you do not defend your mouth against this enemy, it will soon destroy your teeth. A toothbrush, toothpaste, and dental floss are weapons you can use to attack plaque. However, you must use these weapons effectively to keep plaque under control.

Objective: This experiment will show you how effective you are as a plaque fighter and how you can improve your plaque-fighting techniques.

Materials and Method: You will need these materials: toothbrush, toothpaste, dental floss, water, mirror, and food coloring. (Note: Instead of the food coloring, you might use disclosing tablets. These are available from a drugstore.)

Brush and floss your teeth the way you normally do. Then mix the food coloring with water and swish it around in your mouth. Spit it out like mouthwash. Now look at your mouth in the mirror. The places where color sticks to your teeth indicate areas that need more brushing and flossing. Continue the procedure until no color appears in your mouth.

Bad breath, or halitosis, is a condition caused by tooth decay, some illnesses, certain foods, or use of tobacco. Good oral hygiene can control bad breath. However, if it is caused by tooth decay, the cure involves treating the underlying problem.

Lesson 2 Review

Using complete sentences, answer the following questions on a separate sheet of paper.

Reviewing Terms and Facts

1. **Explain** How does the sense of taste work?
2. **Vocabulary** Which of the following terms refers to a gum problem: *gingivitis, abscess, malocclusion?* Describe the gum problem.

Thinking Critically

3. **Evaluate** You have a friend who brushes his teeth "in record time." You noticed that he brushes only the outer surfaces of his teeth. He says that he brushes after every meal and, therefore, doesn't have to brush more carefully. What do you think?
4. **Suggest** List ways you can care for your teeth when brushing them is not convenient.

Applying Health Concepts

5. **Personal Health** Create a poster or puppet show that demonstrates the brushing and flossing techniques described in this lesson. Present it to a preschool class.
6. **Personal Health** Visit your dentist. Ask for any brochures or other printed information about caring for your teeth. Bring them to class. Form small groups and discuss them. Could you improve the way you care for your teeth? Write a short paragraph explaining what you have learned.

Observation and Analysis:
What did you learn about your skill in removing plaque from your teeth? Do you need to improve your brushing and flossing techniques? Plaque that you were unable to remove has hardened into tartar. A dentist or dental hygienist will need to scrape the tartar off your teeth.

Remember that the best time to attack plaque is after eating. That's when the bacteria in plaque reacts with sugar to form the acid that destroys enamel and irritates gums. You will never win the war against plaque, but you can do a great deal to keep it from defeating you.

TEEN HEALTH DIGEST

Myths and Realities

Skin Workout

Nothing beats a good workout to make you look and feel your best. Here are some do's and don'ts to help you make sure that your skin gets the most from a workout, too.

Do's

- Do drink plenty of water while working out. This will keep you from dehydrating.
- Do use two towels when working out in a gym. Use one to wipe the sweat off any equipment you use and the other to wipe sweat off your skin. Sweat contains bacteria that can cause pimples.
- Do take a cool-to-warm shower after working out to wash away sweat and reduce skin redness.

Don'ts

- Don't spray water on your face while working out—it will dehydrate your skin.
- Don't wear sweatbands or makeup. Sweatbands trap moisture next to your skin. Either that or makeup will block your pores.
- Don't use harsh deodorant soaps when you shower. They leave your skin too dry, which may lead to acne.

People at Work

Wanted: Orthodontist

Duties: Corrects malocclusions, or misalignment of the upper and lower jaws, with braces or other appliances.

Qualifications: Must be able to work well with your hands, deal with anxious patients, and spend long hours standing.

Preparation: Two to four years of college, four years of dental school, and an additional two or more years of specialized training.

Contact: American Dental Association
211 East Chicago Avenue
Chicago, IL 60611

Try This:

Write down words that describe your appearance. Pretend that you are a good friend describing your looks. Would a friend want to hurt your feelings? Describe honestly everything that is good about the way you look.

HEALTH UPDATE

Your Eyes Have It

Q. I need glasses, and I'll have to wear them when I play sports. What kind of lenses should I get?

A. Memorize these words: *polycarbonate plastic.* That is the only material used to make truly shatterproof eyeglasses. In recent studies, other materials shattered when struck by objects.

Be warned: polycarbonate plastic lenses may cost significantly more than other lenses. However, they are worth the expense for many active teens.

CON$UMER FOCU$

Goo Guide

Here's a guide to products that make your hair behave.

Gels—Gels can give your hair a wet look or a free-spirited, windblown appearance. Gels work best in full-bodied hair. If your hair is thin, gels can leave it limper than ever.

Mousse—The word means "foam" in French. Mousse can work wonders with short, thin hair. Besides shaping your hair, some mousses will color your hair temporarily in natural or vibrant shades.

Styling Lotions—Want "big hair?" Use a styling lotion. Make your hair look thicker with a lotion, brush, and blow dryer.

Hair Spray—Whether you use gel, mousse, or styling lotion, you may want to keep your hair in place with a spritz or two of hair spray.

Try This: *Choose one of the hair care products listed here. Go to a drugstore and compare several different brands of the product. Do their ingredients vary greatly? What about their prices?*

Personal Trainer

The "Body Image"

Do you think that you are too fat? Too skinny? Chances are you're dead wrong!

Most people have faulty "body images." That means that they have a false impression of how they really look. You can be a buddy to your body by putting your body image into proper focus. Try these three steps to improve your body image:

1. **Know Your Strong Suits.** What's best about your appearance? Great hair? Beautiful eyes? Zero in on what you like about your looks.
2. **Get Active.** Exercise every day. Find an activity you love, and go for it. You'll be healthier and learn to appreciate your body.
3. **Visualize Honestly.** This means seeing yourself as others see you—not as you *think* they see you. Always remember: the most attractive quality a person can have is self-confidence.

Lesson 3

Healthy Eyes and Ears

This lesson will help you find answers to questions that teens often ask about their eyes and ears. For example:

- **How can I keep from getting eye infections?**
- **How do I know if I need glasses?**
- **How can loud music damage my ears?**
- **What is the right way to clean my ears?**

Words to Know

lens
cornea
pupil
iris
aqueous humor
sclera
optic nerve
retina
eustachian tube
vestibule
semicircular canals
cochlea
auditory nerve

Your Eyes

Your eyes are your windows to the world. People with full vision gather about 80 percent of their knowledge through their eyes. Your eyes can distinguish shapes, colors, movements, and light.

The Structure of the Eye

In humans, the eye is similar to a camera. It has an opening to let in light and can focus depending on what is being viewed. Your eye is nearly round and rests in a bony socket in your skull. Eyes work together, yet they are independent of one another. Each eye is made of several parts. **Figure 2.12** shows the parts of the eye.

Figure 2.12
The Eye
The eye has many parts, each of which has a specific function.

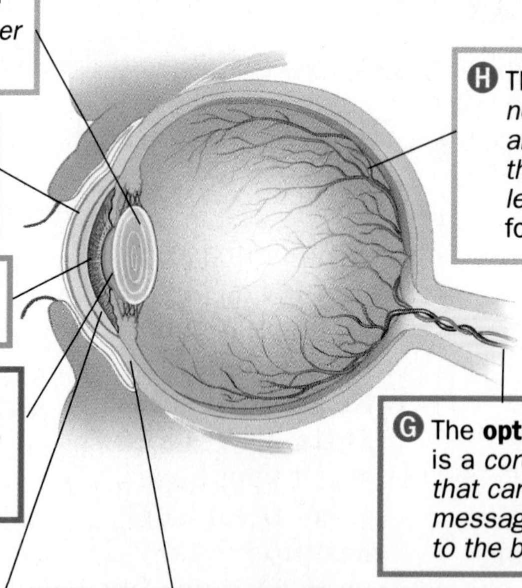

Ⓐ The **lens** (LENZ) is the *structure that allows light to come together in the inner part of the eye.*

Ⓑ The **cornea** (KOR·nee·uh) is a *clear, almost round structure that lets in light.*

Ⓒ The **iris** (EYE·ris) is the *color of the eye seen from the outside.*

Ⓓ The **pupil** (PYOO·puhl) is a *dark opening in the center of the iris.* It controls the amount of light entering the eye.

Ⓔ The **aqueous** (AH·kwee·uhs) **humor** is the *watery fluid between the cornea and lens.* It helps maintain pressure within the eye.

Ⓕ The **sclera** (SKLEHR·uh) is the *tough outer covering*—the white of the eye. It protects the eye.

Ⓖ The **optic** (AHP·tik) **nerve** is a *cord of nerve fibers that carries electrical messages from the retina to the brain.*

Ⓗ The **retina** (RE·tin·uh) is a *network of nerves that absorbs light rays after they pass through the lens.* It is responsible for vision.

How the Eye Sees

The eye does not "see" objects. Instead, it sees the light that objects reflect or give off. **Figure 2.13** shows how the eye sees.

Figure 2.13

How the Eye Sees

Sight is a process that occurs when light enters the eye.

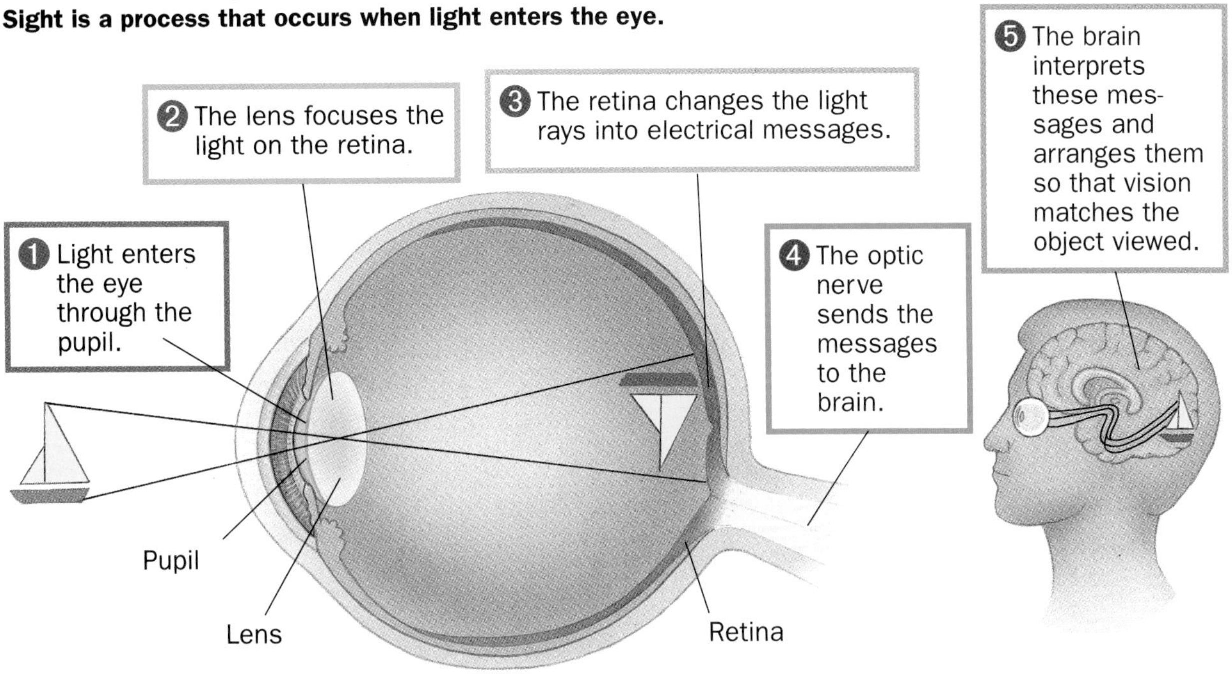

❶ Light enters the eye through the pupil.
❷ The lens focuses the light on the retina.
❸ The retina changes the light rays into electrical messages.
❹ The optic nerve sends the messages to the brain.
❺ The brain interprets these messages and arranges them so that vision matches the object viewed.
Pupil
Lens
Retina

How the Eye Sees Color

Within the retina are millions of nerve endings that contain pigments, or colors. These pigments change when light comes into the eye. Some of these nerve endings distinguish objects in shades of black, white, and gray. These endings are known as rods, and they are used by your eye in dim light. Rods are also used by the eye to perceive motion. Other nerve endings, the cones, distinguish the colors red, blue, and green and their different shadings. Your eyes mix these colors just as you would adjust the color on a television set. Rods and cones send messages to the brain, which interprets the information.

in your journal

Healthy eyes are important to your sense of well-being. Have you ever had an eye problem, such as an eye infection or an eye injury? Perhaps you just had something in your eye, such as an eyelash, that irritated it. How did it affect you and your daily activities? Write a short paragraph about your experience.

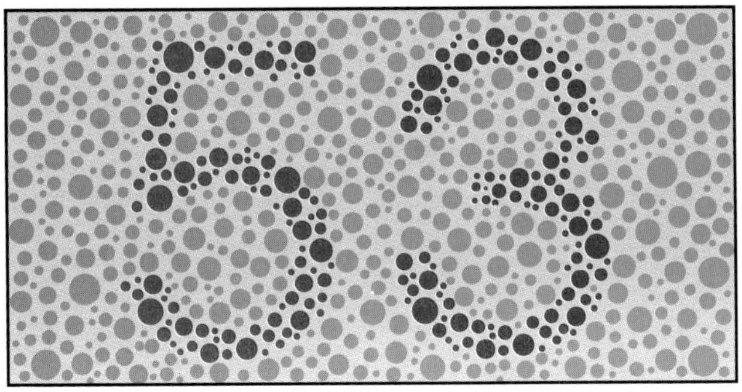

Can you see the number in this box? If so, your color vision is fine. If not, you may be red/green color-blind.

Teen Issues

Which Kind of Shades? ACTIVITY!

Although any sunglasses are better than no sunglasses, some types are more effective in blocking UV rays. If possible, buy ultraviolet-absorbent sunglasses. Look for labels that state "blocks 99 to 100 percent of ultraviolet light." Choose sunglasses that meet the standards of the American National Standards Institute (ANSI). For more information, read recent magazine articles on how to buy sunglasses. Then share your findings with your classmates.

Taking Care of Your Eyes

Your eyes are a vital part of your body. For this reason, you should follow these hints to protect your eyes:

- Read and watch television in a well-lighted room. Shine the light from your reading lamp on what you are reading and not in your eyes. Sit a comfortable distance from the television set.
- Take breaks from using your eyes for long periods of time. Just close your eyes for a short time.
- Avoid exposing your eyes to direct sun or other bright light. When you are outside, wear sunglasses that offer protection from ultraviolet (UV) rays (see **Figure 2.14**). Over the years, exposure to UV rays can damage the lens, retina, and cornea.
- Avoid rubbing your eyes, which irritates or gets dirt in them.
- Keep sharp objects away from your eyes. Beware of pointed sticks, BB guns, and bows and arrows. Avoid throwing sharp items toward another person. Never play with fireworks.
- Wear protective goggles or glasses when engaging in an activity that could cause an eye injury.
- Wear protective equipment when playing such contact sports as baseball and hockey.
- Make sure any towels or washcloths you wipe your eyes with are clean. Diseases such as pinkeye (conjunctivitis) can be spread easily by soiled or dirty towels.
- Be careful not to touch the eyeball when applying eye makeup. Avoid makeup that is old, dirty, or belongs to someone else.

Figure 2.14

What to Look for in Sunglasses

Not all sunglass lenses are created equal. You should keep these differences in mind when purchasing sunglasses.

Ⓐ Sunglasses should block 99 to 100 percent of both UVA and UVB radiation.

Ⓑ Sunglasses should screen out 60 to 92 percent of visible light.

Ⓒ Sunglasses should have gray, green, or brown lenses that are of good quality.

Ⓓ To determine if sunglasses are dark enough, try them on in front of a mirror. You should not be able to see your eyes easily.

Getting an Eye Checkup

An eye checkup by an optometrist (ahp·TAHM·uh·trist) or an ophthalmologist (ahf·thuhl·MAHL·uh·jist) also helps you maintain healthy eyes. If you wear glasses or contact lenses, you should have your eyes checked once a year. If not, an eye examination every two years is sufficient. An eye checkup includes the following:

- **Examination of each eye.** The cornea, pupil, and lens are checked to see if they are clear.
- **Vision check.** Your vision will be determined by the size of the letters you are able to read on the eye chart. If you already wear glasses or contact lenses, your prescription and the fit of your glasses or contact lenses should be checked.
- **Glaucoma check.** Glaucoma (glaw·KOH·muh) is a disease in which the fluid in the eye does not drain properly. Pressure builds up and, if untreated, destroys the optic nerve. Checkups can detect this disease, which is treated with eye drops or pills.
- **Cataract check.** A cataract is a clouding of the lens that may cause some loss of vision. If one is found, an operation can fix the problem. Most cataracts result from aging.

Treating Problems of the Eye

The main job of the eye is to focus images for you. Many people have vision problems, such as farsightedness, nearsightedness, and astigmatism, because their eyes do not focus perfectly. **Figure 2.15** describes these problems, which can be corrected with eyeglasses or contact lenses. The type of lenses suggested by a doctor depends on the condition of your eyes. Today, many people can wear contact lenses, which float on the cornea, to correct a vision problem.

Q&A ?

Eye Exam

Q: I think I have an eye infection. My eyes are full of mucus when I wake up in the morning. They're red and they itch like crazy. What should I do?

A: You need to see an ophthalmologist, a medical doctor who specializes in eye diseases. If you just want to have your vision checked, you could go to an optometrist. An optician, by the way, makes and sells glasses and contact lenses prescribed by an ophthalmologist or an optometrist.

Figure 2.15

Problems of the Eye

Farsightedness, nearsightedness, and astigmatism are common eye problems that involve focusing.

Farsightedness
is a condition in which you can see far objects clearly, but close objects appear blurred. This occurs when the visual images come to a focus behind the retina.

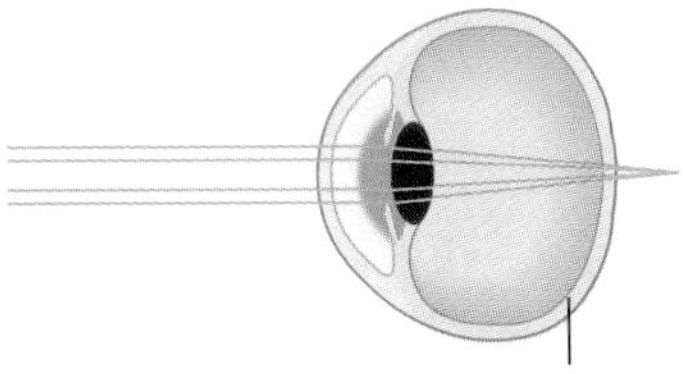

Nearsightedness
is a condition in which you can see close objects clearly, but distant objects appear blurred. It occurs when the visual images come to a focus before they reach the retina.

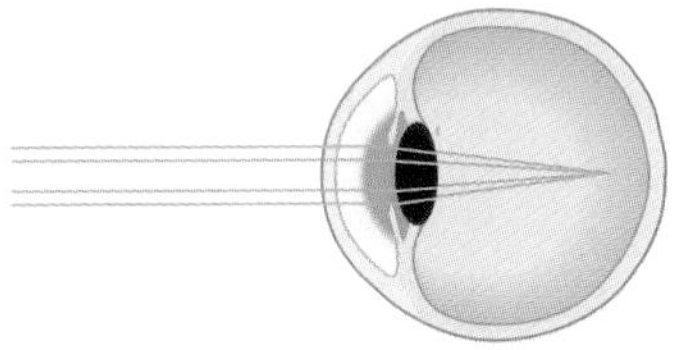

Astigmatism
(uh·STIG·muh·tiz·uhm) is a condition in which images are distorted or blurred because of an irregularly shaped cornea or lens. In this case, visual images do not meet at a single point in the eye.

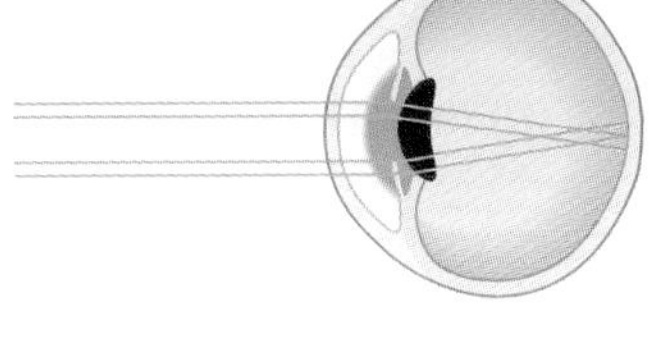

The Structure of the Ear

Your ears allow you to experience the sounds of everyday life. They also help your body keep its balance. Your ears go deep into your skull. **Figure 2.16** shows the parts of the ear.

Figure 2.16

The Ear

The ear has three main parts: the outer ear, the middle ear, and the inner ear.

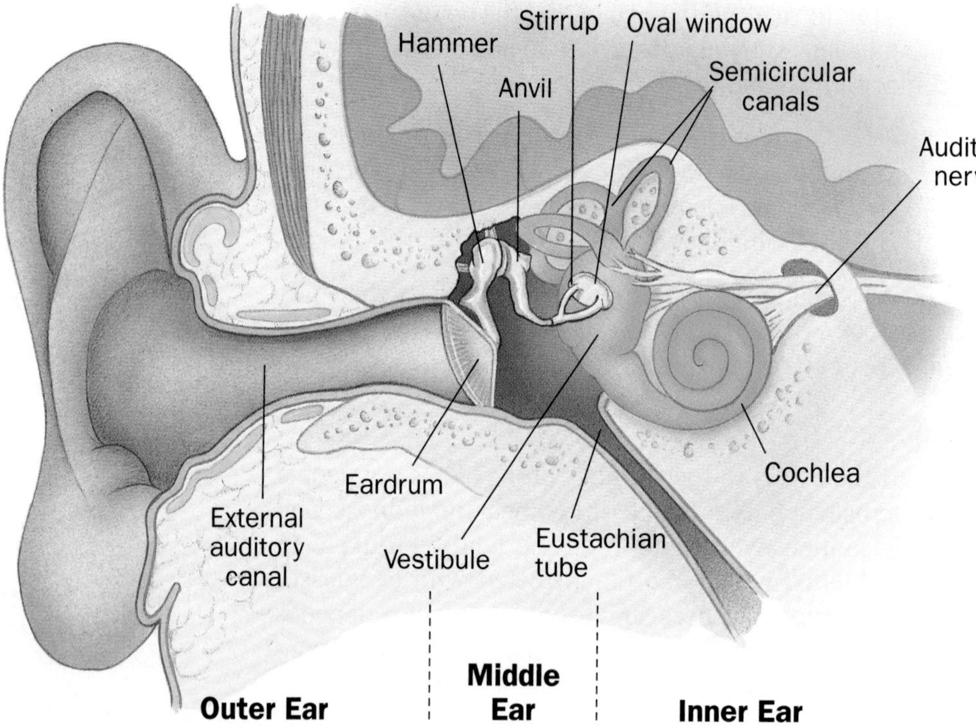

MAKING HEALTHY DECISIONS

Lowering the Boom

Jeff Orner asked Matt to be his partner in a neighborhood yardwork business. Matt gladly accepted the offer. He was looking for a way to make money and to keep busy during the summer.

Jeff provides all the equipment the boys need: rakes, pruning shears, shovels, and boom box. Boom box? Yes, one of those large, portable radios with a four-way speaker system. When the volume is on maximum, the whole neighborhood is alive with the sound of Jeff's music.

Jeff likes to have the radio on full-blast while he works. He says that rap and heavy-metal music energize him and help him work harder. He doesn't think the noise is a problem for his customers, because most of them are not home when he does the yardwork.

Jeff's boom box makes Matt feel uneasy. He learned in health class that all that noise is not good for anyone's ears. On the one hand, Matt would like to tell Jeff to turn the radio off, or at least lower the volume. On the other hand, Matt doesn't want to risk making Jeff angry.

Matt doesn't know what to do. Then he remembers the decision-making process he learned in health class. Matt decides to try it out.

The **eustachian** (you·STAY·shuhn) **tube** *allows air to pass from the nose to the middle ear so the air pressure is equal on both sides of the eardrum.* While not actually part of the middle ear, this tube stretches from the back of the nose to the middle ear.

The inner ear contains three parts. The **vestibule** (VES·ti·byool) is *a baglike structure lined with hair cells that are essential to your hearing.* The **semicircular** (SEM·i·SER·kyuh·ler) **canals** are *responsible for your balance.* The **cochlea** (KOK·lee·uh), *a snail-like structure,* is *made up of three ducts filled with fluid and more than 15,000 hair cells.* The *nerves in the cochlea carry messages to the brain.* These nerves *form a vast network,* which is called the **auditory** (AW·di·tor·ee) **nerve.**

Hearing is a complex process. **Figure 2.17** shows the steps.

Figure 2.17

The Steps in Hearing

Every time your ear hears a sound, these five steps occur.

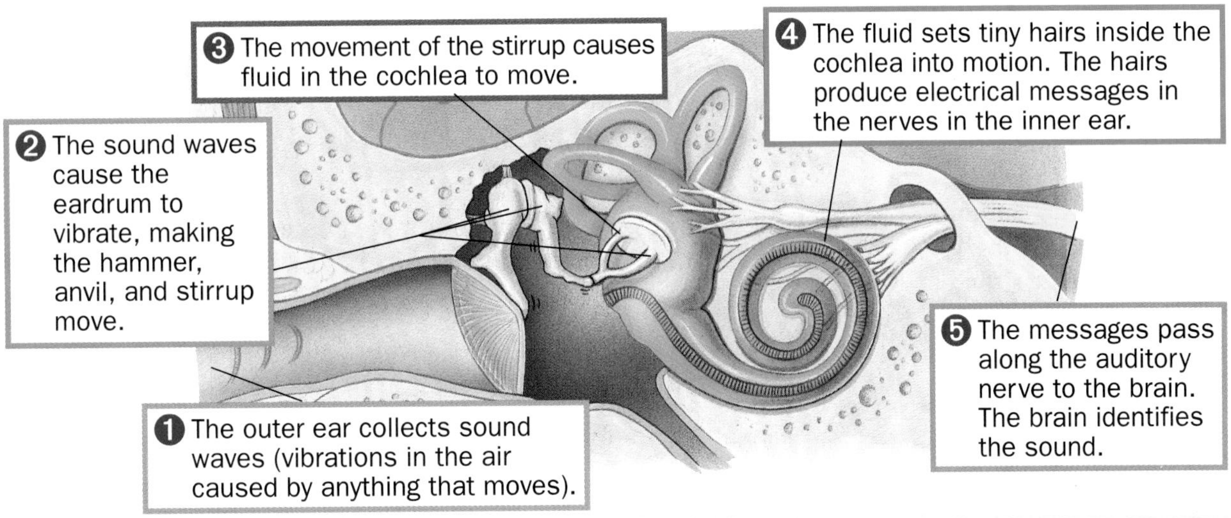

1 The outer ear collects sound waves (vibrations in the air caused by anything that moves).
2 The sound waves cause the eardrum to vibrate, making the hammer, anvil, and stirrup move.
3 The movement of the stirrup causes fluid in the cochlea to move.
4 The fluid sets tiny hairs inside the cochlea into motion. The hairs produce electrical messages in the nerves in the inner ear.
5 The messages pass along the auditory nerve to the brain. The brain identifies the sound.

1. **State the situation**
2. **List the options**
3. **Weigh the possible outcomes**
4. **Consider your values**
5. **Make a decision and act**
6. **Evaluate the decision**

Follow-up Activities

1. Apply the six steps of the decision-making process to Matt's problem. Compare your outcome to the solutions of your classmates.
2. Research the relationship between loud noise and hearing loss so that Matt has some facts to present to Jeff.

Q&A

Motion Sickness

Q: I used to get carsick when I was a young child. Even now I feel dizzy and nauseated when I'm on a boat or on an airplane. What causes motion sickness and what can I do about it?

A: Constant motion causes continuous movement of the fluid in the semicircular canals. As a result, many different messages are sent to the brain at once. After a while, the brain becomes confused and sends distress signals to the body. Medications can control motion sickness. Other solutions include sitting in the front seat, sitting near a window, or focusing on the horizon.

What Is Balance?

When you learned how to ride a bike or roller-skate, you also had to learn how to balance yourself. Balance is the feeling of stability and control over your body. As noted, the semicircular canals in the inner ear control balance.

Fluid and tiny hairs fill the canals. The hairs are connected to nerve cells. When you move or change position, the fluid and hairs move, sending messages to the brain. The brain receives the messages and tells your body how to adjust or change to meet the new situation. Sometimes the canals send too many or too few impulses to the brain, which can result in balance abnormalities. Two such common problems are *vertigo,* or dizziness, and motion sickness.

Taking Care of Your Ears

The ability to hear makes your life more enjoyable. You can take care of your hearing in several ways.

- Avoid loud sounds, which can damage nerve cells in your ears and cause permanent hearing loss. Turn down the volume on your radio and television. Keep the volume low when you use a personal cassette player or other device with speakers close to the ear, or when you are in a closed car.
- Wear hearing protection, such as ear plugs, when you are exposed to loud noises. See **Figure 2.18** for some examples of noises that are dangerous.
- Use a wet washcloth to clean your outer ear. Avoid sticking a cotton swab into your ear canal.
- Keep all sharp objects out of your ears.
- Wear earmuffs or a hat that covers your ears in cold weather to protect the outer ear from frostbite.
- See a doctor if you have an ear infection or other ear problem. Allow a doctor to remove a buildup of wax in your ears.

This teen is taking care of his ears by wearing hearing protection and by turning down the volume of sound.

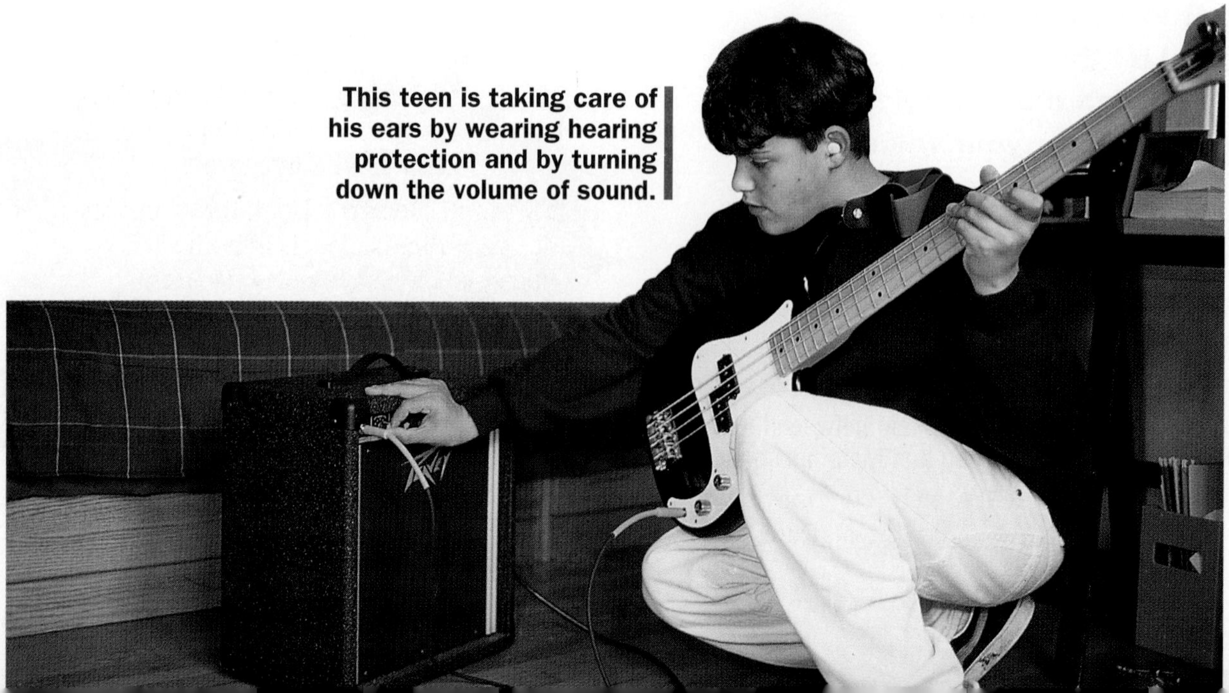

Figure 2.18
Decibel Levels of Common Noises

The decibel measures the loudness of sound. Constant exposure to sounds over 85 decibels can harm your hearing. Serious damage occurs with exposure to sounds over 125 decibels.

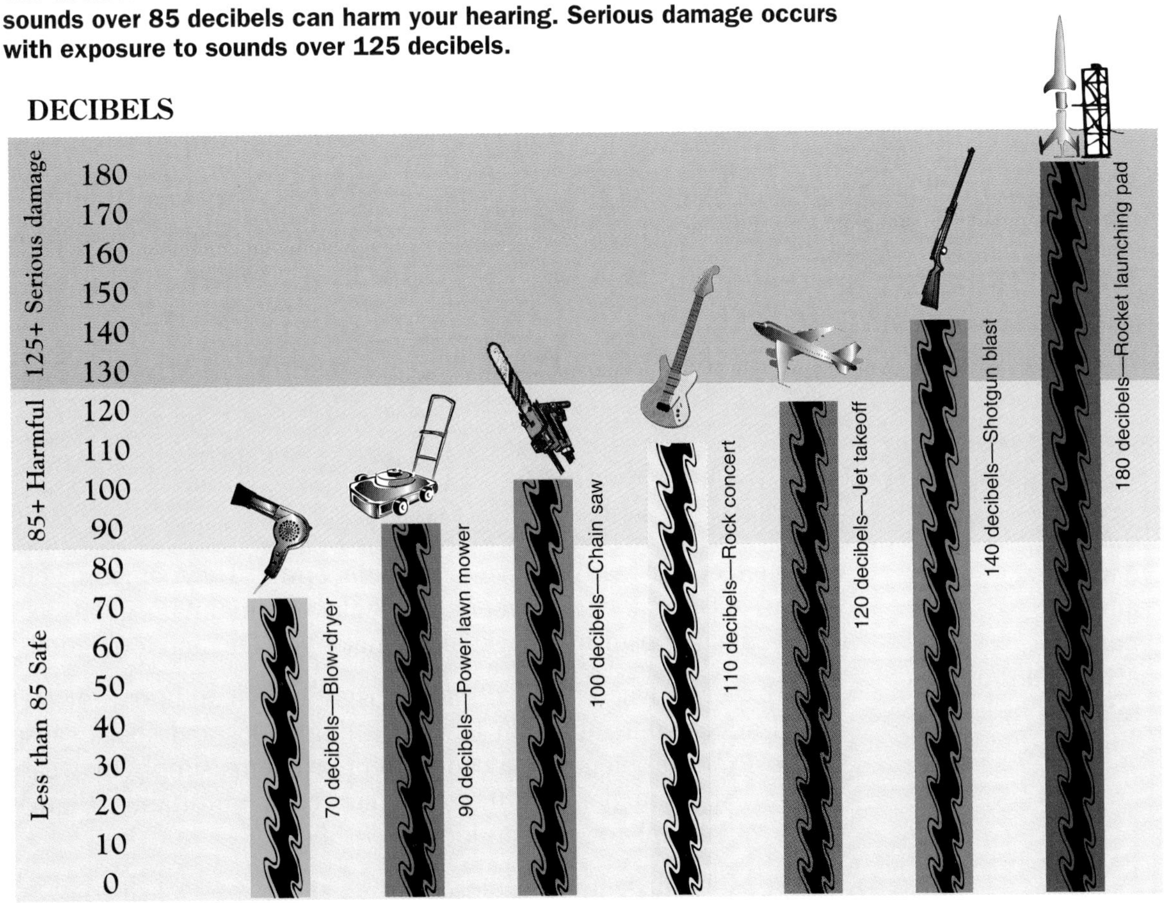

Lesson 3 Review

Using complete sentences, answer the following questions on a separate sheet of paper.

Reviewing Terms and Facts

1. **Vocabulary** Define the term *astigmatism*. Use it in an original sentence.
2. **Recall** How do the semicircular canals in the inner ear help you to maintain balance?

Thinking Critically

3. **Analyze** Your friend Michael never wears sunglasses, even when he is at the beach. He says the sun does not hurt his eyes. What do you think?
4. **Explain** How is the process of hearing like a chain reaction?

Applying Health Concepts

5. **Health of Others** Write a brief guide for teens about protecting their eyes. Display it on a bulletin board.
6. **Personal Health** Look for examples of harmful noise levels at home. Perhaps you have a noisy vacuum cleaner, or a family member has the volume on the television or stereo turned up high. Make a list of the examples you find. Then discuss with family members what can be done to reduce noise pollution in your home. Summarize your findings in a short paragraph.

Lesson 4

Healthy Feet and Posture

This lesson will help you find answers to questions that teens often ask about their feet and posture. For example:

- **How can I select the best-fitting shoes?**
- **Why do I get corns and blisters?**
- **Why do adults always want me to stand up and sit up straight?**

Words to Know

callus
corn
blister
bunion
athlete's foot
fallen arches

Taking Care of Your Feet

Your feet are really marvels of engineering! They support your weight, act as shock absorbers, and help you maintain good posture. Feet and posture go together to make you feel and look good.

However, when shoes do not fit right, they can hurt your feet and affect your mood. In fact, ill-fitting shoes and socks cause most foot problems. You can prevent problems simply by wearing shoes and socks that fit your feet comfortably. **Figure 2.19** explains what to look for in shoes.

Your feet are enclosed inside shoes most of the day, so they perspire. This perspiration can cause the buildup of bacteria. To prevent this buildup, wash between your toes and scrub away dead skin from the heel and ball of your foot. Then be sure to dry your feet thoroughly.

Feet swell during the day. As a result, shoes that fit in the morning may be too tight in the afternoon. If possible, switch to another pair of shoes during the day to relax your feet.

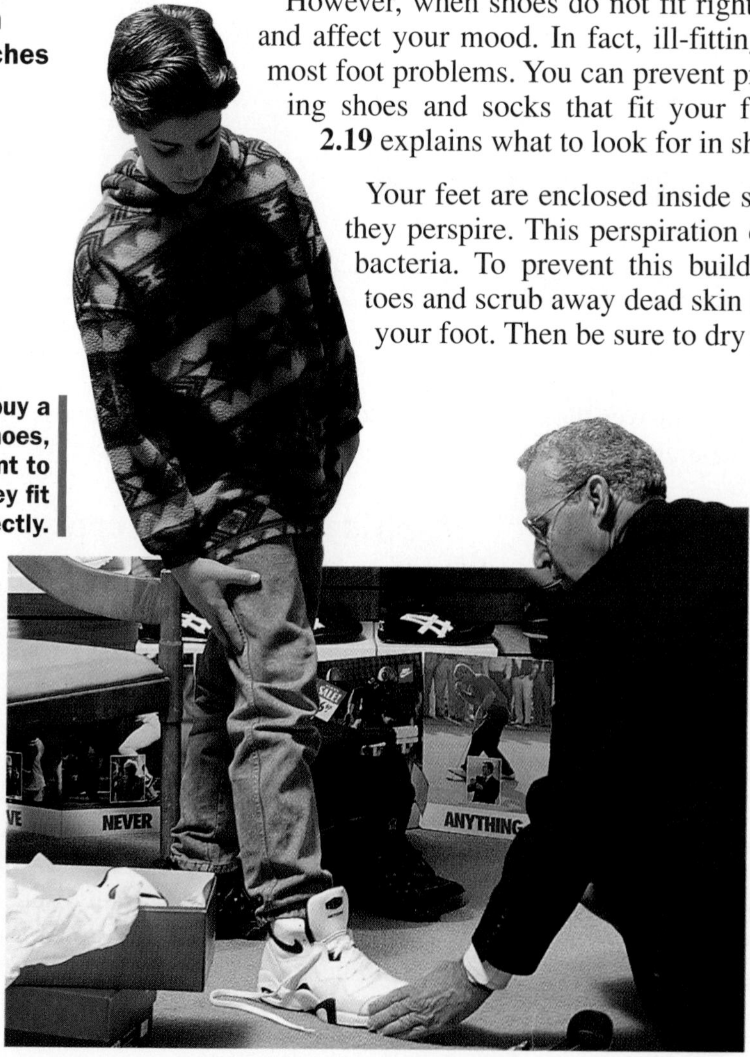

When you buy a new pair of shoes, it is important to make sure they fit correctly.

Some Foot Problems

Proper foot care can eliminate or reduce many of the following uncomfortable foot problems.

- A **callus** is *a hard, thickened part of the skin on the foot.* It results from your foot rubbing against the inside of a shoe. Calluses are often found on the ball of the foot.
- A **corn** is *an overgrowth of the skin at some point on a toe.* It usually appears where the toe rubs against a shoe. Corns can be painful. If they thicken too much, a doctor must cut them away.
- A **blister** is *a fluid-filled pouch on the skin.* Like a corn, a blister is usually caused by an ill-fitting shoe. Blisters usually are painful.
- A **bunion** (BUHN·yuhn) is *an inflammation in the first joint of the big toe.* Tight shoes can cause discomfort.
- **Athlete's foot** is *a problem caused by fungi growing in the warm, damp areas of the foot.* Redness and itching usually appear between the toes. Athlete's foot is contagious. It can be treated with powder or medications.
- **Fallen arches** is another name for *flatness in the bottom of the feet.* Muscles and connective tissues in the arches weaken. The best relief for flat feet is wearing shoes that support your feet well.

in your journal

You have just read about foot care. Do you give your feet as much attention as other parts of your body? Have you ever thought about the important work your feet do for you? How many of your shoes fit your feet well? Write about your foot-care habits in your journal.

Figure 2.19

What to Look for in Shoes

You should look for these qualities in shoes.

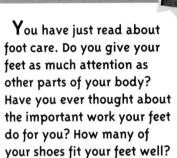

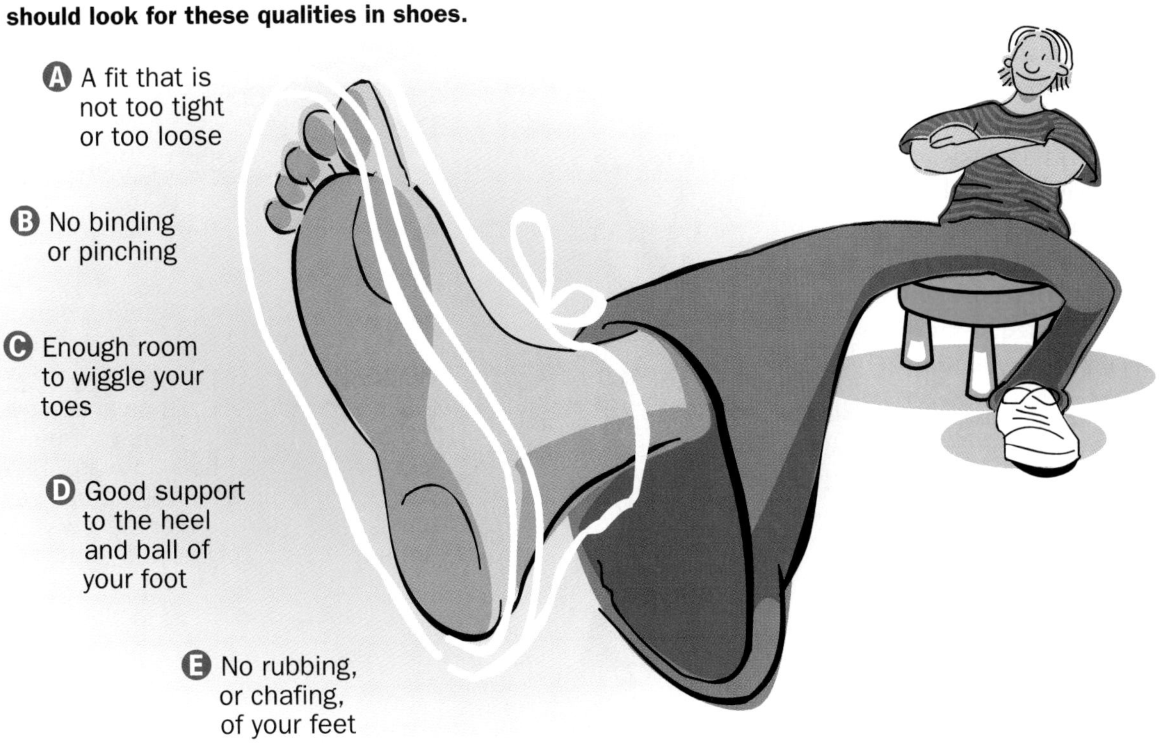
A A fit that is not too tight or too loose
B No binding or pinching
C Enough room to wiggle your toes
D Good support to the heel and ball of your foot
E No rubbing, or chafing, of your feet

How to Build Good Posture

Posture is the way you carry yourself. It involves standing, sitting, and walking. You can work to improve your posture by following the guidelines in **Figure 2.20.**

Figure 2.20

Correct Posture

Your posture has an effect on your overall appearance as well as on your health.

Standing:
Your feet are the key to good posture. Your head, upper body, and lower body should be balanced on the balls of your feet.

Sitting:
Your head and shoulders should be balanced directly over your hips. Make sure your feet are flat on the floor and your back is straight against the chair. Doing this can also help you stay alert.

Teen Issues

Stand Up and Be Counted

Tall teens are sometimes uncomfortable or self-conscious about their height. Because of this, they lean over or slouch, which can harm their posture. Everyone grows at a different rate. If you are a tall teen, stand up and be counted as the special person you are.

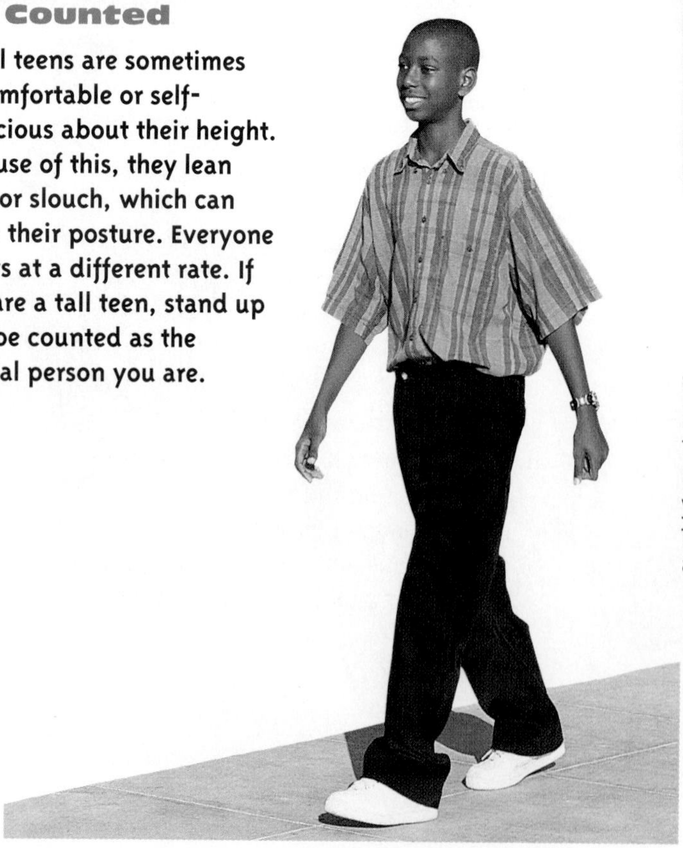

Walking:
Make sure your body is balanced over the balls of your feet. Use your upper legs to move your body forward. Hold your shoulders back in a natural way, tuck in your stomach, and allow your arms to hang freely at your sides.

Here are some easy ways to improve your walking posture.

- Keep your back straight when rising from a chair.
- Keep your feet parallel to one another when walking. Your toes should not point in or out.
- Wear comfortable walking shoes. Walking shoes should be almost flat. High-heeled shoes throw off your balance, creating stress on your ankles and the arches of your feet.

Having Good Posture

Now that you know what good posture is, you have to practice it. Posture can tell as much about you as the appearance of your hair and skin. It can reflect your attitude and affect your health. In fact, poor posture is one of the more common causes of backaches. Good posture is important because it

- helps you move, stand, and sit with ease.
- helps you save energy because you can move more easily.
- allows your internal organs to function properly because you are not hunched over.
- distributes pressure so it does not put added stress on your back.
- helps your bones and muscles grow properly.
- makes your figure and body build look good.

in your journal

How's your posture? Do you make an effort to stand, sit, and walk tall? Think of someone you know who has good posture. What difference does good posture make in the person's attitude and appearance? Write your observations in your journal.

Review Lesson 4

Using complete sentences, answer the following questions on a separate sheet of paper.

Reviewing Terms and Facts

1. **Describe** What are the characteristics of comfortable shoes?
2. **Vocabulary** What is the difference between a *callus*, a *corn*, and a *bunion?*

Thinking Critically

3. **Synthesize** Your friend wants to buy a pair of shoes that are just the right style, just the right price, and just a little tight in the toes. What advice would you give your friend? Why?
4. **Persuade** What advice might you give a friend who stoops because he or she is self-conscious about being tall?

Applying Health Concepts

5. **Personal Health** Along with a classmate, evaluate one another's posture. Then help each other practice the tips for good standing, sitting, and walking posture. Write a short paragraph about what you learned about your posture and any changes you have made to improve it.
6. **Consumer Health** Look through catalogs and magazines for pictures of shoes that can lead to back pain or injury. Cut out and paste the pictures on poster paper. Title your poster.

Chapter 2 Review

Chapter Summary

- **Lesson 1** Proper care of skin, hair, and nails is essential for a healthy appearance.
- **Lesson 2** Good dental habits and a nutritious diet can prevent tooth decay. Flossing removes plaque the toothbrush cannot reach. Regular dental checkups also help keep teeth healthy.
- **Lesson 3** Your eyes and ears provide information about the world around you. To keep your eyes healthy, have regular eye exams, and protect yourself from bright sunlight. To keep your ears healthy, keep them clean, and avoid loud noises.
- **Lesson 4** Your feet are the key to good posture. Properly fitted shoes are an important part of foot care.

Reviewing Key Terms and Concepts

Using complete sentences, answer the following questions on a separate sheet of paper.

Lesson 1

1. Identify the following parts of your skin: *epidermis, dermis, subcutaneous layer, melanin, pores.*
2. Name some common hair and scalp problems.

Lesson 2

3. What are the parts of a tooth and the different types of tissue it contains?
4. Explain the process of tooth decay.

Lesson 3

5. List the parts of the eye.
6. List the parts of the ear.

Lesson 4

7. What are four problems that can be avoided by wearing shoes that fit well?
8. What causes athlete's foot?

Thinking Critically

Using complete sentences, answer the following questions on a separate sheet of paper.

9. **Hypothesize** Why do you think acne is common among teens?
10. **Analyze** Why is it important to floss your teeth even if you brush after every meal?
11. **Give Examples** What might be some symptoms of eye problems?
12. **Suggest** What are some ways to improve your posture while sitting, standing, and walking?

Chapter 2 Review

Your Action Plan

Choose a personal grooming task that you would like to improve. This will be your long-term goal. Look back over the entries you made in your private journal for this chapter for ideas.

Step 1 Write down your long-term goal. For example, perhaps you want to improve the health of your teeth and gums. Getting into the habit of flossing your teeth each day will be your short-term goal.

Step 2 To help you meet your long-term goal, it's a good idea to create a system for checking on your progress. For example, you might put a calendar in your bathroom and make a tally mark on the calendar every time you floss your teeth.

Step 3 After a while, flossing will become a natural part of your day and you will no longer need the calendar.

Once you have reached your long-term goal, reward yourself.

In Your Home and Community

1. **Health of Others** Conduct a dental clinic for younger students. Teach them how to clean their teeth well. Demonstrate brushing and flossing techniques. Show them the proper type of toothbrush to use.
2. **Community Resources** Identify sources of noise pollution in your community. For example, freeway noise or noise from a nearby airport may be a source of concern for neighborhood residents. Keep informed of the issues involved by reading newspaper accounts. Contact community and government groups to see what action they might be taking to reduce noise levels. If possible, join in the action.

Building Your Portfolio

1. **Teen Models** Pretend that you are the director of an agency that hires teen models. You look for teens who radiate good health as well as good looks. Write an advertisement that describes the type of teen you are seeking. Add the advertisement to your portfolio.
2. **Hygiene Tips** Proper care of the skin, teeth, eyes, and ears begins in childhood. Look for newspaper and magazine articles and brochures that inform parents and other caregivers about hygiene and proper care for children. Add these resources to your portfolio. If possible, use the information to teach a good health habit to a young child.
3. **Personal Assessment** Look through all the activities and projects you did for this chapter. Choose one or two that you would like to include in your portfolio.

Chapter 3

Being Mentally and Emotionally Healthy

Student Expectations

After reading this chapter, you should be able to:

1. **Explain how thoughts, feelings, and behavior affect mental and emotional health.**
2. **Describe healthy ways to meet emotional needs and express emotions.**
3. **Identify the dangers of stress, and list healthy ways to cope with it.**
4. **Recognize signs of mental health problems.**
5. **Name types and sources of help for mental and emotional problems.**

Teen Chat Group

Lucy: Hello?

Maureen: Hi, Lucy. Are you busy?

Lucy: Oh, hi, Maureen. Can I call you back in an hour? I'm studying for the big algebra test.

Maureen: You're kidding me! That test isn't until next week!

Lucy: I know, but I don't want to leave studying until the last minute.

Maureen: Well, you can't spend *all* your time studying. You have to have some time to have fun, or you'll just get all stressed out.

Lucy: That's why I figure I need to pace myself. If I study a little bit every day, I'll still have time to relax. Doing well in this class is really important to me.

Maureen: Gee, I haven't even started studying yet. Do you think I could study with you tomorrow?

Lucy: Sure—that way we can help each other. I'll call you when I'm done, okay?

in your journal

Read the dialogue on this page. How do you balance your responsibilities and manage stress? Start your private journal entries on mental and emotional health by answering these questions:

- How do you feel about yourself in general? What do you see as your greatest strengths and weaknesses?
- How well do you think you deal with stress?
- Have you ever been concerned about someone's mental and emotional health? If so, what action did you take?

When you reach the end of the chapter, you will use your journal entries to make an action plan.

Lesson 1

What Is Mental and Emotional Health?

This lesson will help you find answers to questions that teens often ask about mental and emotional health. For example:

- **What is mental and emotional health?**
- **How can I tell if I am mentally and emotionally healthy?**
- **How can my thoughts and behavior affect the way I feel about myself?**

Words to Know

- mental and emotional health
- values
- personality
- self-concept
- self-esteem

Mental and Emotional Health

Just as you need to get along with other people and have a healthy body for overall good health, you also need a healthy mind and healthy emotions, or feelings. **Mental and emotional health** means *the ability to accept yourself and others, adapt to and cope with emotions, and deal with the problems and challenges you meet in life.*

There are several signs you can look for in yourself and others to give you a more complete sense of what it means to be mentally and emotionally healthy. The following are some signs of good mental and emotional health.

When you are mentally and emotionally healthy, you tend to learn from your mistakes rather than see them as signs of failure.

- You see yourself and life in general in positive ways.
- You face life's challenges with confidence.

- You can motivate yourself to achieve long-term goals.
- You recognize and manage your feelings.
- You focus on your strengths.
- You accept honest criticism and learn from your mistakes.

Benefits of Good Mental and Emotional Health

Your mental and emotional health affects every aspect of your life. It influences your happiness, your success in school and in life, and your relationships. When you are mentally healthy, you tend to do what you need to do to be physically and socially healthy. Therefore, your mental health can determine how well you keep your overall health in balance.

What Makes You Who You Are?

As you grow and mature, you are learning more about who you are. You are finding out about your physical and mental abilities and what you do well. You are finding out what makes you unique and who you like to be with. You are discovering *the beliefs and ideas that are important to you,* or what your **values** are. Your family has the most influence on your values, but your friends also influence them.

Your Personality

Your personality has a big impact on your mental and emotional health. Your **personality** is *the unique combination of feelings, thoughts, and behavior that makes you different from everyone else.* Your personality determines in part how you react to problems, new situations, and other events. How do you react to meeting new people, for example? Do you feel confident and excited or unsure of yourself and afraid?

There are several factors that shape your personality. Some aspects of your personality are inherited. Some aspects have been shaped by your environment. Your environment includes your family and friends as well as your school and neighborhood. You cannot control what you inherit, and you can only partly control your environment. However, you *can* change how you behave and how you think.

Your Self-Concept

Your **self-concept** is *the view you have of the unique person you are.* It is basically how you see yourself. How would you describe yourself? Would you describe your strengths as well as your weaknesses? Sometimes teens tend to focus on or exaggerate their flaws and do not focus enough on their strengths. This can lead to an unnecessarily negative self-concept.

interNET CONNECTION

Discover the keys to success, high self-esteem, and healthy stress management with help from the Glencoe Web site.

http://www.glencoe.com/sec/health

Cultural Connections

Culture and Personality

Anthropologists have long been aware that culture plays an important role in shaping personality. All children learn ways of behaving, thinking, and feeling that are appropriate for their culture. Thus, people from different cultures may have different personality traits that are deeply ingrained. For example, in the Asian-American culture, traits such as respectfulness and cooperation tend to be reinforced. Being aware of such basic differences in personality can help you to understand people from other cultures.

in your journal

Almost all people have elements of their personalities that they would like to change. Think of a behavior that you would like to change. Perhaps you'd like to get more exercise or get along better with your parents. Imagine working hard to bring about the change, receiving encouragement for your efforts, and finally accomplishing your goal. In your private journal, describe how you would feel. How do you think your success would make you feel about working to change other behavior?

Self-Esteem

Self-esteem, *the way you feel about yourself, or how you value yourself,* is closely related to self-concept. Often a negative self-concept can lead to low self-esteem. For example, you might forget about how well you swim and see yourself as poor at all sports because you do not play soccer well. This unrealistic picture of yourself could negatively affect your self-esteem. People with low self-esteem generally do not feel good about themselves. They tend to avoid new challenges and worry about what they think of as their faults.

How do you feel when you think about the kind of person you are? Do you like and respect yourself? Do you accept yourself for who you are? Do you feel you are competent in some areas? Do you feel confident to try new things even if it means you may sometimes fail? If you do, you have high self-esteem. **Figure 3.1** shows how high self-esteem leads to success.

Figure 3.1

How High Self-Esteem Leads to Success

If you have high self-esteem, you are more likely to try hard and succeed. This, in turn, reinforces your self-esteem and leads you to make efforts in new areas.

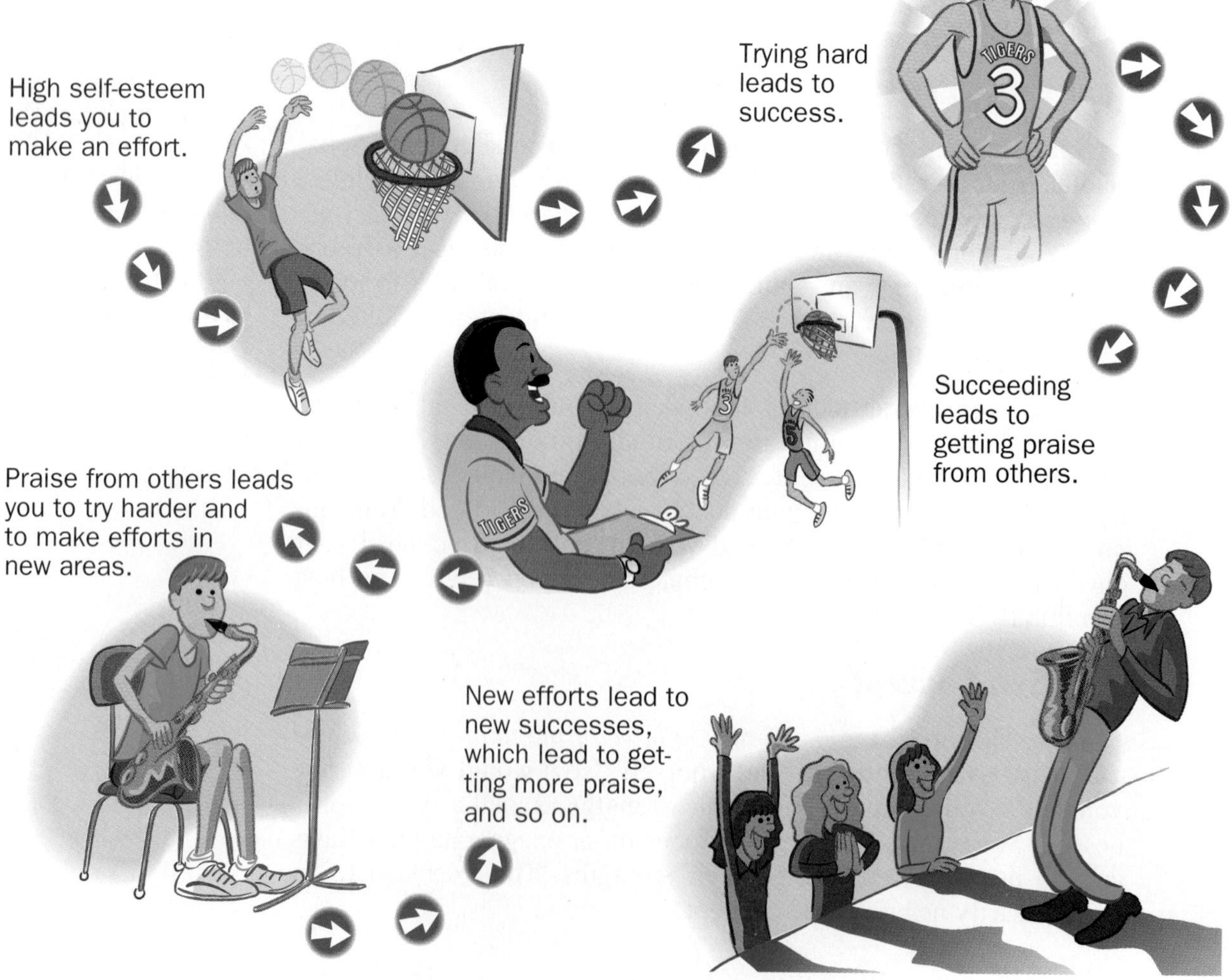
High self-esteem leads you to make an effort.
Trying hard leads to success.
TIGERS 3
Succeeding leads to getting praise from others.
TIGERS
Praise from others leads you to try harder and to make efforts in new areas.
New efforts lead to new successes, which lead to getting more praise, and so on.

The Road to Mental and Emotional Health

The benefits of high self-esteem and being mentally and emotionally healthy are clear. However, like your physical health, your mental and emotional health has its ups and downs. You may not always feel confident and positive about life's challenges. You may feel unsure of how to handle new situations. You can learn skills, however, to help you improve your self-esteem and your level of mental and emotional health.

Motivating Yourself

Being able to motivate yourself is the key to success in almost everything you do in life. It means setting long-term goals and working toward achieving them, even if you must give up something in the short term. For example, you might set the long-term goal of playing in your state youth orchestra. Because you are motivated, you will spend time practicing. Sometimes you may give up going to a movie with a friend or doing something else you enjoy to help you achieve your goal.

Having hope about the future, or being optimistic, can help keep you motivated. If you believe in yourself and think you can get into the orchestra, you will be more likely to work hard and make practicing a priority. Achieving your goal will, in turn, motivate you to keep trying hard, and will lead to more success in the future.

Knowing and Managing Your Feelings

Managing your feelings is an important part of your mental and emotional health. For example, suppose you find yourself snapping at friends for no apparent reason. You may realize that you are anxious because you have a track meet coming up. Recognizing what is causing your anxiety will help you manage your interactions with your friends.

This teen has a strong motivation to succeed and has practiced hard to become a competent diver.

Teen Issues

If You Don't Try, You Can't Succeed

Any time you try something new there is a chance that you will make a mistake. Be willing to take risks; that is the only way you will get the chance to succeed.

There are some who believe that only those with luck or superior talent can achieve success. This is simply not true. Did you know that Michael Jordan was cut from the varsity team when he was a sophomore in high school? Where would Michael be now if he had been too afraid to try again?

Success comes from having the courage to try new things—despite the risk. Success also comes to those who continue to try even when they have failed before—they simply learn from their mistakes and do better the next time.

Did You Know?

The Strength of Superman ACTIVITY!

In 1995, Christopher Reeve, best known for playing Superman in four movies, was paralyzed after a fall from a horse. Since the accident, Reeve's new focus is spinal cord injury research, rehabilitation, and insurance policy reform. He has used his fame as his strength, attracting national attention to a problem that has long been overlooked.

Changing Your Thoughts and Behavior

Your thoughts and behavior have a strong influence on your mental and emotional health. If you see life's challenges as obstacles you can overcome, your mental health will be affected in a positive way. If, however, you feel that you cannot cope with the challenges, your mental health will be affected in a negative way. How do you handle challenges? You can begin by thinking positively. Thinking this way, in turn, will influence the way you feel. These relationships are illustrated in **Figure 3.2.**

Improving Your Self-Esteem

By improving your self-esteem, you are changing the way you think about yourself and what you can and cannot do. There are several things you can do to give your self-esteem a boost. These include focusing on your strengths, accepting criticism constructively, and learning from your mistakes.

Focusing on Your Strengths

Seeing yourself in a more positive way can help improve your self-esteem. Start by making a list of all your strengths and of all your successes. Perhaps you are good at playing tennis or a musical instrument. Working to improve your skills can also improve your self-esteem. Set reasonable, measurable goals, and reward yourself when you achieve them.

Figure 3.2

The Role of Thoughts, Feelings, and Behavior in Mental and Emotional Health

You can improve your mental health by overcoming your fears and thinking positively about new situations. How did this teen's behavior influence his way of viewing new situations?

Behavior Todd fears new situations but attends his first school dance anyway.

Thoughts He has a good time and realizes there was nothing to be afraid of. He then thinks about new situations in a new way.

Feelings Knowing he can handle new situations changes how he feels about them. He feels less afraid and takes on more new situations.

Accepting Criticism Constructively

Another way to improve your self-esteem is to learn how to handle criticism. You can benefit from criticism if you

- focus on the problem itself and not on how the criticism makes you feel.
- listen carefully to the criticism and ask questions if you are unsure what is meant by it.
- ask yourself if the behavior is something you can change and think about how to do it.

This teen had his bike stolen when he left it out unlocked. He is now careful to lock up his bike or put it away when he is not using it. His parents have come to trust him to be more responsible, and their trust reinforces his self-confidence.

Learning from Your Mistakes

You also can improve your self-esteem by learning from your mistakes. This means taking responsibility for your actions and admitting to yourself and others when you are wrong. It also means seeing mistakes as opportunities to grow and improve.

One mistake teens sometimes make is staying up too late. As a result, they may oversleep or have to get through the day feeling tired or sluggish.

Review Lesson 1

Using complete sentences, answer the following questions on a separate sheet of paper.

Reviewing Terms and Facts

1. **List** Identify three signs of good mental and emotional health.
2. **Vocabulary** Define the term *personality.*
3. **Restate** Explain the difference between *self-concept* and *self-esteem.*

Thinking Critically

4. **Infer** How can your values affect your mental and emotional health? Give an example.
5. **Analyze** Explain why high self-esteem tends to reinforce itself.

Applying Health Concepts

6. **Personal Health** With a classmate, role-play how a person with low self-esteem might respond to a critical comment. Then role-play how a person with high self-esteem might respond to the same comment. Switch roles and repeat the exercise. Describe how each role made you feel.
7. **Health of Others** Create an illustrated brochure or poster that gives teens specific, practical tips for increasing their self-esteem.

Lesson 2

Handling Emotions in Healthy Ways

This lesson will help you find answers to questions that teens often ask about handling emotions. For example:

- **How can I express my emotions in healthy ways?**
- **How can I satisfy my emotional needs in healthy ways?**
- **How can I use refusal skills to avoid high-risk behavior?**

Words to Know

emotions
hormones
emotional needs
abstinence
refusal skills

Teen Issues

Gloom Busters ACTIVITY!

Everyone feels down sometimes. The next time the gloom sets in, try one of these tips.

- Do something social—call a friend.
- Do something physical—take a walk, a bike ride, or a swim.
- Do something to calm your mind. Take a few minutes to relax—listen to a favorite CD, write, draw, or read.

What Are Emotions?

Your **emotions** are your *feelings, such as happiness, love, sadness, jealousy, anger, and fear.* They are a natural part of life. Emotions play a major part in your mental and emotional health. They can influence everything you do, including how you behave. For example, if you feel happy when you are with your friends, you probably will want to spend time with them. Likewise, fear of failure may keep you from trying out for a sports team.

During your teen years you may experience physical changes that trigger emotional reactions. One minute you feel happy, the next minute you feel down for no apparent reason. These sudden emotional shifts are due to **hormones** (HOR·mohnz)—*chemical substances, produced by glands, that control many body functions.* Sudden emotional shifts are a natural part of adolescence.

Kinds of Emotions

Some people believe that certain emotions are bad or wrong. They may think that it is wrong to feel anger, for example, or they may be ashamed of feeling afraid. In reality, emotions are neither good nor bad, right nor wrong. They are part of being human.

How emotions are expressed or handled is another matter. Sometimes people handle their emotions in ways that are hurtful to themselves or others. People with good mental health seek healthy, responsible ways of managing their emotions.

An important step in learning how to manage your emotions is learning to be aware of them. **Figure 3.3** shows basic emotions that all people feel at some point in their lives. When have you felt each of these emotions?

Figure 3.3

Basic Human Emotions

People do not always agree on what such emotions as love and joy mean. However, people everywhere in the world would recognize the basic emotions expressed in these photographs.

Happiness is a state of well-being. When you are happy, the world looks brighter, you can make decisions more quickly, and you feel better about things in general. You are also more likely to be considerate to other people.

Sadness is a normal, healthy reaction to unhappy events, such as a pet dying or a good friend moving away. When you are sad, you may feel more easily discouraged and less energetic.

Fear is an emotion that can help keep you safe from danger. However, some fears, such as the fear of failure, may keep you from doing the things you want or need to do.

Anger is a common reaction to being insulted or attacked. It is an emotion that everyone feels from time to time. Lashing out or suppressing anger can be unhealthy ways of coping with this emotion, but you can learn healthy ways to express your anger.

Expressing Emotions in Healthy Ways

People express emotions in different ways. People often learn how to express emotions from watching how those close to them express their emotions. In some families, people are very open and talk frequently about feelings. Some other families do not say much but communicate how they feel by smiling when they are pleased, or by slamming doors, remaining silent, or crying when they are displeased. Some people have difficulty dealing with such emotions as envy, guilt, fear, and anger. Everyone, however, can learn how to deal with and express emotions in healthy ways.

Communicating How You Feel

Good communication is a two-way process. It means speaking in a way that helps others understand you. It also involves being a good listener. Good communication skills can help you let others know what you are thinking and feeling. These skills can also help you understand other people's feelings.

Did You Know?

Feelings from Faces

People feeling the same emotion have such similar facial expressions that a computer system can read emotions by the facial expression. A camera converts smiles, frowns, and other expressions into a form the computer can analyze. In experiments, when people made deliberate expressions of emotion, the computer read the right emotions most of the time.

Managing Fear and Anxiety

Have you ever felt anxious before taking a test, giving a report, or speaking in front of others? When you are anxious or fearful, you are apt to take shorter breaths, your heart beats faster, and your muscles tense. Anxiety can help you do better on a test by releasing energy to help you work harder. However, fear and anxiety can also cause you to lose sleep or even to panic. Some ways in which you can cope with anxious feelings include talking about how you feel, learning to laugh at yourself, using relaxation techniques, and planning ahead.

Expressing Anger

It is normal to feel angry at times, but anger is one of the emotions that are sometimes expressed in unhealthy ways. Some people yell or hit when they are angry; others hold their anger inside. There are healthier ways to express anger. Try these steps when you feel angry.

- Take a deep breath and calm down.
- Focus on exactly what made you angry.
- Think of words to express your true feelings.
- Tell the other person how you feel.

in your journal

In your private journal, describe one healthy way in which you currently meet each of the three emotional needs. Then describe another way to meet each need. For example, you might meet your need to belong by participating in family activities. Another way to meet that need might be to join a club at school. Describe how you could incorporate each of the new ways of meeting your needs into your life.

Understanding Your Emotional Needs

There are certain things that your body must have. They are called physical needs, and they include food, water, and sleep. You also have **emotional needs.** These are *needs that affect your feelings and sense of well-being.* Your basic emotional needs include the following:

- **The need to feel worthwhile.** You need to feel that you make a difference in the world—that you are making a contribution. When you help another person do something or you come up with a useful idea, you are contributing.
- **The need to love and be loved.** You need to feel that you are cared for and that you are special in someone's eyes. You also need to feel that way about others.
- **The need to belong.** You need to know that others like you and accept you as part of a group. The first group that you belong to is probably your family.

Meeting Emotional Needs in Healthy Ways

People with good mental and emotional health try to meet their emotional needs in healthy ways. For example, they may offer to help someone without being asked, or ask a friend how her day went and really listen to the answer. They may do volunteer work for a good cause, or start a club and do their best to make it a success. Meeting emotional needs in healthy ways means making the choice to engage in healthy behavior. It also means saying no to unhealthy behavior.

Practicing Abstinence

You can meet your need to belong without practicing risky behavior.

Some teens may try to fill their emotional needs to be loved and to belong by engaging in behavior that puts them at risk. Meeting emotional needs in healthy ways means practicing **abstinence** (AB·sti·nuhns), which is *refusing to participate in sexual activity* before marriage. Remember that choosing abstinence means that you have made a commitment to yourself to maintain a high level of health. You are choosing to avoid dangerous situations, including the risk of getting pregnant or contracting a sexually transmitted disease. You are choosing to feel better about yourself and have more self-respect by saying no to behavior that goes against your values.

Sometimes others will pressure you to participate in high-risk or unhealthy behavior. This pressure will be easier to deal with if you practice your refusal skills. **Refusal skills** are *ways of communicating that help you say no effectively.* These skills make it easier to practice abstinence when you are under pressure. Ways to say no effectively include

- looking the other person directly in the eye and using a firm, confident voice when you say no.
- giving reasons for saying no. You do not have to give reasons, but doing so will help you convince others that you are serious.
- avoiding situations and people that pressure you to say yes. Choose friends who also practice abstinence.

Review Lesson 2

Using complete sentences, answer the following questions on a separate sheet of paper.

Reviewing Terms and Facts

1. **Identify** List three basic emotional needs.
2. **Vocabulary** Define the term *abstinence.*
3. **List** Name three refusal skills that can help you say no.

Thinking Critically

4. **Contrast** Explain the difference between *emotions* and *emotional needs.*
5. **Synthesize** Give two examples of how emotions can influence behavior.

Applying Health Concepts

6. **Health of Others** Write a public service announcement or make a poster showing how teens can use refusal skills to say no to alcohol or other drugs.

TEEN HEALTH DIGEST

Sports and Recreation

A Champ with a Sense of Balance

"A" not only stands for abstinence, it also stands for All-Star and all-around good guy. What's more, it stands for A. C. Green, Phoenix Suns basketball player, NBA All-Star, and founder of Athletes for Abstinence. Members of this group include David Robinson, giant on the NBA courts, and Barry Sanders, one of the most elusive running backs in NFL history. The group's message is: Choose abstinence from sex until marriage. In addition to being good role models by choosing abstinence themselves, group members have made a video promoting abstinence, called "It Ain't Worth It."

People at Work

Family Counselor

Interview with Dr. Grace Ritchy, family counselor

Q. How do you help the teens who come to see you?

A. I help them find healthy ways to face their problems, so they won't turn to alcohol or other drugs.

Q. Why do you see teens with their families rather than as individuals?

A. An important part of my work is helping teens and their parents communicate effectively with each other. I can't do that if I only talk to individuals.

Q. What did you study to become a family counselor?

A. I earned a doctoral degree in psychology and then did a year of supervised counseling.

Personal Trainer

Feeling Exercise Burnout? Try Cross-Training

Are you bored with your exercise program? Working out less as a result? Why don't you try cross-training, or combining two or more different sports or exercise activities? For example, if you are bored with running every day, you might alternate weight lifting with running throughout the week. You could also substitute bicycling for running on some days. People who cross-train usually have a healthy self-image—so it improves your mental as well as your physical health.

Try This: *Design a cross-training program for yourself that combines two or more different sports or workouts to work muscles throughout the body and provide vigorous exercise. Put your program into practice.*

HEALTH UPDATE

Stress Shrinks the Brain

Learn to deal with stress before your brain shrinks! Using a new way of seeing the brain, called magnetic resonance imaging or MRI, researchers have found significant shrinkage in the brains of people with a history of severe stress or major depression. The part of the brain affected is the hippocampus, which is important for memory and learning. When the hippocampus shrinks, there may be memory loss and problems in reasoning. The shrinkage may be due to continuous high levels of stress hormones, including adrenaline.

CON$UMER FOCU$

"KEN" Can Help

Got a problem? Help may be a phone call or mouse-click away.

The National Mental Health Service Knowledge Exchange Network (KEN) provides free public information and referrals for mental health services. KEN health information specialists answer callers' questions or refer them to federal, state, or local resources for more information.

Lesson 3

Stress and Your Health

This lesson will help you find answers to questions that teens often ask about stress. For example:

- **What causes stress?**
- **How does my body respond to stress?**
- **What can I do to manage the stress in my life?**

Words to Know

stress
distress
stressor
adrenaline
fatigue
physical fatigue
psychological fatigue
defense mechanism

What Is Stress?

No doubt you have heard people say, "I'm stressed out," or "I never have enough time to do everything I need to do." Chances are, you have said something like it yourself. You may think of stress as bad. However, that is not necessarily true. Rather, it is a process that may be positive or negative. **Stress** is *your physical response to change* and a normal part of being alive.

When stress helps you cope with change, it is positive. For example, when your body responds to a dangerous situation by speeding up your heart so that you can either run away or put up a fight, it is positive. Sometimes stress will motivate you to do your best to meet a challenge. Imagine having the last shot in a close basketball game or giving an oral report to your class. Stress in situations such as these can be positive. Positive stress can make your life more exciting.

Sometimes stress can have unhealthy effects. You may lose sleep because you are worried about memorizing your part for a play, or you may forget to return a library book because you and a friend argued. *Stress that interferes with your life and makes you unhappy or sick* is called **distress.** This is what most people mean when they use the word *stress.*

The teen years are a time of many changes. Your body is changing rapidly, and you are gaining new responsibilities and forming new relationships. You may become involved with so many new activities that you need to manage your time more carefully. Because of such changes, teens are often under a lot of stress. This lesson will help you learn how to handle stress in healthy ways.

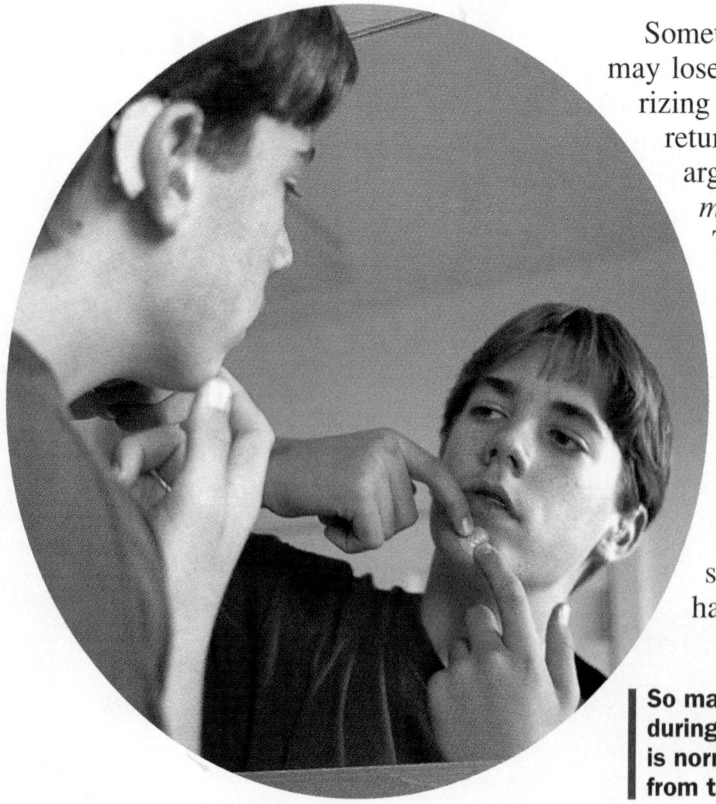

So many changes occur during your teens that it is normal to feel stressed from time to time.

What Causes Stress?

To handle stress, you need to know what causes it. *Anything that causes stress* is called a **stressor.** Not all stressors are the same for everyone. One person may find speaking in front of a group very stressful, whereas another person may enjoy being in the spotlight. **Figure 3.4** shows some of the things that cause most people stress.

Figure 3.4

Common Stressors

People react to stressors in different ways. What is extremely stressful to one person may not affect another person in quite the same way. How would you rate the following events on a scale from *somewhat* to *extremely* stressful?

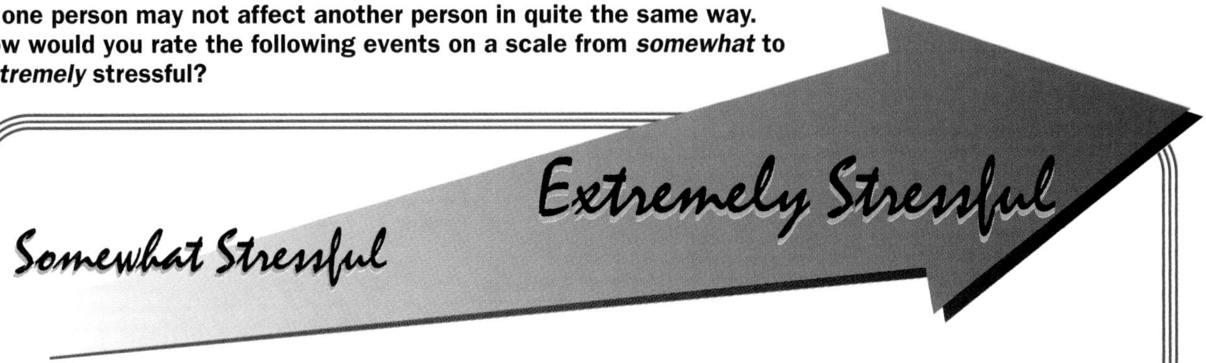

- Arguing with a brother or sister
- Going to a new school
- Getting glasses or braces
- Moving to a new home

- Arguing with a parent
- Parent losing a job
- Worry over weight, height, or acne
- Getting in trouble in school

- Family member having a serious illness
- Loss or death of a pet
- Quitting or being suspended from school
- Starting to use alcohol or drugs

- Death of a close family member or friend
- Divorce or separation of parents
- Failing a subject or grade at school
- Getting arrested

We all have stressors in everyday life—missing a bus, being criticized, doing poorly on a test. When stressors add up, you feel the physical effects of stress.

Physical Effects of Stress

Experiencing a lot of stress can cause your body to react as though you are in danger. It releases **adrenaline** (uh·DRE·nuhl·in), *a hormone that prepares your body either to fight or to flee.* Adrenaline gives you a jolt of energy, speeds up your heart, widens your air passages, tightens your muscles, and sharpens your senses. It can give people the ability to perform amazing physical feats that would otherwise be impossible.

Too much stress can lead to **fatigue,** or *exhaustion.* Repeated spurts of adrenaline can cause **physical fatigue,** or *aches and pains and extreme tiredness of the body.* You need to rest and reduce your stress before it leads to more significant health problems. Over time, repeated stress can cause headaches, high blood pressure, digestive disorders, and lowered resistance to infection.

Q&A

Symptoms of Stress

Q: How can I tell if I am under too much stress?

A: If you regularly have any of these symptoms, you may be overly stressed:

- Difficulty sleeping
- Difficulty concentrating
- Frequent headaches
- Feeling tense, irritable, and overwhelmed
- Overeating or losing your appetite

Teen Issues

Time Management

ACTIVITY!

Constantly feeling as though there are not enough hours in the day is an indication of stress. Follow these tips to manage your time better and lower your level of stress.

- Do not try to be superhuman; pare down your activities so that your schedule is realistic.
- Allow time for interruptions and unexpected events.
- Learn how to say no to people. Use your time for activities that are important to you.
- Set priorities for using your time, and do the most important things first.

Too much stress can also cause **psychological** (sy·kuh·LAH·ji·kuhl) **fatigue,** or *feelings of tiredness caused by your mental and emotional state.* Worrying or feeling upset can wear you out as much as physical activity can. Activities that take your mind off the stress can energize you.

Ways to Cope

People cope with stress in many different ways. Some ways of coping are more effective than others because they help you maintain overall good health. Ways of coping include using a defense mechanism; relaxing and exercising; thinking positively; and planning ahead.

Defense Mechanisms

A **defense mechanism** (duh·FENS·MEK·uh·nizm) is *a mental strategy you use to cope with stress.* Although they are not usually aware of it, people use

I didn't get my homework done because you were making too much noise in the house!

When you make someone else responsible for your own mistakes, you are using a defense mechanism called projection. Why do you think projection can be an unhealthy way to cope with stress?

HEALTH LAB

Thinking and Stress

Introduction: Sometimes you can reduce the stress you feel by relaxing and thinking about a happy time or place. You can actually lower your blood pressure and soothe tense muscles by concentrating on happy thoughts.

Objective: During the next week, make a note of times when you are feeling especially stressed. Follow the directions in the next section to see if this method can help you relieve your stress.

Materials and Method: Each time you feel stressed, take a few minutes to imagine a relaxing scene. You may use the following scene or think of one of your own. You might imagine yourself on a beach near the ocean, hiking in the mountains, or any other place where you would feel good about your surroundings. Keep notes on why you were feeling stressed and how you felt before and after imagining a relaxing scene.

Scene: You are sitting or lying down comfortably in an open field or park surrounded by tall trees. A flower garden is nearby. You can smell the flowers—it is the most wonderful fragrance you have ever experienced. You can hear birds chirping and see squirrels running. The sky is deep blue and accented with small, fluffy clouds. The sun feels like many different defense mechanisms. Defense mechanisms are normal and can provide temporary relief from stress. Many defense mechanisms, however, can be unhealthy when they are used as long-term solutions to stress. Defense mechanisms include:

- **Rationalization**—making excuses instead of admitting mistakes. A teen rationalizes that she did poorly on a test because it was too hard, not because she did not study.
- **Denial**—not recognizing an unpleasant reality. A teen refuses to accept the fact that his dad is dying of cancer.
- **Repression**—blocking out stressful thoughts. A teen blocks out thoughts about going to the dentist and misses her appointment.
- **Projection**—blaming someone or something else. A teen tells himself that his low grade on a test was not his fault—the teacher just does not like him.
- **Regression**—behaving as you did in an earlier, less stressful time. A teen whose parents are divorcing asks them to tuck her into bed.
- **Displacement**—shifting emotions from one person or situation to another. A teen who is angry with his mother transfers his anger to his sister and starts a fight with her.

Some defense mechanisms can be unhealthy. If you depend on them too much, you may avoid dealing directly with the cause of the stress. The following defense mechanisms, however, can be healthy ways of coping with stress:

- **Sublimation**—transforming unacceptable behaviors into acceptable ones. Instead of yelling when she gets angry, a teen lets off steam by running around the block.
- **Substitution**—replacing an unattainable goal with a realistic one. A lanky teen goes out for track instead of gymnastics.

in Your Journal

After reading about the defense mechanisms listed here, keep a log of each time you use one of them to cope with stress. After each incident, describe how using the defense mechanism made you or others feel. What other ways might you have chosen to cope with stress?

a warm embrace, and an occasional breeze keeps you from feeling too warm. You take long, slow breaths, savoring the scene.

Observations and Analysis: Write a comparison of how you felt before and how you felt after thinking about a relaxing scene. Could you feel your muscles relax? Did your breathing slow down? Share your observations and analysis with a group of classmates. Discuss together which methods of dealing with stress each person finds most effective.

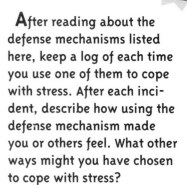

Your Total Health

Stress and Rest

When you have not had enough rest, you begin the day with stress. When you are overly tired, situations that would normally be minor annoyances can seem like major problems. Stress can add up throughout the day until everything is stressful. Be sure to get the right amount of sleep, and start each day right.

Relaxation and Exercise

Relaxation and exercise are both healthy ways to cope with stress. Exercise can bring about physical and emotional changes that can offset the negative physical effects of stress and give you a better outlook. Some of these changes are shown in **Figure 3.5.** There are many different ways to exercise—walking, bicycling, and shooting baskets, to name a few. Often such activities also give you a chance to socialize and have fun, both good stress busters themselves.

Relaxation can give you a better perspective on your problems, slow your heart and lower your blood pressure, and make you feel less tense and anxious. The next time you feel tense, you might try one of the following ways to relax.

- Slow your breathing. Take deep, even breaths for five minutes.
- Shut your eyes and imagine a beautiful scene. For five minutes, think about all the details of your scene—the sights, sounds, and smells.
- Tighten and then relax one group of muscles at a time. Start at your toes, and work your way up to your head.
- Do something that is fun for a while. Read a book, watch a video, listen to your favorite music, or play a game.

Positive Self-Talk and Planning Ahead

How do you react when you have to give an oral report, lose your homework, or other stressful events occur? Do you feel anxious, unhappy, even sick to your stomach? Perhaps you know

Figure 3.5

Exercise and Stress

Exercise can have both physical and psychological benefits when you are under stress.

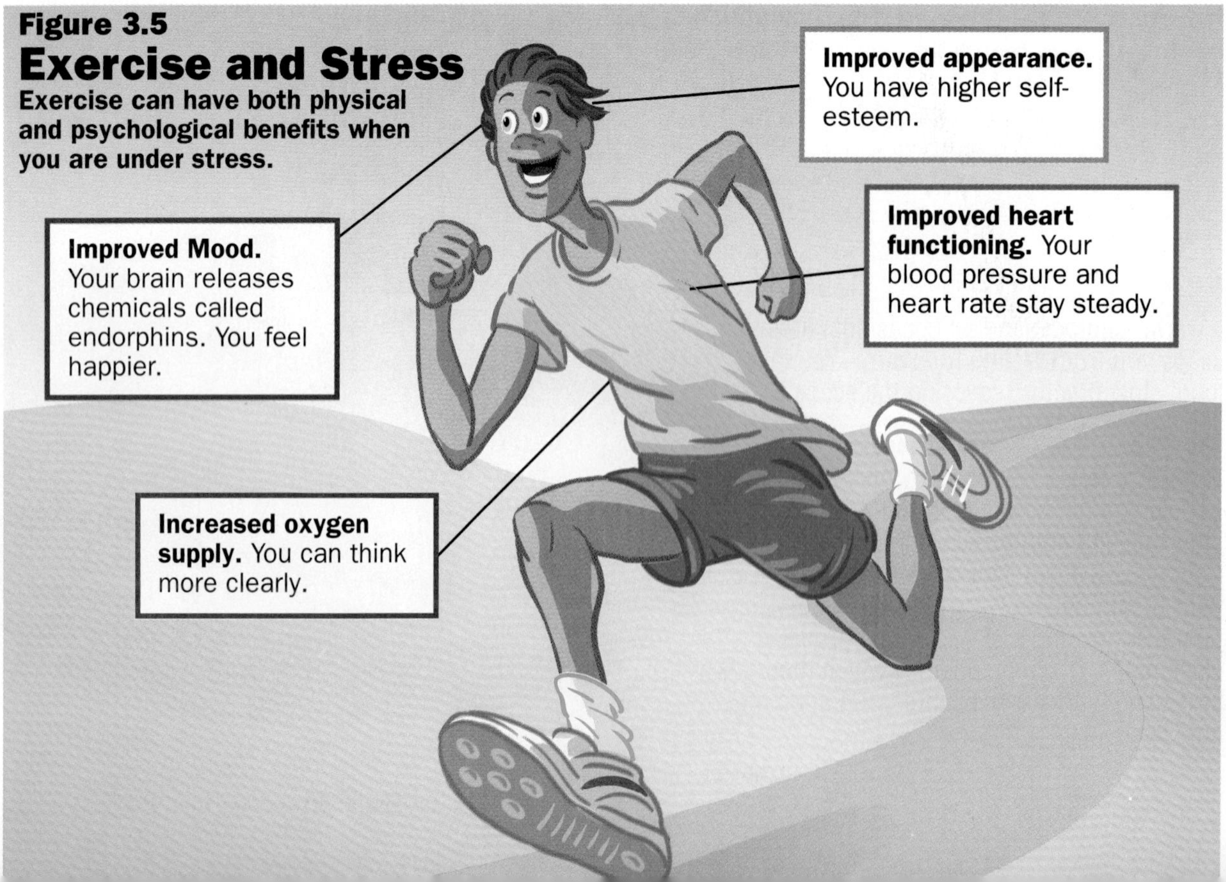

Improved appearance. You have higher self-esteem.
Improved Mood. Your brain releases chemicals called endorphins. You feel happier.
Improved heart functioning. Your blood pressure and heart rate stay steady.
Increased oxygen supply. You can think more clearly.

someone who never seems to be bothered by stress. Why do people react so differently?

The way you react to stressful events depends a lot on your thoughts, or what you tell yourself about the events. If you tell yourself that you will make a fool of yourself whenever you have an oral report to give, you will feel badly stressed. You can help yourself feel less stressed if you plan ahead and prepare well. As you get up to speak, practice positive self-talk by telling yourself you will do well.

The next time you feel stressed, try to identify the exact cause. Is it your own attitude? Can you reduce your stress by planning ahead? By taking positive action and thinking of stress as a welcome challenge rather than as a stumbling block, you will learn to meet and overcome life's stresses.

Did You Know?

Crying Is Good for You

Crying may have evolved as a way to help humans cope with stress. Tears contain a unique combination of chemicals, including hormones that resemble endorphins (brain chemicals that help relieve stress). When tears are absorbed into the nasal cavity, the chemicals can travel to the brain. This may explain why most people feel better after they cry.

This teen used to worry that he would miss every time he had to do a place kick, but he has learned to think instead about succeeding. How do you think his way of thinking has helped him handle stress?

Lesson 3 Review

Using complete sentences, answer the following questions on a separate sheet of paper.

Reviewing Terms and Facts

1. **Distinguish** Explain the difference between *stress* and *distress*.
2. **Vocabulary** Define the term *stressor*, and give three examples.
3. **Restate** What are some physical effects that can result from too much stress?
4. **Identify** Name three defense mechanisms that can be unhealthy ways of coping with stress.

Thinking Critically

5. **Analyze** Explain how stress can save your life as well as put your health at risk.
6. **Suggest** Give an example of how the defense mechanism projection can be an unhealthy way to cope with stress.
7. **Deduce** How do you think that high self-esteem can help you cope with stress?

Applying Health Concepts

8. **Health of Others** Make a videotape that demonstrates how positive thoughts about stressful events can decrease stress and increase self-esteem.

Lesson 4

Mental Health Problems

This lesson will help you find answers to questions that teens often ask about mental health problems. For example:

- **How do I know when mental health problems are serious?**
- **What are the signs of major depression?**
- **What can be done about mental health problems?**
- **How can I help a friend who may be thinking of suicide?**

Words to Know

anxiety disorder
phobia
mood disorder
major depression
schizophrenia
suicide

Kinds of Mental Health Problems

Everyone faces problems and feels stress. The majority of people manage to cope with their problems and stresses and maintain good mental and emotional health. However, at least one out of five people cannot cope. These people seek help handling their mental health problems.

Two of the most common mental health problems are anxiety disorders and mood disorders. People with these disorders are troubled by worries, fears, or other emotions that disrupt their mental and emotional well-being. There are many other types of disorders that can affect mental and emotional health, including schizophrenia, which is a more serious mental disorder.

Anxiety Disorders

Everyone worries sometimes, and most people have healthy fears that keep them safe. However, more than 20 million Americans have unreasonable fears or worries. These people have **anxiety disorders,** *mental disorders characterized by extreme feelings of anxiety or fear.* **Figure 3.6** shows common anxiety disorders and their symptoms.

Figure 3.6
Anxiety Disorders

Disorders	Symptoms
General Anxiety Disorder	vague sense of anxiety constant worries about everything
Obsessive-Compulsive Disorder	extreme specific worries about dangers such as germs rituals like washing hands over and over and over repeated unwelcome thoughts
Phobia (FOH·bee·uh)	*extreme, irrational fears that restrict lifestyle*
Panic Disorder	physical symptoms such as racing heart and shortness of breath feelings of losing control fear of dying

Mood Disorders

People who feel sad when life is good, or happy for no apparent reason, may suffer from a mood disorder. A **mood disorder** is *when a person experiences extreme or prolonged emotions or mood changes that he or she cannot control.* Mood disorders include manic-depressive disorder (also called bipolar disorder) and depression. People with manic-depressive disorder have dramatic mood swings. They go from feeling upbeat and energetic to feeling down in the dumps. These mood swings are much more extreme than the normal mood swings experienced by many teens.

Depression

What doctors call **major depression** (di·PRE·shuhn) is *a mood disorder in which people lose interest in life and no longer find enjoyment in anything they do.* People who suffer from major depression feel more than just sad. They have a feeling of despair that they cannot shake.

Many professionals believe that major depression is caused by a chemical disorder in the brain. Some people inherit a tendency to develop major depression. Other people have anxieties or phobias that isolate them, and they are therefore more likely to develop major depression. In addition, some people have episodes of major depression brought on by major stresses that they face.

Major depression is especially common in teens: as many as four out of ten teens may suffer from major depression from time to time. This is an alarming number, because many people who are depressed abuse drugs or try to harm themselves. Major depression can be treated, so it is important to be aware of its warning signs. These signs are shown in **Figure 3.7.**

Cultural Connections

Body and Soul ACTIVITY!

People in all cultures experience mental health problems, but they may express them in different ways. For example, instead of talking about how depressed they are, people from some Latin American cultures might talk about "losing their souls," a condition called "susto," when mourning the death of someone close. How do you think such cultural differences might affect the diagnosis of depression and other mental disorders?

Figure 3.7

Warning Signs of Depression

People who have most of these symptoms of depression every day for two weeks or longer should seek professional help.

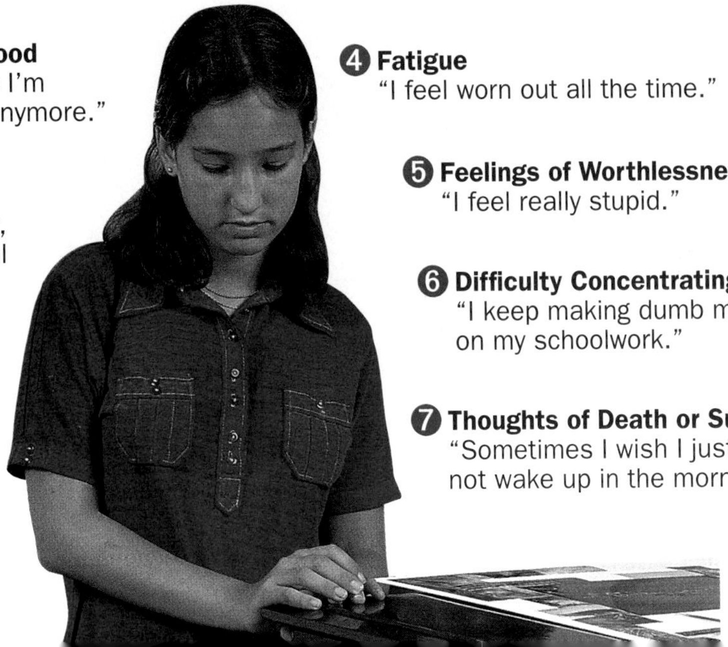

1 Depressed Mood
"It seems like I'm never happy anymore."

2 Change in Appetite
"I've always loved to eat, but food does not appeal to me at all lately."

3 Change in Sleep Patterns
"I've always slept like a log, but lately I keep waking up in the middle of the night."

4 Fatigue
"I feel worn out all the time."

5 Feelings of Worthlessness
"I feel really stupid."

6 Difficulty Concentrating
"I keep making dumb mistakes on my schoolwork."

7 Thoughts of Death or Suicide
"Sometimes I wish I just would not wake up in the morning at all."

Did You Know?

The Brain and Schizophrenia

People who have schizophrenia often hear or see things that other people do not. Now scientists think that they know why. A recent study determined that people with schizophrenia respond to sounds and other signals in the environment differently than those without the disorder. Because of a defect in their brains, they are unable to filter out irrelevant sounds and distractions. This defect leads them to hallucinate and makes it impossible for them to concentrate. The defect is one of several risk factors that work together to bring on the disorder.

Schizophrenia

Schizophrenia (skit·zoh·FREE·nee·uh) is a *severe mental disorder in which people lose contact with reality.* They see or hear things that are not actually there, or have hallucinations. They may also have delusions, or faulty beliefs. People who have schizophrenia are separated from what is really happening, but believe that they are experiencing something real. For example, they may believe that they are someone else, such as a figure from history. Often they behave in very unusual ways. They may remain silent and unmoving for hours on end, or they may talk and behave very agitatedly.

Schizophrenia is believed to be caused by a number of different factors. The disorder tends to run in families, suggesting that heredity plays a part. Environmental influences, such as mental or physical abuse, infection at birth, and even stress, may also contribute to the development of the disease. Schizophrenia usually first affects people in their late teens or early twenties. Although there is no cure, treatment often helps control the symptoms and enables people who have schizophrenia to function more normally. New medications help many such people function well.

Suicide

Suicide, or *killing oneself on purpose,* is a major problem in the United States today, especially among teens. Every year as many as half a million teens and young adults attempt suicide, and more than 5,000 actually succeed in taking their own lives. Suicide is now the third leading cause of death for this age group.

Most people who commit suicide are suffering from major depression. People at greatest risk are those who have tried to kill themselves before. Drugs or alcohol may be another reason.

Teens often help each other when they are feeling sad or depressed. If you have a friend who you think has overwhelming problems, urge him or her to talk to a concerned family member, adult, or a professional counselor.

Warning Signs of Suicide

You may know someone who has said things like, "The world would be better off without me," or "I'd be better off dead." Most people who commit suicide talk about it beforehand, so anyone who talks about suicide should be taken seriously.

Besides talking about suicide, there are several other warning signs. At first, people who are thinking about suicide may show signs of depression. Once they decide to take their own lives, they may feel better for a while and may start giving away possessions they value. People who reach this point are in great danger. The warning signs of suicide include

- dropping usual activities and friends.
- acting lethargic and hopeless.
- letting personal appearance go.
- taking unnecessary risks.
- having a sudden improvement in mood.
- giving away prized possessions.

Students often realize before parents or teachers when a friend is suicidal. If you suspect that someone you know is thinking of suicide, be sure to talk to a responsible adult about your fears. It is important to get help before it is too late.

What To Do

For most people, a suicide attempt is a cry for help. Often people don't really want to die, but they feel so much emotional pain that they do not see any other alternative. They need to be convinced that even though the pain seems unbearable, it will not last forever. They need to realize that with treatment and the support of loved ones, they will feel better in time. If anyone you know talks about suicide:

- Try to react calmly and let the person talk out his or her feelings.
- Never make comments like "You can't be serious" or "You'd never have the nerve."
- Offer comfort and support. Tell the person how important she or he is to you and to other people.
- Never promise to keep a friend's talk of suicide secret. Tell an adult as soon as you can.
- Above all else, urge the person to get help.

Teen Issues

When Is Depression Normal?

It is perfectly normal to feel sad or even depressed for some time after a major upset in your life, such as the divorce of parents or the death of a close friend. If the depression is very deep and prolonged, you should seek help from a professional. Depression for which there is no apparent cause also usually requires treatment.

Things to Remember When You're Down

Everyone has bad times and feels depressed now and then. Remind yourself of the following when problems become difficult to handle.

- You are not alone. There are many others who feel just as you do.
- You, more than anyone else, control the way you feel.
- Take care of the basics. Get enough sleep, eat regular and healthful meals, and get lots of exercise. Believe it or not, taking care of your physical needs will improve your state of mind.
- Avoid alcohol and other drugs, even caffeine. They will only add to the problem.
- It isn't what happens to you that counts as much as how you *view* what happens to you.

If you feel your problems are overwhelming, it is important to seek out the help of family members. People with mental and emotional problems, especially those who may be considering suicide, need the love and support that family members can offer.

Family members can be a source of help and support for teens who are having difficulty handling their problems.

LIFE SKILLS

Thinking Positively

Thinking positively means sending yourself positive messages. Positive messages can improve your mental and emotional health by giving you hope and helping you feel good about yourself. Learn how to change your negative thoughts into more positive ones by studying the following examples. Then put what you learn into practice by doing the follow-up activity.

- Negative message: "I always mess up."
  Positive message: "I will study hard and do better next time."
- Negative message: "I am too serious."
  Positive message: "I am very sincere."
- Negative message: "I am too tall."
  Positive message: "I have athletic potential."
- Negative message: "I can't do anything right."
  Positive message: "I may not be able to bat, but I'm a great runner."
- Negative message: "I am stupid."
  Positive message: "Everybody makes mistakes, but I try to learn from them."

Review

Lesson 4

Using complete sentences, answer the following questions on a separate sheet of paper.

Reviewing Terms and Facts

1. **Vocabulary** Define *phobia.*
2. **List** Name two types of mood disorders.
3. **Identify** What are the symptoms of schizophrenia?
4. **Describe** What should you do if you know someone who is thinking about committing suicide?

Thinking Critically

5. **Describe** Explain how a phobia could negatively affect your lifestyle.
6. **Restate** Tell why major depression is a serious mental disorder.
7. **Depict** Describe the behavior of someone who is thinking about committing suicide.

Applying Health Concepts

8. **Health of Others** Imagine that you have a friend who always seems to see life in a negative way and therefore is often depressed. Write a letter telling the friend what advice you have for him or her.

► Negative message: "I am such a jerk."
Positive message: "Nobody is perfect, but I keep trying to improve."

Follow-Up Activity

Write a list of negative thoughts that you have had about yourself or that you have heard other people express about themselves. Rewrite each thought so that it is positive. How do you think such positive messages would make you feel? Practice sending yourself positive messages in the future.

Lesson 5

Where to Go for Help

This lesson will help you find answers to questions that teens often ask about getting help for mental health problems. For example:

- **How do I know if my problems are serious enough to ask for help?**
- **Who can help me if they are?**

Words to Know

side effect
psychiatrist
psychologist

in your journal

Everyone needs support from time to time. In your journal, make a list of people you feel you can confide in, and describe a problem you might take to each person.

Knowing When to Go for Help

If you really are unhappy or can't seem to cope, you should talk to an adult. Tell a parent, teacher, school counselor, or other trusted adult how you are feeling. Whether it is fear, anger, or shame that is making you miserable, try to describe exactly how you feel.

Talking about your thoughts and feelings can be difficult, especially if you feel frightened, angry, or ashamed. Everybody needs help with emotional problems from time to time. Sometimes all you need to do is let someone know you need help. Needing help is nothing to be ashamed of, but it is a shame not to get the help you need.

Talking to an adult about a problem can be the first step in solving the problem and feeling better.

When to Talk to a Professional

How do you know if a problem is serious enough to consult with a professional? Knowing the warning signs of mental health problems will help. **Figure 3.8** shows some signs that may indicate a mental health problem for which a professional's help may be needed.

Sometimes depression is the result of another mental health problem. For example, a teen may be too nervous in social situations to make friends or go to social events. She may blame herself for her unhappiness and feel depressed. The cause of her depression may be social phobia, but it is her depression that brings her to see a professional.

Methods of Therapy for Mental Health Problems

There are different methods of therapy, or treatment, for mental health problems. They fall into two broad categories: talk therapy and biological therapy. Talk therapy includes a variety of counseling methods. Biological therapy refers primarily to the use of drug treatment, or medication, to treat mental problems.

The goal of all methods of treatment for mental health problems is to help you change so that you can handle problems better. Some professionals use only counseling, others use only medication, and still others use a combination of methods. A teen who is depressed because of her social phobia might be given medication to help improve her mood while she gets counseling to help her overcome her fear.

Your Total Health

Alternative Therapies ACTIVITY!

Some mental health professionals use a holistic, or body-and-mind, approach and alternative therapies. For example, to treat depression, the following therapies might be used:

- Exercise
- Relaxation techniques
- Diet
- Yoga

Find out more about an alternative therapy. What evidence is there that it helps people with major depression feel better?

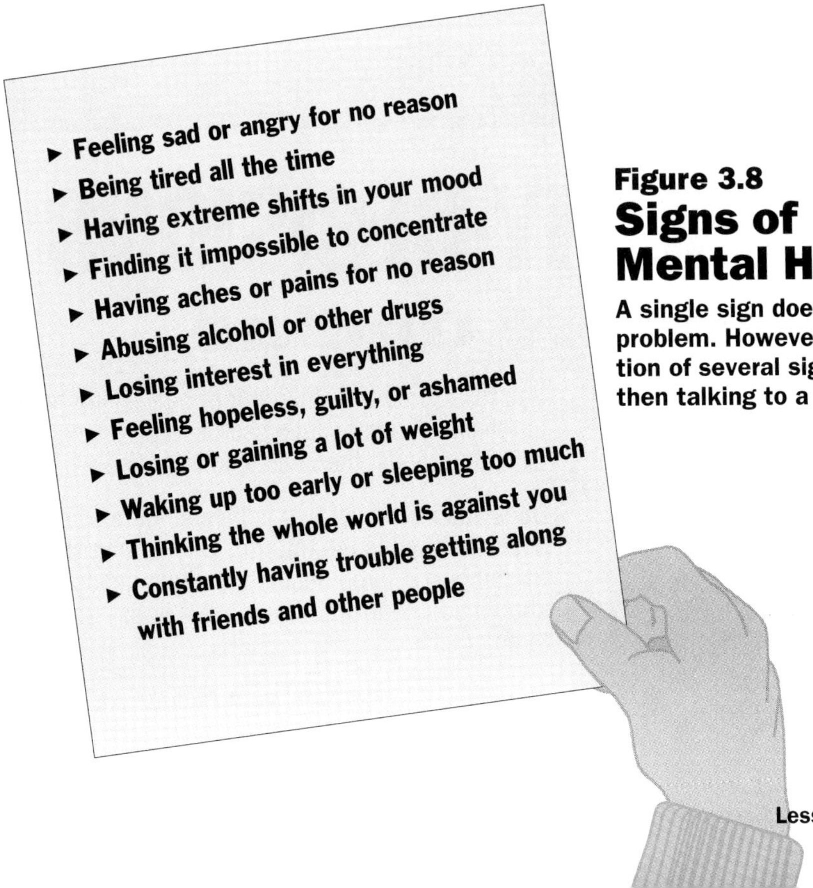

▸ Feeling sad or angry for no reason
▸ Being tired all the time
▸ Having extreme shifts in your mood
▸ Finding it impossible to concentrate
▸ Having aches or pains for no reason
▸ Abusing alcohol or other drugs
▸ Losing interest in everything
▸ Feeling hopeless, guilty, or ashamed
▸ Losing or gaining a lot of weight
▸ Waking up too early or sleeping too much
▸ Thinking the whole world is against you
▸ Constantly having trouble getting along with friends and other people

Figure 3.8

Signs of Mental Health Problems

A single sign doesn't indicate a mental health problem. However, if you experience a combination of several signs, and if they last a long time, then talking to a professional may help.

Counseling Methods

In counseling, you talk with a mental health professional about your problem and learn new ways of thinking or behaving. Changing your thoughts or behavior leads, in turn, to changes in the way you feel. By learning to think and behave in healthier ways, you can improve your mental and emotional health.

Some people feel much better after just a few sessions of talking to a professional. Other people need many sessions. You can talk to a professional individually or in a group with other people who have the same or similar problems. Some people feel more comfortable talking about their problems in private, but many people benefit from the extra empathy and support that comes from other members of a group.

Counseling is helping this teen learn to cope with a problem.

MAKING HEALTHY DECISIONS

Seeking Support On-line

Your friend Julio has always been a computer nut. He was the first one in your crowd to get his own computer, and he spends hours on the Internet. In fact, lately it seems as though that's all Julio does, and you think that may be a problem.

As soon as he gets home from school, Julio logs on and spends most of the evening sharing his problems with new, unfamiliar people he meets on the Internet. He has stopped calling his friends and prefers staying on the Internet, rather than eating dinner with his family.

You're worried that Julio might be seeking help from unreliable sources. Julio seems to be losing contact with his friends, the ones who truly know him.

Does Julio need help, or is he just enthusiastic about a new hobby? Is the Internet where Julio should go for support? If you decide that Julio needs help, should you confront him about it or say something to an adult?

You feel confused by all your options and their possible outcomes. You turn to the six-step decision-making process to help you decide what to do.

One form of counseling focuses on helping people to think more positively about themselves. This form of therapy can be especially helpful for people who suffer from depression. The professional helps the depressed individual identify negative thoughts that are contributing to the depression and shows the individual how to think more positively. A teen who is depressed because she tells herself she is "ugly" or "dumb," for example, can learn to send herself more positive messages. She can learn to focus on her strengths or achievements rather than on her weaknesses or mistakes.

Another form of counseling focuses on changing people's behavior. This form of therapy has been especially helpful for people with anxiety disorders such as phobias. The individual learns how to stay relaxed while facing more and more frightening situations. Someone with a fear of giving speeches might try giving a one-minute talk to a few friends while staying calm. Once he has achieved that, perhaps he could talk for three to five minutes. Eventually he might be able to speak in front of a large group of peers without feeling any fear.

Counseling for a depressed teen with a social phobia might be aimed at changing her thinking *and* her behavior. The teen might have the mistaken belief that her handling of any social situation should be perfect. The counselor might help the teen change her expectations. The counselor might also encourage the teen to try some relatively nonthreatening social situations, such as going to a movie with one close friend. How do you think overcoming her fears would affect the teen's self-esteem and depression?

Teen Issues

When Is Shyness a Sign of Social Phobia?

Although shyness may make some teens unhappy, they probably do not need professional help. How can you tell the difference between normal shyness and a social phobia? If you have a social phobia, you are likely to

- avoid people because you are afraid of being rejected or humiliated.
- feel ashamed about your shy feelings.
- have panic attacks when you are in social situations.
- make up excuses or lie about why you're not socializing.

1. **State the situation**
2. **List the options**
3. **Weigh the possible outcomes**
4. **Consider your values**
5. **Make a decision and act**
6. **Evaluate the decision**

Follow-Up Activities

1. Apply the six steps of the decision-making process to the problem.
2. With a small group of other students, discuss why seeking help on the Internet may not be the best course of action to solve problems. Why might cutting oneself off from friends and family be harmful to one's overall health? Work together to write down your conclusions, based on your discussion.

Drug Treatment, or Medication

Sometimes medication is prescribed to treat mental health problems. The medication used can only be prescribed by a medical doctor. Medication is used to treat major depression and schizophrenia. The kinds of medicine that are used to treat depression affect brain chemistry and improve mood. Counseling is often recommended, too, to prevent the depression from returning when the medication is stopped. The types of medicine used to treat schizophrenia control hallucinations and delusions.

Both types of medication have side effects. A **side effect** of a medicine is *a reaction other than the ones that are intended.* Side effects of the medications used to treat schizophrenia and depression may include upset stomach, headache, and blurred vision, among others.

Q&A

Too Much Talk

Q: My uncle says counseling can take years. I'd like to talk to someone, but I want to feel better soon. What should I do?

A: Most forms of psychological counseling used today work much more quickly than in the past. Sometimes just one or two sessions can put you on the road to better mental and emotional health. By all means, talk to a professional if you have a mental or emotional problem that can't wait.

Sources of Help

There are various people who can help with mental and emotional problems. The person you choose may depend on the type of problem, on who is available in the area to treat that type of problem, and on how comfortable you feel with the person you select.

- **Parent or Other Adult Family Member** Talking about a problem with a parent, older brother or sister, or other adult family member may be all the help that you need. These people care about you. Putting your thoughts and feelings into words can help you see things more clearly. Getting love and support can help you feel better about yourself.
- **Clergy Member** If you feel as if you do not know where to turn, you may want to talk to a leader of your church, synagogue, or mosque. Members of the clergy often have experience in counseling. Many have formal training in counseling.
- **Teacher or School Counselor** A teacher or school counselor can help with learning problems and conflicts at school and can advise about career questions. School counselors specialize in problems that concern students. They usually have a master's degree in counseling.
- **Family Counselor** Instead of counseling individuals, family counselors see the family together. Their goal is to help the members of the family communicate with each other more effectively.
- **School Nurse** If you are not sure what kind of help you need, a good place to start would be your school nurse. School nurses are trained in health care and in the problems of teens. A nurse can guide you in finding the help you need.
- **Psychologist** (sy·KAH·luh·jist) This is *a mental health professional who is licensed to counsel and may have a masters or doctoral degree.* Psychologists treat most types of mental health problems using one or more types of counseling.

- **Psychiatrist** Psychiatrists (sy·KY·uh·trist) are *medical doctors who treat serious mental health problems*. They are the only mental health professionals who can prescribe drugs.

Hot Lines

Teen hot lines are special telephone services that teens can call when feeling stress. Some hot lines are answered by teens; others are answered by adults. Both groups are trained to listen to and help teens experiencing a crisis.

in your journal

Many people find it hard to confide in others. Sometimes journal writing can be a good substitute for talking to another person. Putting problems into words can help you see things more clearly and think of solutions.

Think of something that troubles you, and write down in your private journal whatever comes to mind about it. Explore your feelings, and try to put them into words. When you finish, reflect on how writing in your journal made you feel.

This family is getting along better since meeting with a family counselor. Why do you think it might be important for all family members to be involved in counseling, even when it appears that only one of them has a problem?

Review

Lesson 5

Using complete sentences, answer the following questions on a separate sheet of paper.

Reviewing Terms and Facts

1. **Identify** Name two basic types of mental health treatment.
2. **Vocabulary** What does the term *side effect* mean?
3. **Recall** Which type of mental health professional can prescribe drugs?

Thinking Critically

4. **Restate** What types of behavior might indicate an individual needs to see a professional for a mental health problem?
5. **Explain** How can counseling be used to improve an individual's self-esteem?

Applying Health Concepts

6. **Consumer Health** Check the Yellow Pages of your local telephone book to find out what mental health services are available in your area. What kinds of disorders do different groups and/or individual professionals specialize in? Make a chart of your findings.

Chapter 3 Review

Chapter Summary

- **Lesson 1** Mental and emotional health can affect all aspects of your life. Skills you can learn to improve your mental and emotional health and your self-esteem include changing your thoughts and behavior, motivating yourself, and focusing on your strengths.
- **Lesson 2** Expressing emotions and meeting emotional needs in healthy ways are important for good mental and emotional health.
- **Lesson 3** Stress can cause physical and psychological fatigue and other health problems. Exercise and relaxation are healthy ways to cope with stress.
- **Lesson 4** Mental health problems are serious if they interfere with the quality of life or a normal lifestyle. It is important to be aware of the warning signs of major depression and suicide.
- **Lesson 5** Mental health problems can be treated with counseling, medication, or both. There are many types of professionals who can help with mental health problems.

Reviewing Key Terms and Concepts

Using complete sentences, answer the following questions on a separate sheet of paper.

Lesson 1

1. Define *mental and emotional health.*
2. List two ways to accept criticism constructively.

Lesson 2

3. Define *emotions.*
4. What are *hormones,* and how do they affect emotions?

Lesson 3

5. How does physical fatigue differ from psychological fatigue?
6. Identify two healthy ways of coping with stress.

Lesson 4

7. Identify three types of anxiety disorders.
8. List three warning signs of major depression.

Lesson 5

9. List five signs that could indicate a mental health problem.
10. Name three professionals you could talk to about a mental health problem.

Thinking Critically

Using complete sentences, answer the following questions on a separate sheet of paper.

11. **Relate** How is self-esteem related to self-motivation?
12. **Synthesize** Show by example that emotions are neither good nor bad, but that people's reactions to them may be.
13. **Distinguish** How are anxiety and mood disorders different? How are they similar?
14. **Infer** What advantages do you think counseling has over medication for treating depression?

Chapter 3 Review

Your Action Plan

The journal entries you created throughout Chapter 3 were meant to put you more in touch with your thoughts, behaviors, and feelings and how they are affecting your mental and emotional health. Review these journal entries now, and follow the steps below. Write an action plan to help you improve your mental and emotional health.

Step 1 Write down a realistic long-term goal. You might set a goal of coping with stress in a healthier way.

Step 2 Think of several short-term goals that will help you meet your long-term goal. A short-term goal for coping with stress in a healthier way might be exercising instead of snacking when you are stressed.

Step 3 Put your plan into action, and at the end of one week, evaluate how well you met your short-term goal(s). If you did meet them, how do you feel?

When you reach your long-term goal, reward yourself in a healthy way!

In Your Home and Community

1. **Growth and Development** Role-play and tape-record a typical disagreement with a family member or friend. Replay the disagreement and stop the tape each time one of you expresses a thought or feeling in a way that does not help to resolve the problem. Work together to rephrase statements in a way that does help to resolve the problem. For example, instead of saying, "You never listen to me," you might say, "Could you repeat what I said so that I know that you've heard me?"
2. **Community Resources** Make a list of the mental health departments and agencies in your community that help teens with mental health problems. Use the information you find to create a flier that helps teens locate appropriate sources of help.

Building Your Portfolio

1. **Healthy Traits** Based on the material in the chapter, make a list of five traits that you think are very important to good mental and emotional health. Add the list to your portfolio.
2. **Handling Emotions** Ask at least three other students how they deal with a strong emotion such as fear or anger. Write down any ideas that you think might work for you. Add these ideas to your portfolio.
3. **Personal Assessment** Look through the activities and projects you did for this chapter. Choose one or two that you would like to include in your portfolio.

Unit 2
Social and Public Health

Chapter 4 

Your Social Health

Chapter 5 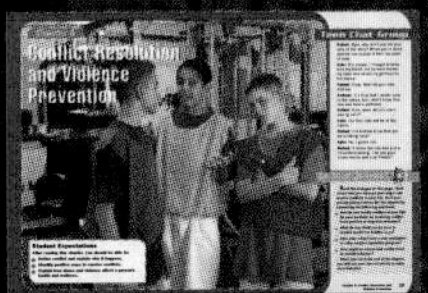

Conflict Resolution and Violence Prevention

Chapter 6 

Consumer Choices and Public Health

Chapter 4

Your Social Health

Student Expectations

After reading this chapter, you should be able to:

❶ Explain how to build healthy relationships with other people.

❷ Identify and practice important communication skills.

❸ List different kinds of families and describe ways in which families are changing.

❹ Describe the role that friendship plays in health.

❺ Discuss dating practices and reasons to choose abstinence.

❻ Describe marriage patterns and the roles and responsibilities of parents.

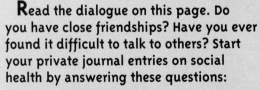

Teen Chat Group

Anne: My mom said I could invite friends over for a movie party this Friday. Would you guys like to come?

Mareika: I'd love to come. I've been studying really hard for my biology test. It will be nice to do something fun with my friends.

Shelley: I'm coming, and I'll bring the popcorn. My parents are having some of their friends over on Friday and I'd rather not be there. I never know what to talk about with my parents' friends.

Anne: I was thinking of inviting that new girl to come. She's already been here for two weeks, but I always see her sitting alone.

Mareika: That's a great idea! Maybe she's really shy and is just afraid to approach anyone.

Shelley: I would feel awful if I didn't have you guys to talk to every day. Who would I tell all my troubles to? Let's tell her about the party today.

in your journal

Read the dialogue on this page. Do you have close friendships? Have you ever found it difficult to talk to others? Start your private journal entries on social health by answering these questions:

- In general, how do you feel you get along with other people?
- What do you like about your friendships? What do you dislike?
- What activities do you enjoy most with your friends? For what activities do you prefer to be with your family?
- What would you like to change about your relationships with family members?

When you reach the end of the chapter, you will use your journal entries to make an action plan.

Lesson 1

Building Healthy Relationships

This lesson will help you find answers to questions that teens often ask about relationships. For example:

- **How can I learn to get along better with others?**
- **What should I do when I disagree with what someone says?**
- **What's the secret of being a successful team player?**

Words to Know

social health
relationships
communication
compromise
cooperation
tolerance

What Is Social Health?

Two sides of your health triangle are physical health and mental health. The third side is social health. **Social health** is *your ability to get along with the people around you.* When you have good social health, you work well as a member of a group. You also know how to make and keep friends and how to offer and get help when it is needed. People with good social health

- can accept differences in other people.
- get along with family members.
- meet people easily.
- have at least one or two close friends.
- can accept other people's ideas and suggestions when they are working in a group.
- can make friends with people of both sexes.
- continue to take part in an activity even when other people disagree about what to do.

Taking part in a group project at school helps you build your social skills.

Social Health and Relationships

Your social health is tied directly to your relationships with other people. **Relationships** (ri·LAY·shuhn·ships) are *the connections you have with other people and groups in your life.* These connections are based on how you relate to, or act toward, others. Your life is full of relationships. **Figure 4.1** shows some of them.

Building Healthy Relationships

Most people do not relate to everyone in their lives in exactly the same way. How you act with a brother or sister, for example, may be very different from how you act with a parent or teacher. You may have a very close relationship with one friend, and more casual relationships with other friends. You may choose not to have any kind of friendship with some people if their values are very different from your own. What is important about all your relationships is that they be as healthy as possible.

You can build healthy relationships by learning three key skills of social health. They are *communication, compromise,* and *cooperation.* These skills will help you get along with others.

interNET CONNECTION

Get acquainted with the Glencoe Web site and learn more about how to establish healthy relationships.

http://www.glencoe.com/sec/health

in your journal

The list on the facing page identifies the characteristics of good social health. Which of those characteristics do you feel you already have? Which do you need to work on? What other qualities do you think contribute to good social health? Write your responses in your private journal.

Figure 4.1
Balancing Relationships

It's not always easy to find the right balance among all the different people in your life. Most people experience conflicts from time to time.

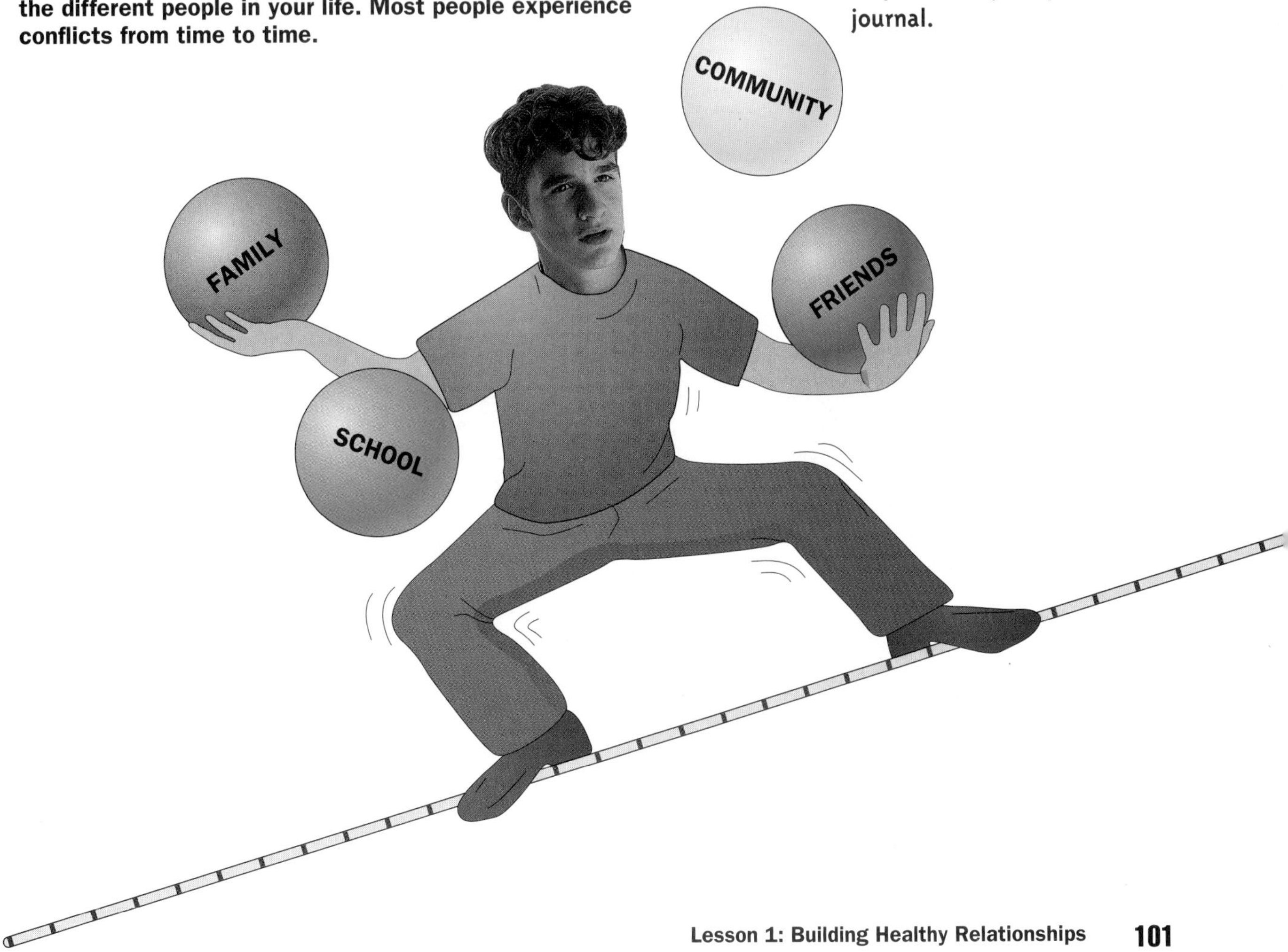

Teen Issues

No Way!

It is important to learn to compromise, but it is just as important to learn never to compromise about matters you believe in strongly. Suppose someone tries to get you to do something you believe is wrong. When you are faced with this situation, the right response is not to compromise. The right answer is to say, "No way!"

Communication

Communication is *the exchange of thoughts, ideas, and beliefs between two or more people.* By communicating, you get to know people. Communication also enables you to share your thoughts and feelings and have a good time with people. Communication also helps you solve problems. You will learn more about developing communication skills in Lesson 2.

Sometimes disagreements occur between two people or groups of people. **Figure 4.2** gives some rules for good communication when these disagreements occur.

Compromise

Have there ever been times when you wanted to see a movie and your friend wanted to play video games but there was not enough money for both? Do you remember how you handled the problem? At such times, compromise might be the answer. **Compromise** (KAHM·pruh·myz) is *the result of each person's giving up something in order to reach a solution that satisfies everyone.* Compromise is also known as "give and take."

Compromise can take many forms. Consider the choice between a movie and video games. The compromise might be that your friend gets to choose the activity this time and you get to choose next time. It may be that the two of you decide to do something completely different. Whatever form the compromise takes, it helps a relationship run smoothly. It also accomplishes something that arguing never will: it leads to positive action.

Figure 4.2
Communication Tips

Stay calm and explain why you are upset. If you shout, the other person may not listen.

To avoid interruption, choose the time and place carefully.

Concentrate on the main problem and avoid raising side issues.

After you have spoken, give the other person a chance to respond.

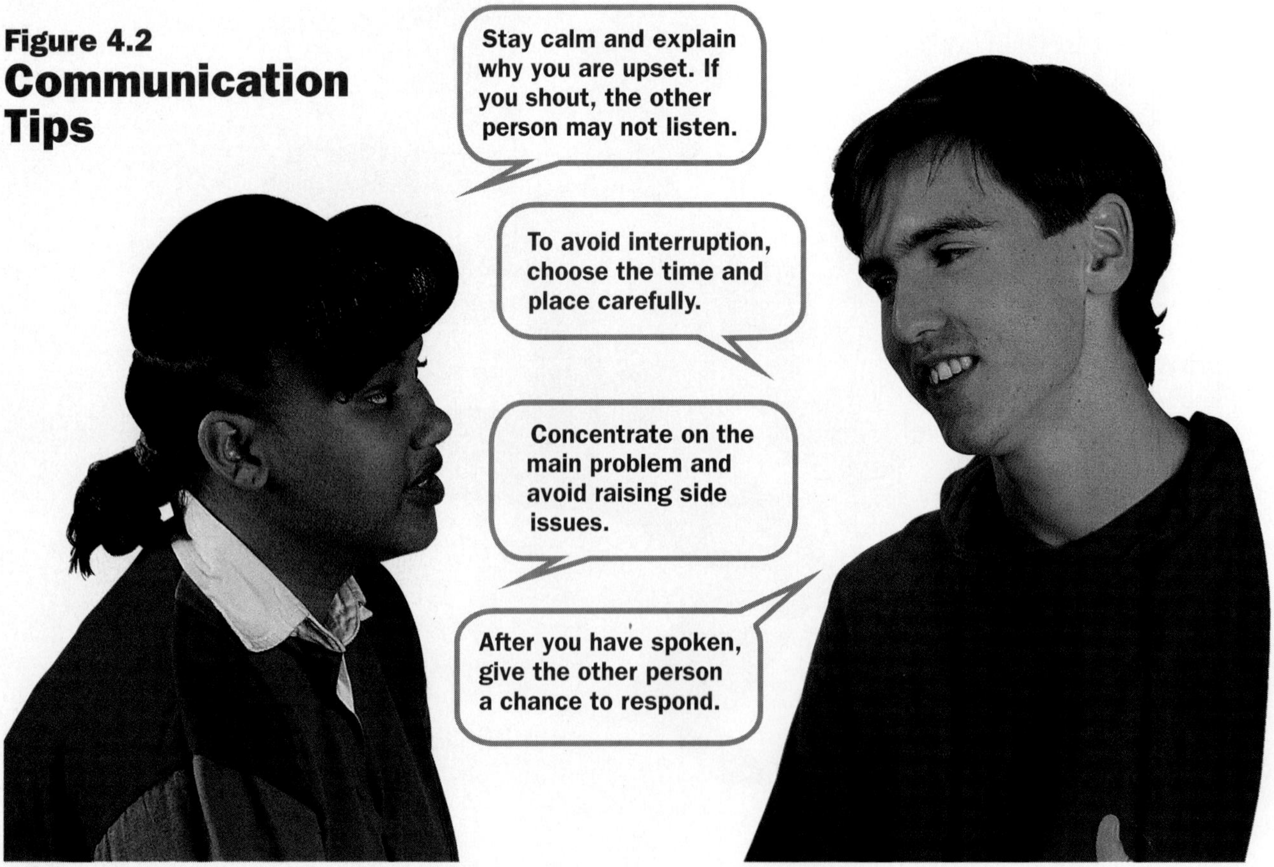

Cooperation

Cooperation is *working together for the good of all.* Another name for cooperation is *teamwork.* Suppose you and a friend are working together to make a science display for the school fair. In order to have the project ready on time, you decide to share responsibilities. By cooperating with each other, you reach a solution. For example, you might design labels and captions while your friend collects samples. Together, you and your friend assemble the display. That's cooperation!

Working as a team builds stronger relationships. To be a good team player, you need to be willing to work with and listen to others. You also need to have a helpful attitude.

Acceptance of Individual Differences

People of many different races, religions, and cultural groups live in the United States. Part of good social health is tolerance of all these individual differences. **Tolerance** (TAHL·er·ens) means *accepting and respecting other people's beliefs and customs.* It helps you recognize that different people have a right to express themselves in ways that may be different from your own. At the same time, you recognize that people are more alike than they are different. Tolerance helps you get along with others.

A person with good social health also shows tolerance of people of all ages. Disagreements sometimes arise between people of different generations. Teens may have difficulty getting along with older adults because they have different ways of talking, dressing, and acting. You need to be willing to accept all people and to develop an understanding of their point of view.

Caring and Respect

You can show tolerance within your family, too. Good social health includes respecting family members. That means listening to your parents' point of view and learning how to communicate your opinions. It means being considerate and polite. It means not teasing your brothers or sisters about mistakes they make. When you have good social health, you can accept family members—faults and all—because you care for them.

Cultural Connections

"Getting to Know You" ACTIVITY!

Learning about the customs and beliefs of various groups of people helps develop tolerance. The more you know about other people, the easier it is to understand and accept them. Get to know another cultural group by attending an event such as the following:

- Cinco de Mayo
- Passover seder
- Kwanza observance
- Native American powwow
- Vietnamese New Year celebration
- A neighborhood block party

Take photographs and share them with your classmates.

Learning about other people's beliefs and customs is an important step toward accepting individual differences.

Belonging to a Group

Have you ever stopped to think about the number of groups to which you belong? You belong to your family, to your class at school, and to your circle of friends. You may be part of a club, a team, or a religious group. Certainly you are a member of a very large group known as society.

The health of each group depends on the social health of each of its members. Each member shares an equal responsibility for maintaining the health of the group. By the same token, the health of every member is affected by the overall health of the group.

You can see how this works if you think about a soccer team. Each member of the team is responsible for showing up for practice, staying healthy, and playing as well as he or she can. That way, the whole team benefits. When the team plays well together, each member benefits. Similarly, when one member lets the team down, the whole team is affected and may not play as well as usual. When the team plays badly, everyone suffers.

Lesson 1 Review

Using complete sentences, answer the following questions on a separate sheet of paper.

Reviewing Terms and Facts

1. **Vocabulary** Explain in your own words what *social health* means.
2. **Recall** What is the term that means "accepting and respecting other people's beliefs and customs"?
3. **Explain** What are some ways of showing respect for members of your family?

Thinking Critically

4. **Compare** Use real-life examples to explain the difference between compromise and cooperation.
5. **Illustrate** What are some ways that teens and older adults can demonstrate greater tolerance toward one another.
6. **Analyze** List the different groups to which you belong. Identify one way you keep one of those groups healthy and one way it keeps you healthy.

Applying Health Concepts

7. **Health of Others** Pretend you are the leader of a group that is planning a community project, such as cleaning up litter in a park, conducting a recycling campaign, or planning a food drive. Decide what tasks are involved and make a plan to show how members of the group can cooperate to meet the overall goals of the group. If possible, carry out your plan.
8. **Growth and Development** Create an illustrated guidebook to cultural events, customs, traditions, organizations, festivals, and historical landmarks in your community. Include specific dates and locations of the events.

Developing Communication Skills

Lesson 2

This lesson will help you find answers to questions that teens often ask about communicating. For example:

- **How can I learn to communicate better?**
- **Why are some people easier to talk to than others?**
- **What is body language and what do I need to know about it?**
- **How do I say no to my friends without offending them?**
- **How can I persuade my friends to make the right decisions?**

Words to Know

verbal communication
active listening
body language
eye contact
refusal skills

The Importance of Communicating

The foundation of any relationship is the ability to communicate. People need to communicate to start a relationship and to keep a relationship strong. Communicating helps you get to know other people. Sharing interests, experiences, feelings, and concerns helps people grow closer together.

Talking is the main way most people communicate. Talking is a form of verbal communication. **Verbal communication** means *using words to express thoughts, ideas, beliefs, and wants.*

Just talking to another person does not guarantee good communication. The listener may be daydreaming and may not actually listen to what the speaker is saying. The speaker may be talking too fast for the listener to follow along. Good communication is a skill. It needs to be learned and practiced.

Communication skills don't just happen. They need to be practiced.

Speaking Skills

Communication is a two-way street—giving and receiving messages. Speaking is the giving part. Good communication involves speaking clearly and carefully. Developing speaking skills takes practice. Here are some tips for improving your speaking skills.

- **Avoid nonstop talking.** Find a balance between sharing your experiences and letting the other person talk. If you do all the talking, the other person may become bored and tune out.
- **Think before you speak.** Avoid embarrassing yourself or hurting the other person by saying something you will later regret. Allow your message to go through your brain before it comes out of your mouth.
- **Be positive.** No one likes to listen to someone who's grumpy all the time. Try to be cheerful and enthusiastic—unless, of course, you have a serious problem to discuss.
- **Be aware of your listener.** Make sure the other person understands what you are saying. Ask for feedback from time to time.
- **Be direct.** Say what you want to say. Be direct about your values and about what's important to you.
- **Be creative.** If your listener doesn't understand you the first time you say something, express the idea in a different way.

A Conversation Tip

You may have less of a problem communicating with family members and friends. Communicating may be more difficult with a person you are just getting to know. For example, you might say, "Do you play basketball?" The other person might reply "No" and that's the end of the conversation! Instead of asking questions that require only a yes or no, ask open-ended questions (see **Figure 4.3**).

Q & A

"When I Was Your Age . . ."

Q: Why do teens sometimes have trouble communicating with adults?

A: Because adults grew up in an earlier generation, they may have ways of thinking, talking, and acting that are different from yours. If you take your time and practice good listening skills, you and these adults can talk. You may even enjoy hearing them say, "When I was your age . . ."

Figure 4.3
Conversation Starters
Ask open-ended questions that encourage communication.

What sports do you like playing?
How can I join the drama group?

For example, you might say, "What hobbies do you have?" Open-ended questions encourage the other person to say more. In the process, the person will reveal information you can use to keep the conversation going—"Oh, yeah? I play the guitar, too."

Listening Skills

Listening is the receiving part of communication. Good communication requires active listening. **Active listening** means *hearing, thinking about, and responding to the other person's message.* Don't just sit back and absorb the sound waves. Make a real effort to understand what the person is saying. Here are some tips for improving your listening skills.

- **Pay attention.** Concentrate on what the other person is saying. Give the speaker your undivided attention. For example, don't try to watch TV and listen at the same time. Don't be thinking about what you're going to say next.
- **Provide feedback.** Let the other person know you're listening by nodding your head, asking questions, or saying to him or her, "Then what happened?"
- **Let the person finish speaking.** She or he will be better able to explain if there are no interruptions.
- **Stay calm.** Even if you're hearing something you don't like, stay calm instead of getting angry. Breathe deeply.
- **Keep an open mind.** Listen even if you disagree. Accept that other people will not always think the same way you do.

in your journal

Look at the lists of speaking skills and listening skills. From each list, choose one skill that you need to work on. Write it in your private journal. Over the next week, concentrate on improving those skills. Record your progress in your journal.

What movies would you recommend?
Who's your favorite rock group?
I heard you went to Alaska. What was it like?

Cultural Connections

Social Rules

ACTIVITY!

Different cultures have different ways of showing social courtesies. For example, in some cultures it is customary to shake hands upon meeting. In others, people hug each other when they meet. Ask members of your community to give you other examples of cultural courtesies and share them with your classmates. Why is it important to know about these social rules?

Body Language

"I'm okay," you say bravely, but your friend knows you are really feeling scared. Your body language—drooping shoulders, downcast look, and trembling lip—gives you away.

Body language is *a form of nonverbal communication.* Without saying a word, people can send messages by the way they hold their bodies (posture), by the expressions on their faces, by the gestures they use, and by the clothes they wear.

Speakers and listeners need to be aware of body language. Body language can be a sign of a person's true feelings, as in the example above. Some body language, such as smiling and nodding, encourage communication. Other forms, such as frowning and crossing arms tightly across the chest, discourage communication.

A special type of body language is eye contact. **Eye contact** is *direct visual contact with another person's eyes.* You can use eye contact to show that you are sincere or listening carefully. In the United States, eye contact is acceptable, but in some cultures, it is seen as a sign of rudeness.

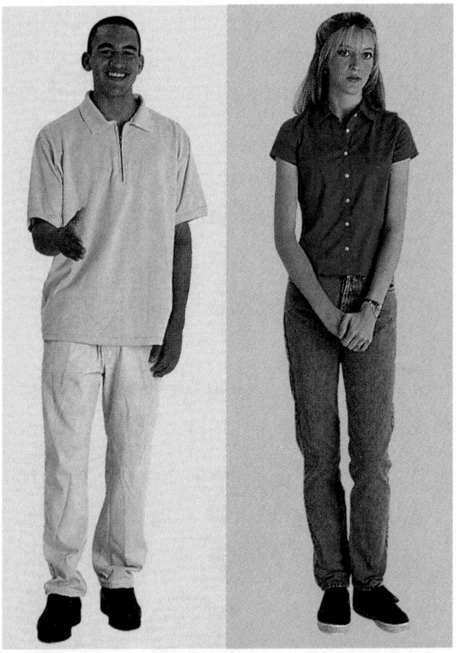

Body language sends powerful messages. If these two teens were applying for a part-time job, who do you think would be chosen?

MAKING HEALTHY DECISIONS

Deciding to Say No

Christy plays goalie on her school's soccer team. Her coach asked her to join a traveling soccer team this summer. At first, Christy was excited at the thought of being on the team. She loves playing soccer. Being able to play during the summer would help improve her skills. Traveling around the state would be fun.

There's a problem, however. Christy has already made a commitment for the summer. The McGuires, who live across the street from Christy, are going away for a month. Christy has promised to feed their cat every day, mow the lawn weekly, and water the houseplants. The McGuires have agreed to pay Christy $20 a week for her work. Christy is looking forward to earning some money. She has been saving for a new bicycle, and that extra money would give her what she needs.

So now Christy is confused. Should she tour with the team this summer or honor her commitment to her neighbors? She decided to use the step-by-step decision-making process to help her evaluate her options and make a decision:

1. **State the situation**
2. **List the options**
3. **Weigh the possible outcomes**
4. **Consider your values**
5. **Make a decision and act**
6. **Evaluate the decision**

Refusal Skills

To develop relationships, you need to be open to the ideas and wishes of other people. However, sometimes friends and acquaintances want you to do something that you do not want to do. Maybe you don't have the time. Maybe it's something that goes against your values or your family's values. Maybe you're just not interested. You might be afraid to say no, fearing that he or she might not like you anymore or might not include you in future activities. You might be afraid of hurting his or her feelings.

No thanks. I'm not interested.

Refusal skills are helpful for these situations. **Refusal skills** are *communication strategies that help you say no effectively.* Using these skills will help you be true to yourself. You can say no without feeling guilty or uncomfortable. Other people will respect you for being honest about your needs and wants.

If you don't want to do something, just say so. You don't have to give a reason.

Follow-up Activities

1. Apply the six steps of the decision-making process to Christy's story.
2. Along with a partner, role-play a scene in which Christy turns down the coach's offer to be on the traveling soccer team. Have her use refusal skills.
3. Now role-play a scene in which Christy explains to the McGuires that she cannot keep her promise. Think about suggestions she can make for helping them deal with the problem she has created.

Teen Issues

Setting Priorities

Knowing your short-term and long-term goals can help you say no to activities that don't fit your plan. Make a list of your goals for this week. Then, if a friend asks you to hang out at the mall on Saturday afternoon, consider how doing so will affect your goals.

How to Say No

When you need to say no to someone, you need to show that you mean what you say. Here are some suggestions you can follow to build your refusal skills.

- **Be honest.** Tell the other person exactly how you feel about the situation. You can explain your decision if you like, but you are not obliged to give an explanation.
- **Be friendly and polite.** Don't insult or yell at the other person.
- **Match your tone to your message.** If your voice sounds wishy-washy, the other person might try to change your mind. Sound firm when you say no.
- **Use eye contact.** This will show that you mean what you say.
- **Offer an alternative.** Suggest something—a different time, a different activity—that would be more acceptable to you.

Lesson 2 Review

Using complete sentences, answer the following questions on a separate sheet of paper.

Reviewing Terms and Facts

1. **Recall** What are six ways of improving speaking skills?
2. **List** Give five tips for being an active listener.
3. **Vocabulary** What is body language? Give some examples of ways people communicate using body language.

Thinking Critically

4. **Analyze** Choose someone you consider to be a particularly good communicator. Identify the skills that person uses to communicate so well.
5. **Describe** Give examples of body language that might indicate a person is not listening attentively.
6. **Synthesize** A friend is participating in a walkathon for a local charity. He asks you to pledge two dollars for every mile he walks. You don't have any extra money right now. How can you say no without making your friend angry?

Applying Health Concepts

7. **Growth and Development** Every day for the next week, make an effort to say something positive to family members, teachers, or classmates. Keep a log of your positive statements. At the end of the week, write a paper describing how giving positive reinforcement can affect people's emotional health.
8. **Personal Health** Pretend you wrote a best-selling book on communication skills. Give the book a title and write a summary of how the book can help improve these skills and why they are important for success. Create and illustrate the book's cover.
9. **Health of Others** Make a videotape that demonstrates the impact of nonverbal communication. Tape the body language of family members and friends, and narrate the tape explaining how body language sends messages. Ask the audience to interpret each person's message from his or her body language.

Lesson 3

Social Health and Your Family

This lesson will help you find answers to questions that teens often ask about families. For example:

- **What makes families different from other groups?**
- **What are some ways my family helps me?**
- **What are some ways I help my family?**
- **How are families different today from the way they used to be?**
- **Whom can I turn to if I have family problems?**

Words to Know

family
couple family
nuclear family
single-parent family
extended family
blended family
stepparent

The Importance of Families

Humans are social beings. Each of us needs to feel that he or she belongs. Most of the time, this need to belong is satisfied by groups. In your lifetime, you will belong to many groups.

The first group to which we belong is the **family,** *the basic unit of society.* All societies in the world are made up of families. It is within the family that you share experiences and develop lifetime bonds. Being part of a family means acquiring values, building traditions, and feeling the comfort of belonging.

In your family, you also begin to develop social skills. Through your family, you form a sense of who you are. Through your family, you also learn to care for and share with others.

Your social health starts with your family. Family members have been influencing your values and attitudes since you were born.

An African Proverb

An African proverb says that it takes the village to raise a child. In other words, child-rearing is such a huge and important responsibility that every adult in the community needs to become involved. This concept can be seen in communities in the United States, where adults are encouraged to provide physical care and emotional support for young people, whether or not they are related.

The Family

Members of a family have special emotional bonds with one another. The family provides for and nurtures its members. It is also responsible for guiding its members and teaching them right from wrong. You learn your values through your family.

Family Roles

In most societies, different family members have different roles, or jobs. In our society, it is the job of the adults of the family to supply food, clothing, shelter, and medical care for the rest of the family. The adults are also responsible for teaching the children right from wrong and helping them grow. Children, in turn, take on more responsibilities as they grow older. In doing so, they learn how to succeed as adults.

Kinds of Families

There are many different kinds of families in our society. **Figure 4.4** shows five of the most common family structures, but many others exist as well. It is not unusual in our society for family structures to change many times. For example, single adults, or adults who are not married, are also part of a family—the family they grew up with.

Also, when people do not live close to other family members, they may look upon close friends as almost a family group. Thus, family structures are very flexible and have many variations. Every family has special characteristics that each member can enjoy.

Figure 4.4
Kinds of Families

Families today come in many shapes and sizes.

Couple Family
A family made up of two adults with no children.

Nuclear Family
A family made up of a mother, a father, and a child or children.

Single-Parent Family
A family in which only one parent lives with the child or children. The parent may be unmarried, divorced, or widowed.

Extended Family
A nuclear or single-parent family plus other relatives—grandparents, aunts, uncles and cousins—living in the same household.

Blended Family
A family consisting of a parent, a stepparent, and the children of one or both parents. (A stepparent is someone who marries a child's mother or father.)

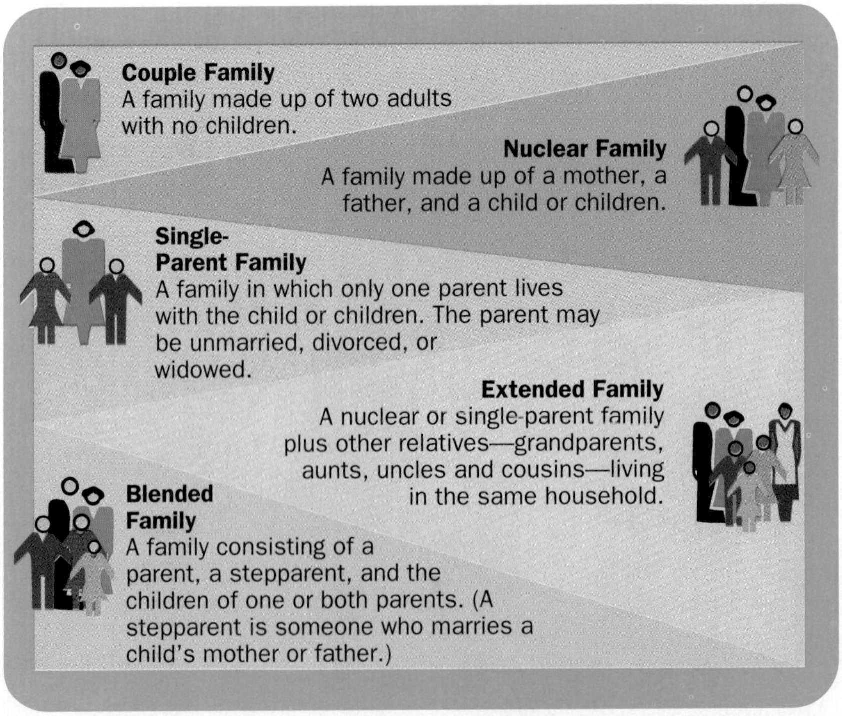

Changing Families

In recent years, many major changes have taken place in family structure, roles, and lifestyles. These changes affect the idea of "family" in our society. They have also affected the ways children in our society are cared for.

Trends Affecting Families

Some of the ways American families have changed include the following trends of recent years:

- **more smaller families.** Married couples are having fewer children. Some of them feel they have time and energy for only one or two children. Other reasons for smaller families include the expense of raising a family and concerns about overcrowding the Earth.
- **more single-parent families.** Twenty-seven percent of the families in the country are now headed by one parent, usually the mother. **Figure 4.5** shows how the number of single-parent families has been increasing in recent decades.
- **more dual-career families.** In more and more families, both parents have jobs outside the home. One reason for this is the expense of supporting a family. Another reason is that some parents like their jobs and want to keep working after they have children.

These trends have changed the ways families operate. Today, many parents take their children to child-care centers during the week. Many communities offer after-school activities and other support programs for families.

Figure 4.5
Changing Families in the United States

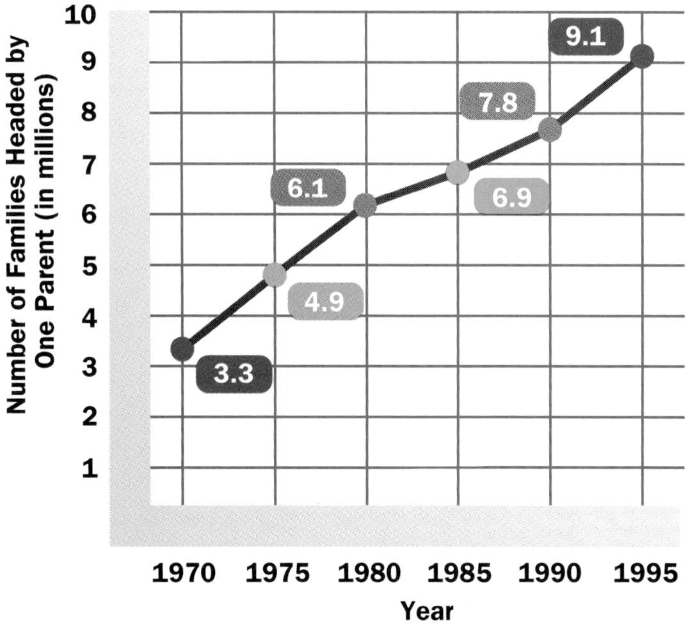

Source: U.S. Bureau of the Census, Current Population Reports, P20–488, "Household and Family Characteristics: March 1995" and earlier reports

With more single-parent and dual-career families, teens often have to do more to help at home.

Sharing celebrations and traditions strengthens family bonds. What traditions does your family observe?

Strengthening Families

Living in a family brings many joys. It also presents certain challenges. For a family to be healthy, it must respond to these challenges. If one family member is troubled or does not get along with another, the family as a whole suffers.

Strong family relationships depend on communication and shared values. In healthy families, members feel free to express their thoughts and feelings. Yet they listen to and value what others have to say.

Dealing with Family Problems

All families have problems from time to time. Good communication within the family can help members deal with many of their problems. For serious problems, such as those listed below, people may need to seek outside help.

Separation and Divorce When parents can no longer get along, they may separate and divorce. Divorcing parents may argue over the care and custody of the children. Family members must adjust to new living arrangements. The divided family may have less money to live on.

Illness A serious illness or accident can disrupt family life. Family members may need to spend a great deal of time caring for the ill or hurt person. Medical bills may drain the family's finances.

LIFE SKILLS

Improving Family Relationships

Do you sometimes get the feeling that you just don't sit down and *talk* with your family anymore? Busy schedules, outside interests, and rushed meals can keep families from spending time together. You can do something to change that and to improve relationships within your family.

Suggest that you have regular family meetings. Just like a student council or 4-H Club, family members can meet to talk about one another's activities, plan events such as weekend outings or vacations, and discuss problems. Family meetings can improve communication and keep the family healthy.

Discuss the idea with your family members and get their help. Together, you can decide when and where to have the meeting. Choose a time that is convenient for everyone. Choose a place free of distractions so that everyone will focus on the conversation. Make sure everyone agrees to turn off the TV during the meeting. Some families hold meetings around the dinner table after sharing a meal together.

Suggest that everyone make notes about items they want to talk about at the meeting. You could start a list and place it on the refrigerator door. That way,

Unemployment A parent may lose her or his job. If that parent provided the family's main or only income, the family may have to change its way of living. Also, an unemployed parent may feel additional stress and may need extra emotional support.

Substance Abuse A family member may become dependent on, or addicted to, alcohol or other drugs. Other family members may live in constant tension, never knowing how the addicted person will act. The addicted family member may cause problems by not carrying out responsibilities.

Abuse of Family Members A family member may mistreat another family member. The abuse may be physical, such as hitting, slapping, or choking, or it may be emotional, such as taunting or being cruel. Sexual abuse occurs when one person forces a sexual act on another.

Your Total Health

Neglect

Another type of abuse is neglect. Neglect occurs when adult family members fail to provide adequate food, clothing, or shelter for children. Neglect also means failure to meet children's emotional and social needs.

Running Away

Serious family problems can cause teens a great deal of stress. Some teens react to family problems by turning inward. They don't feel like talking to anyone or being with anyone.

Some teens try to get away from a problem by leaving home. Running away often leads to other problems, however. Runaways usually have no place to live and no money for food. Some runaways turn to crime. Many become the victims of crime.

The key to getting help is talking about the problem. Teens need to talk with someone they trust. That could be a parent, another family member, or a person in the school or community.

Running away is never the best solution. Do everything you can to urge a friend to get help from a trusted adult.

other family members can add to the list. Everyone will know ahead of time what topics will be discussed.

The family will need to agree on guidelines for the meeting. For example: Everyone is given a chance to speak his or her mind; Everyone is encouraged to express her or his opinion; No one laughs at or puts down the ideas of another person.

Try to stick to a time limit for your meeting. This will encourage everyone to get down to business. Besides, no one likes to sit through meetings that run too long.

Try to have family meetings on a regular basis. Your family will look forward to this time together.

Follow-up Activity

Take a look at the way you and your family communicate. Do you think you set aside enough time to talk things over? Can you think of some ways of improving communication within the family? If so, make a plan like the one described above. Talk it over with your family. Then make it happen.

in your journal

Write a list in your journal of the people you could turn to if you needed to discuss a problem.

Community Counseling

Listed below are some of the people in the community that troubled teens can turn to.

- **Teachers, school guidance counselors, social workers.** They want to help students solve problems and succeed.
- **Peer counselors.** Some schools and religious groups train young people to help peers with problems.
- **Religious leaders.** Ministers, priests, rabbis, and mullahs are trained to counsel people.
- **Doctors, nurses.** Medical workers in clinics can help with health problems.
- **Youth leaders.** Leaders of groups such as Scouts, 4-H, YMCA, and YWCA are ready to help.
- **Crisis center volunteers.** These people offer emergency help.
- **Support group leaders.** In support groups teens can talk with others with similar problems.

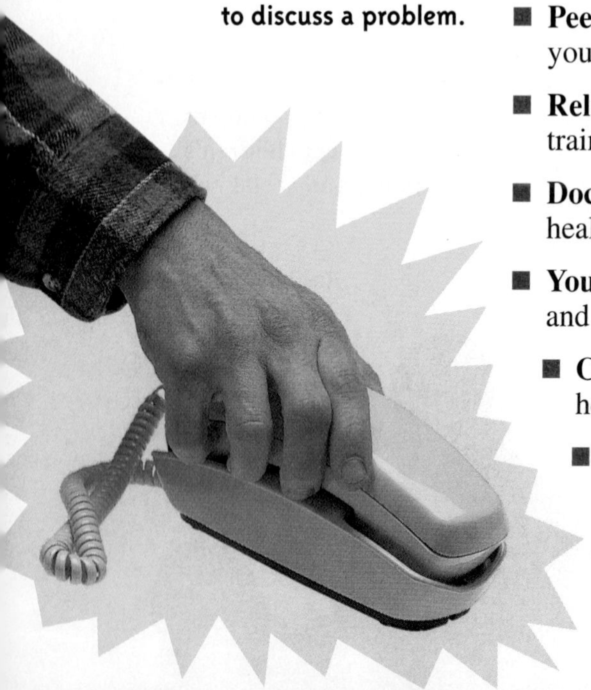

There is always someone who will listen to you. Don't hesitate to call if you think you need help.

Lesson 3

Review

Using complete sentences, answer the following questions on a separate sheet of paper.

Reviewing Terms and Facts

1. **Vocabulary** What is the difference between an *extended family* and a *blended family?*
2. **Recall** What three trends have changed families?
3. **List** Give four examples of people teens can turn to when they and their families are troubled.

Thinking Critically

4. **Analyze** What makes your family different from any other group you belong to?
5. **Explain** What are some ways that your community has responded to changes in American families?
6. **Hypothesize** If a friend told you she was having problems at home or was planning to run away from home, what organizations could you refer her to?

Applying Health Concepts

7. **Growth and Development** With a group of classmates, compile a list of traditions and rituals that families might share. Then discuss your list. Which of the traditions and rituals does your family take part in? Which would you like to have your family practice? Why? How could each of the traditions enhance a family's sense of unity?
8. **Health of Others** Make a list of local sites, events, and outings appropriate for families that include teenagers. Work with classmates to plan, make, and display posters advertising two or three of your choices.

Lesson 4

Social Health and Your Friends

This lesson will help you find answers to questions that teens often ask about friends. For example:

- **What makes a good friend?**
- **How can I make new friends?**
- **What are some good ways of dealing with peer pressure?**

Words to Know

reliable
sympathetic
peers
peer pressure

Friendships

Everyone needs friends. Friends provide us with companionship, and they can be a source of help when we have a problem. Friends are people with whom we can share a common interest or hobby. We cooperate with our friends to get jobs done better and faster. In short, good friendships are important to our social health.

Tips for Making New Friends

Making new friends is sometimes hard, but it is not impossible. Just remember that making friends is a skill that gets better with practice. **Figure 4.6** on page 118 tells you some ways you might try to make friends.

Sharing a hobby or interest with a good friend makes it even more enjoyable.

Qualities of Good Friends

You may have known some of your friends for as long as you can remember. Others may have entered your life just this year. No matter how you met them, or how long you have known them, four qualities are generally true of all good friends:

- **Loyalty.** Good friends stick by you. They like you for who you are. They are there when you need them.
- **Reliability.** Good friends are **reliable**—*able to be counted on.* Have you ever stood outside a movie theater after the picture started, waiting for a friend to show up? A reliable friend will do his or her best to keep dates and promises.
- **Sympathy.** Good friends are usually *aware of how you are feeling,* or **sympathetic** (sim·puh·THE·tik). Most friends will share your happy times, but *good* friends will also share your bad ones. Has a classmate ever comforted you when you were sad? If so, then that person is a good friend.
- **Caring.** Good friends care for and about each other. A friend who cares can accept the other person's weaknesses as well as strengths. Caring friends will value each other's feelings as much as they do their own.

Remember, good friendship points in both directions. It is important to have good friends, but it is just as important to *be* a good friend to others.

Music Connection

Say It with Music ACTIVITY!

Friendship is a frequent subject of popular songs. With your classmates, make a list of songs that deal with friendship. Study the lyrics of these songs. What do the words say about the importance of friends and the qualities of good friends? Write out the lyrics to one of these songs and share them with a friend, or write your own song about friendship.

Figure 4.6

Tips for Making New Friends

A Start a conversation with someone in your class. Ask a question or give a compliment. At the very least, you'll have classwork to talk about.

B Join a club or group. Meeting someone with similar interests is a good start toward making a new friend. If you like biking, join a weekend biking club. If you like acting in plays, join a local theater group or the school drama club. Take part in school activities.

Recognizing Peer Pressure

During your teen years, your friendships take on a special role. Your friends and classmates are your **peers,** or *people your age who are similar to you in many ways.* As a group, your peers have certain attitudes and beliefs. **Peer pressure**—*influence to go along with these beliefs and to try new activities*—may come from the group, either directly or indirectly. This kind of pressure can be hard to resist. There are two types of peer pressure, positive peer pressure and negative peer pressure.

Positive Peer Pressure

Positive peer pressure is what you feel when others your age inspire you to do something worthwhile. If you see your friends working hard at a team sport, their enthusiasm may be catching. You may find yourself exercising more often and practicing a sport in which you are interested.

Your peers can have positive effects on you in other ways. As a young teen, you are becoming more independent. You are making your own decisions more often. This can be scary. Growing up is less frightening when you have your peers to support you. You can try out your ideas on your peers and get their reaction. If you are not sure of yourself, your peers can help give you confidence.

in your journal

Study the tips for making new friends. If you want to make new friends, use your private journal to say how you will do that. If you have someone particular in mind, write down ways you could start a conversation with that person.

C Offer to help someone. If someone in your class is having difficulty with math or needs help fixing something, offer to help. By reaching out to others, you let them know you want to be friends.

D Volunteer to work on a committee or project. Join classmates who are helping with a recycling effort or decorating the gym for a school dance. Working together forms bonds among people.

Negative Peer Pressure

Negative peer pressure is what you feel when others your age try to persuade you to do something you don't want to do. This might be using tobacco or other drugs, including alcohol. It might be doing something dangerous or illegal or something that hurts other people. You may also be pressured to try something you feel you are not ready for and that goes against your values.

Dealing with Negative Peer Pressure

As you grow into a young adult, it is important for you to develop your own identity, one that is separate from that of the group. When someone challenges what you believe in, it is important for you to know how to stand your ground and what you can do to resist negative peer pressure.

One way to deal with negative peer pressure is to avoid getting into difficult situations. That way you prevent problems from occurring in the first place. You also need to ask yourself, "Is this something I need or would I be better off doing something else?" Think about your values, too. Ask yourself, "Am I being asked to do something that goes against my beliefs or my common sense?"

If you do find yourself in a situation in which you need to resist negative peer pressure, you can act in a number of ways. **Figure 4.7** shows some of the refusal skills you can use.

Figure 4.7

Closing the Doors on Negative Peer Pressure

A Get out of the situation. There is no need to defend your position. If you wish, state your reasons clearly, and then leave.

B Don't agree to "meet the person halfway." It is your right to say no. Giving in a little is still giving in.

C If the person persists, make up an excuse. Say anything that will end the conversation.

D Suggest some alternatives to the behavior the other person is suggesting. Create a little positive peer pressure of your own.

E If all else fails, walk away. That's certain to end the debate.

Review

Using complete sentences, answer the following questions on a separate piece of paper.

Reviewing Terms and Facts

1. **Vocabulary** Use the word *reliable* in a sentence to show that you understand its meaning.
2. **Recall** What is positive peer pressure?
3. **List** Give three examples of ways to deal with negative peer pressure.

Thinking Critically

4. **Compare** Look up the words *friend* and *peer* in a dictionary. In what ways are peers and friends similar? In what ways are they different?
5. **Apply** Gina's family just moved to your community. What advice would you give Gina on making new friends?
6. **Interpret** Think about the saying: "One rotten apple spoils the barrel." What do you think this saying means? How might it apply to peer pressure?

Applying Health Concepts

7. **Growth and Development** Write an advertisement for an "ideal" friend, stating the qualities you look for. Include the activities and interests you would like to share with the friend. Display the ad anonymously on a bulletin board. Do other ads list similar requirements?
8. **Personal Health** Working with a classmate, think ahead of a situation in which your peers might try to pressure you into doing something you don't want to do. Plan how you would use refusal skills. Develop a skit and role-play it for the class.

HEALTH LAB

Recognizing Peer Pressure

Introduction: To belong to a peer group, you may feel that you have to think and act the way the group does. This is called peer pressure. Peer pressure may influence your choice of clothes and the way you spend your time. It may also influence your decisions about alcohol, tobacco, and other drugs.

Peer pressure is everywhere in society. All age groups must deal with peer pressure, but it is especially common among young teens. Learning to recognize peer pressure will help you decide whether to go along with the group or to act as an individual.

Objective: During the next week, observe the peer pressure around you. Try to identify one example of peer pressure in each of these areas:

- in your life and the lives of your friends.
- in the lives of your family (parents or brothers and sisters).
- on television or in other media.

Materials and Method: You will need a sheet of paper for each observation. Divide the sheet into two columns. Head the columns with the words *Observation* and *Analysis.* In the Observation column, write just the facts—who, when, where, and what. If possible, include quotes from the people involved to give an idea of their thinking. In the Analysis column, write your interpretation of the event. Answer questions such as these: In what way was peer pressure involved? Was the pressure positive or negative? Did the person handle the pressure correctly? If not, what should the person have done?

Observation and Analysis: At the end of the week, share your observations and analyses with a group of your classmates. See how many different situations of peer pressure the group identifies. Discuss consequences of giving in to negative pressure and ways of resisting it.

TEEN HEALTH DIGEST

CON$UMER FOCU$

The Ad Bandwagon

The scene: A sunny beach

The people: A group of good-looking teens

The action: A volleyball game. The teens laugh, horse around, and drink from bottles of soda . . .

We all know what it takes to have a good time like the one shown in this ad—friends and an enjoyable activity. What *don't* you need? The soda.

Ads like this use the *bandwagon technique.* The expression "Everyone is jumping on the bandwagon" means that everyone is eager to become part of a trend. This ad implies that to have fun, you should drink the soda.

Myths and Realities

Safe Surfing

The World Wide Web offers you amazing opportunities to have fun and expand your mind. To get the most out of the on-line world, though, you should keep in mind the following "netiquette" tips as you surf the Net.

- Treat others as you want to be treated! That means no "flaming"—a term for sending mean messages in chat rooms or by E-mail.
- Keep your privacy! That means not giving out family information (such as a parent's credit card number) to people you meet on-line. Also, don't tell your real name, address, or phone number, or your school's address.
- Don't agree to meet with someone you talk to on-line unless your parents come along.

Try This:

Watch for "bandwagon" ads. Identify the cool or fun behavior each ad shows. Then list what you really need to have the kind of fun shown in the ad. Odds are, the sponsor's product won't be on your list!

HEALTH UPDATE

Shyness: Don't Let It Hold *You* Back

- *You pass a cute new student in the hall.*
- *Tryouts for the school play are coming up—you'd love to get a part.*

Do any of these situations give you butterflies? Just about everyone is shy at some time or another.

However, if you are too timid to make friends or try new activities, then maybe shyness has got the best of you. Psychologists recommend the following process for overcoming shyness:

- **Visualize.** Picture yourself talking to a new friend. Go over the scene a few times. Above all, don't be afraid to fail.
- **Do it.** After you have visualized the scene, try doing it in real life. Maybe things won't go just as you had planned. They just might go better!

Try This: *The next time you face a situation that gives you butterflies, write down all of the positive possible outcomes. Focus on them, and not your fears, as you face the situation.*

Sports and Recreation

Have Fun, Stay Healthy

Sports are fun and can keep you physically fit. Did you know that sports can also help you achieve *social* health?

A recent study from the U.S. Department of Health and Human Services says just that. According to the study, taking part in positive, goal-directed activities like sports gives teens a chance to develop social skills and build character. It may also reduce unhealthy behavior, such as drug abuse.

That's why—whether your game is varsity basketball, church league softball, or in-line skating with your friends—it's smart to get active, set goals, and stay healthy!

Teens Making a Difference

Peer Mediators

Meg and Teri have just started yelling at each other in the cafeteria. Fortunately, they have a way to solve their problem quickly.

Meg and Teri attend Dakota Heights Middle School. The school has 21 peer mediators who help other students resolve conflicts.

Minutes after their shouting match, Teri and Meg sit face to face with Gina, a peer mediator. Each girl has a chance to state her side of the argument. Then Gina helps them talk over possible solutions. Soon Teri and Meg come to a solution that satisfies them both.

Score another solution for peer mediation. Why is it so successful? "Lots of times students talk to me, a peer mediator, more freely than to an adult," says Gina.

Lesson

5 Responsible Peer Relationships

This lesson will help you find answers to questions that teens often ask about dating and marriage. For example:

- **Do most people my age feel more comfortable going out in a group?**
- **What do I need to think about before I go out?**

Words to Know

socializing
group dating
responsible dating

Changing Relationships

During adolescence, your relationships with other people begin to change. You depend less on your parents and other adults to make decisions for you. As you grow in knowledge and experience, you begin to make more decisions for yourself. For example, you begin to decide who you will spend your time with and how you will spend that time.

As a child, you may have had a limited circle of friends. Perhaps you played just with the children in your neighborhood. Now your circle of friends and acquaintances is expanding. By being with different people, you practice your skills at **socializing** (SOH·shuh·ly·zing), *getting along with and communicating with other people.* You become aware of your strengths and weaknesses. You learn how to express yourself and how to work out differences of opinion with others.

As you begin to spend more time with your friends, you'll have a chance to practice and improve your social skills.

Dating Relationships

Dating can help you learn more about relating to people of the opposite gender. It can help you learn about yourself as well.

Not all teens your age want to date or feel ready to date. Some teens have other interests they prefer for the time being. Some teens are shy, and the idea of dating makes them nervous. It is a good idea to date only when you're ready. If anyone pressures you into dating, you probably will not have fun.

Going Out in Groups

Group dating, *going out with male and female friends at the same time,* is popular among teens. There may be an equal number of boys and girls, there may be more girls than boys, or there may be more boys than girls.

Going out in a group is a good way to ease into dating. Many young people are more comfortable going to parties, movies, and dances in groups. You do not have to worry about making conversation with one person. You can get used to being with people in a social situation. What's more, going out with the group can be a lot of fun. **Figure 4.8** shows ways to have fun with a group.

Figure 4.8
Activities to Do with a Group

Sports	Entertainment	At Home
bowling	dancing	board games
in-line skating	spectator sports—football, baseball, basketball	computer games
swimming	picnic	video rental
volleyball	amusement park	pizza party
ice-skating	fair	barbecue
bicycling	movies	
sledding	youth center activities	
hiking		

Cultural Connections

Matchmaker, Matchmaker ACTIVITY!

Dating is not practiced in some cultures because parents arrange the marriages of their children. They might use the services of a matchmaker to find a mate for their son or daughter. In other cultures, adult chaperones accompany young men and women on dates. Do some research in the library or ask people you know for more information on interesting dating and marriage customs around the world. Share your findings with your classmates.

in your journal

Study the list of activities to do when you are out in a group. Can you think of other activities you would like to do? Use your journal to make your own list. Write down the three categories—Sports, Entertainment, At Home—and list ideas that are interesting to you and your friends.

When parents set rules about dating, they are showing their love and concern.

Individual Dating

When you go out with a group, you may begin to develop special feelings about one person. You may want to spend more time with that person alone rather than with the group. Whether you are with a group or with one other person, you are responsible for your behavior. **Responsible dating** means *being trustworthy, showing respect for the other person, and thinking ahead about the consequences of your actions.*

You can be responsible and show respect for your date by choosing an activity that both of you will enjoy. Use good communication skills. Be honest with yourself about your feelings for the other person. Go out with someone because you want to. Sometimes teens spend time with certain people to win the approval of their peer group. Go out with someone because you want to get to know that person and have fun.

Abstinence Before Marriage

Most parents or guardians show love and concern for their children by setting limits and establishing guidelines. Because parents want to protect their teens' self-respect, values, and safety, they do not want their teens to be sexually active. Responsible teens show respect for their parents or guardians when they practice abstinence from sexual activity before marriage.

During your teen years physical attraction for another person can increase. It is easier, however, to decide on what limits you will set before you are in a situation that is difficult to control. You can decide to avoid behaviors that arouse sexual feelings. You can also avoid situations that make it more difficult to use self-control.

These teens are giving themselves time for their friendship to develop through a mutual interest.

Speaking with a parent, guardian, or other trusted adult about this important issue will help. You can talk about the physical and emotional feelings you may be experiencing. These feelings are a normal, healthy part of growing up. He or she can offer suggestions for demonstrating affection in safe and healthy ways, such as:

- hugging or holding hands.
- doing something nice for the other person.
- giving compliments.
- giving cards or small gifts.
- writing poems or letters.

Individuals who choose sexual abstinence know that they will not have to worry about getting sexually transmitted diseases, becoming pregnant, or dying of AIDS. They know that they will gain self-respect by following their values. Also, practicing abstinence makes it easier for them to remain physically and emotionally healthy.

By practicing abstinence you show that you care about your welfare. When you choose abstinence you know that sex will never become the focus of your relationship. Instead, you establish a relationship based on trust, caring, and friendship. There are other ways to show your affection that do not include risking your physical and emotional well-being. More and more teens choose abstinence from sexual activity for the following reasons:

- to avoid the risk of getting sexually transmitted diseases.
- to avoid the risk of unplanned pregnancy.
- because they believe that they should wait until they are married.
- because it makes their relationships less complicated.
- because they want others to respect them and their values.
- to give themselves time to explore other aspects of their relationships.
- to focus on planning and working toward their future.
- for religious and moral reasons.

Ways to Say No

There may be times when you feel pressured by your peers to participate in an unsafe activity. In these instances, remind yourself that it is your life, not anyone else's. You can make your own choices. It will help you to practice how you will say no before you find yourself under pressure. Here are some ways you can say no.

- "I'm just not ready for a sexual relationship."
- "I want to respect my parents' wishes."
- "If you loved me, you wouldn't pressure me."
- "I'm not ready to be a parent."
- "I want to wait until I'm married."
- "I want to concentrate on my studies right now."
- "I don't want to risk getting a sexually transmitted disease."

Don't ever forget that you have the right to say no. You will respect yourself, and others will respect you.

Teens know that there are many ways to show affection and have fun together that do not include sex.

Lesson 5

Review

Using complete sentences, answer the following questions on a separate sheet of paper.

Reviewing Terms and Facts

1. **Restate** Explain how group dating could improve your socializing skills.
2. **Vocabulary** In your own words, explain what is meant by the term *responsible dating*.
3. **Recall** Name three reasons teens may have for abstinence from sexual activity before marriage.

Thinking Critically

4. **Analyze** What are the advantages of group dating over individual dating?
5. **Evaluate** How could practicing how to say no help you remain sexually abstinent?

Applying Health Concepts

6. **Growth and Development** Write a skit in which one teen asks another teen to go to the movies and he or she refuses. Write it so that the teen shows respect when he or she says no. Write several different last lines to your skit, showing different ways a person can handle the disappointment of being turned down.

Lesson 6

Marriage and Parenthood

This lesson will help you find answers to questions that teens often ask about marriage and parenthood. For example:

- **Why do people marry? What makes a marriage work?**
- **What does being a parent involve?**
- **Why are teens discouraged from becoming parents?**

Words to Know

love
commitment
parenting
responsibility

Marriage

"I do" are words most American adults say at some time in their lives. Statistics show that nine out of ten Americans marry. Marriage is a serious decision that is not to be taken lightly.

Reasons for Getting Married

Most people get married because they are "in love." **Love** is *a strong emotional attachment to another person.* By getting married, people demonstrate their desire to live together and care for each other throughout their lives.

People get married for other important reasons. Most people feel that marriage provides a stable environment in which to raise children. Many people enjoy the companionship and comfort that marriage brings. As a contract, marriage entitles the partners to certain financial benefits as well.

Getting married is a serious commitment. Two elements are usually present in all marriage ceremonies. First, the couple declares their willingness to be married, and second, the ceremony takes place in front of witnesses.

Cultural Connections

Happily Ever After

Cultures differ in what parents expect of their children. These differences are sometimes apparent in the stories parents read to their children. For example, the story "The Three Little Pigs" stresses the values of hard work and determination. In the Turkish version of this story, called "The Three Little Hares," the values of tradition and following parents' instructions are emphasized. In this version, the first two hares disobey their parents and build tree houses. Soon after their houses are built, these two hares are eaten by a fox. The third hare follows his parents' wishes and builds an underground den. This hare is safe from the fox and lives happily ever after.

Factors Affecting Marriage

While love is important in a marriage, many other factors affect whether a marriage will be successful. One of the most important of these is emotional maturity. Emotionally mature people bring commitment, effort, compromise, good communication, and understanding to a marriage. A **commitment** (kuh·MIT·muhnt) is *a pledge or a promise.* Emotional maturity includes understanding someone else's needs and feelings and being able, at times, to put the other person's needs ahead of your own.

Parenting Roles and Responsibility

Many people marry to have children. Parenthood can be one of life's most wonderful experiences. Most parents find great joy in loving and caring for a child. They watch excitedly as the child grows and develops over the years. When the child becomes a healthy, well-adjusted adult, they feel a great deal of satisfaction.

A parent is the father or mother of a child. However, there is a difference between being a parent and parenting. **Parenting** means *meeting a child's physical, emotional, social, and mental needs.*

Many people, including grandparents, aunts and uncles, and teachers, use parenting skills. When you take care of younger brothers or sisters or other children, you are probably using some parenting skills.

Parents work hard to see that their children's needs are met. They get great satisfaction from seeing their children grow and change.

Parenthood can be rewarding; it can also be hard, demanding work. Effective parenting requires knowledge of child development. It requires teaching, counseling, and nursing skills. It requires such qualities as patience, understanding, and a sense of humor. As the list below shows, parents must fulfill a number of responsibilities. A **responsibility** is *a duty or an obligation that depends on you.*

Parents' Contract

Although parents do not sign a contract as such, by having children they take on a number of responsibilities. If parents were to sign a contract, it might say something like this.

We, as parents, agree to do the following for our children:

- **Take care of their physical needs.** We promise to give them nutritious meals and snacks, clean clothes, and adequate shelter. We will see that the children get plenty of rest, enough exercise, and good medical care.
- **Take care of their emotional and social needs.** We promise to love them. We will help them feel accepted and valued. We will teach them to know right from wrong and how to get along with others.
- **Take care of their mental needs.** We promise to stimulate their thinking and learning. We will help them get a good education. We will teach them how to make decisions and solve problems so that they can become independent adults.

Besides taking care of their children's needs, parents must make time for themselves as individuals and make time for each other as well. They must look out for their own physical, emotional, social, and mental well-being. Being a good parent takes work!

Q&A

Baby Love

Q: I know a girl who wants a baby so she'll have something to call her own—something she can love and that will love her back. What do you think of this?

A: Many teens have the mistaken idea that a baby will satisfy their emotional needs. Loving a child is a one-way street. Young children are not yet capable of returning love in the way an adult might. Your friend is setting herself up for a major disappointment.

Teen Parenting

In the United States each year, more than 500,000 babies are born to teens. Over 75 percent of those babies are born to unmarried teens. Many unmarried teen mothers choose to keep their babies rather than give them up for adoption.

Under the best of circumstances, parenthood is a challenging task. Teen parents generally lack money, education, and emotional maturity. As a result, raising children is more challenging for teen parents than for older parents.

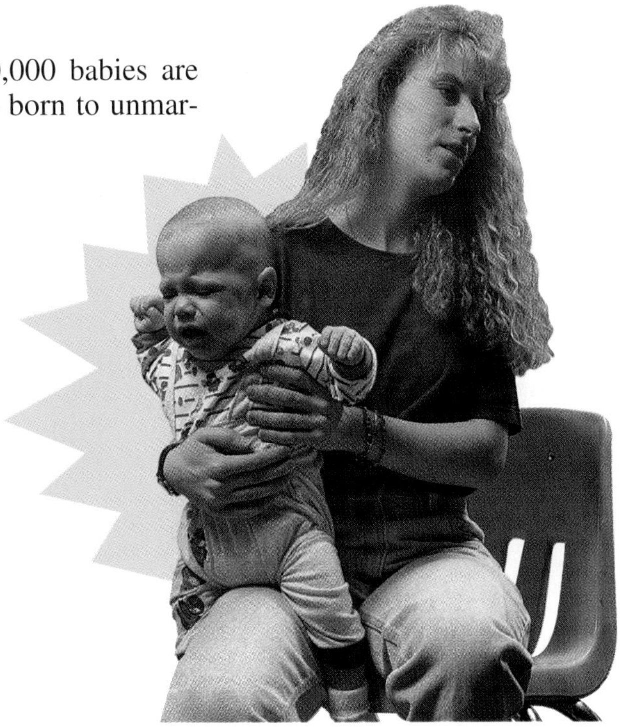

Raising a child is especially challenging for a single parent, especially a teen single parent.

Consequences of Teen Parenthood

Teen pregnancy and parenthood can present health risks, financial problems, and emotional stress. Teen parents may also find themselves with fewer choices in life.

Fewer Choices

Oftentimes, teen parents must put aside their plans for education and a fulfilling career. They may have to drop out of school to take care of their child. They may have to quit school to earn money to support their child. Teen dropouts usually find it hard to go back to school, complete their education, and graduate.

Teens without a high school diploma have a limited choice of jobs and little chance of a well-paying job. Teens who continue in school may find it difficult to take care of a baby and study.

in your journal

You have been reading about the problems teen parents face. Since there are so many of these problems, why do you think so many teens become parents? Use your private journal to write your thoughts about this.

Health Risks

Teen pregnancy and parenthood create health risks for the young mother. In the teen years, the young female body is still developing and may not be completely ready to support and nourish an unborn child. The pregnant teen may not get enough nutrients for herself and her baby, which can harm both of them.

Teen pregnancy and parenthood create health risks for the child, too. Teen mothers may not know how to take care of themselves during pregnancy. One-third of pregnant teens, for example, receive inadequate prenatal care. As a result, children born to teen mothers are more likely to have low birth weight, which can lead to health problems. These children are also more likely to have physical and mental handicaps. Raising a child with health problems is costly and stressful.

Helping Hands

Fortunately, many schools and communities provide help for pregnant teens and teen parents. **Figure 4.9** shows some of the services they offer.

Figure 4.9
Help for Teen Parents

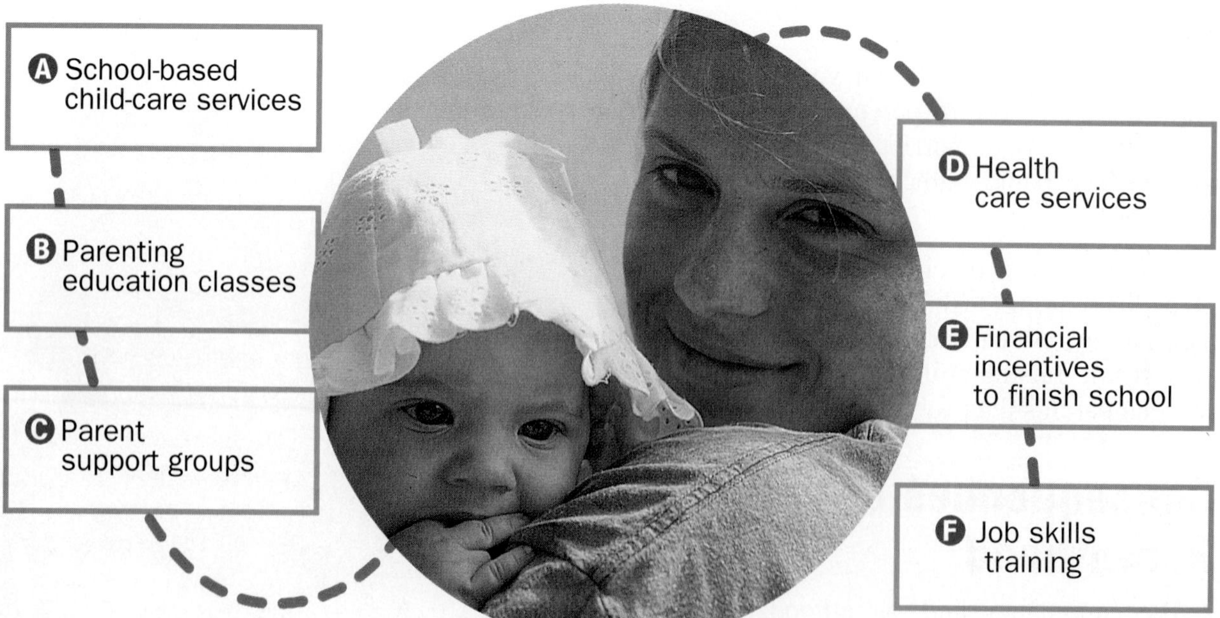

As children of teen parents grow older, they continue to be at risk for health problems. Many teen parents cannot afford to take their children to the doctor. The children do not get shots and other care they need to stay healthy. Also, teen parents may live in run-down housing, which risks accidents and disease.

Financial Problems

Raising a child costs a great deal of money. **Figure 4.10** shows just some of the items that parents need to buy. Teen parents have difficulty meeting expenses. Constantly worrying about money causes great stress. Teen parents may find themselves falling into a cycle of poverty from which they cannot escape.

Emotional and Social Stress

During adolescence, teens struggle to discover who they are and where they fit into the scheme of things. Many teens have all they can do to cope with the normal anxieties of adolescence. Adding the responsibility of caring for a baby creates even more pressure.

Parenting is a time-consuming job. Teen parents will have less time to spend with their friends, or they may be too tired for other activities. Many teen parents eventually become frustrated and resentful of the limits on their personal freedom.

Figure 4.10
Items for Baby

In the first year alone, parents need to buy hundreds of dollars' worth of items.

Review
Lesson 6

Using complete sentences, answer the following questions on a separate sheet of paper.

Reviewing Terms and Facts

1. **Vocabulary** In your own words, explain what is meant by the term *commitment.*
2. **Vocabulary** Use the word *responsibility* in a sentence to show that you understand its meaning.
3. **List** What are the three types of needs in children for which parents are responsible?

Thinking Critically

4. **Evaluate** How does emotional maturity help a marriage succeed?
5. **Explain** How do you use parenting skills? How does this differ from parenthood?
6. **Hypothesize** What factors enable parents to practice effective parenting skills?

Applying Health Concepts

7. **Growth and Development** Observe young children and their parents in a public place such as a park, playground, or shopping mall. Notice instances in which the parent uses effective parenting techniques. Keep a list of these techniques and share your findings with your classmates.
8. **Health of Others** Set up a debate that explores the rights and responsibilities you believe teenage males have when their sexual partner becomes pregnant. How—if at all—does the role of the father-to-be differ from that of the mother-to-be?

Chapter 4 Review

Chapter Summary

- ▶ **Lesson 1** Social health is the ability to get along with the people around you. Communication, cooperation, compromise, and tolerance can all help you build healthy relationships.
- ▶ **Lesson 2** Good communication includes speaking and listening skills, refusal skills, and attention to body language.
- ▶ **Lesson 3** There are many kinds of families in the United States. Good communication can help families work out their problems.
- ▶ **Lesson 4** Good friends are loyal, reliable, sympathetic, and caring. Friends can exert peer pressure on each other in positive or negative ways.
- ▶ **Lesson 5** During your teen years, your relationships will change. Group dating is a good way to begin dating relationships.
- ▶ **Lesson 6** When people marry, they make a lifelong commitment. Parents have the responsibility to provide for their children's physical, mental, emotional, and social needs.

Reviewing Key Terms and Concepts

Using complete sentences, answer the following questions on a separate sheet of paper.

Lesson 1

1. Define the term *relationships.*
2. List three skills that can help you build strong relationships.

Lesson 2

3. List five ways in which you can practice refusal skills.
4. Explain the difference between verbal communication and nonverbal communication.

Lesson 3

5. Describe five different types of families.
6. What are some problems that affect families?

Lesson 4

7. Name four qualities of good friends.
8. What are *peers?*

Lesson 5

9. Give some examples of ways in which you socialize with people you know.
10. What are some ways for teens to say no to sex?

Lesson 6

11. What is the difference between *love* and *commitment?*
12. Define the term *parenting.*

Thinking Critically

Using complete sentences, answer the following questions on a separate sheet of paper.

13. **Suggest** What are some ways in which a school might foster tolerance among students from different cultural backgrounds?
14. **Hypothesize** When might a teen need to use refusal skills with someone other than a peer?
15. **Analyze** What is the difference between positive and negative peer pressure?
16. **Hypothesize** What are some concerns that children whose parents are divorcing might have?
17. **Evaluate** Why is teen parenthood particularly challenging?

Chapter 4 Review

Your Action Plan

You can make an action plan to improve your social health. Look back through your private journal entries for this chapter. What do your comments tell you about areas of your life that you would like to change?

Step 1 Write down your long-term goal. Make sure your goal is achievable. Making new friends is a realistic goal.

Step 2 Think of a series of short-term goals, or what you can do to move toward your long-term goal. Write these down. For example, you might decide to meet people by joining a sports team or another after-school activity.

Step 3 Plan a schedule for reaching each short-term goal. Check your schedule periodically to keep track of your progress.

When you reach your long-term goal, reward yourself with a fun activity.

In Your Home and Community

1. **Growth and Development** Volunteer to be your family's historian. Put photos of family events in an album or a scrapbook. Include stories about the funny, unusual, or special family events.
2. **Health of Others** With your classmates, write a manual or handbook to guide student behavior in your school. Include rules of conduct for the cafeteria and halls and for school dances and other events. The handbook should promote respect for all adults and other students. Make your handbook available to students.

Building Your Portfolio

1. **Cultural Exchange** Arrange to interview an older adult or a person from a different cultural background. Plan some topics to talk about, such as expectations of teens, traditions and cultural celebrations, or jobs and hobbies. Practice good speaking and listening skills during the conversation. Ask the other person for permission to tape-record the conversation, and include the tape in your portfolio.
2. **Peer Pressure** Write a short play about teens and negative peer pressure. You might base the play on something that happened to you or to a friend. Set the scene, and then have a teen character use refusal skills to get out of an unhealthy situation. Ask your classmates to act out the play. Place a copy of your play in your portfolio.
3. **Personal Assessment** Look through all the activities and projects you did for this chapter. Choose one that you would like to include in your portfolio.

Chapter 5

Conflict Resolution and Violence Prevention

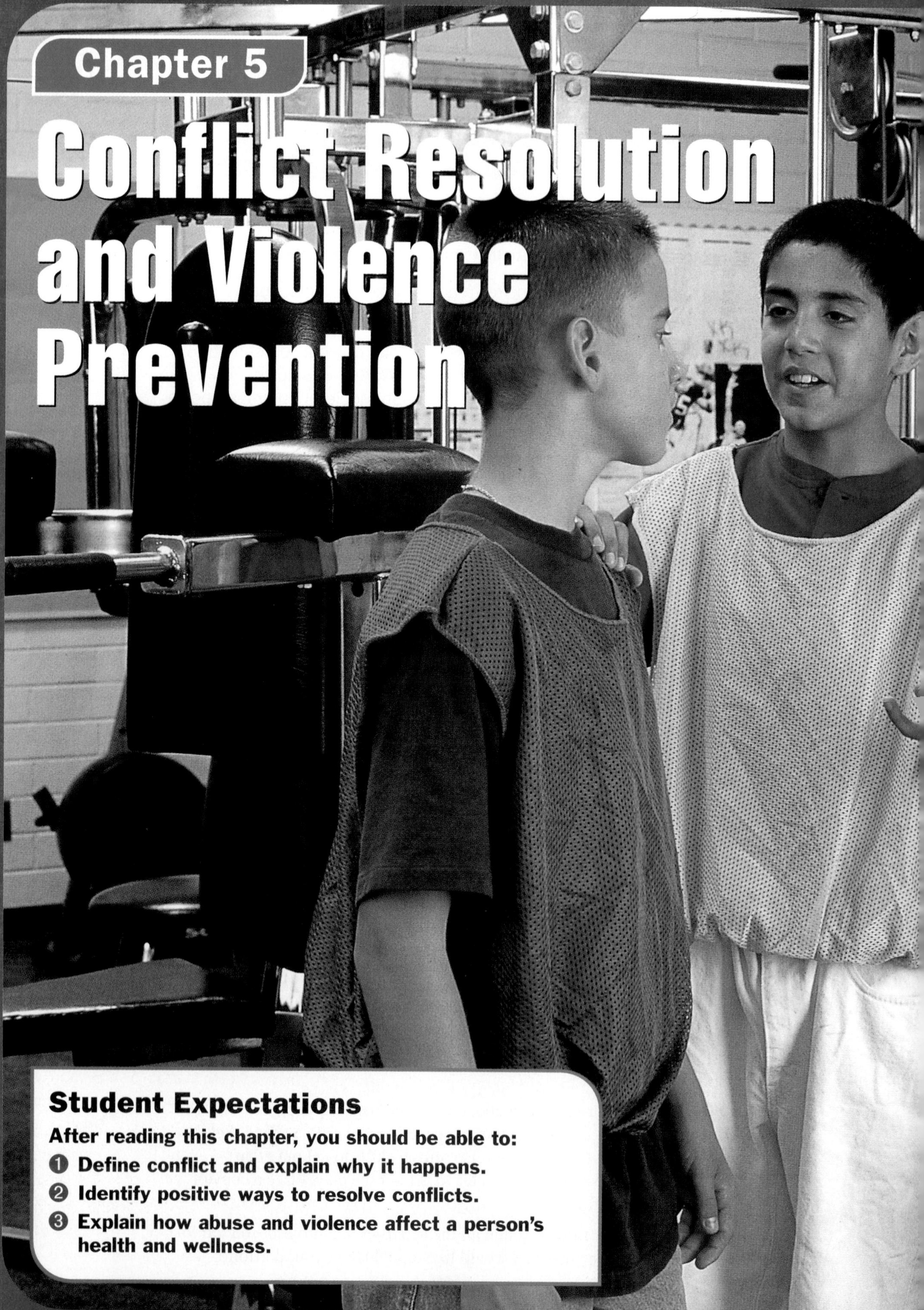

Student Expectations

After reading this chapter, you should be able to:

1. **Define conflict and explain why it happens.**
2. **Identify positive ways to resolve conflicts.**
3. **Explain how abuse and violence affect a person's health and wellness.**

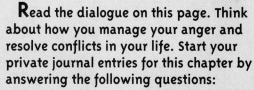

Teen Chat Group

Rafael: Kyle, why don't you tell your side of the story? When you're done, Andrew can explain it from his point of view.

Kyle: It's simple. I thought Andrew was my friend, but he went behind my back and asked my girlfriend to the dance.

Rafael: Okay. Now tell your side, Andrew.

Andrew: It's true that I asked Julia to the dance, but I didn't know that she was Kyle's girlfriend.

Rafael: Kyle, when did you start seeing Julia?

Kyle: Our first date will be at the dance.

Rafael: Did Andrew know that you were taking Julia?

Kyle: No, I guess not.

Rafael: It looks like this was just a misunderstanding. Can you guys shake hands and stay friends?

in your journal

Read the dialogue on this page. Think about how you manage your anger and resolve conflicts in your life. Start your private journal entries for this chapter by answering the following questions:

- How do you handle conflicts in your life? Do your methods for resolving conflict have positive or negative outcomes?
- What do you think can be done to resolve conflict in healthy ways?
- Does your school have a peer mediation or other conflict resolution program?
- How might an unresolved conflict lead to violent behavior?

When you reach the end of the chapter, you will use your journal entries to make an action plan.

Lesson 1

What is Conflict?

This lesson will help you find answers to questions that teens often ask about conflict and anger. For example:

- **What is conflict?**
- **What factors can cause conflict?**
- **What causes some conflicts to become violent?**
- **How can I manage my anger constructively?**

Words to Know

conflict
resource
prejudice

Conflicts Are a Part of Life

What is conflict? **Conflict** is *a struggle, disagreement, or a difference of opinion between opposing viewpoints.* It can involve individuals or groups. Conflicts arise among friends, family members, and groups in a community, as well as among different communities and countries. There are also conflicts that one person can experience within himself or herself. Sometimes a conflict can be positive and can produce needed change.

Conflicts are a part of everyday life, and many can be settled easily. For example, two friends might disagree about which video to watch. They might settle the dispute by deciding to watch one video one night and the other another night. A conflict does not have to be a contest in which one side wins and the other loses. The best solution is a fair one, in which both sides win.

Some conflicts require thought and planning to resolve. Two community groups might have to meet many times before deciding where a new road should be built. Sometimes a conflict ends only when one side accepts the other side's view. A parent and a teen might disagree about how late the teen can stay at a party, but the teen agrees to follow her parent's wishes. In other cases, the people in conflict may just agree to disagree.

Conflicts happen every day. These teens want to spend Saturday afternoon together, but they cannot agree on what to do. What might be one way to resolve their conflict?

Conflicts Over Resources

There are many reasons for conflict, but the three major causes are competition for resources, clashes between values, and exchanges involving emotional needs. A **resource** is *something usable, such as goods, property, money, or time*. At school, you and another student might want to use a computer at the same time. You are in conflict over a resource—the computer. You and a sister or brother might argue over the space each of you can use in a closet you both share.

A conflict over a resource might involve money and how to spend it. Imagine that a club or other school organization has a set amount of money for an end-of-the-year party. Members of the group might be involved in long discussions about how to divide that money between refreshments and entertainment.

Time is also a resource, and teens often have limited amounts of time. Suppose one friend wants you to shop at the mall this afternoon, and another friend wants you to play soccer. You may be in conflict over how to spend your time. You could be in conflict over whether you can participate in sports or band and still keep your paper route after school.

Conflicts Over Values

Your values are the beliefs and ideas you consider important. A conflict over values may involve you and your parents disagreeing about what is an appropriate way for you to dress or do your hair. You might argue with a friend who does not value studying as much as you do, and who keeps urging you to go to the mall with him when you are trying to study for a test. Another example of a conflict over values could involve a student who wants to participate in a school-sponsored event but cannot because it is held on a religious holiday. If you had such a conflict, what would you do? How do you think such a conflict might be resolved?

interNET CONNECTION

Click on the Glencoe Web site for strategies to help you manage conflicts and protect yourself from violence.

http://www.glencoe.com/sec/health

Language Arts Connection

Literary Conflicts ACTIVITY!

Conflict is an important part of most stories. It makes a story interesting and exciting. Sometimes the conflict is within a character, but often it is between two characters. Identify a conflict in a book or story that you are reading. Write a description of the characters involved in the conflict, what the problem is, and how the conflict is or is not settled.

The two teens who share this room disagree on how it should be kept. One values neatness; the other does not.

Cultural Connections

No Head Pats, Please ACTIVITY!

Different cultures have different customs about touching others. In some cultures it is very common to pat or touch a small child or baby on the head. In other cultures touching is viewed as inappropriate. For example, a person from the Vietnamese culture might be deeply offended if you were to pat his or her child on the head. A person from another culture who did not know this could cause a conflict by such an action without even knowing it.

Interview someone in your community who comes from a culture different from yours. Are there differences in customs that you think might cause conflicts? Share your findings with the class.

Conflicts Involving Emotional Needs

People's basic emotional needs include the need to belong and the need to feel respected and worthwhile. Conflicts may arise when people are excluded from groups they would like to join. Also, when people show disrespect to another person or group, disagreements are bound to occur. Sometimes a person may try to build herself up by putting another person down, and conflict results. For example, a student who is disappointed that she is not chosen for the school academic team might make fun of a student who is chosen.

Why Some Conflicts Get Out of Hand

If a conflict is not managed successfully, it may get out of hand. Some conflicts may even become violent. It is important to recognize what can cause conflicts to flare out of control. Recognizing and successfully dealing with conflict can be the key to preventing violence. It is easier to resolve a conflict peacefully in the early stages before the situation escalates.

Anger

Everyone feels angry now and then. When you are angry, hormones are released, causing your heart to beat faster. Blood rushes to your face, and the palms of your hands may feel sweaty as your body prepares to take action. If you manage anger well, these physical changes can energize you to reach a goal.

If anger is not managed well, however, the conflict can worsen. Dwelling on how angry you are does not help you lessen your anger. Instead, the anger builds up and may lead to unreasonable rage. The angry person can no longer think clearly, and violence may result. One way to lessen that anger is to talk about it with someone (see **Figure 5.1**). **Figure 5.2** shows other positive ways to manage anger.

Figure 5.1
Talking It Out

When you dwell on your anger instead of trying to manage it, it can sometimes get the best of you. One way to defuse anger is to talk it out with someone.

Figure 5.2
Positive Ways to Manage Anger

I'm so ANGRY!
Take time to cool down.
Attack the problem, not the person.
PROBLEM
Explain to the other person how his or her actions make you feel.
Brainstorm reasonable ways to handle the situation.
Try to imagine the other person's point of view.
Talk to a trusted friend, adult, or school counselor if you cannot resolve the problem yourself.

Name-Calling and Bullying

Be careful not to resort to name-calling and bullying, which can cause conflicts to escalate. Both behaviors work against settling a conflict because they increase the level of anger, hurt, and fear. Name-calling is attacking the person rather than the problem. When parties in a conflict focus on personal attacks rather than on the problem, finding a solution becomes difficult.

If you are dealing with someone who does resort to bullying, walk away from the situation. Bullying usually involves a threat of physical or mental harm. Bullies often view the world as unsafe and imagine threats where none exist. If you find yourself the victim of a bully, avoid that person, or talk about the situation with a school counselor, parent, or other adult. A counselor or adult may be able to help the bully to see the situation in a better light.

in your journal

Think about times when you have been angry. In your journal, make a list of all the ways in which you express your anger. Decide which of these ways is most likely to escalate a conflict, and draw a line through that one. Then describe an alternative way to manage your anger.

Teen Issues

Why the Violence?

Most students think that drugs and peer pressure lead to violence. In a national survey for the National Crime Prevention Council and the National Institute for Citizen Education in the Law, students were asked what factors contributed to violence among teens. Sixty-one percent blamed drugs, and 52 percent blamed peer pressure. What factors do you think contribute to violence among teens?

Group Pressure

Group pressure can push a conflict toward violence. Imagine two girls arguing over whether one is flirting with the other's boyfriend. Students crowd around the arguing teens and begin shouting, "Fight! Fight!" Pressure from peers can have an impact on conflict, making a small problem escalate into a violent one. Keep in mind that the group that encourages a fight usually has little or nothing to lose.

Sometimes people get caught up in what a group thinks and feels. These people ignore their own thoughts, respond as the group wants them to, and therefore may act in ways that are different from the way they would normally act. Although it does not cause prejudice, group pressure can cause people to act with prejudice, sometimes in ways they normally would not if they were alone. **Prejudice** (PRE·juh·dis) is *an opinion that has been formed without knowledge, usually about a person's race, religion, gender, or country of origin.*

Drugs and Alcohol

Drugs and alcohol affect the central nervous system, including the brain. Drugs and alcohol alter a person's feelings and affect his or her ability to think clearly, to control anger, and to make reasonable judgments. These impairments make settling conflicts more difficult.

The use of drugs and alcohol can also make it more difficult for people to consider the consequences of their behavior. This may explain why nearly half of all violent crimes are committed by people who are under the influence of alcohol or other drugs. Avoiding situations where drugs and alcohol may be present could prevent you from being confronted with violence.

Teens can choose activities that are drug- and alcohol-free.

Review

Using complete sentences, answer the following questions on a separate sheet of paper.

Reviewing Terms and Facts

1. **Vocabulary** Define the term *conflict.* Then use the term in an original sentence.
2. **List** Give three examples of resources that may cause or create a conflict.
3. **Vocabulary** Define *prejudice.*

Thinking Critically

4. **Explain** Prejudice and group pressure often work together to escalate a conflict. Give an example of how this might happen.
5. **Analyze** Look at the ways to manage anger listed on page 141. Describe how each of them would make resolving a conflict easier.

Applying Health Concepts

6. **Health of Others** With other students, brainstorm positive ways to combat name-calling and bullying in your school. Make a poster that tells other teens how to do this. Obtain permission to hang the poster in the school hallway or lunchroom.
7. **Personal Health** Describe situations or remarks that make you angry. Then make a list of healthy activities that will help you release your anger in constructive ways.

HEALTH LAB

A Survey of Conflicts

Introduction: Analyzing past conflicts and how they were managed can give insight into effective ways to manage future conflicts.

Objective: With a small group of classmates, keep a record of conflicts observed at home and in school over a one-week period. Note how the conflicts are managed. Then analyze the conflicts, and suggest better ways to settle those conflicts that were not resolved or managed well.

Materials and Methods: Work together to create a sheet to record information about conflicts that are observed. A recording sheet might be set up as follows.

Conflict number:

Location:

Number of people involved:

Problem:

Was the conflict settled? If yes, how?

Each member of the group should use the sheet to record information about at least four conflicts that he or she observes during the week.

Observations and Analysis: After working on your own and completing the recording sheet, get back together with your group. Discuss what you observed. How many of the conflicts were settled? How were they settled? Discuss at least two conflicts that were not settled or were settled unsatisfactorily. Brainstorm ideas for better ways in which those conflicts could have been settled, and write an action plan.

Lesson 2

Managing Conflict

This lesson will help you find answers to questions that teens often ask about managing conflict. For example:

- **What are some techniques used to manage conflict constructively?**
- **What is mediation?**
- **How does peer mediation work in schools?**
- **Who can become a peer mediator?**

Words to Know

tolerance
mediation
neutrality
confidentiality
negotiation

Conflict Resolution Skills

Each conflict can be considered an opportunity to reach an agreement or positive change. Many conflicts are easily resolved. For example, if two teens both want to use the same CD player, and they agree to take turns, they have resolved their conflict. Conflict can serve a useful purpose and has the potential to be constructive.

Sometimes, however, to resolve a conflict, the parties may have to compromise, or to give up some part of their original positions. Consider the following situation: Carlo and Tomas take turns making supper for their mom. Carlo loves to make spaghetti. Tomas, however, says he hates spaghetti, and he complains loudly every time Carlo makes it. Carlo might agree to make spaghetti less often. Tomas might agree not to complain when Carlo makes spaghetti.

There are some conflicts that are never resolved, but most conflicts can be managed. In this case, the parties respect their differences and agree to disagree. Parents and their teens may never agree on what music they like, but can agree to respect each other's choices.

in your journal

Think about a conflict you have been involved in that was either difficult to resolve or was not resolved. In your journal, describe the factors that made this conflict hard to resolve. Tell what impact you think peer mediation could have had in helping resolve this conflict in a positive way.

Sometimes parties in a conflict have to compromise in order to reach a solution.

Basic Principles of Conflict Resolution

In order for people in conflict to move toward agreement, they must practice good communication skills—using self-control and positive emotional expression to convey their viewpoints. They must cooperate with each other in searching for a solution. They also need to show **tolerance**—that is, *respect for each other's point of view.* Finally, each person must be willing to take responsibility for her or his own actions. **Figure 5.3** illustrates the basic principles of conflict resolution.

Skills That Work

There are skills and techniques that support the principles of conflict resolution. You may already practice some of these skills every day. You may want to try other, new skills the next time you find yourself in a conflict.

- **Use "I" statements.** You can speak only for yourself. Instead of: "You make me feel . . . ," say: "I feel bad when I hear you say . . ."
- **Listen actively.** This means making eye contact with the person who is speaking and repeating what the other person has said so that both parties know that they are understood: "You mean you feel put down when I . . ."
- **Use time-outs.** If necessary, take a break from the discussion to calm down. Go for a walk or listen to some of your favorite music.
- **Manage your anger.** Don't let your anger prevent you from thinking clearly. Calm down and try to keep an open mind.
- **Apologize.** Saying that you are sorry for your part in the conflict can help in finding a solution.

Cultural Connections

Eyeing the Situation

Many people consider direct eye contact friendly, respectful, and a sign of paying attention. However, this is not true for all cultures. People from some Native American and Asian cultures may consider direct eye contact rude. In these cultures it is more respectful to keep the eyes down or to make only occasional eye contact. What impact might cultural differences such as these have on conflicts and their resolution?

Figure 5.3
Principles of Conflict Resolution
Each of these principles must be working for conflicts to reach resolution.

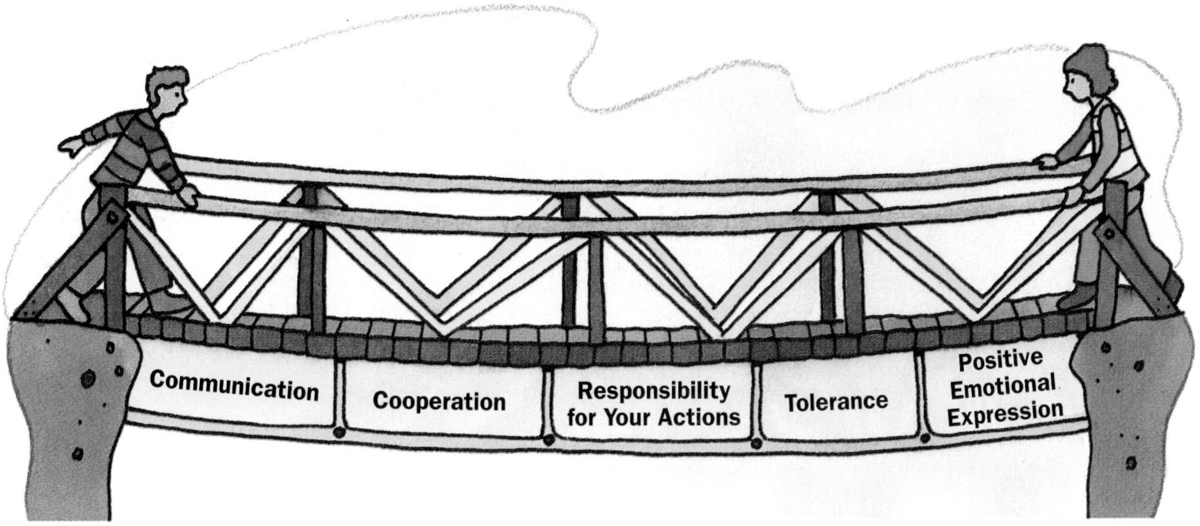

Your Total Health

Fitness Helps Keep You Calm

Studies have shown that people who are aerobically fit are better able to handle emotional stress. Fear and anxiety cause an increase in anyone's heart rate. A person who is fit will have less of an increase in heart rate than a person who is less physically fit. A lower heart rate helps you stay calm and in control of your emotions.

- **Go for a win-win solution.** Brainstorm for solutions. Be creative. There is usually more than one possible solution. If both parties feel that they are getting something they wanted, they are more likely to agree with and be committed to the solution.

Mediation

In many cases, the parties in conflict can find a solution without any outside help. Some conflicts, however, need to go through **mediation** (mee·dee·AY·shuhn), *a process of having a neutral third person, a mediator, help those in conflict to find a solution.* To have confidence in the process, the parties seeking mediation need to know that the mediator will observe **neutrality** (noo·TRA·luh·tee), or make *a promise not to take sides.* They need a private place to talk. They also need to know that the mediator will observe **confidentiality** (KAHN·fuh·den·shee·A·luh·tee), or *secrecy about anything that is said* during mediation. However, mediators *must* report talk of suicide or rape for the safety of the individual. When the mediator can provide neutrality, privacy, and confidentiality, then **negotiation** (ni·goh·shee·AY·shuhn), or *the process of discussing problems to reach an agreement,* can take place. School mediators can be counselors, teachers, or parents, but in many schools, the mediators are students' peers. **Figure 5.4** shows the six steps in the mediation process. Each step depends on successful completion of the previous step.

Figure 5.4
The Mediation Process

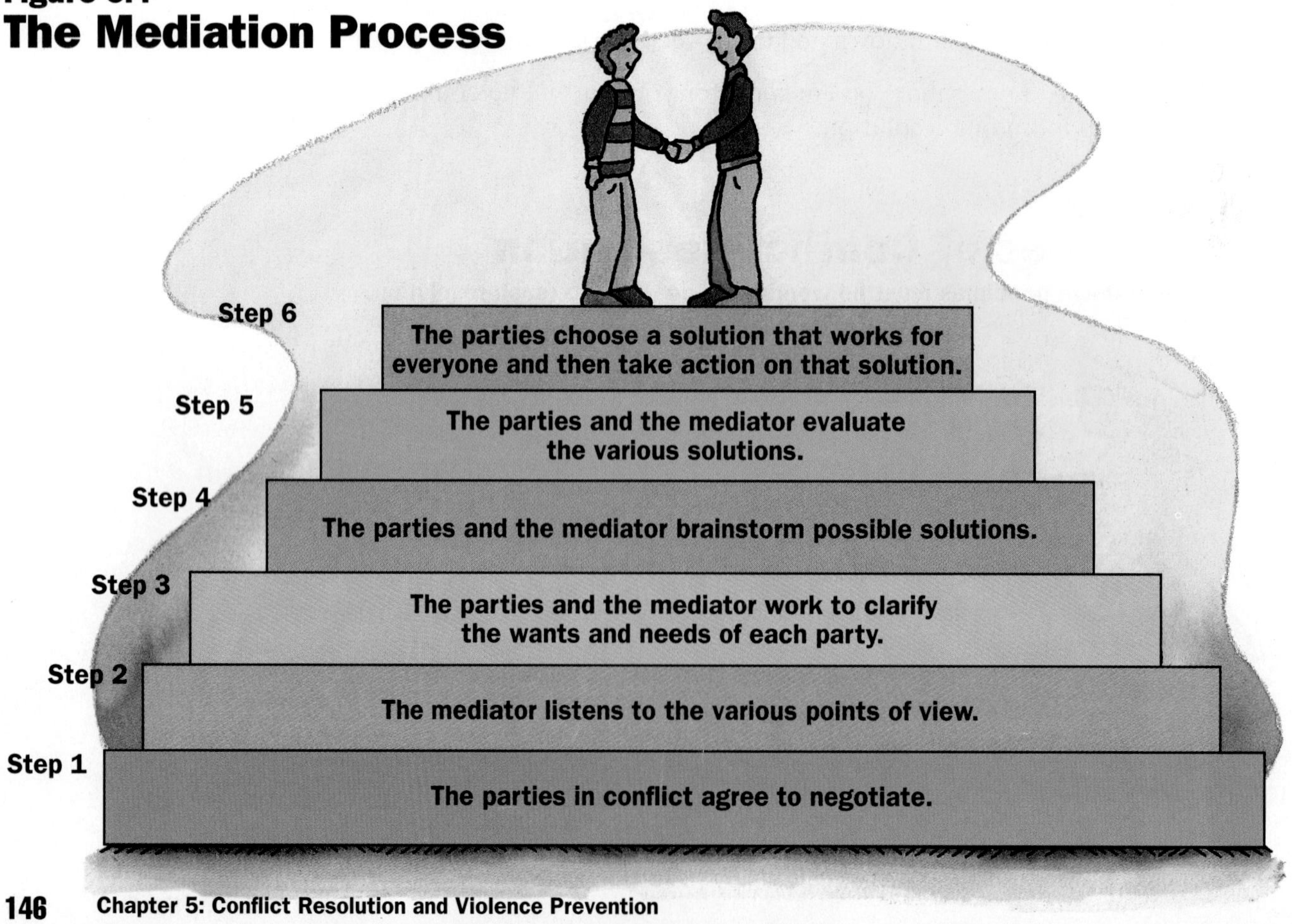

Step 6
The parties choose a solution that works for everyone and then take action on that solution.
Step 5
The parties and the mediator evaluate the various solutions.
Step 4
The parties and the mediator brainstorm possible solutions.
Step 3
The parties and the mediator work to clarify the wants and needs of each party.
Step 2
The mediator listens to the various points of view.
Step 1
The parties in conflict agree to negotiate.

Peer Mediation

Peer mediation programs can help to keep schools safe.

Many schools have peer mediation programs. In peer mediation a student serves as the mediator for students who are involved in a conflict. In many programs peer mediators work in pairs. Some of the situations appropriate for peer mediation are incidents involving name-calling, rumors, students bumping into each other in the hallways, and bullying. Working together, the students are able to solve many conflicts. However, problems involving assault or criminal behavior are not suitable for peer mediation and should be referred to a teacher, counselor, or school administrator.

Peer mediation has benefits for the students involved in the conflict, for the students acting as peer mediators, and for the whole school. The students involved in the conflict have the opportunity to get their conflict resolved in a positive way. Peer mediators learn skills that are useful in many situations throughout life, and because they can make a positive difference in people's lives, their self-esteem gets a boost. The whole school may benefit because a peer mediation program can help keep conflicts from getting out of hand. It can make the school a safer place to be.

MAKING HEALTHY DECISIONS

When to Suggest a Mediator

Marti's friends, Leticia and Tanya, aren't speaking to each other. Leticia tells Marti that Tanya tries to copy Leticia's schoolwork papers and tests. Leticia also says that when she tried to talk to Tanya about it, Tanya was very rude and just denied that she copied anything.

Later, Marti asks Tanya for her side of the story. Tanya says that she thinks Leticia is spreading rumors, and she wants to get even with Leticia. She asks Marti not to get involved.

Marti thinks that maybe she should suggest that Leticia and Tanya try peer mediation to settle their problem, but she remembers that Tanya has asked her not to get involved. She is worried because she is not sure what Tanya meant by "get even." Marti wants to stay friends with both girls. She uses the six-step decision-making process to help her decide what to do.

① **State the situation**
② **List the options**
③ **Weigh the possible outcomes**
④ **Consider your values**
⑤ **Make a decision and act**
⑥ **Evaluate the decision**

Follow-up Activities

1. Apply the six-step decision-making process to Marti's dilemma.
2. With a partner, role-play a scene in which Marti talks to Leticia about using a peer mediator to solve their conflict.
3. Imagine that you are Marti. Write a diary entry for the day she decides what to do.

Did You Know?

Actions Speak Louder Than Words ACTIVITY!

Words make up only 10 percent of the message that you communicate when you are talking. The remaining 90 percent comes from your facial expressions, your tone of voice, and your body movement. From a distance, observe two people talking. Stay far enough away so that you cannot hear what they are saying. Write a paragraph describing what you could tell about their conversation just from observing the facial expressions and body language.

Peer Mediators

Peer mediators need to have certain qualities. They must be neutral and fair so that they can help the parties in a conflict find an agreeable solution. They need to be trustworthy, since what happens during mediation must be confidential. To propose creative solutions, mediators need to be open-minded. Mediators need good communication skills—to be able to listen carefully and to express ideas clearly.

Training for Peer Mediators

Students receive special training to become peer mediators. Training may be provided by the teachers who supervise the peer mediation program at the school or by people from community peer mediation organizations. The training program can take up to 20 hours and usually covers a number of topics. The following is a sample list of topics the trainees study

- **The causes of conflict**—How conflicts start and how each conflict can be turned into an opportunity to reach an agreement.
- **Active listening**—How to restate correctly what the parties in a conflict say and understand how the parties feel.
- **Body language**—How to interpret body language, or what a person can "say" just by the way he or she sits or moves.
- **Ground rules**—Learning the importance of having self-respect and respect for the rights of others, and agreeing to accept responsibility for one's actions.
- **Note-taking**—How to take accurate notes, which are important when writing the agreement.
- **Writing an agreement**—How to write clearly so that parties understand what they are agreeing to.

During training to be peer mediators, students may role-play peer mediation situations.

Peer Mediation at Work

Imagine that Zack trips in the hall and spills his books. He looks up to see Leon laughing at him. Zack accuses Leon of causing the accident and grabs him. Leon forcefully denies having tripped Zack. Before tempers flare out of control, a passerby suggests that Zack and Leon speak to a peer mediator.

The goal of peer mediation is for parties to agree that each will do his or her part to make the solution work so that everyone wins.

After school, Zack and Leon meet with Frank, a peer mediator. Frank explains that their goal is to reach an agreement that both Zack and Leon can feel good about. Frank begins by asking each to tell his side of the story. Frank cautions them not to interrupt each other. Then Frank retells the story to be sure that he understands it.

Frank then summarizes the problem: "The problem is that when he saw Leon laughing, Zack thought Leon had tripped him. Zack grabbed Leon. Leon protested, saying he did not trip Zack." Both Zack and Leon agree that Frank understands the problem.

"Let's brainstorm some solutions," says Frank. Both Zack and Leon suggest that the other person should apologize. Frank points out that it is very crowded in the halls, and it is easy to trip. He also agrees that it feels terrible to have someone laugh at you.

Zack and Leon offer more solutions. They agree on this one: Leon apologizes for laughing at Zack; Zack apologizes for grabbing Leon. Also, they agree to speak in a friendly way to each other at least once each day for a week. Frank writes up the agreement. Zack and Leon sign it. They see Frank in a few days to be sure that the agreement works.

Review — Lesson 2

Using complete sentences, answer the following questions on a separate sheet of paper.

Reviewing Terms and Facts

1. **Vocabulary** Define the terms *neutrality* and *confidentiality.*
2. **List** Identify the basic principles of conflict resolution.
3. **Restate** Describe the process of mediation.

Thinking Critically

4. **Explain** How can a peer mediation program help to make a school a safer place?
5. **Analyze** Why is confidentiality an important part of peer mediation?

Applying Health Concepts

6. **Growth and Development** Choose an age range of children, either preschool (ages 3–5) or early elementary (ages 6–8). Create a poster for that group of children that would show ways to solve conflicts positively.

TEEN HEALTH DIGEST

People at Work

Police Officer

Name: Steve Garcia
Job: Police officer working to control gangs
Education: Training at the police academy; college courses in criminal justice, psychology, and gang sociology

Steve Garcia has a dangerous and important job. As a police officer in a major city, Garcia works with gang members to control violence.

"This is a tough business... gangs will protect their turf at all costs, and they don't care who they have to blow away in the process," says Garcia.

Myths and Realities

Safety: GUARANTEED!

You've seen the ads.

- *This steering wheel lock stops car thieves cold!*
- *Your car stereo is safe when you use our product!*
- *Stop muggers with this pepper-spray key chain!*

What the ads often fail to mention is that no product can replace common sense and caution when it comes to avoiding crime. If you use an antitheft device, read the directions and warning labels carefully. Use it as directed. Above all, don't rely on a product alone to keep you safe.

Try This:

Contact your local police force to find out about gang activity in your community. Is there any? What is being done to control it?

CON$UMER FOCU$

Child See, Child Do?

Does violent television programming lead some children to act violently? A study at the University of Washington found that violent crime doubled within 15 years of the time television began to be sold.

Another study found that some children who watched a lot of violent television shows became more aggressive than children who did not. "They see violence as a way of solving problems," says one psychiatrist.

These studies led to the "V-chip" law. The law requires all makers of television sets to include a computer chip that lets parents block certain programs. All television sets made after February 1998 will have the V-chip.

HEALTH UPDATE

School Uniforms

The U.S. Department of Education wants you to wear a uniform! According to the government, school uniforms will

- decrease violence and theft.
- help prevent gang members from wearing "colors."
- instill students with discipline.
- help parents and students resist peer pressure.
- help students concentrate.
- help school officials recognize intruders.

Try This: *Write what you think about school uniforms. Does your school have a uniform policy? If not, do you think it should? Why or why not? What would you recommend that a school uniform look like?*

Teens Making a Difference

Cooperation Works

To combat violence and gang activity, the Minneapolis, Minnesota, Parks and Recreation Department sponsors a variety of activities. Teens are offered leadership training, leisure time activities, and positive ways to improve their community. As the teens work alongside park and city police, they see that the police work to keep the entire community safe—including teens.

Lesson

3 Violence Prevention for Teens

This lesson will help you find answers to questions that teens often ask about violence. For example:

- **What is abuse?**
- **How does violence affect a person's health and wellness?**
- **What is sexual harassment?**

Words to Know

abuse
victim
battery
sexual harassment
homicide
gang
hate crime

Abuse and Violence in Relationships

In the time it takes you to read this paragraph, someone in the United States has been abused! **Abuse** (uh·BYOOS) is *physical, mental, or emotional injury inflicted on a person.* Abuse occurs across all racial and ethnic groups and all age groups. As hard as it may be to believe, abuse happens in close relationships. Parents or guardians may abuse children. Brothers and sisters sometimes abuse each other. Even a friend may abuse a friend. Remember that abuse is never okay—it is damaging to everyone involved, *and* it is illegal.

The abuser is often someone who is older, physically stronger, or otherwise more powerful than the **victim,** *the person who suffers from the abuser's negative behavior.* Anyone can be a victim, although victims of abuse are most often women, children, and the elderly. Of the children who are abused by their parents or guardians, just over one-fifth are teens 13 to 18 years old. Abuse is *never the victim's fault.*

Figure 5.5
Where to Get Help
These organizations provide information and counseling for child abuse victims and offenders.

Where to Get Help

Child Help USA	General Federation of Women's Clubs	National Committee to Prevent Child Abuse
Provides crisis counseling by mental health professionals for victims, offenders, and parents who fear that they will abuse.	10,000 clubs across the country provide prevention and education programs and support.	Chapters in all 50 states provide information and statistics on child abuse. Maintains a large publication list.

One way in which the cycle of abuse can be broken is for troubled families to get counseling from mental health professionals on better ways to communicate and manage anger.

People can abuse their victims out of hatred or dislike, but often the abusers have been victims of abuse themselves. They may have emotional problems that they do not know how to handle. Learning to communicate well and expressing emotions in nonviolent ways can be the keys to breaking the cycle of abuse. See **Figure 5.5** for sources of help for victims and their abusers.

Effects of Abuse

No one—no matter what—deserves to be treated abusively. Abuse is damaging and harmful to everyone. When children who are abused do not get help, they often will abuse others. They may harm pets or friends. Sometimes teens abuse their dating partners. When abused children grow up, they may abuse their spouses, children, or elderly parents. It is very important that this cycle of abuse be stopped!

Forms of Abuse

Although abuse is not always physically violent, it always hurts. In different ways, abuse hurts the person who is abused, the abuser, and society as a whole. Abuse may occur not only physically, but also in the form of neglect, emotional abuse, and sexual abuse.

Physical Abuse

Battery, or *the unlawful beating, hitting, or kicking of another person,* sometimes resulting in physical injury such as bruises or broken bones, is abusive. Other forms of physical abuse include burning, scalding, and throwing a victim. Shaking a baby or young child is also physical abuse. It can actually cause brain damage or death.

Neglect

Children need love and encouragement, nourishing food, clothing, and housing. A child deprived of any one of these suffers from neglect. Neglect causes physical and emotional harm. The victim may grow up feeling worthless and have difficulty setting or achieving goals. Children, as well as others who need care, such as the elderly and seriously disabled, are vulnerable to neglect.

Teen Issues

Help for Teens

Sometimes teens who suffer from abuse see no solution to their problem, and they run away. Unfortunately, runaways can experience terrible abuse on the streets. If you feel like running away, talk to a parent or a trusted adult. If you can't talk to your parents, see your school counselor, your school nurse, or a trusted clergy member. You will find more help talking to someone you know about your problems than you will find on the streets.

Emotional Abuse

Emotional abuse is hurting with words or gestures. Critical or angry words are abusive when they make the victim feel worthless or helpless. Verbal threats, especially threats of physical violence, always constitute abuse. Sometimes teens who are dating confuse romance with abuse. If a boy threatens his girlfriend with violence when he sees her with another boy, his actions are not romantic or loving. They are abusive.

Sexual Abuse

Children, teenagers, and adults, both male and female, can be victims of sexual abuse. Sexual abuse occurs when one person forces another to be part of a sexual act against his or her will. It is sexual abuse any time an adult commits a sexual act with a child or a teen, whether or not the victim objects. All sexual abuse is illegal.

Often the abuser is a trusted adult, such as a family member or friend, who may talk about love. Sometimes, the victim may feel guilty, as if she or he has done something wrong. It is important to remember, however, that sexual abuse is never the victim's fault.

Victims of sexual abuse often feel depressed, worthless, and angry. They are likely to have trouble in school. Untreated, a victim may begin to abuse others. It is very important for the victim of sexual abuse to tell an adult, such as a teacher, school nurse, counselor, or the police. Both the victim and the abuser need professional help. The right kind of help can break the cycle of abuse.

LIFE SKILLS

How to Recognize an Abusive Relationship

Do you have a dating relationship that is abusive? If you answer yes to *any* of the following questions, you do.

- Does the other person often hurt my feelings?
- Did this person ever hit or physically harm me?
- Do I feel worthless around this person?
- Does this person pressure me for sex?

If you answer yes to *all* the following questions, chances are your relationship is healthy.

- Does this person respect me?
- Do I feel good about myself around this person?
- Does this person care about my feelings and needs?

How do you develop healthy dating relationships and avoid abusive ones? Follow this advice.

- Give yourself time to get to know someone before you call him or her a real "friend."
- Until you really get to know and trust someone, double date or attend only group activities.
- Understand that no one, including you, deserves to be abused.

Follow-up Activity

Do research on abusive relationships. Find out what actions a person can take to get out of an abusive relationship and what resources are available to help you in your community.

Abuse and Violence in School

Although school should be a safe environment, abuse and violence can happen there. Remember, however, that you have the power to make your school safer. In many schools across the country, students' involvement can be the key to forming school policies and activities that promote safety and violence prevention. Peer courts and peer mediation programs are more and more common. In some schools, teams of students, parents, teachers, and administrators have instituted "zero tolerance" policies for weapons at school. That means that anyone who brings a weapon to school, even once, gets a mandatory punishment.

Sexual Harassment

One kind of abuse that may happen at school is **sexual harassment** (SEK·shuh·wuhl huh·RAS·muhnt), which is *any sexual comment, behavior, or contact that the victim does not want or that creates a hostile environment for the victim.* Teens and adults, male or female, can be the victims of sexual harassment. Sexual harassment can be unwelcome touching, noises, jokes, looks, notes, graffiti, pornography on display, or gestures with sexual meaning.

How can you tell the difference between joking or other behavior that is flirtatious and behavior that is harassment? Flirting usually feels good; harassment does not. Flirting is mutual; harassment is not. Flirting is complimentary; harassment is insulting. If the person who is the subject of jokes and other sexual behavior shows that he or she does not like it, and the behavior continues, that is sexual harassment.

Sexual harassment is illegal, and it is no laughing matter. The victim can suffer serious, long-term effects. **Figure 5.6** illustrates some of these effects.

Q&A

I Can't Tell — ACTIVITY!

Q: How can I tell if I'm being sexually harassed at school?

A: If certain behaviors have made you feel uncomfortable or have created a hostile environment for you, you probably are being harassed. Be sure to talk to an adult you can trust. You can also read about it. Check with your librarian for books and pamphlets on sexual harassment.

Figure 5.6

The Effects of Sexual Harassment Are Serious

Sexual harassment can affect the victim's physical and emotional health.

Physical Effects

- Headaches
- Lack of energy
- Skin problems
- Panic reactions
- Difficulty sleeping

Psychological Effects

- Low self-esteem
- Depression
- Feelings of powerlessness
- Feelings of anger and fear
- Feelings of shame and/or guilt

What You Can Do

There are actions you can take if you are being sexually harassed. Take your own feelings seriously, and know your rights under the law. Victims of sexual harassment can

- enlist the aid of trusted adults at home and at school.
- take the necessary steps, together with a supportive adult, to make the harassment stop.
- work toward getting a school sexual harassment policy established if none exists.
- work to educate others about sexual harassment.

Did You Know?

Ex-Gang Members Get Fresh Start

"Fresh Start," a program launched in Chicago, uses laser surgery to remove tattoos from former gang members. Former members can be marked as targets for violence by their gang tattoos. Removing the tattoos has three benefits for these ex-gang members: (1) It reduces their risk of injury; (2) It improves their self-esteem; (3) It enhances their employment opportunities.

Violence in the Community

Violence in the community seriously affects teens. Consider these figures: Young people in the United States are 12 times more likely to die by gunfire than young people in any other industrialized nation. Almost three-fourths of children murdered in the entire industrialized world are killed in the United States. Violent crime is the second leading cause of death for all Americans aged 15 to 24.

Unfortunately, teens are also committing serious crimes. Teens are increasingly involved in **homicides** (HAH·muh·sydz), *the killing of one person by another.* Since 1985, the rate of homicide committed by teens aged 14 to 17 has almost doubled, and the number of juveniles committing homicide with a gun is four times greater.

Gangs

A **gang** is *a group of people who associate with each other.* Gangs may form for improper or illegal purposes. The problem of gang violence is serious and widespread. Many teen gangs are involved in violent criminal activity. When asked, over 80 percent

These teens are meeting their need for companionship and support by joining together to perform positive community service.

of urban school administrators and other leaders listed violence and gang-related activities as their top concern. In some cities, gangs are responsible for over 40 percent of all the homicides. Other serious crimes committed by gang members include drug and weapons trafficking, gambling, smuggling, and robbery.

in Your journal

Describe the personality of someone—another teen or an adult—who would support you if you were in trouble or needed help. What makes that person approachable? What characteristics does that person have that allows you to trust her or him?

Resisting Gangs

Why do teens join gangs? Some teens are pressured into joining by other teens. Young people may think that they will gain respect if they are members of a gang. A gang may seem to offer a sense of power and belonging. Some teens join gangs to be with people of their own racial or ethnic group. Members of these gangs may engage in **hate crime,** that is, *crime against people or property belonging to racial or ethnic groups different from their own.*

Many gang members engage in risky and unhealthy activities. Gang recruiters do not tell recruits that once they join, it is extremely hard to resign. The gang's code is that you are in for life—and death. Teens in gangs are often shot at and jailed. Their risk of being the victims of homicide is very high. Luckily, there are actions you can take to deal with the pressure to join a gang.

- If gang members threaten you, do not overreact. Try not to show fear. Walk away calmly.
- Say that you respect their rights but are just not interested.
- If threats and pressure continue, get protection from parents or guardians, the police, school officials, or other trusted adults.
- Involve yourself in activities you enjoy, such as sports, after-school programs, church groups, or community service activities.

Review

Lesson 3

Using complete sentences, answer the following questions on a separate sheet of paper.

Reviewing Terms and Facts

1. **Give Examples** What serious crimes might a gang member be involved in? Give examples.
2. **Vocabulary** Define the term *abuse.*

Thinking Critically

3. **Explain** Why do you think some people might find sexual harassment funny?
4. **Hypothesize** Why do you think "zero tolerance" policies toward weapons in school have been instituted? How do you think they might reduce or prevent violence?
5. **Analyze** Do you feel safe at school? What measures would you recommend to ensure a safe school environment?

Applying Health Concepts

6. **Health of Others** Gather information from local officials about how to avoid becoming involved with gangs. Counselors at Work, Achievement, Values, and Education (WAVE) or Boys & Girls Clubs of America give advice about gangs, including how to escape from one. From your research, create a guide or handbook explaining how to avoid gangs and how to escape from them.

Chapter 5 Review

Chapter Summary

- **Lesson 1** Conflict often occurs because of competition for resources, clashes between values, or exchanges involving emotional needs. There are actions one can take to prevent conflicts from becoming violent.
- **Lesson 2** Conflicts are often solved through the intervention of a neutral mediator who helps parties negotiate a resolution. Peer mediation in schools has benefits for all people involved.
- **Lesson 3** Abuse, which may occur in the form of physical abuse, neglect, emotional abuse, or sexual abuse, is harmful for both the victim and the abuser. Students can help create or change policies to prevent sexual harassment and violence in their schools.

Reviewing Key Terms and Concepts

Using complete sentences, answer the following questions on a separate sheet of paper.

Lesson 1

1. What are some positive ways to manage anger?
2. Describe behaviors and situations that may cause conflicts to escalate.

Lesson 2

3. Why is tolerance an important principle of conflict resolution?
4. What is the meaning of the term *negotiation?*

Lesson 3

5. What does a victim of battery experience?
6. What kinds of behavior constitute sexual harassment?

Thinking Critically

Using complete sentences, answer the following questions on a separate sheet of paper.

7. **Hypothesize** How might prejudice and group pressure lead to hate crimes committed by individuals or gangs?
8. **Synthesize** Imagine that a classmate has wrongly accused you of taking something from her locker. What would you do to resolve the conflict? Do you think that you would want the help of a peer mediator? How would the mediator help?
9. **Infer** How might an adult who sexually harasses other adults affect teens who witness this behavior?
10. **Explain** Discuss the negative impact of gang membership and the effects that gangs have on others who are not involved.

Your Action Plan

Look over your private journal entries for this chapter. How well are you able to resolve conflicts? An action plan can help you improve those skills.

Step 1 Your long-term goal is to improve your conflict resolution skills. Make a list of ways to improve those skills, such as using "I" statements or taking time out before you speak in anger.

Step 2 Each item on your list is a short-term goal. Make a schedule for adding each short-term goal to your conflict resolution skills. For instance, you may want to use "I" statements in your next disagreement with a friend.

Step 3 Your schedule might be hard to plan, since you do not always know when you will need to use your conflict resolution skills. Make adjustments to your list of short-term goals as you implement them.

Reward yourself when you are able to resolve a conflict successfully.

In Your Home and Community

1. **Community Resources** Research places in your community that offer help to abuse victims. Include shelters, support groups, organizations, and psychological services. Create a poster based on your research, and post it where teens will see it.
2. **Health of Others** Find out what the policy on sexual harassment is in your school. Write up and distribute your findings to other students. If your school has no policy, form a committee of students, teachers, and administrators to develop an effective policy to prevent and resolve cases of sexual harassment in your school.

Building Your Portfolio

1. **Conflict News** Cut out newspaper articles that deal with conflict. Pick two, and summarize the sources of conflict, the different viewpoints, and what is being done to resolve each conflict. Add the summaries to your portfolio.
2. **Mediation Center** Find out more about The Carter Center, founded by former U.S. president Jimmy Carter and former first lady Rosalynn Carter. Write a report on the kinds of conflicts The Carter Center resolves and how many countries are affected by its work. Add your report to your portfolio.
3. **Personal Assessment** Look through all the activities and projects you did for this chapter. Choose one that you would like to include in your portfolio.

Chapter 6

Consumer Choices and Public Health

Student Expectations

After reading this chapter, you should be able to:

1. Describe the benefits of being a wise consumer.
2. Explain how to comparison shop, and name some influences on your consumer choices.
3. Describe the American health care system and the types of health services available to consumers.
4. Identify and avoid quackery, and describe how to handle problems with health goods or services.
5. Tell how government agencies, public health laws, and voluntary organizations promote good health.

Teen Chat Group

Dan: Wow, this bike shop has so much to choose from.

Clarice: It should, considering how long it took us to walk here.

Dan: I think it will be worth the trip. Jesse said this place had the best prices in town.

Clarice: What kind of helmet are you going to buy?

Dan: I want to get one that has the safety approval seal on it. A friend of mine bought one that wasn't safety-approved and it's already cracked from him dropping it.

Clarice: Well, just make sure it fits. Last month my Dad bought me these neat shoes that I wanted, but they're always slipping off.

Dan: That's a good point. I'd better make sure that I make the right choice, otherwise I'll have to walk all the way back here to return it. Which helmets should I try on?

in your journal

Read the dialogue on this page. What kind of factors are influencing the way Dan and Clarice choose to shop? Do you think that any of these factors influence your buying decisions? Start your private journal entries on consumer choices and public health by responding to these questions:

- Are you influenced by ads or peer pressure when you shop?
- Do you plan your purchases, or do you buy on impulse?
- What do you do if you buy something that is broken or defective?

When you reach the end of the chapter, you will use your journal entries to make an action plan.

Lesson 1

Building Healthy Consumer Habits

This lesson will help you find answers to questions that teens often ask about their consumer decisions. For example:

- **How can I be a wise consumer?**
- **What are the benefits of improving my consumer skills?**
- **What government groups protect consumer rights?**

Words to Know

consumer
goods
services

Where Does Your Money Go?

Who is a consumer? You are. So are all of your friends. All together, you and your friends and all other teens buy millions of dollars' worth of products. A **consumer** (kuhn·SOO·mer) is *anybody who purchases goods or services.*

Some of the items you buy—such as music tapes, CDs, food, and clothes—are **goods.** These are *products that are made and purchased to satisfy someone's needs or wants.* You also buy services. **Services** are *activities that are purchased to satisfy someone's needs or wants.* You may pay to hear a concert or to have someone cut your hair. You are also a health consumer. **Figure 6.1** shows some health goods and services you might buy.

Some of the goods and services you buy are not as clearly related to your health, but they still affect it. Sunglasses are an example. You may think of sunglasses as a type of product you buy for

Figure 6.1
Consumer Goods and Services
Which of the health-related items shown here is a service?

their looks, but sunglasses are a health product. Some protect your eyes from the sun's harmful ultraviolet rays, whereas others do not. To make healthy consumer decisions, you need to know which product is best for your health. You can get information from many sources to help you learn the facts about sunglasses and other health products.

in your journal

Do you consider yourself a wise consumer? If so, list the traits that make you wise. If not, list two steps you can take to build your consumer skills.

How to Be a Wise Consumer

- Use your money wisely to get the most out of what you spend.
- Buy useful goods and services—ones that will help you maintain a high level of health.
- Buy safe goods and services, and stay away from goods and services that will harm you.
- Know what to do if you have a consumer problem.

Consider what happened to Natalie. She bought some deodorant to keep her underarms dry. When she applied the deodorant, her skin turned red and began to itch. Natalie knew that she was allergic to an ingredient in some health care products. She should have looked at the label for that ingredient. When she did not, she was not using good consumer skills. If she had read the label, she might not have bought the deodorant. She would have saved herself some money—and spared herself the rash!

interNET CONNECTION

Don't shop in the dark. Become an informed consumer with information you'll find at our Web site.

http://www.glencoe.com/sec/health

Why Be a Wise Consumer?

Being a consumer also means building your consumer skills. These help you choose health products and services wisely. Being a wise consumer benefits you in four ways.

- **You can promote and protect your health.** When you purchase useful goods, you can improve your health. When you buy safe products, you lessen your risk of harm.
- **You can save time and money.** By shopping carefully, you have the best chance of choosing products that work for you. That means you will not waste your money on products that do not work. It can also mean that you will not have to spend more money later trying to fix a problem caused by an unwise purchase. Natalie, for instance, may now have to buy some medicine to clear up the rash.
- **You can build your self-confidence.** As you use your consumer skills well, you become more sure of yourself. This helps build self-esteem, which can carry over to other areas of your life.
- **You protect your rights.** Each of us has certain rights as a consumer. Many groups work with consumers who have problems. You can turn to them for help and advice when you have a problem, but the best defender of your consumer rights is you.

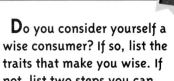

Wise consumers read product labels when choosing health products.

The Rights of Consumers

Many groups have worked hard to establish rights for consumers. The list below summarizes those rights.

- **We have the right to safety.** We have the right to purchase goods and services that will not harm us.
- **We have the right to choose.** We have the right to select from many goods and services at competitive prices.
- **We have the right to be informed.** We have the right to truthful information about goods and services.
- **We have the right to be heard.** We have the right to join in the making of laws about consumers.
- **We have the right to have problems corrected.** We have the right to complain when we have been treated unfairly.
- **We have the right to consumer education.** We have the right to learn the skills necessary to help us make wise choices.

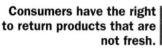

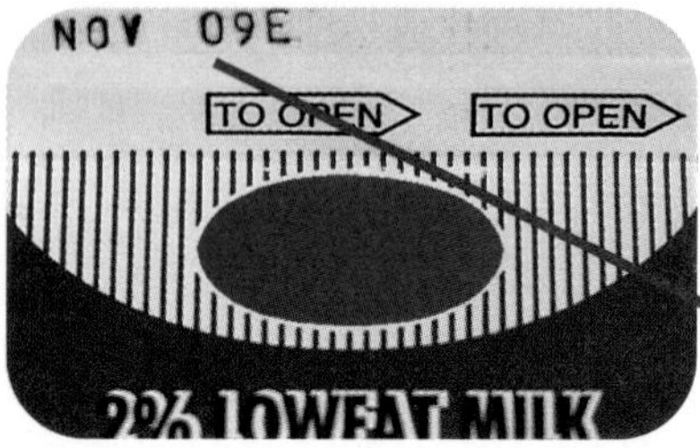

Consumers have the right to return products that are not fresh.

MAKING HEALTHY DECISIONS

Being a Wise Consumer

Mitch has been shopping around, looking for a mountain bike for weeks. Most of them are too expensive for his budget.

Yesterday, his friend Matt called and told him that the Cycle Center is going out of business. Matt said that all bicycles are on sale for 30 percent off. That sounded like a good deal to Mitch.

When Mitch went down to the Cycle Center, he found that one of the models he likes was within his price range. His mother reminded him that if the store goes out of business, Mitch won't have anywhere to go if he has a complaint or needs a repair.

The bicycles are selling fast, so Mitch needs to decide soon. His mother suggested that he use the step-by-step decision-making process to make up his mind.

1. **State the situation**
2. **List the options**
3. **Weigh the possible outcomes**
4. **Consider your values**
5. **Make a decision and act**
6. **Evaluate the decision**

Consumer Protection

Consumers are not completely on their own. Governments at all levels have agencies that are concerned with protecting consumer rights. The federal government has a number of agencies concerned with ensuring that products are safe and that their benefits are represented accurately.

- **Consumer Product Safety Commission (CPSC).** This organization makes sure that appliances, toys, and other products are safe. It can ban products it finds dangerous and can order manufacturers to notify people who have already bought the product with the problem. The CPSC requires that medicines be sold in child-resistant packaging.
- **Food and Drug Administration (FDA).** The FDA is responsible for the safety and purity of cosmetics, medicines, and all foods, except for meat and poultry. It requires that labeling be accurate and complete. It also decides whether a medicine should be sold by prescription from a doctor or whether it is safe to sell it over the counter.
- **Food Safety and Inspection Service (FSIS)** of the Department of Agriculture. The FSIS oversees the safety of meat and poultry. It inspects meat-packing plants.
- **Federal Trade Commission (FTC).** The FTC regulates the advertising of products and services in newspapers and magazines and on radio and television. The goal is to prevent advertisements from presenting false or misleading information.

Did You Know?

Two Sides of the Same Coin ACTIVITY!

Every consumer right comes with a responsibility. Think of the consumer responsibility for each of the rights on page 164. For example, along with the right to safety goes the responsibility to use products as directed. Make a poster or sign for each responsibility.

Follow-up Activities

1. Apply the six steps of the decision-making process to Mitch's story.
2. If Mitch decides to buy the bicycle, do you think he is being a wise consumer? Why or why not?
3. Along with two or three other students, role-play a scene in which Mitch explains his decision to buy the bike.

Consumer Education

Consumer rights have another side: consumer responsibilities. One is to exercise your rights. This starts with consumer education.

Many publications evaluate and report on products. However, you the consumer must do some research to benefit from these studies. Many consumer organizations can help you if you have a problem with a store or a manufacturer. However, you the consumer must know about and use these organizations. It all comes down to this: the educated consumer is the best-protected consumer.

Government agencies test many products for safety and effectiveness. Consumer organizations conduct tests on different brands or models of the same product. Doing some background research before you buy will help you make wise consumer choices.

Lesson 1 Review

Using complete sentences, answer the following questions on a separate sheet of paper.

Reviewing Terms and Facts

1. **Vocabulary** What is the difference between *goods* and *services*?
2. **List** Name the four ways in which being a wise consumer benefits you.

Thinking Critically

3. **Analyze** Some people believe that the right to be an informed consumer is the most important right of all. Explain why that could be true.
4. **Give Examples** Consumers expect people who sell goods and services to treat them honestly. How can they act honestly in turn? Give examples.

Applying Health Concepts

5. **Consumer Health** Take an inventory of health-related goods in your home, such as hair products, deodorants, and first-aid supplies. Based on what you have learned in this chapter, decide which products may have been a waste of money. Make a list of the products and summarize your findings.
6. **Consumer Health** With a group of classmates, look for newspaper and magazine articles that give advice on spending money wisely. Put together a collection of these articles, then discuss them. Which ones are really helpful? What tips do they offer on spending money wisely? Which articles are less useful? Why?

Lesson 2

What Influences Your Choices?

This lesson will help you find answers to questions that teens often ask about the purchases they make. For example:

- **How do I know I'm getting the best buy for my money?**
- **What influences me to buy certain goods and services?**

Words to Know

comparison shopping
warranty
discount store
coupon
generic product
tradition
advertising

Shopping Around

Al thought it would be easy to buy a pair of glasses. However, when he and his mom went shopping, they had to make some choices. Should they buy glass lenses or plastic lenses? How can they decide from among the different kinds of plastics, coatings, and tints that are available?

Like Al, you may need to choose from among several products or services that do the job. Good information will help you choose. You can get information by talking to family members or friends. You can read books or magazines that publish ratings of products or services to learn which are well regarded.

Shopping for Goods

Comparison (kumn·PEHR·i·suhn) **shopping** is *a method of judging the benefits of different goods or services.* Comparison shopping helps you get the best value for your money. **Figure 6.2** shows the factors to consider when you comparison shop.

Figure 6.2
The Factors in Comparison Shopping

Price	Features	Quality	Convenience	Warranty
Staying within a certain cost range is important to most people.	The characteristics of a product are important.	Quality includes how well a product is made, how well it performs its job, and how long it will last.	The labor-saving features of a product affect many consumer decisions. The store's location may also make a difference.	A **warranty** is a *written promise to handle repairs if the product does not work.*

How to Comparison Shop

Figure 6.3 shows an example of comparison shopping. In addition, you can use comparison shopping to find the best place to make your purchase. Ask yourself these questions: Which store offers the best price for the product I want? What are the store's return policies? How helpful are the salespeople? Is the store's location convenient? This is particularly important if return visits are needed for adjustments or repairs. For convenience, many people opt to make purchases through the mail.

Figure 6.3

An Example of Comparison Shopping

After you have gathered information about different products, you can make a chart like this one to see similarities and differences at a glance. Al made this chart to compare glasses. If you know that Al plays a lot of basketball, which factors do you think are important?

Options	Price	Features	Quality	Convenience	Warranty
Regular plastic lenses	Least Expensive	Lightweight	Need scratch protection	Varies	One year
High-index plastic lenses	Moderately Priced	Thinnest plastic; filter UV rays	Very durable	Varies	Lifetime
Polycarbonate lenses	Most Expensive	Almost unbreakable; filter UV rays	Need scratch protection	Varies	Lifetime

Shopping for Services

Before buying new glasses, people need to have their eyes checked. They can choose between two kinds of doctors. An optometrist (ahp·TAHM·uh·trist) examines eyes, diagnoses vision problems, and prescribes eyeglasses and contact lenses. An ophthalmologist (ahf·thuhl·MAHL·uh·jist) is a medical doctor, who provides the same services as an optometrist but can also prescribe medications and perform surgery.

When Al started complaining about blurry vision, his mother took him to Dr. Rodman, an ophthalmologist associated with their health insurance plan. Al's parents think the doctor gives thorough examinations, and her hours are convenient for them. They also like the way she takes time to answer their questions.

Shopping for Price

Different stores charge different amounts for the same products and services, as illustrated in **Figure 6.4.**

- **Discount stores** are *stores that offer few services but have lower prices.* Most discount stores have fewer salespeople than full-price stores and may look less fancy.
- **Coupons** (KOO·pahnz) are *slips of paper that offer savings on certain brands of goods.*
- **Generic** (jeh·NEHR·ik) **products** are *goods sold in plain packages and at lower prices than brand name goods.* Buying generic products makes sense if they are equal in quality to brand name items.

in your journal

Think about a product or service you bought recently. What influenced you to buy it? Cost? Tradition? Advertising? Peers? Salespeople? Were you satisfied with your purchase? Answer these questions in your journal.

Figure 6.4

Comparing Stores' Prices

Have you ever compared a product in two different types of stores? Why is it less expensive in one store than the other?

HEALTH LAB

Generic or Brand Name Products?

Introduction: Generic products can cost a lot less than brand name products. Sometimes the only difference is in the fancy packaging of brand name products.

Objective: Compare prices, ingredients, and other features between generic and brand name products.

Materials and Method: Make a comparison chart with vertical columns for "Name of Generic Product" and "Name of Brand Name Product"; and with horizontal columns for "Price," "Ingredients," and "Other Features." Go to the drugstore or grocery store and compare three different products. Make sure the generic and brand name products are supposed to be the same. Write down all the information in the chart, placing in the "Other Features" column any "extras" that make one product more desirable than another.

Observation and Analysis: After completing your chart, which of the three products would you buy—the generic ones or the brand name ones? Give reasons for your selections. Do you believe that it is wise for consumers to buy generic products? Why or why not?

The Influences on What You Buy

Math Connection

Check It Out ACTIVITY!

Choose a brand name shampoo, toothpaste, mouthwash, or soap. Check out the price of this product at a supermarket with a coupon for 50 cents off. Then check out the price at a discount store. What is the difference? Now check out the price of a generic form of the product at a supermarket and at a discount store. Make sure the size and volume are the same as the original product. What is the difference?

Your consumer decisions are yours alone. You will decide which goods or service you want, but many factors influence you. Those influences include cost, tradition, advertising, peers, and salespeople. You have already learned how prices affect your choices. The other factors are explained below.

Tradition

Tradition (truh·DI·shun) is *the usual pattern of thought, behavior, or action.* Many consumer decisions are based on tradition. Your food choices, for instance, are strongly influenced by the kind of food your family buys and eats.

Advertising

The main influence on your consumer choices is **advertising.** This is *a format for sending out messages (or advertisements) meant to interest consumers in buying goods and services.* Billions of dollars in advertising are spent each year on television, on radio, in newspapers and magazines, and on billboards.

Ads give information. They also try to persuade you to buy a specific product. Different appeals are used to convince you that a product or service will make you healthier, happier, or more popular. Wise consumers get the information they need to make a purchase without being deceived.

This advertisement is trying to convince consumers to buy a specific brand of suntan lotion. Do you think it is effective? Why or why not?

Peers

Your friends and images of teens in the media can strongly influence your consumer decisions. You want to do things your friends are doing. This can mean wearing the latest styles or joining in their activities. Your health, however, is affected by your health decisions—not anyone else's. If friends pressure you to do something that is not good for your health, decide to resist their influence and stick by your decision.

Salespeople

Salespeople can give good information about a product, but they sometimes pressure buyers. To resist sales pressure, give yourself time to make a decision. Use the decision-making process. Also, ask questions. The answers may be useful in helping you make a wise consumer choice, or they may reveal that the salesperson does not know much about the product.

When you get help from a salesperson, ask questions and give yourself time to make a decision.

Lesson 2 Review

Using complete sentences, answer the following questions on a separate sheet of paper.

Reviewing Terms and Facts

1. **Vocabulary** Define the term *warranty.* Use it in an original sentence.
2. **Recall** Identify five factors to consider when comparison shopping for a product.

Thinking Critically

3. **Apply** Leona wants a new exercise bike. What are some things she should consider *before* she begins comparison shopping?
4. **Suggest** Cindy wants to purchase expensive cosmetic products she has seen advertised in teen magazines. What advice would you give her?

Applying Health Concepts

5. **Consumer Health** Choose a health product that many teens buy, such as sunglasses, contact lenses, or blow dryers. Look in consumer magazines for ratings of different brands of the product. Do the magazines include useful tips on what to look for and what to consider when purchasing these items? Share the information you find with your classmates.
6. **Consumer Health** Identify sources of consumer information in your school and community. Which do you think would be most useful to you? Are there any resources specifically for teen consumers?

Lesson

3 Choosing Health Services

This lesson will help you find answers to questions that teens often ask about health services. For example:

- **Where should I go if I get sick or if I am injured?**
- **Why do I need to have health insurance?**
- **How do I shop for health services?**

Words to Know

health care system
primary care provider
specialist
health care facility
health insurance
preferred provider
Medicare
Medicaid
health maintenance organization (HMO)

The Health Care System

Molly fell off her bike and bumped her head. Several weeks after the accident, her head still hurt and she was not sleeping well. Her mother took her to see the family's regular doctor, Dr. Kim. After examining Molly, Dr. Kim sent her to Dr. Miller, a specialist in treating people with head injuries.

When Molly went to see Dr. Kim, she entered our country's health care system. A **health care system** includes *all the medical care available to a nation's people, the way they receive the care, and the way the care is paid for.* The health care system in the United States includes primary care providers and specialists.

Who Provides Health Care?

Doctors play a vital role in the health care system. However, a wide range of other people provide health care. Nurses, dentists, dental hygienists, optometrists, pharmacists, and physical fitness instructors are just a few examples of people other than doctors who work in the health care field.

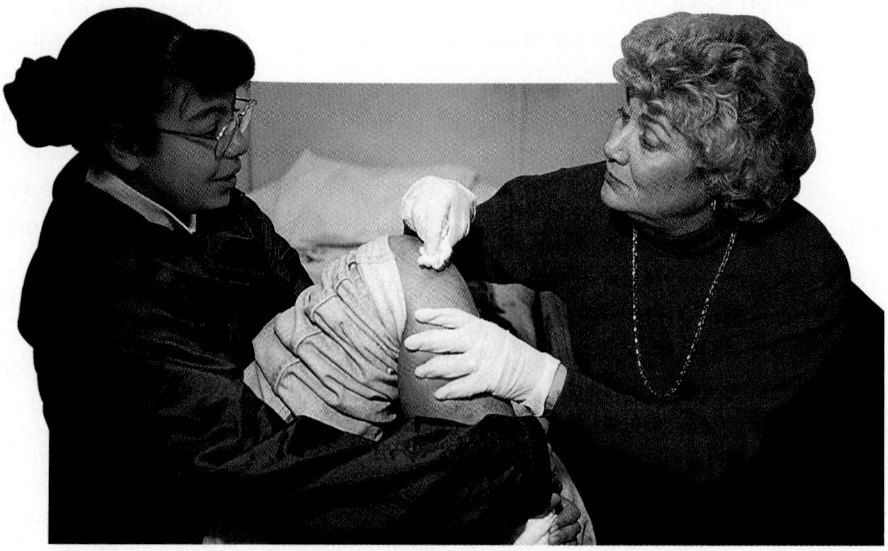

Some people receive health services at a community clinic. In some areas, these clinics are located in schools.

Primary care providers are *the doctors and other health professionals who provide medical checkups and general care.* Patients with more serious conditions or conditions that require specialized equipment may see a specialist. **Specialists** (SPE·shuh·lists) are *doctors trained to handle particular kinds of patients or health matters.* Midlevel practitioners are a relatively new kind of health care professional. Some common ones include nurse practitioners and physician's assistants. They help to keep health costs down by performing many of the routine medical tasks that doctors used to perform. Workers in the health care system have three main goals. They are shown in **Figure 6.5.**

in your journal

Make a list of the people who provide you and your family with health care. Beside each name, write what the person does for you or others in your family.

Figure 6.5

Health Care Goals

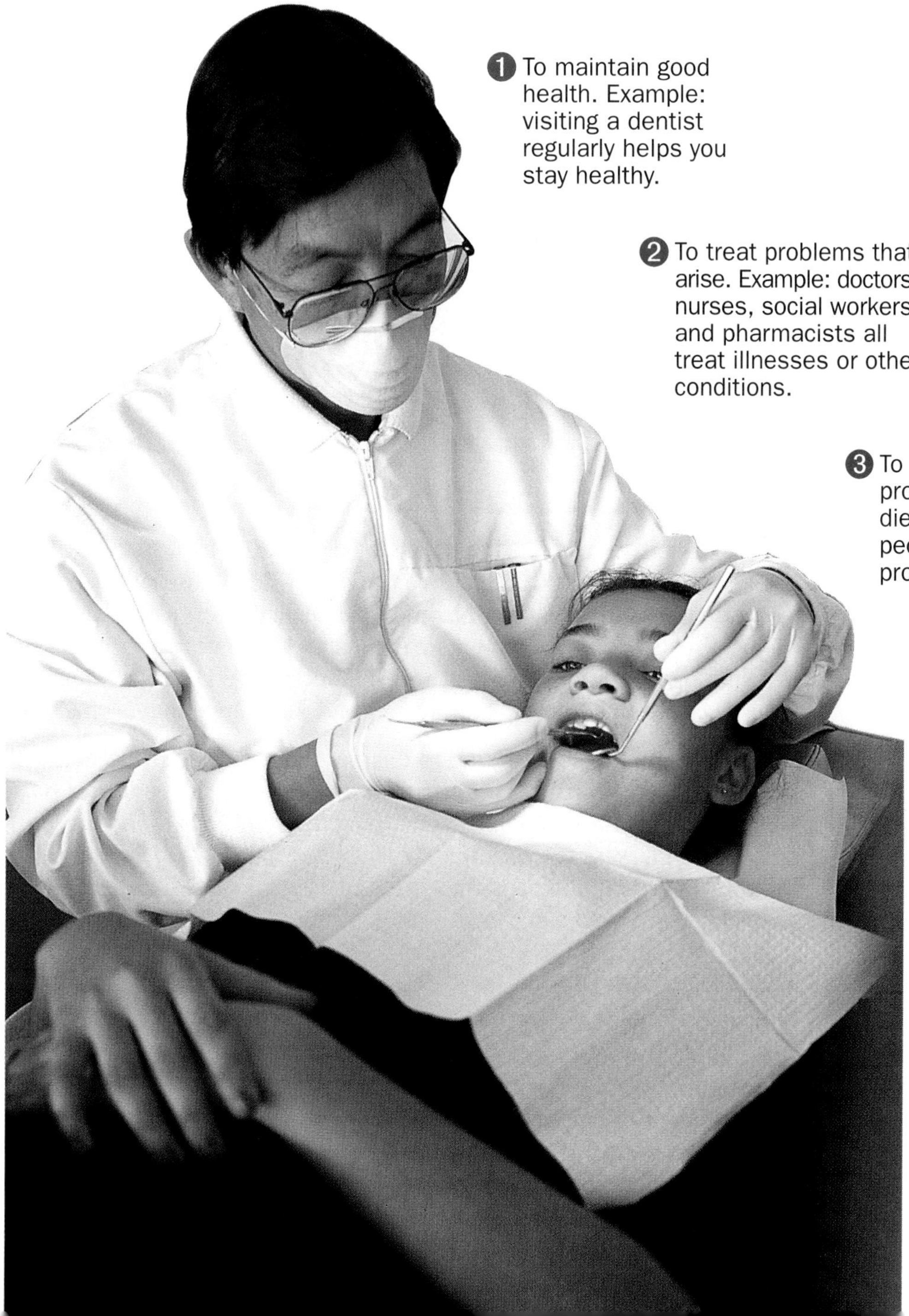

1. To maintain good health. Example: visiting a dentist regularly helps you stay healthy.
2. To treat problems that arise. Example: doctors, nurses, social workers, and pharmacists all treat illnesses or other conditions.
3. To prevent health problems. Example: a diet counselor helps people prevent weight problems.

Types of Health Care Facilities

A **health care facility** is *a place where you can receive health care.* The two basic types are facilities for inpatient care and facilities for outpatient care.

Inpatient Care

Patients need inpatient care when they cannot care for themselves, require treatment that cannot be given on an outpatient basis, or are not in stable condition. Examples are major surgery or a medical condition that may worsen without warning. Patients stay at the facility as long as necessary. The two main types of inpatient health facilities are hospitals and nursing homes.

Outpatient Care

Outpatient care is provided for less serious conditions or simple operations. Examples are treating sprains, putting stitches on serious wounds, extracting teeth, and performing some minor surgery. Patients come to the health care facility, get the treatment they need, and leave for home on the same day. Facilities that provide outpatient care include doctors' offices, clinics, and hospital outpatient clinics.

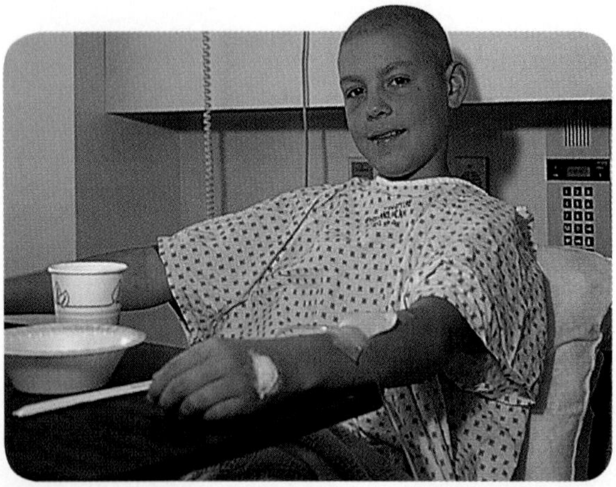

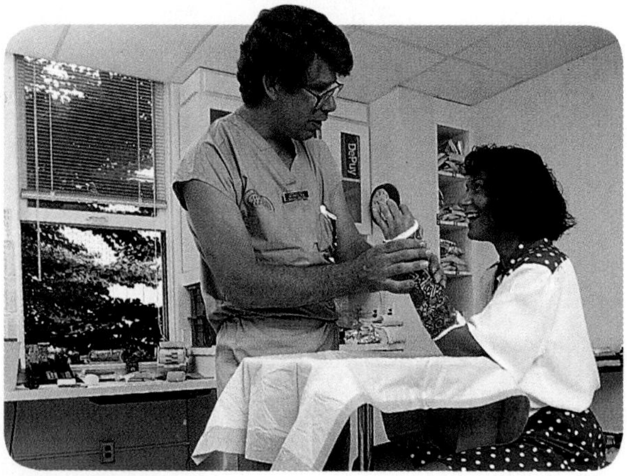

Patients receive either inpatient care or outpatient care depending on their conditions and the types of treatment they need.

Health Insurance

Health care in the United States is costly. In 1994, national health expenditures totaled over $949 billion. Americans might spend thousands on a single medical test, surgery, or a hospital stay. Costs continue to increase each year because of high-technology equipment, organ transplants, the AIDS crisis, and insurance fees that doctors and medical facilities must pay.

Health insurance is a way to ensure that many of these medical expenses can be paid. **Health insurance** (in·SHUR·ens) is *a plan in which private companies or government programs pay for part of the medical costs, and the patient pays for the rest.* **Figure 6.6** shows the breakdown of the different types of medical insurance coverage Americans have.

Private Insurance

Many private companies sell health insurance to consumers. In return for a monthly premium, or fee, the company agrees to pay a portion of the insured person's medical bills. The consumer pays the rest. Some insurance plans require consumers to go to preferred providers. **Preferred providers** are *doctors approved by the health care plan.* They keep their rates within a certain range.

Consumers may purchase private insurance as part of a group or as individuals. Group insurance is sold primarily through places of employment. The employer may pay all or part of an employee's premium as a work benefit. In individual health insurance programs, people pay the premium themselves.

Millions of Americans do not have health insurance. Some are unemployed; others have jobs but their jobs do not include health insurance. In most cases, private insurance is too expensive for them, and they may be ineligible for government programs.

Government Programs

The federal government has two insurance programs for the general public. **Medicare** (MED·i·kehr) provides *health insurance to people 65 years old or older.* People who receive Social Security disability benefits are also eligible, even if they are younger than 65. Medicare covers the costs of hospital care.

The other government insurance program is called **Medicaid** (MED·i·kayd). It provides *health insurance to people who are poor.* People with low incomes and dependent children, people with high medical costs in relation to their income, and people with disabilities usually qualify for Medicaid.

Cultural Connections

The Shaman

Shamans are health practitioners who bring a spiritual dimension to health care for Native Americans. Some health care facilities allow shamans to bring their healing art to their Native American patients.

Obtaining Health Services

Health services are available in most communities in a variety of forms. Those forms include private practices, group practices, clinics, and health maintenance organizations. However, many people receive health care insurance through their work. Increasingly, the type of health services they receive is determined by the insurance program. In many programs, for example, participants must choose doctors from a list of preferred providers.

Figure 6.6

Medical Insurance Coverage

In 1994, Americans' health insurance coverage was broken down into these categories.

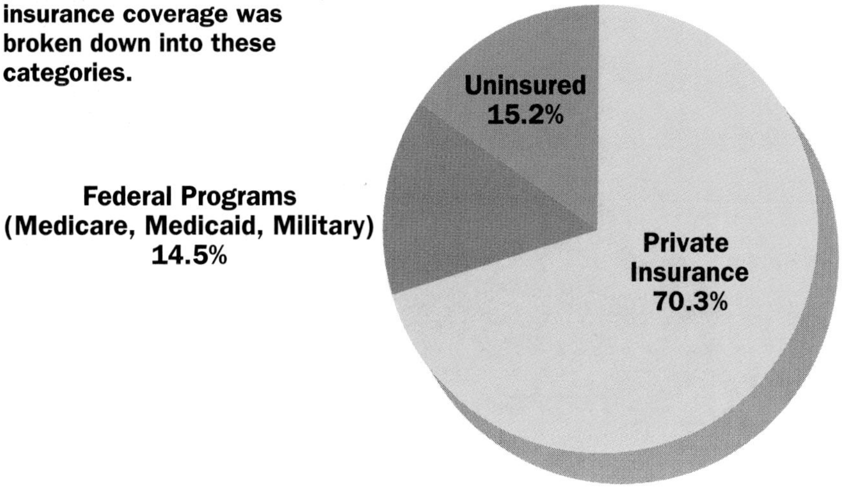

Source: U.S. Bureau of the Census, March Supplement to the 1995 Current Population Survey, unpublished data

Teen Issues

Growing Up ACTIVITY!

One part of growing up is taking more responsibility for your own health. Following the instructions of your dentist or dental hygienist for brushing and flossing your teeth is part of meeting that responsibility. Make a list of your other responsibilities as a consumer of health services.

Private Practices

Primary care providers and specialists may be in private practice. Molly's primary care provider, Dr. Kim, is in private practice. She has her own office and works for herself. When you see a doctor or other health professional in private practice, you are billed for each visit. You pay only for the services you receive.

Group Practices

Often two or more doctors join together to offer health care. They work in a group practice. Doctors in group practice share office space, equipment, and staff. They often consult with one another on the care of their patients. Groups may include a number of doctors with different specialties, or the entire group may specialize in the same area, such as the care of children.

Clinics

Primary care providers and specialists may work for clinics. Clinics provide care for people who are sick or injured. They may operate as part of a hospital or school. Some clinics are run by a group of doctors or community organizations. Clinics often receive government funding to help pay for some of the care given to patients who cannot afford it.

Health Maintenance Organizations

A health maintenance (MAYN·te·nuhns) organization is like a clinic in many ways. A **health maintenance organization (HMO)** includes *many different types of doctors who give health care to members*. You can receive medical care, dental care, and eye care through the HMO.

They are different in several important ways, however. HMOs stress preventive medicine in an attempt to reduce the high cost of medical care. HMOs charge members a yearly or monthly fee. In return, members receive medical care—from routine checkups to major surgery—for little or no additional cost.

Members must choose a primary care physician who belongs to the HMO. In most cases, they are limited to specialists and hospitals that are part of the HMO. To see a doctor outside the HMO, members must get approval.

A health maintenance organization may have a central location where members receive medical care, dental care, and eye care.

Trends in Health Care

Our country's health care system is changing every day. Several trends have developed that aim to improve the quality of health care or reduce its cost.

- **Birthing centers.** These facilities offer several benefits over the traditional hospital setting. They are homelike, and they involve the entire family in the delivery. They are also significantly less expensive than hospitals.
- **Computerized health technology.** This program collects health information on computer. It will allow people to answer their own health questions and will provide visual images of complicated medical procedures.
- **Health centers.** These centers meet the needs of people who are not covered by other health care supports. Some meet the needs of adolescents whereas others serve all the people who are part of a particular community.
- **Hospice care.** This care for the terminally ill combines loving care with techniques for pain and symptom management. Hospices provide for patients' physical and emotional needs.
- **National health care.** On August 21, 1996, President Bill Clinton signed the Health Insurance Portability and Accountability Act. This act set federal minimum standards for health care insurance. The government continues to debate other issues concerning national health care.

Did You Know?

Government Web Sites

Often, the government provides up-to-date, accurate health information on the Web. The Food and Drug Administration, for example, has a Web site which provides articles on topics ranging from acne to tobacco. The articles often include pictures and illustrations.

Review

Lesson 3

Using complete sentences, answer the following questions on a separate sheet of paper.

Reviewing Terms and Facts

1. **Vocabulary** Which of the following terms are types of physicians, and which are types of health insurance? *primary care provider, Medicare, specialist, Medicaid, health maintenance organization, preferred provider?*
2. **List** What are the three main goals of workers in the health care system?

Thinking Critically

3. **Apply** Luis' grandmother recently broke her hip. She lives alone and cannot care for herself while her hip heals. What type of health care facility would be best for her? Why?
4. **Analyze** Would you prefer to go to a doctor in a private medical practice or one who belongs to an HMO? Explain your answer.

Applying Health Concepts

5. **Personal Health** Write a list of suggestions on how to prepare for a visit to the doctor. Along with a classmate, role-play a visit to the doctor.
6. **Personal Health** Find out what health-related services and screenings are offered at your school. Share your findings in a written report.

TEEN HEALTH DIGEST

CON$UMER FOCU$

Bad Breath Blues

It seems too good to be true—a pill to sweeten your breath "from the inside out." The drawback? The price—$6 or more for 50 tiny pills!

Fortunately, you don't need to spend big bucks for beautiful breath. Most bad breath starts in your mouth, not in your stomach.

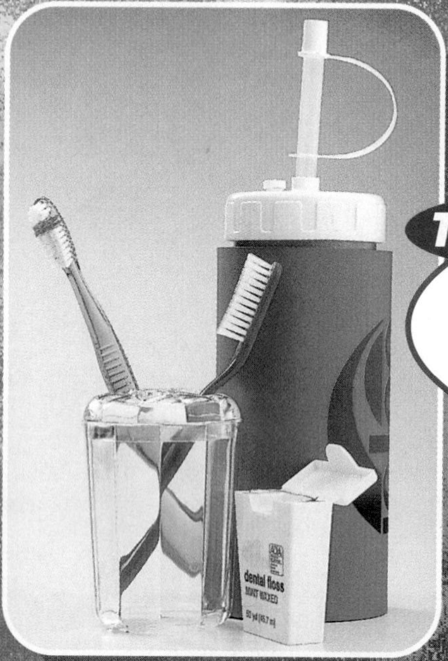

Try This: *Here are the do's and don'ts for beating the bad breath blues.*

Do's ► *Do floss every day.* ► *Do brush after every meal.* ► *Do drink plenty of water.*

Don'ts ► *Don't eat too many hot, spicy foods.* ► *Don't smoke.* ► *Don't be a stranger to your dentist.*

HEALTH UPDATE

Tabloid Medicine

He: I read that scientists say that eating broccoli prevents cancer!

She: I read that pesticides on vegetables *cause* cancer, but eating lots of broccoli can *cure* cancer.

He: It says here that aspirin prevents heart attacks!

She: My magazine says that aspirin causes ulcers.

Sometimes it's hard to know what to believe based on what you read in the media. The American Heart Association offers these tips to help you make sense of medicine and media.

- Make sure that the reports are based on information from respected medical journals.
- Look for balance in the story. Was more than one source quoted?
- Look at the source reporting the news. Is it a credible source, or does it also do stories on outrageous topics?

Sports and Recreation

Go Girls!

Nancy Williams was mad. As coach of the girls' varsity field hockey team at Shore Regional High School in Long Branch, NJ, she saw the boys' teams get huge fan support during prime weekend times. The girls' teams, however, played after school to empty stands.

Williams filed a complaint against her school under Title IX, a program that guarantees equal rights for female and male athletes. As a result, the girls' field hockey team played its final game at night in front of hundreds of fans—and there was even a pep squad!

Myths and Realities

What's For Lunch?

For a long time, a school cafeteria lunch meant potato puffs and gelatin molds. That's all changing. The Federal School Lunch Program recently made big changes in the menus it provides. Look for more fresh fruits and vegetables and greater variety on the menu.

Try This:

Is your school cafeteria serving the new foods? Check it out!

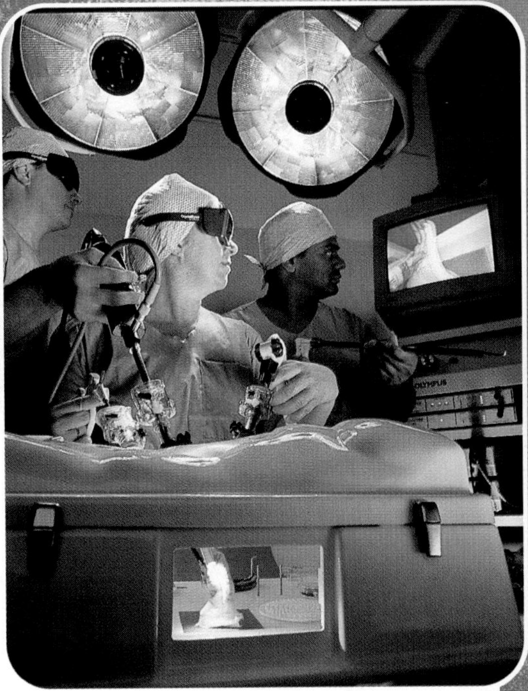

People at Work

"Scalpel... Suture... Mouse..."

Today more and more surgeons practice their skills with computers and "virtual surgery" programs. These powerful computers let doctors poke inside a make-believe body on screen, cut and reattach "virtual organs," and more.

Who benefits? The doctors, of course. Their patients do, too, because the doctors can practice as often as they want so they are prepared for the real surgeries!

Lesson 4

Handling Consumer Problems

This lesson will help you find answers to questions that teens often ask about dealing with consumer problems. For example:

- **How can I keep from buying worthless products and services?**
- **What should I do if I have a problem with something I buy?**
- **What should I do if I have a problem with health services?**

Words to Know

quackery
placebo effect
consumer advocate
small-claims court
second opinion
license
malpractice

Let the Buyer Beware

A centuries-old saying is "Let the buyer beware." This means that consumers have to watch out for goods and services that do not do what sellers claim they will do. Most products *do* work, and most sellers *are* honest. Some businesses, however, sell useless products. Part of being a wise consumer is knowing how to spot them—and avoid them.

Health and Medical Quackery

Quackery (KWA·kuh·ree) is *the sale of worthless products and treatments claimed to prevent diseases or to cure other health problems.* An example is a miracle "cure" for a disease that does not have a cure such as AIDS. Selling weight-reduction programs that are not healthy is also quackery. A quack is a person who makes dishonest claims about products and treatments to make money. Some impostors pretend to have medical skills when, in fact, they have none.

It is against the law to make false claims about drugs and cosmetics. Yet quackery makes millions of dollars a year by selling products that are not cures. This deception takes advantage of people's desire for fast, easy results or their desire to look better. Perhaps the saddest kind of quackery is the kind that offers false hope to people suffering from diseases that do not have effective treatments. **Figure 6.7** describes some of the most common types of quackery.

Do not always believe the claims made about products in television ads. Ask a physician or pharmacist if you have any doubts about health products.

The Placebo Effect

If a person's health improves soon after taking a quack's remedy, it can be due to the **placebo** (pluh·SEE·boh) **effect.** This means that *the person improves because of a strong belief that the "medicine" is helping and not because of anything that the quack provides.*

How to Spot Quackery

To protect yourself from quackery, learn to recognize signs. Some of the common ones follow.

- Quacks tend to work alone—not in clinics—and to sell their products through the mail or door-to-door.
- Quacks often insist on payment by cash.
- Quacks may claim a "medical breakthrough."
- Quacks may say that the health care system is suppressing the news about their miracle cure.

If you have a question about some product or a person selling something, ask an expert—a doctor, a person at a clinic, or someone in your local or state government.

History Connection

Dr. Johnson's Snake Oil

Quackery has been around for centuries. In the 1800s, fast-talking salesmen traveled in "medicine wagons" from town to town. They put on shows and sold "medicinal" potions between acts. These potions, claimed the salesmen, could cure anything from an ingrown toenail to a broken heart. See if you can find other examples of quack remedies and devices from the past.

Figure 6.7

Common Types of Quackery

Type of Product	Typical Advertisement	Facts
Diet Aids		
Pills **Fad diets**	TEEN GIRLS! LOSE WEIGHT FAST! Our Body Shaper program lets you eat all the foods you want. No need for boring exercises. To get started on a totally gorgeous body, send $25 to: P.O. Box 19209, Las Vegas, NV 89109.	A good weight-loss program is based on eating fewer calories and less fat and exercising to burn calories. Losing weight takes time. False diet aids can damage your health.
Beauty Products		
Acne creams **Hair enhancers**	HAVING PROBLEMS WITH YOUR SKIN? Our remarkable new formula can erase pimples and blackheads forever. Try a FREE sample today. Just send $10 for shipping and handling to: Med-Sci Formulas, P.O. Box 70443, Detroit, MI 48243.	Many products can help your skin temporarily. No product, however, can make your skin blemish-free permanently. Quack products have not been approved by the government and may actually harm your skin.
Miracle Cures		
Arthritis **Cancer**	HELEN LAMAR, HEALER Are you sick or in constant pain? Do you suffer from anxiety or depression? Helen Lamar, a gifted healer, can solve your health problems for as little as $25 per visit. Call today. 555-6900.	Quacks sell worthless products and services, often giving seriously ill patients false hope. Even worse, people who take these so-called cures may delay getting the medically approved treatment that could help them.

Problems with Products

Even the wisest consumer has a problem with a purchase from time to time. It can happen to anyone. What can you do if a problem like this happens?

Figure 6.8 shows how to solve a consumer problem. You can usually go to the store where you bought the product if you have a problem with it. You can also write to the manufacturer to get either a replacement or your money back.

In most cases, these steps are enough to solve the problem. Most businesses depend on their customers being satisfied. They will want to solve your problem to maintain your good will as a customer—so you will come back again.

The blow dryer this teen purchased was defective. She took the steps above to solve her problem.

LIFE SKILLS

Evaluating Product Claims

Every day, manufacturers bombard you with claims about their products. Take toothpaste, for instance. Toothpaste X contains fluoride, said to strengthen tooth enamel. Toothpaste Y forms an "invisible shield" around your teeth. Which product claims can you believe?

Knowing something about product ingredients will help you evaluate claims. Different brands of the same product generally contain the same basic ingredients. Other ingredients may make the product look, taste, or smell better—and make the product cost more.

All toothpastes, for example, contain a mild abrasive for cleansing the teeth. Toothpaste is really soap for your teeth, and an abrasive is the only ingredient necessary for cleansing. Manufacturers add other ingredients that supposedly improve your teeth. Of all the additives, however, only fluoride has been proven to have beneficial effects.

Knowing something about healthful practices can help you evaluate product claims. You should use personal grooming products as aids and not as substitutes for healthy habits. Toothpaste must be used along with proper brushing, flossing, proper diet, and regular visits to the dentist.

Knowing something about how the body works can also help you evaluate product claims. Bad breath may be due to diseases of the nose, sinuses, lungs, or stomach and intestines. No toothpaste can prevent bad breath that results from these causes.

You can also ask for the opinions of experts. The seal of approval from the American Dental Association (ADA) on a toothpaste can guide your selection. Often you must simply try several products to see which works best for you—regardless of the claims.

Follow-up Activities

1. Choose a personal grooming product you use every day, such as soap, deodorant, or shampoo. Watch for advertisements for this product. Write down the manufacturer's claims. Decide which ones are probably truthful, which claims are exaggerations or half-truths, and which claims are outright lies. Share your findings with your classmates.
2. Research old catalogs and magazines from the early part of this century. Compare the products, the way they were presented, and the claims about them to present-day ads. Share your findings in a two-page report.

Figure 6.8
Solving a Consumer Problem

(1) START. Your new blow dryer is not working properly.

(2) Read the instructions to see if you followed them correctly.

(3) If the blow dryer still does not work, you have a right to complain.

(4) Gather the information you will need to back up your complaint.

(5) Find the sales receipt proving you bought the blow dryer.

(6) Write down what you did, what happened, and why you are not satisfied.

(7) Decide what you think would be a fair solution. If you want the dryer repaired, GO TO **(8)**. If you want a refund, GO TO **(9)**.

(8) Read the warranty that came with the blow dryer. Follow the directions in the warranty.

(8a) Take the blow dryer to an authorized service center or mail it to the manufacturer for repairs.

(8b) If you are satisfied with the results, STOP. If not, contact a special consumer group.

(9) Go to the store where you bought the blow dryer, and ask to talk to someone who can handle your complaint.

(9a) Tell your story calmly, show your evidence, and offer your solution.

(9b) If the person does not agree with your solution, ask to see a manager and explain your story again.

(9c) If you are satisfied with the results, STOP. If not, contact a special consumer group.

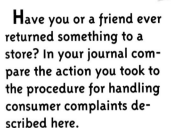

This teen took her faulty hair dryer back to the store, where she explained the problem.

in your journal

Have you or a friend ever returned something to a store? In your journal compare the action you took to the procedure for handling consumer complaints described here.

Language Arts Connection

Letter Perfect

Use the following tips to write a complaint letter.

- Keep the letter short.
- Be firm but polite.
- State the product's name, when you bought it, what you paid, how you used it, and what happened.
- Include copies of related papers, but keep originals.
- Include a request for action—tell the company what you want.
- Include your address and phone number.

Teen Issues

Is the Customer Always Right? ACTIVITY!

Many teens report that salespeople do not treat them with the same courtesy with which they treat adults. Salespeople may even refuse to wait on teens. The situation is even worse if teens try to return defective products or complain about poor service. Discuss with your classmates why this situation exists and what might be done about it.

Did You Know?

Winning Through Communication

Studies show that the way people explain their problems to health care providers affects the care they receive. Vague complaints make it difficult to find out what is wrong. People who have their facts together and act reasonably are likely to be taken seriously and get the best results.

Special Consumer Groups

The actions in **Figure 6.8** on page 183 should take care of most product problems. Sometimes, though, more action is required. Different kinds of groups help consumers with problems if taking the usual steps does not produce a satisfactory result.

- **Consumer advocates** (AD·voh·kets) are *people or groups who devote themselves to helping consumers with problems.* These include the Consumers Union and local consumer groups.
- **Business groups** also help consumers with problems. Among the most useful are the Better Business Bureaus (BBB).
- **Governments** at all levels have workers whose job is to make sure that consumers' rights are being upheld. They work in places like the "consumer affairs office."
- **Small-claims courts** are *state courts that handle cases with problems involving small amounts, usually $2,500 or less, but in some states up to $5,000.* The consumer and the person or store being sued present their own cases. A judge hears both sides and decides who wins.

You can find the addresses and phone numbers of any of these groups or agencies in your local library or in the telephone book. When you go for help, be prepared to tell the whole story and have documentation to prove your case. Describe your problem, how you tried to solve it yourself, and what happened. Many times, the group or agency can get the problem solved. They know what to do and say to convince a business to act.

Problems with Health Services

In addition to having problems with products and personal services, some people have problems with health services. Sometimes these problems are solved simply by discussing them with a physician or other health care professional or by changing physicians. For example, if someone feels that a doctor does not spend enough time answering questions, he or she can change doctors.

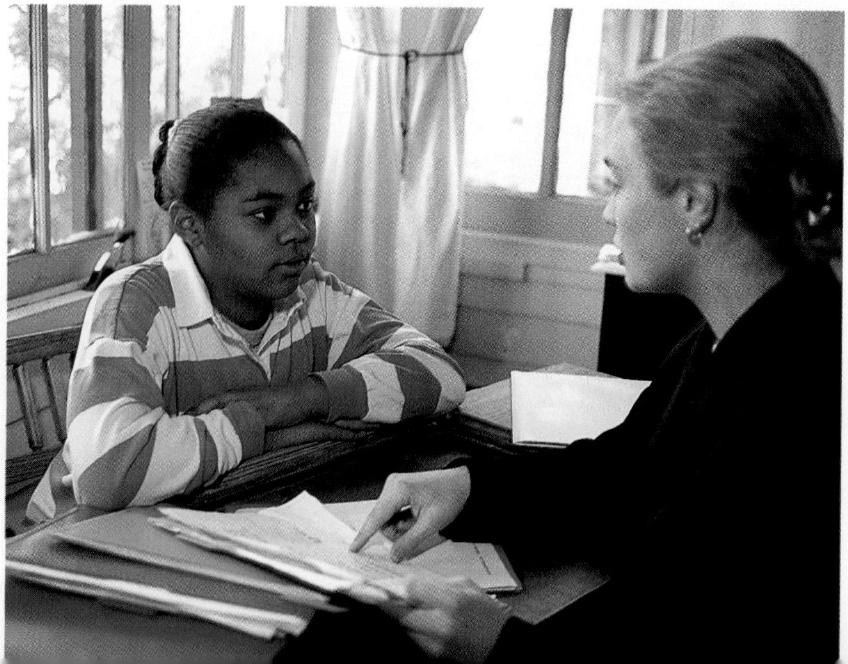

Because this teen could not solve her problem with the blow dryer by going through the usual channels, she consulted a local consumer group.

At other times, however, the question is over the quality of health care. Someone may feel that a doctor did not identify an illness early enough. In another case, a patient may think that a recommended treatment is not really needed.

The first step is to get a **second opinion.** This is a *statement from another doctor giving his or her view of what should be done.* The second doctor may reach a different conclusion or may agree with the first doctor's opinion.

A patient who thinks that a treatment already carried out was performed poorly can take a second step. He or she can complain to a state licensing board. These agencies license certain health workers. A **license** is *a document that gives a person the right to provide health care but holds that person to certain standards.* If a licensing board gets a complaint, it will look into the matter. The board may find that the worker did something wrong, or it may say that what the worker did was reasonable.

After taking these steps, the patient must decide whether to sue the doctor for **malpractice** (mal·PRAK·tis). This is *a failure to provide an acceptable degree of quality health care.* Someone making a decision to sue needs the help of a lawyer. If the case is taken to trial, a judge or jury will decide the case.

If you have a problem with the care or treatment you receive from a physician, there are many ways to try to resolve it.

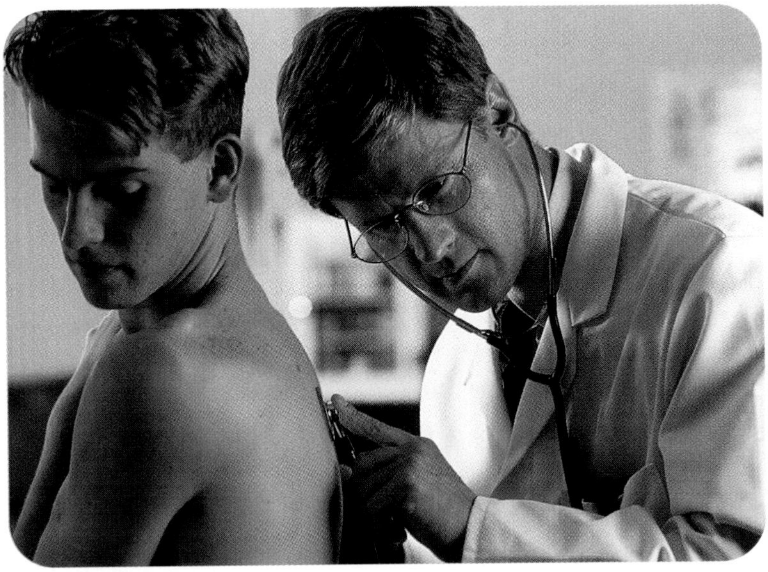

Review Lesson 4

Using complete sentences, answer the following questions on a separate sheet of paper.

Reviewing Terms and Facts

1. **Vocabulary** What is the difference between a *consumer advocate* and *small-claims court*?
2. **Recall** What steps can you take to resolve a problem that you have with your physician?

Thinking Critically

3. **Suggest** Your friend wants to spend $12.95 for a cream with a "secret beauty formula." She saw the cream advertised in a supermarket tabloid. What would you say to your friend?
4. **Apply** Michelle's new curling iron does not heat properly. Michelle says she is going to throw it away. What should Michelle do instead?

Applying Health Concepts

5. **Consumer Health** Write a letter to the manufacturer of a health-related product you like. Tell the manufacturer what you like about the product (or suggest how it could be improved). Include the letter and any response in your portfolio.
6. **Health of Others** Make a directory of local groups or persons you can contact for help in solving consumer problems. Distribute your directory to family members, neighbors, and friends.

Lesson 5

Public Health

This lesson will help you find answers to questions that teens often ask about public health. For example:

- **How do I know the cosmetics, grooming products, and medicines I buy are safe?**
- **Who makes sure that the food I eat and the water I drink are safe?**

Words to Know

public health
ordinance
sanitation

Government Health Departments

You receive health care from health workers such as doctors, nurses, and dentists. You also receive health care from many agencies of the government. Federal, state, and local governments all provide health services.

Government efforts to keep individuals healthy are part of a larger effort to keep the entire community healthy. These efforts are often referred to as public health. **Public health** deals with *the protection and improvement of community health.*

Public health authorities ensure that the water in public swimming pools is safe to swim in and that the water you drink is safe for consumption.

Local and State Health Departments

All states and most cities and counties have health departments. Although the jobs of these agencies differ from place to place, they all help to prevent and control diseases. Some tasks of local and state governments are listed below.

- Making sure that restaurant and hotel kitchens are clean and safe
- Making sure that garbage is taken away
- Making sure that local water is clean
- Offering health education programs
- Enforcing laws aimed at controlling disease
- Making sure that buildings are clean and sanitary
- Keeping birth and death records and records of diseases

Federal Health Departments

Many agencies of the federal government provide services related to health care. They belong to the Department of Health and Human Services. The agencies are described in **Figure 6.9.**

> **Q&A**
>
> **Health Hazard**
>
> **Q:** The water in our city swimming pool seems dirty. The bathrooms and changing areas aren't very clean either. What should I do?
>
> **A:** Contact your local health department right away. Ask them to test the water in the pool. Also tell them about the dirty rest rooms. Get your friends to call too. This sounds like a dangerous situation.

Figure 6.9

The Main Groups of the Department of Health and Human Services

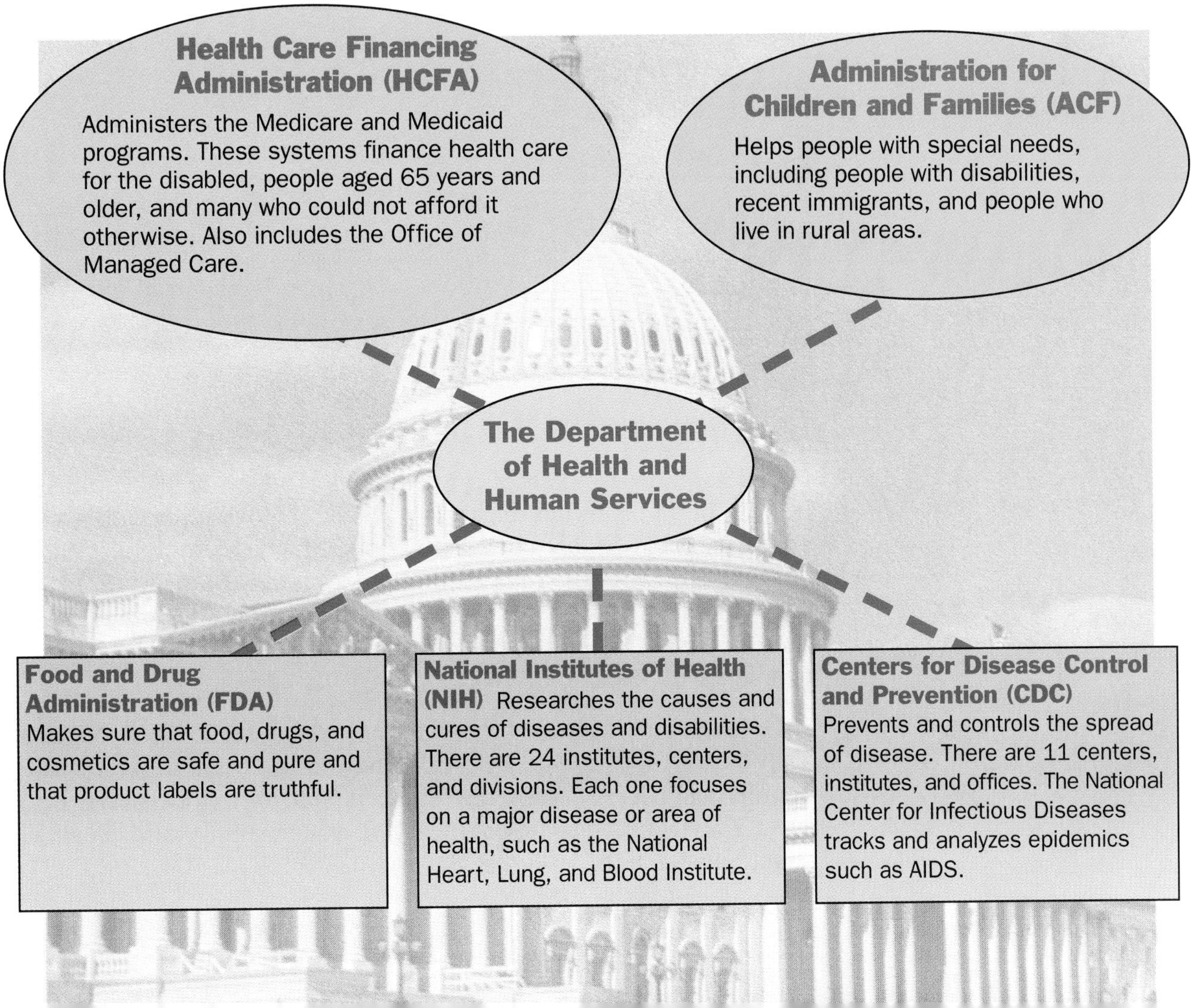

Health Care Financing Administration (HCFA)
Administers the Medicare and Medicaid programs. These systems finance health care for the disabled, people aged 65 years and older, and many who could not afford it otherwise. Also includes the Office of Managed Care.
Administration for Children and Families (ACF)
Helps people with special needs, including people with disabilities, recent immigrants, and people who live in rural areas.
The Department of Health and Human Services
Food and Drug Administration (FDA)
Makes sure that food, drugs, and cosmetics are safe and pure and that product labels are truthful.
National Institutes of Health (NIH) Researches the causes and cures of diseases and disabilities. There are 24 institutes, centers, and divisions. Each one focuses on a major disease or area of health, such as the National Heart, Lung, and Blood Institute.
Centers for Disease Control and Prevention (CDC)
Prevents and controls the spread of disease. There are 11 centers, institutes, and offices. The National Center for Infectious Diseases tracks and analyzes epidemics such as AIDS.

Your Total Health

Legal Protection ACTIVITY!

Choose one or more of the laws in the chart on this page. Write a paragraph to explain how the law affects you. For instance, because of the Food, Drug, and Cosmetic Act, you know that it is safe to use a particular lotion on your skin to prevent chapping.

Laws to Protect Public Health

Governments at all levels pass laws or ordinances that protect people's health. An **ordinance** (OR·di·nuhns) is *a law passed by a city or town.* **Figure 6.10** shows major federal laws that have been passed to protect your health.

Figure 6.10
Federal Laws that Protect Public Health

Food, Drug, and Cosmetic Act (1938)	Prohibits the distribution of unsafe foods, drugs, medical devices, and cosmetics. Forbids false or misleading labeling on such products.
Clean Water Act (1972)	Prohibits discharge of pollutants into rivers and streams.
Resource Conservation and Recovery Act (1976)	Regulates storage, transport, treatment, and disposal of hazardous wastes. Describes cleanup of contaminated sites.
Labeling of Hazardous Art Materials Act (1988)	Requires warning labels on art materials that contain hazardous substances.
Clean Air Act (1990)	Requires industries to reduce the amount of toxic substances they release into the air. Sets standards for release of pollutants by vehicles.
Health Insurance Portability and Accountability Act (1997)	Sets federal minimum standards for health care insurance.

Dealing with Disaster

Federal, state, and local governments work to help people stay healthy on an everyday basis. All levels of government also safeguard people's health during disasters. Hurricanes, floods, earthquakes, and fires disrupt sanitation systems. **Sanitation** (san·i·TAY·shuhn) means *the disposal of sewage and wastes in ways that protect health.* When sanitation systems are disrupted by a disaster, people are exposed to disease.

Government health workers hurry to the scene of a disaster. They bring food and clean drinking water and immunize disaster victims against disease. They show people how to avoid getting sick. They work fast to disinfect the water supply and clean up contaminated areas.

Nongovernmental Health Organizations

The work of nongovernmental groups is an important source of health services. Such groups as the American Heart Association and the American Cancer Society pay for research into ways to prevent and cure diseases. They help people who suffer from these diseases. They teach the public how to avoid these diseases.

The American Red Cross works to relieve human suffering after disasters such as fires and floods. It collects blood from volunteers and distributes it to people who need transfusions. The Red Cross also offers courses on first aid, safety, and health.

These groups need people's help. They are not governments that get money from taxes. They are not businesses that make money by selling goods or services. They can do their work only if they receive money from people. Many people also volunteer their time to help these groups do their jobs.

Both governmental and nongovernmental health workers help people in a disaster area by providing food and clean drinking water.

Lesson 5 Review

Using complete sentences, answer the following questions on a separate sheet of paper.

Reviewing Terms and Facts

1. **Vocabulary** Define the term *sanitation.* Use it in an original sentence.
2. **Recall** Why are nongovernmental health groups necessary?

Thinking Critically

3. **Investigate** Public health concerns become more critical wherever large groups of people are in close contact. What are some actions your school takes to safeguard the health of students?
4. **Explain** How do state and local health departments promote health in your community?

Applying Health Concepts

5. **Health of Others** Interview the manager of your school cafeteria. Find out what state and local health laws the cafeteria must obey.
6. **Personal Health** Take a class in first aid or cardiopulmonary resuscitation (CPR) sponsored by the American Red Cross.

Chapter 6 Review

Chapter Summary

- **Lesson 1** Wise consumers improve their health and get the most for their money. As a consumer, you have certain rights and responsibilities.
- **Lesson 2** Comparison shopping for goods and services helps you find the best buy. Cost, tradition, advertising, peers, and salespeople also influence consumers' decisions.
- **Lesson 3** Many types of professionals and facilities provide health care. Health insurance helps consumers pay for health care costs.
- **Lesson 4** Quacks are people who sell fake health care products and treatments. Consumer groups exist to protect consumers against false claims and faulty products.
- **Lesson 5** Government health departments and nongovernment health organizations work to protect public health.

Reviewing Key Terms and Concepts

Using complete sentences, answer the following questions on a separate sheet of paper.

Lesson 1

1. What are the characteristics of a wise consumer?
2. List your six rights as a consumer.

Lesson 2

3. List three ways to save money on products.
4. What influences your buying choices?

Lesson 3

5. Define *health care system, health care facility,* and *health insurance.*
6. Describe the two basic types of health care facilities.

Lesson 4

7. What are some ways to spot quackery?
8. Define *placebo effect* and give an example.

Lesson 5

9. Name the five main groups of the Department of Health and Human Services.
10. Define the term *ordinance.* Use it in an original sentence.

Thinking Critically

Using complete sentences, answer the following questions on a separate sheet of paper.

11. **Analyze** Some corporations furnish public schools with needed equipment and materials in return for the right to advertise their products in the school. Do you think that this arrangement is beneficial or harmful to students? Explain your answer.
12. **Give Examples** There are some occasions when comparison shopping is not possible. List two instances when that might be the case.
13. **Assess** Should businesses be required to contribute to their employees' health insurance plans? Explain your answer.
14. **Judge** Should people who sell quack remedies be allowed to advertise in newspapers and magazines and on television? Explain your answer.
15. **Analyze** Why do you think the U.S. government passes health-related laws? Are these laws necessary? Why or why not?

Chapter 6 Review

Your Action Plan

If you are like most people, you would like to be a better consumer. You can make an action plan to improve your buying habits.

Step 1 Look back through your private journal entries for this chapter to see what habits you could change. Perhaps you would like to take more control of your spending and not depend so much on advertising or on the opinions of friends.

Step 2 Choose a way you would like to change as a consumer. This is your long-term goal. Your long-term goal might be to become a more informed consumer.

Step 3 Once you have decided on a long-term goal, break it down into a series of short-term goals—steps to help you move toward your long-term goal.

When you have reached your long-term goal, reward yourself.

In Your Home and Community

1. **Consumer Health** Make a list of products your family purchases on a regular basis. Then list factors that influence your product choices. Examine your list and write down ideas on how your family could shop smarter.
2. **Health of Others** Volunteer your services at a local health care facility. You might deliver flowers and gifts to hospital rooms; read to children who are hospitalized; or write letters for disabled residents of nursing homes.

Building Your Portfolio

1. **Personal History** Find out as much as you can about your own health history. What diseases have you had? What immunizations have you had, and when? Are you allergic to anything? Have any relatives had serious illnesses? Write a report on your health history, and put it in your portfolio.
2. **Health Careers** Look in the employment section of your local newspaper for ads for health care workers. Note the kinds of jobs available and the qualifications. Choose a job in health care that you might like to have. Read more about the job in a career encyclopedia. Write a brief job description and put it in your portfolio.
3. **Personal Assessment** Look through all the activities and projects you did for this chapter. Choose one or two that you would like to include in your portfolio.

Unit 3
Fitness and Nutrition

Chapter 7

Your Growth and Development

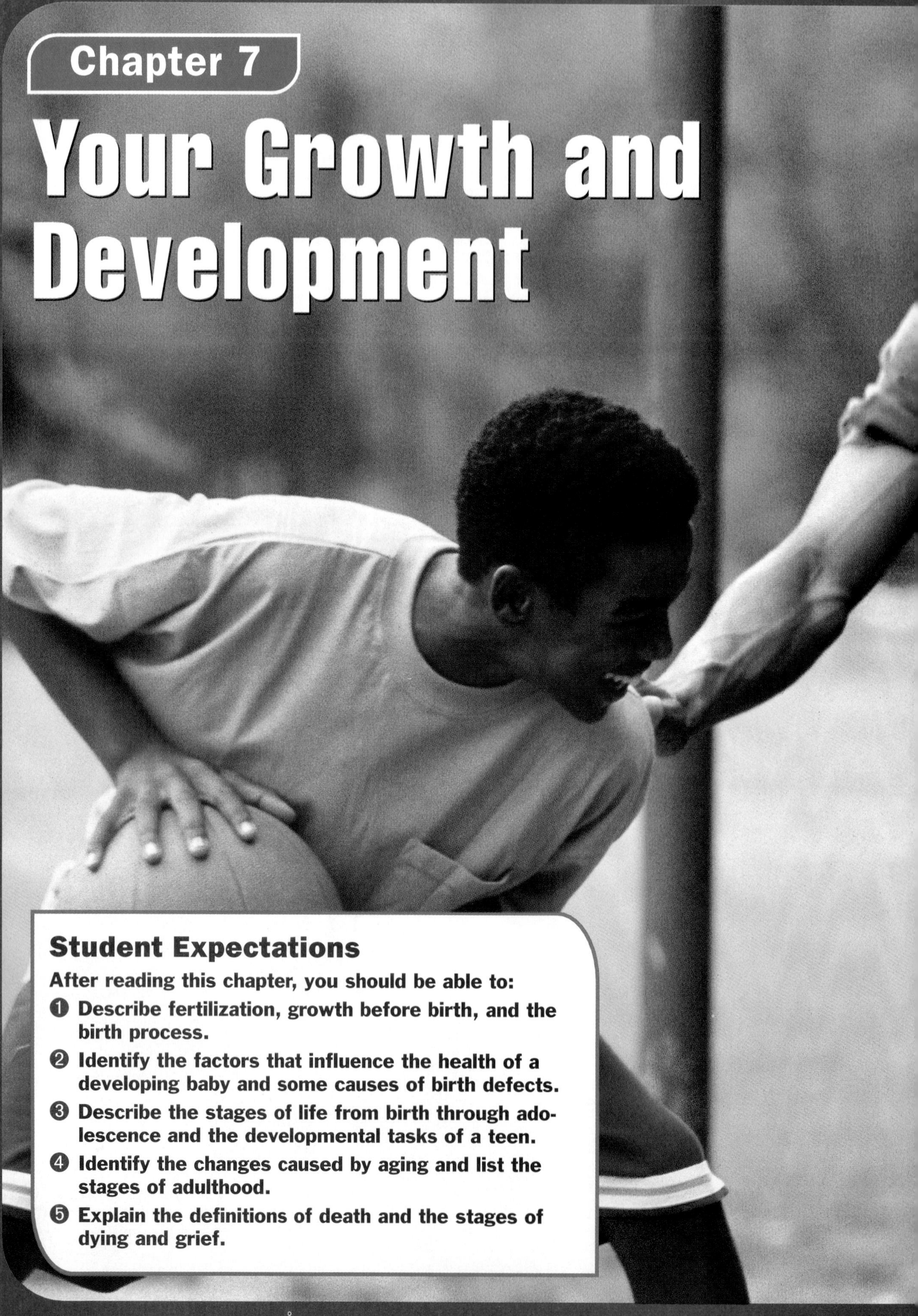

Student Expectations

After reading this chapter, you should be able to:

1. **Describe fertilization, growth before birth, and the birth process.**
2. **Identify the factors that influence the health of a developing baby and some causes of birth defects.**
3. **Describe the stages of life from birth through adolescence and the developmental tasks of a teen.**
4. **Identify the changes caused by aging and list the stages of adulthood.**
5. **Explain the definitions of death and the stages of dying and grief.**

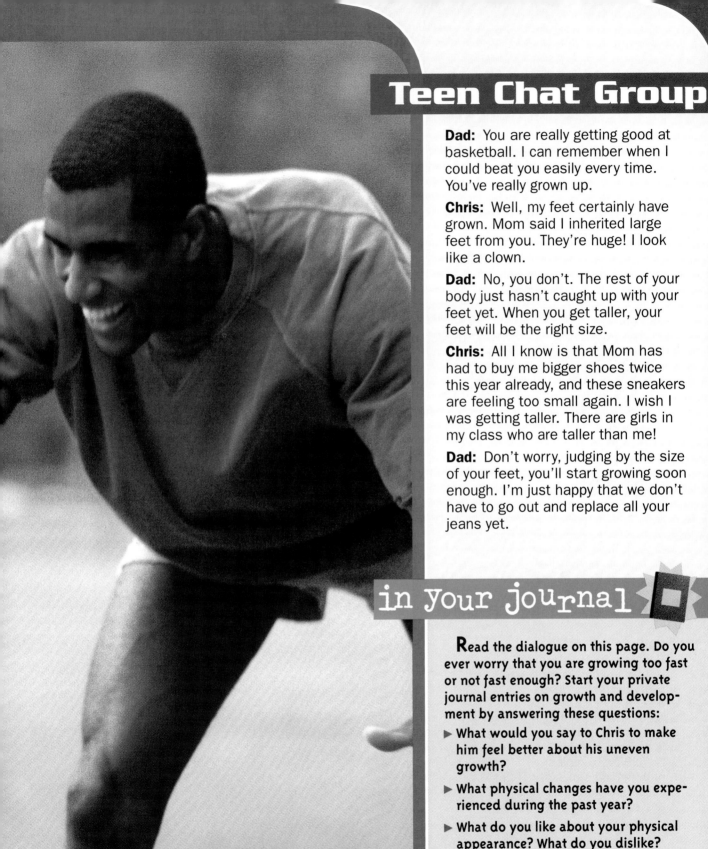

Teen Chat Group

Dad: You are really getting good at basketball. I can remember when I could beat you easily every time. You've really grown up.

Chris: Well, my feet certainly have grown. Mom said I inherited large feet from you. They're huge! I look like a clown.

Dad: No, you don't. The rest of your body just hasn't caught up with your feet yet. When you get taller, your feet will be the right size.

Chris: All I know is that Mom has had to buy me bigger shoes twice this year already, and these sneakers are feeling too small again. I wish I was getting taller. There are girls in my class who are taller than me!

Dad: Don't worry, judging by the size of your feet, you'll start growing soon enough. I'm just happy that we don't have to go out and replace all your jeans yet.

in your journal

Read the dialogue on this page. Do you ever worry that you are growing too fast or not fast enough? Start your private journal entries on growth and development by answering these questions:

- **What would you say to Chris to make him feel better about his uneven growth?**
- **What physical changes have you experienced during the past year?**
- **What do you like about your physical appearance? What do you dislike?**
- **In what ways have you grown mentally and emotionally? In what ways have you grown socially?**

When you reach the end of the chapter, you will use your journal entries to make an action plan.

Lesson 1

The Beginning of Life

This lesson will help you find answers to questions that teens often ask about the beginning of life. For example:

- **How did my life start?**
- **What happens during pregnancy?**
- **How is a baby born?**

Words to Know

cells
tissues
organs
fertilization
egg cell
sperm cell
uterus
embryo
fetus
placenta
umbilical cord
cervix

Beginning of Life

Life begins with a cell—a tiny bit of matter so small that it can be seen only through a microscope. In an astounding process, that cell grows into many cells, and these cells form our tissues, organs, and body systems (see **Figure 7.1**). Each of us is made up of trillions of cells. Cells are the building blocks of life.

The remarkable process of growth continues throughout life. Everyone grows at a different rate, but there are stages of growth that each person goes through.

Figure 7.1
From Cell to System

A Cell
Cells are the *basic units, or building blocks, of life.* Every cell in your body does a specific job. There are many types of cells. The cell shown here is a nerve cell in the brain. Examples of other kinds of cells are blood cells and muscle cells.

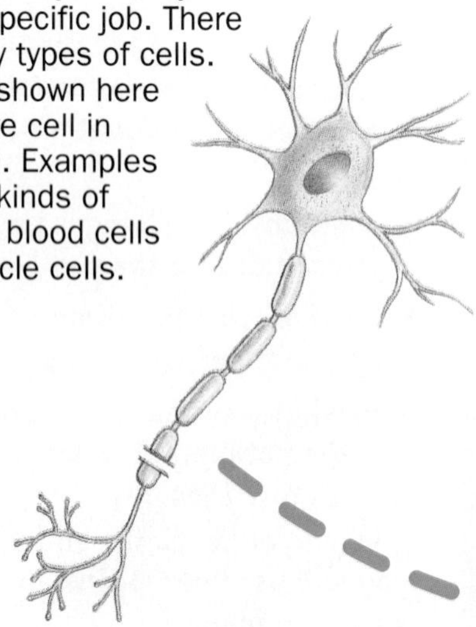

B Tissue
Cells that do similar jobs form **tissues.** Your body is made up of several kinds of tissue. Nerve cells make up the brain tissue shown here. Heart muscle cells make up heart muscle tissue.

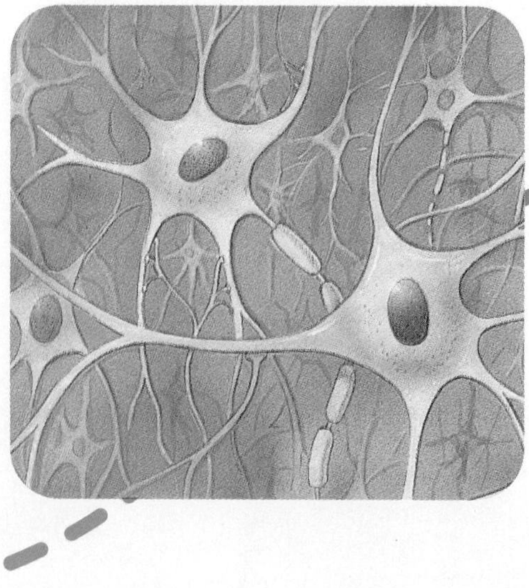

A Single Cell

The body begins with a single cell that is the result of fertilization. **Fertilization** (fer·til·i·ZAY·shuhn) is *the joining together of two special cells, one from each parent.* The *cell from the mother that plays a part in fertilization* is called an **egg cell.** The *cell from the father that enters the egg cell* is called a **sperm cell.** The sperm fertilizes the egg cell. After fertilization, a protective coating forms around the egg cell to prevent other sperm cells from entering. Fertilization takes place inside the mother's body.

Sometimes a newly fertilized egg splits into two complete fertilized eggs, which then copy each other. This produces identical twins of the same gender. If two separate eggs are fertilized at the same time, this produces fraternal (fruh·TERN·uhl) twins. These twins are not identical. They may be two girls, two boys, or a boy and a girl.

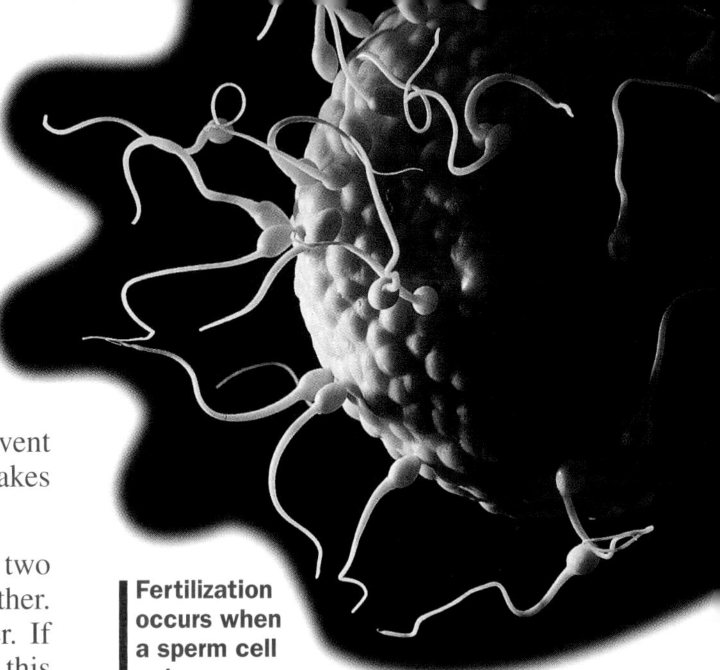

Fertilization occurs when a sperm cell enters an egg cell.

interNET CONNECTION

Let our Web site guide you in learning more about the developmental stages of life from birth to adulthood.

http://www.glencoe.com/sec/health

C Organ
Tissues combine into larger structures called organs. These **organs** are *body parts,* such as the brain, shown here. The main kind of tissue in the brain is nerve tissue. The heart is also an organ.

D System
Groups of organs that work together form systems. Your body has several systems, such as the nervous system, shown here. The brain is the main organ of the nervous system. The heart is the main organ of the circulatory system.

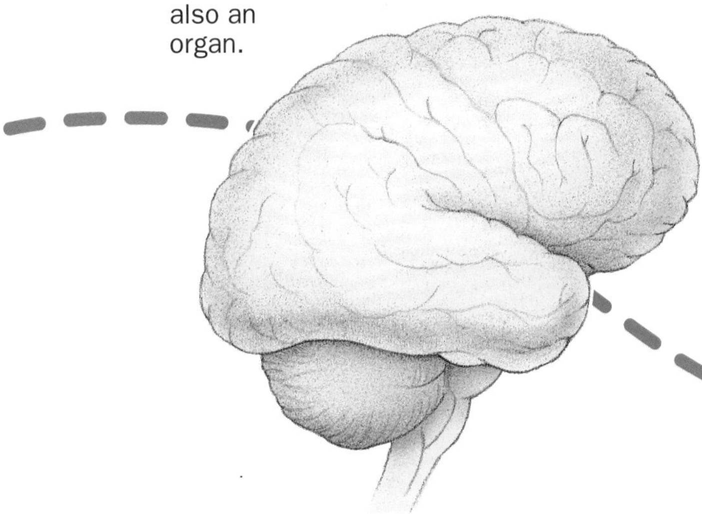

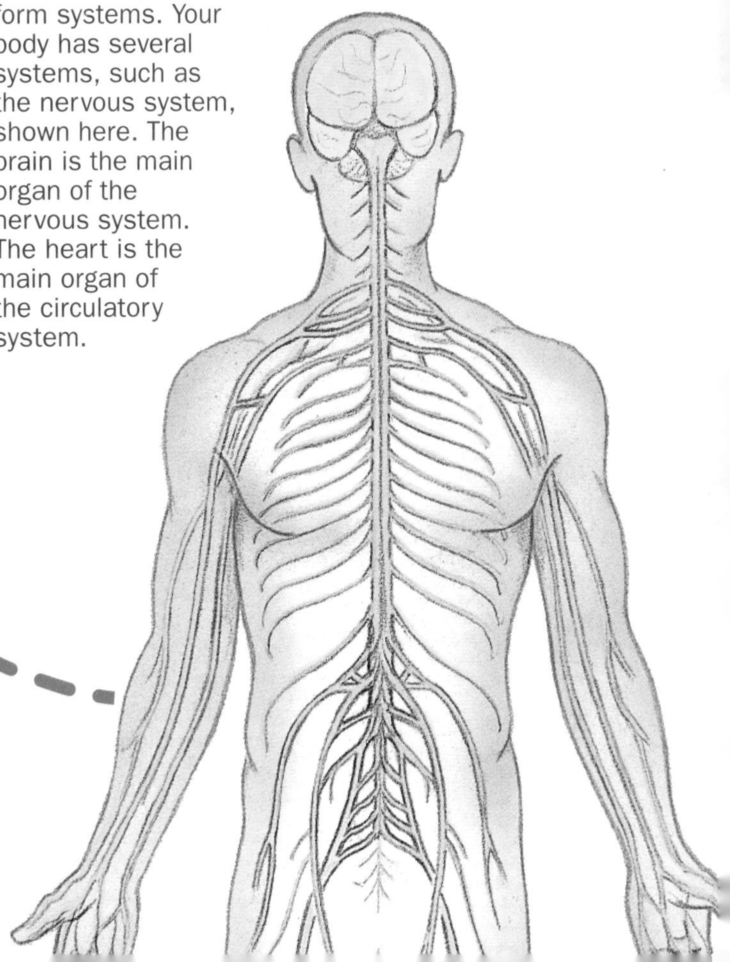

in your journal

Interview your mother or another female family member about any changes in diet during her pregnancy. Did she, for example, change her eating habits? Record her responses in your journal.

Growth During Pregnancy

The newly fertilized cell attaches itself to the wall of a *pear-shaped organ inside the mother's body.* This organ is called the **uterus** (YOO·tuh·ruhs). *As the fertilized cell begins to divide, it is called* an **embryo.** Cells in the embryo continue to divide and eventually join to make tissues, organs, and systems. *After two months, the developing baby is called* a **fetus.** At the end of about nine months, the baby is ready to be born. **Figure 7.2** shows the development of the embryo and fetus during these nine months.

Figure 7.2

Development Before Birth

How a baby develops during the nine months before birth.

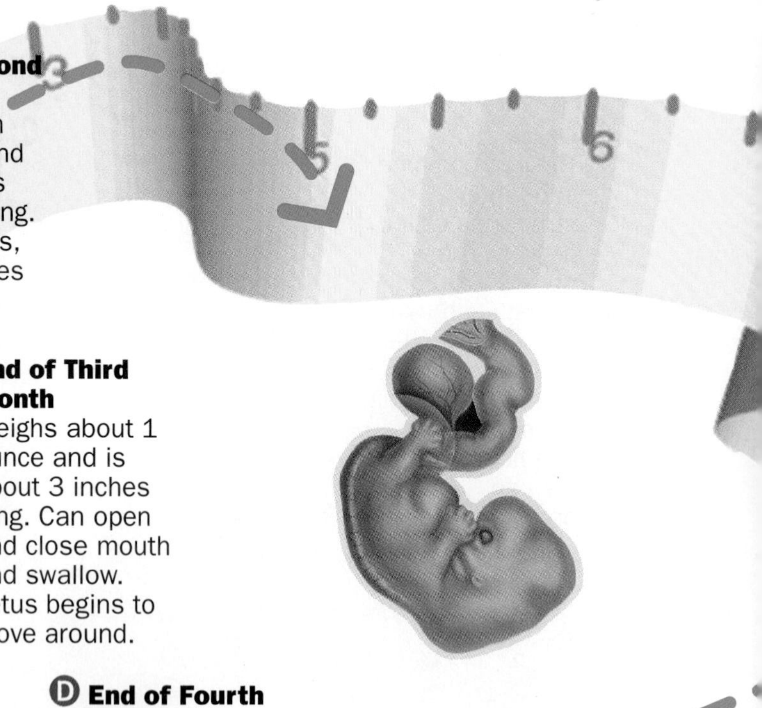

A End of First Month
About ⅓ inch long. Heart, brain, and lungs are forming. Heart begins to beat.

B End of Second Month
About 1 inch long. Skin and other organs are developing. Arms, fingers, legs, and toes are forming.

C End of Third Month
Weighs about 1 ounce and is about 3 inches long. Can open and close mouth and swallow. Fetus begins to move around.

D End of Fourth Month
Weighs about 6 ounces and is 5 inches long. Facial features become clearer. Movement can be felt.

E End of Fifth Month
Weighs about 1 pound and is just under 10 inches long. Eyelashes and nails appear. Heartbeat can be heard.

During pregnancy, it is important to eat healthy foods and to avoid tobacco, alcohol, and other drugs. A baby deserves the best possible start in life.

Growth Inside the Uterus

From the start, the developing fetus needs food to help it grow. It gets this food from a *thick, rich lining of tissue that builds up along the walls of the uterus and connects the mother to the baby.* This tissue is called the **placenta** (pluh·SEN·tuh). The placenta also gives the baby oxygen to breathe. The food and oxygen reach the baby through *a cord that grows out of the placenta.* This tube, called the **umbilical** (uhm·BIL·i·kuhl) **cord,** attaches to what will become the baby's navel. The baby's waste travels through the umbilical cord as well. The waste products are then carried away in the mother's bloodstream.

Cultural Connections

Naming the Baby ACTIVITY!

Choosing a name for a baby is important. In some cultures, parents name babies after relatives. In many Latin American cultures, a baby may receive several names: the family name of the mother and the father and, perhaps, even the place of birth. Babies are sometimes named for qualities their parents hope they will have.

Find out about your own name. Did it come from another language? What does your name mean? Ask someone in your family why you were given your name.

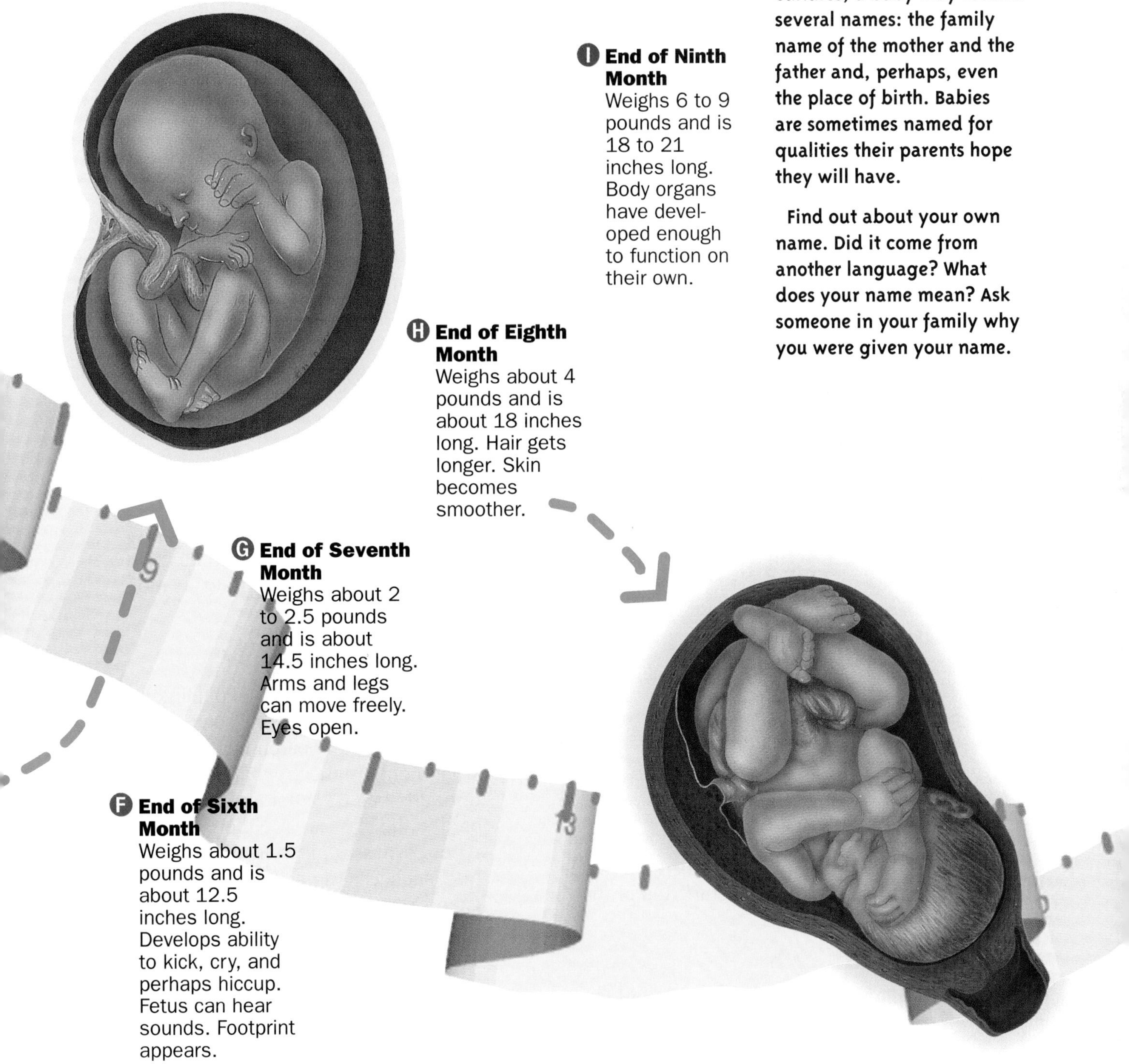

F End of Sixth Month
Weighs about 1.5 pounds and is about 12.5 inches long. Develops ability to kick, cry, and perhaps hiccup. Fetus can hear sounds. Footprint appears.
G End of Seventh Month
Weighs about 2 to 2.5 pounds and is about 14.5 inches long. Arms and legs can move freely. Eyes open.
H End of Eighth Month
Weighs about 4 pounds and is about 18 inches long. Hair gets longer. Skin becomes smoother.
I End of Ninth Month
Weighs 6 to 9 pounds and is 18 to 21 inches long. Body organs have developed enough to function on their own.

The process started with the joining together of the egg and the sperm cell. Now, nine months later, a baby is born.

Birth

By the ninth month, the fully developed baby is ready to be born. Birth happens in three stages.

- **Stage one.** The first stage begins with mild contractions (kuhn·TRAK·shuhnz). These are a *sudden tightening in the muscles of the uterus.* Contractions cause the muscles of the uterus to shorten. This forces the **cervix** (SER·viks), which is *the opening of the uterus,* to open, or dilate.
- **Stage two.** By the beginning of the second stage, the cervix has opened to a width of about 4 inches (10 cm). Contractions are now quite strong. The contractions push the baby through the cervix and out of the mother.
- **Stage three.** In this final stage of birth, several more very strong contractions of the uterus help push out the placenta. If any part of the placenta remains inside the mother's body, she could become ill. The health care professional must make sure that all the placenta comes out.

Lesson 1

Review

Using complete sentences, answer the following questions on a separate sheet of paper.

Reviewing Terms and Facts

1. **Give Examples** List two types of body tissue.
2. **Recall** Identify the main organ of the circulatory system.
3. **Vocabulary** Using your own words, define the term *fertilization.*
4. **Vocabulary** What is the difference between an *egg cell* and a *sperm cell?*
5. **Review** Describe the development of the embryo and fetus during pregnancy.
6. **Identify** What is the function of the placenta?

Thinking Critically

7. **Explain** Cells are often referred to as the building blocks of life. Why is this an appropriate descriptior?
8. **Analyze** A pregnant woman should be careful about what she eats and drinks. Explain why this is important.
9. **Synthesize** Make a list of the main events of pregnancy from fertilization to birth.

Applying Health Concepts

10. **Consumer Health** Find out about classes for preparing expectant parents for childbirth and parenthood. During what month in the pregnancy do classes normally begin? What topics are covered in the classes? Are there different types of classes given in your community, such as early pregnancy classes, exercise classes for pregnant women, childbirth education, baby care classes, and exercise classes for pregnant women? How do they differ?

Lesson 2

Factors in Your Development

This lesson will help you find answers to questions that teens often ask about factors in development. For example:

- **Why was I born with certain traits such as my hair color and the shape of my nose?**
- **Should a pregnant woman continue to exercise?**
- **Why are some babies born with birth defects?**

Words to Know

heredity
chromosomes
genes
genetic disorder
environment
prenatal care
obstetrician
birth defects
fetal alcohol syndrome (FAS)
addiction
rubella

What Makes You Special

Have you ever wondered what makes every person unique? Each person is one of a kind, with his or her own special looks, mannerisms, and personality. A number of factors shape each baby at birth. These factors affect how babies look and how healthy they are. The two most important factors are heredity and environment.

Children inherit certain physical characteristics, such as hair color and eye color, from their parents. Sometimes a child does not look like either parent. Sometimes there is a strong family resemblance.

Teen Issues

Kid Brothers and Sisters ACTIVITY!

Do you have a little brother or sister? If you do, you can make a difference in his or her development. Older brothers and sisters are important people in the lives of children. With your younger brother or sister, make a list of activities you can do together. Then set aside some time each week to do them. Your help will be appreciated by everyone in the family.

Q&A

Unseen Traits

Q: I have straight hair, but neither one of my parents has straight hair. How could that happen?

A: Some of the traits you have may be shown by your mother, some may be shown by your father—and some may be shown by neither one. For example, the trait for straight hair can be carried by a parent's genes, but not be visible in the parent.

Heredity

Heredity is *the passing of traits from parents to their children.* The color of children's eyes and the shape of their faces are examples of traits they inherited from their parents. Structures within cells play important roles in heredity. (See **Figure 7.3.**)

- **Chromosomes.** The *threadlike structures found within the nucleus of a cell that carry the codes for inherited traits* are **chromosomes** (KROH·muh·sohmz). There are 46 chromosomes, or 23 pairs, in most human body cells. One chromosome of every pair is from each parent. A sperm cell or an egg cell each has 23 single chromosomes. A fertilized egg, however, has 46 chromosomes—23 from each parent.
- **Genes.** The *basic units of heredity* are called **genes.** They are located on chromosomes and carry codes for individual traits, such as hair color, eye color, and height. Children of the same parents inherit different combinations of chromosomes and genes.

Heredity and Genetic Disorders

Most of the time the genes that both parents pass on to children produce a healthy, normal baby. Sometimes, however, the genes carried by one parent lead to unexpected results. When this happens, the baby may be born with a **genetic** (juh·NE·tik) **disorder.** This is *a disease or condition in which the baby's body does not work normally because of a problem with genes.* Sometimes the disorder is obvious at birth. Sometimes it does not surface until the child is a few years older.

More than 150,000 babies are born each year with genetic disorders. Some of these disorders are mild, others very severe. They can have a serious effect on a person's health. Scientists have

Figure 7.3

Inherited Characteristics

A The photo shows a single cell with 23 pairs of chromosomes. The genes that determine individual traits are located on the chromosomes.

B The diagram shows how one trait, eye color, is passed on to children. If one parent has brown eyes and the other has blue eyes, the baby could have either brown or blue eyes. However, the chances of the baby having brown eyes are three out of four.

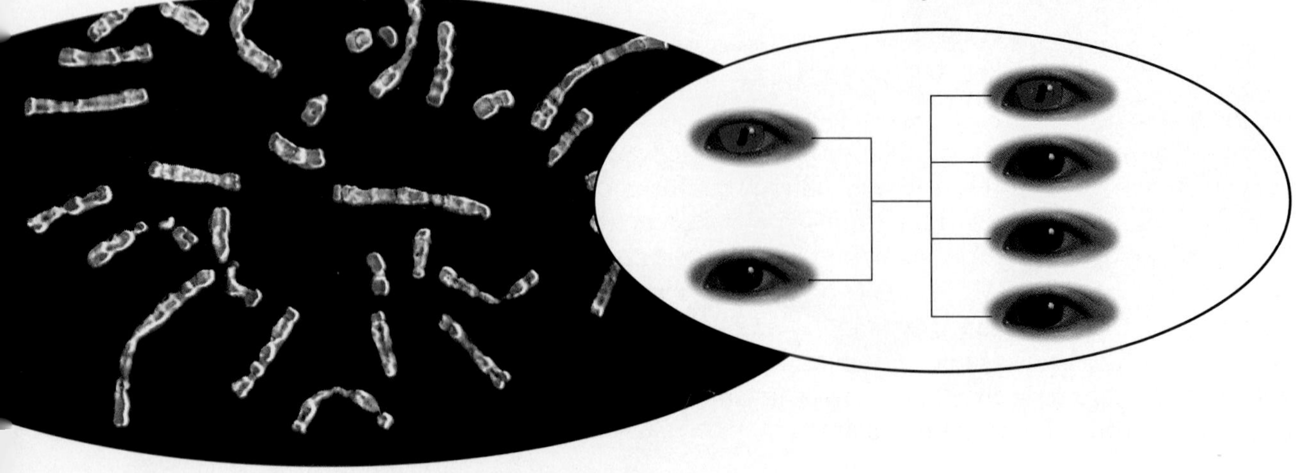

determined that some genetic disorders occur when a cell has more than the usual number of chromosomes. One of these conditions is Down syndrome. However, the cause of almost 60 percent of genetic disorders remains a mystery. Scientists have made many breakthroughs in the last 20 years, and research continues to find ways of preventing and treating many genetic disorders.

Environment

The second factor in the health of a developing baby and a newborn child is environment. **Environment** (en·VY·ruhn·ment) is *the sum total of a person's surroundings.* The environment of the developing baby is the uterus. The baby's health, then, is affected directly by the actions and total health of the pregnant woman.

Care of the Pregnant Woman

Healthy mothers are more likely to have healthy babies. That is why it is extremely important for a woman to begin a program of prenatal care as soon as she finds out she is pregnant. **Prenatal** (pree·NAY·tuhl) **care** includes *a number of steps taken to provide for the health of a pregnant woman and her unborn baby.* One of the most important steps is regular visits by the woman to a health clinic, family doctor, or **obstetrician** (ahb·stuh·TRI·shuhn). This *doctor specializes in the care of a pregnant woman and her developing baby.* The obstetrician will make sure the pregnant woman stays healthy and that her child is developing as it should. When the mother takes good care of her own health and follows the steps listed below, she is giving her baby the best possible start in life.

Steps to Good Prenatal Care

- Visit an obstetrician or other health care professional regularly.
- Eat nutritious foods.
- Get enough rest and participate in moderate exercise.
- Avoid the use of tobacco, alcohol, and all medications and other drugs that have not been allowed by the health care provider. These substances can be very dangerous to the fetus.

Birth Defects

Following these steps to good prenatal care is the best present a mother can give her newborn baby. For example, seeking medical care in the first weeks of pregnancy and continuing with regular checkups will help ensure that problems are identified and dealt with at an early stage. Not following the other steps for good prenatal care—eating properly; avoiding the use of tobacco, alcohol, or drugs—can lead to serious problems in the developing child. In some cases, using alcohol and drugs can result in birth defects. **Birth defects** (DEE·fekts) are *disorders of the developing and newborn baby.* Birth defects may be caused by a genetic disorder or by harmful substances in the fetus's environment. Certain infections can also be harmful during pregnancy.

in your journal

Babies born to very young mothers often have a lower than normal weight. In general, the younger the mother, the greater the risks to the baby's health. Having a baby also causes problems for teenage parents. Write a short paragraph describing how the life of a teenager would change with the added major responsibility of raising a child. Write your paragraph in your private journal.

Did You Know?

Not for Women Only

Research suggests that some birth defects are related to fathers who smoke. The study suggests that men who smoke are more likely to have babies with medical problems than men who do not smoke.

Problems in the Fetal Environment

- **Nutrition.** The baby gets all food from its mother. When a woman fails to eat the right foods during pregnancy, the baby may be born too early or have a low birth weight. These babies have a greater chance of having mental or physical problems. Eating nutritious foods is extremely important for the health of the mother and her developing child.
- **Alcohol.** When a pregnant woman drinks alcohol, it passes through the placenta and enters the developing baby's body. This can lead to a condition known as **fetal** (FEE·tuhl) **alcohol syndrome (FAS),** *a pattern of physical and mental problems that occur in the child of a woman who drinks alcohol during pregnancy.* Women who are pregnant should avoid alcohol.
- **Medications and drugs.** A woman who is pregnant should avoid the use of all medications and drugs—unless she has her doctor's approval. Even drugs that seem harmless, such as over-the-counter cold pills, can affect the developing baby. Illegal drugs can lead to **addiction** (uh·DIK·shuhn), *a physical or mental need for a drug or other substance.* When such substances are taken by a pregnant woman, her baby may be born with an addiction to the drug.
- **Tobacco.** A woman who uses tobacco during pregnancy can seriously harm her unborn baby. Growth before birth can be slowed and the baby may be born prematurely or with a low birth weight. The baby may develop an addiction to nicotine (NI·kuh·teen), a drug found in tobacco. Women who are pregnant should avoid smoking and also try to avoid secondhand smoke from others.

MAKING HEALTHY DECISIONS

Giving Advice

Rachel spots her cousin Maria across the room at a family reunion, and she shouts and makes her way through the crowd. They both start hugging and talking excitedly. It is the first time they have seen each other for several months because Maria moved out of town after she got married. Rachel, who is 14, has always looked up to Maria.

When they sit down to eat, Rachel has a soft drink and Maria takes a glass of wine. Rachel announces that she made the basketball team and asks Maria what's new with her. "I thought you'd never ask," says Maria, "I just found out I'm pregnant, and I'm so happy!"

Rachel has a problem. On the one hand, she respects her cousin's ability to make her own decisions. On the other hand, Rachel knows that Maria will have a better chance of having a healthy baby if she does not drink alcohol during her pregnancy.

What should Rachel do? Should she say nothing, hoping that a glass or two of wine won't matter? Should she tell Maria that even a little alcohol might harm her unborn baby? Rachel uses the step-by-step decision-making process.

1. **State the situation**
2. **List the options**
3. **Weigh the possible outcomes**
4. **Consider your values**
5. **Make a decision and act**
6. **Evaluate the decision**

- **Infections.** If a mother-to-be has **rubella** (roo·BE·luh), *the disease called German measles,* her baby may be born deaf or have other serious health problems. There is a vaccine that protects against rubella. Some sexually transmitted diseases may also pass from the mother to the baby. These can cause such problems as brain damage, blindness, or even death. It is important for a pregnant woman to tell her doctor about any possible infections so they can be treated.

Review

Lesson 2

Using complete sentences, answer the following questions on a separate sheet of paper.

Reviewing Terms and Facts

1. **Give Examples** List at least two traits we inherit from our parents.
2. **Vocabulary** Which of the following are the basic units of heredity? *environment, genes, chromosomes, rubella*
3. **Recall** Identify two causes of birth defects.
4. **Identify** List three problems in the fetal environment.
5. **Recall** Cite two causes of low birth weight in newborns.

Thinking Critically

6. **Explain** Describe how heredity and environment affect the development of the unborn and newborn child.
7. **Analyze** Write a list of questions you think a pregnant woman might ask her doctor about what she could do to have a healthy baby.

Applying Health Concepts

8. **Health of Others** With your classmates, make a poster listing the causes of birth defects. Display the poster in the classroom.

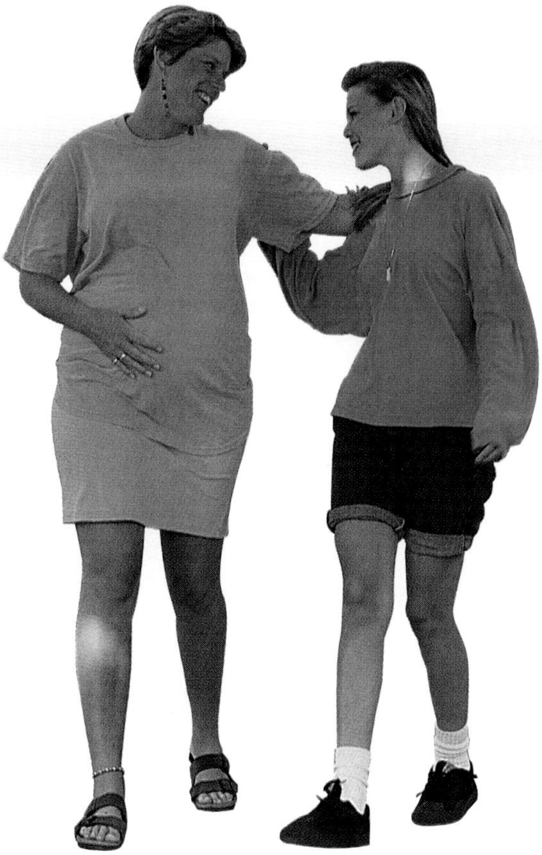

Follow-up Activities

1. Apply the six steps of the decision-making process to Rachel's story.
2. With a partner, role-play a conversation between Rachel and Maria in which Rachel avoids giving any advice to her cousin.
3. Now role-play a conversation in which Rachel tells Maria of her concern and explains why she hopes Maria will not drink during her pregnancy.

Lesson 3

From Childhood to Adolescence

This lesson will help you find answers to questions that teens often ask about the ways people grow and develop. For example:

- **What changes occur during infancy?**
- **What changes will happen to me during adolescence?**
- **Why do my moods seem to change more often than they did before?**

Words to Know

infancy
adolescence
hormones
puberty
developmental tasks

The Growth Years

The period of life from the first years through the teen years is a time of enormous growth. During these growth years, we learn many skills and form many habits. We also go through many physical, mental, emotional, and social changes.

There are many different theories about the way children develop. Some focus on physical growth. Some look mainly at mental or emotional growth. One important view is that of scientist Erik Erikson, who studied the social and emotional development of individuals from infancy to old age. Erikson believed that people pass through eight stages of development. His theories and those of experts on physical and mental growth are combined in the descriptions of the four stages of childhood that follow. These stages—infancy, early childhood, middle childhood, and late childhood—are also illustrated in **Figure 7.4.**

Figure 7.4

From Infancy to Late Childhood

Each individual follows his or her own path of development. Some children, for example, walk or talk at an earlier age than others. However, researchers have found that development occurs in roughly the same order in most children. To study growth and development, researchers divide childhood into four stages.

A Infancy During the first months of life, a child begins to move around and to explore the world.

B Early Childhood Walking, running, and climbing stairs are some of the physical skills learned in early childhood. Children of this age are also beginning to do things for themselves and to communicate with others.

Infancy

During the first year of life, the fastest physical growth takes place. The weight of the child triples, and the height increases by 50 percent. During **infancy** (IN·fuhn·see), as this *first year of life* is called, trust develops. If an infant's needs are met in a loving way, he or she learns to trust and feel safe.

Early Childhood

Between the ages of one and three, children learn to walk and talk. They also learn how to control the removal of wastes from their bodies. Children feel proud of their achievements and eager to do more things for and by themselves. Sometimes a child will fail when trying something new, but that is part of learning and growing. If adults offer love and encouragement and accept the child's individuality, they can help the child develop positive self-esteem.

Middle Childhood

Between the ages of three and five, children's arms, legs, and bodies become longer, and they are able to coordinate their movements better. Children of this age enjoy playing make-believe and imitating adults. They also begin to ask many questions. Once again, the way adults respond to a child's behavior is important. When parents encourage these new abilities and questions, they promote the child's self-esteem. However, if parents are impatient with a child's attempts to do things independently, this may make the child feel guilty about starting new activities and decrease the child's self-esteem.

Late Childhood

From ages six through eleven, children grow at a steadier rate than they did when they were younger. Their physical skills improve and their mental skills increase.

Children of this age often spend a lot of time making things. If the child's creative efforts are appreciated and rewarded, pride in her or his work increases. Children who are scolded for getting in the way or creating a mess may begin to feel worthless. A child's success or failure in any of these stages of growth affects emotional development at that stage. By succeeding at later stages, a child may overcome the setbacks of earlier stages and gain self-esteem.

Literature Connection

Growing Over Time ACTIVITY!

You might enjoy reading the novel "Grandma Didn't Wave Back" by Rose Blue. This is a touching story about the close relationship between a young girl and her grandmother, whose memory is deteriorating. With your family, discuss changes that occur over time. Then write about a special relationship you have and describe how it has changed over time.

C Middle Childhood Children between the ages of three and five can jump and hop and draw simple shapes. Pretend play helps them develop social skills and practice future roles.

D Late Childhood The physical skills of children improve steadily between the ages of six and eleven. Friends are important in building social skills and self-esteem.

Did You Know?

Knowing When to Stop

A growth hormone determines when our bodies stop growing. The pituitary gland, located near the brain, produces the growth hormone. The brain works with the pituitary gland to determine when growth will stop. When the gland stops producing the hormone, the body stops growing.

Adolescence

Next to infancy, the second fastest period of physical growth is adolescence. **Adolescence** (a·duhl·E·suhns) is *the time of life between childhood and adulthood.* It usually begins somewhere between the ages of 11 and 15. Girls often show the physical changes of adolescence earlier than boys.

Perhaps at the start of this school year, you noticed that some of your classmates had grown much taller over the summer, while others looked the same. You may be aware of some changes in yourself as well. Maybe some new hair has begun to appear on parts of your body. These changes are all part of a growth spurt that occurs during adolescence. They are related to the release of **hormones,** which are *chemical substances produced in glands and which regulate many body functions.* These hormones and the changes they cause are preparing you for adulthood.

Growth during adolescence takes place in all three areas of your health triangle. You grow physically, mentally and emotionally, and socially. Keep in mind that there are individual differences in the rate of growth in all three areas.

Figure 7.5

Erikson's Stages of Life

Erik Erikson believed that a person's life could be divided into eight stages of development. Each stage is associated with a developmental task that involves a person's relationship with other people and with the world around. Whether or not a person masters the task of a particular stage, he or she moves on to the next stage of development. If the task was not mastered, it affects the way the individual handles the next stage of development.

Infancy

Birth to 1 Year

Characteristic of stage: child is completely dependent on others to meet his or her needs

Developmental task: to develop trust—a sense that others will be there to help

If not mastered: mistrust—the sense that one is alone

Early Childhood

1 to 3 Years

Characteristics of stage: child is learning to control own body, to do things on his or her own, and to separate from parents

Developmental task: to develop autonomy—confidence in one's ability to do tasks oneself

If not mastered: shame and doubt—a lack of confidence

Middle Childhood

3 to 5 Years

Characteristics of stage: child begins to make decisions and to think of and carry out projects

Developmental task: to develop initiative—ability to create one's own play

If not mastered: guilt—feeling guilty about the actions one takes

Late Childhood

6 to 11 Years

Characteristics of stage: child explores surroundings and must master more and more difficult skills

Developmental task: to develop industry—interest in making objects and performing activities

If not mastered: inferiority—feeling that one is unable to succeed

Physical Growth

Adolescence begins with **puberty** (PYOO·ber·tee), *the time when you begin to develop certain traits of adults of your own gender.* The exact age at which puberty begins is different in different people. Girls tend to start puberty at an earlier age than boys. No two people grow in exactly the same way.

Physical growth during puberty is rapid. Many girls begin their growth spurt between the ages of 11 and 14, adding about 3 inches in height during those years. Boys tend to start their growth spurt later, between the ages of 13 and 16. They may add 6 to 7 inches in height at that time. Growth for boys and girls often continues for several years after the first growth spurt.

Growth during adolescence is rapid and uneven. Among girls and boys of the same age, there is great variation in size and shape.

Adolescence

12 to 18 Years

Characteristic of stage: adolescent searches for his or her identity

Developmental task: to develop one's own identity—a sense of who one is

If not mastered: role confusion—being mixed up over the many roles one plays

Young Adulthood

19 to 30 Years

Characteristic of stage: person tries to develop close personal relationships

Developmental task: to develop intimacy—forming a strong relationship with another person

If not mastered: isolation—being alone

Middle Adulthood

31 to 60 Years

Characteristics of stage: person tries to achieve something in work and is concerned with the well-being of children and community

Developmental task: to develop generativity—the sense that one has contributed something to society

If not mastered: self-absorption—being concerned only with one's own needs

Maturity and Old Age

61 Years to Death

Characteristic of stage: person tries to understand meaning of own life

Developmental task: to develop integrity—feeling complete and satisfied with one's life

If not mastered: despair—feeling that one's life has not been satisfying

Cultural Connections

Coming of Age

Throughout history, puberty has been marked in many cultures by ceremonies. The Apache, a Native American group, had a ceremony that marked puberty in girls. In the ceremony, each girl who was entering puberty shared a blanket with an old woman. The woman then became the girl's guardian and was sworn to protect the girl for life.

Physical growth during puberty is very uneven. The outer parts of your body—head, hands, and feet—generally grow first. As a result, your hands and feet may suddenly seem too large for the rest of your body. You may feel awkward. Some young people feel unhappy or self-conscious about their bodies during this stage. These developments, however, are perfectly normal.

During puberty, many other changes take place. Boys may find their voices growing deeper. Girls may find that their figures are developing. Some of the other changes are shown in **Figure 7.6.**

Mental and Emotional Growth

Thinking skills develop during adolescence. As a child, you were able to solve only very basic kinds of problems. As an adolescent, you are able to solve more complex problems. You can see degrees in situations and understand other points of view. You can also think ahead to what might happen if you act in a certain way. You understand that you often have a choice. When friends dare you to walk into an old boarded-up house, you can weigh the consequences of accepting or refusing the dare.

During adolescence, your emotions, or feelings, also go through changes. These changes include the following:

- **Mood swings.** You may feel very happy one minute and moody or unhappy the next. Like the physical changes in your body, these mood swings are related to the release of hormones.

Figure 7.6
Physical Changes During Puberty

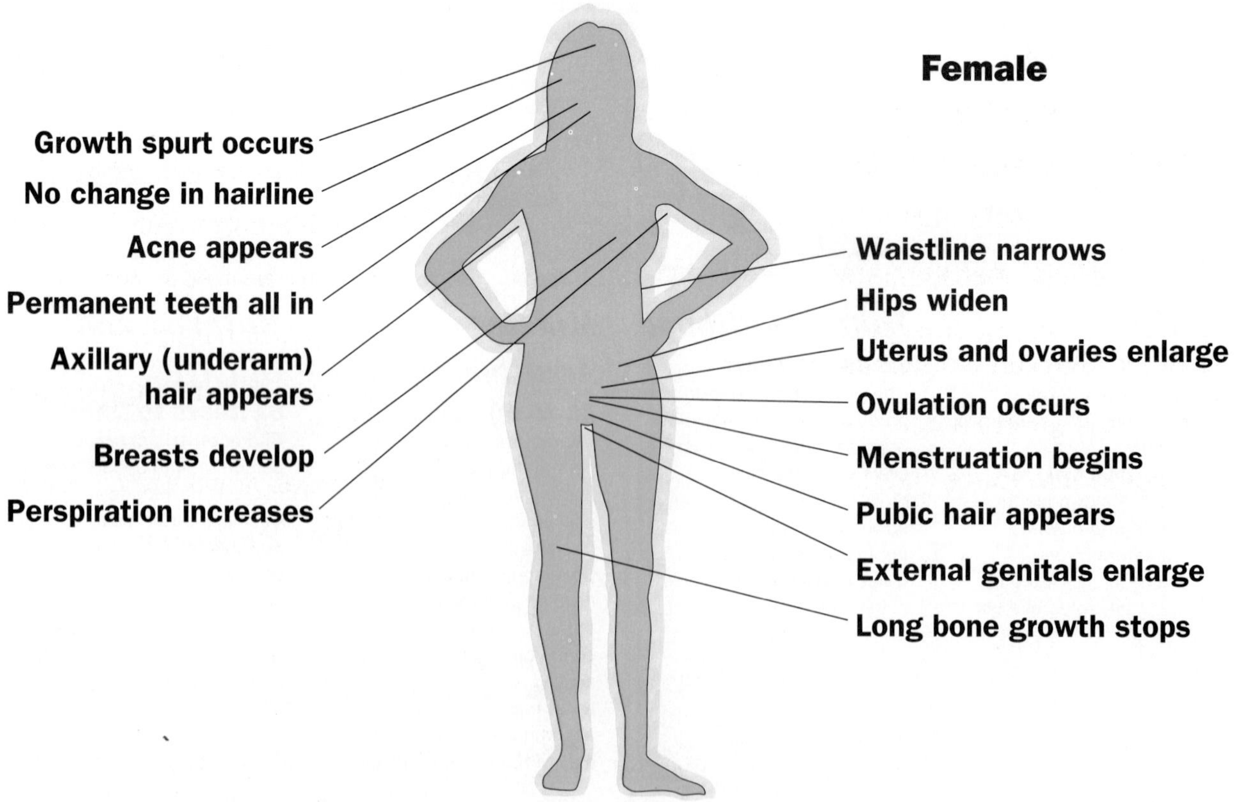

- **Feelings toward others.** You may see family and friends in a new way. People around you are no longer just "givers," as they were when you were a child. You now see these people as having needs, just like yourself. Sometimes you are able to help meet the needs of others. You can listen, for example, when a friend has a problem.
- **Increased interest in the opposite gender.** You may begin to feel a desire to spend time with members of the opposite gender. These new feelings can be confusing, even frightening. Having them, however, is a normal part of growing up.

Going out as a group gives boys and girls the opportunity to get to know members of the opposite gender in a relaxed setting.

Social Growth

During adolescence, your friends become very important to you, and you want to spend a lot of time with them. At the same time, you will be meeting many new people and forming new relationships. You will also become more aware of other people's needs. These developments are all part of social growth, an important part of adolescence.

Many aspects of social growth are defined by **developmental** (di·vel·uhp·MEN·tuhl) **tasks,** *events that need to happen in order for you to continue growing toward becoming a healthy, mature adult.* Experts have identified nine developmental tasks that are basic to adolescence. They are shown in **Figure 7.7** on page 212.

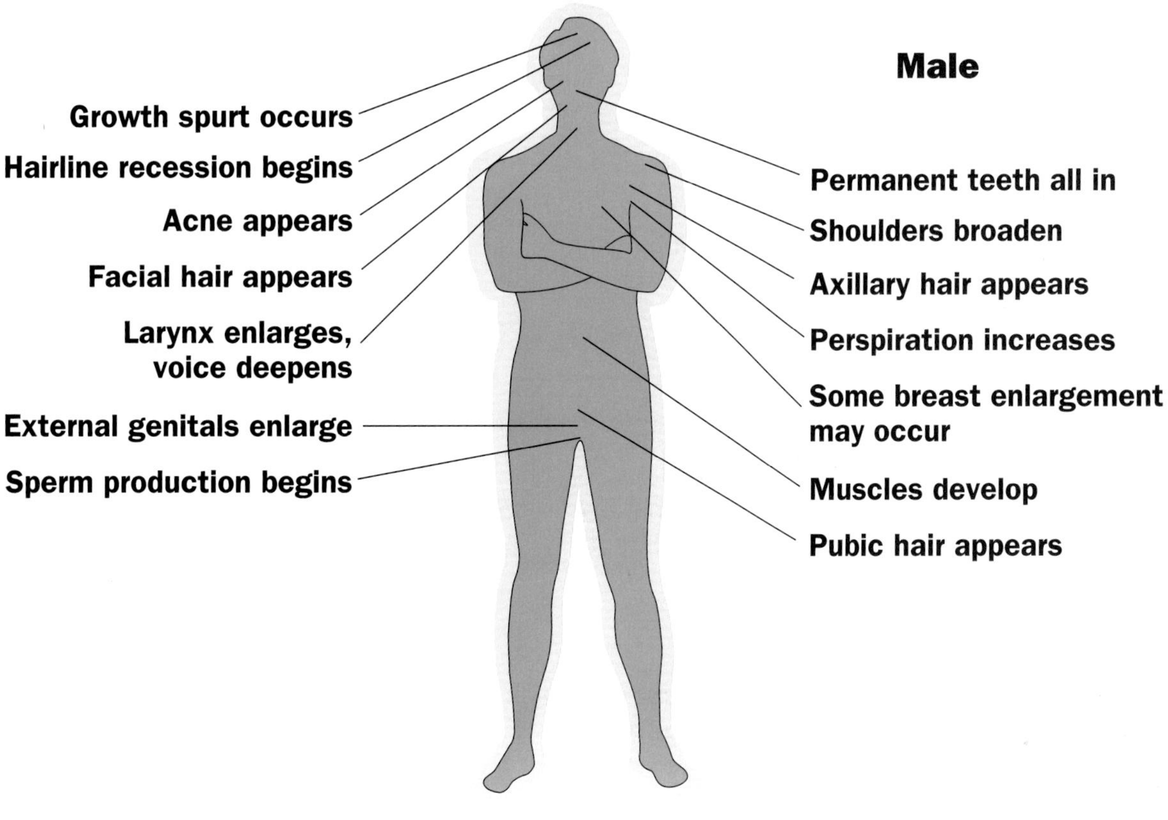

Figure 7.7

Developmental Tasks of Adolescence

The nine developmental tasks of adolescence are important steps in the process you go through to develop into the person you want to become.

Accept your body and its characteristics.
Become more independent of parents and other adults for your emotional health.
Form more mature relationships with people of both genders.
Learn more about who you are.
Develop a set of your own values.
Gain a masculine (MAS·kyuh·lin) or feminine (FEM·uh·nin) view of yourself.
Develop an interest in and a concern for your community.
Get ready for marriage and family life as an adult.
Learn how to solve problems in an adult way.

Personal Inventory

YOUR DEVELOPMENTAL RATE

How successful are you at the nine developmental tasks at this point in your life? The following quiz will help you find out. For each statement, write true or false on a separate sheet of paper.

1. I try to think through problems, looking at all possible solutions.
2. There are several jobs I think I would do well as an adult.
3. I have more adult discussions with my parents or other grown-ups than I used to have.
4. I am able to list my four most important beliefs.
5. I act in a way that goes along with my beliefs.
6. I can describe at least two ways that my life would be different if I were a parent.
7. I am successful most of the time at making male and female friends.
8. I do some things alone or with friends that I used to do with my family.
9. The choices I make promote my overall health and well-being.
10. I know and accept my physical strengths and weaknesses.
11. I listen to other people's ideas even when they are different from mine.
12. I am concerned about local and national problems in the news today.
13. I have one or two close friends with whom I can talk about almost anything.
14. I have an idea of what kind of man or woman I want to be as an adult.

Look at all the statements for which you wrote false. Find the developmental task in Figure 7.7 that each one relates to. These are tasks you will need to work on in the coming years.

During adolescence, your friends and their views become more important than ever. However, you also need to find out who you are, separate from the group. You begin looking, often without knowing it, for an answer to the question, "Who am I?" This search for yourself is a normal part of the developmental tasks that you take on in adolescence.

The choices you make over the next few years will affect your success in these tasks. As you grow throughout your life, your choices will shape how healthy that growth will be.

in your journal

Which of the developmental tasks of adolescence do you think is the most difficult? Which is the easiest? Explain your feelings about these tasks in your private journal.

During the next few years, you will be spending a lot of time on your own—at school, with your friends, and pursuing personal interests. This growing independence from parents and other adults is one of the developmental tasks of adolescence.

Lesson 3 Review

Using complete sentences, answer the following questions on a separate sheet of paper.

Reviewing Terms and Facts

1. **Vocabulary** What is meant by the term *infancy?*
2. **Vocabulary** Which of the following is the second fastest period of physical growth? *infancy, late childhood, adolescence, developmental tasks*
3. **Summarize** Describe Erikson's eight stages of life.
4. **Recall** List seven physical changes that occur during puberty.
5. **Recall** List three emotional changes that occur during adolescence.
6. **Review** Cite seven of the developmental tasks of adolescence.

Thinking Critically

7. **Observe** What stages of development do you observe in the infants and children in your family and neighborhood or in the infants and children that you baby-sit?
8. **Synthesize** Recall some of the activities you were involved in during your childhood. Explain how they reflected Erikson's stages of life.

Applying Health Concepts

9. **Growth and Development** Create a poster titled "The Tasks Ahead," using pictures and articles from magazines and newspapers that show teens successfully meeting the developmental tasks of adolescence. Include a sentence describing each picture.
10. **Health of Others** Compare adolescence in the 1970s or 1980s with adolescence today. Interview people who were teens during that time. Find out what were their concerns, their favorite songs, their role models. Tape the interviews and share them with the rest of the class.

TEEN HEALTH DIGEST

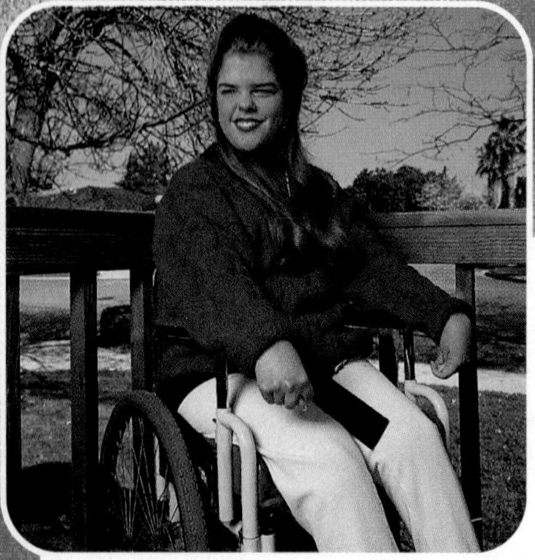

Teens Making a Difference

Meet Michele Troutman

She was born prematurely and weighed just 2½ pounds at birth. Doctors soon discovered that she had cerebral palsy, a medical condition affecting her speech and muscle control. None of this has stopped Michele Troutman!

"[Cerebral palsy] affected the way I can move," says Michele, "but not the way I *think*."

After eight years at a school for students with physical disabilities, Michele attended a mainstream school—Gunderson High in San Jose, California. Michele's education took off. She became a top student, worked on school plays, and joined the staff of the school newspaper. Today Michele is a successful student at San Jose State University.

"There will always be detours in everyone's path of life," says Michele. "You just have to find your way around them to fulfill your dreams."

Myths and Realities

Growing Pains Got You Down?

Do you ever get mysterious dull aches in your legs, back, or arms? How about sharp pains in your limbs for no apparent reason? You're not alone. Doctors say that "growing pains" such as these are common among people in their early teen years.

Although we call them "growing pains," no one knows for sure what causes these mystery aches. It may be that your skin, muscles, and tendons shift as your bones grow, thus causing the pains.

Try This:

If growing pains bother you, try these suggestions.

- *Massage the sore spot.*
- *Put warm compresses or ice packs on the area.*
- *Perform light stretching exercises using the sore muscles.*

People at Work

Nurse Midwife

Nurses are taking more and more responsibility in our health care system. One growing role within the nursing profession is that of the nurse midwife. These specialists are trained to deliver babies. They may deliver babies in the homes of the mothers, or in hospitals or birthing centers.

Nurse midwives must first become registered nurses, which usually requires a four-year college degree. In addition, nurse midwives take extra courses to learn more about pregnancy and birth. This training can take 8 to 24 months and may lead to a master's degree.

Nurse midwives must be experts in *prenatal care,* or the care that a woman needs before giving birth. Prenatal care means taking care of the health of the unborn child as well as that of the mother. For example, the nurse midwife will tell the mother about nutritious foods and safe exercises that will help her and her baby before the child is ever born.

Personal Trainer

Chomp that Charly Horse

Ouch! Just about everyone has felt a "Charly horse"—the shooting pain of a muscle cramp during exercise. What causes those nasty aches?

Cramps can occur when you don't warm up enough before you exercise. Lack of fluids, salt, or other minerals can also cause your muscles to cramp.

Try This: *To prevent muscle cramps, eat foods that are high in potassium, such as bananas, dried apricots, and dried peaches. Be sure to drink plenty of fluids, and don't skip your stretches—both before and after you exercise.*

CON$UMER FOCU$

Vitamin Claims

"They can help you grow!"

"Stressed out? These will help you cope."

"They stop the aging process!"

Some of the claims you hear for vitamins sound too good to be true. Unfortunately, that's exactly what many of the claims are—too good to be true!

Vitamin supplements *can* benefit your health—but only as one part of an overall healthy lifestyle. Before you take any vitamins, make sure that you are eating a well-balanced diet. If you do take vitamin supplements, be sure to follow the recommended doses and take them along with your regular meals. Large doses of vitamins and minerals can actually make you sick!

Lesson 4

Adulthood and Aging

This lesson will help you find answers to questions that teens often ask about aging. For example:

- **What are the stages of adulthood?**
- **What happens to the body and mind as a person gets older?**
- **What is it like to be an elderly person?**

Words to Know

chronological age
biological age
social age
Alzheimer's disease

From Adolescence On

Adolescence prepares you to become a young adult able to be independent and responsible for yourself. As you look to the future, you may think of adulthood as the time when growth finally ends. In fact, young adulthood is the beginning of another stage of life. There are several stages beyond that, too.

Americans today are living longer than ever before. As **Figure 7.8** shows, life expectancy in the United States has increased over the past few decades.

Did You Know?

The Aging of America ACTIVITY!

In the late 1700s, about half the population of the United States was 16 and under. By 1995 less than 16.1 percent of the population in the United States were under 16, and half were 34 or older. Discuss the implications for society of the aging of America.

Figure 7.8

Life Expectancy in the United States

For the years shown, what is the difference in life expectancy between males and females? What do you think might account for the difference?

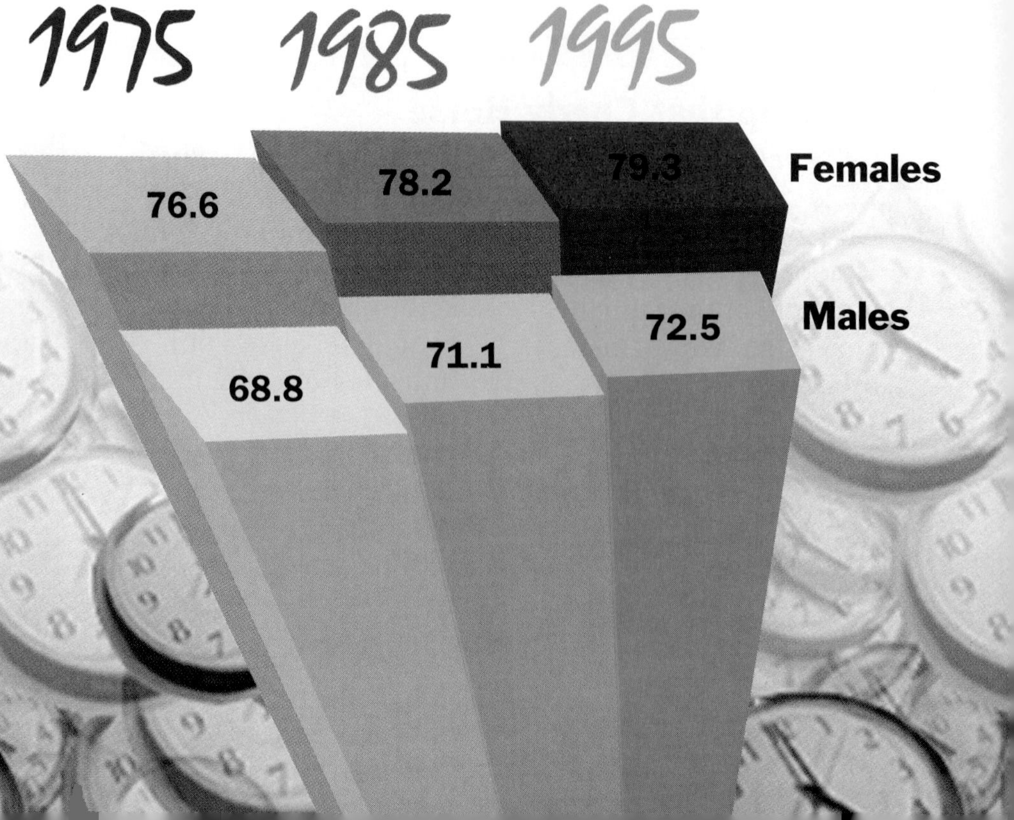

The Adult Years

Like the early years of life, the adult years—the period from the twenties on—are made up of stages.

Early Adulthood

In their twenties, most people begin a career. This is also the time when people start to feel the need to share their lives with another person. For many people, that need is met by marrying and beginning a family.

Middle Adulthood

Advancing in their jobs is a key goal for many people in their thirties, forties, and fifties. People in their middle adult years often gain satisfaction from helping young people. Doing so adds to their feelings of self-worth. Many people get this satisfaction from raising their children.

Late Adulthood

People in their mid-sixties and beyond often look forward to retirement. They also look back on their lives as a whole. If they can feel they have made a contribution, they enter these years feeling good about themselves.

Individual Choices

While most people in our society follow the stages described above, not everyone does. Some people choose to marry later on or not to have children. Others never marry at all. Some begin new careers well into their middle adult years. Others choose not to retire. Each person must do what is best for him or her. Doing so helps that person feel the sense of well-being that comes from living a full and healthy life.

Teen Issues

No Time Like the Present

The teen years are a time to enjoy. There is no reason, however, why you can't enjoy yourself and prepare for your future. Your decisions now will affect the person you become as an adult. You can invest in your future by thinking responsibly when you are faced with tough choices.

Adulthood is marked by different rewards and challenges. You can learn a great deal from the adults in your life.

Most adults marry during the early adulthood stage, but some choose to wait until a later stage.

in your journal

Imagine that your grandmother or another elderly relative is coming to live with you. What could you do to help the person be comfortable and lead a happy, active life? Write your ideas in your journal.

How Age Is Measured

You have probably heard the expression, "Act your age." You may also have heard certain people described as "looking younger than their years." Actually, age is measured in three different ways. These are described in **Figure 7.9**.

Physical Aging

When you think of aging, you may think of wrinkled skin and gray hair. Actually, physical aging begins when people are in their twenties. Starting in this period and going on through adulthood, the body cells divide and replace themselves more slowly.

Figure 7.9

Three Ways of Measuring Age

Chronological Age
Age measured in years is called **chronological** (krah·nuh·LAH·ji·kuhl) **age.** This is the number of your most recent birthday.

Biological Age
How well various body parts are working determines your **biological** (by·uh·LAH·ji·kuhl) **age.** This age is affected by heredity and by your health habits, exercise, and diet.

Social Age
A person's lifestyle is his or her **social age.** Social age has to do with the activities that society expects you to perform at a particular point in life. As a teen, you are expected to be in school, learning. Later you will be expected to be working, having a family, and helping others in your community.

Other signs of aging include a slow weakening of the five senses and a stiffening of the joints and weakening of the muscles. In addition, there is a loss of calcium in the bones, which causes them to become more brittle.

Although aging is a part of life, the signs differ from person to person. The signs also have much to do with a person's lifestyle. A person who makes healthy choices in diet, rest, and exercise throughout life may show fewer signs of aging.

Mental Aging

Mental aging also depends on the individual. Many people have active and alert minds well into old age. A healthy lifestyle not only reduces the signs of physical aging but can also reduce the signs of mental aging.

Some people, however, suffer from a *form of mental slowdown* called **Alzheimer's** (AHLTS·hy·merz) **disease.** This disorder may strike people in their forties and fifties, but most victims are over 65. People with Alzheimer's lose their memories over a period of time. They may also lose the power of speech and control of body movement. The cause of Alzheimer's disease is not yet known.

Teen Issues

Charity Begins at Home

Do you want to get involved in helping senior citizens but don't know where to turn in your community? Think of family first, and not just grandparents. Are there older people in your family such as aunts and uncles who could use some company?

HEALTH LAB

Responsibilities of Parenthood

Introduction: In early and middle adulthood, many people devote their time to raising children. Caring for children can satisfy some of the developmental needs of adults: to form intimate relationships and to make an impact on the world. For adolescents, however, parenthood can create problems. Adolescents are still developing their own identities. The responsibility of caring for a child can interfere with this developmental task.

Objective: In this lab you will learn about some of the responsibilities of parenthood by caring for an egg. Your egg will represent a baby for whom you are responsible. You must carry the egg around with you for one week and ensure that it is not damaged in any way.

Materials and Method: You will need an ordinary hen's egg and a container to carry it in. Whatever container you use for your egg must be padded so that the egg—your "baby"—will be protected from damage.

For one week, take the egg with you everywhere you go. You must never leave your egg unattended; if you need to let it out of your sight at any time, you must get some other responsible person to look after it. If you go anywhere in a car, the egg and its container must be safely buckled in. If you play a sport, you must find someone to take care of your egg while you are at practice.

Observation and Analysis: During the week that you spend caring for your egg, make daily journal entries, recording your thoughts and feelings about the experiment. At the end of the week, examine all your journal entries. Then write a summary of the experiment. Answer the following questions.

- Did you succeed in keeping your egg intact for the entire week?
- How did caring for the egg affect your life? Was it frustrating to have to limit your own activities because you had to provide a safe environment for the egg? Was looking after the egg a bigger responsibility than you had expected?
- Do you think it would be easier or more difficult to take care of a real baby? Explain your answer.

Meeting the Needs of the Elderly

Older people have the same emotional needs that younger people have. These include the need to love and be loved, the need to feel worthwhile, and the need to feel they are making a contribution. Several key factors can help make old age a rewarding and productive stage of life.

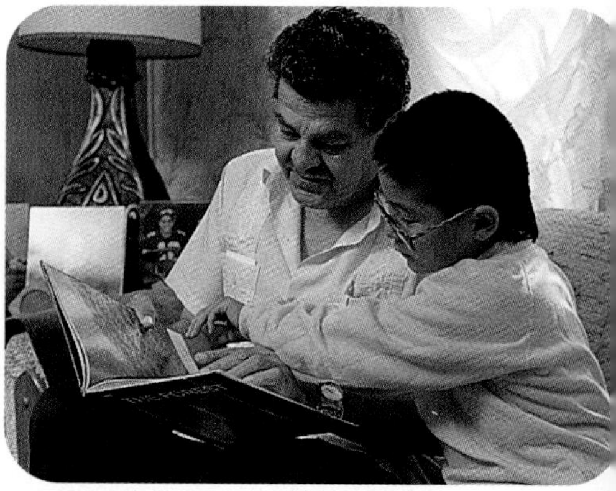

- **Having dealt with changes effectively throughout life.** People who learn early in life to accept change often have less difficulty accepting the changes that are part of growing old.
- **Maintaining contact with family and close friends.** Older people who have their loved ones close by tend to adjust much better than those who live alone.
- **Getting involved with younger people.** Some communities keep their older people involved through programs like Adopt a Grandparent. Such programs keep the elderly active and, at the same time, make them feel useful and needed.

Lesson 4 Review

Using complete sentences, answer the following questions on a separate sheet of paper.

Reviewing Terms and Facts

1. **Select** According to the information in Figure 7.8, which have the greater life expectancy—males or females?
2. **Summarize** Describe the three stages of adulthood.
3. **Give Examples** Cite at least three individual choices that people in a certain stage of development may make that may not be part of that stage of development.
4. **Vocabulary** What is the difference between *chronological age* and *biological age?*
5. **Vocabulary** What is meant by a person's *social age?*

Thinking Critically

6. **Illustrate** Create a poster showing the changes that people undergo in the three stages of adulthood.
7. **Analyze** Why might a person's age measure differently based on chronological, biological, and social age?
8. **Evaluate** What benefits might there be for teens who make an effort to know and help some older people in the community?

Applying Health Concepts

9. **Health of Others** Visit a senior citizen center, and talk with participants in several different programs. Make an audiotape of your interviews. Identify parts of the tape that portray positive aspects of your visit. Play your tape for the class.
10. **Growth and Development** In the library, find out about gerontologists, people who work in and study the area of aging. What kind of education is needed for this job? What personal characteristics would be helpful for a career in that field? Write a job description and share it with the class.

Lesson 5

Facing Death and Grief

This lesson will help you find answers to questions that teens often ask about death. For example:

- **What is death?**
- **What are the stages of dying and grieving?**
- **How do people cope with a loved one's death?**

Words to Know

clinical death
brain death
hospice
grief
coping strategies

The End of Life

Of all the creatures on earth, humans alone go through life knowing that someday they will die. This is not a fact that healthy people spend a great deal of time thinking about. Yet healthy people learn to accept the reality of death as a natural part of the cycle of life. Learning to face this reality becomes a little easier when we better understand the nature of death.

Two Meanings of Death

There is no single definition of death. In **clinical** (KLI·ni·kuhl) **death,** *a person's body systems shut down.* Sometimes people who are declared clinically dead can be brought back to life. For example, a person who dies on the operating table may be saved through the efforts of doctors. Another example is the use of cardiopulmonary resuscitation to revive a drowning victim.

Brain activity is usually considered the difference between life and death. **Brain death** occurs *when oxygen is cut off from all the brain cells.* When the brain ceases to function, a person is said to be medically dead.

Q&A

Declaring Death ACTIVITY!

Q: How do doctors know when brain death has occurred?

A: A person is considered brain dead when an electroencephalogram shows no brain activity for 30 minutes with no other explanation. Find out how an electroencephalograph records brain activity.

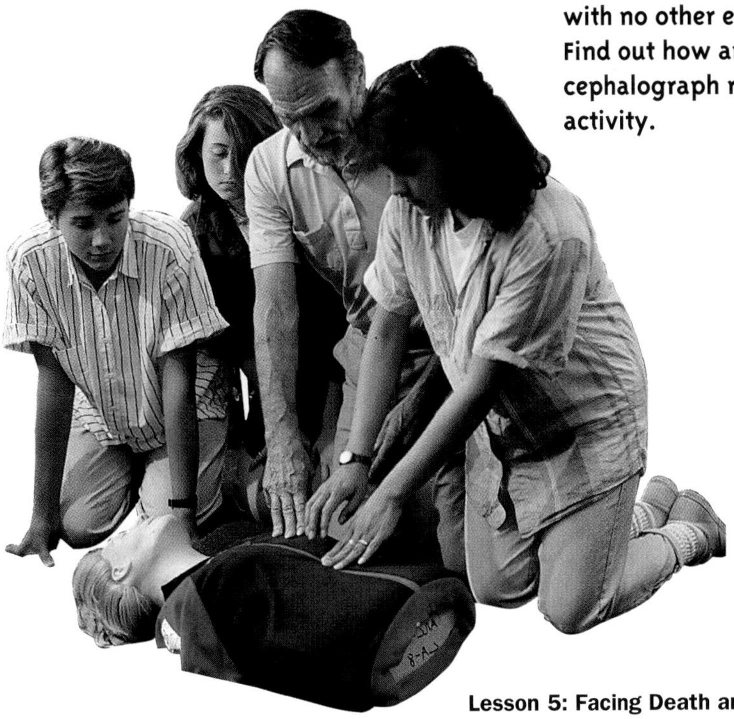

In some cases, CPR (cardiopulmonary resuscitation) can revive people who are clinically dead. CPR is an emergency procedure that is used to get the heart beating again and to restore breathing. Learning how to perform CPR can be a life-saving skill. It must be taught by a health care or rescue professional.

Did You Know?

Hope for Life

Dr. Elisabeth Kübler-Ross found one emotion to be typical of dying people throughout all the stages of death: hope. The dying patients she talked to all hoped a cure would be found so they would not have to die.

Accepting Death

For some people, the end of life comes peacefully while they are asleep. For others, death comes after a long struggle with a disease. For still others, it is sudden and unexpected.

Elisabeth Kübler-Ross, a noted doctor, has studied the experiences of dying people and their families. Dr. Ross identified five stages that people go through in facing death. These stages are listed below. Not all people experience the five stages. However, they are general guidelines we can use to understand how people experience dying.

- **Stage 1: Denial**
  Refusing to accept that one is dying. Telling oneself "it is all a mistake" and hoping to wake up from this "nightmare."
- **Stage 2: Anger**
  Angrily asking, "Why me?" Often directing the anger toward anyone close by—friends, family members, doctors, nurses.
- **Stage 3: Bargaining**
  Looking for ways to prolong life. Hoping for a medical miracle or praying to be spared in exchange for living a better life.
- **Stage 4: Depression**
  Feeling deep sadness for loss of life and other losses. Realizing that one will not live to keep promises or realize goals.
- **Stage 5: Acceptance**
  Accepting the reality of death and making peace with the world.

The family of a dying person often finds great strength and comfort in the dying person's acceptance of death. In this way, the dying sometimes teach the living about life.

As a teen, you are capable of understanding the concept of death. Children do not see death as final, but adolescents do. Because you now understand death, the death of someone close to you may hurt even more. However, knowing how to grieve can help you handle that hurt.

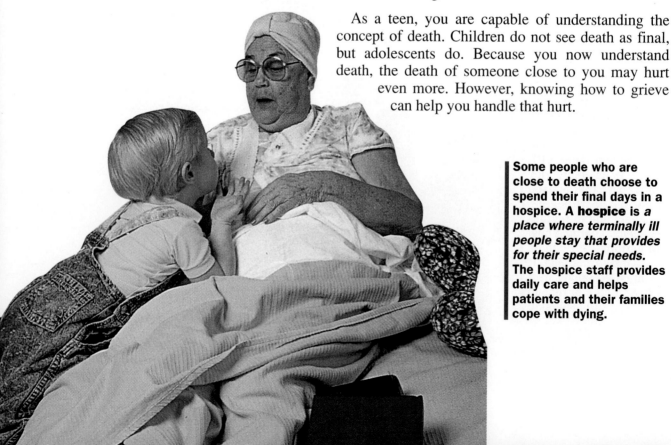

Some people who are close to death choose to spend their final days in a hospice. A hospice is *a place where terminally ill people stay that provides for their special needs.* The hospice staff provides daily care and helps patients and their families cope with dying.

The Grief Process

The death of someone we care deeply about brings out many different feelings. The *sum total of feelings caused by the death of a loved one* is known as **grief.** The length of time that people grieve after a loved one dies varies with the individual. It also varies with the circumstances of the death. When a loved one's death is sudden and unexpected—as in the case of a fatal accident—the grief process tends to take longer.

Some experts have observed that grief has several stages similar to Dr. Kübler-Ross's stages of dying. As with dying, grief reactions vary from person to person. However, five reactions are common.

- **Shock.** Shortly after the death of a loved one, people tend to feel separated from their emotions. They are often numb. If they have any feeling at all, it is an emptiness.
- **Anger.** Sometimes the survivors feel angry. The anger may even be directed toward the dead person for having died.
- **Yearning.** The survivors ache. The loss of the loved one has left a great emptiness in their lives. They wish the loved one could come back, if just for a moment.
- **Depression.** The survivors begin to accept the reality of their loss. The person has died and will not be coming back.
- **Moving on.** The survivors are able to go forward with their lives. They have not forgotten the one who died, but the deep pain over the loss has lessened.

Teen Issues

Shedding a Tear

Some people think that if they haven't cried over a death or loss, they haven't been hurt by it. That isn't true. Grieving can take many forms. When you or someone you know suffers a loss, it is important to let the feelings come. The hurt needs to be expressed in order for healing to begin.

Different cultures deal with death in different ways. Most cultures have rituals that celebrate the life of the person who has died or encourage survivors to recall personal memories. These ceremonies help people cope with the death of a loved one.

Dealing with the Death of a Loved One

Everyone, at one time or another, loses a loved one to death. The one who dies may be a friend, a relative, or a pet. Regardless of the type of relationship, the death of someone close can be a terribly painful experience.

Funeral services, memorial services, and other kinds of services help people deal with their loss. For many people, the service offers an opportunity to celebrate the life of the person who has died. At the same time, the service brings people together to share their grief. Most cultures have special rituals that they observe when somebody dies. These rituals vary from elaborate parades to simple grave-side ceremonies.

Mental health experts have come up with a number of **coping strategies.** These are *ways of dealing with the sense of loss people feel at the death of someone close.* They include the following:

- **Remember what was good about the person.** Focusing on happy times and on ways in which the person was special can help ease the pain.
- **Don't run away from your feelings.** The hurt from the loss is there and cannot be denied. It is best to let the feelings out.
- **Share your feelings with other people.** If nothing else, telling someone else about the hurt you are feeling will remind you that you are not alone.
- **Join a support group.** Most communities have support groups in which people who have suffered a loss can share their pain with others. These groups are usually sponsored by churches, synagogues, and other associations.

LIFE SKILLS

Helping Another Person Cope with Loss

Have you ever had a serious disappointment or lost something that meant a lot to you? Perhaps you lost the friendship of someone close after the two of you had a serious argument. You may have felt very sad when a good friend moved away. Possibly you were depressed because you did not make the basketball team. If you have had such an experience, do you remember how you felt?

The feelings people have after a loss or disappointment are often similar to grief. When someone you care about suffers a loss, there are ways you can help that person cope.

- **Let the person set the speed of recovery.** Everyone handles these feelings differently. Some people get over losses quickly. Others do not.
- **Let the person decide how you can be the most helpful.** Some people simply need to feel the presence of someone close. Don't insist on talking or giving the person advice when he or she just wants to sit quietly.

Review

Using complete sentences, answer the following questions on a separate sheet of paper.

Reviewing Terms and Facts

1. **Vocabulary** What is the difference between *clinical death* and *brain death?*
2. **Give an Example** Cite an emergency procedure that can revive a person who is clinically dead.
3. **Vocabulary** Write an original sentence of your own using the term *grief.*
4. **Recall** List three coping strategies for dealing with the loss of someone close.

Thinking Critically

5. **Compare** How are the stages of dying and the stages of grief similar and how are they different?
6. **Explain** How do funeral services and other rituals relating to death help those who are grieving?
7. **Synthesize** How might you help a younger brother, sister, or other child you know whose pet hamster had died?

Applying Health Concepts

8. **Health of Others** Research hospice care. Find out when it is used and how it is different from hospital care. Then visit a hospice and talk with staff and patients. How does the staff feel about its work? How do the patients feel about their treatment? If a visit is not possible, find an article about hospice care that includes first-person accounts by staff and patients. Write a report of your findings.
9. **Growth and Development** Look in your library for books or poetry on death and grief. Choose one that seems interesting to you. Read it and write down your thoughts about what you have read. Examples that you might look for include the poem "Death Be Not Proud" by John Donne, and the books *A Taste of Blackberries* by Doris Buchanan Smith and *A Bridge to Terabithia* by Katherine Paterson.

- **Respect the person's right to feel sad.** Don't tell the person she or he is wrong or silly to feel bad or that the loss is not important. To her or him, the loss may be very important. The best help is to deal with the grief, not to pretend it will go away.

Follow-up Activity

Think about an experience that a friend or an acquaintance might have had with a loss. How did you help that person cope with it? Do you think you should have handled the situation differently? If so, use the suggestions above to describe what you could have done to help that person cope.

Chapter 7 Review

Chapter Summary

- **Lesson 1** The body develops from a single cell, which divides to form the body's tissues, organs, and systems. The developing fetus gets its food and oxygen through the umbilical cord.
- **Lesson 2** The developing baby is affected by both heredity and environment. Good prenatal care, including proper diet and regular checkups by a health professional, helps to keep the mother and baby healthy.
- **Lesson 3** The growth years include the stages of infancy, early childhood, middle childhood, late childhood, and adolescence. During adolescence, a person's physical, mental, emotional, and social abilities develop rapidly.
- **Lesson 4** During early, middle, and late adulthood, people work on developing relationships with others. Aging is a process that begins in early adulthood and progresses at different rates for different people.
- **Lesson 5** People who are dying usually go through five stages: denial, anger, bargaining, depression, and acceptance. People who are grieving over a death go through similar stages.

Reviewing Key Terms and Concepts

Using complete sentences, answer the following questions on a separate sheet of paper.

Lesson 1

1. Which word refers to the tube that connects a developing baby to its mother: *uterus, umbilical cord,* or *cervix?*
2. Define *cell* and *organ.*

Lesson 2

3. What is the difference between *genetic disorders* and *birth defects?*
4. Name two elements of good prenatal care.

Lesson 3

5. During which stage of development does the fastest growth occur?
6. How do hormones affect physical and emotional development during puberty?

Lesson 4

7. What kinds of changes are caused by Alzheimer's disease?
8. What three basic emotional needs do the elderly share with people in other stages of life?

Lesson 5

9. Define the term *hospice.*
10. List the five stages of grieving.

Thinking Critically

Using complete sentences, answer the following questions on a separate sheet of paper.

11. **Hypothesize** Why are teen mothers less likely to have healthy babies?
12. **Give Examples** Name some ways in which teens become more independent of parents and other adults.
13. **Analyze** Which is most under a person's control: chronological age, biological age, or social age?
14. **Apply** How might you help a friend cope with the death of a friend or relative?

Chapter 7 Review

Your Action Plan

You can make an action plan to help you work toward becoming the kind of adult you want to be. Start by looking back through your private journal entries for this chapter. Review the tasks listed in Figure 7.7.

Step 1: Make a list of the tasks you think you need to work on. Mastery of each task is a long-term goal. You can focus on one task at a time or on a few at a time. For example, you might decide to focus on developing your values.

Step 2: Set short-term goals to help you with each developmental task. For example, if your values include preserving the environment, you might take part in local cleanup campaigns and make an extra effort to reduce waste by reusing bags and recycling bottles and cans.

Step 3: Establish a schedule for reaching your short-term goals. Check your schedule regularly to keep yourself on track.

When you feel that you have reached your goal, reward yourself.

In Your Home and Community

1. **Health of Others** With your classmates, put together a handbook about how to help people cope with a loss. Include the three coping strategies, and provide examples to show how each strategy can be used. You might make your handbook available in the library or counselor's office for other students to see.
2. **Community Resources** Find out what parks or playgrounds in your community are suitable for use by parents with young children. Make a map that highlights these areas, and briefly describe what is available at each place to stimulate a child's physical and social growth. Display the map at a local child care center or clinic.

Building Your Portfolio

1. **An Album of Stages** Create a picture album of Erikson's eight stages of life. Assemble a collection of illustrations (from magazines or family photos) for each stage. Write captions explaining each stage's developmental task. Add your album to your portfolio.
2. **Personal Assessment** Look through all the activities and projects you did for this chapter. Choose one or two that you would like to include in your portfolio.

Chapter 8

Reaching Your Fitness Goals

Student Expectations

After reading this chapter, you should be able to:

1. Explain what physical fitness is.
2. Determine how physically fit you are.
3. Design a fitness program to meet your fitness goals.
4. Describe different types of sports that can help you meet your fitness goals.

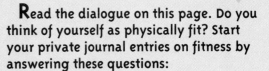

Teen Chat Group

Gina: What's the matter, Jason? Are you out of breath already? We just got started!

Crystal: What happened to "Step aerobics is a piece of cake—anybody can do it," Jason?

Jason: Well, I guess it's not as easy as I thought.

Gina: That's okay. Crystal and I didn't last very long on our first day, either.

Jason: I thought I was in shape, though. It's not like I'm overweight or anything.

Crystal: Don't be too hard on yourself. Gina and I have been taking this class for a whole year. It takes daily exercise to become physically fit.

Gina: Just keep on coming to our class, Jason. It's never too late to get started!

in your journal

Read the dialogue on this page. Do you think of yourself as physically fit? Start your private journal entries on fitness by answering these questions:

- Jason thought that fitness meant not being overweight. What does fitness mean to you?
- In general, are you as fit as you want to be?
- What areas of your personal fitness would you like to improve?

When you reach the end of the chapter, you will use your journal entries to make an action plan.

Lesson 1

What Is Physical Fitness?

This lesson will help you find answers to questions that teens often ask about fitness. For example:

- **What does *being fit* really mean?**
- **What is my physical fitness potential?**
- **Is exercising really all that is needed to be fit?**

Words to Know

totally fit
physically fit
aerobic exercise
anaerobic exercise

Being Fit

Many people think of fitness as they do health, in only physical terms. They think fitness means being in good shape or being able to play a sport well. In part, fitness does mean those things, but total fitness means a lot more. In addition to its physical part, total fitness has a mental part and a social part. When you are **totally fit,** you are *able to handle physical, mental, emotional, and social day-to-day challenges without feeling exhausted.*

Having good physical fitness is a key part of total fitness. One meaning of the word *physical* is "of the body," and the basis of physical fitness is a healthy body. When you are **physically fit** your body is *ready to handle whatever comes your way from day to day.*

Figure 8.1
Fitness Benefits
Being totally fit gives you physical, mental, emotional, and social benefits.

For example, a physically fit person can get through the school day, get at-home chores done, do a good job on homework, and still have enough energy to join in a neighborhood softball game or snowball fight. **Figure 8.1** summarizes some of the benefits of physical fitness. Which are most important to you?

Benefits of Fitness

Being fit keeps your body working at its best to help you feel good and do what you want to do. Fitness benefits the "physical you." Your heart delivers enough blood with each beat to supply your body cells with all the oxygen they need to work well. You don't run out of breath during active work or play. Your blood pressure stays low. Your appetite levels off—you are more likely to take in only the calories you use for energy.

Fitness benefits the "mental and emotional you." Because being physically fit makes you look better and feel better, your self-esteem rises. You find that you like the physically fit *you.* Staying fit also reduces depression and helps you manage the stress in your life. Exercise improves your mood and clears your mind. You may also find that exercise can be a healthy outlet for tension, anger, or frustration.

Fitness benefits the "social you." Being physically fit helps you be at ease with yourself and with others. You have the energy to join in activities with your friends and get the most out of active sports and games. You can meet new people when you participate in organized exercise activities. Organized sports provide a great opportunity for you to work with others toward a common goal.

interNET CONNECTION

Don't just sit there; put your computer in motion to help you find ways to stay fit for life!

http://www.glencoe.com/sec/health

in your journal

The following questions will help you decide whether you need to improve your physical fitness. Write your answers in your journal.

- Do you tire easily from physical or mental activities?
- Do you often "run out of steam" before your friends do?
- Do you have poor posture?

Personal Inventory

ASSESSING YOUR FITNESS BEHAVIOR

Most people have a fitness level that is below their potential level. However, there are actions people can take to increase their fitness. How many of the following physical fitness-building actions do you take?

Regular exercise helps develop physical fitness traits.

1. I walk or bike to school.
2. When my friends are trying to decide what to do, I suggest an active game or activity, such as swimming, basketball, hiking, or bike riding.
3. I take the stairs rather than the elevator or escalator when I have a choice.
4. When traveling by bus a distance too far to walk, I get off early and walk part of the way. If I'm being driven, I suggest that we park and walk part of the way.
5. I participate in an active game, sport, or work activity every day, either with others or alone.

Good nutrition helps develop physical fitness traits.

6. Generally, I eat a balanced diet.
7. When I snack, I choose healthful foods such as fruit, rather than sweets or snacks high in fat or salt.
8. I choose portion sizes that are reasonable: not too large, not too small.
9. I never starve myself to lose weight.

Enough rest and relaxation helps develop physical fitness traits.

10. I get eight to nine hours of sleep each night.
11. I take time to sit and rest for a while after a vigorous game or activity.
12. I allow time daily to relax and do nothing.

Give yourself 1 point for each yes answer. A score of 10-12 is very good. A score of 6-9 is good. If you score below 6, your fitness behavior needs work.

Everyone can develop physical fitness—the strength and energy to continue an activity over time without tiring. Of course all people cannot develop those traits to the same level. Each person's body has a fitness potential level, which is the highest possible level of fitness that person's body can develop. Each person has his or her own fitness potential level determined by the body's limitations. Even when those limitations are great, there is room for development. For example, a person who must use a wheelchair can still develop his or her arm strength.

Each person can strive to reach his or her fitness potential level.

Fitness and You

How many statements in the Personal Inventory apply to you? If most of them do, you are probably already committed to being physically fit. If some of the statements do not apply to you, then you may want to make some changes in your lifestyle. Look at the statements you answered with a *no*. Think about what you can do to fit those activities into your day. For example, if you have trouble running for the bus, put some more vigorous activity into your life. If you are too tired to pay attention in school, think about getting more rest and relaxation.

One factor to consider when deciding to raise your physical fitness level is your physical fitness potential. In Lesson 2, you will learn how to determine your fitness potential. Every person's body has limits. Keep your goals challenging, but realistic. Not everyone can break athletic records, but everyone can improve.

Deciding to raise your physical fitness level is only the first step. Actually getting started in a fitness program is the next step. To motivate yourself, review the benefits of physical fitness on pages 230–31. Do these benefits appeal to you? Which of the benefits would you like to achieve first?

Another way to get started with fitness is to get some help. There are a lot of people who can help you improve your physical fitness. Parents, friends, brothers and sisters, teachers, and coaches are a few. The most important person, however, is you. You must take responsibility for your physical fitness. You can ask other people for advice or encouragement. You can ask someone else to join you in an activity. In the end, however, the level of physical fitness that you reach is up to you.

Did You Know?

Awards of Fitness ACTIVITY!

The Presidential Physical Fitness Award Program was started in 1966. The program, which is designed for young people from the ages of 6 to 17, including students with special needs, increases awareness of the importance of physical fitness. Ask your physical education teacher how you can participate and be a "winner."

What can you do to improve your physical fitness level?

Exercise: A Key to Fitness

Cars, home appliances, and other technologies have removed the need for physical activity to carry out many daily activities. Most people do not get very much exercise unless they make a special effort to do so. Yet, as you have learned, exercise is an important key to fitness. There are two categories of exercises: aerobic and anaerobic. Later in this chapter, you will learn more about how each type of exercise helps you.

Ⓐ **Aerobic** (e·ROH·bik) **exercise** is *nonstop, repetitive, vigorous exercise that increases breathing and heartbeat rates.* Swimming, running, and cross-country skiing are examples.

Ⓑ **Anaerobic** (an·e·ROH·bik) **exercise** involves *great bursts of energy in which the muscles work hard to produce energy.* Examples are gymnastics, push-ups, and sprinting.

Lesson 1

Review

Using complete sentences, answer the following questions on a separate sheet of paper.

Reviewing Terms and Facts

1. **Vocabulary** Define the term *totally fit* using your own words.
2. **Give Examples** List at least five ways to increase your fitness level.
3. **Vocabulary** What kind of exercise is vigorous and sustained, and increases breathing and heartbeat rates?
4. **Recall** Give examples of the two categories of exercise.

Thinking Critically

5. **Analyze** Would you describe yourself as physically fit? Every day for one week write down your activities and how you felt at the end of the day. Tell why you would describe yourself as physically fit or not.
6. **Analyze** How might staying fit help you manage stress? Has physical exercise ever provided you with an outlet for tension or anger?
7. **Explain** Describe how one person's physical fitness level may be different from that of another person.

Applying Health Concepts

8. **Personal Health** Make a list of your physical activities during the last week. Which were aerobic? With a partner, think of ways that both of you can increase your aerobic activity.
9. **Health of Others** Survey adult friends, classmates, and family members who exercise regularly. Ask each why he or she exercises. Write down their answers and compare them to the list of benefits of physical fitness listed on pages 230–31. Share your findings with your classmates.

Elements of Fitness

Lesson 2

This lesson will help you find answers to questions that teens often ask about physical fitness. For example:

- **What are the parts of physical fitness?**
- **How can I test my own physical fitness?**
- **How can I set reasonable physical fitness goals for myself?**

Words to Know

muscle strength
muscle endurance
flexibility
heart and lung endurance
body composition

Determining Physical Fitness

Use your imagination to picture a physically fit male and a physically fit female. Did you picture a young, slim girl and a tall, muscular young man? Perhaps you pictured both as being very skilled at active games and spending a lot of their time playing competitive sports. Many advertisements in magazines and newspapers and on television associate those images with physical fitness. People who match those descriptions may be physically fit, but the truth is that a lot of people who are quite different from those descriptions are also physically fit.

Everyone can develop a level of physical fitness. Some people are short; others are tall. Some people are naturally thin; others have a broader body structure. In addition, some people are naturally good at sports. They seem to be good at every sport they try. Many others have less natural ability, and still others seem to be "all thumbs" at most sports. People of all body types, ages, ability levels, and levels of general health can reach their own potential levels of physical fitness.

The first step in reaching your physical fitness potential is to determine just how physically fit you are now. Physical fitness can be divided into several parts. This lesson explains the major parts of fitness and shows you ways to test yourself for each part. On which parts do you think you will test best?

In Your Journal

Predict your scores on the tests in this lesson. Write your predictions in your journal. Then record your actual scores. How well did you predict?

Whatever your shape or size, you can be as fit as your ability level allows.

Muscle Strength and Endurance

The ability of your muscles to exert a force is called strength. Lifting a weight and pushing a load are acts of strength. *The most weight you can lift or the most force you can exert at one time* are measures of your **muscle strength.**

The ability of your muscles to exert a force over time without becoming overly tired is called **muscle endurance** (en·DER·uhns). Raking a yard takes muscle endurance. **Figures 8.2, 8.3,** and **8.4** show some tests for muscle strength and endurance.

Figure 8.2

Determining Leg Muscle Strength

You can test your leg muscle strength by measuring your ability to do a standing broad jump.

1. Put a piece of tape on the floor or ground and stand behind it with your toes touching the tape.
2. Bend your knees and jump forward as far as you can, landing with your weight on both feet. Mark where you land.
3. Measure from the tape to your landing point to find the distance of your jump. Use the table to rate your muscle strength by comparing the distance you jumped to your height.

Scoring

Distance Jumped	Rating
About 6 inches more than your height	Excellent
Between 2 and 4 inches more than your height	Good
Equal to your height	Fair
Less than your height	Poor

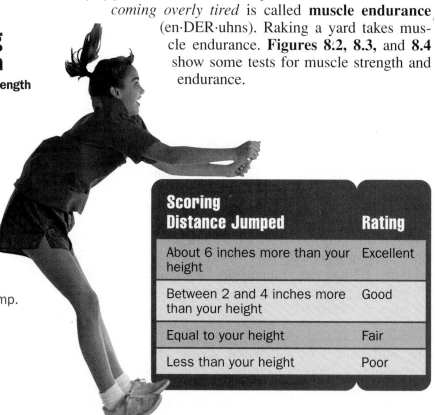

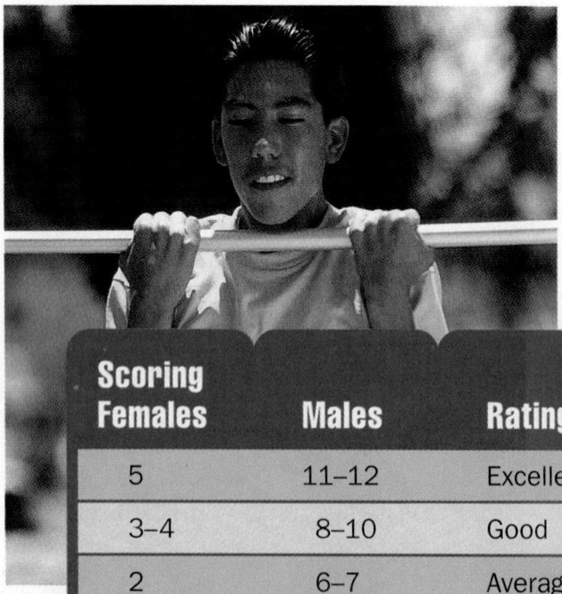

Scoring

Females	Males	Rating
5	11–12	Excellent
3–4	8–10	Good
2	6–7	Average
1	3–5	Fair
0	1–2	Poor

Figure 8.3

Determining Upper Body Strength and Endurance

You can test your upper body strength and muscular endurance by counting the pull-ups you can do. Find a horizontal bar from which you can hang by your hands without touching the ground or floor.

1. Grasp the bar with your palms facing away. Hang without bending your elbows. Pull yourself up until your chin clears the bar.
2. Lower your body to the starting position to finish one pull-up.
3. Your score is the number of pull-ups you can do in one session. Resting between pull-ups and kicking are not allowed.

Figure 8.4

Determining Abdominal Strength and Endurance

You can test the endurance of the muscles of your abdomen by counting the number of bent-knee sit-ups you can complete in one minute. You will need a partner and a watch with a second hand. During the test, remember to breathe freely. Do not hold your breath. Your partner should keep the time and count your sit-ups.

Scoring Females	Males	Rating
30+	40+	Excellent
24–29	33–39	Good
18–23	29–32	Average
11–17	21–28	Fair
10 or less	20 or less	Poor

1. Lie on your back with your knees slightly bent. Place your hands behind your head. Have your partner hold your ankles for support. Raise your upper body from the floor until you touch one elbow to the opposite knee.

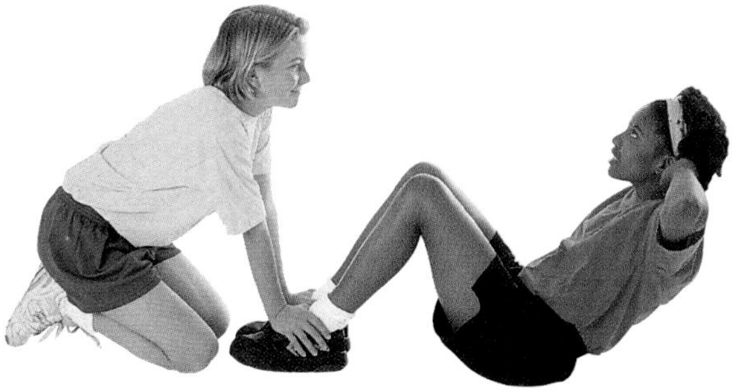

2. Return to the start position to do one complete sit-up. Your score is the number of complete sit-ups done in one minute.

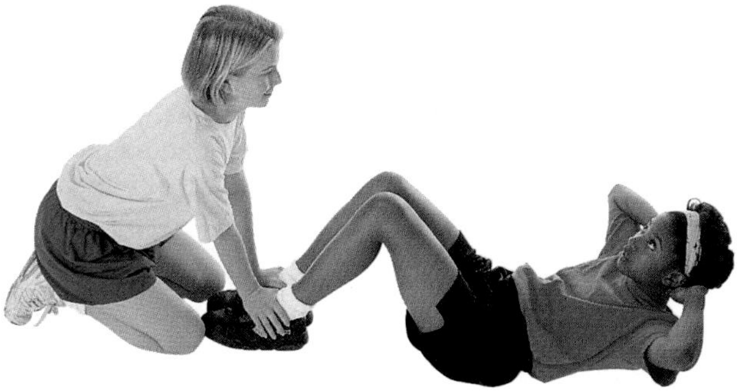

Flexibility

When you move, you bend your body joints and stretch your muscles. *Your ability to move within the range of motion for each joint* is your **flexibility.** People with good flexibility can bend, stretch, and turn their bodies easily. People with poor flexibility feel stiff when they move. You may be more flexible in one part of your body than in another. You can test the flexibility of the major muscles in your lower back and the back of your legs by doing the sit-and-reach test (see **Figure 8.5**).

Figure 8.5

Determining Flexibility

Begin this test by doing some light stretching to protect your muscles from injury. During the test, move smoothly. Avoid quick, jerking motions. Your reach should be gradual and slow.

Sit on the floor with your legs straight in front of you. Your heels should touch a piece of tape on the floor and be about 5 inches apart. Place a yardstick on the floor between your legs so that the 36-inch end points away from your body, and the 15-inch mark is even with your heels. With fingers straight, slowly reach with both hands as far forward as possible and hold your position. Look at the yardstick to see how many inches you reached, which marks your score. Try the test three times. Use your longest reach to find your score.

Scoring Females	Males	Rating
23+	22+	Excellent
19–23	16–22	Good
16–19	12–15	Average
14–16	9–11	Fair
less than 14	less than 9	Poor

Math Connection

Graphic Story ACTIVITY!

Make a line graph of your fitness test scores. For the vertical scale, use poor, fair, average, good, excellent. For the horizontal scale, use the names of the tests. Analyze your scores. Do you have mostly the same score in every test?

Heart and Lung Endurance

Your power to move your whole body over time is called your heart and lung endurance. You can move your body while staying pretty much in the same place, such as when you jump rope. You can move your body while moving from place to place, such as when you walk or run. Either way, *how effectively your heart and lungs work during exercise and how quickly they return to normal after exercise* is a measure of your **heart and lung endurance.** You can get a general idea of your heart and lung endurance by trying the step test shown in **Figure 8.6.**

Caution: Forcing yourself to go on if you become exhausted can be dangerous. People with diseases of the heart or lungs should check with their doctors before trying this test.

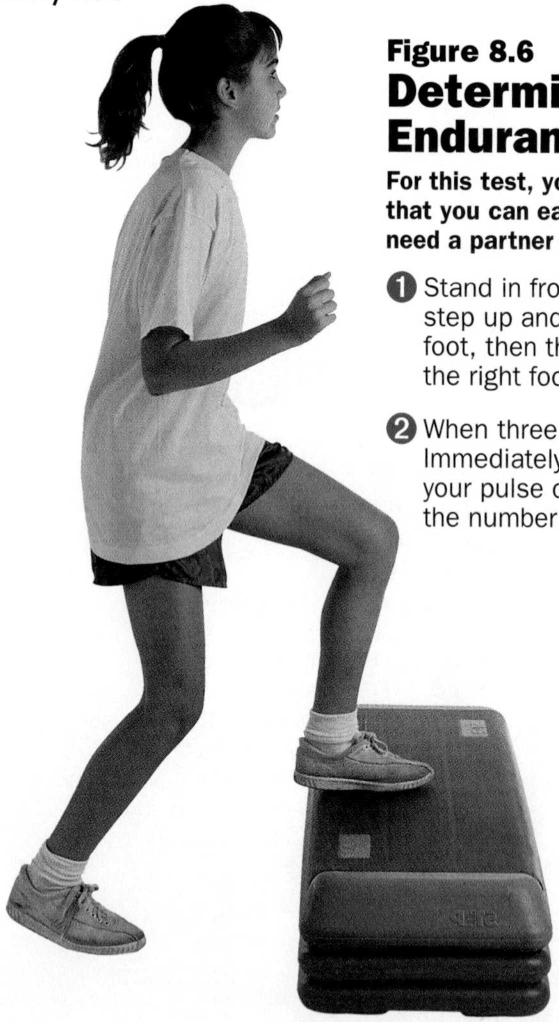

Figure 8.6

Determining Heart and Lung Endurance

For this test, you need a step or a sturdy bench about 8 inches high that you can easily step onto without it wobbling or breaking. You also need a partner and a watch with a second hand to time you.

1. Stand in front of the step or bench. When your partner says "go," step up and down on the step repeatedly. Step up with the right foot, then the left, extending each leg fully. Then step down with the right foot and then the left. Do about 24 steps per minute.
2. When three minutes are up, your partner should say "stop." Immediately stop and sit down. Do not talk. Have your partner take your pulse on your wrist or on the side of your neck. Your score is the number of heartbeats he or she counts in one minute.

Scoring Heartbeats	Rating
70–80	Excellent
81–105	Good
106–119	Average
120–130	Fair
131+	Poor

Body Composition

Another part of physical fitness is your **body composition,** or *the proportion of body fat in comparison with lean body tissue, such as muscle and bone.* People with too high a percentage of body fat are said to be obese. One generally accepted way to measure body composition, and to estimate obesity, is to find Body Mass Index (BMI). BMI is found by dividing a person's weight by the square of his or her height (see **Figure 8.7**).

The U.S. government has defined overweight statistics for various ages, including adolescent boys and girls whose BMI is equal to or greater than certain numbers. The BMI numbers for being overweight are as follows. Ages 12 through 14: males 23.0; females 23.4. Ages 15 through 17: males 24.3; females 24.8. Ages 18 through 19: males 25.8; females 25.7.

If your BMI falls at or above the limit for your gender and age, you may need to change your diet or exercise habits. Before you take action, talk it over with a parent, fitness instructor, or family physician. There may be other factors to consider.

Did You Know?

Thin Is Not Necessarily Fit

Many people consider being thin a sign of fitness. How thin you are, however, is not a good measure of fitness. If you are thin but do not exercise, you could have poor heart and lung endurance and poor muscle strength and endurance. When you want to judge your fitness, your heart and lung endurance is a much better measure than your appearance.

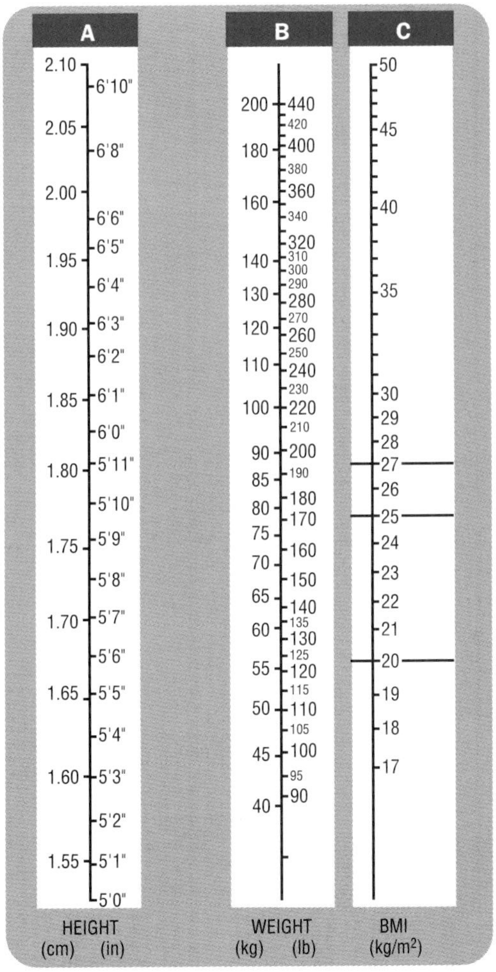

Figure 8.7

Body Mass Index

You can easily find your BMI by using this chart. Mark an x at your height on scale A. Mark an x at your weight on scale B. Use a ruler to draw a straight line through both x's. Make sure the line extends through scale C. The point where the line meets scale C is your BMI.

Your Fitness Level

After completing the tests on the major parts of physical fitness described in this lesson, you should have a good idea of your present levels of muscle strength and endurance, flexibility, heart and lung endurance, and body composition. From the Personal Inventory in Lesson 1, you should have identified your present physical fitness traits. In other words, you know if you have a healthy diet, get enough relaxation and sleep, and exercise every day. Together, this information gives you a data image of your present level of physical fitness. Now it is time for you to decide if you want to improve that image. If you do, you need to set goals and decide how to achieve these goals.

Cultural Connections

Running Potential to Spare

Author John Douillard wrote about the running potential of the Tarahumara Indians of Mexico, who live about 90 miles south of Phoenix, Arizona. Some of these remarkable people "can run 50 to 100 miles in a day with ease, and up to 150 miles seemingly without effort."

Consider Your Limits

Before you set goals for improving your physical fitness, you must consider your limits. Recall from Lesson 1 that everyone has a physical fitness potential—the highest level of fitness he or she can achieve. Your fitness potential is unique. It is probably higher than that of some people you know and lower than that of some others.

Many factors influence fitness potential. Inherited traits are one factor. Long-lasting illnesses and conditions are other major factors. For example, people with asthma, a lung disorder, often become short of breath when they exercise hard. People with weak body joints or other bone problems are also limited in their ability to take part in certain activities. Before setting goals to improve your physical fitness, it is a good idea to check with your doctor. If you have a long-lasting illness or condition, you should definitely ask your doctor to help you set realistic goals.

Setting Your Goals

When setting your physical fitness goals, keep in mind what you want to improve. For example, if you want to increase your heart and lung endurance, choose exercises designed to give your heart and lungs a workout. You can find out which exercises are best for various parts of physical fitness in Lesson 3. The following guidelines can help you set your physical fitness goals.

- Set goals based on your fitness test results, your Personal Inventory results, and your personal preferences. Set goals that you really want to achieve.
- Set goals based on how much time you really can exercise.
- Set goals that you can reach. Remember your limits. Set short-term goals based on where you are now. If you tested "fair," a reasonable goal is to reach a "good" rating.

HEALTH LAB

Finding Your Target Pulse Rate

Introduction: To improve your physical fitness, you must make your heart and lungs work at higher-than-normal rates for at least twenty minutes, three or four times per week. At these higher rates, your heart beats faster, your blood flows faster, and your breathing is deeper. Done regularly, working at this higher-than-normal level makes your body stronger and more fit.

Every person has a maximum heartbeat rate, which gradually decreases with age. Your heart cannot beat faster than its maximum rate. Exercise that causes your heartbeat to go above 85 percent of its maximum rate may be dangerous. On the other hand, exercise that does not raise your heartbeat rate to at least 60 percent of your maximum rate won't do your heart and lungs much good.

The heartbeat rate that will safely give you the most benefit out of exercise is between 70 and 80 percent of your maximum heartbeat rate. This rate is called your target *pulse* rate, also referred to as target *heart* rate.

Objective: Follow the directions on the next page to find your target pulse rate.

Review

Lesson 2

Using complete sentences, answer the following questions on a separate sheet of paper.

Reviewing Terms and Facts

1. **Vocabulary** What is the difference between *muscle strength* and *muscle endurance?*
2. **Vocabulary** Use the term *heart and lung endurance* in an original sentence.
3. **Recall** List three ways to test muscle strength and endurance.
4. **Recall** What information do you need to evaluate your level of fitness?

Thinking Critically

5. **Evaluate** After testing *poor* on muscle strength and endurance, Kim set a goal to "test *excellent* in three weeks." Kim can exercise three days a week and is in good health. Is this a realistic goal? Why or why not?
6. **Analyze** Suppose you knew that a friend of yours often exercised hard enough to raise his heart rate above the upper number of the target pulse rate range for his age. What advice would you give him? Why?

Applying Health Concepts

7. **Health of Others** Make a list of the parts of physical fitness. Review the tests for each part. As you go through your day at school and around your community, look for people engaged in work and other activities that require a good level of at least one of the parts. For example, a carpenter doing a lot of nailing would require good muscle strength and endurance. Make a poster explaining your findings and share it with your classmates.
8. **Health of Others** With one or two classmates, make up a song that tells the benefits of each part of physical fitness. Perform your song for your classmates.

Materials and Method: To find your target pulse rate, first determine your maximum heartbeat rate. Your maximum heartbeat rate is the number *220* minus your age. Your target pulse rate is a range. Multiply your maximum pulse rate by 70 percent and by 80 percent to find the two ends of your range. Check your figures with the chart.

Observation and Analysis: Over the next week or two, take your pulse while exercising. Does your heartbeat rate fall within the range of your target pulse rate? Record your observations and analysis in your journal.

Age	Maximum Pulse Rate	Target Pulse Rate
11	209	146–167
12	208	146–166
13	207	145–166
14	206	144–165
15	205	143–164
16	204	142–163

TEEN HEALTH DIGEST

Myths and Realities

No Pain + No Gain = No Brain

"No pain, no gain," you often hear. Many people who are involved in athletics seem to believe that the only good exercise is painful exercise.

The fact is, "no pain, no gain" works better as a rhyme than as a piece of advice. Pain is a signal from your body that something is wrong.

Sure, exercise can leave you with mild soreness or a few minor aches and pains. However, sharp, shooting, or intense pain when you exercise is a sign that you are over-doing it—or doing it wrong!

If you feel pain when you exercise, *slow down.* If the pain continues, *stop the exercise.* If you keep exercising when you feel pain, you could sustain a serious injury.

Try This: *Survey friends and family about their exercise routines. Find out if any of these people have experienced pain. Was the pain minor, or did it signal a problem? What did they do about the pain?*

Personal Trainer

Power Walking

Here's a great way to get exercise—grab a friend and take a hike!

"Power walking" is more than just a leisurely stroll. When you walk for exercise, take long smooth strides, swing your arms freely from your shoulders, and head for the hills. (Going up and down hills greatly increases the aerobic benefits of a walk.)

A brisk power walk offers many of the benefits of jogging or aerobic dance, without the muscle strain or pounding on your joints.

Try This: *Map out a variety of routes for your power walks. Be sure to include plenty of hills.*

HEALTH UPDATE

Shin Splints

Many athletes have felt it—a painful burning sensation along the front of the lower leg. Doctors call it "medial tibial stress syndrome." The rest of us know it by a simpler name: shin splints.

What causes shin splints? There are three main causes:

- **Too much, too soon.** If an athlete increases the level of activity too quickly, he or she may pay the price with shin splints.
- **Changing routines.** If you make any change to your routine—such as running on a cement sidewalk instead of your usual dirt track—shin splints can result. Even changing to different shoes can cause the painful splints.
- **Poor form.** Exercising improperly can put strain on the tendons in your shins. For example, do you stay on the balls of your feet throughout an aerobic dance class? If so, you're risking shin splints!

People at Work

Personal Trainer

Name: Yvonne Blue

Education: Four-year degree in exercise physiology and education

Job: Personal fitness trainer at a large health club

Yvonne works one-on-one with club members to help them improve their fitness. The process starts when Yvonne interviews her clients and finds out their goals.

"Once I know where the client is and where he or she wants to be, it isn't hard to develop a fitness program to achieve those goals."

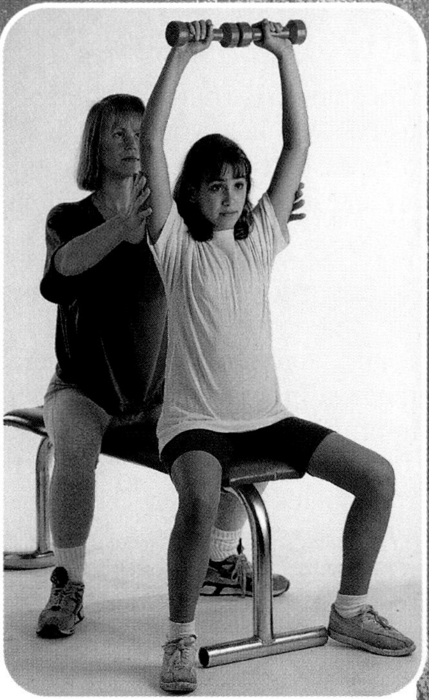

One important part of Yvonne's job is to keep her clients motivated.

"I have to know when to push, when to praise, and when to just be quiet."

Sports and Recreation

Buff Brandi

You've seen her on ESPN and Prime Sports. No doubt about it, teen ski queen Brandi Hunt is one of the top female athletes anywhere.

Brandi has been ranked as the world's number one water skier under the age of 18. She helped bring home the Junior World Championship and was named 1996 Athlete of the Year by *'TEEN* magazine.

What is Brandi's advice to other athletes? Simple: Pick your sport and go for it. "Girls can be just as athletic as guys," Brandi says. "We don't have to sit on the sidelines."

Lesson 3

Planning a Fitness Program

This lesson will help you find answers to questions that teens often ask about designing their own fitness programs. For example:

- **What are the best exercises to help me meet my fitness goals?**
- **How can I find time to exercise?**
- **How often and how hard should I exercise?**
- **How can I keep from being hurt during exercise?**
- **What clothes and shoes should I wear?**

Words to Know

warm-up
exercise frequency
exercise intensity
exercise time
cool-down

Choosing the Right Exercise

Once you have set your fitness goals, you can choose the exercises that will help you reach them. In Lesson 1, you learned about two types of exercise: aerobic (vigorous exercise that gives your heart and lungs a workout) and anaerobic (intense, short bursts of activity).

To improve your heart and lung endurance, flexibility, and body composition, you need to do aerobic exercises. For muscle strength, you need to do anaerobic exercises. For muscle endurance, a program that is part aerobic and part anaerobic is most helpful. **Figure 8.8** shows how various activities rate in each area of fitness. Ratings show the benefits of an activity when done for thirty minutes or longer. The highest score possible is 21.

Figure 8.8
How Exercise Activities Rate
You can choose the kind of exercises that will help you meet your fitness goals.

Exercise	Flexibility	Muscle Strength and Endurance	Heart and Lung Endurance
Handball	16	15	19
Swimming	15	14	21
Jogging	9	17	21
Bicycling	9	16	19
Tennis	14	14	16
Walking	7	11	13
Softball	9	7	6

Figure 8.9
An Exercise Plan
Having a written plan makes it more likely that you will follow it.

Sunday	Monday	Tuesday	Wednesday	Thursday	Friday	Saturday
29	30	31	1	2	3	4
• Bike ride 1 hr. Total: 1 hr.	• Gym class 30 min. • Soccer practice 1 hr. • Walk home from practice 20 min. Total: 1 hr. 50 min.	• Tennis or jog after school 40 min. Total: 40 min.	• Gym class 30 min. • Soccer practice 1 hr. Total: 1 hr. 30 min.	• Tennis or jog after school 40 min. Total: 40 min.	• Gym class 30 min. • Walk home from school 20 min. Total: 50 min.	• Soccer game 50 min. Total: 50 min.

When and Where to Exercise

Whatever your fitness goals include, you should plan on doing at least one form of exercise every day. It is also a good idea to balance your activities throughout the week. One way to be sure that you meet your goals is to make a weekly fitness schedule like the one in **Figure 8.9.**

To begin your schedule, write in all the present times you have to be active. For example, if you have gym class two or three times a week, write that on the correct days. If you ride your bike to and from school all or part of the time, put it down. If you take part in an organized sport, make a note of it on your calendar plan.

When you have written down all of the set times you exercise, try to balance your days by adding, subtracting, or rearranging activities. You want to arrange your activities so that you do something every day and so that you are not overloaded on any one day. Fill in light days with exercises and activities that will help you meet your fitness goals. You don't need to have a specific activity for every exercise session. For example, you may want to plan a forty-minute session twice a week when you will either walk, ride your bike, or play basketball with your friends. The time stays the same, but the activity changes to suit your mood or the weather.

Your exercise schedule should help you meet your personal fitness goals and be healthy. The schedule you make up should be right for you. Your friends' schedules may differ from yours.

in your journal

For two days, keep track of how you spend your time. In your private journal, make a chart that divides your day up into fifteen-minute segments. As the day passes, note what you are doing during each segment. After two days, analyze your chart. How do you spend most of your time?

Exercise Session Stages

Every exercise session should have three stages—the warm-up, the workout, and the cool-down. Every stage is important, and none of the stages should be skipped. Each of the stages is discussed on the following pages. As you study the stages, apply what you learn to your own fitness plan.

Teen Issues

Pumping Iron

The best way to develop muscle strength is through weight training. For it to be helpful, however, you must follow some guidelines. If you lift weights incorrectly, you can injure yourself. The weight should be light enough so that no fewer than 10 lifts can be performed. To build strength, the weight should be heavy enough so that no more than 15 lifts can be performed. Get help from a fitness expert such as a coach or a fitness instructor before you start lifting.

Stage 1. Warm-up

A **warm-up** is *a period of mild exercise that gets your body ready for vigorous exercise.* You should warm up at the beginning of every exercise session for five to ten minutes.

During the warm-up stage, your body gradually changes. Your temperature begins to rise. Your heartbeat rate increases. As more blood flows to your muscles, they become more elastic. The more elastic your muscles are, the less likely they are to become injured when you are exercising.

Some physical fitness trainers recommend warming up by going through the motions of your planned activity at a slowed-down pace. For example, if you are planning to run, walk first. If you are planning to shoot baskets, do shoulder stretches.

Stretching exercises such as those shown in **Figure 8.10** are good warm-up exercises that will increase your overall flexibility. Try doing each exercise two to five times.

Caution: Stretching should be an even, gradual pull on the muscles on both sides of your body. As you stretch, you should feel tension but not pain. Overstretching can damage your joints and the body tissues that hold your bones in place.

Figure 8.10
Warm-up Exercises

A Hip stretch
Lie on your back. Relax and straighten both legs. Pull knees, one at a time, toward chest.

B Shoulder stretch
For support, lean against something at about shoulder level. Keep arms straight while moving your chest downward. Keep feet under hips, with knees slightly bent.

C Calf stretch

Stand close to a wall and lean toward it. As you lean, keep one leg bent and the other extended as shown. Keeping the heel of the extended leg on the ground, move hips forward until you feel a stretch in the calf muscle.

D Hamstring stretch 1

Keep knees slightly bent as you bend slowly from the hips. Bend until you feel a stretch in the back of the legs.

E Hamstring stretch 2

Sit on the floor as shown. Bend front leg slightly while keeping other foot next to the inside of the leg. Bend forward until you feel slight tension.

F Achilles tendon stretch

Lean forward with one leg extended as in the calf stretch. Bend the extended knee slightly, keeping the heel flat.

G Groin stretch

Sit as shown with soles of feet together. Hold onto feet and pull yourself forward.

Stage 2. Workout

In this stage you work to reach your specific fitness goals. It takes a full day for your muscles to recover from exercises that build muscle strength. If you decide to spend time on both muscle and heart and lung exercises during a workout session, do your heart and lung exercises first. For you to benefit from exercise, you must work out often enough, hard enough, and long enough during each session to improve your health (see **Figure 8.11**).

Here are some important points to keep in mind:

- When starting any exercise program, it is best to begin at a comfortable level and build up gradually.

in your journal

Recall the last time you exercised or took part in an active sport. What did you do to warm up? Write your answers in your journal. If you did not warm up, tell why.

Figure 8.11
Factors of Your Workout

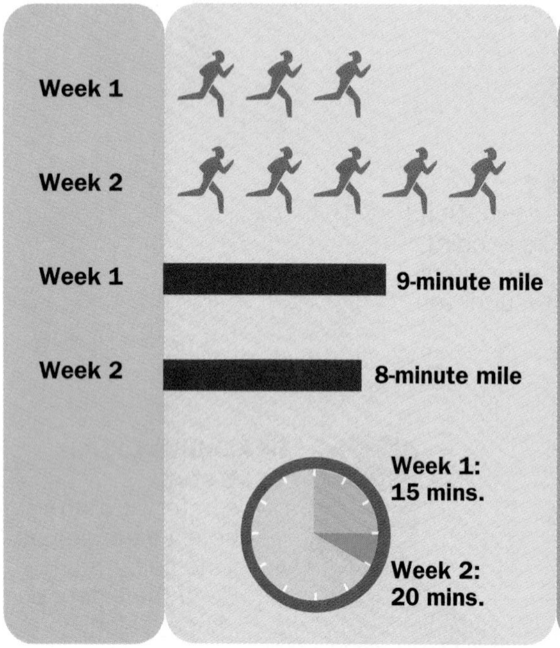

Frequency
The number of times you exercise each week is your exercise frequency. Begin by exercising three times the first week. Then increase to five times by the end of the second week.

Intensity
The amount of energy you use when you exercise is your exercise intensity. Intensity is usually measured by your pulse rate. One way to increase the intensity of your workout is to increase the speed—for example, running a mile in nine minutes the first week to running a mile in eight minutes the second week.

Time
The amount of time you spend exercising during one session is your exercise time. Limit your workout to about 10 to 15 minutes the first week. Then, increase your program by 5 minutes the second week.

MAKING HEALTHY DECISIONS
Too Rushed to Cool Down

Everyone would describe Meredith as extremely busy. She is involved in student government, is captain of the field hockey team, and bikes every day after school. Her friends often ask, "How do you find the time to do everything?" Meredith always just smiles and says, "Planning."

Meredith rides her bicycle with her friend Mark. Warming up and cooling down have always been part of their exercise sessions together. Lately, however, Meredith has decided to skip the cool-down so that she can fit other activities into her evening schedule.

Following their workout this afternoon, Meredith felt a pain in her calf muscle. She tried to ignore it, saying that a little pain now and then is the price an athlete must pay. Mark knew that Meredith was risking injury by not cooling down. He also knew that Meredith liked doing things her own way. What should Mark do? Should he say nothing, hoping that she will realize on her own that she

- One way to increase the intensity of some exercises is by slowing down. For example, in one exercise you lie on your back while raising and lowering your legs. The more slowly you lower your legs, the greater the intensity of the workout.
- The way to increase the intensity of other exercises, such as sit-ups, is to do them faster than before.
- As your endurance improves, increase the time or distance of your workout. Increase running distance by no more than 10 percent a week.

Stage 3. Cool-Down

The warm-up stage of your fitness session gradually gets your heart and muscles working faster and faster. The workout stage brings them up to top speed. **Cool-down** is *a period of gentle exercise that gets your body ready to stop exercising*.

During the workout stage of your fitness session, your increased heartbeat rate sends more blood than usual to your muscles. Your muscles are stretching. If you stop exercising suddenly, your muscles tighten and blood flow slows down. Blood can collect in your muscles. If that happens, you may not get enough blood flow to your brain and heart. This condition could make you feel ill.

When blood collects in your muscles, something else can occur. Waste made by your body cells during exercise can build up in your blood. This waste can result in muscle pain.

The best way to cool down is to continue the motions of the workout stage at a slower and slower pace. If you have been jogging, jog slower and then walk. If you are biking, go slowly and then get off and walk your bike a little. If you are swimming, do stretching exercises in the water. Cool-down should last from five to ten minutes.

Music Connection

Set to Music ACTIVITY!

Try exercising to different types of music. Does the type of music you listen to during exercise affect your exercise intensity? Does the type of music you listen to during exercise affect the length of time you spend exercising? Compare your results with your classmates'. Does one type of music have the same effect on most or all of you?

might be risking injury by not cooling down? Should he remind her about the importance of cooling down? Mark uses the six steps of the decision-making process to help him come to a decision:

1. **State the situation**
2. **List the options**
3. **Weigh the possible outcomes**
4. **Consider your values**
5. **Make a decision and act**
6. **Evaluate the decision**

Follow-up Activities

1. Apply the six steps of the decision-making process to Meredith's situation.
2. Along with a partner, role-play a conversation between Meredith and Mark in which he gives her advice.
3. What decision would you probably make if you were Mark? Explain your decision.

Did You Know?

Water, Please

Drinking water during exercise will not lead to bloating or cramping during your exercise session. In fact, drinking water can actually reduce your risk of overheating when exercising, especially during hot, humid weather. Drink one or two 8-ounce glasses of water about an hour before you begin to exercise. Then, during exercise, stop for water breaks.

Drinking plenty of fluids helps avoid dehydration.

Safety First

Whenever you exercise, you increase your risk of injury. Following the safety tips below will help you keep that risk to a minimum. A few moments spent to prevent injury can save you recovery time and pain. Better safe than sorry!

- **Choose a safe place.** Exercise on soft, even surfaces, such as a track, grass, or dirt. A soft surface is better for a runner's knees than is a hard surface. The street is not a safe place to exercise.
- **Choose a safe time.** During hot, humid weather, exercise less than you normally do. Hot, humid weather puts an extra strain on your body. You could become dehydrated, or dried out. You could become exhausted. On hot days, exercise in the early morning or early evening.
- **Choose proper, loose-fitting clothing.** The looseness helps your skin to breathe. You will stay cooler and avoid overheating.
- **Wear light-colored clothing and reflective coverings if you exercise outside at dusk or at night.** The light-colored clothes and the reflective coverings will make you visible to drivers.
- **When exercising in cold weather, wear one layer less of clothing than you would otherwise wear.** Because you will be making heat when you work out, you won't need as much clothing as you would if you weren't exercising. Wearing layers allows you to take off or add layers as needed.
- **Wear shoes and equipment that fit correctly and are suitable for the activity.** Speak to a coach or a fitness instructor. Try to get the best that you can. Good equipment and shoes that fit comfortably can protect you from injury. Remember that the best is not always the most expensive.
- **Drink plenty of fluids.** Sweating while exercising removes water from your body. You must keep replacing the lost fluid so that you do not become dehydrated. Water and juice are healthy drinks during exercise. Soda pop is not.
- **Protect your feet and legs.** To prevent injury to your feet and legs, try to land on your heels rather than the balls of your feet during active sports and exercise.
- **Pay attention to signals from your body.** Increase your exercise level gradually. If you begin exercising muscles in a new way, it is normal to feel a little discomfort in those muscles. Feeling pain is not normal. If you feel pain anywhere, stop exercising and see a doctor.
- **Begin your exercise session by warming up and end it by cooling down.** You will help prevent serious injury by gradually getting your body ready to begin exercising and by gradually getting it ready to stop exercising.
- **Never exercise when injured.** It is all right to get better by resting. Try alternative activities.

Checking Your Progress

You can check your progress by reviewing your fitness goals and retesting the areas of fitness you want to improve. If you are sticking to your program and not reaching those goals, ask a coach or gymnastics teacher to help you figure out why. Perhaps your goals are not realistic. Maybe you just need more time. Most people do not notice any significant changes as a result of a fitness program for four to six weeks or more.

Even before you reach your fitness goals, you may notice some positive changes of another kind. People who start exercising regularly tend to feel better, sleep better, and have more energy than they did before exercising. After several weeks, you may have less body fat and more muscle. (You may weigh more because muscle tissue is heavier than fat, but you will look trimmer.) You might also feel more confident.

Another way to measure your progress is by measuring your resting heartbeat rate. Your resting heartbeat rate is the number of times your heart beats in one minute while you are resting. The average heartbeat rate is between 72 and 84 beats per minute. A resting heartbeat rate below 72 beats per minute usually indicates a healthy level of physical fitness.

You can check your progress by reviewing your list of exercise goals.

Review Lesson 3

Using complete sentences, answer the following questions on a separate sheet of paper.

Reviewing Terms and Facts

1. **Vocabulary** Which of the following is the amount of energy used with exercise: *exercise time, exercise frequency, exercise intensity?*
2. **Recall** Name the three stages of every exercise session.
3. **Give Examples** List four stretching exercises that are good warm-ups.
4. **Recall** Cite at least six safety tips that will help you decrease your risk of injury during exercise.

Thinking Critically

5. **Analyze** Tom wanted to improve his muscle strength and his heart and lung endurance. He has been lifting weights at the YMCA for a month. Does his fitness program match his fitness goals? Why or why not?
6. **Distinguish** Helen does weight training three times a week. She warms up and cools down at every session. What part of her sessions will probably help most to improve her flexibility?

Applying Health Concepts

7. **Personal Health** Make a fitness schedule like the one in Figure 8.9 on page 245. Analyze your schedule with a partner. Are your days balanced? What can you do to improve your schedule? When can you start?
8. **Health of Others** Find and read an article on fitness routines. Ask two classmates to read the same article. Then discuss the article and write an essay on how it does or does not relate to teens.

Lesson 4

Individual and Team Sports

This lesson will help you find answers to questions that teens often ask about individual and team sports. For example:

- **What are the advantages of individual sports?**
- **What are the advantages of team sports?**
- **What do I need to know about sports equipment and facilities?**
- **What are the benefits of lifetime sports?**

Words to Know

individual sports
team sports
lifetime sports

Individual Sports

To choose an exercise program that is right for you, you need to ask yourself an important question. Do you prefer to exercise on your own or do you prefer to join a team? To answer that question you need to examine your needs and preferences. Doing so will help guide you toward the best kind of exercise for you.

Many people prefer **individual sports.** These are *sports that you can do on your own or with a friend.* You don't have to be part of a team to take part in individual sports. Examples of individual sports are running, swimming, hiking, skating, and biking. Can you think of other examples?

What are the advantages of individual sports? They are more flexible than team sports. You can do them whenever you feel like it. You don't have to show up at a specified time. Also, you can do them for as long as you wish. For example, you can run for twenty minutes or for an hour. It's up to you.

That's also one possible disadvantage of individual sports. It *is* up to you. You have to find the time and the motivation to take part in your chosen sport. There are no set times and no team members to meet. For some people, that is not a problem. They prefer making their own plans. Others, though, find it hard to stick to an exercise plan if they have to do it on their own. You need to decide which kind of person you are.

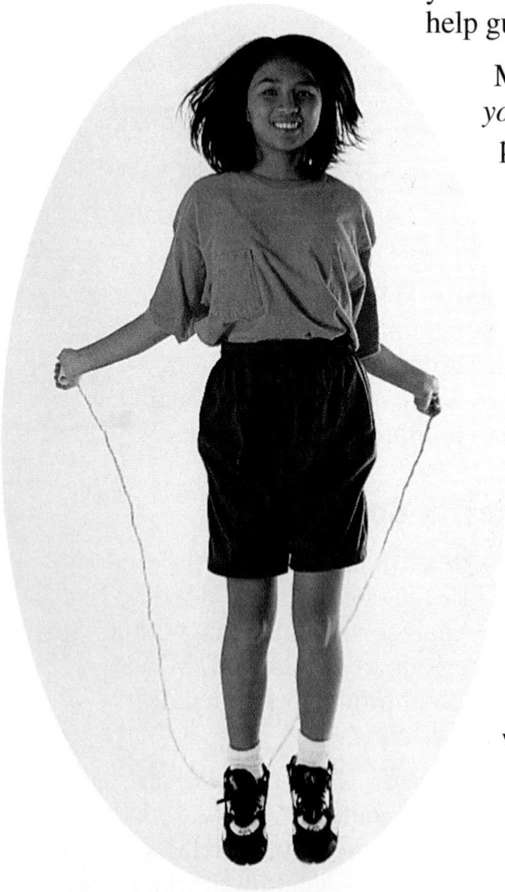

Some teens prefer the flexibility that individual sports offer.

Team Sports

Many teens enjoy taking part in **team sports**—*organized physical activities involving skill, in which a group of people play together on the same side.* By joining a team, you sign up for a regular exercise program. You also give yourself an opportunity to make new friends and get to know people better.

There are many team sports including volleyball, softball, soccer, football, hockey, baseball, and basketball. Check out these places in your community for team sports opportunities:

- Local schools
- Community centers
- Local park district
- Teen clubs
- Sport and fitness centers
- Church and synagogue youth programs

Team sports offer a number of advantages over individual sports. Exercising with other people can be fun. When exercise is fun, you are more likely to keep doing it. Team sports can improve your mental and social health as well as your physical health. They provide you with opportunities to be with other people, and to work together toward a goal. Team sports give you a chance to practice your communication skills and to learn more about cooperation and compromise, which are important social skills.

Of course, team sports are not right for everyone. Some teens dislike the discipline of certain team sports. They do not want to commit themselves to regular practices and weekly games. Perhaps their family circumstances prevent them from committing themselves to a team. For these people, individual sports offer a better alternative that still leads to fitness.

Teen Issues

Going Pro

Some young people dream of professional sports careers. An individual's chance of such a career is low. Only one in 10,000 high school athletes becomes a professional athlete.

Your Total Health

Fuel for Energy ACTIVITY!

The best pregame meal is mostly carbohydrates such as bread, pasta, rice, and potatoes. These foods supply both extra energy and vitamins needed to release it. Write a plan for a balanced meal rich in carbohydrates. Share your plan in class.

Team sports offer opportunities to exercise, make friends, and have fun—three great ways to reduce stress.

Equipment and Facilities

When choosing an exercise program, you should find out about the equipment you will need. Different sports require different equipment. The equipment for some sports is quite expensive. You will need to discuss the cost of equipment with your family before you make a decision.

Some activities require a lot of equipment; others require very little. For example, to do in-line skating safely, you need the skates, a helmet, knee and elbow pads, and gloves, as well as a smooth surface on which to skate. On the other hand, walking requires only good sports shoes.

Sporting goods stores display many varieties of equipment in different price ranges. Check with your coach at school before you buy any equipment. He or she will be able to tell you what is essential and what kind of price you should pay. It may be that the shoes you bought for tennis are just fine for aerobics, too.

The sports you can take part in will also be determined by the sports facilities in your community. You need to find out what facilities are available for sports at local community centers and parks as well as at your school. Some of these public facilities may charge a fee. For example, you may be required to purchase a special badge in order to use the community tennis courts or swimming pool. Private clubs also charge for the use of their facilities. You will need to discuss the cost of using specific facilities with other people in your family.

Cultural Connections

Bicycling Habits

Most bicycles in the United States are used for sport, recreation, or competition. In many European countries, towns and cities are set up to make riding and parking easier for bicyclists. In China, bicycles are the main method of personal transportation, and they are used to carry goods as well as people.

LIFE SKILLS

Getting Fit and Staying Fit

This chapter has provided you with information about setting fitness goals. You have learned how to test your fitness and choose exercises that will help you get fit. Staying fit is a different challenge.

Once you reach your fitness goals, you need a plan for staying fit. Variety, balance, and fun are three exercise factors that can motivate you to keep exercise as a regular part of your life.

- **Variety.** Everyone gets bored doing the same thing over and over. Put some variety into your exercise program. Don't just do the same activity or set of exercises day after day, week after week. Add a different activity now and then, or change your program entirely every few months.
- **Balance.** Don't set up an exercise program that takes too much time or overloads you on one or more days. If your program is too difficult to do, you are less likely to follow it.
- **Fun.** The very best way to stay interested in your exercise program is to have fun doing it. Choose activities that you enjoy. Another way to put fun into your exercise sessions is to get a friend or family member to join you.

Follow-up Activity

Look at your exercise schedule and program. Do they have the variety, balance, and fun to keep you exercising all year? Think of at least one way to improve your program and take action!

Canoeing is just one of many forms of exercise that a person can learn when young and enjoy throughout a lifetime.

Lifetime Sports

Research has shown that exercise helps people of all ages be healthier than they would be without it. The most important fitness goal you can have is lifelong exercise. As people age, their exercise opportunities, abilities, and interests change. Most team sports, for example, are played by young people during their school years. You can keep practicing some sports, however, throughout life. *Exercise activities that can be continued throughout life* are called **lifetime sports.** Learning to enjoy these sports now can help you keep fit for life. Canoeing, hiking, dancing, and cross-country skiing are four lifetime sports. Can you name some more?

in your journal

Choose a lifetime activity that you think you are most likely to enjoy. Use your journal to explain how you plan to participate in this activity. List people you know who already do this activity. Make a note to talk to them about equipment needs and local facilities.

Lesson 4 Review

Using complete sentences, answer the following questions on a separate sheet of paper.

Reviewing Terms and Facts

1. **Give Examples** List three individual sports.
2. **Recall** Identify two advantages of participating in a team sport.
3. **Recall** What is the most important fitness goal you can have?
4. **Vocabulary** Use the term *lifetime sports* in an original sentence.

Thinking Critically

5. **Hypothesize** What are some reasons that a person might have trouble sticking to an exercise program?
6. **Analyze** Susan has the opportunity to play basketball on a team or to join a friend for tennis twice a week. Susan, however, has a very busy schedule and sometimes volunteers to tutor students after school. Which sport would be better for her? Why?
7. **Analyze** Why is it important for teens to learn lifetime sports while they are young?

Applying Health Concepts

8. **Health of Others** With a partner, make a list of all of the places that provide opportunities to join a sports team in your community. Include on your list information about the hours they are open and fees charged. Share your list with your classmates.
9. **Growth and Development** Research the details of one lifetime sport. Find information that describes how to do it, where to do it, equipment needed, and cost. Make a poster explaining what you learned. Display your poster in your classroom.

Chapter 8 Review

Chapter Summary

- **Lesson 1** Total fitness includes physical, mental and emotional, and social fitness. Every person has his or her own physical fitness potential.
- **Lesson 2** Several types of physical fitness combine to make up your total physical fitness level. It is important to consider your limits when setting fitness goals.
- **Lesson 3** Different types of exercise build different areas of fitness. A healthy exercise schedule should be balanced and should include warm-up and cool-down stages.
- **Lesson 4** Many exercise activities require little or no special equipment. The most important fitness goal you can have is lifelong exercise.

Reviewing Key Terms and Concepts

Using complete sentences, answer the following questions on a separate sheet of paper.

Lesson 1

1. List three ways in which physical fitness contributes to total fitness.
2. Nutrition is one area to consider when you want to develop physical fitness. What other two areas should you consider?

Lesson 2

3. What is a good way to test flexibility?
4. What is meant by the term *body composition?*

Lesson 3

5. About how long should you warm up before a workout?
6. Why is the cool-down stage important?

Lesson 4

7. List three advantages of individual sports.
8. What are three exercise activities that require little or no special equipment?

Thinking Critically

Using complete sentences, answer the following questions on a separate sheet of paper.

9. **Identify** Mavis jumped rope. Beatrice lifted weights. Who did an aerobic exercise? Explain your answer.
10. **Analyze** Helen scores well on physical fitness tests but does not always eat a balanced diet or get enough sleep. What does this tell you about her physical fitness level?
11. **Explain** Nicole does all of her exercising on weekends. "This schedule is healthy because I have five days in a row to rest up," she explains. Is Nicole right? Why or why not?
12. **Compare and Contrast** Carl wants to build skills for lifetime fitness. He is interested in joining a mountain hiking club and a skateboarding workshop. Which do you think will best help Carl meet his goal? Why?

Chapter 8 Review

Your Action Plan

You can make an action plan to raise your physical fitness level. Look back at your private journal entries for this chapter.

Step 1: Decide on a long-term goal and write it down. You may want to build endurance, reduce body fat, or improve a sports skill.

Step 2: Create a list of short-term goals to help you reach your long-term goal. If your long-term goal is to build endurance, a good short-term goal is to run 2½ miles three times a week. Start slowly and gradually increase the distance by no more than 10 percent a week, and increase the frequency of your running.

Step 3: Write up a schedule for reaching your short-term and long-term goals.

When you feel you have reached your long-term goal, share your accomplishments with family and friends.

In Your Home and Community

1. **Health of Others** If you have access to a video camera, film family members involved in fitness activities. Include parents and grandparents. Ask their permission to show the film in health classes. Ask your audience if watching the film inspired them to participate in physical fitness activities.
2. **Community Resources** Volunteer to work with young children in your district's fitness programs. If your area has no programs, ask your coach or gym teacher about starting one.

Building Your Portfolio

1. **Fitness Magazines** Examine some fitness magazines at a library. Write down a description of each cover, including the titles of articles on the cover. Then make a chart with two columns, labeled *Health* and *Appearance.* Write each magazine's title in the column that best describes the focus of its articles. Which column is longer? Write a paragraph about what you have learned. Add the summary and chart to your portfolio.
2. **Health Club Facilities** Pretend that you are the manager of a health club. Write an advertisement that explains how joining your health club can help people increase their total fitness. Include the ad in your portfolio.
3. **Personal Assessment** Look through the activities and projects you did for this chapter. Choose two that you would like to include in your portfolio.

Chapter 9

Eating Healthy, Eating Well

Student Expectations

After reading this chapter, you should be able to:

1. Discuss the impact good nutrition has on health.
2. Describe the Food Guide Pyramid and how its use can help ensure a nutritious, balanced diet.
3. Explain how to control weight healthfully.
4. List the steps you would take to help someone with an eating disorder.

Teen Chat Group

Heather: Thanks for coming over and helping me take care of my cousins today.

Samantha: Your cousins are a lot of fun to play with.

Heather: After lunch we can go over to the park.

Samantha: What should we make for lunch?

Heather: I know we have some potato chips in the cupboard.

Samantha: Let's see what's in the fridge. Look at all this yummy fruit—strawberries, grapes, apples. Let's make a fruit salad.

Heather: That's a great idea. Fruit is delicious, and it's better for us than potato chips.

Samantha: Ever since my mom's doctor told my mom to eat foods with less cholesterol, my whole family has been trying to eat healthier. Eating fruit is a good way to start because it's very low in fat.

Heather: It's hard to believe that food can taste so good and be good for us, too!

in your journal

Read the dialogue on this page. Do you eat healthful foods? Start your private journal entries on healthful eating by answering these questions.

- What influences you to choose one food rather than another?
- Do you think that your diet is well balanced? Why or why not?
- If you learned that your diet was not properly balanced, what would you do?

When you reach the end of the chapter, you will use your journal entries to make an action plan.

Lesson 1

Building a Nutritious Diet

This lesson will help you find answers to questions that teens often ask about healthful eating. For example:

- **What can eating the right foods do for me?**
- **What influences the choices people make about food?**
- **What nutrients do I need to be healthy?**
- **How can I use the Recommended Dietary Allowances list?**

Words to Know

nutrition
diet
nutrients
carbohydrates
proteins
amino acids
vitamins
minerals
fats
saturated fats
unsaturated fats
water
Recommended Dietary Allowances (RDA)

Food for Life

Food, along with air and water, is one of life's basic needs. When you go without food for a long time, you feel hungry. This is your body's signal that it needs more food. After you eat, the hunger disappears. Your body has received the fuel it needs to keep going. When that fuel is used up, you will be hungry again.

Although the most important reason for eating is physical, eating is also a social experience. For example, what foods do you associate with sports events, holidays, or picnics? Eating is tied to your emotions as well. Eating to relieve tension or not eating because of stress may result in some unhealthy habits.

Eating the foods your body needs helps ensure proper growth and development. Family background can be a strong influence on your food choices.

By eating healthful foods in recommended amounts, you make sure that you will grow and be healthy. *Eating foods the body needs to grow, develop, and work properly* is called **nutrition** (noo·TRI·shuhn). Good nutrition is one of the main factors in good health. Because you make food choices every day, good nutrition can have a powerful impact on your overall health and well-being.

Good nutrition is especially important in your teenage years. During this time, you are growing faster than you grow at any other time after early childhood. A well-balanced, nutritious diet will provide the fuel you need for energy and growth.

interNET CONNECTION

How can you plan a well-balanced diet—even when you're on the go? Log on to our Web site to find out.

http://www.glencoe.com/sec/health

Are You on a Diet?

What do you think of when you hear the word *diet?* Most people think of a weight-loss diet but that's only one type of diet. A **diet** is something we all follow—*it's the food and drink that we regularly choose to consume.* Think of the foods that you eat each day, each week. Think of the beverages you drink. You will begin to get a picture of the diet that you follow. Many factors affect your choice of foods. **Figure 9.1** shows some of these factors.

Figure 9.1

Factors That Influence Your Diet

The choices you make about what to have for lunch are influenced by the region you live in, your cultural background, convenience, and a number of other factors.

Factor	Influences	Examples
Geography	Local products	South: grits, okra Coastal area: fish
Family	Traditions	Vegetarian meals Meat and potatoes meals
Cultural background	Ethnic foods	Vietnamese: rice, fish Mexican: beans, corn, tortillas
Convenience	Time available for food selection and preparation	Choosing easy-to-prepare foods and takeout meals
Cost	Family budget affects choices	Chicken legs or breasts Pasta or steak
Advertising	Creates demand for products	Selecting one brand over another
Friends	Peer pressure	Choosing snack foods or places to go to eat
Personal taste	Preference for some foods, dislike for others	String beans rather than brussels sprouts Beef rather than lamb

Cultural Connections

Yummy Grubs and Other Bugs

Culture has a big influence on what we choose to eat. Take insects, for example. In some parts of Australia, certain kinds of ants are considered a delicacy. In Japan, fried silkworm larvae are favorites. Why do you think insects are completely absent from American diets?

The Six Types of Nutrients

Q&A

Vitamins and Energy

Q: I've been feeling tired a lot lately. Would vitamin pills give me more energy?

A: The answer is no. You get energy only from fats, carbohydrates, and proteins. In addition, taking too much of vitamins A and D can be very harmful to your body.

Though you have a diet, you may not have a healthful one. A healthful diet provides the nutrients you need to grow and develop. **Nutrients** (NOO·tree·ents) are *substances in foods that your body needs.* Scientists have found some 50 nutrients, which can be grouped into six main types.

The six types of nutrients are carbohydrates, proteins, vitamins, minerals, fats, and water. Each one plays a vital role in your body.

- **Carbohydrates** (kar·bo·HY·drayts) are *the starches and sugars that provide the body with most of its energy.* There are two kinds of carbohydrates—simple and complex. Both are important sources of energy for your body. Simple carbohydrates are found in fruit, sugar, and milk. Complex carbohydrates are found in starchy foods, such as breads, cereals, dry beans, potatoes, and other starchy vegetables. They also provide fiber to aid digestion. Health experts generally recommend that you get about 55 percent of the calories you eat from carbohydrates, mainly from complex carbohydrates.

- **Proteins** (PROH·teenz) are *needed to build, repair, and maintain body cells and tissues,* particularly muscle. They also provide energy. Proteins are especially important during childhood, adolescence, and other periods of growth. Meat, fish, poultry, eggs, milk, cheese, nuts, and dry beans are sources of protein.

  Proteins are made up of **amino** (uh·MEE·noh) **acids.** Of the 22 amino acids in proteins, your body can make 13. The other nine, called *essential amino acids,* must come from the foods you eat. Foods from animal sources are *complete proteins*—they contain all eight essential amino acids. Foods from plants are *incomplete proteins*—they lack at least one essential amino acid. It's important to get all these essential amino acids in your diet. Vegetarians can combine plant foods to make complete protein. Beans and rice is one such combination.

- **Vitamins** (VY·tuh·minz) are *substances needed in small quantities that help regulate body functions,* including helping the body process other nutrients and fight infections. Vitamins fall into two groups—*water-soluble vitamins,* such as vitamin C and many B vitamins, and *fat-soluble vitamins,* such as vitamins A and D. Water-soluble vitamins cannot be stored in the body, so they must be included in your daily diet. Fat soluble vitamins, on the other hand, can be stored in the body until needed, so they don't have to be eaten daily. Since vitamins cannot be made in the body, they must be provided by the diet. Fresh fruits and vegetables, whole-grain breads and cereal products, and fortified milk are rich sources of vitamins. **Figure 9.2** contains more information about vitamin sources.

- **Minerals** are *elements needed in small quantities for sturdy bones and teeth, healthy blood, and regulation of daily elimination.* Whole grains, fruits, peas, spinach, raisins, and milk are good sources of minerals.

- **Fats** are *a source of energy and are essential for vital body functions.* They insulate the body from temperature changes, cushion body organs, carry fat-soluble vitamins, and promote healthy skin and normal growth. Excess fat is stored in the body as extra weight. Fats can be found in butter and margarine, whole milk, egg yolks, most cheeses, and salad dressings.

  Some fats, such as *fats found in meats and dairy products,* are called **saturated fats.** They tend to be solid at room temperature. Eating too much saturated fat can raise blood cholesterol levels, increasing the risk of heart disease. **Unsaturated fats,** *found mainly in vegetable oils, such as olive, corn, or canola oil, are fats that remain liquid.* Most experts recommend that you choose unsaturated rather than saturated fats.

- **Water** is *the most common nutrient,* making up about 60 percent of the body. It carries other nutrients through the body, helps digestion, removes wastes from the body, lubricates the joints, and keeps the body from overheating. You must constantly replace the water your body loses.

A healthful diet contains the right amount, or balance, of nutrients. That is where the term *balanced diet* comes from. A diet that is out of balance may cause health problems. Too much fat may lead to heart disease. Too little protein hinders growth. You need a variety of foods to get all the nutrients.

Your Total Health

Preventing Broken Bones ACTIVITY!

A calcium intake slightly greater than the RDA during the teen years may help lower the risk of fractures from bone loss in old age. It does so by storing added minerals in bones while they are still forming. Find out the RDA for calcium, and estimate your intake of this important mineral by reading food labels. Are you getting enough?

Figure 9.2

Vitamins and Minerals: Sources and Functions

Nutrients	Sources	Functions
Vitamin A	Carrots, eggs, liver	Promotes healthy skin, normal vision
Vitamin C	Oranges, tomatoes, leafy green vegetables	Helps muscles, heart function well
Vitamin D	Fortified milk, oily fish, egg yolks	Promotes strong bones and teeth
Vitamin K	Cabbage, spinach, cereals	Helps blood clot
Calcium	Milk, cheese, shellfish, spinach	Needed to build bones and teeth
Fluoride	Fluoridated water, fish	Promotes strong bones and teeth
Iron	Red meat, nuts, dried fruits	Needed for hemoglobin in red blood cells
Potassium	Oranges, bananas, dry beans, molasses	Helps regulate water balance in tissues

in your journal

In your journal, record a sample menu for one day that reflects your typical food choices for breakfast, lunch, dinner, and snacks. Write down the primary nutrients you think each food choice contributed to your diet. Indicate whether you think you may be getting too little or too much of any nutrient.

Putting Nutrients in Your Diet

Scientists have developed *guidelines for the amounts of vitamins, minerals, and protein you should get from the food you eat.* These guidelines are called the **Recommended Dietary Allowances (RDA).** Percentages of Daily Values for these and other nutrients are listed on nutrition labels. A nutrition label, as shown in **Figure 9.3,** can help you plan nutritious meals.

Nutrition Facts

Serving Size 1/2 cup (114g)
Servings Per Container 4

Amount Per Serving

Calories 90	Calories from Fat 30
	% Daily Value*
Total Fat 3g	**5%**
Saturated Fat 0g	**0%**
Cholesterol 0mg	**0%**
Sodium 300mg	**13%**
Total Carbohydrate 13g	**4%**
Dietary Fiber 3g	**12%**
Sugars 3g	
Protein 3g	

Vitamin A	80% •	Vitamin C	60%
Calcium	4% •	Iron	4%

* Percent Daily Values are based on a 2,000 calorie diet. Your daily values may be higher or lower depending on your calorie needs:

Calories		2,000	2,500
Total Fat	Less Than	65g	80g
Sat Fat	Less Than	20g	25g
Cholesterol	Less Than	300mg	300mg
Sodium	Less Than	2,400mg	2,400mg
Total Carbohydrate		300g	375g
Dietary Fiber		25g	30g

Calories per gram:
Fat 9 • Carbohydrate 4 • Protein 4

Ⓐ The stated serving size is the basis of the nutrient content of the food.

Ⓑ Major nutrients are listed in milligrams or grams and as a percentage of the recommended diet for a person consuming 2,000 calories per day.

Ⓒ The amount of total fat in a serving is listed with the number of calories supplied by that amount of fat. The amount of saturated fat in the total fat is also listed.

Ⓓ Dietary fiber and sugar are listed under Total Carbohydrate.

Figure 9.3
Reading a Nutrition Label

LIFE SKILLS

Reading Nutrition Labels

By law, packaged foods must now carry a Nutrition Facts label so that consumers can make healthful food choices. The labels use Daily Values (DVs) for proteins, vitamins, and minerals. They also list recommended amounts of fat, sodium (salt), carbohydrates, and fiber (also called dietary fiber) in your daily diet:

Fat	less than 65 g
Sodium	less than 2,400 mg
Carbohydrate	300 g
Fiber	25 g

The DVs are based on a 2,000-calorie daily diet. The percent Daily Values on the label show how a food's nutritional content fits into a 2,000-calorie diet. For example, if the label tells you that one serving of a food contains 10 grams of fat, the percent DV column will tell you that 10 grams is 15 percent of 65 grams (your total daily fat allowance).

Follow-up Activities

The new Nutrition Facts labels are designed to help you choose foods for a more healthful diet. Using the labels, however, requires some practice. Refer to the sample label in **Figure 9.3** and the information presented here to answer the following questions. (Assume that you eat about 2,000 calories a day.)

1. How many grams of fat does one serving contain? How much of the fat is saturated?
2. What percentage of your total daily sodium allowance does one serving of the product contain? Would the product be a good choice if you were on a low-salt diet?
3. If you ate two servings of the product, how many grams of fiber would you need to obtain from other foods to get your daily value for fiber? Is the product a good source of fiber?

No two people need exactly the same amount of each type of nutrient. For example, teens need more calcium than adults do for building growing bones. In addition to age, several other factors affect the amount you need of each type of nutrient. To be sure that you get enough of the nutrients you need, scientists have set the RDA nutrient levels fairly high. They estimate that a diet that meets the RDA nutrient levels will be a healthful diet for 95 out of every 100 Americans.

Nutrient needs change throughout your life. Four factors affect your nutrient needs.

Ⓐ Age
Children need more nutrients than adults do for growth and activity.

Ⓑ Body size
Larger people need more nutrients than smaller people do.

Ⓒ General health
Illness increases the amount you need of many nutrients.

Ⓓ Exercise
The more active you are, the more nutrients you need.

Review Lesson 1

Using complete sentences, answer the following questions on a separate sheet of paper.

Reviewing Terms and Facts

1. **Vocabulary** What is a *diet?* What do people often mean when they use the word?
2. **List** Identify the six main types of nutrients your body needs for proper growth and development. List a few sources for each nutrient.
3. **Identify** Which nutrient provides the body with most of its energy?
4. **Explain** What is the difference between complete protein and incomplete protein? How can people who do not eat meat get complete protein in their diet?
5. **Recall** What is the most common nutrient? What is the function of this nutrient?
6. **Vocabulary** What do the initials *RDA* stand for? Explain what information the RDA provides.

Thinking Critically

7. **Analyze** Too much fat can lead to heart disease and other health problems. Should fat be eliminated completely from your diet? Why or why not?
8. **Evaluate** What are some ways that advertising and convenience influence your choice of foods in your diet?

Applying Health Concepts

9. **Personal Health** Find a cookbook at home or in the library. Choose a main course from the cookbook. List all the ingredients. Plan the rest of the menu for that meal. Identify what nutrients are supplied by the foods you chose. Did you plan a balanced meal?
10. **Consumer Health** Go to the supermarket and compare the nutrients contained in several different breakfast cereals. Based on your comparisons, decide which product is the best choice for a healthful breakfast. Write a brief summary and analysis of your observations.

Lesson

2

Making Healthful Food Choices

This lesson will help you find answers to questions that teens often ask about healthful eating. For example:

- **How can I plan a balanced diet?**
- **What are nutritious snacks?**
- **What's unhealthy about eating foods with a lot of fat?**

Words to Know

Food Guide Pyramid
fiber
cholesterol
caffeine

Teen Issues

Ching! Ching!

If you're like most teens, your snacks often come from vending machines. Be aware that many vending machine snacks are high in fat. One study found that the fat content of 33 popular vending machine snacks averaged almost 45 percent. The recommended amount of fat in the diet is 30 percent or less of total calories.

The Food Guide Pyramid

The easiest way to make sure that you are eating a balanced diet is to use the Food Guide Pyramid (see **Figure 9.4**). The **Food Guide Pyramid** is *a guide to daily food choices from five groups of healthful foods.* The basic idea behind the food pyramid is that all foods can be part of a healthful diet if they are eaten in the right proportions. The pyramid illustrates these food choices graphically. At the bottom is the large base of carbohydrates that should form the bulk of your diet. At the top in the small triangle are fats, oils, and sweets; these should be limited in your diet.

To get the most benefit from using the Food Guide Pyramid, keep the following tips in mind:

- **Pay attention to serving sizes.** It is just as important to eat the right amount in each serving of food as it is to eat the right number of servings in a meal.
- **Keep meats lean.** Before cooking, remove skin from poultry and all visible fat from meat.
- **Read the labels on dairy products.** Choose skim, or 1 percent, milk and nonfat or low-fat yogurt and cheese.
- **Use whole-grain or enriched grain products.** Check package labels, and choose these more nutritious breads and cereals.
- **Cook it right.** The way food is prepared really matters. Broiled foods have less fat than fried foods; steamed vegetables retain more vitamins than vegetables cooked in water.
- **Consider nutritive values.** Certain foods supply plenty of nutrients for the calories. The foods at the tip of the pyramid do not and should be used sparingly or not at all.
- **Consume sufficient complete proteins.** This is a special challenge for some vegetarians. Sources of complete proteins are combinations of legumes and grains, eggs, or dairy products.

Figure 9.4

The Food Guide Pyramid

Foods within each group of the pyramid supply similar nutrients. By eating the suggested number of servings from each group, you automatically eat a balanced diet. Because each food group contains a variety of foods, it's easy to find a number of healthful choices that appeal to your taste.

in Your journal

Are you eating a balanced diet? In your private journal, make a list of everything you eat and drink each day. After three days, review your diet.

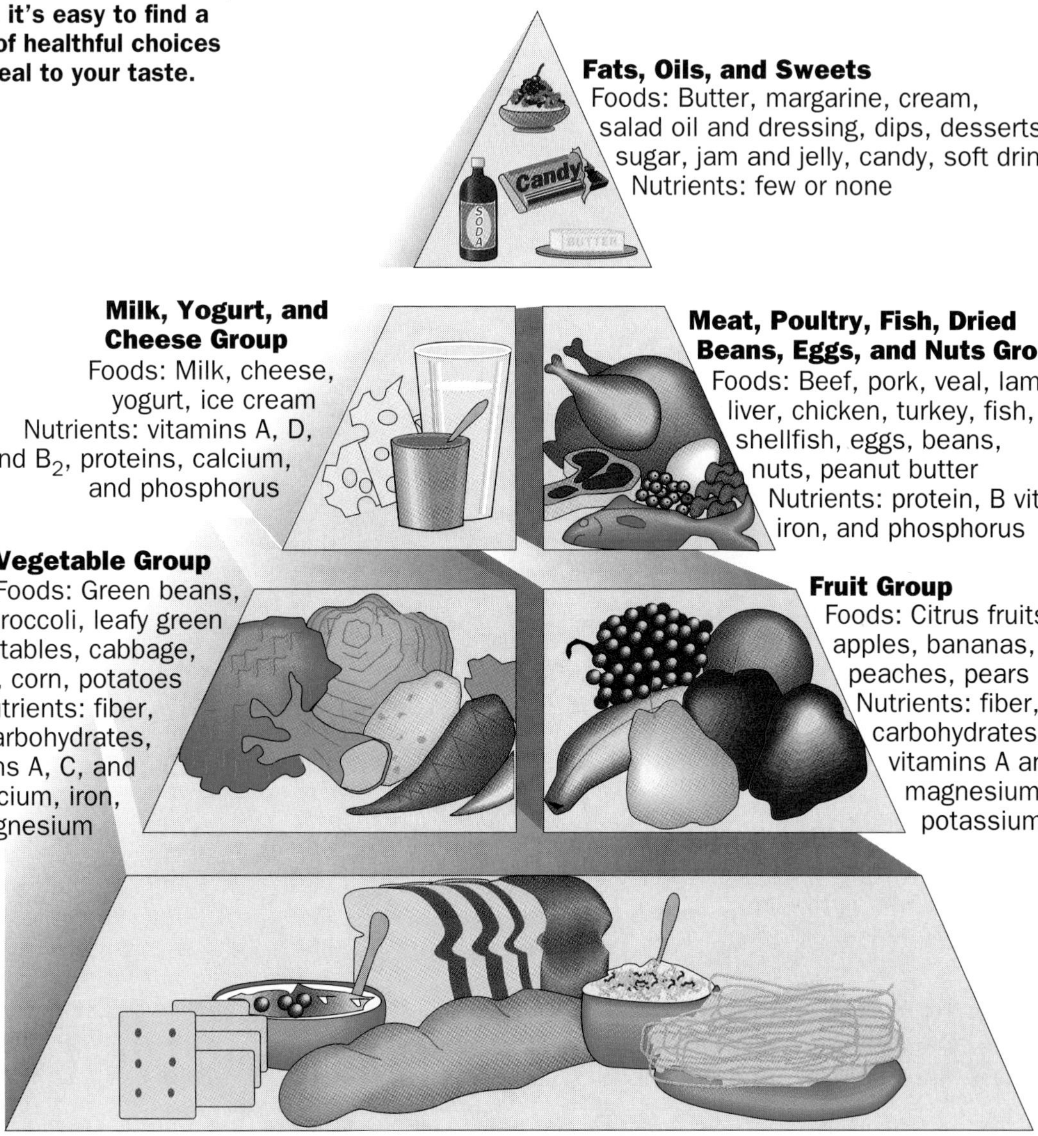

Fats, Oils, and Sweets
Foods: Butter, margarine, cream, salad oil and dressing, dips, desserts, sugar, jam and jelly, candy, soft drinks
Nutrients: few or none

Milk, Yogurt, and Cheese Group
Foods: Milk, cheese, yogurt, ice cream
Nutrients: vitamins A, D, and B_2, proteins, calcium, and phosphorus

Meat, Poultry, Fish, Dried Beans, Eggs, and Nuts Group
Foods: Beef, pork, veal, lamb, liver, chicken, turkey, fish, shellfish, eggs, beans, nuts, peanut butter
Nutrients: protein, B vitamins, iron, and phosphorus

Vegetable Group
Foods: Green beans, broccoli, leafy green vegetables, cabbage, carrots, corn, potatoes
Nutrients: fiber, carbohydrates, vitamins A, C, and K, calcium, iron, and magnesium

Fruit Group
Foods: Citrus fruits, apples, bananas, peaches, pears
Nutrients: fiber, carbohydrates, vitamins A and C, magnesium, and potassium

Bread, Cereal, Rice, and Pasta Group
Foods: Whole-grain or enriched breads, cereals, rice, pasta
Nutrients: carbohydrates, fiber, B vitamins, and iron

Planning—The Way to Health

Each morning think about what you'll eat during the day. Ask the person who prepares the meals in your family what you'll be having for dinner. Then plan to get the other servings you need from the five food groups during breakfast and lunch. Suggested servings are shown in **Figure 9.5.**

Figure 9.5
Food Pyramid Servings
How much of each food group should you eat to achieve a balanced diet? You need to take into account both the number of servings and the size of servings.

MAKING HEALTHY DECISIONS
Choosing Healthful Snacks

Jamie had put on 10 pounds during the course of the school year. None of her clothes fit properly, and she decided that the summer would be a good time to do something about it. She discussed the problem with her mother, and together they worked out a plan for eating healthful, low-calorie meals. She also decided to take the dog for a walk every day and to go swimming at least four times a week at the recreation center pool.

Jamie felt she was making some real progress toward her goal. Then her friend Suzanne called to suggest that they go to the movies with Brian and Felicia. Jamie wants to go, but she knows that they usually stop at a fast-food place after a movie.

Jamie doesn't know what to do. She wants to stay on her weight-loss diet, but she is afraid that if she chooses a salad they will make fun of her for eating "rabbit food." Jamie wonders whether she should

What About Snacks?

When you think about snacks, do potato chips, candy bars, and soft drinks come to mind? Snack foods such as these may be convenient and taste good, but they aren't very good for you. They contain fat and sugar, but few nutrients. They fill you up without helping you grow and stay healthy.

Snacks can be healthful and great energy boosters between meals. Some ideas for healthful snacks are provided in **Figure 9.6.**

Teen Issues

Switching Snacks

If the word snacks means candy bars and soft drinks to you, you need to rethink your snacking habits. Try to work nutritious snacks into your daily routine. For example, you might bring a bagel and juice to school instead of a soft drink.

Figure 9.6

Healthful Snacks

Healthful snacks such as these should be part of a nutritious diet.

A Milk, Yogurt, and Cheese Group
Low-fat or nonfat milk, yogurt, cottage cheese

B Meat, Poultry, Fish, Dried Beans, Eggs, and Nuts Group
Slices of boiled ham or lean roast beef, peanut butter, dry-roasted peanuts

C Fruit Group
Dried fruits such as raisins, any raw fruits

D Vegetable Group
Carrot or celery sticks, tomato wedges, salad

E Bread, Cereal, Rice, and Pasta Group
Whole-wheat crackers, graham crackers, plain bagel, air-popped popcorn (without butter), instant oatmeal, rice cakes, tortillas

just say she is busy. Then she thinks about the step-by-step decision-making process she learned in school.

1. **State the situation**
2. **List the options**
3. **Weigh the possible outcomes**
4. **Consider your values**
5. **Make a decision and act**
6. **Evaluate the decision**

Follow-up Activities

1. Apply the six steps of the decision-making process to Jamie's situation.
2. Role-play the situation in which Jamie explains to Suzanne that she can't go to the movies.
3. Role-play the situation in which Jamie decides to have a salad at a fast-food restaurant.
4. List several healthful snack foods that might appeal to someone who is concerned about gaining weight.

Substances in Food

In addition to the six types of nutrients, you need to be aware of other substances in the foods you eat. Some of these substances are important to include in your diet, and some should be eaten only in limited quantities. Others should be avoided. Fiber is one food substance you need to eat plenty of for good health. Refined sugars, fats, cholesterol, salt, and caffeine are food substances you should limit to stay healthy.

Did You Know?

Bran or Beans?

Not all foods proclaimed to be "high fiber" supply the same amount of this important food substance. For example, a single cup of cooked beans has the same amount of fiber as six bran muffins do.

Fiber

Fiber, also referred to as dietary fiber, is *the part of fruits, vegetables, grains, and beans that your body cannot digest.* Fiber is not a nutrient, but it is very important to good health, helping to carry other food particles through your digestive system. A diet high in fiber can help lower your risk of colon cancer.

Most Americans have too little fiber in their diets. You need about one ounce (25–30 grams) of fiber each day. Whole-grain breads and cereals, raw fruits and vegetables, and beans are all high in fiber.

Sugar

It's hard to believe, but the average American eats about 100 pounds of sugar a year! Almost three-fourths of the sugar we eat is hidden in prepared foods (see **Figure 9.7**). Too much sugar can cause health problems. It contains only negligible amounts of nutrients, and it can promote tooth decay and contribute to added pounds. So avoid eating too many foods that are high in sugar, especially if you eat them in place of foods with more nutrients.

Figure 9.7

Sugar in Common Foods

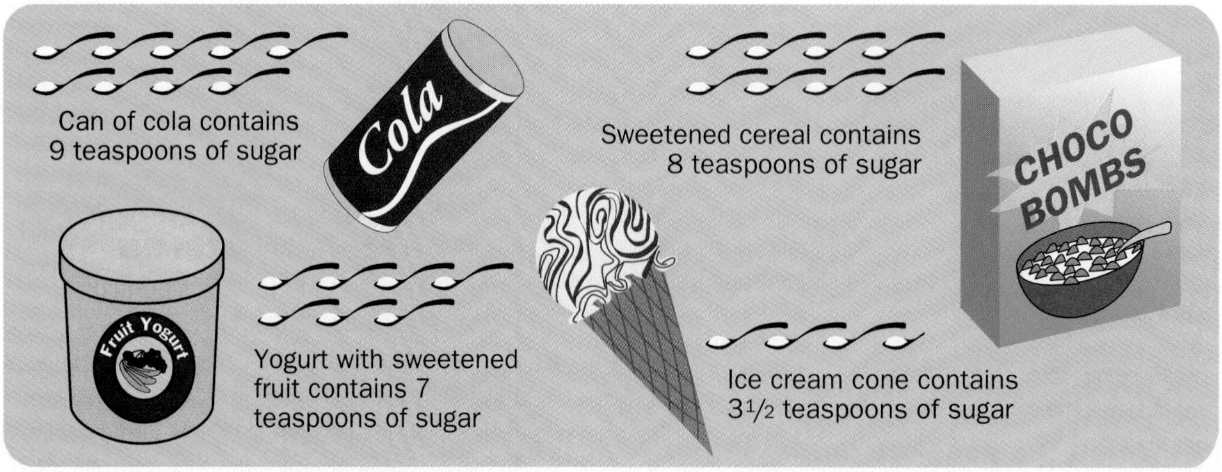

Can of cola contains 9 teaspoons of sugar
Cola
Sweetened cereal contains 8 teaspoons of sugar
CHOCO BOMBS
Fruit Yogurt
Yogurt with sweetened fruit contains 7 teaspoons of sugar
Ice cream cone contains 3½ teaspoons of sugar

Hidden Fats

Most Americans choose diets that are too high in fat content. Fat in your diet should be limited to 30 percent or less of your total calories each day. The foods you eat probably contain more fat than you realize, because most fats are hidden.

It's easy to cut down on the fats you can see—don't butter your baked potato and avoid fried foods. It's harder to cut down on fats that are hidden, but it can be done. Read the labels on cans and packages, and learn which foods are high in fat. **Figure 9.8** provides some information about a few choices you can make to lower the fat content in your diet.

Cholesterol

Cholesterol (kuh·LES·tuh·rawl) is *a fatty, wax-like substance that helps your body make other substances that it needs.* Cholesterol also helps protect nerve fibers. There are two types of cholesterol: *serum cholesterol,* which is produced in your body and circulates in the blood, and *dietary cholesterol,* which comes from food. Cholesterol circulates through the blood in two forms. *LDL* is the bad form of cholesterol because it tends to leave deposits on the walls of the blood vessels. *HDL* is the good form because it carries excess cholesterol to the liver for excretion.

Foods, such as meats, eggs, and dairy products, that come from animals contain cholesterol. Dietary cholesterol is not an essential nutrient since the body produces its own. In fact, too much dietary cholesterol can increase a person's risk of heart disease. To keep your blood cholesterol levels low, you should avoid too much animal fat and choose foods that are low in cholesterol or cholesterol-free.

Your Total Health

Low-fat Choices ACTIVITY!

The best way to lose your taste for fat is not by replacing fatty foods with lower-fat substitutes. Instead, use naturally low-fat choices that will train your taste buds to prefer low-fat foods. Plan to select low-fat foods for two weeks. Keep a log of each time you replace a fatty food with a natural low-fat substitute. Record the fat content of the food you chose and the one you replaced. At the end of two weeks, calculate the amount of fat you didn't consume.

Figure 9.8
Fat Content in Foods

High-Fat Foods (grams of fat)	Moderate-Fat Foods (grams of fat)	Low-Fat Foods (grams of fat)
Fried chicken (3.5 oz.): 17.4 g	Roasted chicken with skin: 13 g	Broiled chicken without skin: 3 g
Whole milk (1 cup): 8 g	2% milk: 5 g	Skim milk: less than 1 g
French fries (14): 11 g	Baked potato with butter (1 pat): 4 g	Baked potato, plain: trace
Danish or donut: 12 g	Bagel with cream cheese (1/2 oz.): 7 g	Bagel, plain: 2 g

Fresh herbs are great taste boosters. Instead of adding butter, sour cream, and salt to your baked potato, try parsley or chives.

Did You Know?

Sodium Sources

Ten percent of the sodium in the average American's diet occurs naturally or is added by the cook. Fifteen percent comes from a saltshaker at the table. The rest, a whopping 75 percent, comes from processed foods.

Sodium

Although *sodium* (SOH·dee·uhm) is a mineral nutrient, most Americans eat far more sodium than is healthful. You can get all the sodium you need by eating less than one-third ounce (3 to 8 grams) of salt a day. This amount is found in the natural foods you eat without adding any salt. Also, people with high blood pressure almost always benefit from a sodium-restricted diet. However, the average American eats double or even triple the amount of sodium they need!

Most of the sodium in our diets comes from processed foods. Some salt is added to foods when they are cooked or at the table with a saltshaker. To reduce the amount of sodium in the food you eat, read food labels and choose products with the least added sodium (see **Figure 9.9**). Don't add salt when cooking foods, and keep the saltshaker off the table.

Figure 9.9

Sodium in Common Foods

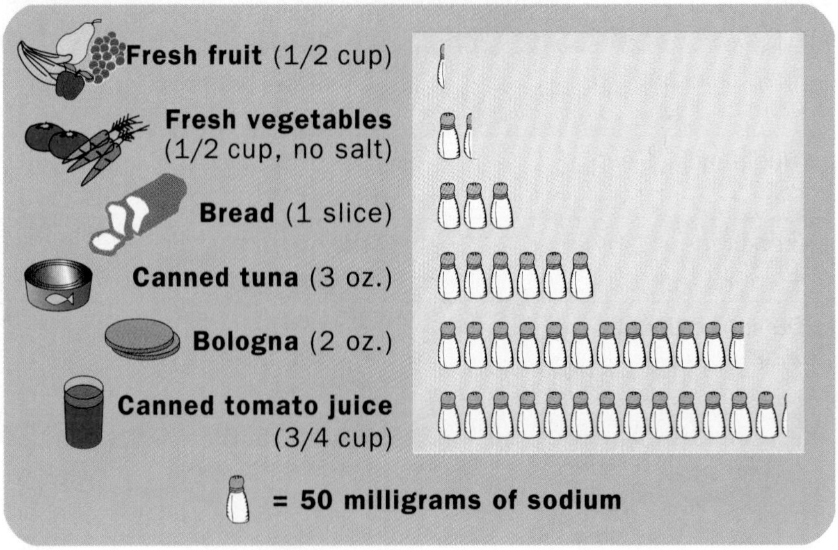

Caffeine

Caffeine (ka·FEEN) is *a chemical, found in some plants, that can make your heart beat faster.* Caffeine can perk you up, but too much of it can make you tense. Like some drugs, caffeine can be habit-forming. For these reasons, you should limit the amount you consume. **Figure 9.10** shows the amount of caffeine in some common beverages.

History Connection

Caffeine Consumption

Coffee originated in Africa around 575 A.D. The beans were used as money and eaten as food.

Figure 9.10
Caffeine Count
To limit the amount of caffeine you consume, you need to know how much caffeine different drinks contain.

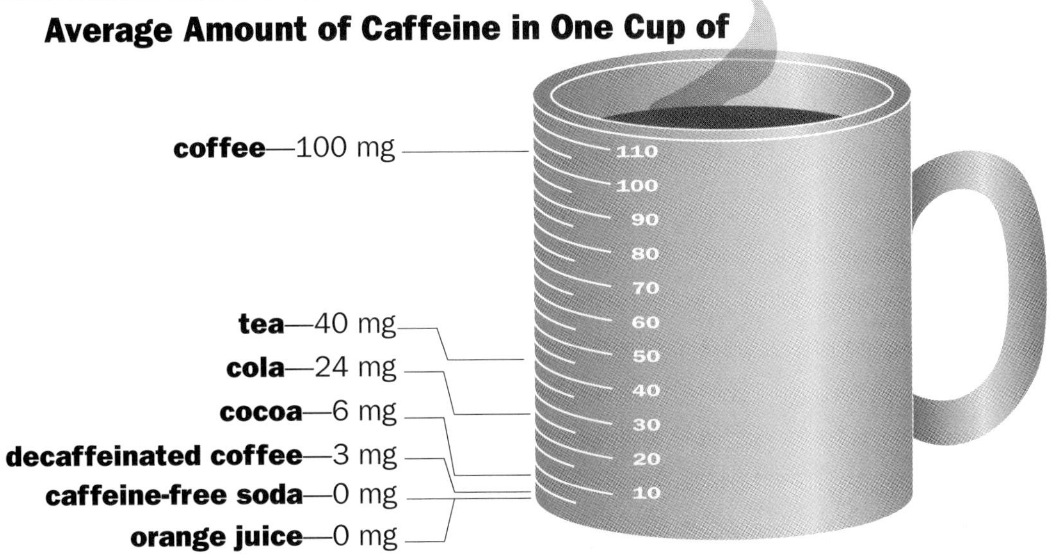

Review
Lesson 2

Using complete sentences, answer the following questions on a separate sheet of paper.

Reviewing Terms and Facts

1. **Explain** Why is it better to broil rather than fry foods? Why is it better to steam vegetables than to cook them in water?
2. **Recall** What nutrients are found in the bread, cereal, rice, and pasta group?
3. **Give Examples** Suggest a healthful snack from each of the five food groups in the Food Guide Pyramid.
4. **Vocabulary** What is *fiber?* Why is it important to a healthy diet? List three sources of fiber.

Thinking Critically

5. **Analyze** Explain how the shape of the Food Guide Pyramid helps make it easier to choose a balanced diet.
6. **Explain** How can planning ahead help improve your daily food choices?
7. **Evaluate** Think about your own diet. What food groups do you need to increase in your diet? What food groups do you need to cut down on?

Applying Health Concepts

8. **Health of Others** Cut out pictures of snack foods from magazines and newspapers or make your own drawings. Use the illustrations to make a snack food "Do's" and "Don'ts" poster.

TEEN HEALTH DIGEST

CON$UMER FOCU$

Got Fiber?

Grandpa goes out of his way to include fiber in his diet. Teens and children should do the same.

Fiber is important to the health of young people. You can determine the amount of fiber you should eat per day by counting your daily calorie intake. If you eat 2,000 calories per day, you should take in 25 grams of fiber daily. If you have a 2,500 calorie-daily diet, you should eat 30 grams of fiber each day.

Here are the amounts of fiber found in servings of common grains:

Whole-wheat bread	*2 grams/slice*
White bread	*0.5 gram/slice*
White rice (0.5 cup)	*1.2 grams*
Brown rice (0.5 cup)	*3.2 grams*

Try This:

Keep track of everything you eat for a day. Use the nutrition labels on the various food packages to see how much fiber you consume.

Myths and Realities

Fat Food Facts

Here are some common myths about fat and foods.

- *Some foods burn fat.* This is simply not true. No food "burns fat."
- *Margarine is low in fat.* Margarine is slightly lower in calories than butter. Still, both deliver most of their calories in the form of fat.
- *Two-percent milk is very low in fat.* Actually, 37 percent of the calories in 2 percent milk come from fat. (The "2 percent" refers to the amount of fat by weight. Most of the weight of milk is water, which has no calories or fat!)
- *Salad bars are low in fat.* This is true only if you avoid the salad dressings. Leafy greens and vegetables *are* low in fat. However, two tablespoons of regular salad dressing have just as much fat as a fast-food burger.

HEALTH UPDATE

Don't Flunk Breakfast

It's scientifically proven—breakfast can make you smarter!

A recent study by doctors in Israel concluded that most students who eat breakfast a half hour before a test do better than students who have not eaten up to two hours beforehand.

"Children running on empty is not an ideal situation for learning," says Keith Ayoob, a professor at the Albert Einstein College of Medicine.

To prepare for that next big test, study the night before—and eat breakfast the morning of the test!

Try This: *Create some special "test day" menus. Treat yourself to nutritious breakfasts on the days when you have important exams.*

People at Work

Dietitian

Name: Tony Herrera

Education: Four-year college degree in nutrition, followed by a six-month internship at a hospital. Tony then passed a test given by the American Dietetic Association.

Job: Food service manager at Hillcrest House, a home for more than 100 senior citizens.

Tony has always loved food and cooking. Today he combines his talents for cooking with his scientific training. Tony's most rewarding challenge is meeting the residents' diet restrictions while creating delicious, tempting meals.

The best part of Tony's job is hearing the people at Hillcrest House rave about his recipes!

Teens Making a Difference

A Peer Who's Been There

As a child, Maria was a shy, self-conscious loner. Today, she is a popular, outgoing teen. What happened?

Maria used to be seriously overweight. She saw herself as the "fat kid" and retreated from her peers. After enrolling in a weight-loss program at a local hospital, Maria slowly began to shed the pounds. She realized that she could conquer her weight problem.

Today Maria is a peer counselor at the weight-loss program. She helps others lose weight by helping them meet the first and toughest challenge—to overcome their own negative self-image.

Lesson 3

Managing Your Weight

This lesson will help you find answers to questions that teens often ask about weight management. For example:

- **How much should I weigh?**
- **How can I lose weight without damaging my health?**
- **What can I do to keep my weight the same?**

Words to Know

weight control
desired weight
overweight
obesity
calorie
nutrient density

What Is Weight Control?

We all want to keep our weight under control. **Weight control** means *reaching the weight that is best for you and then staying at that weight. The weight that is best for you* is called your **desired weight.** It's based on your sex, height, and body frame (small, medium, or large). People who stay at their desired weight tend to be healthier than those who are either underweight or overweight.

Weight control probably receives more attention than almost any other health issue. Fad diets are popular for short periods of time. Diet gimmicks are often expensive, unsafe, and ineffective. Check with your doctor before starting any weight-loss program and remember that there is no easy way to lose weight quickly and safely.

The Pressure to Be Thin

Many of us feel strong pressure to be thin. Most young people, however, don't need to lose weight. In fact, unwise dieting may interfere with normal growth and development.

HEALTH LAB

Counting Calories

Introduction: In this lesson you'll learn about the role of calories in weight control. Knowing your calorie intake is an important component of any weight-loss or weight-gain plan. Yet most people have little idea how many calories they take in.

Objective: In this health lab, you will learn how to keep track of the calories you eat and how to use this information to improve your food choices for successful weight management.

Overweight or Obese?

A person who is **overweight** weighs *more than the desired weight for his or her sex, height, and frame size.* This is not the same as being obese. **Obesity** (oh·BEE·suh·tee) is a more serious condition than being overweight. It means *having too much body fat.* Obese people weigh at least 20 percent more than their desired weight. Their obesity puts them at greater risk of disease and other physical problems. Unfortunately, obesity is a common health problem in the United States. **Figure 9.11** shows how excess weight affects the body.

Figure 9.11

How Excess Weight Affects the Body

Obesity places an extra burden on the body and increases a person's risk of developing certain disorders, such as diabetes and high blood pressure. It also affects a person's self-image.

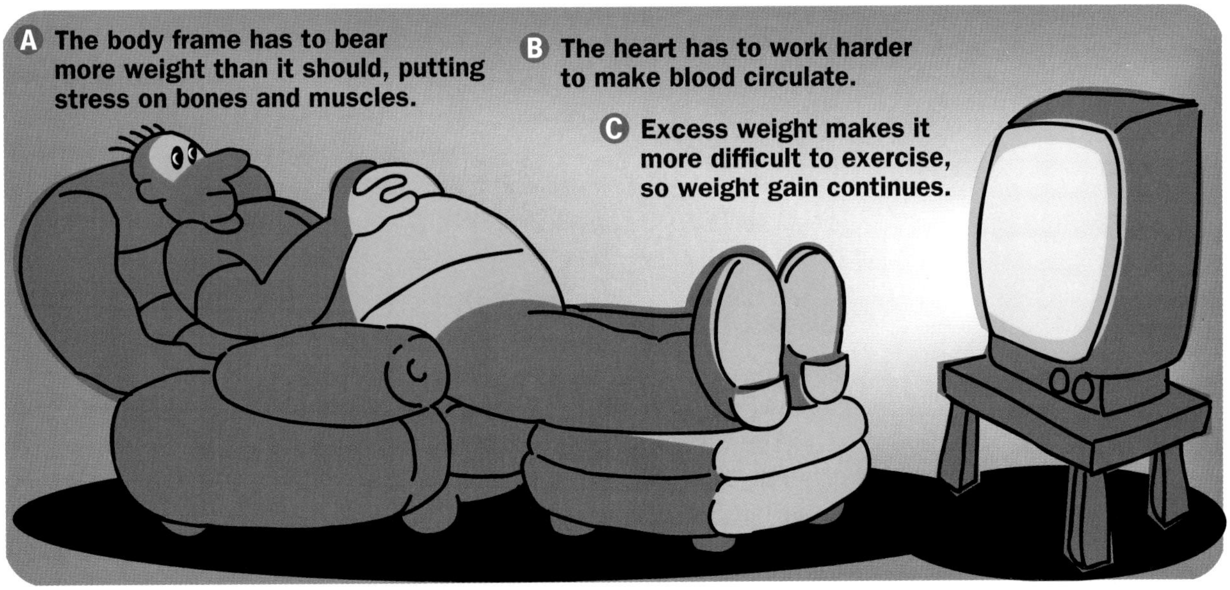

A The body frame has to bear more weight than it should, putting stress on bones and muscles.
B The heart has to work harder to make blood circulate.
C Excess weight makes it more difficult to exercise, so weight gain continues.

Materials and Method: You will need a notebook, pencil, and calorie-counting guide. You will also need some measuring cups and spoons. In the notebook, record everything you eat and all serving sizes for at least one day and preferably for three or more days. Don't forget snacks, beverages, and meals eaten away from home.

Observation and Analysis: At the end of this period, look up the calorie content of each food you recorded. For prepared foods, see the calories-per-serving information on the package label. For foods made from scratch, consult a cookbook and estimate calories per serving from the ingredients. Many fast-food restaurants will provide you with calorie and nutrient content information for their products. Add up your daily calorie intake. If you have kept track of your calories for more than one day, calculate your average daily calorie intake.

Which food group is the largest single source of the calories in your diet? Do most of the calories come from the bread, cereal, rice, and pasta food group, or do many of the calories in your diet come from foods that contain a lot of fat and sugar?

Did You Know?

Cookies and Cola

To burn off the calories in just one chocolate chip cookie, you need to walk for 10 minutes or run for 3 minutes. To burn off the calories in one 12-ounce cola, you need to walk for 29 minutes or run for 8 minutes.

The Role of Calories

A **calorie** (KA·luh·ree) is *a unit of heat.* Calories are used to measure the energy available in different foods. The more calories in a food, the more available energy it has. Calories are also used to measure the energy your body uses.

Whenever you eat, you take in calories. Growth and exercise burn up calories. When you take in the same number of calories that you burn up, your weight stays the same. When you take in more calories than you burn up, your body stores the extra calories as fat, and you gain weight. **Figure 9.12** shows how your calorie intake, physical activity, and weight are related.

Figure 9.12
Calories and Your Weight

Food Consumed (per day)	Energy Used (per day)	Effect on Weight
2,000 calories	2,000 calories	Same
2,000 calories	1,700 calories	Gain
2,000 calories	2,300 calories	Loss

However, planning your diet involves more than counting calories. You also need to consider the nutrient value of the foods you eat. For example, most high calorie foods contain a lot of fat or sugar but few other nutrients. A healthful diet is built around foods that have high **nutrient density.** These are foods that *contain large amounts of nutrients relative to the number of calories they provide.* The following are examples of nutrient-dense foods from each of the five food groups.

- **Meat group:** chicken and tuna
- **Milk group:** low-fat and nonfat milk, yogurt, and cheese
- **Grains:** whole-wheat pasta, whole-grain breads, and rice
- **Fruit group and vegetable group:** includes almost every fruit and every vegetable

Teen Issues

Lose Weight Safely

Many people on weight-loss diets skip meals or eat only one type of food in their efforts to drop pounds quickly. Keep in mind that any diet, even a weight-loss diet, must have adequate servings of foods from each of the five main food groups in the Food Guide Pyramid. Any weight-loss diet should also be approved by a doctor.

Gaining or Losing Weight

Someone who is overweight or obese needs to lose weight. Someone who is underweight may need to gain weight. Although it is often difficult in practice, losing or gaining weight is simple in principle. To lose weight, you must take in fewer calories or burn up more calories than you usually do. To gain weight, you must take in more calories than usual. It is important to select foods that have high nutrient density.

Adjusting Calorie Intake

To reduce the number of calories you take in, eat smaller servings or lower-calorie foods. Switch from fried to broiled or steamed foods. They not only have fewer calories but also contain less fat. To increase the number of calories you take in, eat larger servings of complex carbohydrates such as bread and pasta. See **Figure 9.13** for sample menus.

Math Connection

Burning Calories

You have to use up an extra 3,500 calories to lose 1 pound of fat. To lose 5 pounds in a month, how many extra calories do you have to burn per day?

Figure 9.13

Menus for Weight Loss and Weight Gain

Menu for Weight Loss

Breakfast
2 pieces of whole wheat toast
fresh fruit
1 cup of skim milk

Lunch
Tuna salad sandwich made with 2 oz. of canned tuna packed in water, low-fat mayonnaise, lettuce, and tomato on rye bread
1 cup of skim milk

Snack
Vegetable sticks (1/2 cup)

Dinner
Green salad with low-fat vinaigrette
Skinless broiled chicken (2–3 oz.)
Steamed green beans (1 cup) with lemon
Boiled or baked potato (1/2) with no butter
Fresh fruit compote (1/2 cup)

Menu for Weight Gain

Breakfast
3 waffles with fresh fruit and yogurt
1 cup milk (2%)
1 cup of orange juice

Lunch
Tuna salad sandwich with 3 oz. of tuna, mayonnaise, lettuce, and tomato on rye bread
1 cup milk (2%)
An orange

Snack
Vegetable sticks (1/2 cup) with yogurt dip
Whole-wheat crackers
1 slice of vegetable pizza

Dinner
Tossed salad with blue cheese dressing
Baked chicken (6 oz.) with rice (1-1/2 cups)
Green beans (1 cup) with oil and lemon
2 slices of bread with butter (1 pat)
Fresh fruit compote (1 cup) with yogurt

Exercising

The fastest way to burn up calories is to exercise more. You should also exercise when trying to gain weight to be sure the weight you add is muscle and not fat.

Exercise is a great way to control your weight because it has many benefits besides burning calories.

Ⓐ Exercise helps your heart and lungs to work better.

Ⓑ Exercise helps tone your muscles.

Ⓒ Exercise increases the rate at which your body changes nutrients into energy, making it easier for you to control your weight.

Dieting Concerns

Many people want to lose weight fast. Dieting safely, however, is a gradual process. It requires eating a balanced diet and losing no more than 1 to 2 pounds a week. Every year a new diet that promises people amazing results becomes popular. In magazines, you can see ads of various pills and other "procedures" that promise quick weight loss.

Some of the popular fad diets are limited to a few foods or food groups. Some are extremely low in calories. There are also diets that consist entirely of a liquid formula. Any of these may lead to serious nutritional deficiencies. Furthermore, such diets do not deal with the main cause of excess weight, which are the eating and exercise habits of the individual. For this reason, they do not result in permanent weight loss.

Fasting, or not eating for a long period of time, is an extremely dangerous way of losing weight. Long-term fasting has the same effect on the body as starvation. It can result in loss of muscle tissue, heart damage, digestive problems, and stunting of growth.

Diet aids such as pills and body wraps may also be ineffective and harmful. Diet pills, which are supposed to reduce your appetite, can have serious side effects and may be addictive. Sweating in body wraps encourages water loss rather than loss of body fat.

To lose weight and maintain your weight loss, you need to change your eating behavior and exercise habits. Otherwise, you will regain the weight you lost once you return to your old eating habits. Moreover, quick weight loss can lead to a cycle of weight gain and loss called seesaw or yo-yo dieting, which can be even more dangerous than being overweight.

The following is a list of "Do's" and "Don'ts" that you can follow to achieve safe weight-loss dieting.

Teen Issues

Keeping It Off ACTIVITY!

One of the keys to maintaining weight loss successfully is getting support from family, friends, a counselor, or a support group. Find out what counseling services and support groups are available in your school or community to support teens with weight-control problems.

Dieting Do's

- Follow a diet and exercise program under the supervision of a doctor to ensure that the plan is safe.
- Set realistic goals (1 to 2 pounds of weight loss per week).
- Exercise to help burn calories.
- Change poor eating habits.
- Consider food preferences when planning your diet.
- Eat nutrient-dense foods.
- Eat mainly low-calorie foods from the five food groups.
- Eat slowly and wait before taking a second helping.
- If you are tempted to snack, try doing something else—take a walk or visit a friend.
- Weigh yourself only once a week at the same time of day.
- Focus on your progress.

in your journal

Do you eat "on the run" and gulp down your food, or do you eat slowly and chew each mouthful thoroughly? Eating too quickly can lead to indigestion and can contribute to weight gain. In your journal describe how you usually eat, and analyze your eating behavior.

Dieting Don'ts

- Don't be taken in by diets promising quick results.
- Don't rely on special formulas or products.
- Don't lose more than 2 pounds a week.
- Don't eat fewer than 1,400 calories a day.
- Don't skip meals.
- Don't weigh yourself every day.
- Don't reward yourself with food.
- Don't become discouraged if you have a setback.

Choosing healthful foods is an essential part of maintaining your desired weight.

Maintaining Your Desired Weight

To maintain your weight, plan your meals and snacks so that you take in the same number of calories you burn up. Keep track of your weight. If you start gaining pounds, eat less or exercise more. If you start losing weight, eat more. Your goal should be to develop good eating and exercise habits that keep you healthy.

Review

Lesson 3

Using complete sentences, answer the following questions on a separate sheet of paper.

Reviewing Terms and Facts

1. **Vocabulary** Define *weight control.*
2. **Vocabulary** Who has a more serious problem, a person who is *overweight* or one who is *obese?* Why?
3. **Vocabulary** Define *nutrient density.*
4. **Recall** How does exercise help you to control your weight?
5. **List** Name four dieting "Do's" and four dieting "Don'ts."
6. **Review** Summarize the guidelines for maintaining your desired weight.

Thinking Critically

7. **Contrast** Explain how weight control differs from weight loss.
8. **Relate** Explain how calories are related to both diet and exercise.
9. **Analyze** Kevin went to a fast-food restaurant for lunch. He ordered a cola drink; a taco with chicken, cheese, shredded lettuce, and tomato; and ice cream. Which of these foods has high nutrient density, and which has low nutrient density?

Applying Health Concepts

10. **Consumer Health** Look through several teen magazines and count how many times you see thin models in an advertisement. Then walk through your local shopping mall or supermarket and note how many teens and adults you see who are as thin as the models in the advertisements. How do your two sets of observations compare? How do your observations relate to the pressure that many young people feel to be thin?

Lesson

4 Eating Disorders

This lesson will help you find answers to questions that teens often ask about eating disorders. For example:

- **Why do some people develop eating disorders?**
- **Can people with eating disorders do permanent damage to their bodies?**
- **Where can a teen with an eating disorder get help?**

Words to Know

eating disorders
anorexia nervosa
malnutrition
bulimia

Taking Weight Loss to Extremes

There's no question that Americans spend a lot of time worrying about losing weight. An army of doctors and thousands of diet books prove it. Some people get carried away with losing weight and becoming thin. Others may have serious underlying psychological problems that require professional treatment. They develop **eating disorders**—*extreme and damaging eating behaviors that can lead to sickness and even death.*

Anorexia Nervosa

Anorexia nervosa (a·nuh·REK·see·uh ner·VOH·suh) is *an eating disorder characterized by self-starvation leading to extreme weight loss. Anorexia* means "without appetite," and *nervosa* means "of nervous origin." Most people suffering from anorexia nervosa are female. It's particularly common among teenage girls and young women. However, men and boys can also have the disorder. There are many theories about the specific causes of anorexia nervosa, but experts agree that the disorder is related to how an individual sees herself and to her ability to cope with the stresses of everyday life.

People with anorexia nervosa see themselves as fat even when they are thin.

Teen Issues

Mind and Body ACTIVITY!

Anorexia nervosa is a psychological disorder affecting the mind and the body. It is caused by outside pressures, high expectations, the need to achieve, or the need to be popular. People with anorexia nervosa have an irrational fear of becoming obese. Find out about famous people—singers, gymnasts, actors—who have had this disorder. Prepare an oral report on one of these people.

People with anorexia nervosa may eat so little they develop **malnutrition,** the *condition in which the body doesn't get the nutrients it needs to grow and function properly.* Treatment for anorexia nervosa may include a stay in the hospital, where the patient is fed nutrients and receives counseling. Untreated, anorexia may lead to serious illness—and even to death.

Bulimia

Bulimia (boo·LEE·mee·uh), also called bulimia nervosa, is *a condition in which people repeatedly eat large amounts of food and then try to get rid of the food they have eaten.* Like anorexia nervosa, bulimia is more common among young women and teenage girls than it is among men or boys. People with bulimia are extremely concerned about being thin and beautiful. The disorder grows out of their desire to control their bodies. For example, after they eat a gallon of ice cream and a bag of potato chips, they panic, thinking they are losing control of their bodies. They may force themselves to vomit the food, believing that this will put them back in control. They may also take laxatives (LAK·suh·tivs). Laxatives make food speed through the digestive system with little time to release nutrients. Other people who are bulimic may go on crash diets to make up for overeating. The result of any of these methods is that the person does not get enough nutrients. **Figure 9.14** shows the many ways that bulimia can damage the body.

in Your Journal

You have just learned that anorexia and bulimia are more common in girls than in boys. Do you think that our society contributes to this? Use your journal and suggest some reasons for this situation.

Figure 9.14

How Bulimia Damages the Body

The behavior of someone with bulimia can do a great deal of damage to the body.

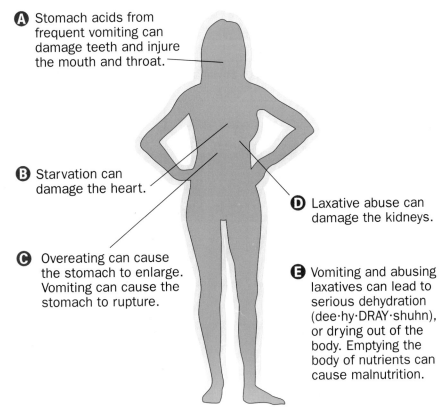

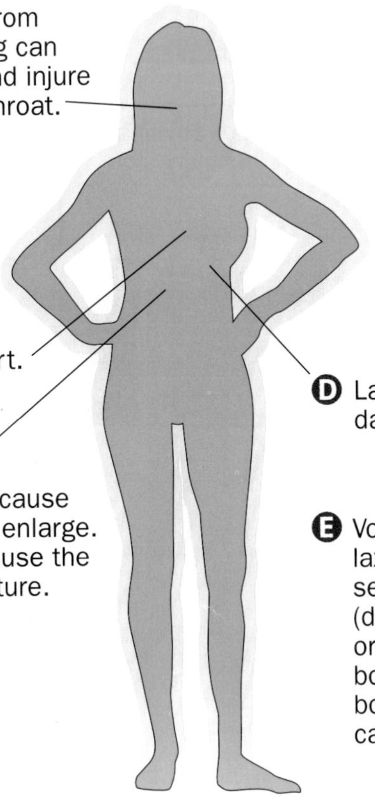

A Stomach acids from frequent vomiting can damage teeth and injure the mouth and throat.
B Starvation can damage the heart.
C Overeating can cause the stomach to enlarge. Vomiting can cause the stomach to rupture.
D Laxative abuse can damage the kidneys.
E Vomiting and abusing laxatives can lead to serious dehydration (dee·hy·DRAY·shuhn), or drying out of the body. Emptying the body of nutrients can cause malnutrition.

Overeating and Obesity

People overeat for a variety of reasons, including boredom, stress, and habit. Overeating is not as severe an eating disorder as anorexia nervosa or bulimia. However, if overeating leads to obesity—being 20 percent or more over your desired weight—it can result in serious health problems.

Excessive body fat puts a strain on the heart and lungs. The obese person may exercise less, resulting in more weight gain and increased health risks. These risks include high blood pressure, stroke, diabetes, heart disease, and even cancer. Obesity may also lead to low self-esteem or even to psychological and social problems associated with obesity. **Figure 9.15** shows the factors involved in adolescent obesity.

Losing excess weight is important to a person's overall health. Although heredity is a factor, overeating and a lack of exercise often cause obesity. The obese person needs to replace poor eating and exercise habits with healthful ones. Regular exercise, a diet approved by a physician, and a basic change in eating behavior are the keys to successful long-term weight loss.

Help for People with Eating Disorders

People with eating disorders rarely get better on their own. This is because they do not have a realistic view of themselves. Although family and friends can play an important role, professional help is usually required. In addition, many communities

Q&A

Recognizing Anorexia Nervosa

Q: I have a friend who is very thin. How can I tell if she has anorexia nervosa?

A: Your friend may have anorexia nervosa if she eats very little yet shows an abnormal interest in food, exercises obsessively, or thinks she's fat when she's actually thin. If you suspect anorexia, follow the steps in the diagram to get her professional help.

Figure 9.15
Factors Contributing to Obesity

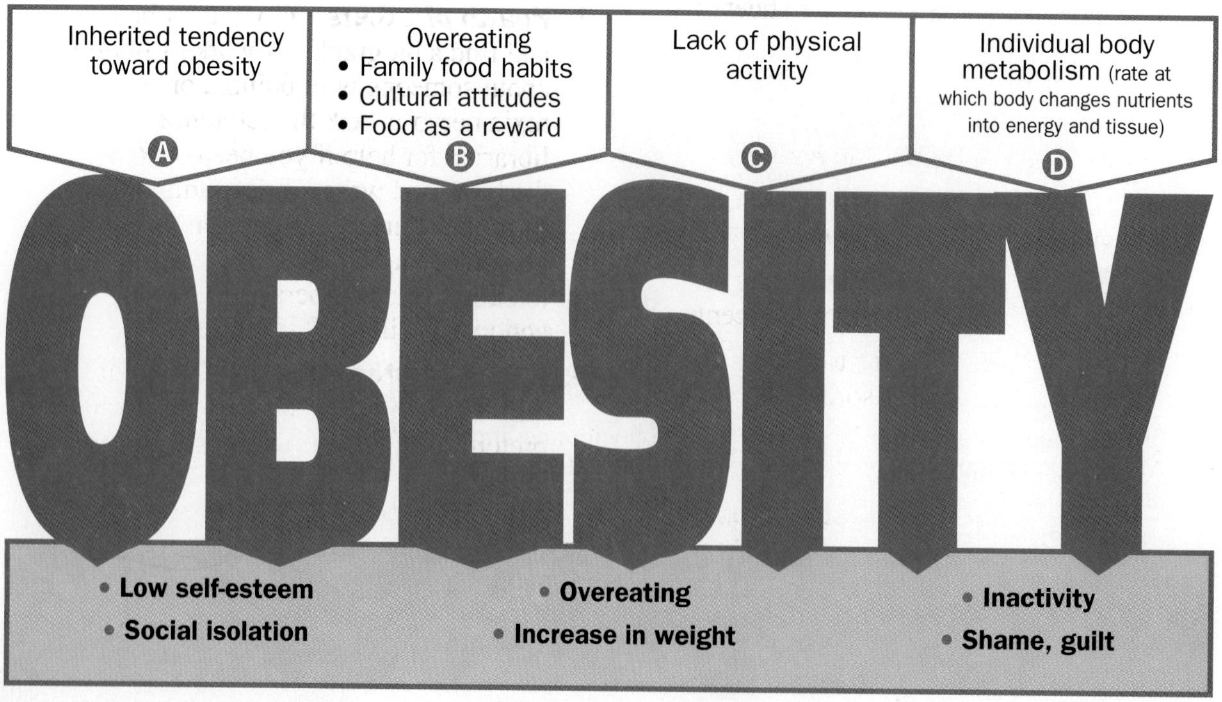

have clinics and support groups, such as Overeaters Anonymous, that can help. It may be difficult, however, to convince a person with an eating disorder, particularly someone with anorexia, to seek help. It is important that he or she get treatment, though.

Treatment and recovery is usually a long-term process. People with eating disorders need the support of family and friends to continue treatment and to remain healthy (see **Figure 9.16**).

Figure 9.16

Helping Someone with an Eating Disorder

To help a person with an eating disorder, follow these steps.

1. **Convince the person to get help.** A person with an eating disorder may not be aware of the seriousness of the condition.
2. **Tell an adult.** The school nurse, a counselor, parents, or another adult must know about the problem so that the person will get the help needed.
3. **Get professional help.** A person with an eating disorder has psychological problems and requires professional help. Sometimes other family members are also encouraged to meet with the counselor.
4. **Encourage the person to join a support group.** A support group can offer important support and encouragement to a person with an eating disorder.
5. **Recommend a follow-up.** People who are treated for eating disorders may need to return for follow-up visits to be sure that the problem does not recur.

Lesson 4 Review

Using complete sentences, answer the following questions on a separate sheet of paper.

Reviewing Terms and Facts

1. **Vocabulary** What is an *eating disorder?*
2. **Vocabulary** What is *bulimia?*
3. **Review** Name the main factors contributing to obesity in adolescents.
4. **Outline** List the steps to take to overcome an eating disorder.

Thinking Critically

5. **Analyze** What are some characteristics of people who develop anorexia nervosa?
6. **Explain** Why are people who suffer from eating disorders at risk of dying from these disorders?

Applying Health Concepts

7. **Health of Others** Go to the library and find a biography or work of fiction about someone with bulimia or anorexia nervosa. Ask the reference librarian for help if you need it. Read the book and write a brief summary of it. In your summary, focus on the person's struggle with the eating disorder. Was this person able to conquer the illness? If so, how?
8. **Health of Others** Role-play a skit with a classmate in which one of you pretends to have an eating disorder and the other is a concerned friend. The friend should convince the person with the eating disorder to seek professional help.

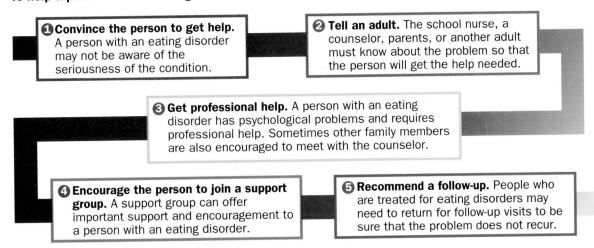

Chapter 9 Review

Chapter Summary

- **Lesson 1** Eating a healthful diet can help you look and feel your best. A healthful diet provides the right amounts of the six types of nutrients.
- **Lesson 2** The Food Guide Pyramid shows how many servings of the five basic food groups you should eat each day to ensure a balanced diet.
- **Lesson 3** Overweight or obese people are at risk of developing many more health problems than people of normal weight. Losing weight depends on burning more calories than are consumed.
- **Lesson 4** An obsession with being thin can lead to eating disorders such as anorexia nervosa and bulimia. People who have eating disorders need professional help to deal with the underlying psychological problems.

Reviewing Key Terms and Concepts

Using complete sentences, answer the following questions on a separate sheet of paper.

Lesson 1

1. Define *nutrition*.
2. What is the difference between saturated and unsaturated fats?

Lesson 2

3. What is the meaning of the term *cholesterol?*
4. Why should you limit your intake of caffeine?

Lesson 3

5. What is the meaning of the term *desired weight?*
6. What role do calories play in weight loss and gain?

Lesson 4

7. What is the main characteristic of the diet of a person with anorexia nervosa?
8. Define *malnutrition*.

Thinking Critically

Using complete sentences, answer the following questions on a separate sheet of paper.

9. **Analyze** Why would a completely nonfat diet not be a healthful diet?
10. **Apply** Explain the idea behind the Food Guide Pyramid and why its shape is so important.
11. **Evaluate** Why might nutrient-dense foods be better for a weight-loss program than other foods that are higher in fat but have the same number of calories?
12. **Hypothesize** How do current advertisements contribute to the prevalence of eating disorders among teen girls and young women in our country?

Your Action Plan

Now that you know more about planning a healthful diet, make an action plan to improve your diet.

Step 1: Choose one or two long-term goals for improving your diet. One long-term goal could be to eat a diet low in fat.

Step 2: Write down several short-term goals to reach your long-term goal. For example, you could stop drinking soft drinks or choose yogurt instead of ice cream for dessert.

Step 3: Keep track of your eating patterns so that you can check if you are meeting your goals.

When you feel that you have reached your goal, reward yourself with a fun activity.

In Your Home and Community

1. **Community Resources** Work with several classmates to draw up a list of sources of professional help available in your community for people with eating disorders. Look for support groups, counselors and psychologists, clinics, and hot lines that specialize in the treatment of eating disorders. Distribute this list at your school and other places where teens go.
2. **Health of Others** As a class, develop a skit for children in first through third grades that demonstrates the use of the Food Guide Pyramid. Have your teacher arrange for you to present your skit to a group of young children. After the skit, ask volunteers in the audience to choose foods to make up a nutritious meal.

Building Your Portfolio

1. **Body Size and Weight** Prepare a questionnaire on body size and weight. Include several open-ended questions, such as: "If you could change one part of your appearance, what would it be?" Let your classmates fill out the questionnaire anonymously. Write a paragraph summarizing and interpreting the results of your survey to add to your portfolio.
2. **Personal Assessment** Look through all the activities and projects you did for this chapter. Choose one or two that you would like to include in your portfolio.

Unit 4
Your Physical Health

Chapter 10

Wellness and Your Body Systems

Student Expectations

After reading this chapter, you should be able to:

1. List eight major body systems and describe what each one does.
2. Identify the parts of each body system and describe the job of each part.
3. Describe how to care for each of your eight body systems.
4. Identify problems that may affect each of your body systems and describe how these problems may be treated or prevented.

Teen Chat Group

Ramon: Congratulations, Troy! You ran a great race.

Troy: Thanks! I felt pretty confident that I could win it today. I felt like my whole body was working together—my mind, my arms, and my legs.

Josh: You looked like you knew what you were doing out there. How did you train?

Troy: I run every day, of course. I also think it's really important to take good care of my body. I make sure to eat the right foods and get enough sleep.

Ramon: That really makes a difference?

Troy: Sure. If I don't eat right or get enough sleep, then I don't do my best on the track.

Josh: Well, you're obviously doing something right because you sure blew away the competition!

in your journal

Read the dialogue on this page. How well do you understand your body systems? Start your private journal entries on your body systems by answering these questions:

- Do you agree with Troy that it is important to take good care of all of your body systems? Why or why not?
- What personal habits or activities might harm your body systems?
- What changes can you make in your daily routine that will help you have a healthier, better-looking body?

When you reach the end of the chapter, you will use your journal entries to make an action plan.

Lesson 1 Your Nervous System

This lesson will help you find answers to questions that teens often ask about their nervous system and how it works. For example:

- **How are my senses connected to my nervous system?**
- **Why is damage or injury to the nervous system so serious?**
- **What can I do to protect my nervous system?**

Words to Know

neuron
central nervous system (CNS)
peripheral nervous system (PNS)
brain
spinal cord
somatic system
autonomic system

The Control Center

What do brushing your teeth, riding a bicycle, and solving a math problem have in common? They all result from instructions from your body's control center—your nervous system. This complex group of specialized cells controls your thoughts and actions.

The specialized cells that make up the nervous system are called nerve cells, or **neurons** (NOO·rahns). Unlike other body cells, they cannot repair or replace themselves if they are damaged. Neurons carry messages to and from different parts of the body (see **Figure 10.1**). These messages are in the form of very weak electrical signals.

Figure 10.1
How the Nervous System Works

Neurons are more sensitive than other cells, and they work quickly. The action described here occurs in less than a few seconds.

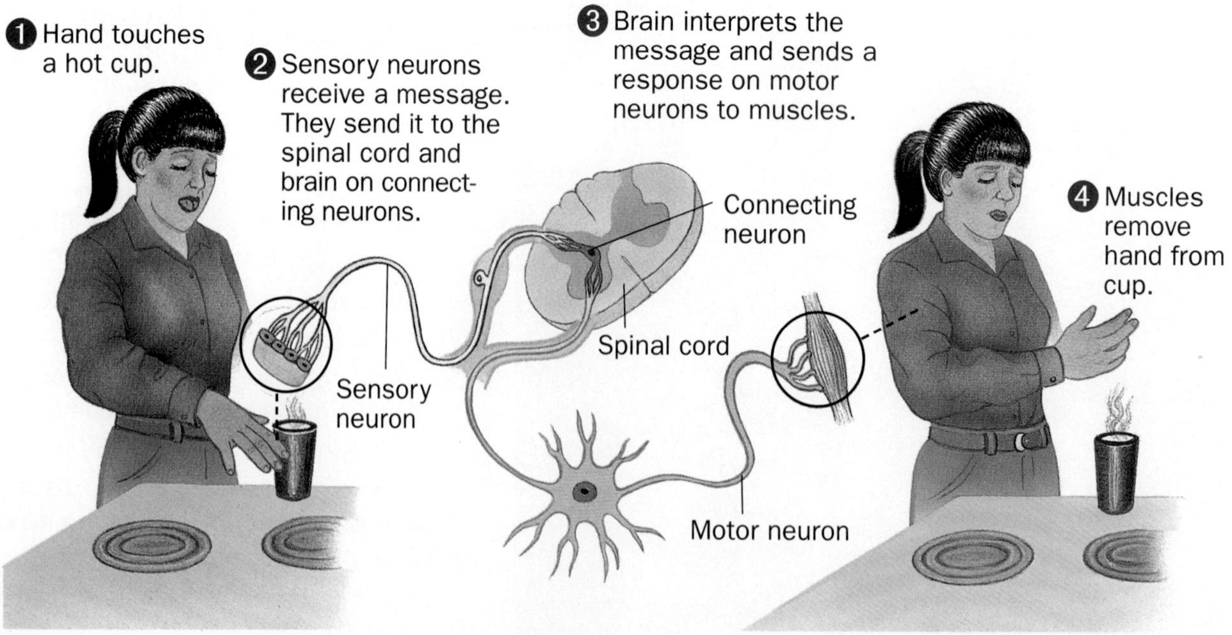

1 Hand touches a hot cup.
2 Sensory neurons receive a message. They send it to the spinal cord and brain on connecting neurons.
3 Brain interprets the message and sends a response on motor neurons to muscles.
Connecting neuron
4 Muscles remove hand from cup.
Spinal cord
Sensory neuron
Motor neuron

Parts of the Nervous System

Your nervous system consists of your brain, spinal cord, and many nerves. It is divided into two main sections (see **Figure 10.2**).

- The **central nervous system (CNS)** includes *the brain and the spinal cord.* It is your body's main control center.
- The **peripheral** (puh·RIF·uh·ruhl) **nervous system (PNS)** includes *the nerves that connect the CNS to all parts of the body.* It carries messages to and from the CNS.

interNET CONNECTION

Tap into the World Wide Web and discover the secrets to the complex workings of your body systems.

http://www.glencoe.com/sec/health

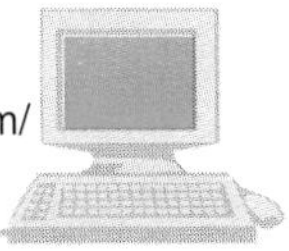

Figure 10.2

The Nervous System

The nervous system controls all of your body's actions. The central nervous system (yellow) and the peripheral nervous system (blue) work together. Shown here are 31 pairs of spinal nerves that branch off from the spinal cord. Each pair serves a particular part of the body.

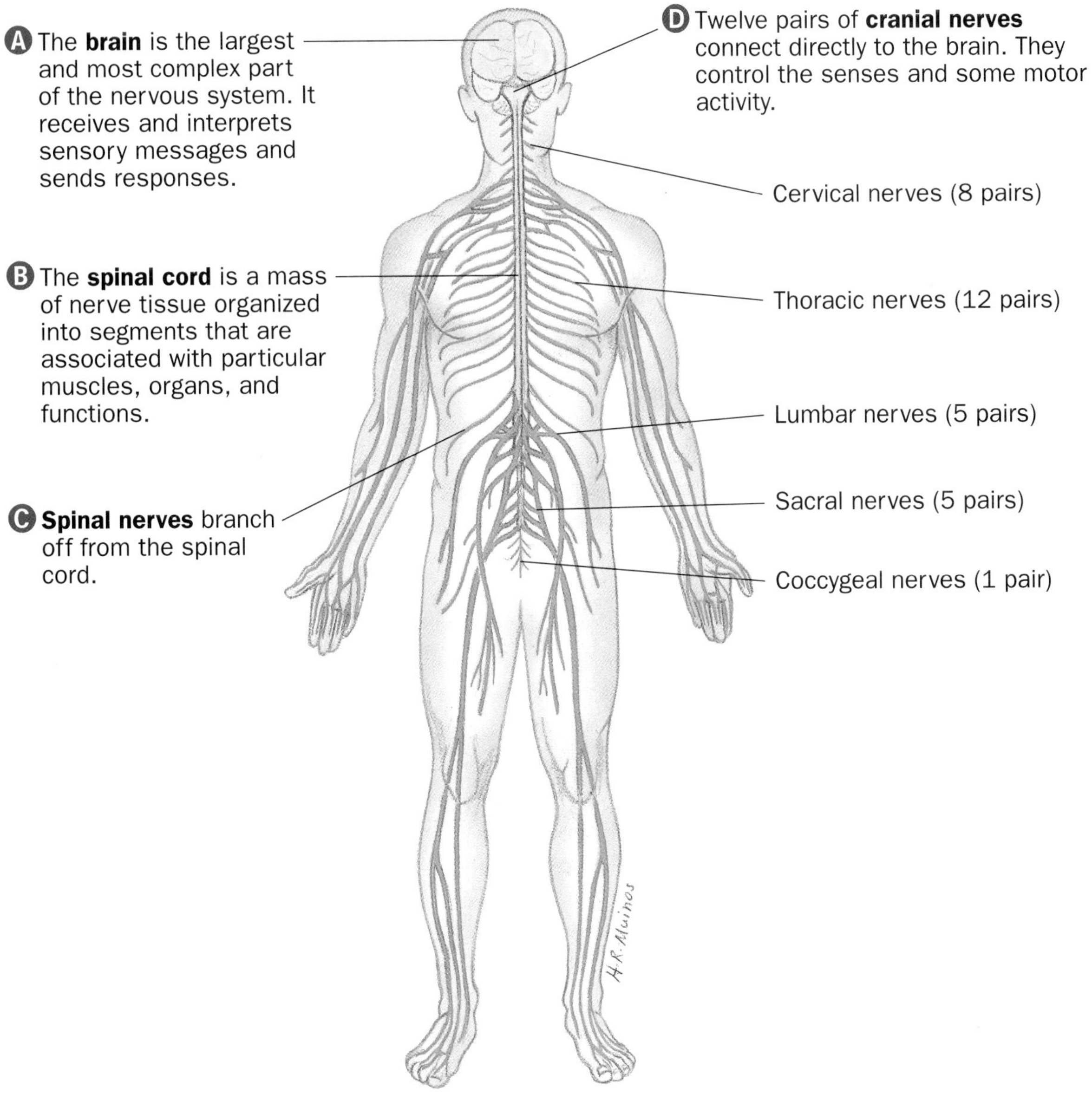

A The **brain** is the largest and most complex part of the nervous system. It receives and interprets sensory messages and sends responses.
B The **spinal cord** is a mass of nerve tissue organized into segments that are associated with particular muscles, organs, and functions.
C **Spinal nerves** branch off from the spinal cord.
D Twelve pairs of **cranial nerves** connect directly to the brain. They control the senses and some motor activity.
Cervical nerves (8 pairs)
Thoracic nerves (12 pairs)
Lumbar nerves (5 pairs)
Sacral nerves (5 pairs)
Coccygeal nerves (1 pair)
H.R. Muinos

The Central Nervous System

The central nervous system (CNS) controls your body's actions. These actions are divided into two types—voluntary and involuntary. Voluntary actions are those that you control, such as walking and smiling. Involuntary actions are those that you cannot control, such as the beating of your heart.

The CNS consists of your brain and spinal cord. Neurons carry messages back and forth between the CNS and nerves found in all parts of your body.

- The **brain** is *the mass of neurons that controls all actions, emotions, thoughts, and memory.* It is made up of about 10 billion neurons and weighs about 3 pounds. Blood vessels cover your brain, carrying the food and oxygen it needs to work. Your brain is well protected. It is encased in the bones of your skull. It is also suspended in a fluid, which serves as a shock absorber.
- The **spinal cord** is *a long bundle of neurons that extends almost the entire length of the body.* It plays an important role. The spinal cord *relays messages from all parts of the body to the brain and from the brain to muscles and glands.* Your spinal cord, which is less than 2 feet long and about the same diameter as your index finger, is protected by your backbone.

Figure 10.3 shows the three main parts of the brain, the *cerebrum* (suh·REE·bruhm), the *cerebellum* (ser·uh·BE·luhm), and the *brain stem.* Each of these parts controls many important body actions. Also shown are the *meninges,* which protect the CNS.

Did You Know?

Taking Sides

The brain is divided into two halves, or hemispheres. The right side of your brain controls the left side of your body. The left side of your brain controls the right side of your body. The left side of the brain of a right-handed person is more dominant than the right side.

LIFE SKILLS

Caring for Your Body Systems

Think of your body as a complex machine made up of several simpler machines. In this case, the simpler machines are your body systems. For the body to function properly, all of its systems must be healthy and in good working order. You can play an important part in keeping the body systems at their best by making healthy choices.

- **Rest.** Get plenty of rest. Your body parts work hard, and you need the proper amount of rest to keep them in good working order.
- **Exercise.** Regular exercise strengthens your heart and muscles, and helps keep the lungs working well. Exercise also helps bones grow properly.
- **Diet.** Food is the fuel that provides energy for all the cells in your body. Eat meals at regular times each day. Choose foods wisely. Eat a balanced diet and avoid foods that are high in fat, cholesterol, and salt. Keep your weight at a level that is right for you.
- **Stress.** Reduce your level of stress when you can. Stress that goes on too long or happens too often can harm your body. Try to think and plan ahead, and learn to relax.

Figure 10.3
The Brain

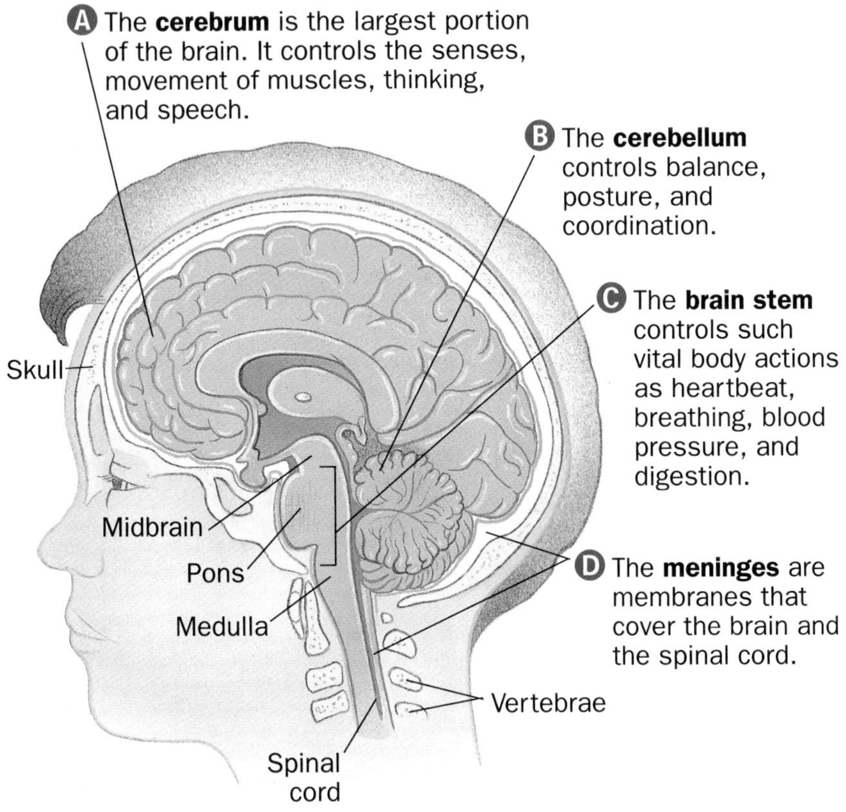

A The **cerebrum** is the largest portion of the brain. It controls the senses, movement of muscles, thinking, and speech.
B The **cerebellum** controls balance, posture, and coordination.
C The **brain stem** controls such vital body actions as heartbeat, breathing, blood pressure, and digestion.
D The **meninges** are membranes that cover the brain and the spinal cord.
Skull
Midbrain
Pons
Medulla
Vertebrae
Spinal cord

in your journal

Write two column headings in your journal—voluntary and involuntary. Define each one and list several activities that you carry out in the next few hours in each column. Find out which part of the brain controls each activity listed.

- **Smoking.** Say no to smoking. Cigarette smoke harms the nose, throat, and lungs. It reduces the ability of red blood cells to carry oxygen. Smoking can also lead to cancer and heart disease.
- **Drugs.** Don't use drugs, including alcohol. Drugs affect nerve cells and can damage or destroy brain cells. Damage to the nervous system cannot be undone.

Follow-up Activity

Nobody is perfect. We can all do better at making healthy choices. Which of the areas listed above do you need to work on most? Plan and carry out healthy actions in that area. Then tackle other areas on which you need to work.

The Peripheral Nervous System

The peripheral nervous system (PNS) is made up of many nerves that connect the CNS to all parts of your body. Peripheral nerves carry messages to and from your muscles or various body organs. With this system, the brain is able to control the body.

The PNS has two main parts. One part, called the **somatic** (soh·MA·tik) **system,** *deals with actions that you control.* The second part, the **autonomic** (aw·tuh·NAH·mik) **system,** *deals with actions you do not usually control.* Such actions include your heartbeat, breathing, and digestion.

Did You Know?

Speedy Messenger Service

Nearly 45 miles of nerves run through your body. They receive and send the messages that control all your body's movements and processes. These messages travel as fast as 248 miles an hour.

Problems of the Nervous System

Figure 10.4 describes several diseases and disorders of the nervous system. Some can be prevented; others cannot. However, treatment and therapy can help people who have these problems.

Figure 10.4

Diseases and Disorders of the Nervous System

Disease or Disorder	Description	Treatment or Prevention
Infections		
Polio	Caused by a virus; can result in paralysis (inability to use muscles)	Vaccination
Rabies	Caused by a virus transmitted by bite of infected animal; may be fatal if untreated	Series of shots; avoid contact with strange animals
Meningitis	Inflammation of the membranes that cover the brain and spinal column	Vaccine; antibiotics
Structural Disorders		
Brain tumor	Uncontrolled cell growth; may be cancerous	Surgery; additional treatment
Head injury	Caused by a blow to the head; blood collects in damaged area and may cause pressure	Rest; surgery if necessary
Spinal cord Injury	Results in paralysis of a part or most of the body	Physical therapy
Seizure Disorder		
Epilepsy	Brain disorder that causes uncontrollable muscle activity	Controlled by medication
Degenerative Disorders		
Cerebral palsy	Caused by damage or injury to the cerebrum; symptoms may vary	No cure; therapy can help victims live active lives
Multiple sclerosis	Caused by damage to protective outer coating of some nerves; symptoms may vary, but become progressively worse with time	No cure; medication and therapy can help somewhat in the early stages

Nervous System Injuries

Injuries are the most common cause of damage to the nervous system. Blows to the head can damage the brain. The most common and mildest form of brain injury is a concussion, which temporarily disturbs brain function. Injuries to the neck or back can cause spinal cord damage. Such damage can result in partial, or even total, paralysis. A pinched nerve happens when one part of the spine is displaced by a sudden movement or blow and presses on a nerve. Such injuries can be very painful.

Most injuries result from accidents or carelessness. You can prevent them by acting safely and wearing protective gear when necessary, as shown in **Figure 10.5.**

Teen Issues

It's the Law ACTIVITY!

The number of people who enjoy bicycling, skateboarding, and in-line skating is large. Many state and local agencies have passed laws requiring the use of helmets and other safety gear. Organize a class debate to discuss the issue.

Figure 10.5
How to Avoid Injuries

Avoid neck and back injuries. Be sure to take all necessary precautions and use common sense when diving and lifting.

Wear a helmet. When you are bicycling, skateboarding, or playing a contact sport, always wear a helmet.

Wear a safety belt. Whenever you are in a moving vehicle, fasten your safety belt.

Obey all traffic safety rules. Whether you are in a car, on a bicycle, or just walking, obey all traffic rules.

Review — Lesson 1

Using complete sentences, answer the following questions on a separate sheet of paper.

Reviewing Terms and Facts

1. **Vocabulary** Define the *somatic* and *autonomic systems.*
2. **List** Identify four ways to avoid injury.

Thinking Critically

3. **Analyze** What takes place in the nervous system when you catch a ball?
4. **Hypothesize** Why do spinal cord injuries often result in paralysis?

Applying Health Concepts

5. **Health of Others** Volunteer to work at a hospital or clinic helping people with nervous system injuries or disorders. Give a talk to your class about your experiences and how they add to your understanding of the problems of the nervous system.
6. **Personal Health** Think about how many health choices involve forming good habits. In the library, read about the part played by the nervous system in habit formation. Then write an answer to this question: Why is forming a habit often difficult at first but easier as you keep trying?

Lesson 2

Your Circulatory System

This lesson will help you find answers to questions that teens often ask about their circulatory system. For example:

- **How does my heart work?**
- **Why does the doctor check my pulse and blood pressure when I have a physical examination?**
- **What is my blood type and why is it important?**

Words to Know

circulatory system
cardiovascular system
arteries
veins
capillaries

The Transport System

The **circulatory** (SER·kyuh·luh·tohr·ee) **system** is your body's transport system. The circulatory system *keeps the body working well by delivering essential materials to body cells and removing waste materials from the cells.* This body system is also known as the **cardiovascular** (KAR·dee·oh·VAS·kyoo·ler) **system.**

How the Circulatory System Works

The blood carries various substances throughout your circulatory system (see **Figure 10.6**). Different organs of the body serve as transfer stations. At some stations, blood picks up needed nutrients and other materials and delivers them to the cells. Blood also picks up waste products and carries them to other transfer stations, where they are removed from the body.

Figure 10.6
How the Circulatory System Works

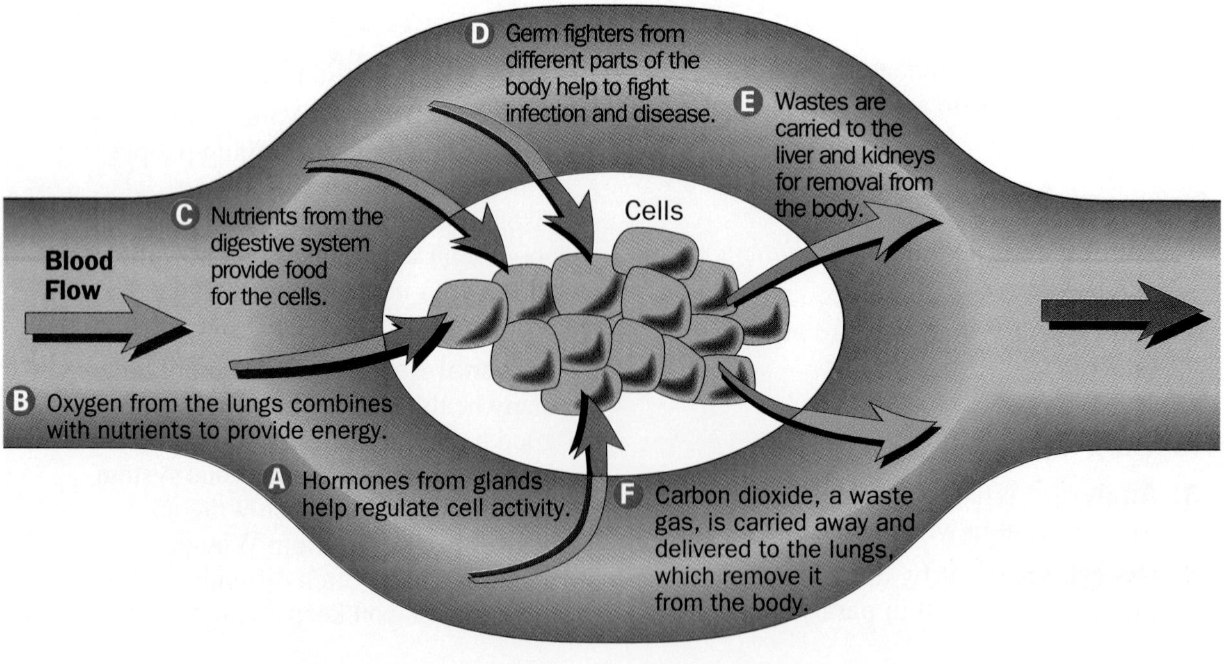

D Germ fighters from different parts of the body help to fight infection and disease.
E Wastes are carried to the liver and kidneys for removal from the body.
Cells
C Nutrients from the digestive system provide food for the cells.
Blood Flow
B Oxygen from the lungs combines with nutrients to provide energy.
A Hormones from glands help regulate cell activity.
F Carbon dioxide, a waste gas, is carried away and delivered to the lungs, which remove it from the body.

Parts of the Circulatory System

Your circulatory system includes your heart, blood vessels, and blood. Your heart is a pump that moves blood in two major pathways—pulmonary circulation and systemic circulation. **Figure 10.7** shows the two pathways.

Did You Know?

A Demanding Organ

The heart uses more nutrients and oxygen than any other organ in the body.

Figure 10.7
The Circulatory System

Systemic circulation **moves blood to all the body tissues except the lungs.** ***Pulmonary circulation*** **is the flow of blood from the heart to the lungs and back to the heart. In these drawings, red represents oxygen-rich blood, and blue represents blood containing carbon dioxide.**

Ⓐ Your **heart** is divided into four chambers. Each upper chamber is called an **atrium** (AY·tree·uhm), and each lower chamber is called a **ventricle** (VEN·tri·kuhl). **Valves** open and close to control the flow of blood in a one-way direction through your heart.

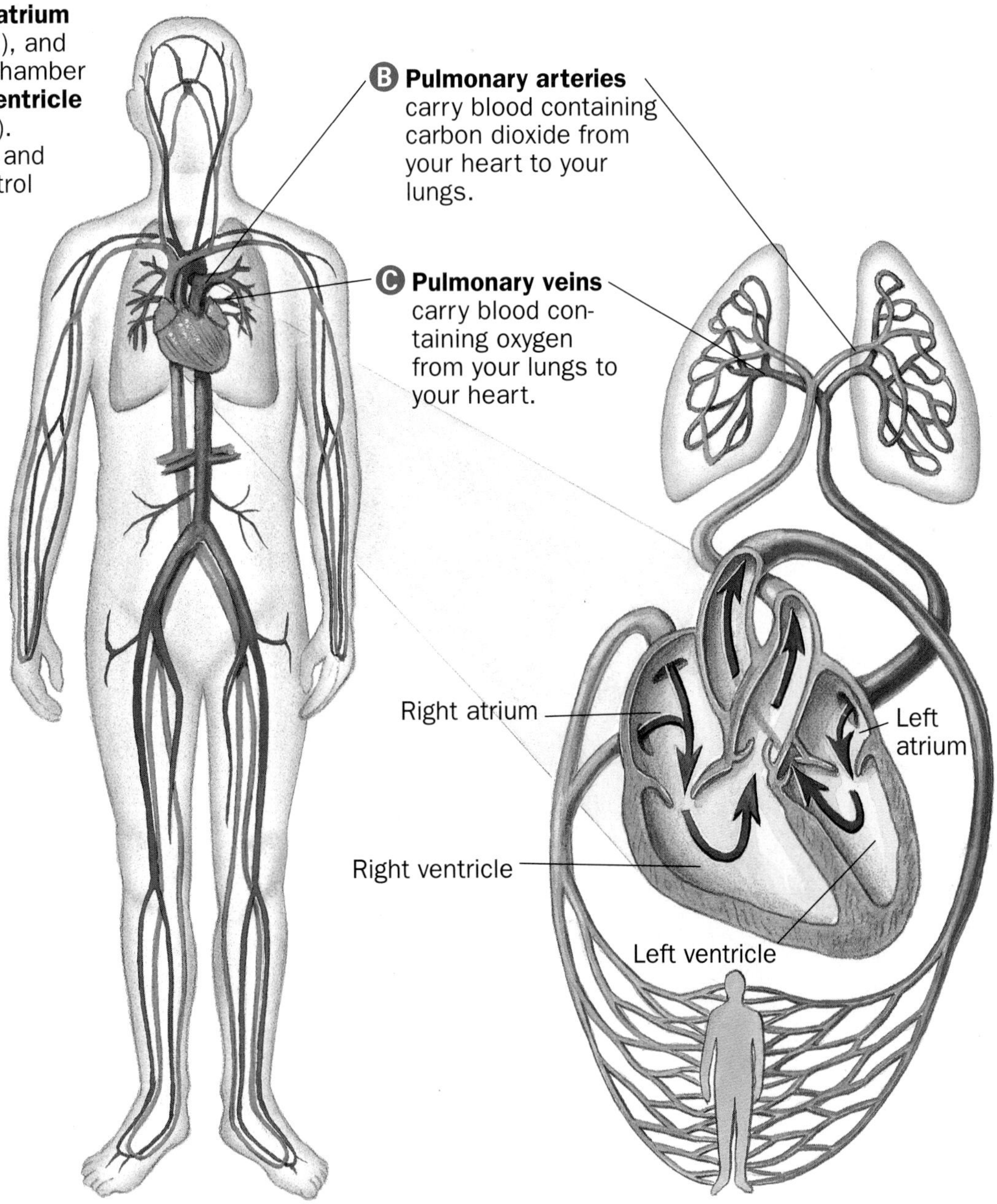

Ⓑ Pulmonary arteries carry blood containing carbon dioxide from your heart to your lungs.
Ⓒ Pulmonary veins carry blood containing oxygen from your lungs to your heart.
Right atrium
Left atrium
Right ventricle
Left ventricle

The Blood

Blood is a mixture of solids in a large amount of liquid called *plasma* (PLAZ·ma). Plasma is about 92 percent water. The solids are red blood cells, white blood cells, and *platelets* (PLAYT·luhts). **Figure 10.8** describes the role of each part of the blood.

Figure 10.8

The Parts of the Blood

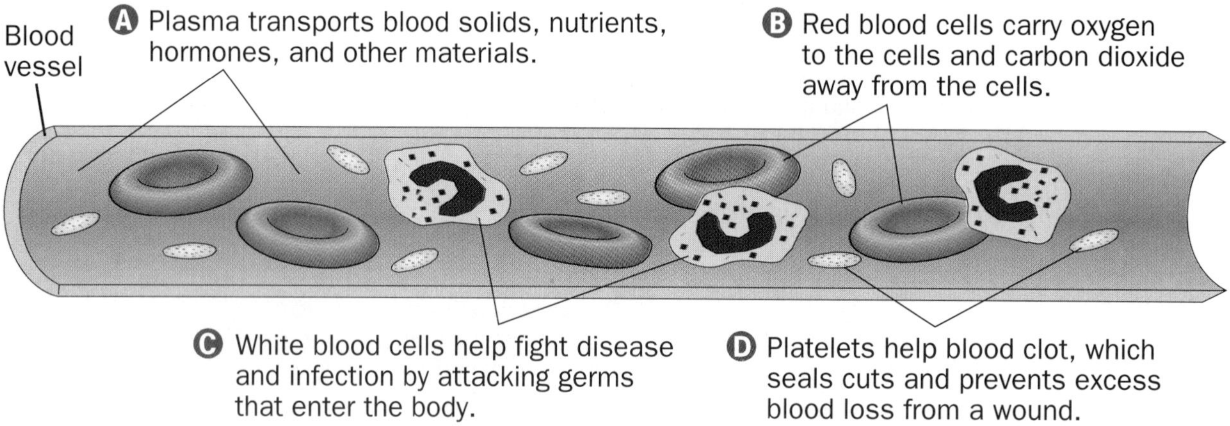

Blood vessel
A Plasma transports blood solids, nutrients, hormones, and other materials.
B Red blood cells carry oxygen to the cells and carbon dioxide away from the cells.
C White blood cells help fight disease and infection by attacking germs that enter the body.
D Platelets help blood clot, which seals cuts and prevents excess blood loss from a wound.

Blood Types

Blood is essential to life. Sometimes people lose some of their blood during surgical procedures or in accidents. If you lose too much blood, you will die. Fortunately, doctors can replace lost blood with blood from another person. Such a procedure is called a blood transfusion (trans·FYOO·zhuhn).

Your blood is not the same as everyone else's. In fact, there are four major blood types: A, B, AB, and O. Your type depends on the presence or absence of certain substances in the blood. For a transfusion to be successful, the blood from the person giving the blood, the donor, must mix safely with the blood of the person receiving it. Mixing certain blood types can have serious side effects. These include high fevers, difficulty breathing, and even death.

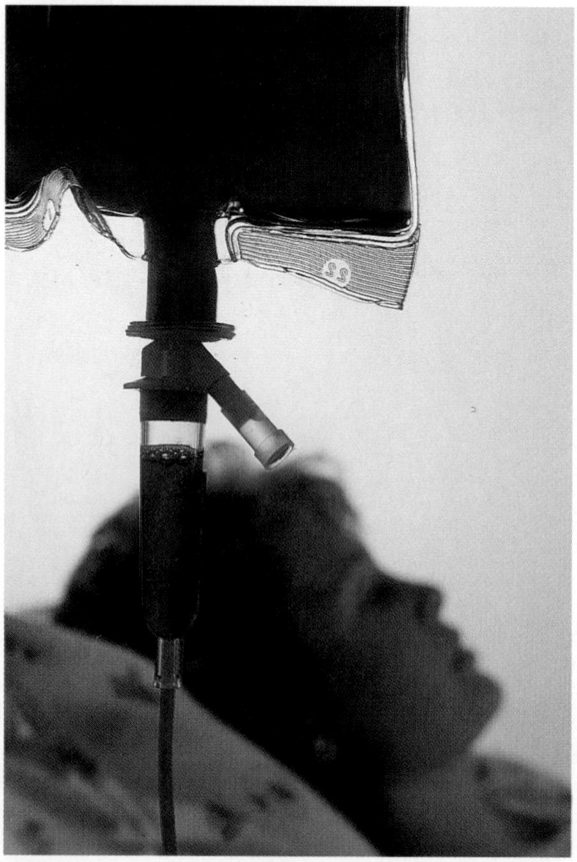

Before giving a transfusion, hospitals take extreme care in checking blood types.

Doctors must consider another factor, called the *Rh factor,* before a transfusion. Most people are positive for this factor, or Rh+, meaning that their blood contains the factor. The rest are negative for the factor, or Rh–. Their blood does not contain the Rh factor.

Q&A

What's My Blood Type?

Q: How can I find out my blood type?

A: Blood can be tested for type in a doctor's office.

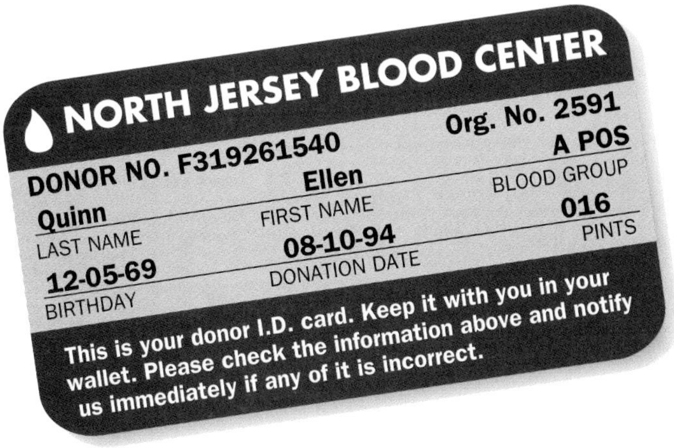
NORTH JERSEY BLOOD CENTER
Org. No. 2591
DONOR NO. F319261540
A POS
BLOOD GROUP
Quinn
LAST NAME
Ellen
FIRST NAME
016
PINTS
12-05-69
BIRTHDAY
08-10-94
DONATION DATE
This is your donor I.D. card. Keep it with you in your wallet. Please check the information above and notify us immediately if any of it is incorrect.

Adults who give blood usually receive a blood donor card that gives their name, blood type, and the number of pints donated.

Blood Banks

People who are old enough and in good health can give the gift of life—their blood. Every day, thousands of people donate blood to the Red Cross and other charitable organizations. This blood is stored in blood banks for use when needed.

Many people are concerned about the safety of blood stored in blood banks. Only people in good health are allowed to give blood. A new needle is used every time blood is taken and every time someone receives blood. All donated blood is tested for a variety of diseases, including HIV. Blood that fails the tests is discarded.

Teen Issues

Personal Savings ACTIVITY!

Concern about the safety of blood stored in blood banks has led many people to donate their own blood to be stored for personal use at some later date. How do you feel about this practice? Write a paragraph to explain your feelings.

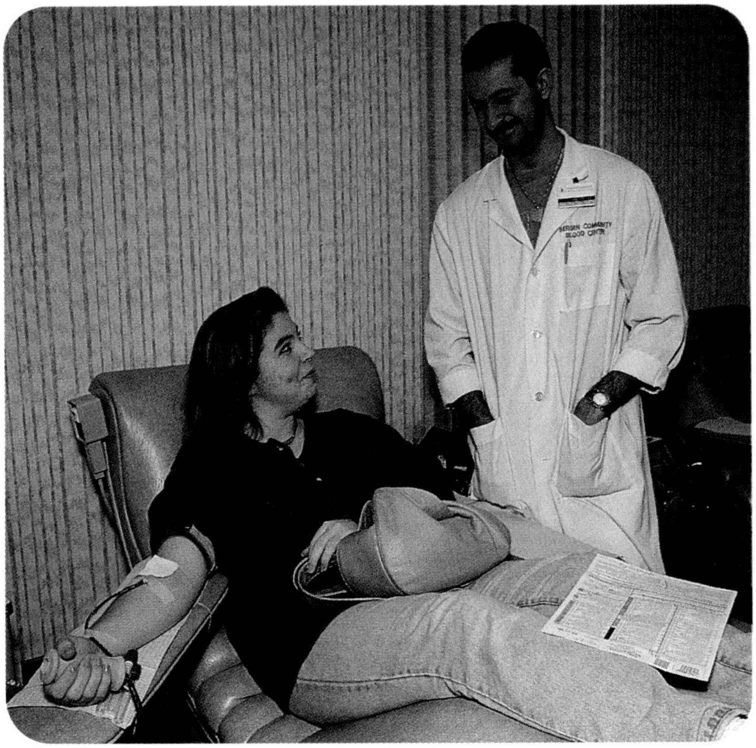

Adults who give blood are not at risk for contracting diseases of the blood.

Your Blood Vessels

Over 80,000 miles of blood vessels move your blood throughout your body. There are three types of blood vessels.

- **Arteries** (AR·tuh·reez) *carry blood away from the heart.*
- **Veins** (VAYNZ) are *the blood vessels that carry blood from the body back to the heart.*
- **Capillaries** (KAP·uh·lehr·eez) are *tiny tubes that carry blood from the arteries to the body's cells and from cells to the veins.*

in your journal

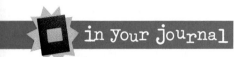

Does someone you know have one of the diseases listed in Figure 10.10? In your private journal, describe his or her symptoms and treatment.

Cultural Connections

Sickle-Cell Anemia

Sickle-cell anemia is an inherited condition that affects the ability of blood to circulate properly. The condition is found mainly among people whose cultural roots are in Africa, India, and Mediterranean and Middle Eastern countries.

Blood Pressure

As blood moves through your body, it exerts pressure against the walls of blood vessels. This is called *blood pressure.* **Figure 10.9** explains how blood pressure is measured.

Health professionals use an instrument called a sphygmomanometer (sfig·mo·muh·NAH·muh·ter) to measure blood pressure. They wrap a soft, rubbery cuff around your upper arm and inflate it until it is tight enough to stop the flow of blood. The air is gradually deflated until, through a stethoscope, they can hear blood flowing through your arm. This maximum amount of pressure is called systolic pressure. The cuff is then deflated until blood flows steadily, giving a reading of the diastolic, or lowest, pressure.

Figure 10.9

Measuring Blood Pressure

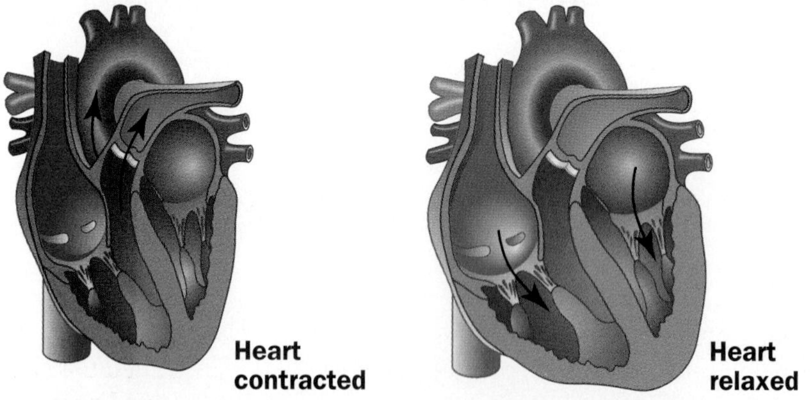

A As the ventricles of your heart contract to push the blood into your arteries, the pressure is at its highest point (systolic pressure).

B As the heart relaxes to refill, the pressure is at its lowest point (diastolic pressure).

Problems of the Circulatory System

Figure 10.10 gives information about some problems of the circulatory system. Those that affect the heart or blood vessels are known as *cardiovascular disorders.* Other circulatory problems affect the blood itself.

Figure 10.10

Diseases and Disorders of the Circulatory System

Disease or Disorder	Description	Treatment or Prevention
Hypertension (high blood pressure)	Blood pressure higher than normal for a long time; can lead to heart attack, stroke, kidney failure	Reduce stress; change diet to reduce intake of sodium, fats, and cholesterol; medication; regular checkups
Stroke	Cluster of blood cells blocks blood vessel in brain	Same as for hypertension
Heart attack	Stoppage in flow of blood to heart	Same as for hypertension
Arteriosclerosis	Artery walls harden; caused by diet high in fat and cholesterol	Same as for hypertension
Anemia	Lack of red blood cells or cells that do not carry enough oxygen; causes weakness, low energy	Iron supplements; rest
Sickle-cell anemia	Blood unable to circulate properly	Blood transfusions and medication
Mononucleosis	Viral infection; symptoms are sore throat, swollen glands, and fatigue	Bed rest and a well-balanced diet
Leukemia	Abnormal white blood cells	Medication; radiation
Hemophilia	Blood does not clot properly	Transfusions of blood-clotting factors

Review

Lesson 2

Using complete sentences, answer the following questions on a separate sheet of paper.

Reviewing Terms and Facts

1. **Vocabulary** What are *arteries, veins,* and *capillaries?* Explain their functions.
2. **Recall** Identify the three solids that make up blood. What is the liquid portion of blood called?

Thinking Critically

3. **Review** What steps are taken to make sure that donated blood is safe?
4. **Suggest** Why is high blood pressure called the silent killer? How can high blood pressure be detected before it leads to serious health problems?

Applying Health Concepts

5. **Consumer Health** Do research to find out how the following substances in food affect your circulatory system: salt, fats, and cholesterol. Prepare a brief paper on the information to present to the class.

Lesson 3

Your Respiratory System

This lesson will help you find answers to questions that teens often ask about their respiratory system. For example:

- **Why is breathing so important to staying alive?**
- **What does smoking do to my respiratory system?**

Words to Know

respiratory system
epiglottis
trachea
bronchi
diaphragm
alveoli

The Breath of Life

Did you know that you can live only a few minutes without air? Air contains oxygen, a gas your body needs to maintain life. Breathing—inhaling and exhaling—is carried out by your **respiratory system.** This system consists of *the organs that provide the body with a continuous supply of oxygen and rid the body of carbon dioxide.* **Figure 10.11** shows the important parts of the respiratory system and tells what each part does.

Figure 10.11

The Respiratory System

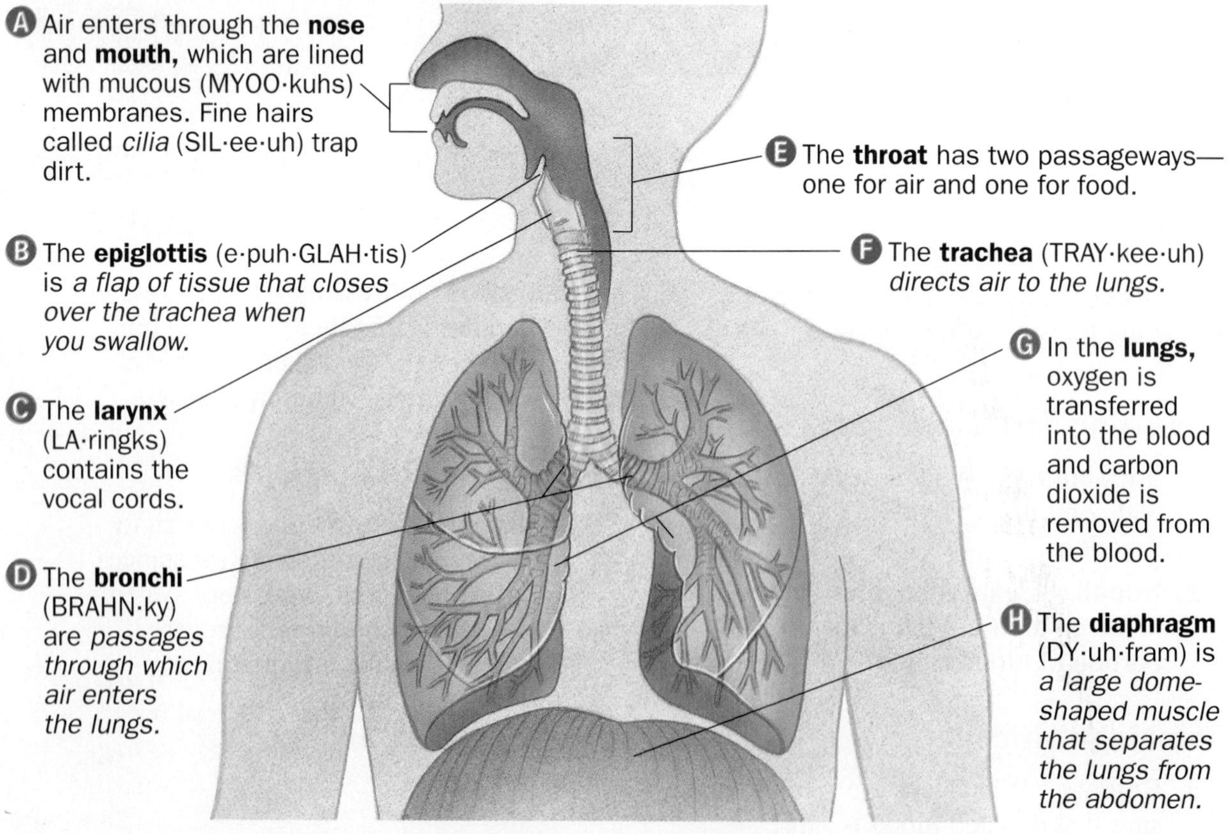

A Air enters through the **nose** and **mouth,** which are lined with mucous (MYOO·kuhs) membranes. Fine hairs called *cilia* (SIL·ee·uh) trap dirt.
B The **epiglottis** (e·puh·GLAH·tis) is *a flap of tissue that closes over the trachea when you swallow.*
C The **larynx** (LA·ringks) contains the vocal cords.
D The **bronchi** (BRAHN·ky) are *passages through which air enters the lungs.*
E The **throat** has two passageways—one for air and one for food.
F The **trachea** (TRAY·kee·uh) *directs air to the lungs.*
G In the **lungs,** oxygen is transferred into the blood and carbon dioxide is removed from the blood.
H The **diaphragm** (DY·uh·fram) is *a large dome-shaped muscle that separates the lungs from the abdomen.*

How the Respiratory System Works

The respiratory system has two important jobs. First, it supplies oxygen to the blood. This oxygen is carried to all cells of the body. In the cells, oxygen combines with nutrients to provide the energy the cells need to do their jobs. When oxygen combines with nutrients, the waste gas carbon dioxide is produced. The second job of the respiratory system is to remove carbon dioxide from the blood and release it outside the body.

How Breathing Works

Breathing consists of two actions—inhaling and exhaling. When you inhale, you bring in air from outside your body. When you exhale, you release air to the outside. The air you exhale contains more carbon dioxide and less oxygen than the air you inhale. **Figure 10.12** shows what happens when you breathe. The exchange of oxygen for carbon dioxide takes place inside your lungs. For this reason, the lungs are the most important organs of your respiratory system.

in Your Journal

Do you breathe more with your rib muscles or with your diaphragm? To find out, place your hand just beneath your rib cage and breathe normally. Can you feel your chest rise or fall? If so, you are mainly a rib breather. For more healthful breathing, strengthen your diaphragm muscle by using good posture and by exercising. In your journal, write a plan for doing so.

Figure 10.12
The Action of Breathing

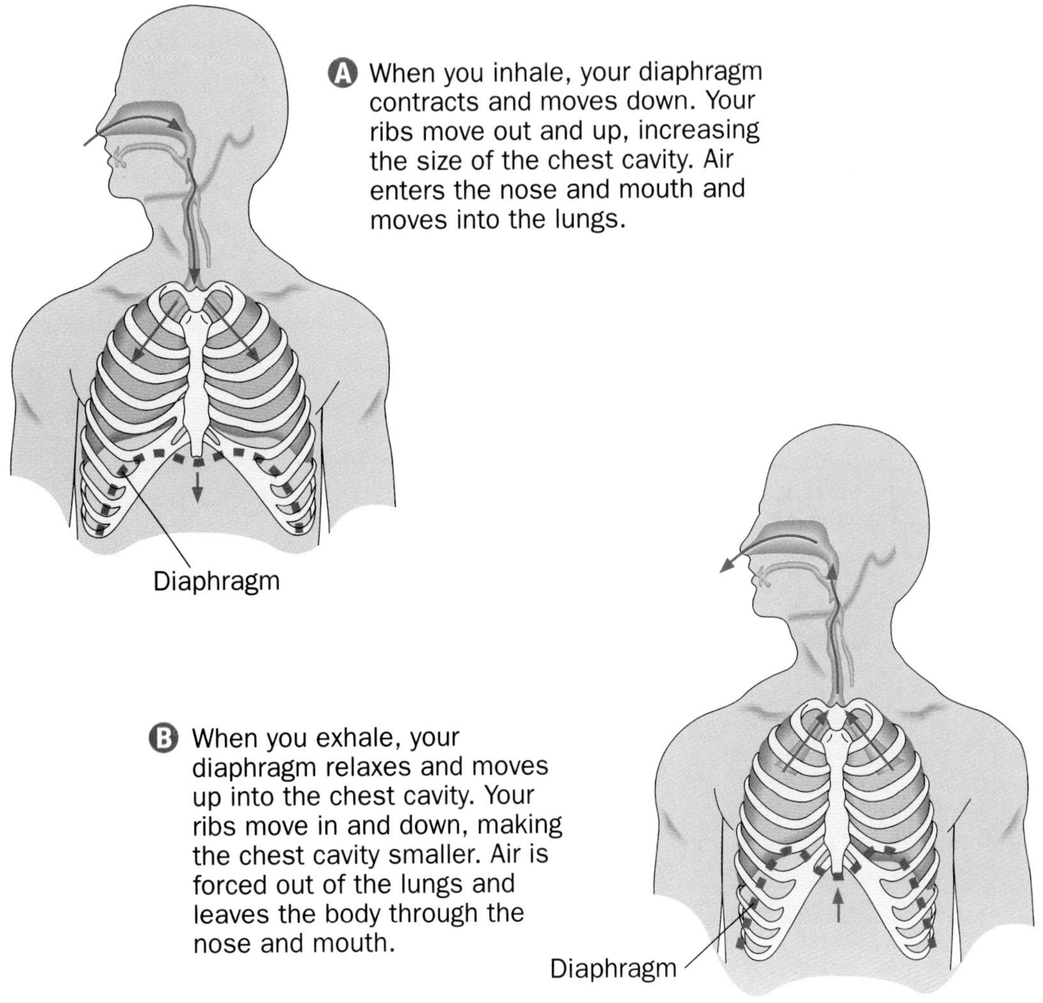
A When you inhale, your diaphragm contracts and moves down. Your ribs move out and up, increasing the size of the chest cavity. Air enters the nose and mouth and moves into the lungs.
Diaphragm
B When you exhale, your diaphragm relaxes and moves up into the chest cavity. Your ribs move in and down, making the chest cavity smaller. Air is forced out of the lungs and leaves the body through the nose and mouth.
Diaphragm

What Happens in the Lungs?

Your lungs consist of clusters of *microscopic air sacs* called **alveoli** (al·vee·OH·ly). These sacs are at the ends of the smallest branches of the bronchi. **Figure 10.13** shows how oxygen and carbon dioxide are exchanged in the alveoli.

Problems of the Respiratory System

The respiratory system is a common site of infection because germs can easily enter the body through your nose and mouth. **Figure 10.14** lists some of the problems of the respiratory system. Bronchitis, emphysema, and lung cancer have been linked to smoking. The best way to prevent them is to not smoke.

Figure 10.13

The Exchange of Oxygen and Carbon Dioxide

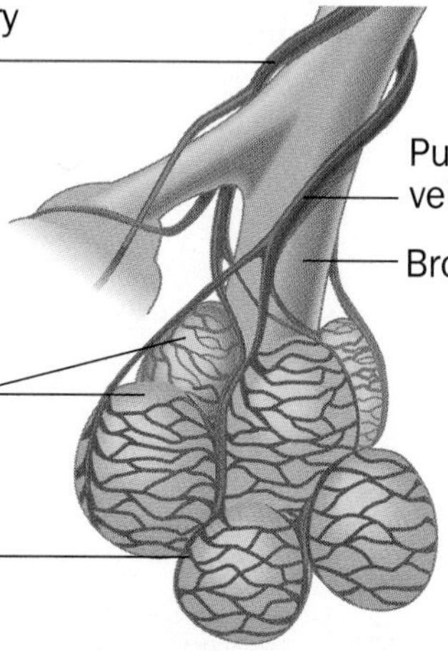

Ⓐ Blood from the heart enters the lungs through the pulmonary arteries and capillaries. This blood contains carbon dioxide from the body's cells.

Ⓑ Carbon dioxide passes from the blood into the alveoli where it is exchanged for oxygen.

Ⓒ Oxygen passes from the alveoli into the capillaries, where it is picked up by the blood and carried back to the heart through the pulmonary veins.

MAKING HEALTHY DECISIONS

Choosing Health

All during Lenny's school years, he and several close friends did everything together. Then the unthinkable happened.

Last year, Lenny and his family had to move to another part of the country. The move was temporary, though, and after a year the family moved back.

Lenny now had a problem. His friends had taken up smoking. They urged him to smoke, too.

Lenny was confused. He enjoyed being with his friends. He knew smoking was bad for his health, but he felt uncomfortable being one of the nonsmokers. He also knew that for anyone under the age of 18, buying cigarettes was illegal. He decided to use the step-by-step decision-making process to make up his mind.

1. **State the situation**
2. **List the options**
3. **Weigh the possible outcomes**
4. **Consider your values**
5. **Make a decision and act**
6. **Evaluate the decision**

Follow-up Activities

1. Apply the six steps of the decision-making process to Lenny's situation.
2. Along with several other class members, role-play a scene in which Lenny decides not to smoke. Have him use his refusal skills.

Figure 10.14

Problems of the Respiratory System

Disease or Disorder	Description	Treatment or Prevention
Flu/Colds	Caused by virus; cough, runny nose, aches, fever	Bed rest and fluids; flu vaccine can prevent some types
Tuberculosis	Bacterial lung infection; dry cough in early stages, chest pain later	Medication
Allergies	Sneezing, itchy eyes, runny nose, hives; caused by reaction to substances	Antihistamines may relieve symptoms; avoid contact with irritating substances
Pneumonia	Lung infection by bacteria or viruses; fever, chest pain, difficulty breathing	Antibiotics for bacterial type; bed rest for viral type
Bronchitis	Swelling of the bronchi due to infection; cough, fever, tightness in chest	No known cure; symptoms usually disappear after time
Asthma	Bronchial swelling and blockage; wheezing, short breath, coughing	No known cure; medication to reduce swelling
Emphysema	Alveoli destroyed; extreme difficulty breathing; often fatal	No known cure; pure oxygen to ease breathing
Lung cancer	Alveoli destroyed; often caused by smoking	Low survival rate; surgery, radiation, chemotherapy

Review

Lesson 3

Using complete sentences, answer the following questions on a separate sheet of paper.

Reviewing Terms and Facts

1. **Vocabulary** Define the term *trachea*. Use it in an original sentence.
2. **Recall** Why are respiratory infections so common?

Thinking Critically

3. **Explain** What happens when you inhale? What happens when you exhale?
4. **List** Make a list of all the reasons you can think of for not smoking.

Applying Health Concepts

5. **Consumer Health** Conduct a survey of your class about smoking. Ask each student to give reasons why one should or should not smoke. Present the results of your survey to the class.
6. **Health of Others** Record an interview with a person who has breathing problems, asthma, or allergies. Ask the person to tell what brings on the problem and to describe how he or she feels during an attack. Ask what actions he or she takes to bring the attack under control. Ask permission to present your taped interview to the class.

Lesson 4

Your Skeletal System

This lesson will help you find answers to questions that teens often ask about their skeletal system. For example:

- **Do bones have other jobs in the body besides supporting it and giving it shape?**
- **If bones are hard and inflexible, how is movement possible?**
- **What is the difference between a sprain and a fracture?**

Words to Know

skeletal system
cartilage
joint
ligament
tendon

The Body's Framework

All structures need some sort of framework to give them strength and shape. Your body's framework, which is called the **skeletal system,** is *a system made up of bones, joints, and connecting tissue.* **Figure 10.15.A** shows the skeletal system. In addition to supporting your body, it allows movement and protects your internal organs. It also produces red and white blood cells in the marrow, the center part, of your long bones. **Figure 10.15.B** shows two kinds of marrow in a long bone.

The Bones

Your skeleton consists of bone and **cartilage** (KAR·tuhl·ij), which is *a strong, flexible tissue that provides cushioning at your joints.* When you were a baby, your skeleton was mostly cartilage. As your body grew, the cartilage was replaced by bone.

Bones are living tissue composed of cells. Like all body cells, bone cells need food and oxygen to grow, strengthen, work, and repair themselves. Providing a framework for your body is just one job of your bones. They do many important jobs.

- **Movement.** Bones provide points of attachment for muscles. Body parts, such as your arms and your legs, move when muscles pull on bones.
- **Support.** Your backbone is made up of 24 bones called vertebrae (VER·tuh·bray). The backbone supports your head and upper body and protects your spinal cord.
- **Protection.** The bones of your skull protect your brain. Your ribs protect your lungs and heart from injury.
- **Blood cell formation.** Bones play a role in your circulatory system, too. Red and white blood cells are formed by tissue called marrow (MEHR·oh), which is in the center of some bones.
- **Storage.** Bones store minerals, such as calcium and phosphorus, for use when needed by your body.

Teen Issues

Safe or Cool? ACTIVITY!

Medical and health officials recommend that you wear a safety helmet and other protective gear when you go skateboarding or in-line skating. This is even required by law in some states. Many teens ignore this advice. They think that wearing such gear is not cool. Write a paragraph to explain how you feel about this issue.

Figure 10.15A

The Skeletal System

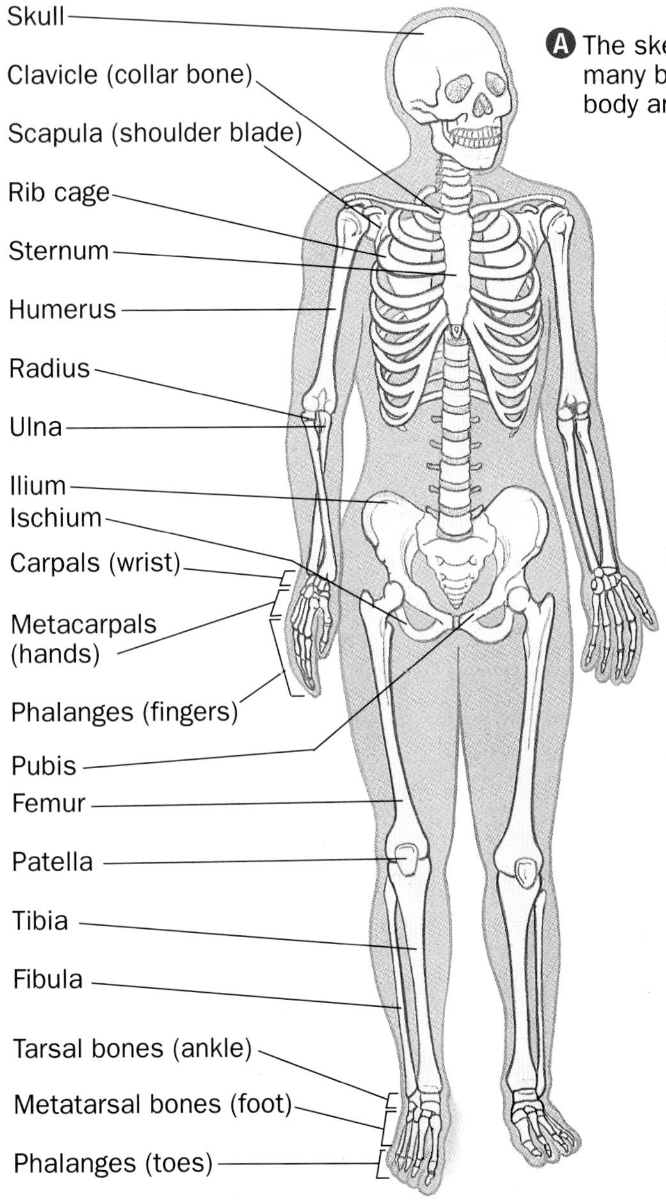

A The skeletal system includes many bones that support the body and protect the organs.

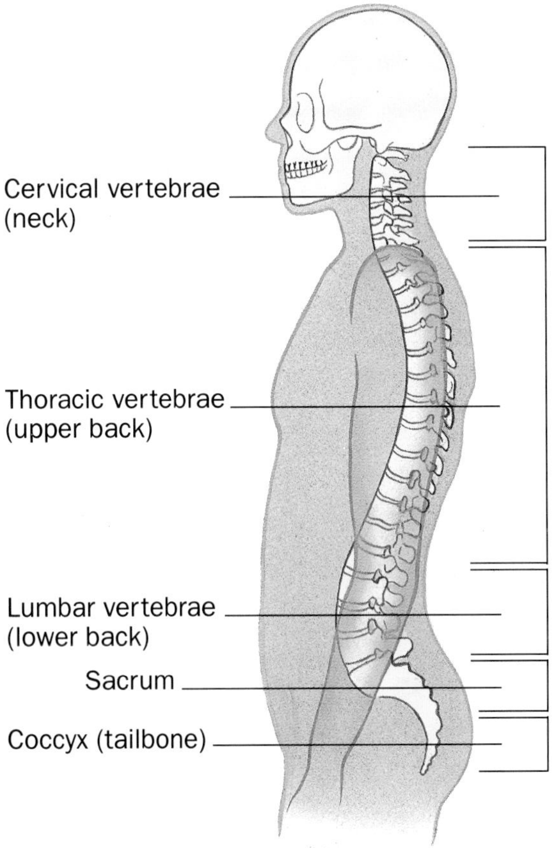

B The backbone, or spinal column, is made of 24 separate bones called vertebrae. This enables you to bend your back in several different directions. The bones form curves, as shown in this side view.

Figure 10.15B

Cross-Section of a Long Bone

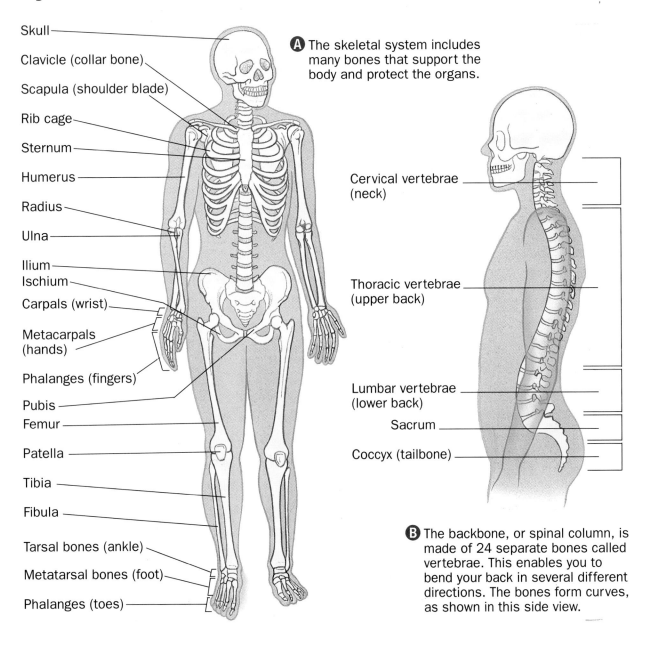

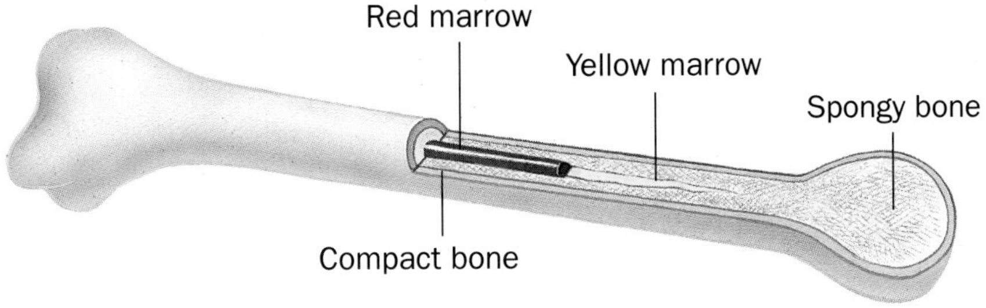

The inner cavity of your long bones, such as the femur, contains yellow marrow, which is a fatty tissue, and red marrow at the ends. Red marrow produces red blood cells and most of the white blood cells in your blood.

Figure 10.16
Types of Joints
Each type of joint allows a certain kind of movement. What type of joint is in your fingers?

The Joints

Joints are *the points at which bones meet.* Joints differ from one another in the type of movement they allow. **Figure 10.16** shows the various types of joints in your body.

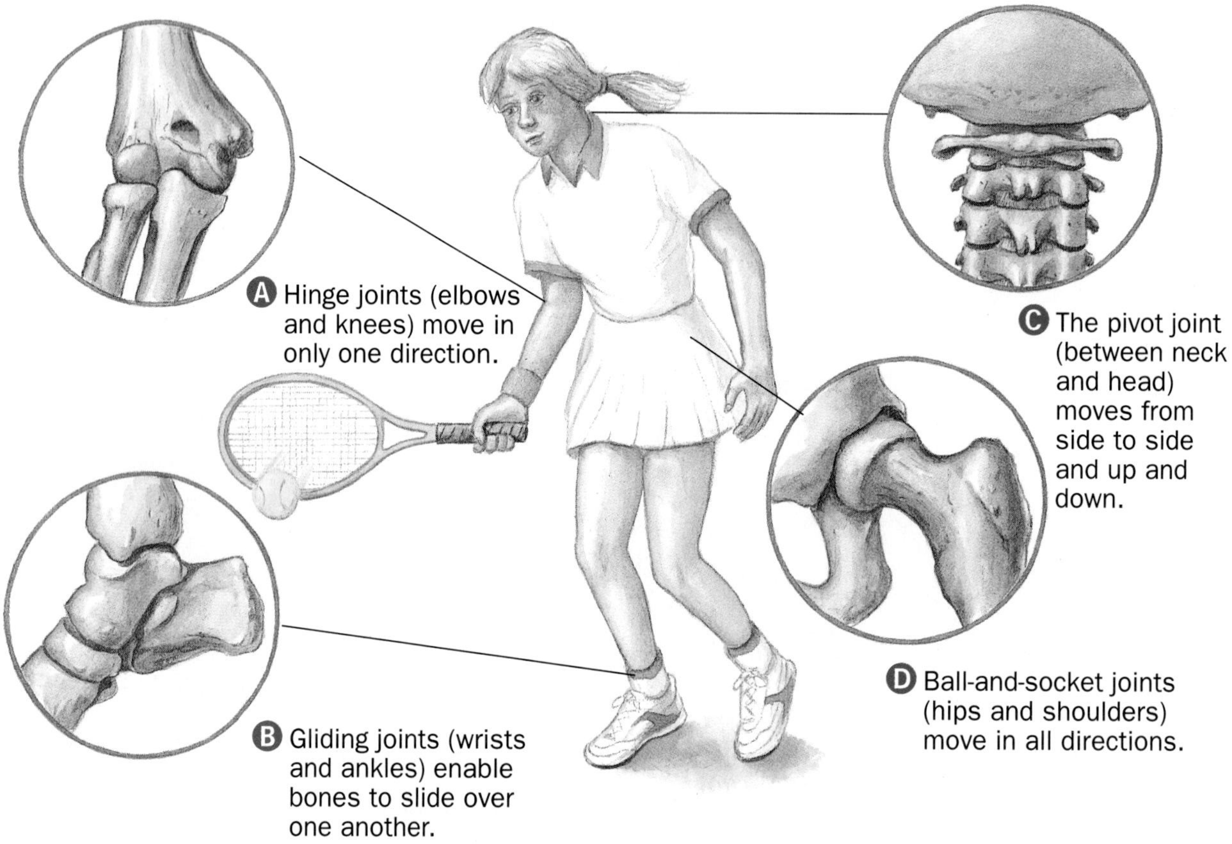

A Hinge joints (elbows and knees) move in only one direction.
B Gliding joints (wrists and ankles) enable bones to slide over one another.
C The pivot joint (between neck and head) moves from side to side and up and down.
D Ball-and-socket joints (hips and shoulders) move in all directions.

The Connectors

Movement is made possible by three kinds of tissues.

- **Cartilage** is a tough, flexible tissue that is similar to bone. It acts as a cushion between bones at a joint and protects the bones. Your nose and ears are made of cartilage.
- **Ligaments** (LI·guh·ments) are *strong cords of tissue that connect bones at the joints.* Ligaments hold the bones in place.
- **Tendons** (TEN·duhns) are *tough bands of tissue that attach your muscles to bones.* You can feel a large tendon called the Achilles tendon on the back of your leg just above your heel.

in your journal

Look at snapshots of yourself taken when you were about six years old and at your present age. Which bones have grown longer? Which have changed shape in another way? Write your observations in your journal.

Problems of the Skeletal System

Problems of the skeletal system can result from accidents, viral infections, poor posture, and poor diet (see **Figure 10.17**).

Figure 10.17
Problems of the Skeletal System

Disease or Disorder	Description	Treatment or Prevention
Fracture	Break in bone caused by falls or accidents; swelling, extreme pain	Bones are set and kept from moving, usually by enclosing in a cast
Dislocation	Bone pushed out of its joint, usually includes stretching or tearing of a ligament	Bones are reset into proper position and kept from moving
Sprain	Swelling of a joint caused by stretching or twisting ligaments	Rest; elevation of joint to reduce swelling
Arthritis	Swelling and stiffness of joints caused by wear and tear; usually affects older people	Pain relievers and exercise may help; if severe damage, may replace with artificial joints
Scoliosis	Curvature of spine	Exercise may help if mild; if severe, may need braces or surgery
Osteomyelitis	Bacterial infection of the bones	Medication
Osteoporosis	Bones become brittle and porous; associated with deficiencies of calcium, protein, and certain hormones	Regular exercise and a diet rich in calcium may prevent osteoporosis

Lesson 4 Review

Using complete sentences, answer the following questions on a separate sheet of paper.

Reviewing Terms and Facts

1. **Vocabulary** Explain the difference between *ligaments* and *tendons*.
2. **Identify** What two parts of your body are made up mostly of cartilage?

Thinking Critically

3. **Compare and Contrast** Describe the similarities and differences between fracturing, spraining, and dislocating your finger. Describe how each problem is treated.
4. **Give Examples** What are some ways you can act now to prevent osteoporosis later in life?

Applying Health Concepts

5. **Growth and Development** Working with a classmate, plan a way to construct a model skeleton. What materials would you use for the bones, cartilage, tendons, and ligaments? Describe the steps you would follow in making your model.
6. **Consumer Health** Do research to find out about artificial joints. Write a brief paper about these joints to present to the class.

Lesson 5

Your Muscular System

This lesson will help you find answers to questions that teens often ask about their muscular system. For example:

- **How can I have stronger muscles?**
- **Why do my muscles sometimes ache?**
- **What causes muscles to cramp?**

Words to Know

muscular system
contract
extend
smooth muscle
skeletal muscle
cardiac muscle

Moving Body Parts

Your bones serve as a framework that gives your body shape and support. Your muscles allow you to move that framework. Your **muscular** (MUHS·kyuh·ler) **system** is *the group of tough tissues that make your body parts move.*

You control the muscles that move your body. However, your muscular system also includes muscles that you do not control. Many organs, such as your stomach and intestines, are lined with muscles that move without your being aware of them. Your heart is the strongest and, perhaps, most important muscle in your body.

How Muscles Work

You have over 600 major muscles in your body, and they all work the same way. Working in pairs, they **contract,** or *shorten,* and they **extend,** or *lengthen.* When one muscle in a pair contracts, the other muscle extends. This activity produces movement at a joint. **Figure 10.18** shows how your muscles work together to produce movement.

Figure 10.18
Muscles Working Together

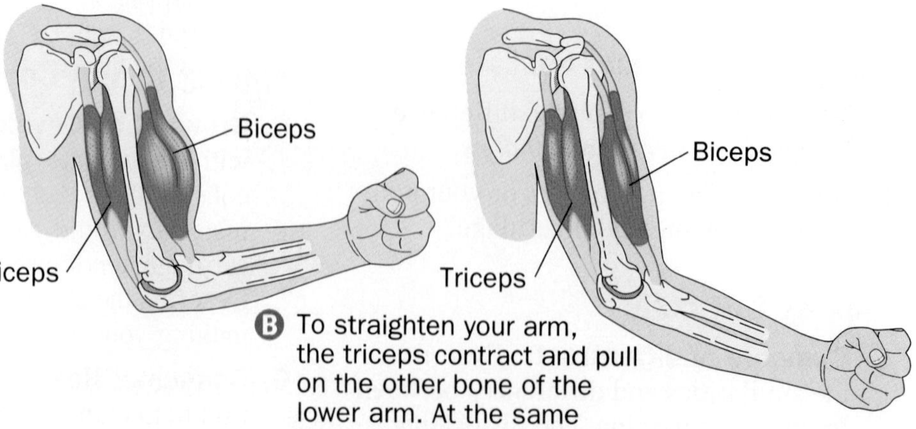

Ⓐ To bend your arm, the biceps (flexors) contract and pull on a bone of your lower arm while the triceps (extensors) extend.

Ⓑ To straighten your arm, the triceps contract and pull on the other bone of the lower arm. At the same time, the biceps extend.

The muscles in your body are responsible for moving your bones, pumping blood, moving food through your digestive system, and controlling the air that moves in and out of your lungs (see **Figure 10.19**).

in Your Journal

List your daily activities that include exercise. Identify the major muscles used in each activity.

Figure 10.19
The Muscular System

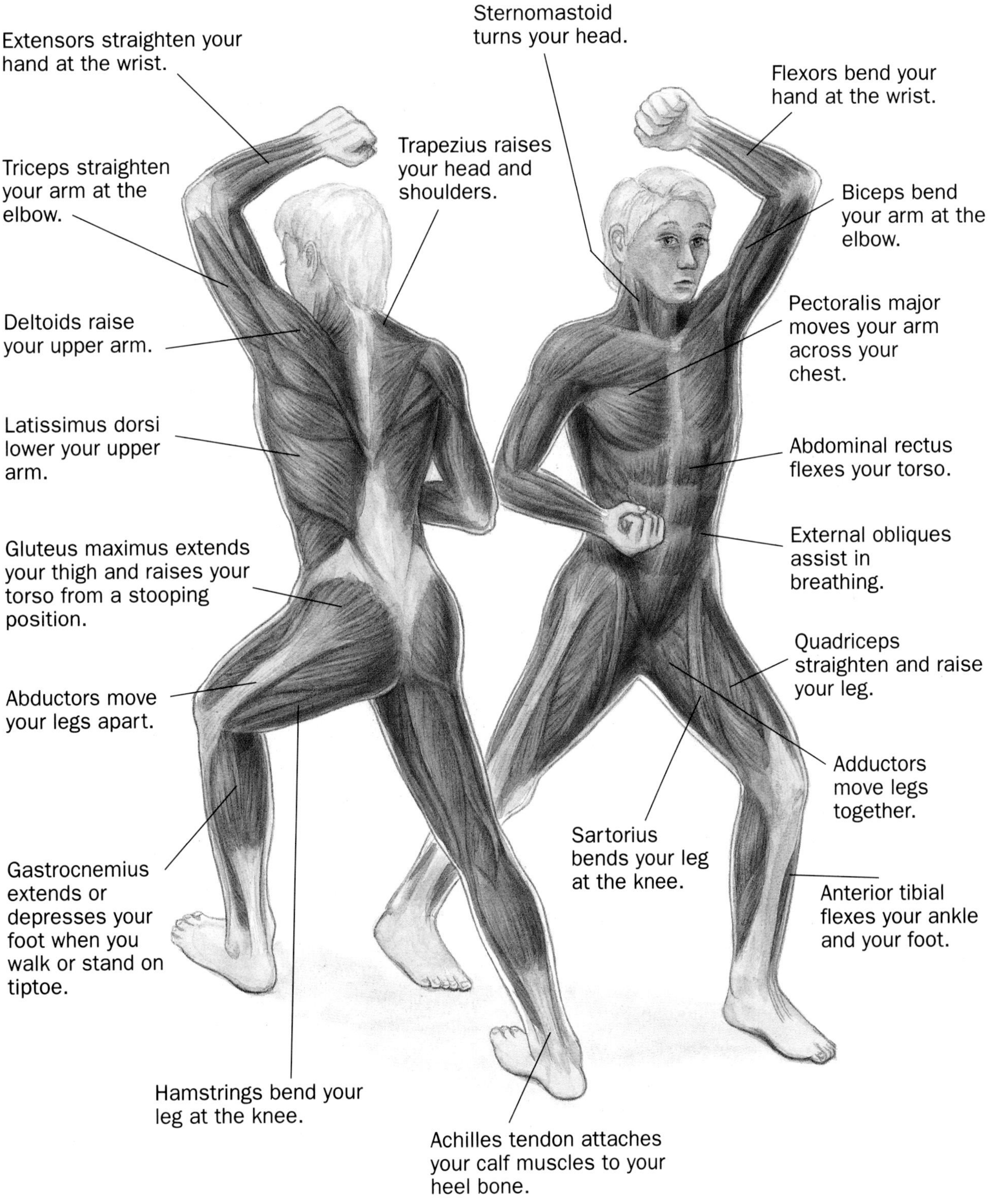

Extensors straighten your hand at the wrist.
Triceps straighten your arm at the elbow.
Deltoids raise your upper arm.
Latissimus dorsi lower your upper arm.
Gluteus maximus extends your thigh and raises your torso from a stooping position.
Abductors move your legs apart.
Gastrocnemius extends or depresses your foot when you walk or stand on tiptoe.
Hamstrings bend your leg at the knee.
Achilles tendon attaches your calf muscles to your heel bone.
Trapezius raises your head and shoulders.
Sternomastoid turns your head.
Flexors bend your hand at the wrist.
Biceps bend your arm at the elbow.
Pectoralis major moves your arm across your chest.
Abdominal rectus flexes your torso.
External obliques assist in breathing.
Quadriceps straighten and raise your leg.
Adductors move legs together.
Sartorius bends your leg at the knee.
Anterior tibial flexes your ankle and your foot.

Kinds of Muscle

Your muscular system consists of three different types of muscle tissue. Each type is designed to carry out certain tasks. **Figure 10.20** shows the three types.

Figure 10.20
Types of Muscle

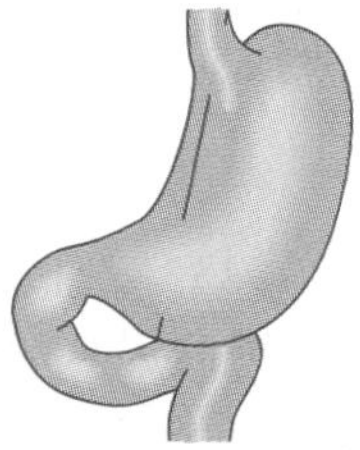

Ⓐ **Smooth muscles** are *found in various organs in the body, such as the stomach and intestines.* You do not control these muscles. For example, once you have swallowed your food, smooth muscles move it through the digestive system.

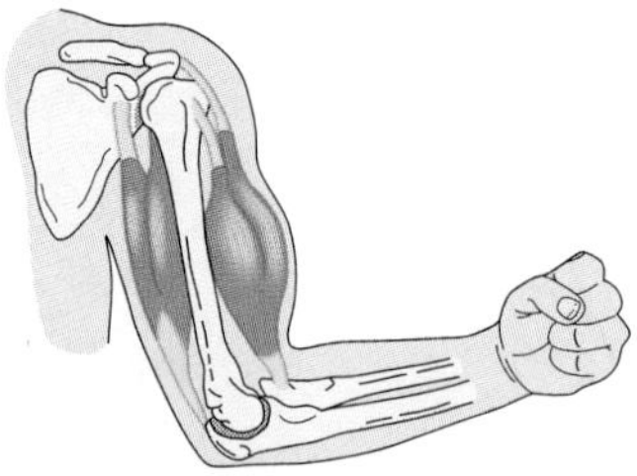

Ⓑ **Skeletal muscles** are *attached to bones.* They work with the bones of the skeleton to allow you to move. You control skeletal muscles. For example, you can make your arms and legs move whenever you wish. Skeletal muscles make up about 40 percent of your body weight.

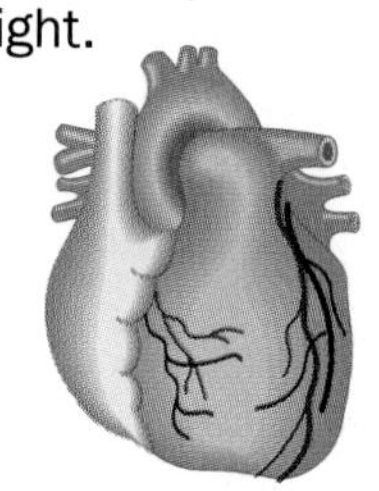

Ⓒ **Cardiac muscle** is *a special type of muscle that is found only in the walls of the heart.* Controlled by your brain, Cardiac muscle constantly contracts and relaxes, causing your heart to pump blood to all parts of your body.

HEALTH LAB

Testing Your Strength and Endurance

Introduction: What kind of shape are you in? Perhaps you can easily lift a certain weight or do a few pull-ups. Such actions show that your muscles have strength, but how many times can you lift the weight before you are too tired? How many pull-ups can you do before you have to stop and rest? The length of time shows endurance.

The following activity will help you test your strength and endurance.

Objective: Determine the effects of regular exercise on your strength and endurance.

Materials and Method: You will need a horizontal bar and a sheet of paper. On the sheet of paper, prepare a data table like the one shown here. You will record the results of each exercise session in the table.

Grasp a bar with an overhand grip. Feet should not touch the floor and legs should hang straight. Begin by hanging with your arms straight. Pull your body up with a steady movement until your chin is over the bar and extend back down. Do as many pull-ups as you can. There is no time limit, and the pull-ups must be done with straight legs. Repeat this exercise twice a day, once in the morning and once in the afternoon, for five consecutive days.

Observation and Analysis: Compare your performance at the end of the five days with that of the first day. Do you see any improvement? Share your results with a group of your classmates. Think of an exercise routine to improve the strength and endurance of your legs and lower body. If you want to try your routine, get your teacher's approval before doing so.

DATA TABLE

DAY 1		DAY 2		DAY 3		DAY 4		DAY 5	
AM	PM	AM	PM	AM	PM	AM	PM	AM	PM

Problems of the Muscular System

Almost everyone has experienced sore muscles after overworking them. This is usually a temporary condition. With rest, sore muscles recover. Some muscular conditions are not temporary. **Figure 10.21** lists some of the disorders that can have an effect on the body's muscular system.

Teen Issues

No More Gym! ACTIVITY!

Some students think that physical education classes waste time. They want to be excused from them. Write an essay to explain what you think.

Figure 10.21
Problems of the Muscular System

Disorder	Description	Treatment
Pulled or torn muscle	Muscle torn from bone	Medical help
Strain	Soreness due to overwork	Rest; application of cold pack, then heat
Cramp	Muscle unable to relax; feels very tight and sore	Massage; application of heat
Tendinitis	Stretched or torn tendon; very painful	Varies according to severity; may range from rest and a cold pack to surgery
Muscular dystrophy	Most common type is an inherited disorder characterized by a weakening of the skeletal muscles; eventual inability to walk and stand	No known cure; muscle therapy as long as it is effective

Lesson 5 Review

Using complete sentences, answer the following questions on a separate sheet of paper.

Reviewing Terms and Facts

1. **Vocabulary** Define *cardiac muscle.* Use it in an original sentence.
2. **Synthesize** Explain how muscles help you move.

Thinking Critically

3. **Analyze** Why is the heart the most important muscle in your body?
4. **Evaluate** Why do muscles sometimes ache after you exercise?

Applying Health Concepts

5. **Growth and Development** Organize an exercise group. Have interested classmates meet at regular times to exercise. Ask your physical education teacher to suggest exercises to help the members of your group strengthen and tone their muscles.
6. **Consumer Health** Find out how aerobic exercises benefit your muscular system. If possible, observe or participate in an aerobics class at a local gym or health club. Write a report about the benefits of this popular fitness routine.

TEEN HEALTH DIGEST

Sports and Recreation

Hoop Dreams

Okay, you're not seven feet tall, you can't slam-dunk, and your jump shot is not so sweet. You can still have fun playing basketball!

Basketball is a great way to keep in shape and develop basic physical skills. It is also a team game, so it teaches players how to work together—a true life lesson.

Here are some tips for anyone who wants to play hoops—either intramurally, in a church or community league, or on a school team.

- Show up on time. If you are reliable, people will count on you.
- Trust your coach and teammates. Every one of you is part of the team.
- Be a courteous winner and a mature loser. A good attitude will earn you respect.
- Try to learn from your mistakes.
- Always do your best. As long as you keep trying, you are bound to improve.

Personal Trainer

Aquacize!

Want all of the benefits of an aerobic workout, without all of the strain on your body? Then get wet!

"Aquacize" is another name for aerobic exercise done in a swimming pool. Aquacize has several advantages over workouts on dry land.

- Waist-deep water supports over half of your body weight. Your aquacize routine won't pound joints that can be hurt by a rigorous land routine.
- Water has 12 times the resistance of air. Your muscles get a better workout with aquacize.
- Aquacize can tone your body and increase your aerobic endurance and flexibility while you exercise at a lower heart rate.

Try This:

When it's time to exercise, jump in the pool, and have fun as you get fit.

HEALTH UPDATE

Mind Your Bones

How do people break bones? Skating? Falling off bikes? Playing football? About 25 million Americans risk breaking a bone just by rolling over in bed!

Those 25 million people suffer from osteoporosis. This is a disorder in which bones become porous and brittle.

Osteoporosis may not show up for several years, but to prevent it, it's important to get plenty of calcium in your diet—starting now! Teens should take in between 1,200 and 1,500 milligrams of calcium a day. Look for the calcium content on the nutrition labels of the foods you eat. (Hint: Is the amount given as a percentage? That shows what percentage of 1000 milligrams of calcium are in a serving. Just add a zero to the number, and that will tell you how many milligrams there are.)

Try This: *Record the amount of calcium you eat each day for a few days. Do you meet the 1,200-milligrams-a-day minimum?*

CON$UMER FOCU$

Healthfinder On-Line

The Internet is a great place to find information, including advice on health. However, the Internet is so big that you can get lost looking for the information you need.

Now you can navigate the Net for health tips with the help of a Web site created by the government. It links Web-surfers with hundreds of sites created by health organizations and government agencies. Do you want to find out about smoking and its effect on your circulatory system? Do you want to know how the amount of rest you get is related to the amount of stress you feel? A search function on the site will steer you to the answers.

Myths and Realities

Don't Sizzle Your Skin

Myth #1: You can get a safe tan by using an indoor tanning lamp.

Indoor sunlamps can be more dangerous than sunbathing. Skin cancers caused by lamps can be worse and may spread more quickly than those caused by the sun. Indoor tanning will also damage your eyes unless you wear protective goggles.

Myth #2: It's important to get a protective base tan.

A tan provides at best the screening power of an SPF 4 sunscreen. You increase the damage to your skin and the risk of developing skin cancer the longer that you are exposed to the sun's rays.

Lesson 6 Your Digestive System

This lesson will help you find answers to questions teens often ask about their digestive system. For example:

- **Why does my mouth water when I smell food cooking?**
- **Why does food have to be digested?**
- **What causes indigestion?**

Words to Know

digestive system
digestion
saliva
stomach
small intestine
liver
gallbladder
pancreas
excretion
colon
kidney

The Body's Engine

Your **digestive** (dy·JES·tiv) **system** *changes the food you eat into nutrients that your cells can use.* Food is your body's fuel, or source of energy. The digestive system is something like a car's engine. The engine changes stored energy in gasoline into a form of energy that moves the car. The digestive system changes the energy stored in food into a form of energy the body can use to work properly and to grow and develop.

How the Digestive System Works

As food moves through your digestive system, it is chemically changed. It is changed into particles that can be absorbed into the bloodstream. *The process of changing food* in this way is called **digestion** (dy·JES·chuhn).

The Mouth and Teeth

Digestion begins in your mouth. There, your teeth cut and grind food into smaller pieces. At the same time, food is being mixed with **saliva** (suh·LY·vuh). Saliva is *a liquid produced by the salivary glands.* It consists of about 99 percent water and contains an enzyme that starts the digestion of carbohydrates. Saliva also moistens and softens food so it can be swallowed easily. **Figure 10.22** shows what happens when you swallow.

Figure 10.22
The Process of Swallowing

A Before Swallowing Passages from the nose and throat to the trachea are open, allowing air to pass to the lungs.

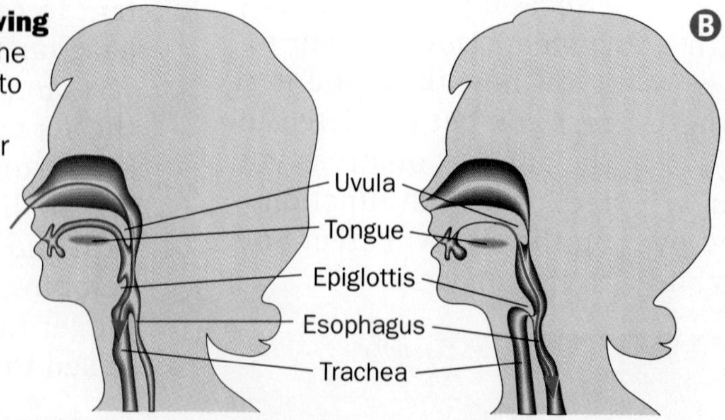

B During Swallowing Air passages are closed by two flaps of skin. The *uvula* (YOO·vyuh·luh) closes the airway to the nose. The epiglottis closes the opening to the trachea, or windpipe.

The Stomach and the Small Intestine

After being swallowed, your food enters your esophagus, a muscular tube that pushes food down into your stomach. The **stomach** is *a muscular organ in which food is held while digestion continues*. The muscular walls of the stomach churn the food and mix it with gastric juice, a mixture of acid and enzymes. Glands in the stomach wall produce gastric juice. The enzymes in the stomach begin the digestion of proteins.

Partially digested food moves from your stomach to your **small intestine,** which is *a coiled, tubelike organ about 20 feet long*. Most digestion takes place in the *duodenum* (doo·uh·DEE·nuhm), which is the first section of the small intestine. **Figure 10.23** shows the parts of the digestive system.

Did You Know?

Taste Buds

Taste buds are sensory organs located on your tongue. They can detect sweet, salty, sour, and bitter tastes.

Figure 10.23

The Digestive System

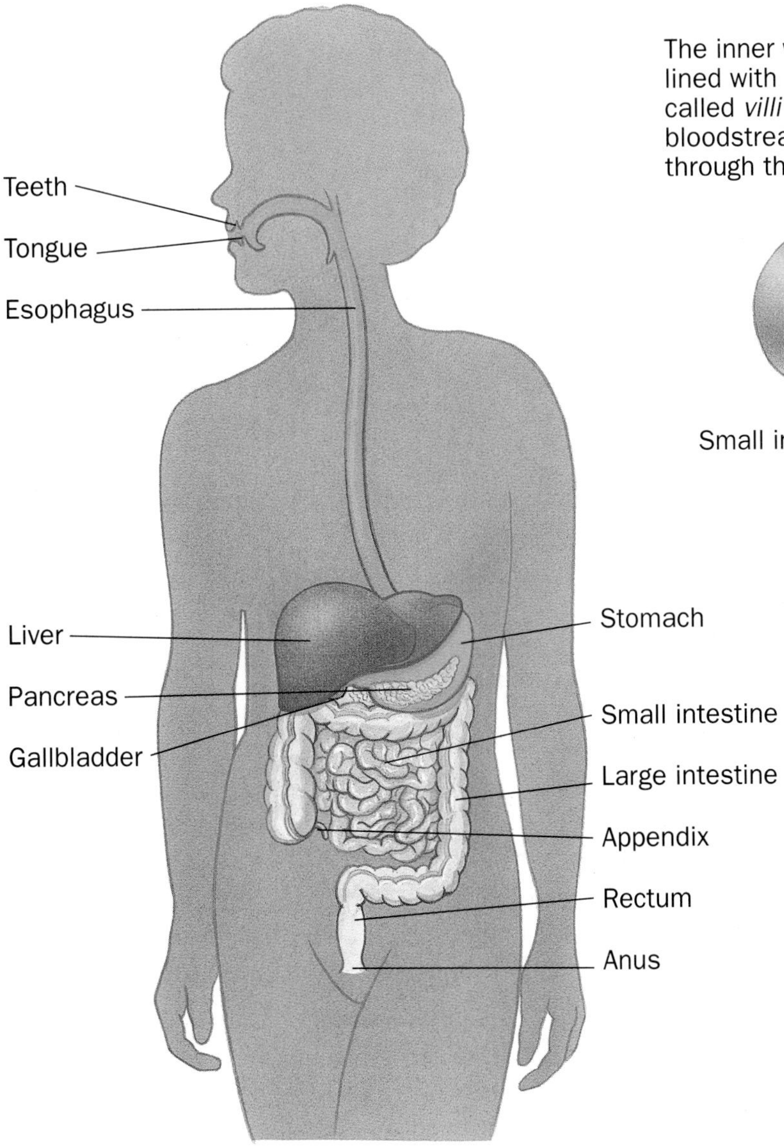

The inner walls of the small intestine are lined with tiny, fingerlike projections called *villi* (VIL·eye). Nutrients enter the bloodstream from the small intestine through the villi.

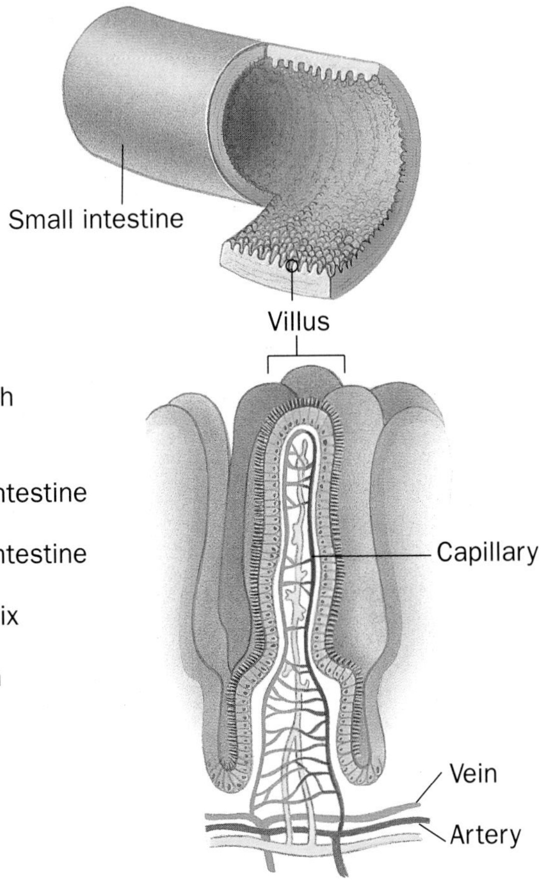

Finger-Licking Good

Q: Why does my mouth water when I smell something good to eat?

A: Your smell sensors send a signal to your brain telling it that something tasty is nearby. Your brain then signals the salivary glands, telling them to get ready.

The Liver, Gallbladder, and Pancreas

Three other organs are included as part of the digestive system, even though no food passes through them. These organs—the liver, gallbladder, and pancreas—are shown in **Figure 10.24.** The pancreas is also part of your body's endocrine system (see the next lesson to learn more about that system).

▪ Changes sugar into a form of starch that can be stored in the body until needed.

▪ Helps maintain blood sugar levels.

▪ Removes worn out red blood cells.

▪ Changes toxic waste materials into less toxic substances.

▪ Stores fat-soluble vitamins.

Figure 10.24
The Liver, Gallbladder, and Pancreas

Ⓐ The **liver** is *the largest gland in the body.* The liver produces bile, a substance that aids in the digestion of fats.

Ⓑ The **gallbladder** is *a small baglike organ.* It stores the bile produced by the liver and releases it into the small intestine when needed.

Ⓒ The **pancreas** *produces three digestive enzymes.* These are released into the small intestine.

Science Connection

The Water Cycle

You need water to survive—lots of it. Your cells are mostly water, and your body systems need water to do their jobs. Working in small groups, discuss fresh water as Earth's most important natural resource. Review the water cycle and draw a sketch to show the different stages. Label each stage and draw arrows to show how water moves through the stages.

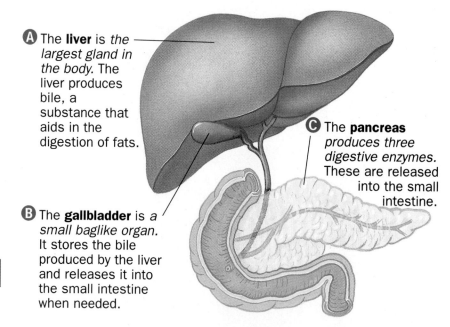

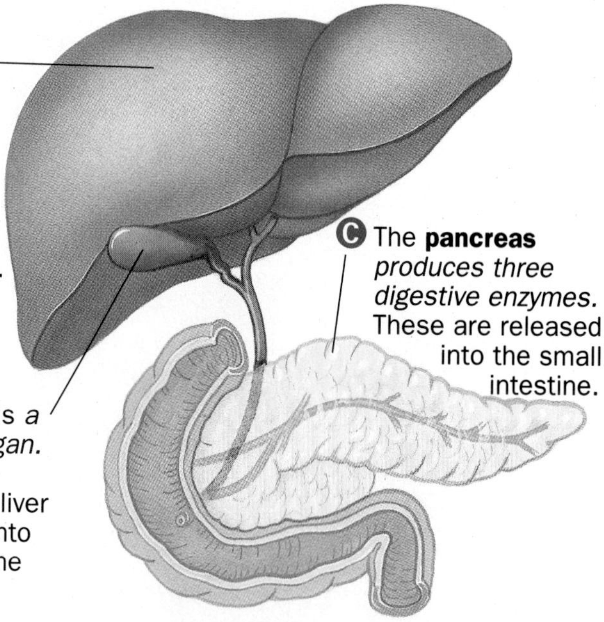

Removing Wastes

Your body produces three kinds of wastes that need to be removed. Solid wastes are made up of foods that have not been digested. Liquid wastes and carbon dioxide gas are products formed by the activities of your cells.

Your skin removes some wastes through its pores when you sweat. Carbon dioxide is removed by your lungs when you exhale. The remaining wastes are removed by your liver, kidneys, bladder, and large intestine.

The Kidneys, Bladder, and Large Intestine

Many wastes produced in your body are dissolved in water. *The process of removing liquid wastes from the body* is called **excretion** (ek·SKREE·shuhn). **Figure 10.25** explains which parts of the body work together to remove these liquid wastes, which are called *urine,* from your body.

Water and undigested food that your body cannot use pass into your *large intestine,* which is also known as the **colon** (KOH·luhn). The lining of the colon absorbs almost all of the liquid. The solid wastes that remain are called *feces* (FEE·seez). When the large intestine is full, nerves signal muscles in the walls of the large intestine to contract. As a result, the feces pass out of the body through the *anus* (AY·nuhs).

Figure 10.25

The Process of Removing Wastes

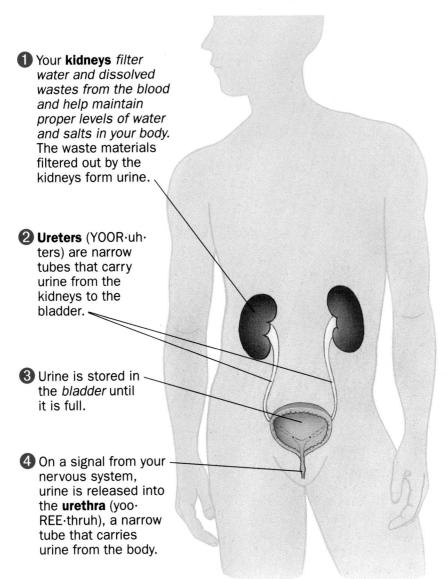

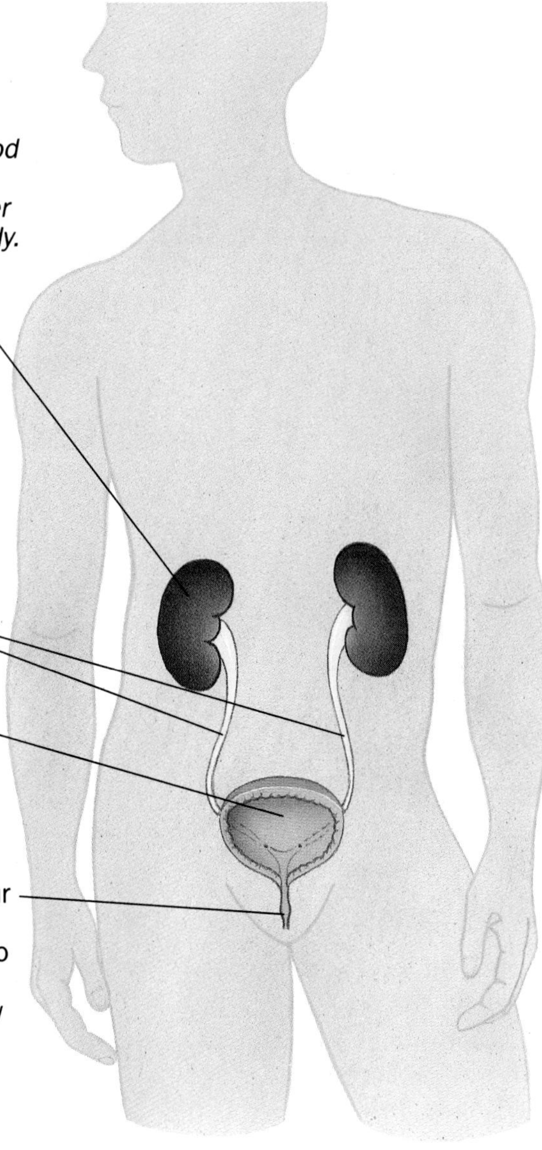

1 Your **kidneys** *filter water and dissolved wastes from the blood and help maintain proper levels of water and salts in your body.* The waste materials filtered out by the kidneys form urine.
2 **Ureters** (YOOR·uh·ters) are narrow tubes that carry urine from the kidneys to the bladder.
3 Urine is stored in the *bladder* until it is full.
4 On a signal from your nervous system, urine is released into the **urethra** (yoo·REE·thruh), a narrow tube that carries urine from the body.

in your journal

To have healthy kidneys you need to drink plenty of water—6 to 8 glasses a day. In your journal, keep track of the amount of water you drink each day. Are you getting enough?

Did You Know?

Kidney Machines

A person whose kidneys are not working properly can be helped by a machine that does the work of the kidneys. The person's blood is sent through the machine, which filters the blood, removes wastes, and returns the blood to the person's body. This treatment is called hemodialysis.

Care of the Digestive System

The best way to care for your digestive system is to practice healthful eating habits. These include the following.

- Eat a variety of foods from all food groups, especially foods that are low in fat and high in fiber.
- Eat complete meals at regular intervals during the day. Eating breakfast is especially important.
- Do not hurry through your meals. Take the time to relax and enjoy them rather than eating in a rush.
- Eat enough food to satisfy your hunger. Do not stuff yourself.
- Drink plenty of water. Your digestive system needs a lot of water to work properly.
- Have regular dental checkups. Strong teeth are necessary to break food into smaller pieces to start digestion.

The best way to promote the health of your digestive system is to eat a variety of foods, especially those that are high in fiber.

Q&A

How Sweet It Is!

Q: If I hold a piece of starchy food, like a cracker, in my mouth, it begins to taste sweet. Why?

A: As part of the digestion process, enzymes in your saliva change the starch in the food to sugar.

Problems of the Digestive System

Most digestive problems are related to eating habits and the kinds of foods eaten. They are usually temporary and minor. However, if the problems persist or if they are accompanied by a fever, a medical checkup may be necessary. **Figure 10.26** lists some of the problems of the digestive system.

Figure 10.26
Problems of the Digestive System

Disorder	Description	Treatment
Indigestion	Stomach too acidic, may be caused by eating too fast or too much or by spicy or acidic foods	Tablets to neutralize stomach acids
Diarrhea	Watery feces; caused by bacteria, virus, food poisoning, nutritional deficiencies	Usually clears up when cause has been eliminated
Ulcers	Sores on inner walls of stomach or small intestine	Medication, special diet, perhaps surgery
Cirrhosis	Destruction of liver tissue; caused by drinking too much alcohol	Medication and blood transfusions
Gallstones	Crystals in gallbladder; may block passage of bile to small intestine	Medication, special diet, perhaps surgery
Kidney stones	Crystals in kidney; may block passage of urine to bladder	Sound waves to break up large stones
Appendicitis	Inflammation of the appendix	Surgery
Hemorrhoids	Swelling of veins near opening of anus	Exercise, change in diet, perhaps surgery
Colon cancer	Uncontrolled growth of abnormal cells in large intestine	Chemotherapy, radiation, surgery

Review

Lesson 6

Using complete sentences, answer the following questions on a separate sheet of paper.

Reviewing Terms and Facts

1. **Vocabulary** Describe the function of the stomach and what takes place in the stomach.
2. **List** Identify six functions of the liver.

Thinking Critically

3. **Synthesize** Trace the path of a meal through the digestive system.
4. **Analyze** Why might a person take an antacid tablet for an upset stomach?

Applying Health Concepts

5. **Consumer Health** In the past, it was assumed that the main cause of ulcers was negative emotions. Find a recent article in a magazine, health newsletter, or newspaper about the causes of ulcers. What is the current thinking about the main causes of ulcers? How are ulcers treated? Share your findings with the class.
6. **Consumer Health** Do research on the role that water plays in maintaining health. Then survey your classmates about their water-drinking habits. Do you and your classmates generally drink the amount of water that is recommended?

Lesson 7

Your Endocrine System

This lesson will help you find answers to questions that teens often ask about their endocrine system. For example:

- **Why does my heart beat faster when I am frightened or excited?**
- **Why am I shorter (or taller) than most of my classmates?**
- **Why do some people have diabetes?**

Words to Know

endocrine system
gland
pituitary gland

The Regulator

Your nervous system has been described as your body's control center. Your **endocrine** (EN·duh·krihn) **system** *works closely with your nervous system to regulate body functions.*

The endocrine system consists of several glands located throughout your body. A **gland** is *a group of cells, or an organ, that secretes a chemical substance.* The substances secreted by the endocrine glands are called *hormones.* Hormone comes from a Greek word that means "to set in motion." The endocrine glands secrete their hormones directly into your bloodstream, where they are carried to various parts of the body and activate these parts in specific ways. Some hormones are produced continually; others are produced only at certain times.

The Glands of the Endocrine System

Each hormone produced by the endocrine glands regulates one of your body's activities. **Figure 10.27** shows the locations of the endocrine glands and tells what each one does.

A gland in your endocrine system, the pituitary gland, controls your growth.

The endocrine glands work on signals from the brain or from other glands. The brain tracks the presence of substances in the blood. For example, when the brain senses too little thyroid hormone in the blood, it signals the pituitary. The pituitary, in turn, signals the thyroid, which releases more of the hormone.

Did You Know?

Small and Important

The pituitary gland is one of the smallest, but most important, glands in your body. It is about the size of an acorn.

Figure 10.27

The Endocrine System

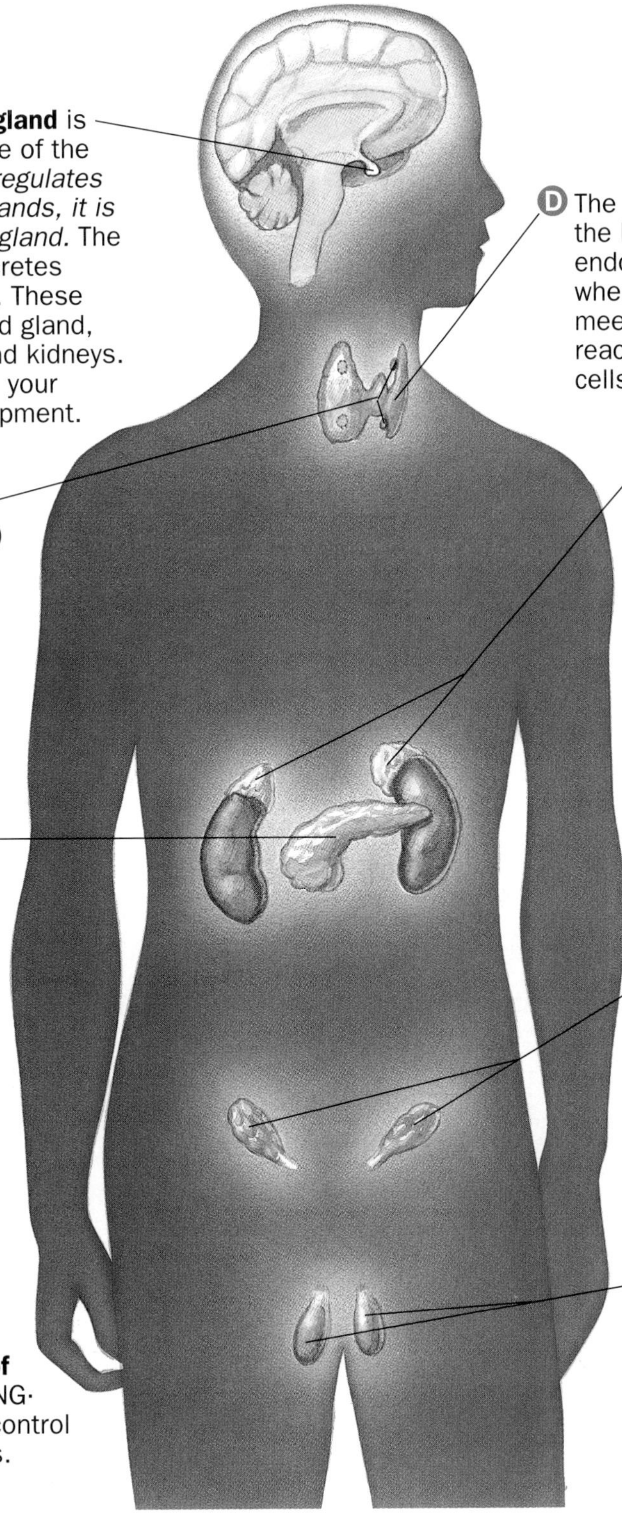

A The **pituitary** (pi·TOO·i·tehr·ee) **gland** is located at the base of the brain. *Because it regulates other endocrine glands, it is called the master gland.* The pituitary gland secretes several hormones. These regulate the thyroid gland, adrenal glands, and kidneys. They also regulate your growth and development.

B The **parathyroid** (pehr·uh·THY·royd) **glands** regulate the distribution of certain minerals in your body.

C The **pancreas** (PAN·kree·uhs) is part of two body systems—the digestive system and the endocrine system. The pancreas is located behind the stomach and supplies the small intestine with digestive juice. The pancreas contains small clusters of cells called the **islets of Langerhans** (LAHNG·er·hahnz), which control blood sugar levels.

D The **thyroid** (THY·royd) **gland** is the largest gland in the endocrine system. It is located where the larynx and trachea meet. It regulates the chemical reactions of nutrients in the cells.

E The **adrenal** (uh·DREEN·uhl) **glands** are located on your kidneys. They secrete hormones that help the body maintain its levels of sodium and water, aid the digestive process, and control your body's response to emergencies.

F The **ovaries** (OH·vuh·reez) are the female reproductive glands. They control the development of secondary sex characteristics during adolescence.

G The **testes** (TES·teez) are the male reproductive glands. They control the development of secondary sex characteristics during adolescence.

Your Total Health

Learn to Relax

ACTIVITY!

Relaxation is one way to relieve stress. What do you do to relax? Do you lie down, listen to some music, or go for a leisurely walk? Keep a list for a week of how many times a day you relax, and what you did each time. Do you think you need to relax more often? If so, plan ways to include more relaxation time into your schedule.

Activities That Hormones Control

Medical experts are still uncertain about the functions of the pineal and thymus glands. The other glands do the following jobs.

- The pituitary gland controls physical growth; controls other glands; controls the movements of smooth muscles.
- The parathyroid regulates calcium and phosphorous levels.
- The islets of Langerhans regulate your blood sugar level.
- The thyroid gland controls the rate at which food is converted to energy in the cells.
- The adrenal glands control the body's water balance and use of carbohydrates, proteins, and fats; start the stress response.
- Ovaries and testes control secondary sex characteristics.

Good health habits are important for a healthy endocrine system, especially during the teen years.

The Stress Response

Whenever you are excited or anxious, your body is under stress. Your adrenal glands then release the hormone *adrenaline* (uh·DRE·nuhl·in). **Figure 10.28** shows how adrenaline prepares your body to respond to stress. This response ends when the cause of the stress is gone, or when your body slows down because it cannot maintain the high level of activity.

The stress response can be harmful if it goes on too long or happens too often. You can avoid harm caused by the stress response by learning to manage stress.

Figure 10.28

The Effects of Stress on the Body

Various changes occur as the body responds to stress. Some of them are listed here.

Body Part	Under Stress	After Stress
Brain	Blood flow to brain increases	Blood flow to brain decreases
Sweat glands	Sweat production increases	Return to normal
Lungs	Air passageways expand	Air passageways contract
Circulatory system	Heart rate increases; blood pressure rises; blood to skeletal muscles increases	Returns to normal
Digestive system	Digestion slows	Digestion increases
Adrenal gland	Releases adrenaline	Returns to normal
Liver and gallbladder	Gallbladder stimulates liver to release sugar	Return to normal

Disorders of the Endocrine System

Most endocrine disorders are related to the production of a hormone—too much or too little. **Figure 10.29** describes some disorders of the endocrine system.

Q&A

A Fishy Solution

Q: I don't think I eat foods that contain iodine. Why don't I have a goiter?

A: You don't need much iodine in your diet. Since seawater contains iodine, eating seafood can provide all the iodine needed to keep your thyroid healthy. Also, the table salt you use may have small amounts of iodine added.

Figure 10.29
Disorders of the Endocrine System

Disorder	Description
Diabetes mellitus	Loss of nutrients and energy due to inadequate insulin production by the islets of Langerhans; symptoms include lack of energy, extreme thirst, and frequent urination
Goiter	Enlargement of the thyroid gland; visible as a swelling of the lower neck; caused by too little iodine
Growth extremes	Caused by the release of abnormal amounts of growth hormones; too little growth hormone causes dwarfism (results in a very small person); too much growth hormone causes gigantism (results in a very large person)

Review Lesson 7

Using complete sentences, answer the following questions on a separate sheet of paper.

Reviewing Terms and Facts

1. **Vocabulary** What is a *gland?* Explain the role of glands in the endocrine system.
2. **Identify** What gland is part of the endocrine system and also plays an important role in the digestive system?

Thinking Critically

3. **Explain** What is the largest gland? Where is it located? What is its function?
4. **Analyze** Why is caring for your endocrine system especially important during the teen years?

Applying Health Concepts

5. **Personal Health** Think of a situation when you experienced a stress response. Describe what caused the response, the changes your body underwent, and how the situation was resolved.
6. **Health of Others** There are two main forms of diabetes—juvenile and adult. Do research to find out how these two types of diabetes and their treatments differ. Make a chart comparing the two types. Share your findings in class.

Lesson 8

Your Reproductive System

This lesson will help you find answers to questions that teens often ask about their reproductive system. For example:

- **What happens when a male ejaculates?**
- **Why do females menstruate and males do not?**
- **At what age do females begin to menstruate?**

Words to Know

reproductive system
sperm
menstruation
menstrual cycle

The Producer of New Life

Reproduction is the process by which life is maintained from one generation to the next. All human life results from the union of two cells, one from the mother and one from the father. These cells are produced in the **reproductive** (ree·pruh·DUHK·tiv) **system.** The human reproductive system *consists of body organs that are involved in the production of offspring.* **Figure 10.30** shows the cells produced by the male and female reproductive systems.

Unlike other human body systems, organs in the male and female reproductive systems are not the same. As a result, each system requires different care. In addition, the potential problems of each system are different.

Figure 10.30
Cells of the Reproductive Systems

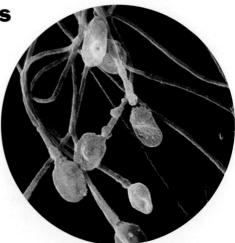

A The sperm in this photograph are magnified. Approximately 400 million sperm are present in the semen released during a single ejaculation.

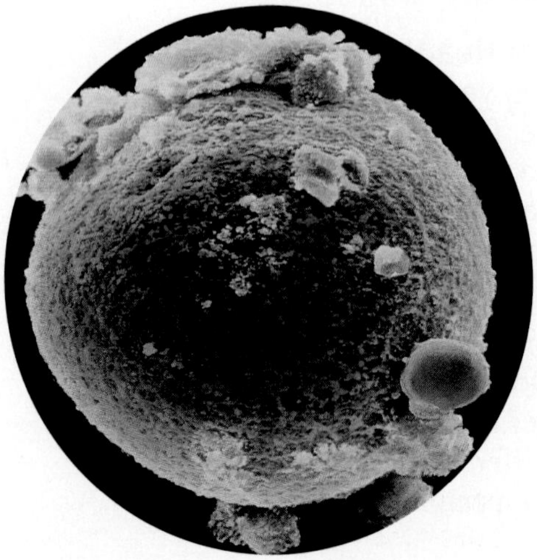

B The egg cell in this photograph is magnified. At birth, a female has hundreds of thousands of immature egg cells in her ovaries.

The Male Reproductive System

The male reproductive system produces **sperm.** Sperm are *male reproductive cells.* These cells join with female reproductive cells to produce new life. The union of male and female reproductive cells is called fertilization. Males begin to produce sperm when they reach puberty, usually between the ages of 12 and 15.

The male reproductive system includes the different organs involved in the production and storage of sperm and the release of sperm to the outside. **Figure 10.31** shows the male reproductive organs and describes what they do.

Sperm are produced in the testes and stored in the epididymis. When they leave the epididymis, they travel to the vas deferens. There they mix with seminal (SE·mi·nuhl) fluid produced by the seminal vesicles, the prostate glands, and the Cowper's glands. The mixture of sperm and fluids is called semen (SEE·muhn). The action that forces the semen through the urethra and out of the body is called ejaculation (i·ja·kyuh·LAY·shuhn).

in your journal

How might knowing the correct names for the parts of your reproductive system help when you have a medical checkup? Write your answer in your private journal.

Figure 10.31
The Male Reproductive System

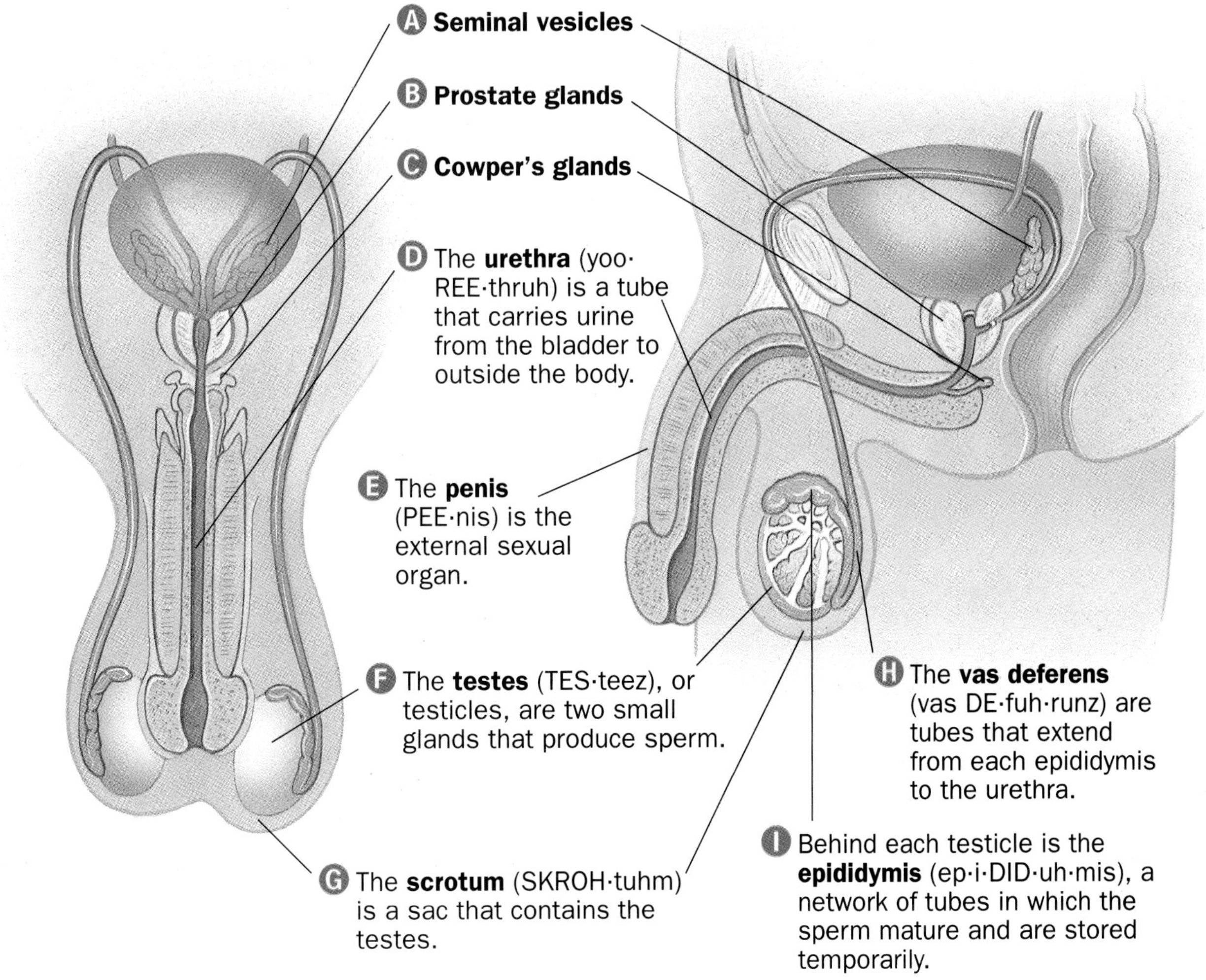

A Seminal vesicles
B Prostate glands
C Cowper's glands
D The urethra (yoo·REE·thruh) is a tube that carries urine from the bladder to outside the body.
E The penis (PEE·nis) is the external sexual organ.
F The testes (TES·teez), or testicles, are two small glands that produce sperm.
G The scrotum (SKROH·tuhm) is a sac that contains the testes.
H The vas deferens (vas DE·fuh·runz) are tubes that extend from each epididymis to the urethra.
I Behind each testicle is the epididymis (ep·i·DID·uh·mis), a network of tubes in which the sperm mature and are stored temporarily.

The Female Reproductive System

The female reproductive system has three important functions. They are to produce and store egg cells, to allow fertilization to occur, and to nourish and protect the fertilized egg until it is ready to live outside the female's body. **Figure 10.32** shows the female reproductive organs and describes what they do.

Figure 10.32

The Female Reproductive System

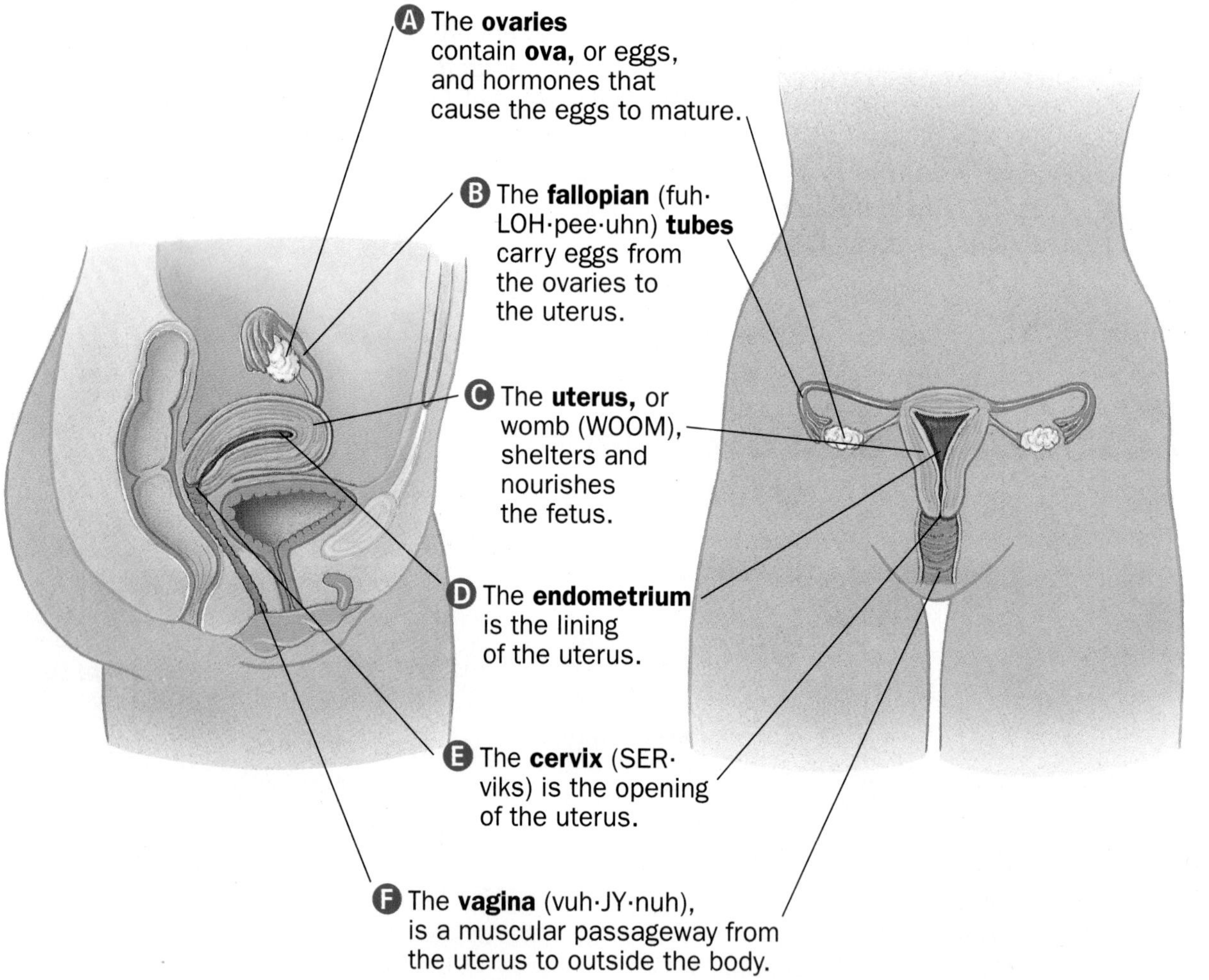

A The **ovaries** contain **ova,** or eggs, and hormones that cause the eggs to mature.
B The **fallopian** (fuh·LOH·pee·uhn) **tubes** carry eggs from the ovaries to the uterus.
C The **uterus,** or womb (WOOM), shelters and nourishes the fetus.
D The **endometrium** is the lining of the uterus.
E The **cervix** (SER·viks) is the opening of the uterus.
F The **vagina** (vuh·JY·nuh), is a muscular passageway from the uterus to outside the body.

The Menstrual Cycle

As a female reaches puberty, hormones cause egg cells to mature. The ovaries begin to release one mature egg cell each month. As a result of this process, called *ovulation* (ahv·vuh·LAY·shuhn), the uterus thickens in preparation to receive and begin to nourish a fertilized egg. If fertilization does not occur, the thickened lining breaks down. This material is then expelled from the female's body. *The flow of the lining material out of the female body* is called **menstruation** (men·struh·WAY·shuhn).

Menstruation usually lasts from 5 to 7 days. The **menstrual** (MEN·struhl) **cycle** is *the time from one menstruation to another.* A cycle usually is about 28 days, but it may vary from one female to another. In addition, stress or illness may affect the hormones that control the menstrual cycle. **Figure 10.33** shows what happens during the menstrual cycle.

Most girls begin menstruation between the ages of 9 and 16. For the first year or two, the ovulation and menstrual cycles may not be regular. That is not a cause for concern. The menstrual cycle normally varies greatly from one female to another. Some girls experience cramps, nausea, or dizziness when they menstruate. Some always have cycles of the same length. Others have irregular cycles.

Your Total Health

Self-Examination ACTIVITY!

Find out how to perform a self-examination. Boys should find out about examining their testicles. Girls should find out about examining their breasts. Write the steps on a sheet of paper and perform them, self-testing on a regular basis.

Figure 10.33

The Typical Menstrual Cycle

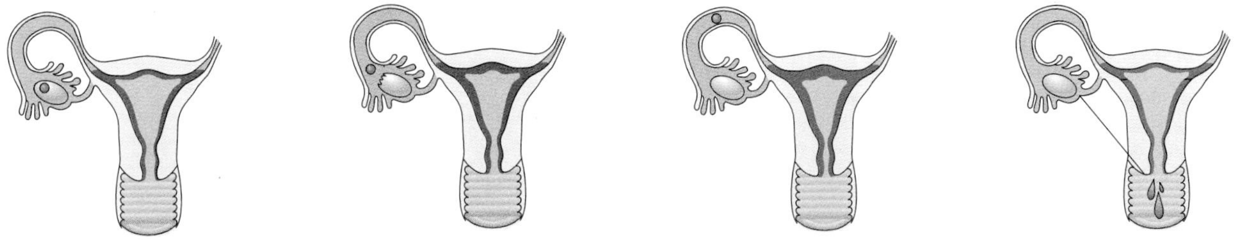

1 On days 1 through 13 of the cycle, even while menstruation is occurring, a new egg cell is maturing inside the ovary.

2 On day 14 of the cycle, ovulation occurs and the mature egg is released into one of the fallopian tubes.

3 From day 15 through day 20, the egg travels through the fallopian tube.

4 On day 21 the egg enters the uterus. After 7 days, if the egg has not been fertilized, menstruation begins.

Fertilization

When a male's sperm enters a female's vagina, it travels to a fallopian tube. Fertilization may occur, especially if there is a mature egg waiting. A sperm cell unites with an egg cell to produce a fertilized egg, and small hairs lining the fallopian tube move the egg through the tube into the uterus.

The fertilized egg attaches itself to the wall of the uterus. There it begins to grow and develop into a baby. The uterus has several layers of tissue and a rich supply of blood to nourish the baby during its months of development. The mother's body provides the baby with food and oxygen as it develops.

After about 40 weeks in the uterus, the baby is ready to be born. At that time, muscles in the wall of the uterus begin to contract. These contractions open the cervix. The baby is pushed out of the uterus through the cervix. It passes through the vagina until it is outside the mother's body.

Caring for Your Reproductive System

You can care for your reproductive system by taking the following actions.

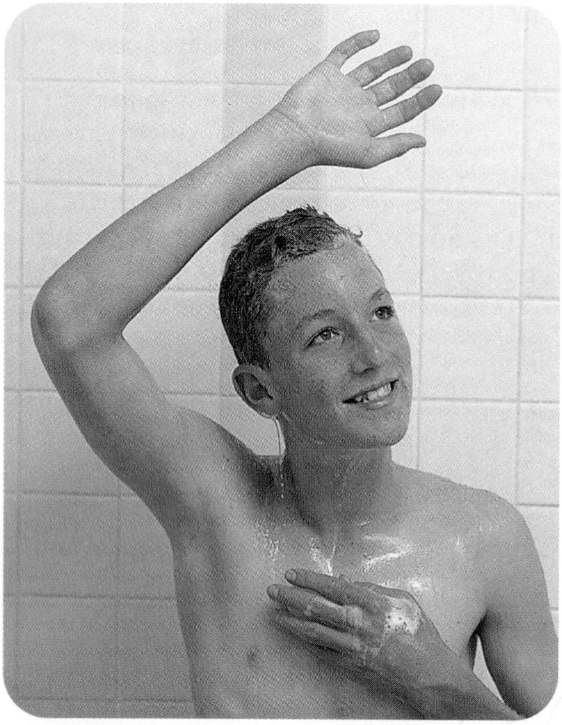

Taking regular showers is one way to care for your reproductive system.

- Bathe or shower daily to keep your external reproductive organs clean.
- Males should avoid underwear or clothing that is too tight. They should wear protective gear when playing contact sports. Males should do self-examinations of their testes to check for lumps, swelling, or soreness and have regular physical checkups. **Figure 10.34** lists some problems of the male reproductive system.
- For females, cleanliness is especially important during menstruation. Sanitary pads and tampons should be changed often. Females should have regular checkups by a *gynecologist* (gy·nuh·KAH·lah·jist), a physician who specializes in the care of the female reproductive system. Females should also do breast self-examinations. **Figure 10.35** lists some problems of the female reproductive system.

Figure 10.34

Problems of the Male Reproductive System

Disorder	Description	Treatment or Prevention
Testicular or prostate cancer	Uncontrolled cell growth that destroys glands and surrounding tissue	Surgery is usually required; self-testing and regular checkups can identify these diseases in early stages
Inguinal hernia	Part of the intestine pushes into the scrotum; caused by improperly lifting heavy objects	Surgery to repair weak spot in the abdominal wall; avoid lifting heavy objects
Sterility	Inability to produce healthy sperm in sufficient numbers to reproduce; caused by exposure to certain drugs or illness	No known cure
Enlarged prostate gland	A common problem associated with aging	Surgery

Figure 10.35

Problems of the Female Reproductive System

Disorder	Description	Treatment or Prevention
Premenstrual syndrome	Physical and emotional changes before menstruation; headaches, moodiness, irritability	May be relieved by regular exercise and changes in diet
Toxic shock syndrome	Rare, but serious bacterial infection associated with tampon use	Change tampons every 4–8 hours; consult package instructions or physician about proper use of tampons
Infertility	Inability to reproduce due to blockage in fallopian tubes or failure of ovaries to produce eggs	May be corrected by surgery or hormone treatment
Vaginitis	Infection of vagina; pain, itching, and discharge	Medication
Ovarian cysts	Growths on outside of ovary	Surgery to remove large cysts
Cancer	Can affect breasts, ovaries, uterus, cervix	Surgery, radiation, chemotherapy; self-examinations and check-ups can spot it early

Review

Lesson 8

Using complete sentences, answer the following questions on a separate sheet of paper.

Reviewing Terms and Facts

1. **Vocabulary** Define *menstruation.* Use it in an original sentence.
2. **List** Identify common disorders of the male and female reproductive system.

Thinking Critically

3. **Compare and Contrast** What happens if an egg is not fertilized? What happens if it is fertilized?
4. **Review** What are the three important functions of the female reproductive system?

Applying Health Terms

5. **Consumer Health** Pretend you are the author of a best-selling book about caring for the male or female reproductive system. Write a brief overview describing how the book can help improve the reader's chances for having and maintaining a healthy reproductive system.
6. **Health of Others** With a partner, write a skit in which you describe a discussion you might have with a younger brother or sister about growing up. Include questions and answers about the body changes to expect when he or she reaches puberty.

Chapter 10 Review

Chapter Summary

- **Lesson 1** The nervous system is the body's control center. It controls all of the body's actions. The nervous system consists of the brain, spinal cord, and many nerves. The work of the nervous system is done by neurons, which carry messages to and from all parts of your body. The best way to maintain your nervous system is to avoid head, neck, and back injuries.
- **Lesson 2** The circulatory system is the body's transport system. It delivers essential materials to body cells and removes wastes from them. The circulatory system is made up of the heart, blood vessels, and blood. Special white blood cells fight disease and infection by attacking germs that enter the body.
- **Lesson 3** The respiratory system provides the body with the oxygen it needs and rids the body of carbon dioxide. The lungs are the main organs of the respiratory system. The body takes in oxygen by inhaling and releases carbon dioxide by exhaling. The respiratory system is a common site of infection because germs can easily enter the body through the mouth and nose.
- **Lesson 4** The skeletal system is the body's framework. It gives the body shape and support, protects the internal organs, allows the body to move, produces blood cells, and stores minerals. The skeletal system consists of bone, joints, and connecting tissue.
- **Lesson 5** The muscular system is the group of tough tissues that work with the skeletal system to move the body. Working in pairs, muscles contract and extend to produce movement. Muscles also help pump blood, move food through the digestive system, and control the air that moves in and out of the lungs.
- **Lesson 6** The digestive system changes the food a person eats into nutrients the body can use and removes wastes. The digestive system consists of the mouth, teeth, stomach, small intestine, liver, gallbladder, pancreas, kidneys, bladder, and large intestine.
- **Lesson 7** The endocrine system controls and regulates many important activities of the body. It consists of glands located throughout the body. The chemicals released by these glands activate body processes, such as growth, and maintain the body's blood sugar level.
- **Lesson 8** The organs of the reproductive system carry out the processes that are necessary to produce offspring and maintain life from one generation to the next. Unlike other body systems, the reproductive systems for males and females are different.

Chapter 10 Review

Reviewing Key Terms and Concepts

Using complete sentences, answer the following questions on a separate sheet of paper.

Lesson 1

1. Identify the parts and describe the functions of the central nervous system and peripheral nervous system.
2. Define *neuron.* Explain why it is particularly important to protect neurons from damage. Define *brain,* and list its three main parts.

Lesson 2

3. Define the terms *circulatory system* and *cardiovascular system.* Identify the three main parts of the circulatory system.
4. Identify four materials transported by the circulatory system.

Lesson 3

5. What is the function of the respiratory system? Define each of the following respiratory system terms: *epiglottis, bronchi,* and *diaphragm.*
6. Define the term *alveoli.* What substance is passed from the blood to the alveoli? What substance is passed from the alveoli to the blood?

Lesson 4

7. Describe the role that the skeletal system plays in blood cell formation. Describe two other functions of the skeletal system.
8. Define the terms *cartilage* and *joint.* Identify four kinds of joints and three problems that occur in joints.

Lesson 5

9. Define *muscular system.* What is the function of the triceps and hamstring muscles?
10. What is a muscle strain? What is the treatment for a muscle strain?

Lesson 6

11. What is the function of the digestive system? Explain what each of the following terms has to do with the digestive system: *digestion, saliva, small intestine, gallbladder,* and *pancreas.*
12. Define *excretion.* Explain the role of the kidneys and colon in removing wastes from the body.

Lesson 7

13. What is the function of the endocrine system? Describe the role of hormones in the endocrine system.
14. What functions are regulated by the pituitary gland? Why it is sometimes called the master gland?

Lesson 8

15. What is the function of the reproductive system? What are the male reproductive cells called?
16. Explain what happens during the menstrual cycle.

Chapter 10 Review

Thinking Critically

Using complete sentences, answer the following questions on a separate sheet of paper.

17. **Analyze** How are voluntary actions, such as wriggling your toes, and involuntary actions, such as breathing, related to your brain?
18. **Explain** Why is it important to wear a helmet when riding a bike or playing contact sports?
19. **Distinguish** What is the difference between pulmonary and systemic circulation?
20. **Apply** Why is it important to know your blood type and Rh factor?
21. **Explain** What is the difference between the ways in which bacterial and viral pneumonia are treated?
22. **Analyze** Why is smoking harmful to your respiratory system?
23. **Summarize** In what ways do the bones change as a person grows from an infant to an adult?
24. **Synthesize** How would a person's ability to move change if the backbone were a single bone instead of 24 separate bones?
25. **Compare and Contrast** How are smooth muscle and skeletal muscle alike and different?
26. **Recommend** Suggest some ways to avoid and relieve muscle cramps.
27. **Analyze** How does eating meals in a relaxed manner help digestion?
28. **Apply** Why are regular dental checkups an important part of maintaining a healthy digestive system?
29. **Synthesize** What is the relationship between the brain and the endocrine system?
30. **Deduce** Why is the stress response sometimes harmful instead of helpful?
31. **Recommend** List some ways in which males can protect their reproductive organs.
32. **Explain** Why does the menstrual cycle stop when a woman is pregnant?

Chapter 10 Review

Your Action Plan

You can make an action plan to improve the health of one or more of your body systems. Review your journal entries for this chapter.

Step 1: Select a long-term goal, and write it down. Perhaps you would like to improve your muscular system by implementing and maintaining an exercise plan.

Step 2: Choose short-term goals to help you reach your long-term goal. One way to improve your muscular system, for instance, is to join an exercise class.

Step 3: Establish a schedule for reaching your short-term goals. For example, "By the end of one month, I will find an affordable exercise class that I can attend regularly."

Check your schedule to keep yourself on track. When you have achieved your goal, reward yourself.

In Your Home and Community

1. **Community Resources** Collect from hospitals and other community centers information about lectures and classes on caring for the body. Find out if any offer free medical tests to check the functioning of body systems. Display the pamphlets, class listings, and other information you collected.
2. **Personal Health** Work in groups of three or four to write a handbook that describes actions teens can take regularly to keep their bodies healthy. Include information from this chapter and from other sources.

Building Your Portfolio

1. **Body Systems Scrapbook** Clip articles that discuss body systems from magazines or newspapers. Topics may include new medical treatments and people who have overcome disease. Share your scrapbook with the class, and add it to your portfolio.
2. **Organ Transplants** Research information about organ transplants. Find out which organs can be transplanted and how problems of infection and rejection are handled. Learn about the availability of organs. Write a report about your findings, and add this report to your portfolio.
3. **Personal Assessment** Look through the activities and projects you did for this chapter. Choose one that you would like to include in your portfolio.

Chapter 11

Communicable Diseases

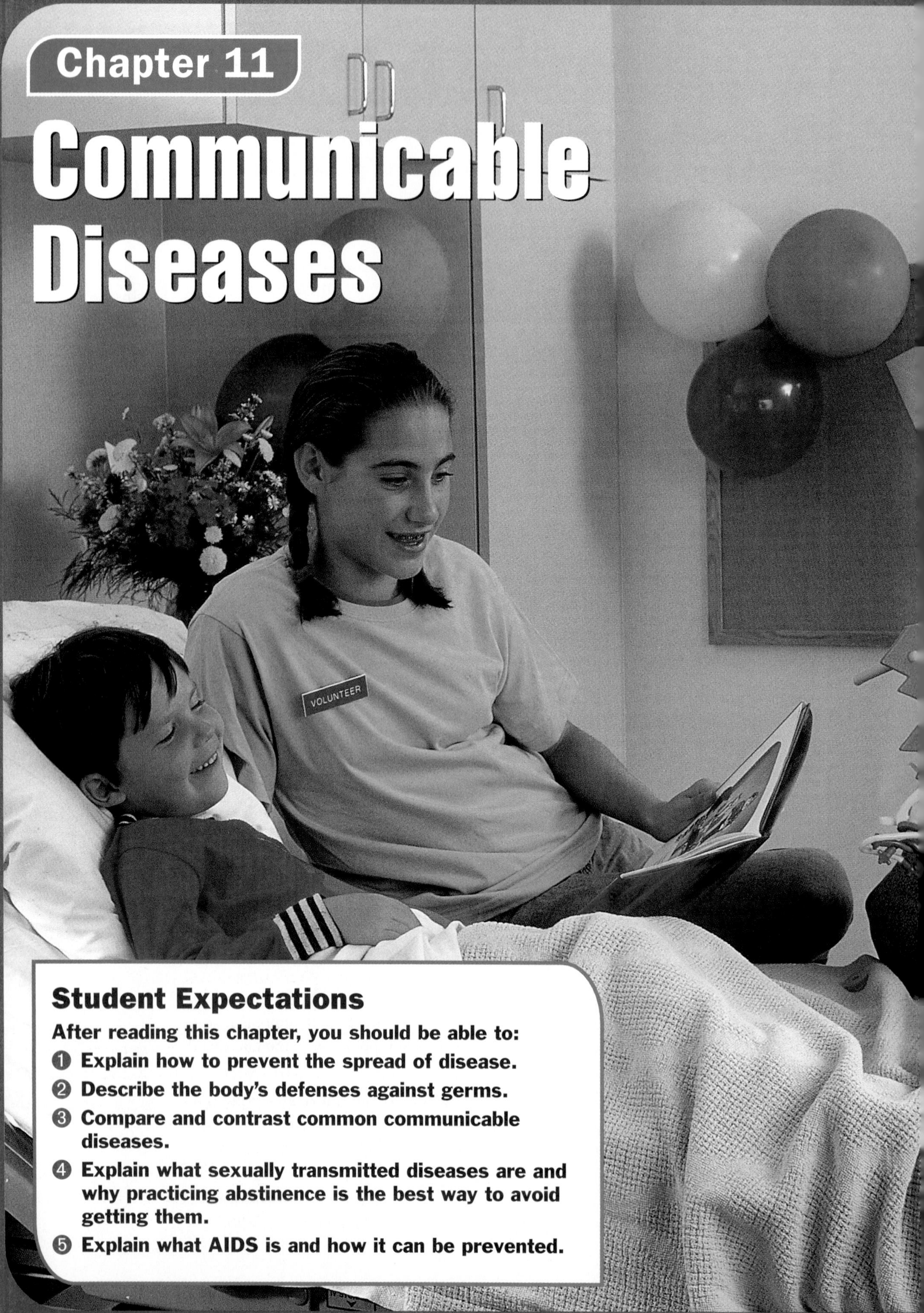

Student Expectations

After reading this chapter, you should be able to:

1. Explain how to prevent the spread of disease.
2. Describe the body's defenses against germs.
3. Compare and contrast common communicable diseases.
4. Explain what sexually transmitted diseases are and why practicing abstinence is the best way to avoid getting them.
5. Explain what AIDS is and how it can be prevented.

Teen Chat Group

Emily: I don't understand why we had to get a medical exam and shots before we could become hospital volunteers. We're not sick!

Nicholas: That's just it. We had to get an exam to make sure that we were healthy. The shots will help keep us from *getting* sick.

Emily: So, the hospital wants to make sure that we don't catch any diseases from the patients.

Nicholas: That's not the only reason for the shots, though. The hospital also wants to make sure that we don't spread our germs *to* the patients.

Emily: I bet that's why we're supposed to wash our hands a lot, too. Staying clean helps prevent the spread of diseases.

Nicholas: Being a hospital volunteer is going to be harder than we thought! It feels good, though, to know that we're helping.

in your journal

Read the dialogue on this page. Do you know how diseases are spread? Start your private journal entries on communicable diseases by answering these questions:

- Do you think that it was necessary for these hospital volunteers to get physical exams and shots? Why or why not?
- What diseases do you think you can catch from others?
- What do you think you can do to protect yourself from catching diseases when other people around you are sick?
- What do you think you can do to protect others from catching what you have when you are sick?

When you reach the end of the chapter, you will use your journal entries to make an action plan.

Lesson 1

Preventing the Spread of Disease

This lesson will help you find answers to questions that teens often ask about the spread of disease. For example:

- **What are germs?**
- **How are germs spread?**
- **How can I avoid picking up or passing on germs that cause disease?**

Words to Know

disease
communicable disease
germs
infection
bacteria
virus
rickettsias
fungi
protozoa
contagious period

What Is Disease?

When you are healthy, you feel good both physically and mentally. Sometimes, though, disease gets in the way of feeling good. A **disease** is *an illness that affects the proper functioning of the body or mind.* **Communicable** (kuh·MYOO·ni·kuh·buhl) **diseases** are *those that can be passed from one person to another.* Other diseases are not spread by contact with other people. Those diseases are caused by how people live, conditions they are born with, or environmental hazards. They are called noncommunicable diseases and are discussed in Chapter 12.

What Causes Communicable Diseases?

Communicable diseases are caused by *organisms so small you can see them only through a microscope.* These are called **germs.** *When germs invade the body and its cells, they grow, reproduce, and often produce poisonous waste products.* The result is an **infection** (in·FEK·shuhn), which damages or destroys body cells. **Figure 11.1** explains the difference between a communicable disease and a noncommunicable disease with similar symptoms.

Figure 11.1
The Difference Between Communicable and Noncommunicable Diseases

A If your runny nose, watery eyes, and sore throat are caused by a cold, you have a communicable disease.

B If your runny nose, watery eyes, and sore throat are caused by an allergy, you have a noncommunicable disease.

Types of Germs

The types of germs that cause communicable diseases include *bacteria, viruses, rickettsias, fungi,* and *protozoa.* Viruses are the most common cause of human communicable diseases. They cause such diseases as the common cold and the flu. They also cause some diseases, like AIDS, that can kill people. Viruses and bacteria together account for most illness in the United States. The following list describes the types of disease-causing organisms.

- **Bacteria** (bak·TIR·ee·uh) are *tiny one-celled organisms that grow virtually everywhere.* Bacteria can be harmless or harmful. There are three types of bacteria: cocci, bacilli, and spirilla.
- **Viruses** (VY·ruh·sez) are *the smallest and simplest form of life.* Many viruses are harmful to humans.
- **Rickettsias** (ri·KET·see·uhs) are *small bacteria that are spread by the bites of insects, such as ticks and lice.*
- **Fungi** (FUHN·jy) are *simple life forms that are unable to make their own food.*
- **Protozoa** (proh·tuh·ZOH·uh) are *simple, animal-like organisms.*

Countless bacteria live in the world around you—and even inside you. Most bacteria do not cause disease. In fact, many are helpful. Bacteria that live in your intestines help you digest food. Bacteria become harmful when they go places where they do not belong. Bacteria that is harmless in your mouth can enter your middle ear. Once there, they can cause an ear infection. To grow, bacteria need a food supply, warmth, and moisture. The body—which provides these three needs—makes an ideal home for them.

There are many different types of germs. Some common ones such as the bacteria *cocci* can cause such diseases as an abscess, gonorrhea, bacterial pneumonia, strep throat, and scarlet fever. *Bacilli* are responsible for botulism (food poisoning), diphtheria, tetanus, tuberculosis, whooping cough, and leprosy. *Spirilla* can cause polio, syphilis, and Lyme disease.

Viruses are very specialized. Some attack only certain kinds of animals. Some attack only certain cells of animals' bodies. The rabies virus, for instance, only affects the nervous system. Viruses are responsible for AIDS, measles, chicken pox, colds, the flu, mumps, polio, viral pneumonia, and mononucleosis.

Rickettsias are found in lice, mites, and ticks. They enter the human body when a person is bitten by an infected animal. Rocky Mountain spotted fever is caused by rickettsias. People who enjoy camping or hiking in the woods should guard against tick bites.

Fungi that attack the body often live in the hair, nails, and skin. Athlete's foot and ringworm are two diseases caused by fungi. Athlete's foot affects the feet. Ringworm appears on other body parts.

Many protozoa are harmless, but some cause disease. Malaria is caused by protozoa that live in certain kinds of mosquitoes. If an infected mosquito bites a person, the person will be infected.

interNET CONNECTION

Investigate the ways your body defends itself against germs, and how you can protect yourself from disease.

http://www.glencoe.com/sec/health

Science Connection

Beneficial Bacteria

Many bacteria are harmless and some are even essential for life. Without intestinal bacteria, for example, we could not digest food. Even harmless bacteria, however, can cause infection if they go where they don't belong. Bacteria from the intestines, for example, can cause infection if they get into the urinary tract or the bloodstream.

How Germs Are Spread

Germs can enter the body in four ways. Each type of germ is spread in one of these ways.

- **Close contact with a person who has the germ.** You can breathe in germs if someone coughs or sneezes near you. The germs travel in water droplets in the air, you inhale them, and they enter your body. Diseases such as colds, flu, measles, and tuberculosis can be spread this way. You also can get colds and other communicable diseases when you share eating utensils and drinking glasses.
- **Direct contact with a person who has the germ.** You can pick up germs on your hands and skin through direct contact with others. You also can pick up germs through sexual contact. This is the way people get diseases such as AIDS, gonorrhea, syphilis, and herpes.
- **Contact with animals.** You can get germs if you are bitten by some insects and other animals. Mosquito bites spread malaria, for example. Bites from animals infected by rabies spread that disease. Tick bites spread two serious diseases—Rocky Mountain spotted fever and Lyme disease.
- **Other contacts.** Germs can enter your body if you drink water or eat food that contains them. Food that is improperly stored or undercooked is dangerous for this reason. Giardia (an intestinal infection) comes from contaminated water, for example, and botulism from spoiled food.

in Your Journal

In your journal, list some of the ways you have heard you can get colds (for example, by getting a chill or too little sleep). Indicate whether you think each way is a possible cause, a contributing factor, or just a myth. Explain your responses.

Did You Know?

How Small Are Germs?

Most germs can be seen only with a microscope. In fact, viruses are so small they are visible only with a special microscope called an electron microscope. Until the electron microscope was invented in 1932, no one had ever seen a virus. Bacteria were first seen when the light microscope was invented. Do you know what year that happened?

How to Prevent the Spread of Disease

Practicing good health habits keeps you strong and better able to resist germs. Practicing good health behaviors helps prevent the spread of germs between you and others.

Practice Good Health Habits

- Eat a balanced diet.
- Get plenty of rest.
- Exercise regularly.
- Bathe or shower daily to keep your skin and hair clean.
- Avoid substances and behaviors that can harm your health.

Practice Good Health Behaviors to Protect Yourself

- Prepare food in safe ways. For instance, cook it thoroughly to kill bacteria.
- Store unused food quickly and properly.
- Do not use the same utensils or drinking glasses as someone else.
- Wear the right clothing and protective gear for your activities.
- Avoid having sex to prevent sexually transmitted diseases.
- Make sure your vaccination schedule is up to date for diseases that have *vaccines* (see Lesson 2).

Did You Know?

Dirty Water ACTIVITY!

An estimated 80 percent of all diseases in developing countries are caused by contaminated water.

Contact someone in your local public health department to find out what is done in your community to make water clean.

Practice Good Health Behaviors to Protect Others

- If you are sick, find out about the **contagious period,** which is *the period of time when your illness can spread to others.*
- During the contagious period, stay home from school so you cannot spread your germs to others.
- Cover your mouth and nose when you cough or sneeze.
- Seek medical treatment so you can get over the illness more quickly.
- If a doctor prescribes medication, follow the instructions and take the full amount prescribed.
- Encourage your family and friends to practice the good health habits you have learned.

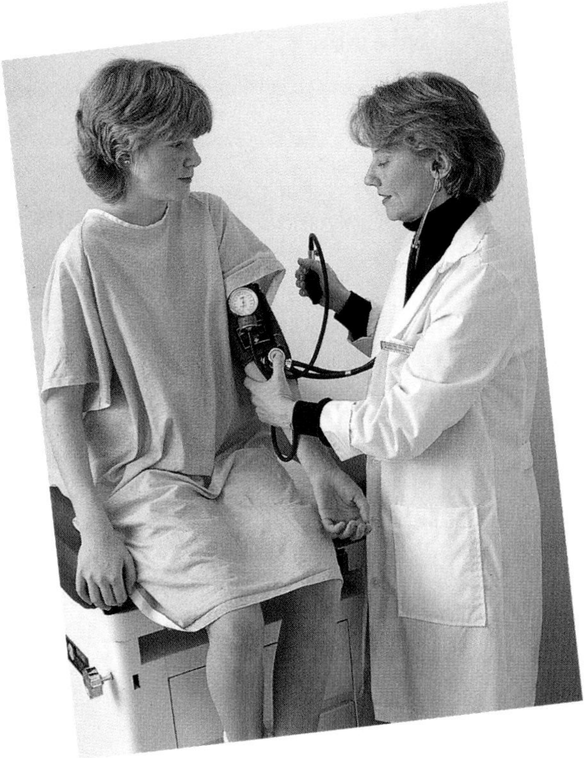

Personal Inventory

BEHAVIORS FOR GOOD HEALTH

Good health behaviors help you stay healthy, recover from illness faster, and prevent spreading germs. How healthy are your behaviors? To find out, write yes or no for each statement below on a separate sheet of paper.

1. I wash my hands after I use the bathroom and before preparing or serving food.
2. I cover my nose and mouth when I cough or sneeze.
3. I avoid sharing unwashed eating utensils or drinking glasses with others.
4. I avoid sharing combs, towels, or toothbrushes with others.
5. I make sure food is properly stored and cooked.
6. I avoid drinking water from streams and lakes.
7. When I'm sick, I stay home from school.
8. When I'm sick, I do not go out during the contagious period.
9. When I'm well, I avoid contact with people who have diseases that I could catch.
10. When I'm very sick, I get medical treatment.
11. I examine myself for ticks after being outdoors.
12. I have had all the necessary vaccinations.

To rate yourself, give yourself 1 point for a yes. A score of 10–12 is very good. A score of 8–10 is good. A score of 6–8 is fair. If you score below 6, you need to work on improving your health behavior.

Lesson 1

Review

Using complete sentences, answer the following questions on a separate sheet of paper.

Reviewing Terms and Facts

1. **Vocabulary** Define the term *communicable diseases*, using your own words.
2. **Recall** List four good behaviors to protect yourself from disease.

Thinking Critically

3. **Analyze** You have a friend who coughs and sneezes without covering his mouth and nose whenever he has a cold. What advice would you give him?
4. **Explain** Tell how exercise and a balanced diet can help prevent diseases caused by germs.

Applying Health Concepts

5. **Health of Others** Contact a local veterinarian or check out a library book to find out how ticks and fleas affect pets. Find out what you can do to help prevent a pet from getting ticks and fleas. Share your findings with your class.

Lesson 2

The Body's Defenses Against Germs

This lesson will help you find answers to questions that teens often ask about how the body fights germs. For example:

- **If germs are all around me, why am I not sick all the time?**
- **What is immunity and how do I know if I am immune?**
- **What vaccines do I need and why do I need them?**

Words to Know

immunity
lymphatic system
lymph nodes
lymphocytes
B-cells
T-cells
antibodies
vaccine

The Body's Defenses

Although germs are always around you, they seldom make you sick because of your body's defenses. Your body's first line of defense (your skin and body fluids) is described in **Figure 11.2.** If germs do enter your body, your body's main line of defense is activated. This is your **immunity** (i·MYOO·nuh·tee)—*your body's resistance to germs and the harmful substances they produce.*

Figure 11.2
The First Line of Defense
Your body's first line of defense works to protect you from germs.

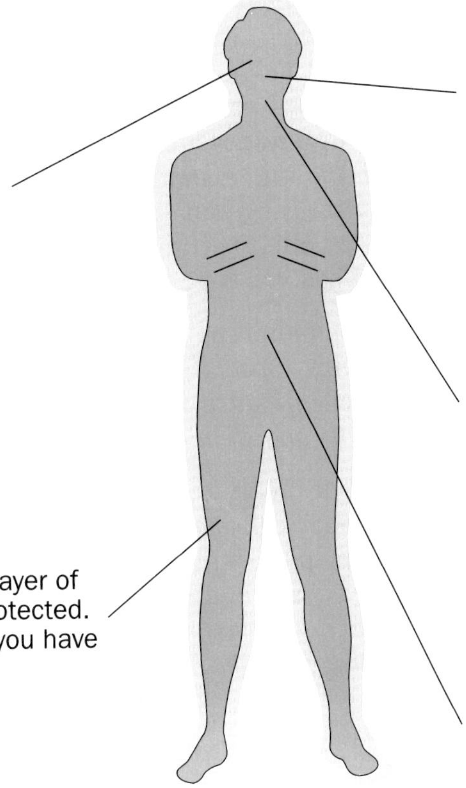
Mucous Membranes
These membranes line your nose, mouth, and throat and secrete a fluid called mucus (MYOO·kuhs) that traps germs. You get rid of the trapped germs when you sneeze, cough, or blow your nose.
Tears
Tears wash germs from your eyes. They also contain chemical compounds that kill germs.
Saliva
Saliva washes germs from your teeth and helps keep your mouth clean. It also contains chemical compounds that kill germs.
The Skin
As long as the tough, outer layer of skin is unbroken, you are protected. Germs can enter only when you have a cut, burn, or scrape.
Gastric Juice
Gastric juice produced by the mucous lining of your stomach destroys germs that enter through food or drink.

The Main Line of Defense

Sometimes harmful germs get through your first line of defense. Then your body's immune system takes over. Invading germs are attacked first in general immune reactions. Later, other immune responses occur that are tailor-made for specific germs.

in Your Journal

Before reading further in this chapter, describe in your journal how you think your body defends itself against germs. After you read the rest of the chapter, look back at your entry to see how much your understanding has improved.

General Reactions

- When germs enter your body, blood vessels nearby release special white blood cells called *phagocytes* (FAG·uh·syts). These cells engulf germs and destroy them in a process called *phagocytosis* (fag·uh·suh·TOH·suhs), which means "eating up cells."
- When certain body cells are invaded by viruses, they release a chemical substance called *interferon,* which stops the viruses from reproducing and infecting other cells.
- Fever, or elevated body temperature, kills germs that cannot survive body temperatures that are higher than normal.

Specific Immunity

If germs survive the general immune reactions, *specific immunity* takes over. This involves immune responses to specific germs and the poisons they produce. Specific immunity often gives the body the ability to remember how to destroy the same germs if they invade the body again. The next time they invade, the body can respond quickly so the germs won't have a chance to multiply—and you won't get sick.

The Lymphatic System

Specific immunity involves the **lymphatic** (lim·FA·tik) **system**—*a secondary circulatory system of vessels and nodes that carry a fluid called lymph.* This system helps maintain the balance of fluids in the body and helps your body fight germs. Lymphatic vessels carry lymph to a vein near the heart, where it enters the bloodstream. **Lymph nodes** are *small lumps of lymphatic tissue located throughout the system that act as filters to keep germs from invading body tissues.* When the body has been infected by a germ, lymph nodes often become swollen. Have you felt them in your neck area when you have been ill?

Teen Issues

Fever Reliever ACTIVITY!

If you have a fever, do not take aspirin or products that contain aspirin. In people under 18, taking aspirin for fever can result in Reye's syndrome, a potentially fatal disorder of the nervous system. Check the labels of fever-reducing medicines in the drugstore. Which ones should you avoid because they contain aspirin?

Specific immunity is carried out by two types of **lymphocytes** (LIM·fuh·syts)—*special white blood cells that circulate in the lymph.* **B-cells** *produce substances that fight germs.* **T-cells** *attack germs directly and stimulate B-cells to work* (see **Figure 11.3**).

Lymphocytes react to *antigens,* which are the parts of germs that connect to body cells and harm them. With bacteria, these antigens are toxins, or poisons, that the bacteria release. To fight antigens, B-cells release **antibodies.** These are *proteins that attach to germs or to the toxins germs produce, thus preventing the germ or toxin from harming your body.* B-cells produce a specific antibody for each specific antigen.

Figure 11.3

How the Immune System Responds to Viruses

B-cells and T-cells respond somewhat differently to bacteria in two ways. First, antibodies attack the toxins that bacteria release, killing those poisons. Second, antibodies force the bacterial cells to bunch together. Then they call on phagocytes to eat the bunches.

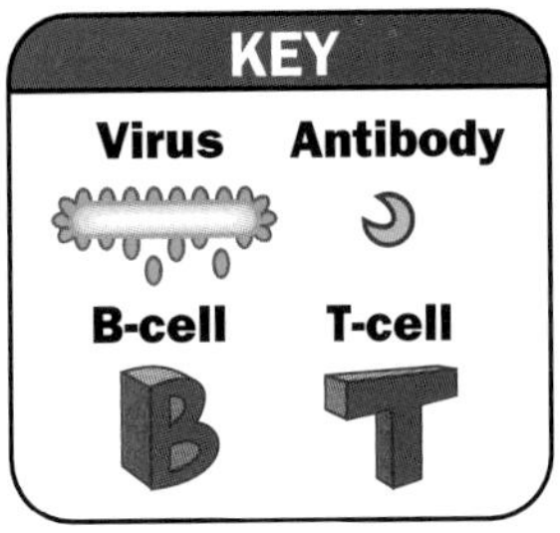

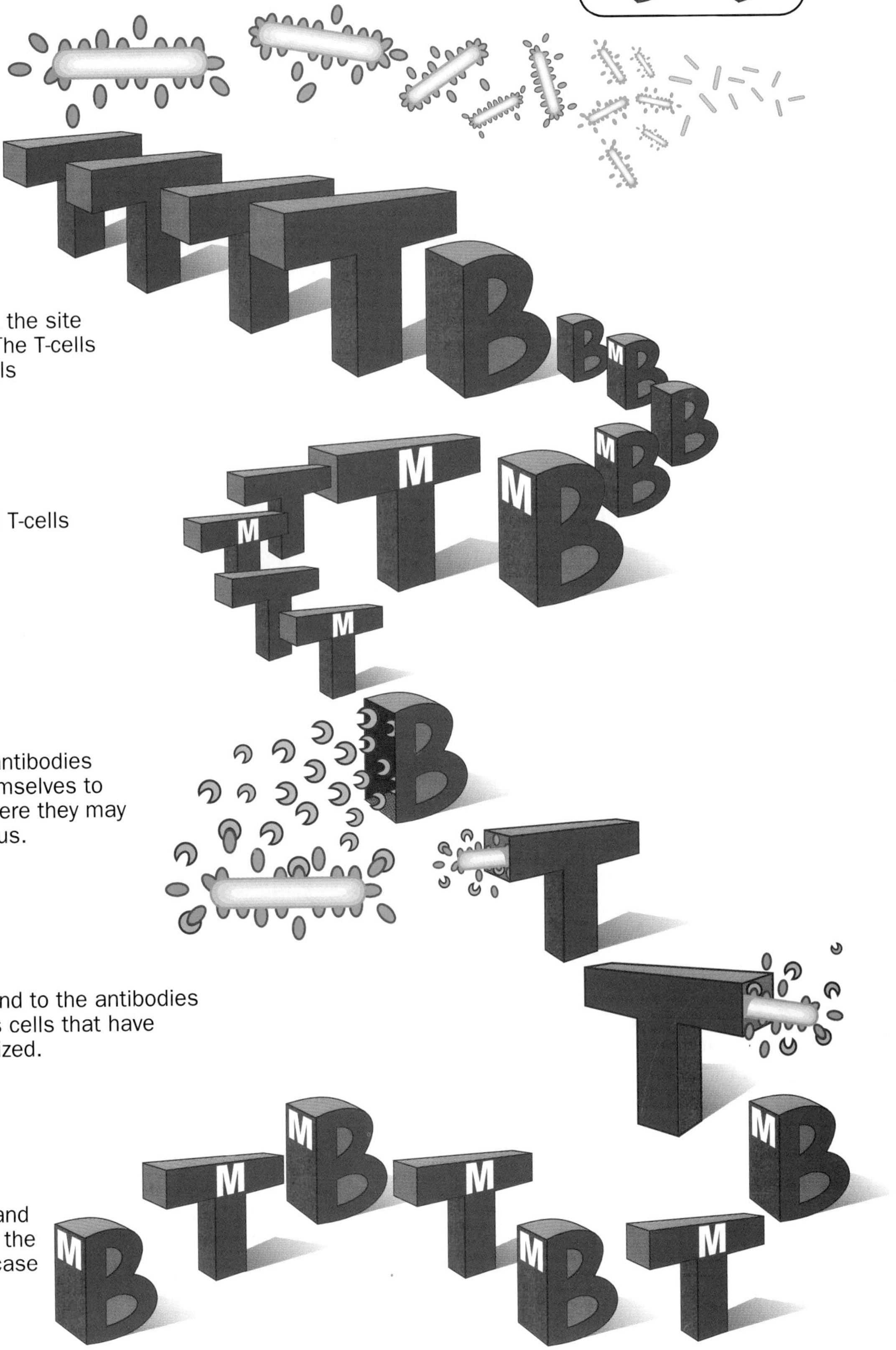

1. Virus enters the body.
2. T-cells identify the virus
3. T-cells multiply at the site of the infection. The T-cells activate the B-cells
4. B-cells multiply. Some B-cells and T-cells become memory lymphocytes.
5. B-cells produce antibodies which attach themselves to the virus cell, where they may neutralize the virus.
6. Special T-cells bind to the antibodies and destroy virus cells that have not been neutralized.
7. Memory B-cells and T-cells remain in the bloodstream in case the same virus invades again.

Immunity and Vaccines

Having a disease is one way you may become immune to it. Another way is through a **vaccine** (vak·SEEN). A vaccine is *a preparation of dead or weakened germs that is injected into the body to cause the immune system to produce antibodies.* Vaccines for each disease follow a specific schedule (see **Figure 11.4**). Some people have reactions to vaccines, such as rashes or fevers. Reactions usually are much less severe than the disease itself.

Figure 11.4
Vaccination Schedule

Vaccine	Recommended Ages for Vaccination
Diphtheria, whooping cough, tetanus	2 months, 4 months, 6 months, 12–18 months, 4–6 years
Polio	2 months, 4 months, 12–18 months, 4–6 years
Measles, mumps, rubella	15 months, 4–6 years (some experts postpone this dose to 10–11 years)
Influenza B	2 months, 4 months, 6 months (optional), 12–15 months
Adult tetanus and diphtheria	14–16 years, and every 10 years thereafter
Hepatitis B	birth–2 months, 1–4 months, 6–18 months; *or* 11–12 years if not previously immunized

HEALTH LAB

Tracking Temperatures

Introduction: While the average body temperature in healthy people is 98.6 degrees Fahrenheit, temperature varies from person to person and even in the same person from time to time. If temperature is taken orally, a reading from 97.6 to 99.6 is considered normal. (The normal range for temperature taken under the arm is 96.6 to 98.6.)

Objective: Learning how to read and interpret body temperature is an important health skill. By taking the same person's temperature repeatedly for several days, you can practice this skill.

Materials and Method: Take your own temperature or that of a family member at least twice a day for a week. Body temperature may be measured by mouth (oral) or under the armpit (axillary). You may use a glass thermometer or a disposable thermometer. If the thermometer is glass, it should be wiped with alcohol after each use. This kills any germs on it. (You can also use a thermometer sheath. This paper sleeve covers the thermometer while the temperature is taken and is then thrown away.) Disposable thermometers are used only once and then thrown away. Here are the steps.

Review

Lesson 2

Using complete sentences, answer the following questions on a separate sheet of paper.

Reviewing Terms and Facts

1. **Recall** Name the parts in the body's first line of defense.
2. **Recall** How does fever fight disease?
3. **Vocabulary** Which term refers to the lymphocyte that makes antibodies: *B-cell* or *T-cell*?

Thinking Critically

4. **Explain** Tell how general immune reactions differ from specific immune reactions.
5. **Analyze** Why does the law require vaccines for school-age children?
6. **Analyze** Shawn became ill with a cold. His friend Jorge caught his cold, but another friend did not. Why do you think that happened?

Applying Health Concepts

7. **Personal Health** Plan a vacation to countries in Africa, Asia, or South America. Ask your local health department what vaccinations are required to travel to those countries. Write a report explaining why each one is needed.

To read a mercury thermometer, hold the thermometer by the top. Twirl it in your fingers until you can see the column of mercury inside.

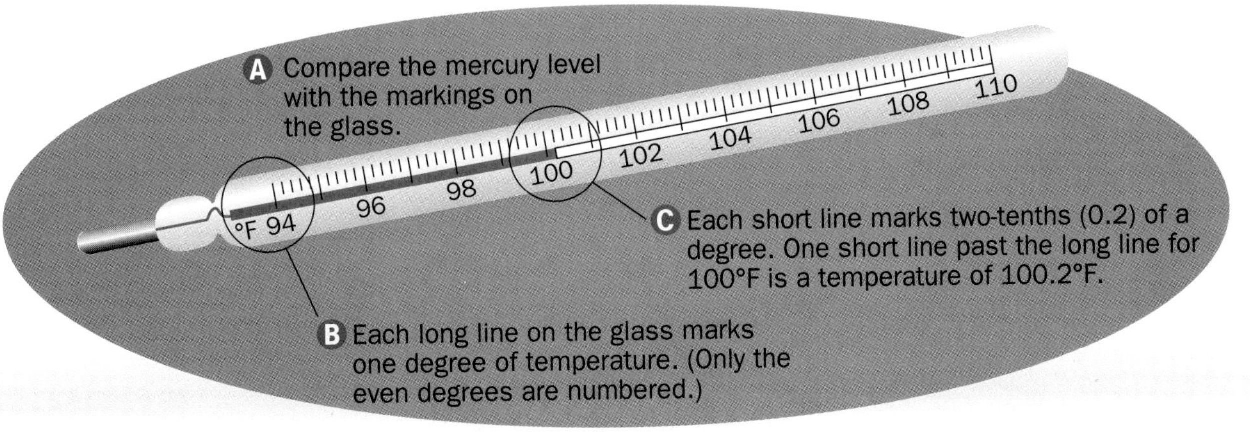

A Compare the mercury level with the markings on the glass.
°F 94
96
98
100
102
104
106
108
110
C Each short line marks two-tenths (0.2) of a degree. One short line past the long line for 100°F is a temperature of 100.2°F.
B Each long line on the glass marks one degree of temperature. (Only the even degrees are numbered.)

1. Holding the thermometer by the top, shake it enough to put the mercury below 96 degrees.
2. Place the mercury end of the thermometer under the person's tongue with the rest sticking out of the mouth. Tell the person to hold it in place for three minutes with his or her lips. (To take axillary temperature, put the bulb end of the thermometer under the person's armpit and keep it there for three minutes.)

Remove the thermometer carefully and record the temperature. Note the conditions of each test. Record whether the person is well or ill; how warmly dressed he or she is; whether or not the person was sleeping, exercising, showering, or eating shortly before you took the temperature; and how warm or cool the room is.

Observation and Analysis: At the end of the week, add up all the readings and then divide by the total number of readings. The result gives you the person's average temperature. How much does each reading vary from the average? Look at your notes about each temperature-taking session. What conditions are associated with high and low values? How can you apply what you have learned to monitoring your own temperature the next time you are sick?

Lesson

3 Common Communicable Diseases

This lesson will help you find answers to questions that teens often ask about common communicable diseases. For example:

- **What causes colds, and how can they be cured?**
- **What other common diseases are communicable?**

Words to Know

influenza
hepatitis
mononucleosis

The Common Cold

The most common communicable disease is the cold. Colds are caused by any of 200 or more different viruses. Symptoms of colds include mild fever, runny nose, itchy eyes, sneezing, coughing, mild sore throat, and headache.

Following healthy behaviors is the best way to prevent colds (see **Figure 11.5**). Get plenty of rest and drink lots of liquids. Some medicines can relieve cold symptoms. Even if they make you feel better, however, you should stay home for at least 24 hours after cold symptoms first appear. That is when your cold is most contagious, and you may pass the virus on to other people.

Figure 11.5
Preventing a Cold
Prevent colds by limiting your exposure to cold viruses and keeping yourself healthy enough to resist germs.

A Don't share eating utensils.
B Exercise regularly.
C Eat a balanced diet.
D Wash your hands frequently.
E Avoid smoking.
Hacks
F Get eight hours of sleep each night.

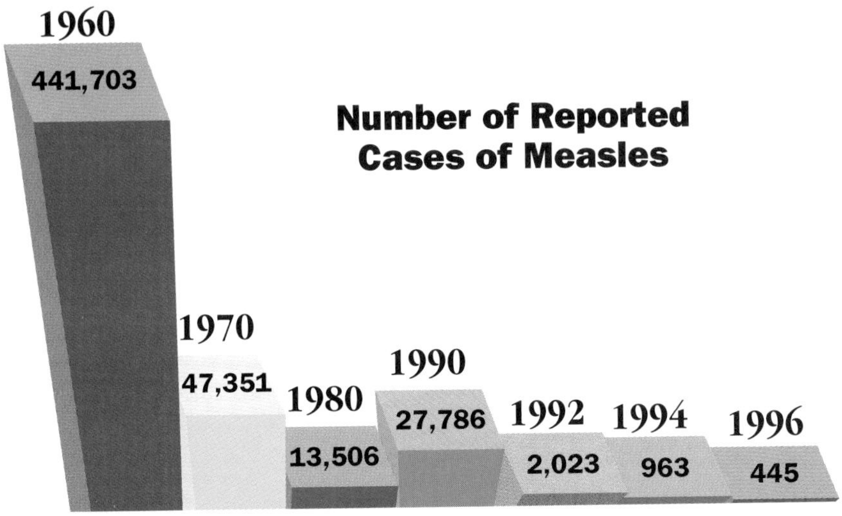

Source: Centers for Disease Control and Prevention

Figure 11.6
Decline of Measles in the United States

Measles is an extremely contagious disease that usually affects children. However, people of any age may get it. Measles was once a very common disease. A vaccine first used in the early 1960s had sharply decreased the number of cases. Then, in the late 1980s, outbreaks of measles began to occur. Experts believe that these outbreaks were due to the failure to vaccinate many infants.

Other Communicable Diseases

Several communicable diseases—rubella, measles, mumps, polio, and whooping cough—were once fairly common childhood illnesses. Most of these diseases have been nearly eliminated by the use of vaccines. See **Figure 11.6** for measles statistics. Some communicable diseases are discussed in **Figure 11.7.**

Figure 11.7
Some Communicable Diseases

Disease	Symptoms	Contagious Period	Vaccine
Chicken pox	Rash, fever, headache, body ache	One day before symptoms appear to six days after	Yes
Pneumonia	Chills, high fever, chest pain, cough	Varies	For some types
Rubella	Headache, swollen lymph nodes, cough, sore throat	Seven days before rash starts to five days after	Yes
Measles	Fever, runny nose, cough, rash	Seven days before rash starts to five days after	Yes
Mumps	Chills, fever, headache, swollen lymph nodes	Seven days before symptoms to nine days after	Yes
Hepatitis A & B	Fever, fatigue, mild chills, loss of appetite, headache, muscle pains	**A:** Unknown, possibly up to 1 week after onset **B:** Varies; may persist in carrier state for years	Yes
Whooping cough	Fever, runny nose, sneezing, dry cough (with) whooping sound	From inflammation of mucous membranes to four weeks after	Yes
Tuberculosis	Fever, fatigue, weight loss, coughing blood	Varies	Yes

A blood test can determine if you have hepatitis.

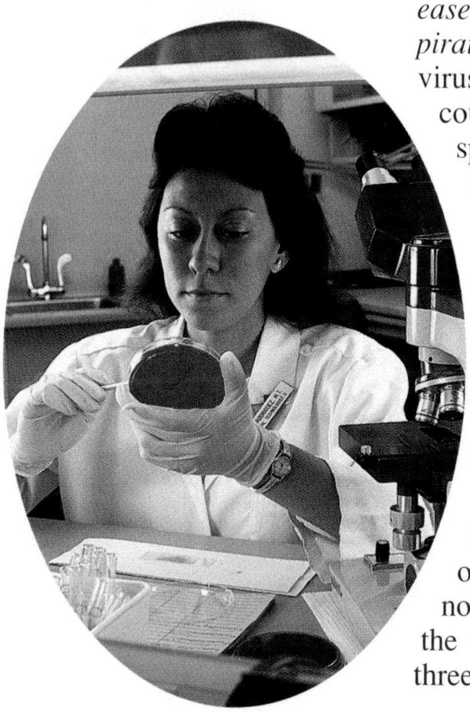

Influenza

Influenza (in·floo·EN·zuh), or "the flu," is *a communicable disease characterized by exhaustion, chills, headache, body ache, respiratory problems, and fever.* There are three types of influenza virus, each with several different strains. Influenza is spread by coughing and sneezing. Vaccines cannot completely stop its spread. Because the virus changes frequently, a vaccine that kills an old strain may not harm a new one. Yearly vaccination is recommended for the elderly and for people who have chronic diseases. Treatment includes plenty of rest and fluids, a balanced diet, and medicines to help relieve symptoms.

Hepatitis

Hepatitis (he·puh·TY·tis) is *a viral disease of the liver characterized by yellowing of the skin and the whites of the eyes.* The two major types—*hepatitis A* and *hepatitis B*—are each caused by a different virus. A person who has hepatitis A is immune for life. Therefore, the vaccine for it is given only to people who have not been exposed to the virus. There is no cure for hepatitis B, but the vaccine provides protection from the virus in 80–95 percent of persons who have been given all three doses.

Mononucleosis

You've probably heard of "the kissing disease," or "mono." These terms refer to **mononucleosis** (MAH·noh·noo·klee·OH·sis), *a viral disease that shows up as swelling of the lymph nodes in the neck and throat.* In addition to being spread by kissing, mono is spread by sharing eating utensils, drinking glasses, or toothbrushes with someone who has the disease. Mononucleosis is most common in teens and young adults.

LIFE SKILLS

Shopping for Cold Medicines

There are so many over-the-counter medicines for treating the symptoms of a cold that choosing the one that is best for you can be difficult. One important guideline to follow is to make sure the product you choose treats the symptoms you have and not those you do not have. Some medicines relieve runny noses, for example, whereas others relieve nasal congestion. Taking the wrong one for your symptoms may leave you feeling worse instead of better.

Most over-the-counter drugs have side effects or can cause allergic reactions, so it is important to read labels carefully. In addition, over-the-counter medicines may differ considerably in cost. Name brands are usually more expensive than generic brands.

Think about the last time you had a cold. Make a list of the symptoms you had when you felt your worst. Now, go to a drugstore and read package labels of cold medicines to find a name brand product that should help your worst symptoms. Then try to find a generic product that helps the same symptoms. Record the following information for each product:

Symptoms begin several weeks after exposure to the virus. They include fever, sore throat, swollen lymph nodes, and tiredness. Treatment is bed rest for three to six weeks. Symptoms gradually disappear after about six to eight weeks. The patient may remain contagious for a period of up to one year.

Review

Lesson 3

Using complete sentences, answer the following questions on a separate sheet of paper.

Reviewing Terms and Facts

1. **Identify** Cite four good health behaviors that reduce your chances of getting a cold.
2. **Vocabulary** Which is a viral disease of the liver: *influenza, hepatitis,* or *mononucleosis*?
3. **Recall** What has been the effect of widespread use of the measles vaccine?

Thinking Critically

4. **Synthesize** Based on your study of contagious periods, describe how to protect others from infection with communicable diseases.
5. **Analyze** Why is it difficult to develop a vaccine against colds and flu?

Applying Health Concepts

6. **Health of Others** With a group of classmates, demonstrate to the rest of the class how germs on the hands can be passed from one person to another. Use a small piece of double-faced tape to represent a germ. Ask the rest of the class to point out ways the germ's spread could be interrupted.
7. **Health of Others** Work with a group of classmates to write and illustrate a brochure informing other teens about mononucleosis. Include such topics as how it is spread, what ages are most at risk, what the symptoms are, and how it is treated.

- What symptoms is the product supposed to relieve?
- What are the product's side effects and warnings?
- How much of each active ingredient does the product contain?
- What is the recommended dosage for your age?
- How much does the product cost?

Follow-up Activity

Back at home or school, compare the two products. How are the products the same? How are they different? Which product would you choose if you had the same symptoms again? Why?

TEEN HEALTH DIGEST

HEALTH UPDATE

Tuberculosis Q & A

At one time tuberculosis (TB) was the most feared disease in the United States. Then, for decades, the disease declined. It seemed as if TB had been beaten. About ten years ago, though, cases of TB began to increase in number in the United States. Today health officials believe that tuberculosis is an enormous public health problem worldwide.

Q: What are the symptoms of TB?

A: Symptoms include weight loss, fever, night sweats, and a weak or sick feeling—as well as coughing, chest pain, and coughing up blood.

Q: What causes TB?

A: TB is caused by bacteria that are spread through the air when a person who has TB coughs, sneezes, laughs, or sings. Not everyone who is infected with the bacteria develops the disease.

Q: How many people have TB?

A: In the United States alone, about 22,000 people a year develop the disease. Worldwide, there are about 8 million new cases a year. In addition, 10 to 15 million people in this country are infected with the TB bacteria and could develop the disease.

Q: Who is most at risk for developing TB?

A: Those with the highest risk are poor and homeless people, alcoholics, intravenous drug users, and people who are infected with HIV.

Teens Making a Difference

AIDS Education Activist

Name: Michael Smith

School: Minnechaug Regional High School, Wilbraham, Massachusetts

Accomplishments:

- State-certified HIV/AIDS peer educator
- Member, Governor's Peer Leadership Council, Massachusetts
- Northeast Region Youth of the Year of the Boys & Girls Clubs of America

Quote: "I go to homes or community centers and hold 'safety net' parties. . . [it's] a lot of straight talk about what can happen if they aren't careful about what they're doing."

Since fall 1994, Michael has talked with more than 150 teens about the dangers of STDs and about methods to avoid contracting them.

People at Work

Medical Laboratory Technician

Do you want to help fight illness? Do you also like working with high-tech equipment? Then a career as a medical laboratory technician might be for you.

Roberta Imann works as a technician in a medical lab. At one time Roberta thought that she would become a nurse. Then, while taking high school biology, Roberta discovered that she loved working in a laboratory. After high school she earned a two-year associate's degree at a local community college.

Today, Roberta works in a hospital lab. She tests patients' blood and other tissues to help doctors diagnose diseases and recommend treatments.

Try This: *For two or three Sundays, check the classified advertising section of your local paper for ads for medical laboratory technicians and other health-related workers. What do the ads say the job requirements are? Share your findings with your classmates.*

Personal Trainer

Gym Hygiene

Playing a sport is a great way to get healthy and stay that way. Still, you may be exposed to infections—viruses, fungi, and bacteria—when you participate in sports. Here are some rules that can help you stay well as you play sports:

- Don't share water bottles.
- Dispose of paper drinking cups immediately after use.
- Don't treat injuries with ice taken from a drinking container—use ice packs.
- Wear gloves when touching or wiping up body fluids.
- Securely cover all skin wounds with clean bandages.

CON$UMER FOCU$

Worm Alert

What's cuter than a sweet little puppy? Who can resist a playful kitten? Pet owners should take care, however—that cuddly critter may carry worms!

Intestinal roundworms can be spread from animals to people when pet owners accidently ingest the eggs of the pet's worms. The eggs hatch inside a person's body, and the worm larvae spread to the liver, lungs, and other organs.

Here's how to prevent your pet from contracting—and spreading—worms.

- Have a veterinarian check your pup or kitten for worms. The vet can also prescribe medicines to prevent your pet from getting worms.
- Make sure that your older pets continue to receive regular tests for worms.
- Clean up after your pet. This means making sure a cat's litter box is fresh and removing dog waste from areas where people play.

Lesson 4

Sexually Transmitted Diseases

This lesson will help you find answers to questions that teens often ask about sexually transmitted diseases. For example:

- **Which diseases are sexually transmitted?**
- **How can I get a sexually transmitted disease?**
- **Why is abstinence the best way to avoid getting a sexually transmitted disease?**
- **How can sexually transmitted diseases be treated?**

Words to Know

chlamydia
gonorrhea
genital warts
genital herpes
syphilis

Teen Issues

Planning Ahead

It is a good idea to carry money for a phone call when you go out with friends, or on a date. If your date pressures you to have sex and you want to leave early, you can call home for a ride. Many public phones also allow you to make direct and/or operator-assisted emergency calls without money. However, the next time you go out, be sure to take some change.

What Are STDs?

STD is short for *sexually transmitted disease.* STDs are illnesses that pass from one person to another through sexual contact, but they can be prevented. Young people are at greatest risk of getting STDs because they lack knowledge about the diseases. See **Figure 11.8** for statistics about STDs. To avoid STDs, teens need to know more about them (see **Figure 11.9** on pages 360 and 361).

- **STDs are dangerous.** Permanent effects can include sterility, blindness, deafness, insanity, and death.
- **STDs may have no symptoms or some that come and go.**
- **Most STDs can be treated.** Early diagnosis is important.
- **STDs recur.** The body cannot build up an immunity to any STD.
- **Most STDs can be spread only through sexual contact.**

Figure 11.8
Statistics About STDs
Of the 12 million STD cases reported in the United States in 1995, nearly one-fourth were teens.

STD	Total
Trichomoniasis	3 million
Urethritis	1.2 million
Gonorrhea	392,848
Chlamydia	477,638
Genital Warts	500,000
Genital Herpes	200,000
Syphilis	16,500

Practicing Abstinence

Sexually transmitted diseases are different from other communicable diseases in two important ways. First, no vaccines are available to prevent them. Second, the body does not build up an immunity to any STD. Therefore, the only sure way to avoid getting most STDs is through abstinence from sexual activity. It's as simple as that. Saying no to sex before marriage will be one of the most important health decisions you ever make.

Dates may pressure you to have sex, but they cannot decide for you. You must take responsibility for your own health. Here are some ways to help you practice abstinence from sexual activity.

Smart Behaviors

- Choose your friends carefully—those who will support your decision to practice abstinence from sexual activity until marriage.
- Avoid being alone with a date.
- Seek advice from trusted adults.
- Say no through your words *and* your actions.

Smart Words

- If your date says, "You would have sex with me if you really loved me," you should say, "You would respect my wishes if you really loved me."
- If your date says, "Everybody's doing it," you should say, "Most teens *aren't* doing it. Anyway, it's my decision that matters to me and should matter to you."
- If your date says, "Sex can be safe," you should respond with, "Abstinence is the only sure way to be safe."

Group social activities are a good way to have fun while eliminating the pressure to have sex.

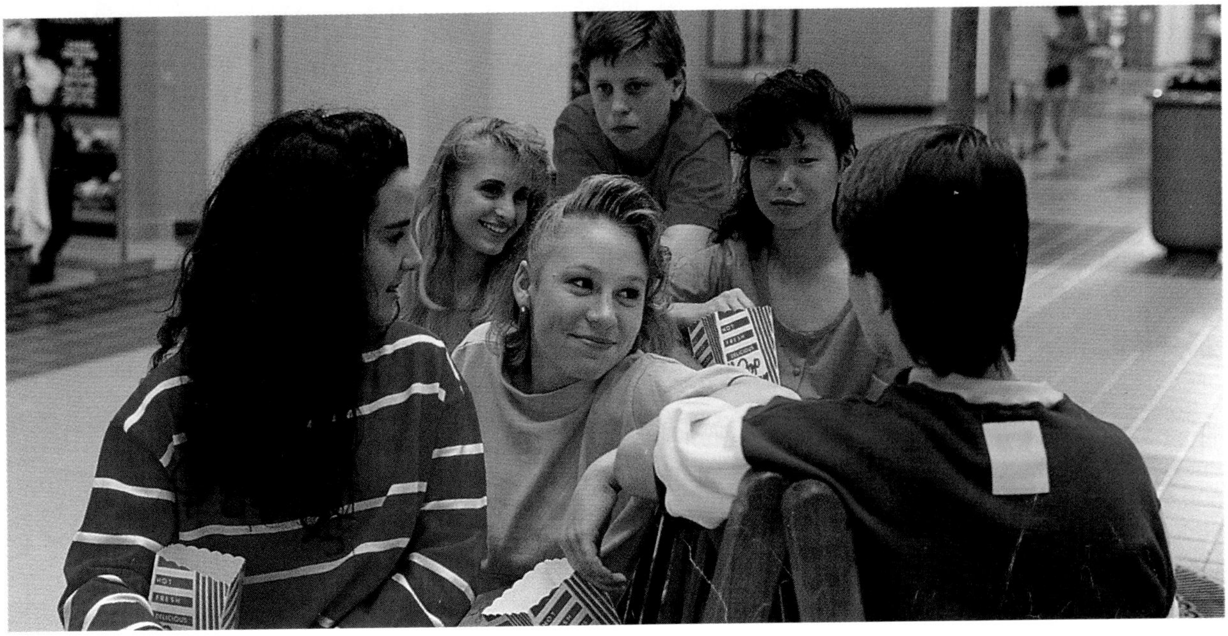

Did You Know?

The "Silent" STD ACTIVITY!

About 75 percent of females and 20 percent of males with chlamydia show no early signs of the disease. The lack of early signs of infection makes prevention crucial.

Write a public service announcement telling other teens the single best way to prevent getting chlamydia.

in your journal

In your journal, write down reasons you think STDs are more likely to go untreated in teens than in other age groups. Describe how you would feel and what you would do if you thought you had an STD.

Feeling Good About Your Decision

You may worry that by choosing abstinence, you may lose your boyfriend or girlfriend to another person. Dating should be fun. If it is full of tension over the pressure to have sex, it is no longer fun. If your date won't stop pressuring you, it may be best to end the relationship. This is a difficult decision to make, one that can hurt at the time. However, the alternative will hurt more when agreeing to have sex goes against your values. By sticking to your decision to say no to sex, you can live honestly and comfortably. You can still find company—and have fun without pressure—with other friends.

Help from Others

A parent or another trusted adult may offer some sound advice. In addition, people in government who are responsible for public health prepare and distribute brochures that explain the STDs and their prevention. Some public health workers give talks at schools and community centers to answer the questions teens have about these diseases. Others place public service announcements in the media—radio, television, and magazines—to explain that the safest way to avoid an STD is to say no to sex.

Common STDs

Each year, thousands of teens contract an STD. Many fail to seek medical attention because they are embarrassed or unwilling to take responsibility for their actions. Some ignore their symptoms. In some cases the symptoms are not obvious, and the teen doesn't know he or she has a disease. The symptoms and effects of many common and serious STDs are shown in **Figure 11.9** on pages 360 and 361. Another very serious STD, AIDS, is covered in Lesson 5.

MAKING HEALTHY DECISIONS

Helping a Friend Choose Abstinence

Lillian and Tamara have been best friends since they were in elementary school. They spend a lot of time together on weekends and after school. Since the beginning of the school year Tamara has been dating a classmate, Tommy.

Tamara and Tommy are usually together at school activities and at parties. Tamara really likes Tommy and enjoys their dates together. She always talks about him to Lillian.

Today, however, Tamara is especially quiet. When Lillian asks her what is wrong, Tamara finally explains that Tommy has been pressuring her to have sex. Tamara says that her dates aren't fun anymore. She says she doesn't feel ready for sex, but she's worried Tommy will leave her if she doesn't give in—and that would "hurt too much." She asks Lillian what she should do.

What should Lillian say to her? Should she stress the dangers of sexually transmitted diseases? Should she urge Lillian to choose abstinence? Should she urge her to stop seeing Tommy?

Chlamydia

Chlamydia is one of the most common STDs in the United States. It is very hard to detect because signs of the disease may not show up until it is well advanced. **Chlamydia** (kluh·MI·dee·uh) is *an STD caused by a bacterium called Chlamydia trachomatis that affects the reproductive organs, urethra, and anus in both males and females.* If left untreated, chlamydia can cause sterility and/or other serious damage to reproductive and other organs.

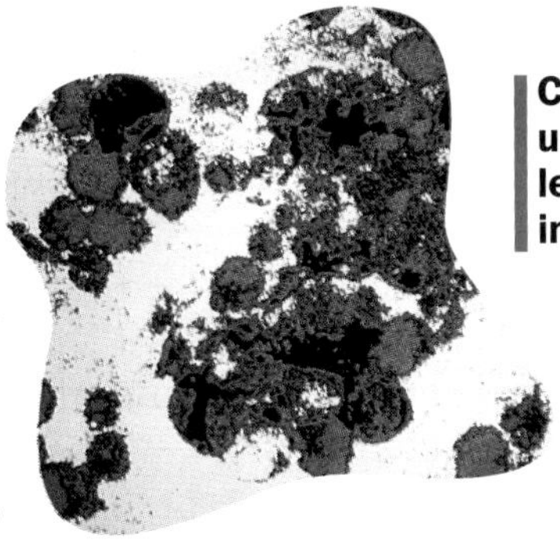

Chlamydia, shown here under a microscope, can lead to sterility (the inability to reproduce).

Gonorrhea

Another common STD is gonorrhea. **Gonorrhea** (gah·nuh·REE·uh) is *an STD caused by bacteria that affects the genital mucous membrane and possibly other body parts such as the heart, throat, or joints.* The bacteria cannot live outside the body. Like chlamydia, the signs and symptoms may not occur until the disease is advanced, especially in females.

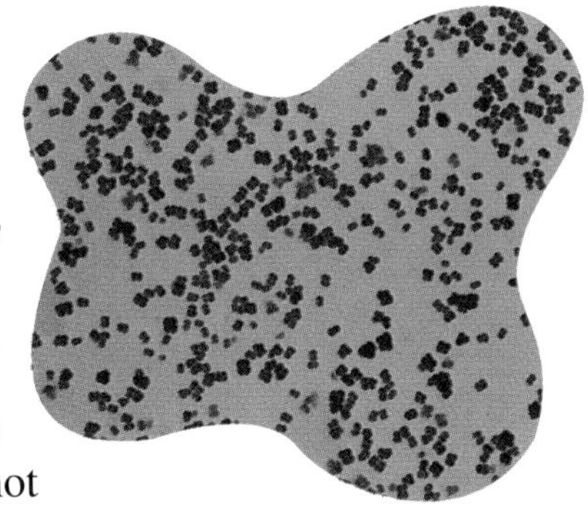

Gonorrhea can also cause sterility, as well as damage to the heart or other organs.

Genital Warts

Genital warts are *growths that develop in the genital area caused by the same virus that causes common warts.* They are generally harmless, but if left untreated they will multiply. They are easily transmitted to another person through sexual contact. This STD is one of the major causes of cervical cancer in women.

Lillian uses the six steps of the decision-making process to help her come to a decision:

1. **State the situation**
2. **List the options**
3. **Weigh the possible outcomes**
4. **Consider your values**
5. **Make a decision and act**
6. **Evaluate the decision**

Follow-up Activities

1. Apply the six steps of the decision-making process to Lillian's story.
2. With a partner, role-play a conversation between Lillian and Tamara in which Lillian gives her advice.
3. What would you do if you were Tamara?

Genital Herpes

Genital herpes (HER·peez) is *an STD that is caused by a virus and produces painful blisters in the genital area of males and females.* The signs and symptoms of this disease may go away temporarily even though the virus remains in the body. The disease is contagious when the signs and symptoms are present, and it may be contagious for a period of time before they appear and after they disappear. At present, there is no cure for genital herpes.

Syphilis

Syphilis (SI·fuh·lis) is *an STD caused by bacteria. If untreated, syphilis may spread to the central nervous system, causing insanity, paralysis, and death.* Syphilis was once the most common

Figure 11.9
Basic Facts About STDs

Anyone who suspects that he or she has an STD needs medical help. The worst thing to do is to ignore the signs.

Disease	Cause	Signs and Symptoms	Treatment	Complications
Chlamydia	Bacteria	Pain, burning during urination; genital reddening and discomfort; discharge	Oral antibiotics	Scarring of reproductive organs; sterility; infections of fetus in pregnant women
Gonorrhea	Bacteria	Discharge; swollen lymph nodes in groin; burning during urination; abnormal menstrual cycles in females	Antibiotics, although some strains are drug resistant	Sterility; permanent damage to joints, heart, and other organs; infection of fetus in pregnant women
Genital Warts	Virus	Warts in genital area one to six months after sexual contact with an infected person	Topical medication; cryotherapy (freezing); surgery to remove warts	Cancer of reproductive system; obstruction of urinary tract in males; can be passed to newborns during birth
Genital Herpes	Virus	Painful, itchy blisters in genital area; discharge; fever; burning during urination	No cure; medications to relieve symptoms	Cervical cancer in females; brain damage or death in infants of infected mother
Syphilis	Bacteria	Reddish sores in genital area; body rash; flu-like symptoms	Antibiotics, usually penicillin	Damage to heart, blood vessels, liver, kidneys, nervous system; blindness; insanity; death

sexually transmitted disease. Syphilis is less common today, with decreasing incidence since 1990.

Syphilis occurs in three stages. Between the stages, the signs and symptoms may disappear. As a result, the affected person may mistakenly think that he or she is cured. The second stage may not occur until months after the first stage. The third stage may not occur for up to 20 years after the second stage.

Other Sexually Transmitted Diseases

Several other serious diseases are transmitted through sexual contact. They are vaginitis, pubic lice, and scabies. *Vaginitis* is an infection of the vagina. Its symptoms include pain, itching, and a burning sensation during urination. It can be treated with antibiotics and proper hygiene. *Pubic lice* are insects that look like tiny crabs. They attach to the skin and hair of the pubic area and suck a person's blood. This causes severe itching. *Scabies* is caused by mites, tiny animals that burrow themselves into the skin and lay their eggs. They can live on clothes and towels for a short time and can infect another person who uses these items.

Disease	Cause	Signs and Symptoms	Treatment	Complications
Trichomoniasis	Protozoa	Yellowish discharge with strong odor; itching in females; males may have slight or no symptoms	Antibiotics	Infections of the bladder and urethra
Vaginitis	Bacteria, fungi, or protozoa	Itching; burning during urination; discharge in females; males may have no symptoms, but can transmit the disease	Antibiotics or fungicide creams	Urinary-tract infections
Nongonococcal Urethritis (NGU)	Bacteria	Sterility; swollen testicles and/or prostate infection	Antibiotics	Sterility; swollen testicles and/or prostate infection
Pubic Lice	Small, crablike insects	Presence of lice and eggs in pubic hair; itching	Medicated shampoo; washing all bed linens and clothes	No lasting effects
Scabies	Tiny animals called mites	Rash; itching where mites have burrowed under the skin	Insecticide cream; washing bed linens and clothes	Scratching can cause bacterial infections

A Final Word

There are more than 30 different sexually transmitted diseases. Some have no cure, and all are serious, even deadly. STDs harm not only the person who has one, but that person's sexual partner.

In recent years, STDs have been spreading rapidly. According to the Centers for Disease Control and Prevention, about 12 million new cases appear every year. More than one-fourth of these cases are occurring among teens.

You can avoid getting an STD. Learn all you can about these diseases. Most important, remember that abstinence is the only sure way to avoid getting an STD. By putting off having sex until marriage, you are protecting yourself and others.

The most effective protection from STDs is to avoid sexual contact.

Lesson 4

Review

Using complete sentences, answer the following questions on a separate sheet of paper.

Reviewing Terms and Facts

1. **Recall** List four facts about STDs that teens need to know.
2. **Recall** Cite two ways in which STDs are different from other communicable diseases.
3. **Give Examples** Name six STDs.
4. **Vocabulary** Which of the following STDs, if left untreated, may spread to the central nervous system: *syphilis, chlamydia,* or *gonorrhea*?

Thinking Critically

5. **Synthesize** Why should you seek medical help if you think you have been exposed to an STD even though you have no symptoms?
6. **Explain** Why is saying no to sex one of the most important health decisions you can ever make?
7. **Compare and Contrast** Discuss how genital herpes and genital warts are similar and how they are different.

Applying Health Concepts

8. **Health of Others** Make a poster that shows teens the potential dangers of STDs.
9. **Health of Others** With another student, present a skit to the rest of the class in which one teen urges another to have sex. Ask the class to suggest convincing responses.

HIV/AIDS

Lesson 5

This lesson will help you find answers to questions that teens often ask about AIDS. For example:

- **What is AIDS, and what causes it?**
- **Do I have to worry about being around someone with AIDS?**
- **What can I do to avoid getting AIDS?**

What Is AIDS?

AIDS, or **acquired immunodeficiency** (im·yoo·noh·di·FI·shuhn·see) **syndrome,** is *a deadly disease that interferes with the body's natural ability to fight infection.* The *virus that causes AIDS is* called **HIV,** or **human immunodeficiency virus.**

- **AIDS is a deadly disease.** There is no vaccine to prevent infection with HIV, and there is no cure for AIDS; it is fatal.
- **You can be a carrier of HIV without having AIDS.** A **carrier** is *an apparently healthy person who has HIV in the blood and can pass it to others.* People infected with HIV have the virus for an average of 10 years before showing any symptoms of AIDS. **Figure 11.10** shows how many teens can be carrying HIV for many years without knowing it. As teens grow older, many begin to show symptoms or are diagnosed with AIDS.
- **AIDS is easy to prevent through abstinence.**

Words to Know

acquired immunodeficiency syndrome (AIDS)
human immunodeficiency virus (HIV)
carrier
opportunistic infection

Figure 11.10
U.S. AIDS Cases at Age of Diagnosis, 1996

Being infected by HIV is not the same as having AIDS. The average length of time from infection to the onset of symptoms and/or diagnosis of AIDS is 10 years. What do these statistics say about high-risk behavior among teens?

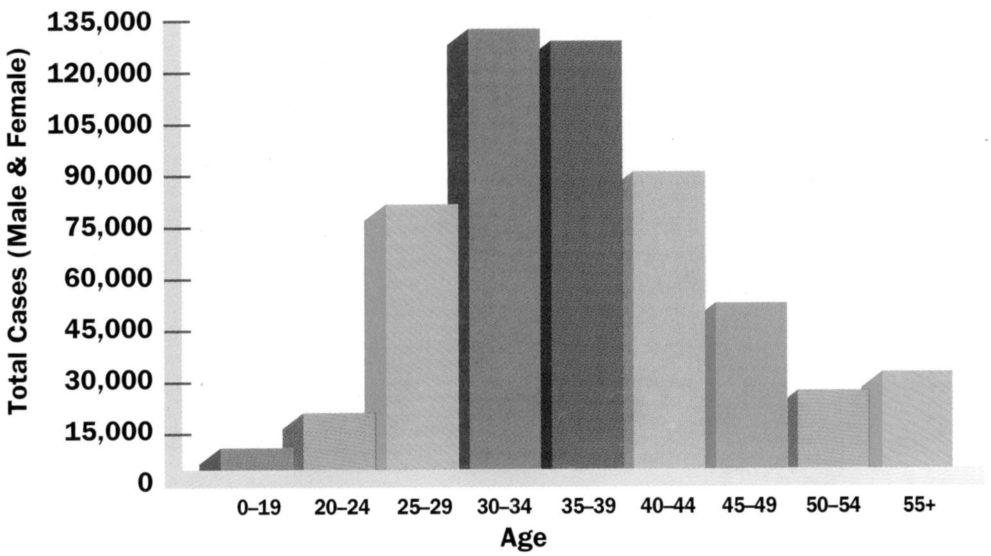

Source: Centers for Disease Control and Prevention, HIV/AIDS Surveillance Report

What HIV Does to the Body

AIDS is a relatively new disease. The first cases in the United States were reported in 1981. Currently, there is no cure for AIDS and no vaccine against HIV.

HIV attacks the immune system (see **Figure 11.11**), leading at first to swollen lymph nodes, tiredness, diarrhea, weight loss, and fever. Eventually, the weakened immune system cannot fight off the germs a healthy immune system could destroy. It is these other germs that usually cause the death of a person with AIDS.

HIV Lets Other Germs Attack the Body

A low T-cell count is one important sign of AIDS. Another criterion for diagnosing AIDS is the presence of certain other diseases. With an impaired immune system, a person with AIDS is susceptible to many *infections that otherwise rarely occur.* Such infections are called **opportunistic infections.** For example, a form of cancer called *Kaposi's* (KA·puh·seez) *sarcoma* was extremely rare until the AIDS epidemic began in the early 1980s. Another opportunistic infection that is common in AIDS patients is a rare form of pneumonia called pneumocystic pneumonia.

Figure 11.11

Comparing Healthy and HIV-Infected Immune Systems

Once in the body, HIV works differently than other viruses.

A Normal Immune Response
In a healthy person, T-cells identify the virus. B-cells produce antibodies that may neutralize the virus. T-cells destroy virus cells that have not been neutralized and stimulate B-cells to produce more anitbodies.

B Immune Response in a Person with HIV
In a person with HIV, the virus seeks out and destroys T-cells. With fewer T-cells, the B-cells stop producing antibodies. With a weakened immune system, the body is open to other infections.

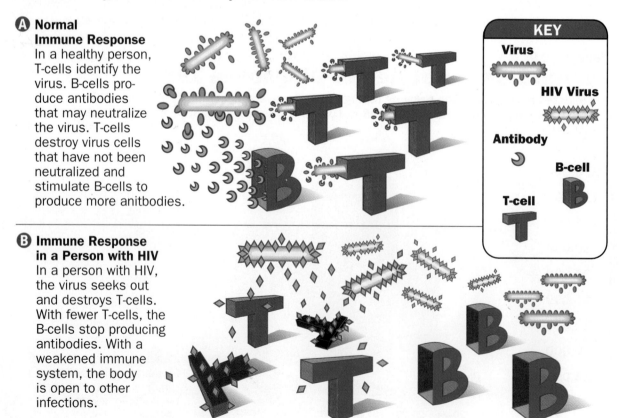

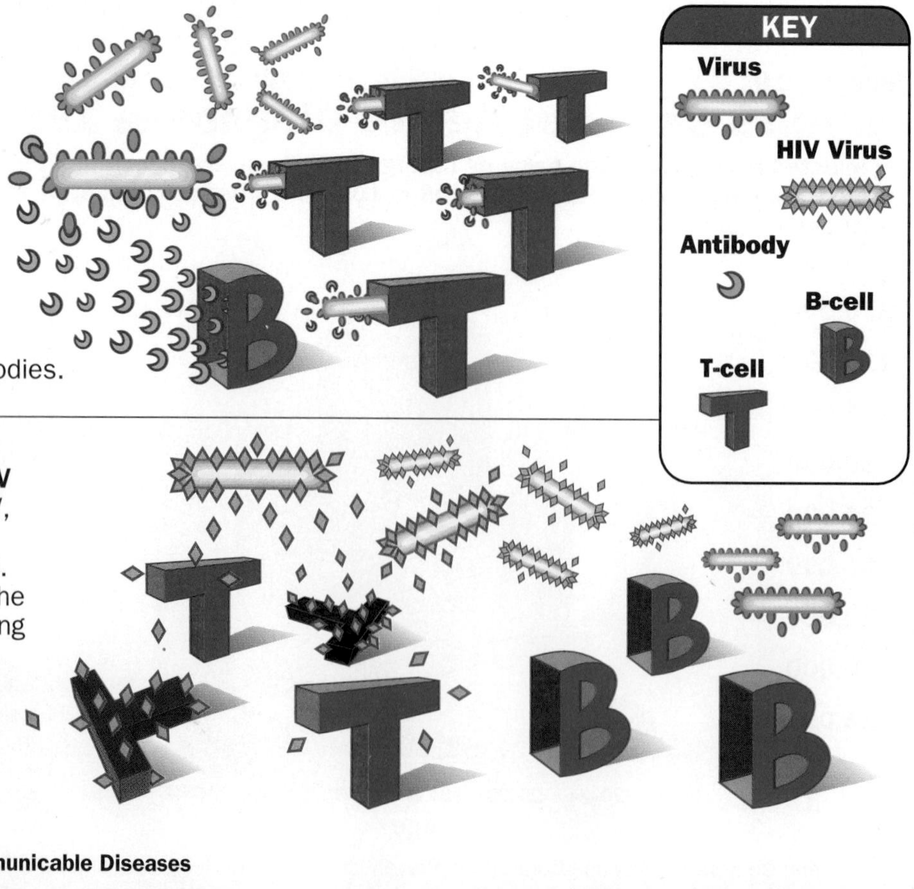

Testing and Treating

A blood test can tell you if you are infected with HIV. A positive test result indicates the presence of HIV antibodies in your blood. However, it may take six months after infection before antibodies show up. If you think you might be infected, even though your test result is negative, have the test repeated at a later date.

Most of the treatments given to AIDS patients are for opportunistic infections, such as antibiotics for pneumonia. There is no drug available that kills HIV and cures AIDS. The drug AZT does delay the onset of AIDS symptoms in some patients by slowing the reproduction of the virus. AZT has serious side effects, however. The FDA has also approved eight other drugs to treat HIV.

How HIV Is Spread

Because HIV is too fragile to survive in the atmosphere, it can be passed from one person to another only in body fluids—blood, semen, and vaginal secretions. Therefore, HIV infection can only occur in the following ways:

- **Sexual relations with an infected person.** People who have sex with multiple partners are at greatest risk.
- **Using the same needle to inject drugs that was previously used by an infected person.** Tiny amounts of blood that remain in the needle can be injected along with the drug. An accidental prick with a used needle is the main way health care workers get HIV infection.
- **Transfusions and other medical treatments using blood from an infected person.** All donated blood is tested for HIV. If it tests positive, the blood is not used. However, the tests are not 100 percent safe. The blood of a newly infected person may not yet contain the antibodies that indicate the presence of HIV.
- **Passing the virus from infected mother to fetus.** This occurs in about half of all pregnancies to HIV-infected women and usually leads to death of the child by age two.

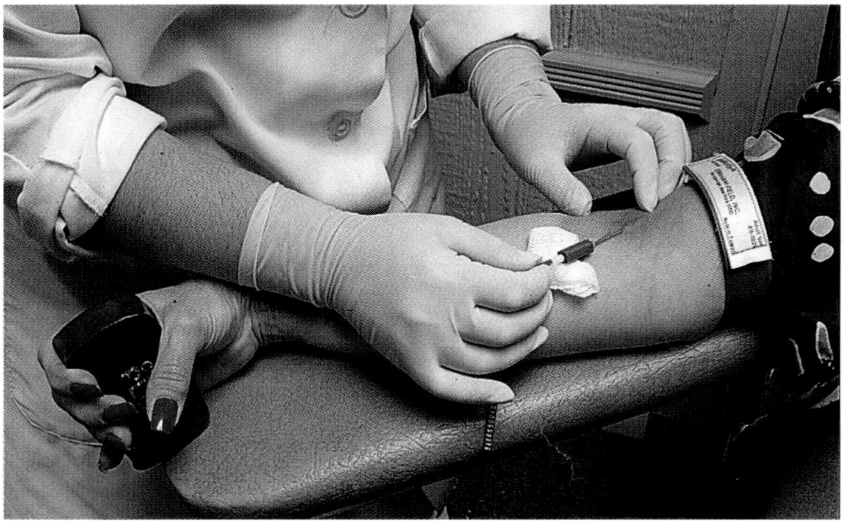

Because clean equipment is used for each blood donor, you cannot get HIV from giving blood or plasma.

Biology Connection

T-Cell Gateway

Scientists have long puzzled over how HIV gets inside T-cells to destroy them. Researchers now think they have found the answer—a molecule on T-cells, called CD26, may provide the gateway the virus needs. This discovery could lead to a vaccine that works by blocking the CD26 gateway. Why would this prevent AIDS?

Teen Issues

Steroids and AIDS

Seventy-two percent of steroid users surveyed at an Illinois high school admitted that they obtained needles illegally from drug dealers. Sharing drug needles is a major cause of HIV infection, so it is only a matter of time before new AIDS cases start showing up in teen bodybuilders. If anyone you know injects steroids, make sure they know about the risk of AIDS as well as the serious consequences of steroid use. These dangers include sterility and impaired liver function.

How HIV Is Not Spread

You have probably heard some myths about ways in which HIV is spread. Myths have led to unnecessary social isolation of people with AIDS. **Figure 11.12** lists six myths about how HIV is spread. Remember—HIV is *not* spread in any of these ways.

in your journal

In your journal, describe how your knowledge of the spread of HIV has changed by reading this chapter. Will your increased knowledge affect how you would interact with a person with AIDS? Explain your response.

How to Prevent the Spread of HIV

Preventing the spread of HIV is simple. Here are the two important behaviors you must practice.

- **Avoid all sexual contact.** There is no way to be sure that another person is not a carrier of HIV. Saying no to sex is the *only* sure way to avoid HIV.
- **Avoid illegal drugs, especially those taken by intravenous needles.** Drugs impair your good judgment, making you less careful. Drug users who share blood-contaminated needles account for a large proportion of HIV infections.

HIV infection is incurable and AIDS is fatal. People who test positive for HIV will probably develop AIDS at some point. For these reasons, it is especially important to refrain from activities that place you at high risk.

Figure 11.12
Exploding the Myths About HIV

Myth	Truth
HIV is spread through the air.	Breathing the same air as an infected person, even being coughed or sneezed on by an infected person, poses no risk of HIV infection.
HIV is spread through kissing.	"Dry" kissing (kissing with mouths closed) is considered safe. In theory, kissing in which saliva is exchanged can transmit HIV. To date, only one such case has been confirmed. In that case, HIV was transmitted by the exchange of blood during deep kissing.
HIV can be spread through casual contact with an infected person.	Although it is a likely way to pick up cold germs, shaking hands with an infected person or having other casual contact poses no risk of HIV infection.
HIV is spread by mosquitoes that have bitten an infected person.	Although some blood parasites can spread through mosquito bites, HIV is not one of them.
HIV is spread by sharing eating utensils with an infected person.	This is another way to catch a cold, but not HIV.
HIV is spread by donating blood.	The needles used to take blood are used only once, then thrown away. There is no risk of catching HIV by donating blood.

AIDS Research and Education

Millions of dollars are spent each year to find a cure for AIDS, to develop a vaccine to prevent HIV infection, and to educate the public about how to prevent its spread. Spearheading these efforts are the federal Centers for Disease Control and Prevention (CDC). CDC scientists gather and publish statistics on AIDS, support AIDS research, and help educate the public about AIDS.

We have learned a lot from this research, and the FDA has approved AZT and eight other drugs for slowing the progress of the virus. Prospects for a cure or a vaccine are not yet in sight. Until a cure or vaccine is found, our only weapon against AIDS is prevention. To prevent AIDS requires knowledge of how it is spread. This means that education is still the key to preventing the spread of AIDS.

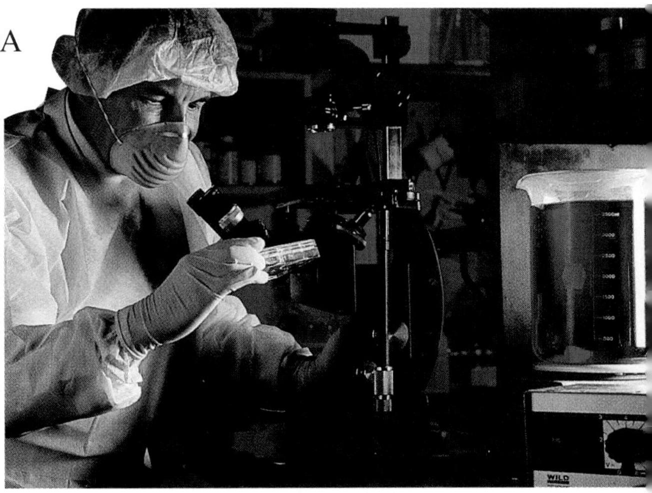

Scientists are working to find a cure for AIDS.

Review

Lesson 5

Using complete sentences, answer the following questions on a separate sheet of paper.

Reviewing Terms and Facts

1. **Vocabulary** Which of the following is a deadly disease that interferes with the body's natural ability to fight infection: *HIV, Kaposi's sarcoma,* or *AIDS*?
2. **Vocabulary** What is a person called who has HIV but has not developed AIDS?
3. **Recall** Cite three facts about AIDS.
4. **Recall** Identify four ways that HIV infection can occur.
5. **Recall** List four ways that HIV infection cannot occur.

Thinking Critically

6. **Differentiate** Explain the difference between HIV and AIDS.
7. **Explain** Tell why AIDS cannot be spread through casual contact with an infected person.
8. **Synthesize** The campaign against AIDS is concentrated on education, because prevention is the only way to stop the spread of the disease. What would be the focus of the campaign against AIDS if there were a vaccine to prevent it?

Applying Health Concepts

9. **Health of Others** Write an essay describing how you think society's view of AIDS would change if an effective vaccine or a cure were found for this fatal disease. What other diseases could it be compared to? What effect do you think such a discovery would have on risky behaviors such as unprotected sex and shared IV needles?
10. **Health of Others** Do some library research on mandatory AIDS testing. Find out why some people are for it and others against it. Organize a class debate with other students and discuss both sides of the issue. Select one student to be moderator.

Chapter 11 Review

Chapter Summary

- **Lesson 1** Communicable diseases are caused by germs that enter the body and damage its cells. Many communicable diseases can be prevented by developing good habits that keep you healthy and prevent the spread of germs.
- **Lesson 2** Your body's own defenses against germs include your skin and body fluids, general immune reactions, and specific immune responses. Vaccines are available to prevent many communicable diseases.
- **Lesson 3** The most common communicable disease is the cold. Other common communicable diseases include influenza, hepatitis, and mononucleosis.
- **Lesson 4** STDs can do great damage to the body. Although early treatment can cure most STDs, the most effective protection is abstinence.
- **Lesson 5** AIDS is a deadly disease caused by HIV. There is no cure or vaccine for AIDS, but it can be prevented.

Reviewing Key Terms and Concepts

Using complete sentences, answer the following questions on a separate sheet of paper.

Lesson 1

1. Define the following terms: *disease, infection, and contagious period.*
2. Define *germ.* Identify and describe five types of germs that cause diseases.

Lesson 2

3. Define *immunity.*
4. Explain how the *lymphatic system* works. Make clear the meaning of *lymph nodes* and *lymphocytes* in your answer.

Lesson 3

5. Define *influenza* and *mononucleosis?*
6. List three communicable diseases that can be prevented by vaccines.

Lesson 4

7. Describe the STDs genital warts and genital herpes. How is each treated?
8. Explain why a person can get the same STD more than once.

Lesson 5

9. How does HIV affect the immune system?
10. Why would a person need to be tested twice to be sure that she or he was not infected with HIV?

Thinking Critically

Using complete sentences, answer the following questions on a separate sheet of paper.

11. **Summarize** What are the most common ways in which germs are spread?
12. **Analyze** Why does washing your hands lower your risk of catching a cold?
13. **Deduce** Since many STDs have no early symptoms, how can people make sure that they don't have one?

Chapter 11 Review

Your Action Plan

Create an action plan, as outlined below, to reduce your risk of catching or transmitting communicable diseases.

Step 1 Your long-term goal is to reduce your risk of catching and transmitting communicable diseases.

Step 2 Write down the behaviors you want to change as your short-term goals. One short-term goal might be to make a habit of washing your hands before handling food.

Step 3 Make a schedule for achieving each short-term goal. Concentrate on handwashing before meals for one week, for example, and then move on to your next short-term goal.

Step 4 Check your schedule often to keep track of your progress.

When you notice that you are regularly practicing habits that reduce your risk of catching and transmitting germs, reward yourself.

In Your Home and Community

1. **Health of Others** Interview several family members, especially older people, about how they take care of themselves when they are sick. Do they use particular brands of medication? Do they rely on chicken soup or hot tea with honey? Share your findings with the class.
2. **Community Resources** Create a poster or pamphlet that explains the signs and symptoms of AIDS, how HIV is and is not spread, and how and where in your community to get tested for HIV. Ask permission to display your work in local pharmacies, hospitals, and other places.

Building Your Portfolio

1. **Preventive Health** Find out what vaccinations you have had. Make a chart that lists the types of vaccinations and the dates when you were vaccinated. Find out when or if you will need another shot for each disease, and include this information on your chart. Decide what to do if you find out that your immunizations are not up to date. Include this chart in your portfolio.
2. **Treatment Advances** Make a scrapbook of newspaper and magazine articles that discuss the latest information about treatments for AIDS and/or other STDs. Summarize what you learn from these articles in a short essay, and include the essay in the scrapbook. Add this scrapbook to your portfolio.
3. **Personal Assessment** Look through the activities and projects you did for this chapter. Choose one that you would like to include in your portfolio.

Chapter 12

Noncommunicable Diseases

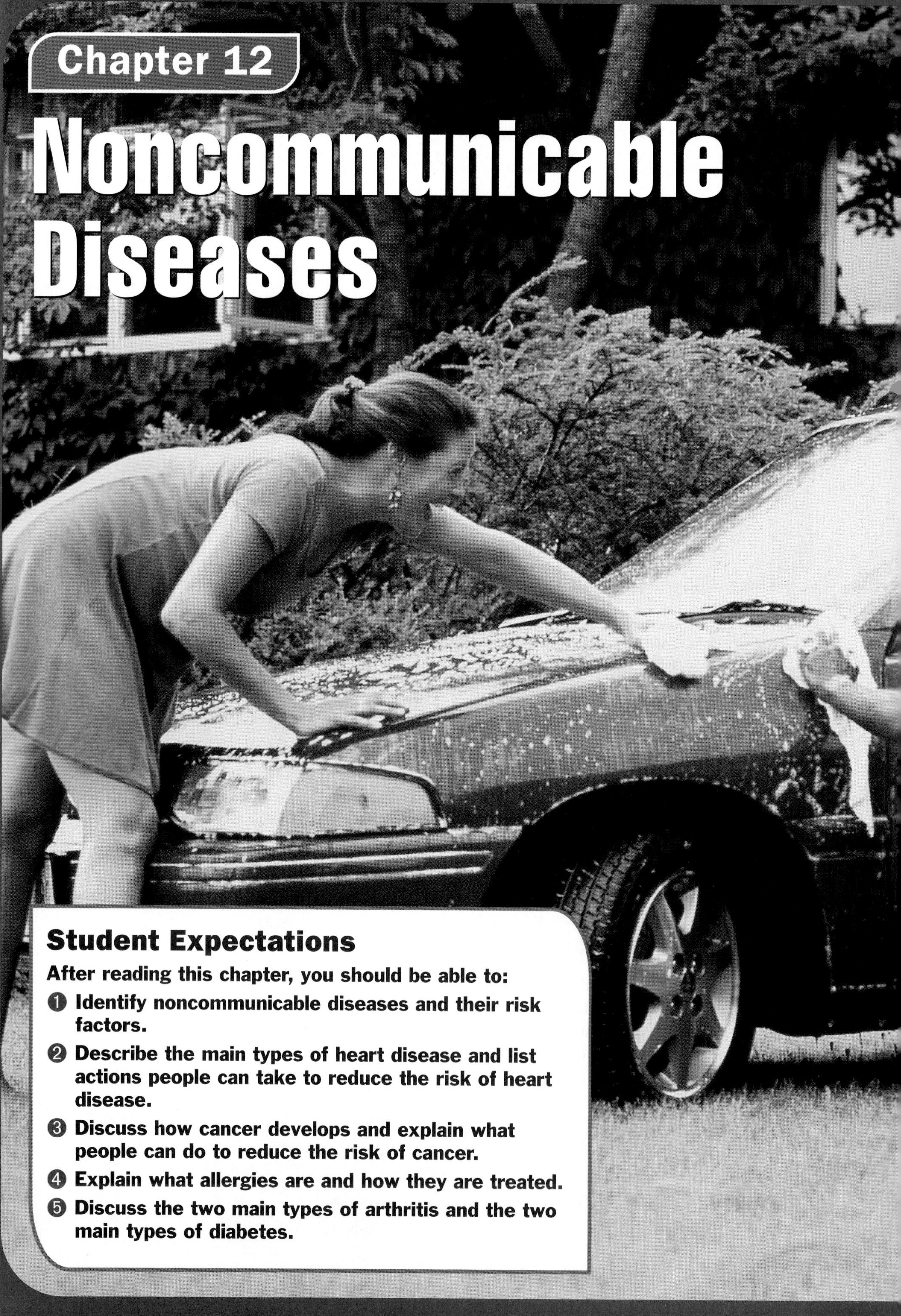

Student Expectations

After reading this chapter, you should be able to:

1. Identify noncommunicable diseases and their risk factors.
2. Describe the main types of heart disease and list actions people can take to reduce the risk of heart disease.
3. Discuss how cancer develops and explain what people can do to reduce the risk of cancer.
4. Explain what allergies are and how they are treated.
5. Discuss the two main types of arthritis and the two main types of diabetes.

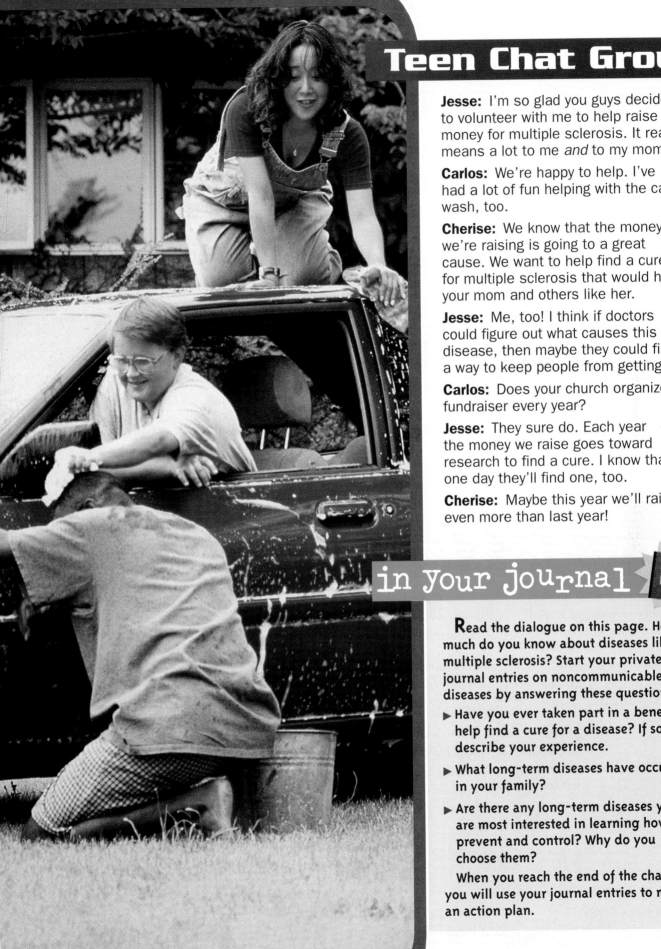

Teen Chat Group

Jesse: I'm so glad you guys decided to volunteer with me to help raise money for multiple sclerosis. It really means a lot to me *and* to my mom.

Carlos: We're happy to help. I've had a lot of fun helping with the car wash, too.

Cherise: We know that the money we're raising is going to a great cause. We want to help find a cure for multiple sclerosis that would help your mom and others like her.

Jesse: Me, too! I think if doctors could figure out what causes this disease, then maybe they could find a way to keep people from getting it.

Carlos: Does your church organize a fundraiser every year?

Jesse: They sure do. Each year the money we raise goes toward research to find a cure. I know that one day they'll find one, too.

Cherise: Maybe this year we'll raise even more than last year!

in your journal

Read the dialogue on this page. How much do you know about diseases like multiple sclerosis? Start your private journal entries on noncommunicable diseases by answering these questions:

- Have you ever taken part in a benefit to help find a cure for a disease? If so, describe your experience.
- What long-term diseases have occurred in your family?
- Are there any long-term diseases you are most interested in learning how to prevent and control? Why do you choose them?

When you reach the end of the chapter, you will use your journal entries to make an action plan.

Lesson 1

Noncommunicable Diseases

This lesson will help you find answers to questions that teens often ask about noncommunicable diseases. For example:

- **What is the difference between communicable and noncommunicable diseases?**
- **Why do some diseases seem to run in families?**
- **Can anything be done to prevent noncommunicable diseases?**

Words to Know

noncommunicable disease
chronic disease
genetic disorder
birth defect
risk factor

Did You Know?

Leading Cause of Death

Accidents are the number one killer of children and young adolescents (5 to 14 years of age). The second leading cause of death among people in this age-group is cancer.

What Is a Noncommunicable Disease?

When you hear that someone you have recently been with has developed the flu—or some other communicable disease—you may worry about catching it. Your concern is understandable because most communicable diseases are caused by germs that are easily passed from one person to another. A second group of diseases, called **noncommunicable diseases,** includes all diseases that *are not spread through contact.* Asthma is one example. You cannot catch asthma by being with someone suffering an asthma attack. Heart disease, another noncommunicable disease, is the leading cause of death in the United States (see **Figure 12.1**).

The reason noncommunicable diseases cannot be passed to other people by contact is that most of these illnesses are not caused by germs. Instead, they are caused by a breakdown in body cells and tissues. The breakdown may begin because of the effects of certain traits a person has inherited or because of that person's lifestyle habits or environment. Some diseases cause further breakdown, or degeneration, in body cells and tissues as they progress. These are called degenerative (di·JE·ne·ruh·tiv) diseases.

Figure 12.1

Leading Causes of Death

In 1995, the four leading causes of death in the United States were noncommunicable diseases.

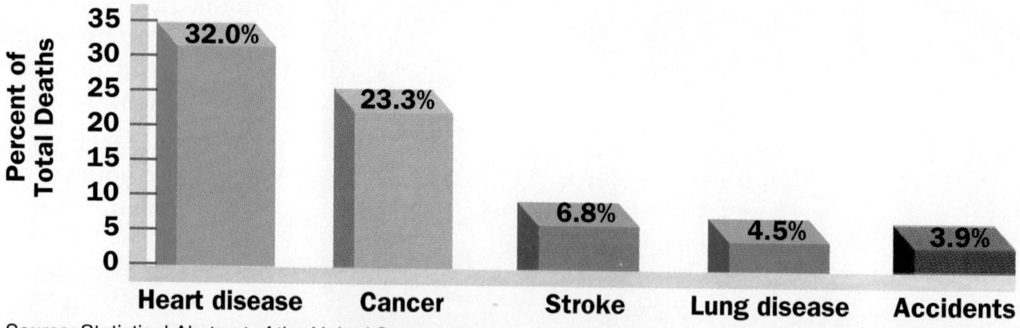

Source: Statistical Abstract of the United States, 1996.

Most noncommunicable diseases are **chronic** (KRAH·nik) **diseases,** which means they *are present either continuously or off and on over a long time.* A person may be born with the disease or a tendency to develop it. The disease may develop as a result of a person's lifestyle behaviors. Sometimes the disease develops because of substances in the person's environment. Some of the most common noncommunicable diseases are described in **Figure 12.2.**

interNET CONNECTION

Reduce your risk of developing diseases with healthy lifestyle behaviors outlined at the Glencoe Web site.

http://www.glencoe.com/sec/health

Diseases Present at Birth

Some babies are born with serious health problems. If a baby does not have a communicable disease, the problem may be caused by a genetic disorder or a birth defect. A **genetic** (juh·NE·tik) **disorder** is *one in which the body does not develop or function normally because of an inherited problem.*

Figure 12.2

Common Noncommunicable Diseases

Disease	Description
Allergies	Bodily reactions to particular substances; common forms include hay fever, eczema, and allergic digestive problems
Alzheimer's disease	Affects the brain and causes increasing loss of memory and other mental functions; affects people 40 and over
Arthritis	Group of diseases that causes body joints to swell, making movement painful and difficult
Asthma	An attack that partially blocks the air passages and results in serious breathing difficulty
Cancer	Group of about 100 diseases; in all types of cancer, abnormal body cells multiply out of control and destroy healthy tissue
Cerebral palsy	Group of disorders caused by damage to the brain that occurs during birth or in the first few years of life
Cystic fibrosis	Causes certain glands of the body to produce large amounts of thicker-than-normal mucus; over time, mucus may damage body organs, especially lungs, pancreas, and liver
Heart disease (cardiovascular disease)	Group of diseases that affects the heart and blood vessels; includes hardening of the arteries, clogged arteries, and high blood pressure; can cause heart attacks and strokes
Multiple sclerosis (MS)	Affects the nervous system; can cause paralysis of limbs or some vision loss
Muscular dystrophy	Affects the skeletal muscles; four common types
Sickle-cell anemia	Blood disorder that causes tiredness and breathlessness

The term **birth defect** refers to various *disorders of the developing and newborn baby.* The causes of many birth defects are unknown. Others can be traced to harmful substances in the environment or to a combination of environmental and genetic causes. For example, if a pregnant woman is exposed to X-rays, the developing baby may be injured. Some serious birth defects are the result of unhealthy lifestyle habits of the mother-to-be. If a pregnant woman drinks alcohol, for example, it may cause fetal alcohol syndrome (FAS) in her developing baby. Babies with fetal alcohol syndrome may have malformed body organs or mental retardation.

In most cases, there is no cure for either genetic disorders or birth defects. However, many people born with health problems can be treated with drugs or surgery. In addition, people with some disorders can be helped by therapy and training.

Did You Know?

Lifestyle Choices

Following are some of the noncommunicable diseases and disorders that are often related—directly or indirectly—to lifestyle behaviors.

- Cancers of the mouth, throat, lung
- Cirrhosis of the liver
- Dental caries
- Diabetes
- Heart disease
- High blood pressure
- Peptic ulcer

Diseases Resulting from Lifestyle Behaviors

Generally, scientists are unable to predict who will develop a particular disease. For some diseases, however, they have identified *certain characteristics that increase a person's chances of developing the disease.* These characteristics are called **risk factors.** Environment, heredity, ethnic group, age, and lifestyle behaviors are examples of risk factors.

A person's lifestyle behavior has a significant effect on his or her health. Many diseases are the direct or indirect result of harmful lifestyle behaviors. Healthful lifestyle behaviors, on the other hand, can help prevent or control certain diseases and disorders. Six healthy lifestyle behaviors that can help you lower your risk of certain diseases and disorders are described in **Figure 12.3.** Which behaviors are part of your lifestyle?

LIFE SKILLS

Evaluating Personal Risk from Media Reports

Featured news reports about health often contradict other reports. This is confusing. Some people throw up their hands and decide to ignore all health information. Others take every report seriously and try to change their behavior. Being able to evaluate health information that comes from the media is an important life skill.

Should you consider changing your behavior because of information in a health news report? Only if it meets four standards: Is the source reliable? Is the scientific research reliable? Is the report or article reliable? Does the information have some relevance to you? To help evaluate these four factors, ask yourself the following questions.

1. The Source

- Does the newspaper, magazine, or program that is the source of the news have a high standard or reputation?
- Did you get the information firsthand, or did you hear it from another person? Can you rely on that person's understanding and memory?

Figure 12.3

Six Healthy Lifestyle Behaviors

Eat a healthy diet	Include plenty of whole grains, fruits, and vegetables in your diet. Avoid eating too much fat, salt, and sugar.
Exercise regularly	Regular vigorous exercise strengthens the heart and helps it do its job better.
Maintain your desirable weight	Keep your weight at the level indicated for your height and body frame.
Learn to manage stress	Get plenty of rest and learn to manage stress in your daily life.
Avoid smoking	Tobacco causes heart and lung diseases, cancer, and strokes.
Avoid using alcohol and other drugs	These substances harm your body, impair your judgment, and may cause permanent damage.

Following the healthy lifestyle behaviors described here is no guarantee that you will avoid developing noncommunicable diseases, but it can help. Even people who have a family history of a disease may get some benefit from these lifestyle behaviors. For example, if several members of your family have high blood pressure, you may be at greater risk of developing it yourself. Following healthy lifestyle behaviors may help you avoid the disease altogether or at least minimize its effects.

The Special Olympics provides an opportunity for people with disabilities to compete in athletic events.

2. **The Scientific Research**
   - ▶ Is the research complete? Has it been repeated with the same results?
   - ▶ Reliable research takes time and involves many subjects. How long has the study been going on? How many people were tested?
3. **The Report**
   - ▶ Does the report focus on scientific facts rather than opinions? Does the report discuss other studies? Does it explain opposing views?
4. **The Relevance to You**
   - ▶ Do you have the same characteristics—age, race, and gender—of the people said to be affected by the information? According to this report, can your behavior now affect your health in the future?

Follow-up Activity

Find a recent health news item. After reviewing the item, answer the above questions. If you cannot answer them all, find more information on the topic.

Diseases Caused by the Environment

Many diseases are caused by hazards in the environment. Lung cancer is an example. Although most cases of lung cancer are caused by smoking, some are caused by breathing in harmful substances such as asbestos. The environmental hazards listed below can cause health problems for some people or make existing health problems worse in others.

- Fumes from chemical waste in landfills can seep into houses that have been constructed over them. Illness can occur years after the waste has been covered.
- Gaseous wastes from automobiles create or add to air pollution that can cause serious illness.
- Certain construction materials, such as asbestos and urea-formaldehyde insulation foam, cause disease after long exposure. They are now restricted.
- Indoor air can be polluted by solvents, paints, and household chemicals.
- Nonsmokers are exposed to dangerous secondhand smoke in restaurants, businesses, and homes.
- The manufacturing of household items such as plastics and paint products can create dangerous air and water pollution.
- Radon is a colorless, odorless gas produced by uranium. It can seep into homes from the surrounding soil. It can cause serious illnesses.

Nonsmokers must be on the alert to avoid exposure to secondhand smoke in restaurants and other settings.

Lesson 1

Review

Using complete sentences, answer the following questions on a separate sheet of paper.

Reviewing Terms and Facts

1. **Vocabulary** Using your own words, define *chronic disease.*
2. **Explain** What causes noncommunicable diseases? How does someone get a noncommunicable disease?
3. **Give Examples** Name five noncommunicable diseases.
4. **Recall** What is cancer?
5. **Vocabulary** What is the difference between a *genetic disorder* and a *birth defect*? Give an example of each.

Thinking Critically

6. **Compare** Point out similarities and differences between noncommunicable diseases and communicable diseases.
7. **Hypothesize** What are three harmful lifestyle behaviors?

Applying Health Concepts

8. **Personal Health** Do you engage in any lifestyle behaviors that are unhealthful? If so, what are they? Which, if any, of these behaviors would you like to change? What are some healthy behaviors that are part of your lifestyle as well?

Understanding Heart Disease

This lesson will help you find answers to questions that teens often ask about heart disease. For example:

- **What is a heart attack?**
- **Can I do anything to prevent heart disease?**
- **Can a person with heart disease get well?**

Number One Killer

Heart disease is the number one killer of adults in the United States. Someone dies as a result of heart disease every 33 seconds. (See **Figure 12.4.**) Many people think that this is a disease of the elderly, but each year more than 2000 children and young adults through age 25 die of heart disease.

The term *heart disease,* also called cardiovascular disease, includes any condition that lessens the strength or function of the heart or blood vessels. Healthy lifestyle behaviors can lower a person's risk of heart disease.

Figure 12.4
Frequency of Heart Disease
About 263 million people live in the United States. Roughly 1 out of every 5 of these people has some form of heart disease.

Words to Know

atherosclerosis
arteriosclerosis
heart attack
stroke
blood pressure
pacemaker

in your journal

Do you think you and members of your family are at a low risk, average risk, or high risk of heart disease? Why? Write your answers in your private journal and explain your observations.

Atherosclerosis and Arteriosclerosis

Like other body cells, the cells of your heart muscle need oxygen and nutrients. These are carried by the blood. The arteries that supply your heart muscle with blood are called coronary (KAWR·uh·nehr·ee) arteries, as shown in part C of **Figure 12.5.**

When the coronary arteries are clear, blood flows freely through them. If the flow slows or stops, a serious health problem can result. **Atherosclerosis** (a·thuh·roh·skluh·ROH·sis) is *a condition in which fatty substances in the blood are deposited on the walls of the arteries.* Part B of **Figure 12.5** shows how atherosclerosis can clog arteries and reduce the blood flow.

One fatty substance that causes atherosclerosis is cholesterol (kuh·LES·tuh·rawl). Some cholesterol is produced by your body. Certain foods also contain cholesterol. Many people lower their intake of foods high in cholesterol and fats to lower their blood cholesterol level.

Healthy artery walls are elastic. As people get older, their arteries naturally tend to become less elastic. This *hardening of the arteries* is called **arteriosclerosis** (ar·tir·ee·oh·skluh·ROH·sis). Arteriosclerosis slows the flow of blood through arteries. It is also a major cause of high blood pressure. Atherosclerosis speeds up hardening of the arteries and makes its harmful effects worse.

When the flow of blood is reduced, blood clots may form within the blood vessels. These clots can block the flow of blood altogether. Blockage is especially likely to happen when a clot sticks in a part of an artery where there is a buildup of fatty deposits. When a coronary artery is blocked, the result can be a heart attack. When an artery in the brain is blocked, the result can be a stroke.

Did You Know?

Good Cholesterol

Small particles called lipoproteins carry cholesterol and other fat molecules in the blood. Two kinds of lipoproteins carry cholesterol. They are high-density lipoproteins (HDL) and low-density lipoproteins (LDL). HDLs are sometimes called good cholesterol because they take cholesterol away from artery walls. On the other hand, LDLs deposit cholesterol in the arteries and increase the risk of atherosclerosis.

Figure 12.5

Heart Attack and Stroke

Healthy coronary arteries are clear and flexible. Enough blood flows to the heart tissue to keep it well supplied with the oxygen needed for life. *If the blood flow slows or stops, heart muscle tissue dies from lack of oxygen,* causing a heart attack. *If the blood supply to the brain is disturbed, part of the brain may be damaged.* The resulting body reaction is called a stroke.

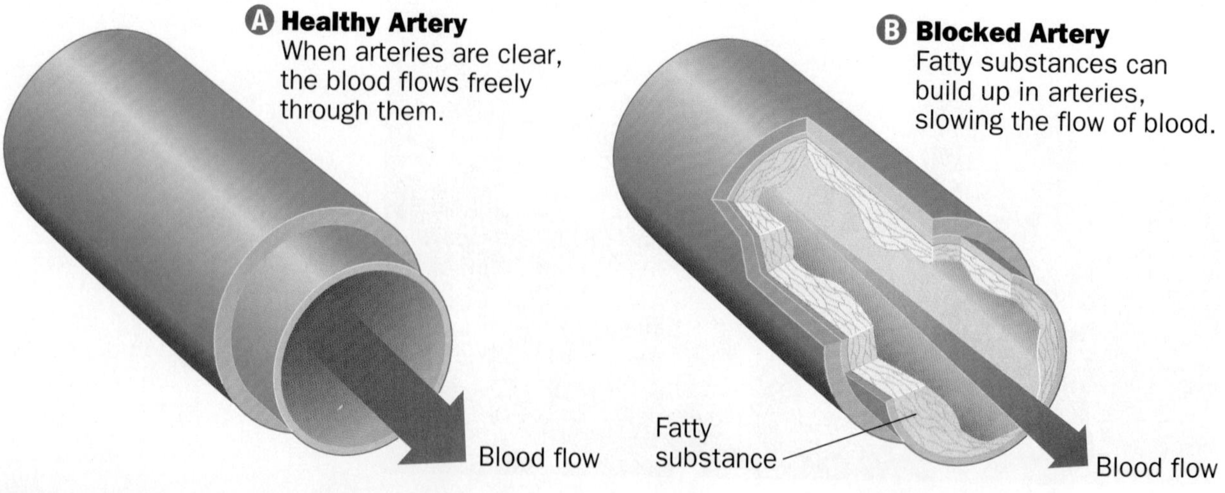
A Healthy Artery
When arteries are clear, the blood flows freely through them.
Blood flow
B Blocked Artery
Fatty substances can build up in arteries, slowing the flow of blood.
Fatty substance
Blood flow

High Blood Pressure

Your heart pumps blood throughout your body. **Blood pressure** is *the force of the blood on the inside walls of the blood vessels.* Blood pressure is expressed as two numbers. A typical blood pressure for a teen might be 110 over 70, often written 110/70. The top, higher, number is the measure of the pressure exerted when the heart contracts, sending blood throughout the body. The bottom, lower, number is the measure of the pressure when the heart relaxes between beats.

Your blood pressure is not the same at all times. When you are feeling stress or exercising, it may be higher than usual. When you are resting, it may be lower than usual. These changes are normal. When a *person's blood pressure is usually higher than normal* for his or her age, that person is said to have high blood pressure, or *hypertension* (hy·per·TEN·shuhn). High blood pressure can lead to heart attack, stroke, and kidney failure.

The cause of high blood pressure is often unclear. However, doctors know that four factors may increase your chance of having high blood pressure.

- Eating a large amount of salt
- Being overweight
- Feeling extreme stress for long periods of time
- Having a family history of high blood pressure

There are no outward signs of high blood pressure until it has caused serious damage. For this reason, high blood pressure is called the silent killer. A regular checkup can detect whether your blood pressure is too high.

Cultural Connections

Blood Pressure and Location

High blood pressure is a national epidemic in some developed countries, such as the United States, but not in many less developed countries. Variations in lifestyle, including diet and exercise, seem to make the difference. People in developed countries are more likely to eat processed foods high in fat and salt and less likely to get enough exercise.

C Heart Attack
A heart attack occurs when heart muscle tissue dies from lack of oxygen and nutrients because of reduced or stopped blood flow.

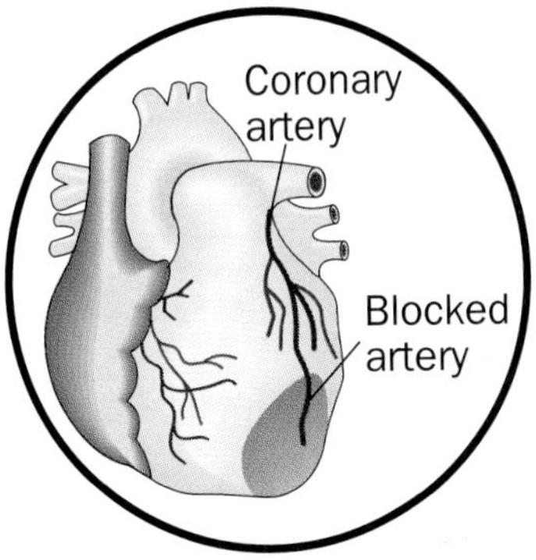

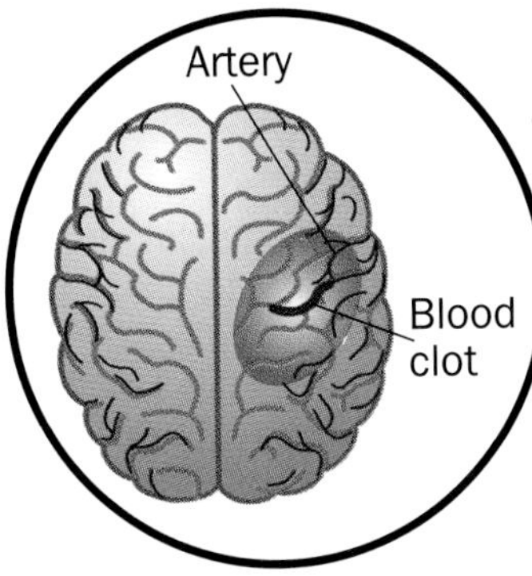

D Stroke
Most strokes are caused by a blood clot blocking an artery that supplies blood to the brain. The clot may develop in any part of the body and travel with the blood to the brain, or it may develop in the brain itself.

More About Strokes
Some strokes are caused by the breaking of an artery in the brain. This type of stroke is known as a *brain hemorrhage*. A stroke can cause a person to lose feeling or the ability to move. A serious stroke can result in death.

Treating Heart Disease

There have been many advances in the treatment of heart disease. If a patient's heart has been greatly damaged by heart disease, doctors may recommend a heart transplant. A heart transplant involves surgically replacing the patient's diseased heart with a healthy heart from a donor. In many more cases, three other treatments are used: bypass surgery, the dissolving of blood clots, and—as shown in **Figure 12.6**—angioplasty (AN·gee·uh·plas·tee).

- **Going around the blockage.** Surgeons create new paths for blood to flow around a blocked artery. They remove a vein from the patient's leg and attach it above and below the blocked area to form a detour through which the blood can flow freely. The procedure is called bypass surgery.
- **Dissolving clots.** Blood clots tend to form in blocked blood vessels where blood flow is affected. Medications are used to help dissolve clots and to keep clots from forming.

Your Total Health

Stress of Being a Teen ACTIVITY!

Teens who feel that their efforts are constantly frustrated may develop high blood pressure. Learning to manage stress is therefore important for teens. Write down five ideas for reducing your stress.

Figure 12.6

Clearing the Blockage in Arteries

Surgeons use instruments with tiny balloons attached near the end to clear blocked arteries. The procedure is called *angioplasty.*

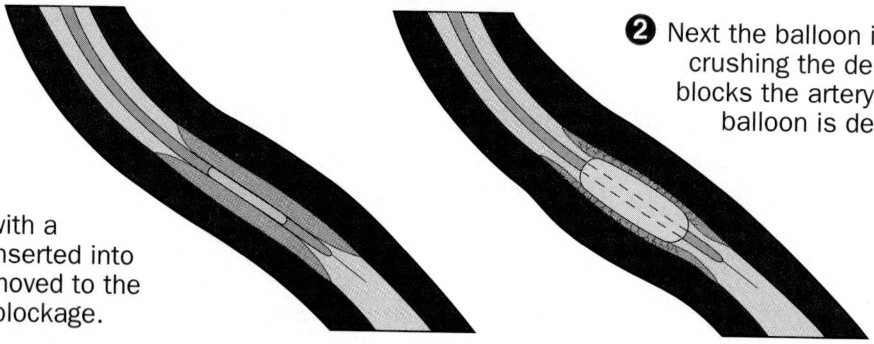

1 An instrument with a tiny balloon is inserted into the artery and moved to the location of the blockage.
2 Next the balloon is inflated, crushing the deposit that blocks the artery. Then the balloon is deflated and removed.

HEALTH LAB

Measuring Blood Pressure

Because blood pressure is an important health factor, many people check it regularly.

Objective: To learn how blood pressure is read.

Materials and Method: This activity should be done by a health practitioner and two or three volunteers. Each volunteer will be checked twice—once at rest and once after physical activity.

Both a stethoscope and a sphygmomanometer are needed to measure a person's blood pressure. A sphygmomanometer has three parts: a cuff, or wide rubbery band, that can be filled with air; a hollow rubber bulb used to pump air into the cuff; and a gauge with a glass tube filled with mercury.

First the health practitioner loosens the screw-valve on the rubber ball to deflate the cuff. The cuff is wrapped snugly, but not too tightly, around the arm of the volunteer. The cup of the stethoscope is placed between the cuff and the inner elbow.

The health practitioner uses the stethoscope to listen for the person's pulse. With the stethoscope in

Treating High Blood Pressure

People with high blood pressure may be given medicines to lower their blood pressure. In addition, researchers have found that certain lifestyle behaviors play an important role in lowering blood pressure. These include eating a balanced diet low in salt and fat and exercising regularly. Learning to manage stress and maintaining a healthy weight are also important factors. If someone with high blood pressure smokes, quitting is always his or her doctor's first recommendation.

in Your Journal

Suppose you wanted to make an argument that preventing heart disease is wiser than trying to cure it. Write the major points of your argument in your journal.

Treating Other Heart Problems

Some people have problems with the valves of their hearts. The heart has four chambers through which the blood moves. Healthy valves open only one way and allow the blood to move in only one direction. Damaged valves allow blood to leak back into the chamber it has left. Doctors can correct some damaged valves with surgery, or they may replace a damaged valve with a mechanical one.

Irregular heartbeat is another common health problem. Healthy hearts beat at a strong, regular pace. If a person's heartbeat is irregular or weak, doctors may insert a **pacemaker** (PAYS·may·ker). This *small device sends steady electrical pulses to the heart to make it beat regularly.*

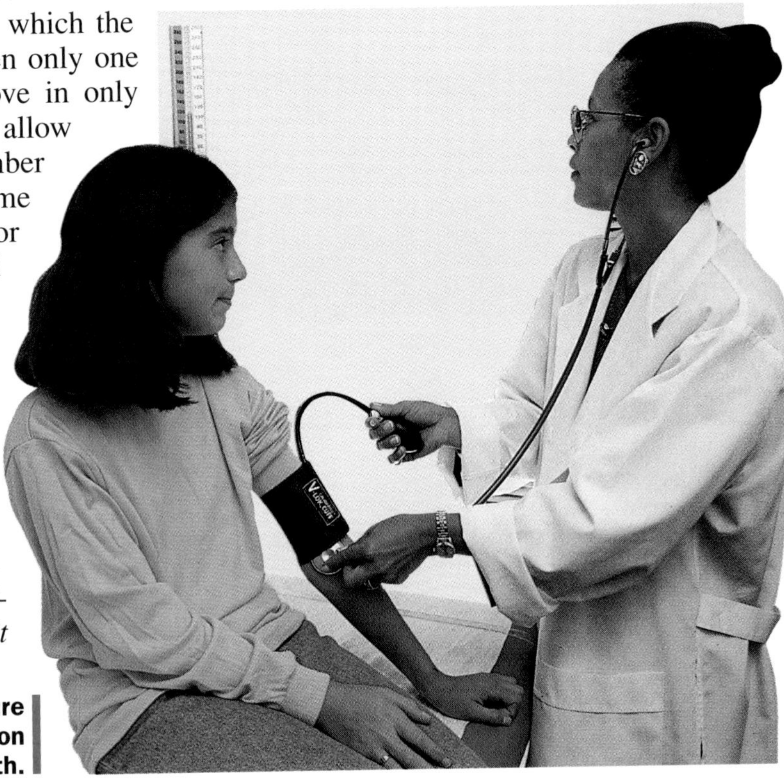

A person's blood pressure is an important indication of his or her health.

place, the screw-valve is tightened. The hollow ball is then pumped to fill the cuff with air until the mercury reaches about 130. Then the screw is loosened enough for the column to let air escape. The mercury starts dropping slowly. The health practitioner listens and watches the mercury as it drops, waiting until there is a steady thumping sound. The location of the mercury at the first thump is the top number of the volunteer's blood pressure—the reading when the heart is contracting to pump blood.

The thumping sound will grow faint and then stop. The location of the mercury at the last thump is the bottom number of the volunteer's blood pressure, when the heart is at rest.

Observation and Analysis: Compare the readings of the volunteers' blood pressure before and after physical activity. What differences do you note?

Preventing Heart Disease

Heart disease can be a lifestyle disease—it can result from how a person lives. Doctors have identified nine risk factors for heart disease. Four of them are not within a person's control. These factors are age, gender, race, and a family history of heart disease. The other five risk factors are well within a person's control. They are matched in **Figure 12.7** with appropriate lifestyle behaviors.

Figure 12.7
Controlling Risk Factors

Risk Factor	Healthy Behavior
Weight	Maintain a desirable weight. Being overweight makes your heart work harder.
Exercise	Regular exercise strengthens your heart and helps you control your weight.
Diet	Follow a diet that is high in fiber and low in salt, fat, and cholesterol. Too much salt can lead to high blood pressure. A diet that is high in fats and cholesterol can contribute to the buildup of fatty deposits in arteries.
Stress	Learn to cope with stress in your life. Constant stress can increase your blood pressure.
Tobacco	Don't smoke. Even one pack of cigarettes a day doubles your chance of heart disease.

Lesson 2 Review

Using complete sentences, answer the following questions on a separate sheet of paper.

Reviewing Terms and Facts

1. **Vocabulary** Compare and contrast *atherosclerosis* and *arteriosclerosis*.
2. **Vocabulary** What is the difference between a *heart attack* and a *stroke*?
3. **Describe** Outline the course of a heart attack or stroke.
4. **Explain** What is angioplasty and what is it used for?
5. **Identify** What are six ways to reduce high blood pressure?
6. **Vocabulary** What is a *pacemaker?* What is it used to treat?
7. **Identify** What are four risk factors for heart disease that are not affected by changing your lifestyle?

Thinking Critically

8. **Analyze** Explain why a blocked coronary artery may lead to damage to heart tissue.
9. **Synthesize** Why is it a good idea to check your blood pressure regularly, even if you have no signs of high blood pressure?

Applying Health Concepts

10. **Personal Health** With a family member or friend, try some low-salt, low-fat versions of the foods you normally eat. For example, try low-salt soup, low-fat cookies, low-fat salad dressing, or low-fat frozen yogurt instead of ice cream. Try a variety of these foods. Which ones did you like and which ones did you dislike? Report your findings to your classmates.

Lesson 3

Understanding Cancer

This lesson will help you find answers to questions that teens often ask about cancer. For example:

- **What causes cancer?**
- **How does cancer harm the body?**
- **What can I do to avoid getting cancer?**

Words to Know

cancer
tumor
benign tumor
malignant tumor
metastasis
carcinogen
biopsy
radiation
chemotherapy

What Is Cancer?

The second leading cause of death for adults in the United States is cancer. Cancer is actually a group of many different diseases. These diseases can affect most parts of the body, including the lungs, blood, skin, brain, and breasts. All types of **cancers** involve *abnormal body cells growing out of control.*

The human body has trillions of cells. Most cells, such as those that form blood, grow and reproduce all the time. The human body forms many trillions of new cells each year. Many thousands are abnormal, but most abnormal cells are destroyed by the body's defenses. However, sometimes an abnormal cell lives on and begins to copy itself at an out-of-control rate. This out-of-control growth of abnormal cells is cancer.

Benign and Malignant Tumors

When an abnormal cell survives and starts to reproduce itself, the cells grow much more rapidly than normal cells grow. *Groups of abnormal cells form in masses* called **tumors** (TOO·mers). There are two kinds of tumors—benign or malignant. **Benign** (bi·NYN) **tumors** are *not cancerous.* **Malignant** (muh·LIG·nuhnt) **tumors** are *cancerous.*

Cancer is a disease characterized by abnormal body cells growing out of control. Describe the difference between the cells shown in the two photographs—the normal cells (left) and the cancer cells (right).

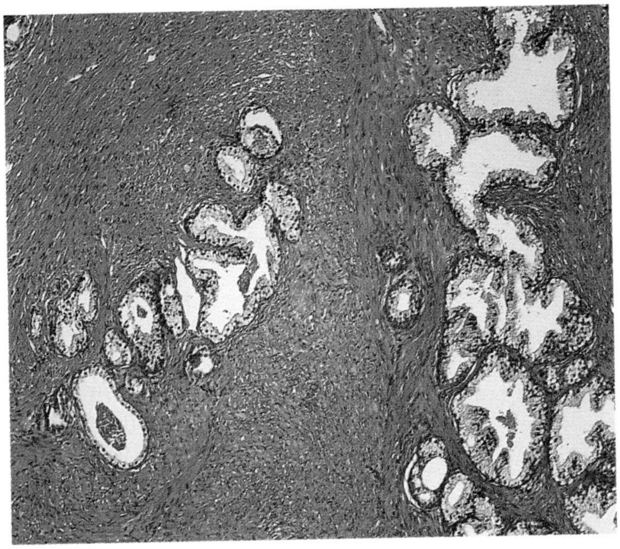

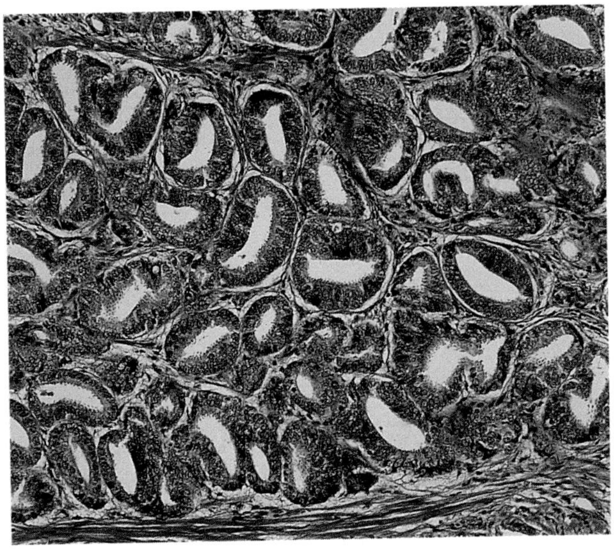

Cancer progresses in stages. In the final stage, cancer cells from malignant tumors may enter the bloodstream or lymph system and travel to other parts of the body and form new tumors. *The spreading of cancer cells* is called **metastasis** (muh·TAS·tuh·sis). Some types of cancer are described in **Figure 12.8.**

Figure 12.8

Common Types of Cancer

Cancer can affect almost any part of the body. Although different types of cancer may develop for different reasons, all types are caused by abnormal body cells growing out of control.

Ⓐ **Skin cancer** is most likely to develop in fair-haired, fair-skinned, and light-eyed people. Exposure to sunlight is the major cause.

Ⓑ **Lung cancer** is the number one cause of cancer deaths. Smoking is considered a factor in 90 percent of all cases of lung cancer in men and 79 percent of all cases in women.

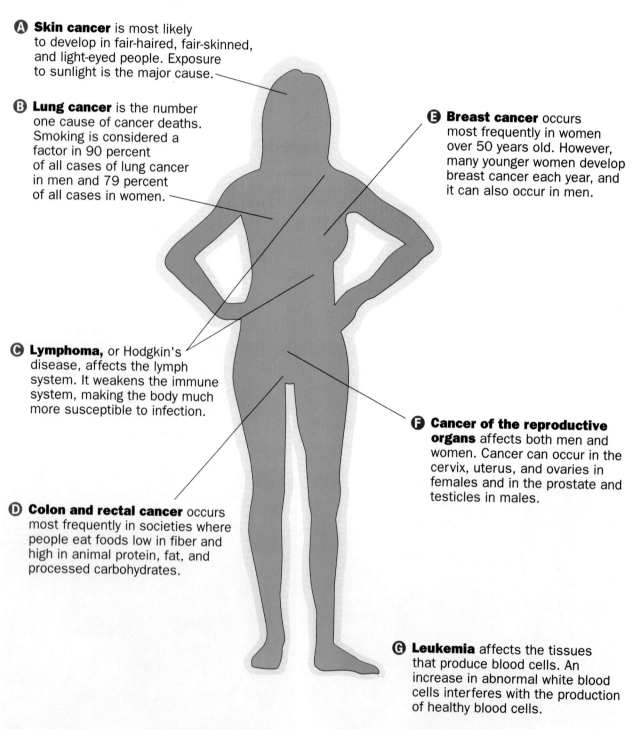

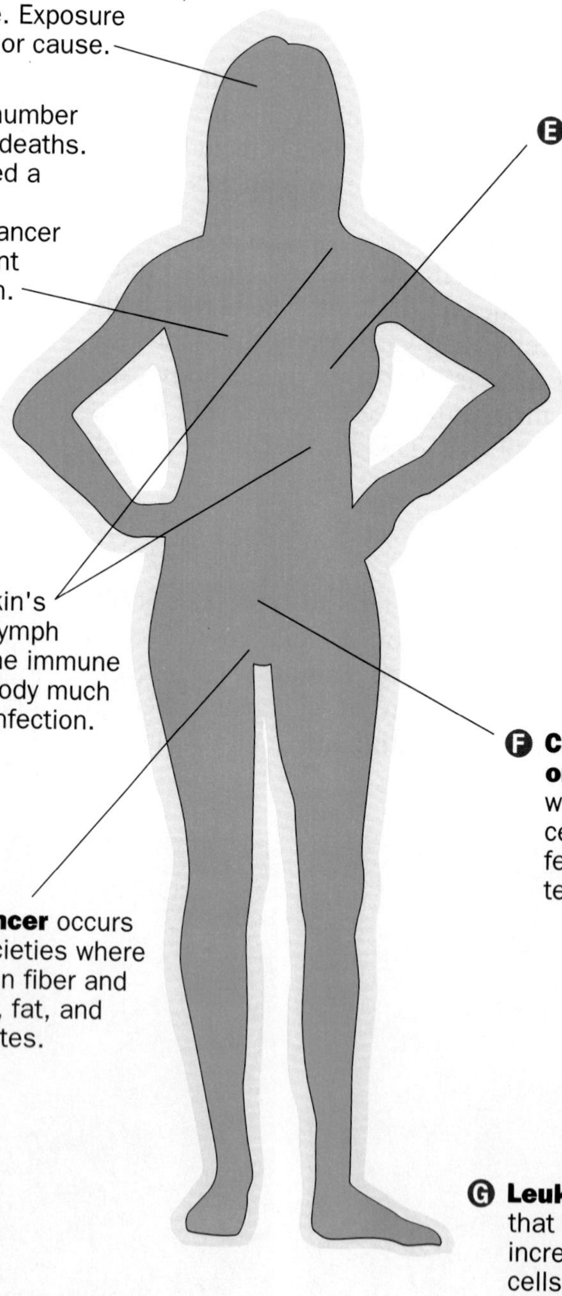

Ⓒ **Lymphoma,** or Hodgkin's disease, affects the lymph system. It weakens the immune system, making the body much more susceptible to infection.

Ⓓ **Colon and rectal cancer** occurs most frequently in societies where people eat foods low in fiber and high in animal protein, fat, and processed carbohydrates.

Ⓔ **Breast cancer** occurs most frequently in women over 50 years old. However, many younger women develop breast cancer each year, and it can also occur in men.

Ⓕ **Cancer of the reproductive organs** affects both men and women. Cancer can occur in the cervix, uterus, and ovaries in females and in the prostate and testicles in males.

Ⓖ **Leukemia** affects the tissues that produce blood cells. An increase in abnormal white blood cells interferes with the production of healthy blood cells.

What Causes Cancer?

Some types of cancer seem to be caused by factors that are inherited. Other types are related to lifestyle behaviors, such as smoking. Some types of cancer are caused by **carcinogens** (kar·SIN·uh·juhns) which are *substances that cause cancer*. Common sources of carcinogens are identified in **Figure 12.9.**

You can avoid some carcinogens. You can choose not to smoke or sunbathe. However, a few carcinogens, such as the chemical pollution from factories, are more difficult to avoid. This type pollution is monitored by government agencies. The Environmental Protection Agency (EPA), the Food and Drug Administration (FDA), and other agencies have regulations that are designed to protect the public from environmental carcinogens.

Diagnosing and Treating Cancer

Doctors can often find some types of cancer during a routine physical exam. They use tests to find others. A blood test, for instance, shows whether the blood cancer leukemia is present. If some tissue appears to be abnormal, the doctor may order a **biopsy** (BY·ahp·see). In this test, *a small piece of tissue is removed for testing in a lab.* The earlier cancer is found and treated, the better the chance of the person's survival.

Figure 12.9
Common Sources of Carcinogens

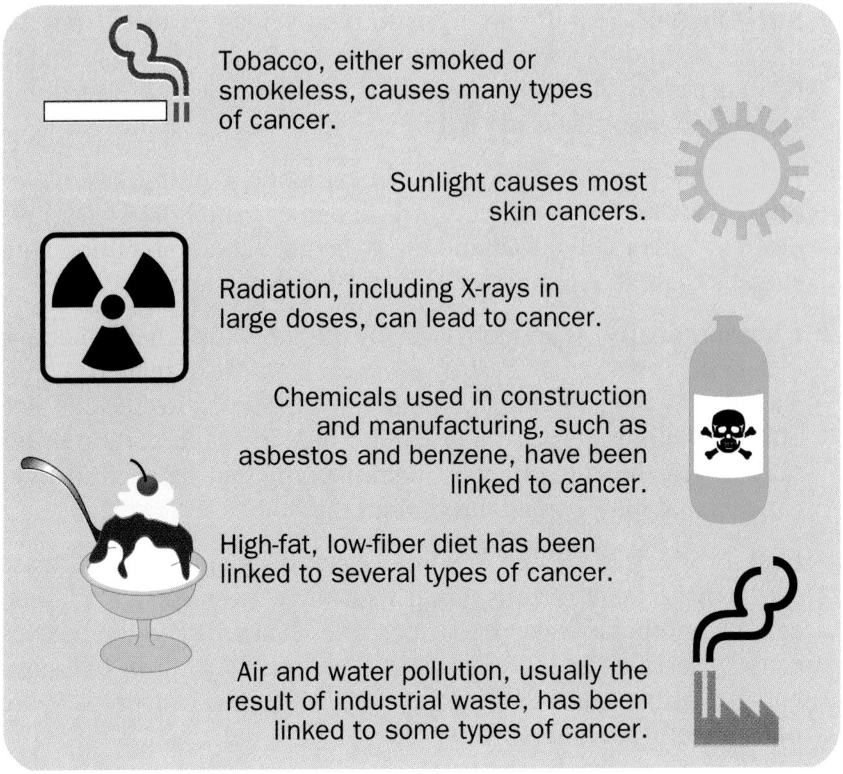

Tobacco, either smoked or smokeless, causes many types of cancer.
Sunlight causes most skin cancers.
Radiation, including X-rays in large doses, can lead to cancer.
Chemicals used in construction and manufacturing, such as asbestos and benzene, have been linked to cancer.
High-fat, low-fiber diet has been linked to several types of cancer.
Air and water pollution, usually the result of industrial waste, has been linked to some types of cancer.

Cultural Connections

Cultural Change and Cancer Risk

The average Japanese diet is much lower in animal fat and higher in fiber than the average American diet. Japanese women living in Japan and eating the traditional Japanese diet have a very low rate of breast cancer. The rate of breast cancer increases dramatically in Japanese women who have moved to the United States and adopted a Western diet high in fat. Of course, diet is only one factor in the lifestyle changes of these women.

in your journal

Do you think you and members of your family are at low risk, average risk, or high risk of developing cancer? Why? Write your answers in your private journal and explain your observations.

Art Connection

Poster Time! ACTIVITY!

Now that you know the seven warning signs of cancer, make a poster that encourages students—and adults—to watch for them.

Warning Signs of Cancer

People can play an important role in protecting themselves from cancer by watching for it. Females, for example, can examine their breasts for lumps, which may be a sign of breast cancer. Males can examine their testicles. Everyone can look for the seven warning signs of cancer identified by the American Cancer Society.

C Change in bowel or bladder habits

A A sore that does not heal

U Unusual bleeding or discharge

T Thickening or lump in breast or elsewhere

I Indigestion or difficulty swallowing

O Obvious change in a wart or mole

N Nagging cough or hoarseness

Watch for the seven warning signs of cancer. If you see one, don't wait. Check with your doctor.

Treatment of Cancer

The key to treating cancer is finding it early. Once cancer spreads, treatment is more difficult. The main ways to treat cancer are surgery, radiation, and chemotherapy. Doctors often draw up a treatment plan for the patient. This plan may involve a combination of these methods.

- **Surgery.** The goal of surgery is to remove cancer cells from the body. This method works best on cancers that have not spread to other parts of the body. Surgery is used for skin, breast, lung, colon, and many other types of cancer.
- **Radiation** (ray·dee·AY·shuhn)**.** In radiation therapy, *X-rays or other radioactive substances are aimed at a tumor.* These rays destroy cancer cells. Radiation may be used in combination with surgery to treat a number of different types of cancer.
- **Chemotherapy** (kee·moh·THEHR·uh·pee)**.** In chemotherapy, *chemicals are used to destroy cancer cells.* More than 100 anti-cancer drugs are used in chemotherapy. Some cause serious side effects, including severe nausea and hair loss, but certain drugs may lessen the side effects. Chemotherapy can be used to fight cancers that have spread throughout the body.

Each type of cancer treatment has some disadvantages. All three can damage healthy cells along with the cancer cells. Radiation and chemotherapy used to treat one cancer may themselves cause a second cancer years later. The goal is to limit the number of healthy cells that are harmed while the cancer cells are being destroyed.

Preventing Cancer

Many factors that cause cancer are connected to lifestyle choices you make. You can lower your risk of developing some types of cancer by making certain healthy choices. These include avoiding tobacco, eating healthful foods—such as fruits, vegetables, and whole grain cereals—and avoiding high-fat foods, and limiting your exposure to the sun. Although making healthy choices does not guarantee that you will not get cancer, it does give you a greater chance of staying healthy.

Skin cancer is the most common form of cancer in the United States. To lower your risk, you should limit your time in the sun, wear a hat, and use a sunscreen with a SPF (Sun Protection Factor) of at least 15.

Review — Lesson 3

Using complete sentences, answer the following questions on a separate sheet of paper.

Reviewing Terms and Facts

1. **Vocabulary** What is a *tumor*? Which type of tumor is a more serious health problem: a *benign* or a *malignant tumor*?
2. **Recall** What is the major cause of skin cancer? What is the major cause of lung cancer?
3. **Vocabulary** Define *carcinogen*. List two common sources of carcinogens.
4. **Vocabulary** What is a *biopsy*?
5. **Identify** List the seven warning signs of cancer.
6. **Recall** What are the three main ways of treating cancer?

Thinking Critically

7. **Hypothesize** What type of diet is best for reducing the risk of colon and rectal cancer?
8. **Analyze** Why is it important to try to discover cancer in its early stages?

Applying Health Concepts

9. **Health of Others** With a partner, role-play trying to convince a friend of the advantages of following the healthy choices for lowering the risk of cancer. Imagine the following situations: that your friend is a smoker, that your friend eats a high-fat diet, that your friend spends every possible moment outdoors without any protection from the sun.

TEEN HEALTH DIGEST

Personal Trainer

Heart Healthy

Exercise tones your muscles—and your heart is the most important muscle in your body. Most people should make a point of doing some aerobic exercise (such as running, bicycling, and swimming) for 30 minutes three times a week. In addition, here are some ideas for daily habits to keep your heart in shape.

- Use the stairs instead of an elevator or escalator.
- When you ride in a car, ask to be dropped off a few blocks from your destination. Then you can walk the rest of the way.
- If you ride the bus or subway, get off a stop or two early.
- Mow the lawn.
- When you study, take an exercise break—walk around to loosen your muscles and relax your brain.

CON$UMER FOCU$

Beat the Allergy Blues

Spring is in the air! So are pollen, molds, and other allergens.

How can you relieve your suffering if you have allergies? The American College of Emergency Physicians suggests the following do's and don'ts for people with allergies.

Do

- Avoid your allergen. Allergic to shellfish? Don't eat them! Cats make you sneeze? Don't pet them!
- Stay indoors as much as you can on windy days. The wind stirs up pollen.
- Keep the windows rolled up when traveling in a car.

Don't

- Don't mow the lawn or be nearby when someone else is mowing.
- Don't hang laundry to dry outdoors. Pollen and molds can collect on clothes and sheets.
- Don't go outside at dawn or dusk. Those are high pollen exposure times.

Try This:

Make a poster of tips for allergy sufferers. Illustrate each tip. Ask permission to display your poster in a public place.

HEALTH UPDATE

Tea for Two (Two Health Benefits, That Is)

Thirsty? Try tea—your body may thank you. Recent studies have linked two tangible health benefits to tea.

First, tea may reduce your risk of getting certain kinds of cancers. Recent studies have linked tea drinking to reduced risks of skin, liver, lung, and esophageal cancer.

Second, another study has found that a substance in green tea, called hexanes, can help protect your teeth from cavities.

Teens Making a Difference

A Teen Role Model

When Matthew Brown graduated from high school, he was at the head of his class. Unfortunately, he never had the opportunity to speak at his graduation. Matthew received his diploma in the intensive care unit of a Minneapolis hospital, where he was awaiting a liver transplant.

Matthew was diagnosed with liver disease as a child. He missed a year of school when he had his first liver transplant in the eighth grade. Rather than repeat the year, he made up his schoolwork over the summer and started high school with his classmates. He kept up an A average and was named valedictorian of his class.

Although he could not attend his graduation, he was able to watch the ceremony. A local TV station, WBGU, donated time and equipment to transmit the graduation live to his hospital room. Instead of listening to a speech made by the valedictorian, Matthew's classmates spoke to him —praising him for his achievements and courage and offering him best wishes for his surgery.

Myths and Realities

Diabetics vs. Sugar

Sugar is poison—a single candy bar could be deadly!

That's just one myth surrounding the disease called diabetes.

It's true that people who have diabetes must control the level of glucose in their blood. That doesn't mean that sugar is forbidden, though. Check with your doctor to find out the amount of sugar you are permitted to have. Fat may be even more dangerous than sugar to a person with diabetes, since this condition carries an increased risk of heart disease. It is very important for people who have diabetes to eat a healthful, balanced diet, planned with the help of a doctor.

Lesson 4

Understanding Allergies and Asthma

This lesson will help you find answers to questions that teens often ask about allergies and asthma. For example:

- **Why do some people develop allergies and others do not?**
- **How can allergies be treated?**
- **What is asthma?**

Words to Know

allergy
allergen
pollen
histamine
hives
antihistamine
asthma
bronchodilator

What Are Allergies?

The human body has a natural, built-in defense system that fights germs that enter the body. This defense system is called the immune system. When germs enter the body, the immune system senses danger and starts a process to destroy or eliminate the germs. In some cases, the immune system also reacts to substances to which a person is sensitive. An **allergy** is *the body's sensitivity to certain substances.* A *substance that causes an allergic reaction* is called an **allergen** (AL·er·juhn).

For example, many people are allergic to **pollen,** *tiny grains from plants.* Pollen can cause sneezing, itchy eyes, and other disagreeable reactions in people who are sensitive to it. Although most allergies develop during childhood and youth, anyone can become allergic to practically anything at any age. **Figure 12.10** shows how allergens affect the body.

Figure 12.10
Allergic Reactions

Some allergens, such as poison ivy, cause allergic reactions in many people. Almost any substance, however, can set off an allergic reaction in a person who is sensitive to it.

1. Contact with allergens happens in three ways: by breathing (pollen, dust, smoke, mold spores); by swallowing (milk, strawberries, aspirin); and by touching them (poison ivy, cosmetics, wool).

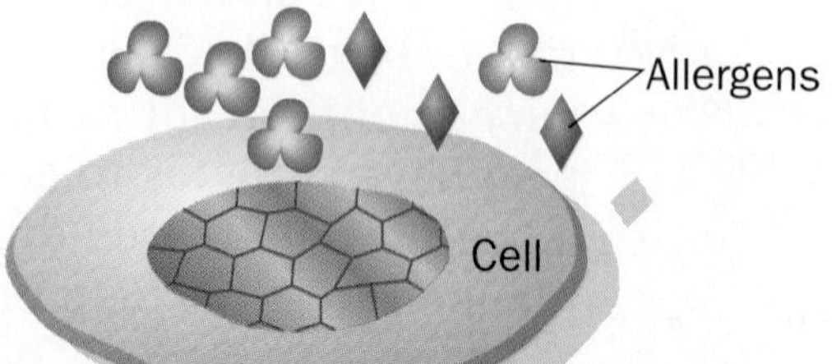

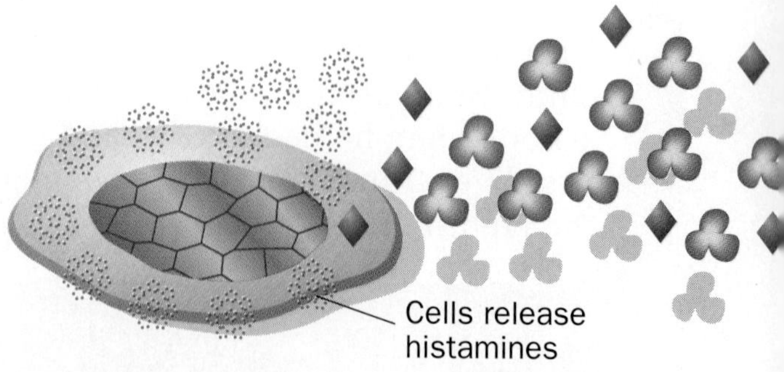

2. When an allergen enters the body, special cells release histamines. These are chemicals that cause the symptoms of an allergic reaction.

Reactions to Allergens

The body's response to allergens is to release histamines. **Histamines** (HIS·tuh·meenz) are *chemicals in the body that cause the symptoms of the allergic reaction.* Two common symptoms are difficulty in breathing and a skin rash. Some people get **hives,** *raised bumps on the skin that are very itchy.* Common allergic reactions are shown in part 3 of **Figure 12.10.**

Diagnosing and Treating Allergies

Discovering the cause of an allergic reaction can be quite simple. Perhaps you break out in a rash when you eat strawberries, or your eyes begin to itch and water when you get close to a cat. If, however, the cause of an allergic reaction is not known, a doctor can perform various tests. In the most common test, the patient's skin is scratched and tiny doses of possible allergens are inserted. If the patient is allergic to one of the substances, the skin at that particular place will turn red and swell slightly.

There is no cure for allergies, but there are several ways of dealing with them. The first is to avoid the allergen as much as possible. When this is not possible, a person's symptoms may be relieved by taking **antihistamines.** These are *medications that work against the effects of the histamines,* which cause the symptoms of the allergy. In severe cases, treatment may involve exposing the allergic person to extremely small quantities of the allergen to build up immunity to it.

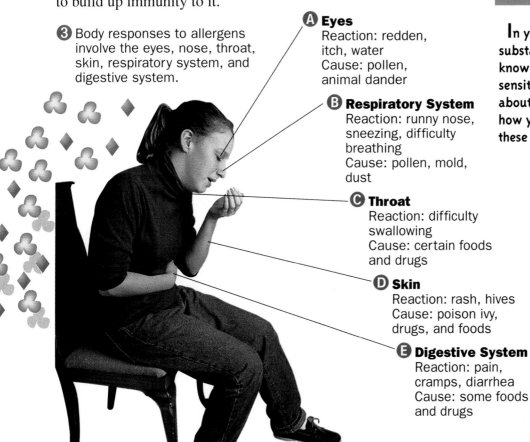

3 Body responses to allergens involve the eyes, nose, throat, skin, respiratory system, and digestive system.

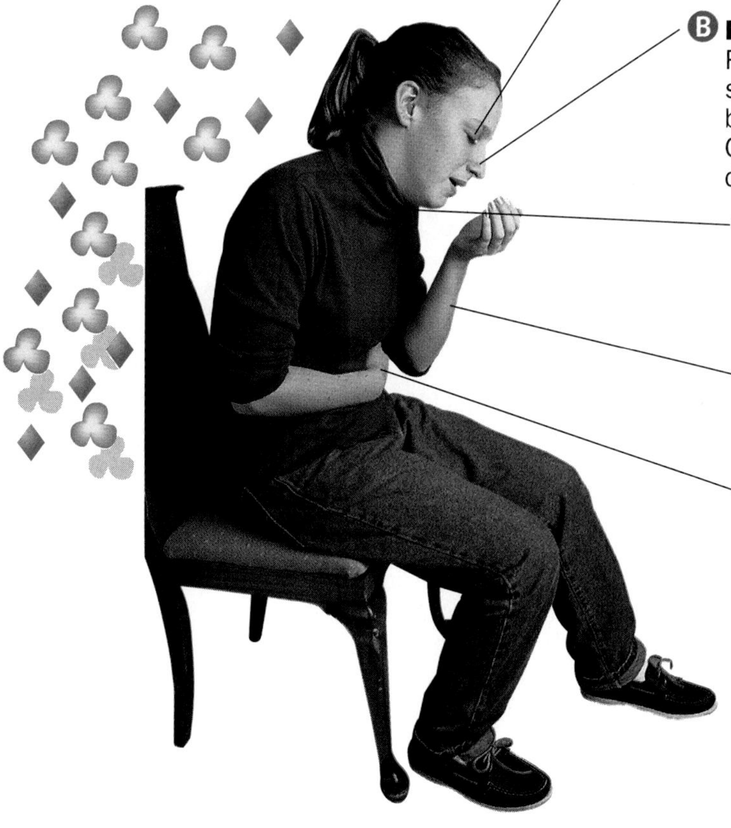

Math Connection

Pollen Count ACTIVITY!

People allergic to pollen can monitor the amount of pollen in the air by checking reports in the newspapers and on radio and television. The daily pollen count is based on the number of ragweed pollen grains in one cubic yard of air.

In the library, check back issues of a newspaper for the pollen count on one day of each month in the past year. Make a graph. What time of year is the count highest? When is it lowest?

in your journal

In your journal, list any substances to which you know or suspect you are sensitive. (Don't forget about poison ivy.) Describe how your body reacts to these allergens.

What Is Asthma?

More than 10 million people in the United States have asthma. One-third of these people are under 18 years old. **Asthma** (AZ·muh) is *a serious chronic condition that causes tiny air passages in the respiratory system to become narrow or blocked.*

Periods when asthma symptoms are being experienced are called asthma attacks (see **Figure 12.11**). Substances or events that start the attacks are called asthma triggers. Something that triggers an asthma attack in one person may or may not affect another person with asthma. Common triggers of asthma include exposure to allergens, cold air, cigarette smoke, air pollution, certain foods or drugs, and strenuous exercise. Sometimes strong emotions or stress can trigger an asthma attack. This usually happens when other triggers are also present.

Figure 12.11

Asthma Attack

Symptoms of an asthma attack are wheezing, a high-pitched whistling sound made by forcing air through narrowed airways; shortness of breath; a gagging or choking sensation; and tightness in the chest.

Ⓐ During normal breathing, air passes through the bronchial tubes. The alveoli expand to take in air.

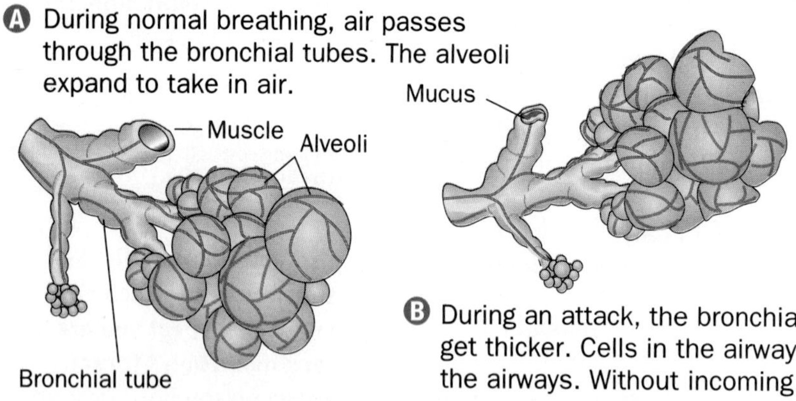

Symptoms of an Attack
Wheezing, a high-pitched whistling sound made by air being forced through narrowed airways; shortness of breath; gagging or choking sensation; tightness in chest.

Ⓑ During an attack, the bronchial muscles tighten and the tubes get thicker. Cells in the airways make extra mucus, which blocks the airways. Without incoming air, the alveoli collapse.

MAKING HEALTHY DECISIONS

Managing Chronic Conditions

Jesse has asthma. He has worked out a treatment plan with his doctor, and as long as he follows the plan, Jesse manages fairly well. The plan includes taking preventive medication before exercise and using an inhaler at the first sign of an attack. Jesse also has to avoid exercise during times when there is a lot of pollen in the air.

Jesse started going to a new school this year and had trouble at first making friends. Now things are better. Jesse joined the track team and gets along fine with his teammates. His asthma has not been giving him much trouble, and for one reason or another, Jesse hasn't told the coach or his friends about his condition.

Today there is a major track meet. However, Jesse woke up this morning with some tightness in his chest, and he felt short of breath after walking to school. Jesse is worried. He doesn't want to let his team down. He doesn't want his new friends to think he is a quitter. Should he try to tough out the track meet or tell his coach that he may be experiencing the start of an asthma attack?

Learning relaxation techniques is also often helpful. People normally breathe faster when they are under stress or excited. This increase in breathing rate often worsens the breathing difficulties for people with asthma.

Several different types of medication are used for treating asthma. Some block swelling in the bronchial tubes and decrease the amount of mucus being produced. Others, called **bronchodilators** (brahn·ko·dy·LAY·terz), are used to *relax the muscles that have tightened around the airways.* When inhaled in a spray, bronchodilators can often bring relief within a few minutes. These different medicines may be taken regularly on a preventive basis or used during an asthma attack. As with all medication, it is important to be cautious while using the bronchodilator.

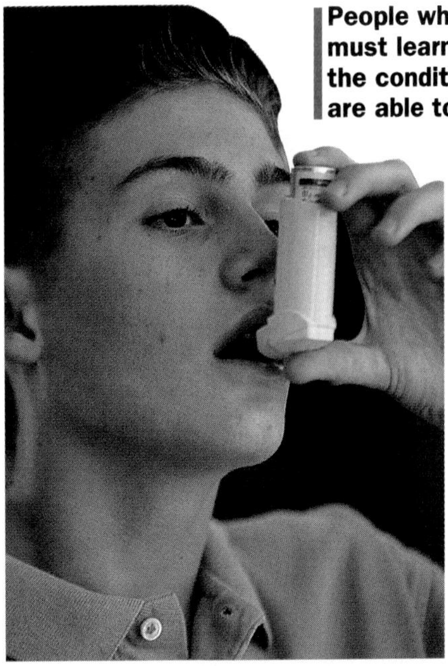

People who have asthma must learn how to manage the condition. Most of them are able to lead active lives.

Review

Lesson 4

Using complete sentences, answer the following questions on a separate sheet of paper.

Reviewing Terms and Facts

1. **Vocabulary** Define *allergen.* List three examples of allergens.
2. **Explain** Describe what happens when a person comes in contact with a substance he or she is allergic to.

Thinking Critically

3. **Synthesis** What is usually the most helpful step in managing allergies and asthma?

Applying Health Concepts

4. **Health of Others** Interview several people with allergies or asthma. Compile a list of how they manage their conditions. Display your list in your classroom.

Jesse remembers the step-by-step decision-making process.

1. **State the situation**
2. **List the options**
3. **Weigh the possible outcomes**
4. **Consider your values**
5. **Make a decision and act**
6. **Evaluate the decision**

Follow-up Activities

1. Apply the six steps of the decision-making process to Jesse's problem.
2. With a group of classmates, discuss who is responsible for managing Jesse's chronic condition.
3. With a partner, role-play telling someone about a chronic health condition.

Lesson 5

Other Noncommunicable Diseases

This lesson will help you find answers to questions that teens often ask about arthritis and diabetes. For example:

- **Do only old people get arthritis?**
- **Is there any way to prevent arthritis?**
- **What is diabetes?**
- **Can diabetes be cured?**

Words to Know

arthritis
rheumatoid arthritis
osteoarthritis
diabetes
insulin
Type I diabetes
Type II diabetes

Did You Know?

How Many Are Affected?

Nearly 40 million people of all ages in the United States are thought to have some form of arthritis.

What Is Arthritis?

Arthritis is not one disease, but many. A person with **arthritis** (ar·THRY·tuhs) may have *one of more than 100 conditions marked by pain and swelling in body joints.* About one person in seven suffers from one of these conditions. Many people think that arthritis affects only older people, but this disease can affect people of any age, from infancy on.

Rheumatoid Arthritis

The more serious of the two main kinds of arthritis is **rheumatoid** (ROO·muh·toyd) **arthritis.** In this condition, *body joints become swollen and painful, and cartilage that separates the bones is destroyed.* Affected joints often become deformed and stiff, and they no longer function normally. Joints usually affected are those of the hands, feet, elbows, knees, hips, and spine. Usually, the effects of rheumatoid arthritis are symmetrical—both hands develop the symptoms at the same time and in the same pattern.

The cause of rheumatoid arthritis is not known. It may follow infection or injury. A person's immune system may be reacting to and attacking the body's own tissues.

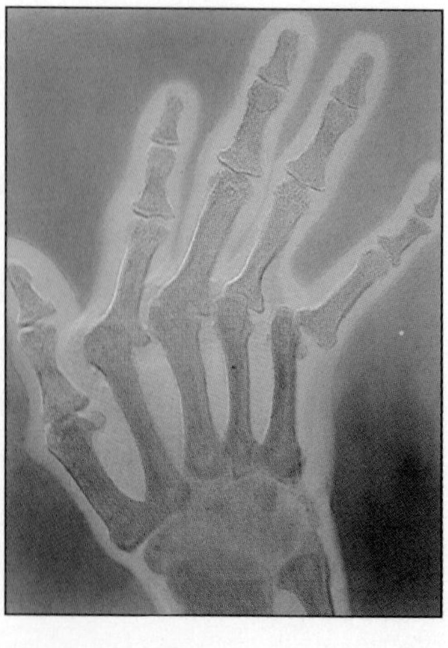

This X-ray shows the joints of a hand affected with rheumatoid arthritis.

Treating Rheumatoid Arthritis

There is no cure for rheumatoid arthritis. When a joint has been severely damaged, the joint may be reconstructed or replaced by surgery. For the most part, treatment centers on relieving pain and preserving or improving joint function. People with rheumatoid arthritis are often given the following advice.

Actions to Take

- **Rest.** Get plenty of rest to reduce stress on affected joints.
- **Medicine.** Take medication as prescribed.
- **Posture.** Develop good posture habits to maintain a healthful positioning of the body.
- **Heat.** Take hot baths or use a heating pad for pain.
- **Exercise.** Exercise daily to prevent further stiffness.
- **Diet.** Eat a healthy balanced diet, including foods that furnish protein and calcium to help prevent further loss of bone tissue.

Daily exercise can help prevent further stiffness.

Osteoarthritis

Osteoarthritis (ahs·tee·oh·ahr·THRY·tuhs) is a more common type of the disease. *This condition results from the wearing away of the body joints.* It affects the joints of the hip and knee most often. These are the joints that bear much of the body's weight. Osteoarthritis is a natural part of aging. Your risk of osteoarthritis increases with age, but this disease can affect people of all ages.

Pain and stiffness in the morning, pain or swelling in a joint, and pain and stiffness in the lower back or knees are warning signs of osteoarthritis. Early medical attention can help lessen its effects.

Treatment for osteoarthritis usually includes ibuprofen or aspirin to ease the pain and swelling. A doctor may also suggest specific exercises to prevent the damage from becoming worse. If the disease has severely damaged a patient's knee or hip joint, a doctor may recommend an operation to replace the diseased joint with a mechanical one.

in your journal

Arthritis often affects the joints of the hands. In your journal, write a list of the everyday tasks, such as writing, that require strong, flexible hands and fingers.

What Is Diabetes?

Did You Know?

Who Gets It? ACTIVITY!

Although in some families there is a tendency to develop Type II diabetes, another factor usually must be present for the disease to develop. Obesity is a major risk factor that can trigger Type II diabetes. Find out if anyone in your family has had diabetes.

Diabetes (dy·uh·BEE·teez) is *a disease that prevents the body from converting food into energy.* About 16 million people in the United States have diabetes. Many of those affected do not know they have it. The tendency to develop diabetes can be passed along in families through the genes. Diabetes is caused by problems with the production and function of a hormone called insulin. **Insulin** (IN·suh·lin) *regulates the level of glucose in the blood.* **Figure 12.12** explains the role of insulin in the human body.

Types of Diabetes

Diabetes affects people of all ages and occurs as either Type I or Type II. **Type I diabetes** is *the result of little or no insulin produced by the pancreas.* Type I is also called insulin-dependent because the person must always take insulin to maintain life. This is the type of diabetes that usually develops in children and young adults and affects more males than females.

Type II diabetes is *the result of too little insulin produced by the pancreas or the inability of the body to use insulin.* About 90 percent of all diabetes cases are Type II. This type of diabetes usually develops in people who are overweight and more than 40 years old, although the age of developing it varies.

Figure 12.12
Insulin and Diabetes

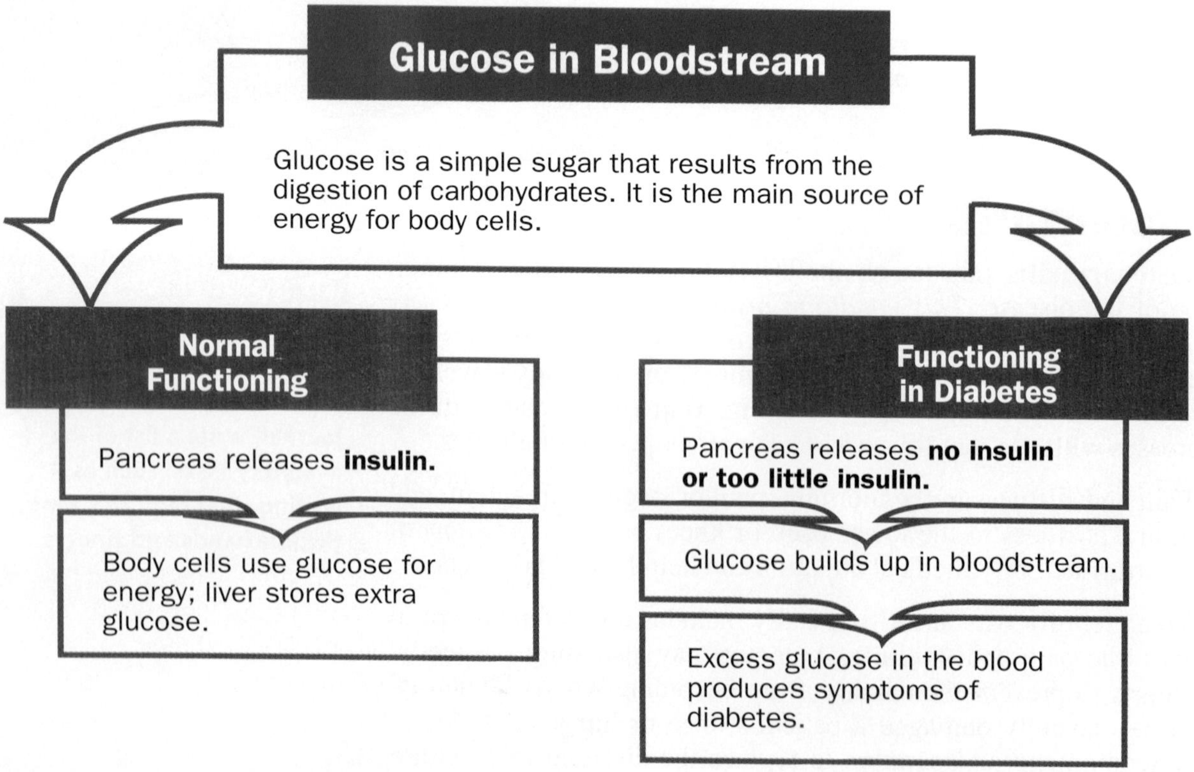

Glucose in Bloodstream
Glucose is a simple sugar that results from the digestion of carbohydrates. It is the main source of energy for body cells.
Normal Functioning
Pancreas releases insulin.
Body cells use glucose for energy; liver stores extra glucose.
Functioning in Diabetes
Pancreas releases no insulin or too little insulin.
Glucose builds up in bloodstream.
Excess glucose in the blood produces symptoms of diabetes.

Treating Diabetes

The symptoms of diabetes occur when a person's body cells are deprived of a source of energy. Anyone experiencing the following symptoms should be checked by a doctor.

Some people with diabetes need to give themselves insulin injections every day.

Symptoms of Diabetes

- Excess production of urine
- Excess thirst
- Excess hunger
- Weight loss
- Shortness of breath
- Dry, itchy skin
- Lack of energy

People with Type I diabetes need to take insulin every day. Insulin is taken by injection with a hypodermic needle. These people must learn how to inject themselves and how to manage their diet. Some people with Type II diabetes take a medicine that helps them use the insulin their body makes.

Diabetes cannot be cured. If left untreated, it can lead to blindness, loss of feeling or severe pain in the feet and hands, kidney failure, and hardening of the arteries. In many cases, however, with medication and proper diet, people with diabetes usually can lead fairly normal lives.

Review Lesson 5

Using complete sentences, answer the following questions on a separate sheet of paper.

Reviewing Terms and Facts

1. **Recall** Which is a more serious condition—rheumatoid arthritis or osteoarthritis? Why?
2. **Compare** How are rheumatoid arthritis and osteoarthritis treated?
3. **Vocabulary** What is *insulin*?
4. **Identify** What are the symptoms of diabetes?

Thinking Critically

5. **Synthesize** What do you think would be most challenging about having diabetes as a teen? Explain your thinking in a brief essay.

Applying Health Concepts

6. **Consumer Health** Look in magazines and newspapers and on television for advertisements of products for people with arthritis. With several classmates, discuss the ads. Decide what the major point of each ad is. Decide which age-group the manufacturer is trying to appeal to. Do you think this is wise? Why?
7. **Consumer Health** Look in magazines and newspapers and on television for advertisements of products for people with diabetes. Compare the number of these ads to the number of ads for arthritis products. Why do you suppose there is a difference?

Chapter 12 Review

Chapter Summary

- **Lesson 1** Noncommunicable diseases are not spread through contact with other people. They are caused by genetic, lifestyle-related, or environmental factors.
- **Lesson 2** Heart disease is the leading killer of adults in the United States. Healthy lifestyle behaviors can help prevent heart disease.
- **Lesson 3** Cancer is a group of many diseases in which there is abnormal growth of body cells. Healthy lifestyle choices can reduce the risk of cancer.
- **Lesson 4** Allergies are sensitivities to certain substances. Asthma is a serious condition that affects the respiratory system. Asthma attacks are triggered by a number of substances and activities.
- **Lesson 5** Arthritis is a disease that can affect people of all ages and is characterized by pain and swelling in body joints. Diabetes is a disease that prevents the body from converting food into energy.

Reviewing Key Terms and Concepts

Using complete sentences, answer the following questions on a separate sheet of paper.

Lesson 1

1. Define *risk factor.* Identify three types of risk factors.
2. List six lifestyle behaviors that lower your risk of developing certain diseases.

Lesson 2

3. Explain why it is important to maintain a low blood cholesterol level.
4. What is *bypass surgery?*

Lesson 3

5. Define *cancer* and *metastasis.*
6. What type of cancer kills the most people?

Lesson 4

7. Define *allergy* and *asthma.* Define *pollen, hives,* and *bronchodilator,* and explain how each term is related to allergies or asthma.
8. Define *histamine* and *antihistamine.*

Lesson 5

9. Define *arthritis.* What type of arthritis is a natural part of aging?
10. Define *diabetes.* Explain the difference between *Type I* and *Type II diabetes.*

Thinking Critically

Using complete sentences, answer the following questions on a separate sheet of paper.

11. **Apply** Joel does not want to visit his uncle who has cancer. He is afraid that he might catch it. Why is his fear unrealistic?
12. **Synthesize** There is a strong family history of high blood pressure in Rhea's family. How can she lower her own risk of developing high blood pressure?
13. **Recommend** What are some ways to keep from developing skin cancer?
14. **Suggest** Paul wants a cat, but he thinks that he may be allergic to them. How can he find out whether or not this is true?
15. **Hypothesize** Why might it be difficult for a person who had rheumatoid arthritis to play the violin?

Chapter 12 Review

Your Action Plan

Choose a lifestyle behavior you would like to improve. Then make an action plan, as outlined below, to lower your risk of heart disease or cancer.

Step 1 Choose a long-term goal. Perhaps you would like to eat a more balanced diet that is lower in fat.

Step 2 Select some short-term goals that will help you reach your long-term goal. A short-term goal for improving your diet might be to replace your favorite fried chicken filet sandwich with a grilled chicken filet sandwich.

Step 3 Make a schedule for reaching each short-term goal.

Step 4 Check your schedule to keep yourself on track.

Your reward for achieving your long-term goal will be a longer, healthier life.

In Your Home and Community

1. **Personal Health** Speak to an allergist. Find out about the most common sources of allergies. Ask if there are allergens in your local area that are not found in other parts of the country. Write a paragraph describing what you have learned. Share your findings with your classmates.
2. **Health of Others** Type I diabetes is a disease that occurs in young people. Find out more about the disease and how it is controlled. Use the information in this chapter, and add facts from other sources. Prepare a handout or pamphlet that lists symptoms and treatments for the disease and make it available through the school nurse's office.

Building Your Portfolio

1. **Building Health Knowledge** Asthma is on the increase, particularly in certain parts of the country. Find out more about this condition and why rates are rising. Collect current newspaper and magazine articles on the subject. Write a short essay summarizing your findings. Add the articles and essay to your portfolio.
2. **Health Profile** Collect stories of people who have survived, or learned to live with, a serious noncommunicable disease or disorder. Clip articles from magazines and newspapers and/or record interviews with people you know. Tape-record the advice you would give, based on these stories, to someone with such a disease. Add the stories and tape to your portfolio.
3. **Personal Assessment** Look through all the activities and projects you did for this chapter. Choose one or two that you would like to include in your portfolio.

D.A.R.E.

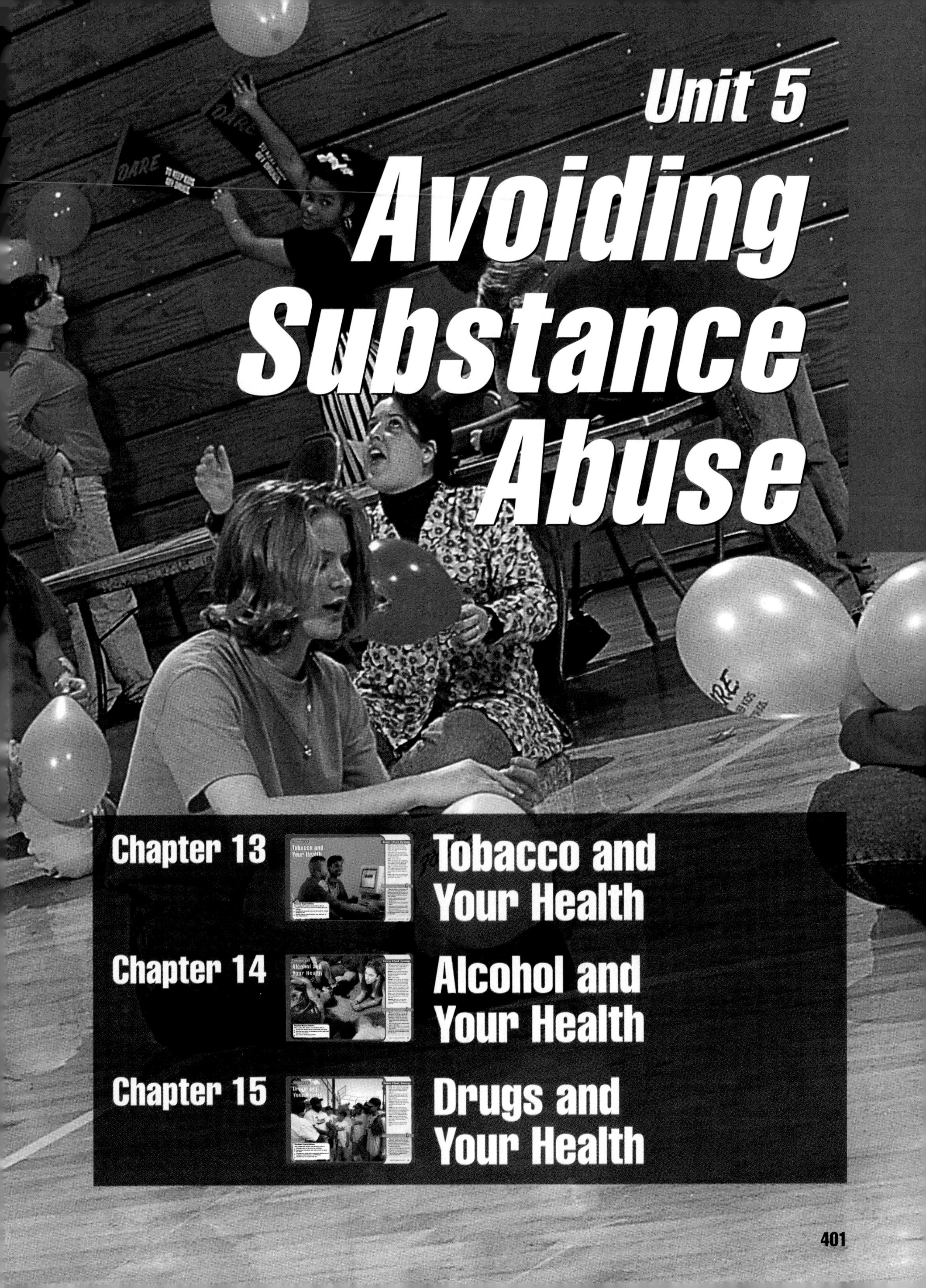

Unit 5
Avoiding Substance Abuse

Chapter 13

Tobacco and Your Health

Student Expectations

After reading this chapter, you should be able to:

1. Explain what tobacco is and how it affects the body systems.
2. Describe the personal costs and the costs to society of tobacco use.
3. Identify ways to remain tobacco free and ways to stop using tobacco.

Teen Chat Group

Sean: I can't believe how many Web pages there are about tobacco.

Anita: There's so much material here, I don't see how we can cover it all in our paper.

Sean: Maybe we should narrow it down to one specific health problem, like lung cancer. Hey, look—a picture of a diseased lung!

Anita: That is *so* gross.

Sean: This stuff is all so disgusting. I don't understand why anyone would ever decide to smoke. Who would want their lungs to look like that?

Anita: I guess they think smoking is cool. Maybe they don't know what it's doing to their bodies, or else they just think it'll never happen to them.

Sean: They'll know better when they see our report. Print out this page—we can use the picture.

in your journal

Read the dialogue on this page. How much do you know about the health problems caused by tobacco use? Start your private journal entries on tobacco and its effect on health by answering these questions:

- **Do you, or does anyone close to you, smoke? If so, how has that habit affected you?**
- **Why do you think some young people smoke?**
- **Have you ever felt pressured to smoke by friends but resisted the pressure? If so, how did you do it?**

When you reach the end of the chapter, you will use your journal entries to make an action plan.

Lesson 1

How Tobacco Affects Your Body

This lesson will help you answer questions that teens often ask about tobacco. For example:

- **What is tobacco?**
- **In what forms is tobacco sold?**
- **What substances are in tobacco?**
- **How does tobacco affect body systems?**

Words to Know

nicotine
tar
carbon monoxide
cilia

What Is Tobacco?

Tobacco is a plant grown in the United States, China, Brazil, and India, among other countries. In the United States, tobacco is grown primarily in southeastern states. The leaves of a tobacco plant are dried, aged for two or three years, and then used to make cigarettes, cigars, pipe tobacco, chewing tobacco, and snuff. Most of the tobacco grown in the United States is made into cigarettes.

Tobacco is a powerful drug. When smoked, sucked, or chewed, it changes the brain's chemistry. This change makes the tobacco user want more and more tobacco. About 50 million people in the United States smoke tobacco on a regular basis.

Cultural Connections

Labeling in Canada

In Canada, labels on all tobacco products include very explicit health warnings. The following labels are used, in both English and French.

- Smoking can kill you.
- Cigarettes are addictive.
- Cigarettes cause fatal lung disease.
- Tobacco causes fatal lung diseases in nonsmokers.
- Cigarettes cause strokes and heart disease.

The tobacco plant is processed in a variety of ways and sold in several different forms.

Chemicals in Tobacco

Thousands of harmful chemicals, some of them deadly, are present in tobacco smoke. Over 40 of these chemicals are known to cause cancer. The three main harmful substances are nicotine, tar, and carbon monoxide.

- **Nicotine** is *an addictive drug that is found in all tobacco products.* It affects a smoker's brain in the same way as heroin and cocaine. The tobacco user constantly craves more nicotine. In addition, nicotine affects the brain in a way that may make the user feel either more alert or more relaxed.
- **Tar** is *a dark, thick, sticky liquid that forms when tobacco burns.* Several of the substances in tar are known to cause cancer. When smokers inhale, tar gets into their lungs, where it can cause cancer, emphysema, and other diseases.
- **Carbon monoxide** is a *colorless, odorless, poisonous gas that is produced when tobacco burns.* The carbon monoxide in smoke passes through the lungs into the bloodstream. The presence of carbon monoxide in the bloodstream reduces the amount of oxygen the blood cells can carry.

As **Figure 13.1** shows, tar, carbon monoxide, and other chemicals that are found in tobacco smoke are harmful to the body. In some cases they are deadly.

interNET CONNECTION

Don't let your health go up in smoke. Learn more about how tobacco can harm you, and how you can remain tobacco free for life.

http://www.glencoe.com/sec/health

Figure 13.1

Puffing Poisons

The chemicals in tobacco smoke are found in items which people would never put into their bodies. Although the amounts of these poisons in tobacco are too small to kill a smoker instantly, they can cause great damage over time.

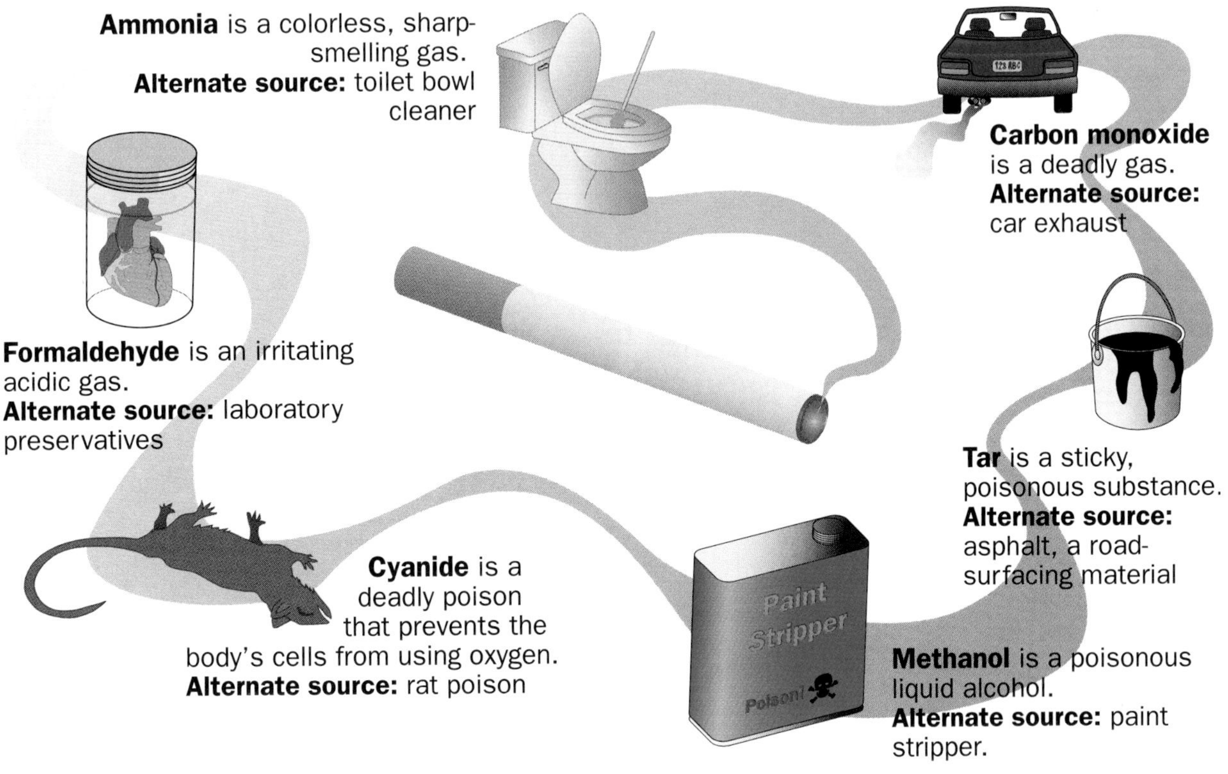

Ammonia is a colorless, sharp-smelling gas.
Alternate source: toilet bowl cleaner
Carbon monoxide is a deadly gas.
Alternate source: car exhaust
Formaldehyde is an irritating acidic gas.
Alternate source: laboratory preservatives
Tar is a sticky, poisonous substance.
Alternate source: asphalt, a road-surfacing material
Cyanide is a deadly poison that prevents the body's cells from using oxygen.
Alternate source: rat poison
Methanol is a poisonous liquid alcohol.
Alternate source: paint stripper.
Paint Stripper
Poison!

Different Forms of Tobacco

Tobacco is sold and consumed in different forms. All forms of tobacco present serious health risks for users. **Figure 13.2** gives the amounts of various tobacco products that are produced in a year.

Cigarettes

Cigarettes are the most common form in which tobacco is used. They are usually sold in packs of 20. A typical smoker may go through at least one pack of cigarettes a day.

Because of the smoke that passes through their lungs, cigarette smokers are at risk for several dangerous lung diseases, including lung cancer and emphysema. Lung cancer is roughly ten times as common among smokers as it is among nonsmokers.

Cigars and Pipes

Pipes and cigars are other forms in which tobacco is smoked. Cigars and pipes produce more tar than cigarettes. Cigar and pipe smokers are more likely than cigarette smokers to develop cancers of the lip, mouth, and throat.

Smokeless Tobacco

Chewing tobacco is made up of coarsely ground tobacco leaves. Users suck and occasionally chew it. Snuff is tobacco made into a fine powder. It is sniffed or placed between the lower lip and gum, where it mixes with saliva and is absorbed into the body.

Figure 13.2
How Much Tobacco?
Here are the amounts of tobacco products that were produced in the United States in 1995.

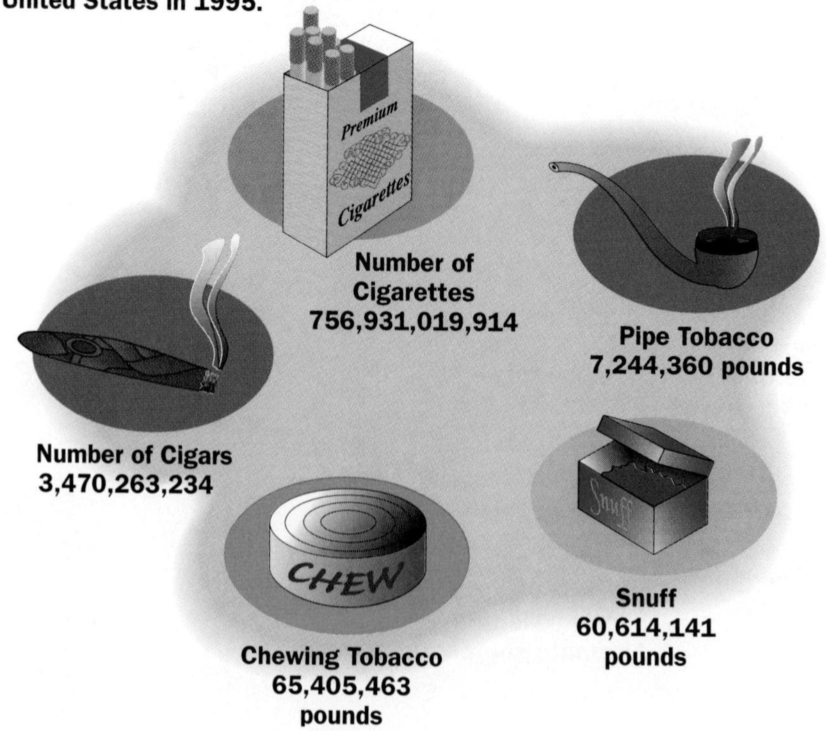

Did You Know?

Recent Invention

Although people have used tobacco for centuries, cigarettes are a relatively recent invention. The first machines to roll cigarettes were made in the 1880s. Cigarette smoking became widespread only after World War I. In the years since, death rates from lung cancer have increased more than tenfold.

Math Connection

Per Capita Tobacco ACTIVITY!

Look at the numbers in Figure 13.2. There are approximately 250 million people in the United States. How many cigarettes were made for every person in the country in 1995? If only 20 percent of these people smoked, how many cigarettes were produced for each smoker in that year? How many would each smoker have had to smoke every day to use them all up? Use a calculator to do the math.

Smokeless tobacco is messy to use. It causes bad breath, inflamed gums, and yellow teeth. Smokeless tobacco has also been linked to cancers of the esophagus, larynx, mouth, and pancreas.

How Tobacco Affects the Body Systems

No matter what form is used, tobacco harms the body in many ways. The chemicals in tobacco cause damage to just about every one of the body's systems. Tobacco is harmful both in the short term and in the long term.

Figure 13.3

Short-Term and Long-Term Effects of Tobacco Use

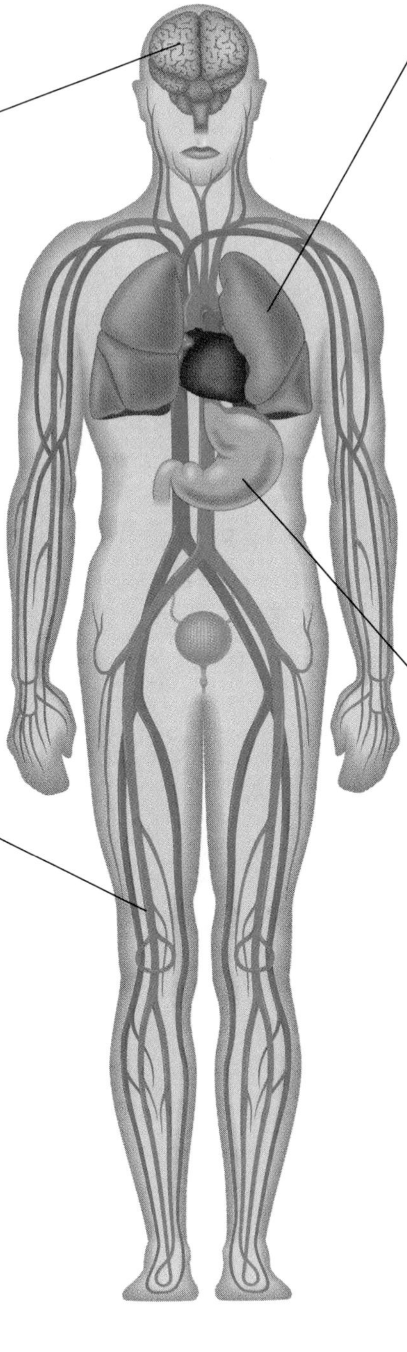

Ⓐ Nervous System

Short Term: Nicotine changes the brain's chemistry and is addictive. Withdrawal symptoms (nervousness, shakes, headaches) occur as early as half an hour after the last cigarette. The change in the brain's chemistry also causes an increase in adrenaline, which leads to increased heart rate and blood pressure.

Long Term: Smoking reduces the flow of oxygen to the brain, increasing the chances of a stroke.

Ⓑ Circulatory System

Short Term: Tobacco constricts blood vessels, which reduces the oxygen supply to body tissues. Tobacco also increases the heart rate.

Long Term: Besides weakening blood vessels, smoking also causes a fatty buildup that clogs blood vessels. Reduced oxygen flow to the heart can damage the heart muscle. Smokers therefore run a far greater risk of heart disease and stroke than nonsmokers.

Ⓒ Respiratory System

Short Term: Smoking causes shortness of breath, thus affecting a smoker's ability to walk, run, climb, bicycle, and so forth.

Long Term: Tar and other chemicals in tobacco smoke leave a sticky residue that destroys the cilia in the bronchi. **Cilia** are the *tiny hairlike projections that line the respiratory passage and filter out dust and foreign matter.* Smoking also damages the alveoli, the tiny air sacs in the lungs. Over time, smokers are far more likely than nonsmokers to suffer from lung cancer, emphysema, and other major lung diseases.

Ⓓ Digestive System

Short Term: Tobacco can cause stomach upset and bad breath. More frequent use stains teeth, dulls the taste buds, and increases the risk of cavities.

Long Term: Cigarettes, pipes, cigars, and smokeless tobacco can cause cancer of the mouth and throat. Tobacco use can cause tooth decay and has been identified as one possible cause of stomach ulcers. The risk of bladder cancer increases up to ten times with long-term tobacco use.

How Smoking Affects Personal Appearance

in your journal

Make a list of the short-term and long-term consequences of using tobacco. Which ones do you find most disturbing? Write a personal statement of your views on tobacco use. Use your list to support your opinions.

Most of the damage caused by smoking occurs inside the body. However, smoking also harms a person's outer appearance in very noticeable ways. The longer a person uses tobacco, the more likely it is that his or her appearance will suffer. These are a few of the effects of smoking on appearance:

- Stained teeth
- Stained fingers
- Clothing damaged by cigarette burns
- Bloodshot eyes
- Wrinkles

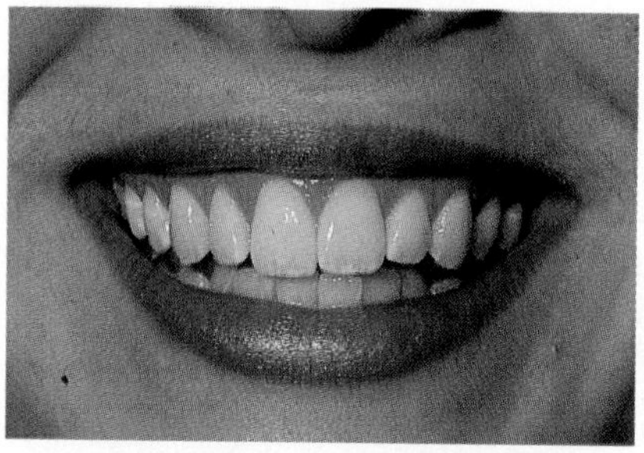

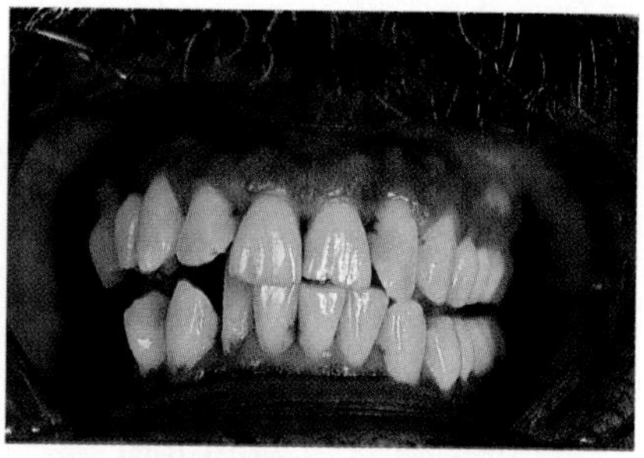

Smokeless tobacco also affects the user's appearance. Compare the teeth and gums in a clean, healthy mouth with the yellow teeth and inflamed gums in the mouth of a smokeless tobacco user.

MAKING HEALTHY DECISIONS

Healthy Ways to Handle Stress

Paula's friend Nancy seemed to have it all. She got good grades in school and played first violin in the school orchestra. Her parents even joked that they had already picked out the college she was going to attend. Paula was very surprised to see Nancy, her studious, talented friend, smoking cigarettes after school.

Paula confronted Nancy about her smoking habit. "I know I should quit," Nancy told Paula. "I started this fall, when I was up for first chair in the orchestra." Nancy said that in the beginning she had used smoking to give herself a break from practicing. Now, though, Nancy has found it hard to stop smoking, even though she really wants to stop.

"I've tried to quit," Nancy explained. "But when I stop, I get all jumpy and nervous. I have enough stress in my life as it is, without asking for more. It seems like the only time I really feel relaxed these days is when I smoke."

Paula thought about Nancy's problem. She did not think that Nancy was taking a healthy approach to handling stress. She knew that smoking was unhealthy and that often people who begin by smoking a few cigarettes a day end up becoming addicted. She also knew that there are much better ways to deal with stress, such as exercise, relaxation techniques, and additional sleep.

Review

Lesson 1

Using complete sentences, answer the following questions on a separate sheet of paper.

Reviewing Terms and Facts

1. **Vocabulary** Define *nicotine, tar,* and *carbon monoxide.*
2. **Restate** Describe some long-term effects that tobacco has on the respiratory system, circulatory system, and digestive system.

Thinking Critically

3. **Suggest** What arguments against smoking do you think would most effectively convince teens never to try smoking? Make a list of the strongest arguments, and share your list with other classmates. What arguments do you agree on?
4. **Hypothesize** Why do you think cigarettes are so much more commonly used than other forms of tobacco?

Applying Health Concepts

5. **Health of Others** Write to a local chapter of the American Cancer Society and request information about the effects of smoking or using smokeless tobacco. Share this information and the facts in this lesson with a friend, neighbor, or family member who smokes or uses smokeless tobacco.
6. **Personal Health** List, in order of their importance to you, your personal top ten reasons for remaining tobacco free.

Paula knew that Nancy liked making her own decisions. She wanted to tell Nancy about other, healthier ways to handle stress, but she was afraid that Nancy would be angry if she thought that Paula was trying to tell her what to do. Paula used the six-step decision-making process to help her make up her mind.

1. **State the situation**
2. **List the options**
3. **Weigh the possible outcomes**
4. **Consider your values**
5. **Make a decision and act**
6. **Evaluate the decision**

Follow-Up Activities

1. Apply the six steps of the decision-making process to Paula's situation.
2. With a classmate, role-play a scene in which Paula recommends other options to Nancy, explaining the benefits of each one.

Lesson 2

The Costs of Tobacco

The lesson will help you find answers to questions that teens often ask about tobacco users. For example:

- **Who uses tobacco?**
- **Why do people use tobacco?**
- **What are the personal costs of tobacco use?**
- **What are the costs to society of tobacco use?**

Words to Know

addiction
physiological dependence
psychological dependence
withdrawal
secondhand smoke
passive smoker
mainstream smoke
sidestream smoke

Who Uses Tobacco?

Tobacco is big business. In one recent year there were over 750 billion cigarettes manufactured in the United States. Tobacco companies spend almost $4.6 billion a year to promote and advertise their products. In other words, about $500,000 is spent every hour of every day!

In spite of all of this advertising, the fact is that the majority of people do not smoke. In the United States the number of adults who smoke has declined by more than 40 percent since 1965. Most teens never smoke. A large majority of adults—about 75 percent—never even try tobacco.

However, a significant proportion of people—27 percent of men, 23 percent of women—do smoke. It is estimated that 25 percent of adolescents are smokers. These tobacco users, and society as a whole, pay a high price for their habit.

A cigarette habit is like throwing your health away, as well as your money.

Personal Costs of Tobacco Use

You have learned how tobacco harms the bodies of people who use it. Their appearance suffers, and in the long run, they damage all of their body systems. Their risk of diseases—such as heart disease, cancer, and stroke—is significantly higher than that of nonusers—so high that some insurance companies refuse to insure tobacco users.

Tobacco is not only an unhealthy habit but an expensive one. A pack of cigarettes costs $2.50 or more, and many smokers go through a pack a day. There are many hidden costs of tobacco as well—money spent on replacing clothes that are ruined by cigarette burns, on extra trips to the dentist to have teeth cleaned, and on higher health insurance rates, to name only three. In fact, a tobacco habit can cost up to $105,000 over the course of a lifetime. Given the high cost of tobacco use, why do so many people continue to use it?

Tobacco Addiction

Most people who use tobacco find it difficult or impossible to stop. They form an **addiction,** *a physical or mental need for a drug or other substance.* According to the Centers for Disease Control and Prevention, nicotine addiction is the most common form of drug addiction in the United States. Nicotine is as addictive as heroin, cocaine, and alcohol. **Figure 13.4** shows how nicotine affects the brain.

Q&A

Smoke Now, Quit Later?

Q: If I smoke now, I can always quit later, can't I?

A: Probably not. Check out these statistics.

- Four out of every ten young people who smoke as few as three cigarettes become regular smokers.
- Each year only 3 percent of all smokers who try to quit will experience long-term success.
- Most alarming of all, half of all smokers who lose a lung or need heart surgery still find it impossible to quit.

Figure 13.4

Nicotine's Addictive Cycle

About 20 seconds after a cigarette is smoked, the nicotine in the cigarette stimulates the neurons to release adrenaline and other chemicals in the smoker's brain. About 30 minutes after the cigarette is smoked, the chemicals have left the brain. The smoker begins to have symptoms such as difficulty concentrating, headache, and irritability. The one-two punch of pleasure followed by discomfort causes the smoker to crave another cigarette.

The Brain Immediately After Smoking
Many stress-reducing chemicals

The Brain About 30 Minutes Later
Few stress-reducing chemicals

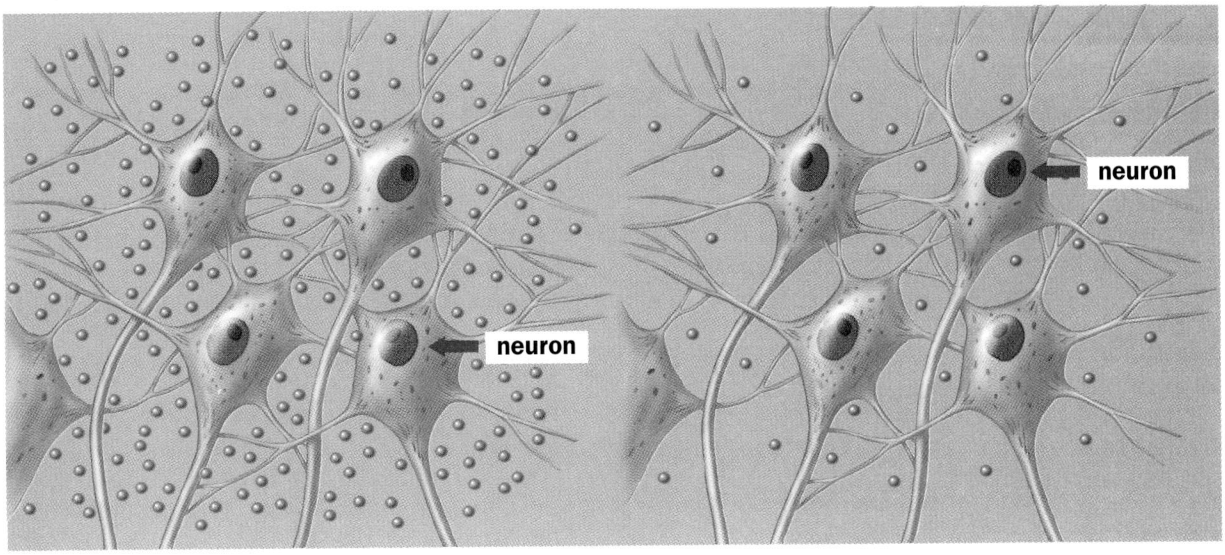

Teen Issues

Working Together

ACTIVITY!

Teens across the country are banding together to stop tobacco use. They are helping police find vendors who sell tobacco illegally to teens; getting their state legislatures to raise the tobacco tax; and getting their school libraries to cancel subscriptions to magazines that print cigarette advertisements. Which of these measures do you think is most likely to be effective in reducing tobacco use? Write a paragraph explaining your viewpoint.

Nicotine causes two types of addiction.

- **Physiological dependence** is *a type of addiction in which the body itself feels a direct need for a drug.* When smoked or ingested, nicotine takes about 20 seconds to reach the brain, where it causes the adrenal glands to produce adrenaline. Once the nicotine leaves the body's systems, the body craves more. Tobacco users don't feel normal unless their bodies are under the influence of nicotine.
- **Psychological dependence** is *an addiction in which the mind sends the body a message that it needs more of a drug.* Psychological dependence can result from habit. Many smokers form the habit of smoking at certain times of day. They smoke

Smokers also may develop rituals that create psychological dependence. For example, some smokers reach for a cigarette when they begin certain activities. Others talk with an unlit cigarette in their mouth before lighting it. These rituals can become as difficult to stop as the actual habit of smoking. One key to breaking the habit is to change the ritual. Instead of reaching for a cigarette, think of something else to do.

LIFE SKILLS

Avoiding Secondhand Smoke

You may have been in this situation: You are shopping at the mall. You decide to stop by the food court for a pretzel, but the area is crowded with people smoking. The smoke in the air is so thick, you can't even think about eating. All you want to do is leave.

Situations like that can make you feel helpless. You may feel as if you have no control over the air you breathe. However, there are actions you can take to stay away from secondhand smoke.

- Seek out stores, restaurants, and other businesses that have a smoke-free environment. Look for a sign on the door that says that smoking is not permitted inside. If you do not see a sign, ask a member of the staff what the store's policy is.
- If people are smoking in a place that is supposed to be smoke free, or if smoke is drifting from the smoking section into the nonsmoking section, you can approach the smokers politely and ask them to stop. If they refuse, you can complain to the manager.

after meals, when using the telephone, or during other everyday occurrences. Habit can make it extremely difficult for tobacco users to quit.

People who break the nicotine addiction go through **withdrawal,** *the physical symptoms that occur when someone stops using an addictive substance.* Withdrawal symptoms include nervousness, moodiness, and difficulty sleeping. The intensity of withdrawal symptoms and the amount of time they last vary from person to person.

Users Want to Quit

Two-thirds of the adults who smoke say that they would like to quit, and teen smokers are as eager to quit as adults are. According to a Gallup poll, seven out of ten teen smokers say that they would not start smoking if they could choose again. Unfortunately, teen and adult smokers find it difficult to beat the addiction. Although only five percent of teen smokers surveyed by the Centers for Disease Control and Prevention said that they would still be smoking in five years, in actuality almost three-quarters of them continued to smoke seven to nine years later.

Teens choose their own friends and pastimes. Being independent also means choosing to be free of addictions such as smoking.

THANK YOU
FOR NOT
SMOKING

- If you regularly go to establishments that allow smoking, you can put pressure on the management to start a no-smoking policy. Make it clear that you will stop eating or shopping there if the business does not become smoke free. Get your friends and family to join you in writing letters or a petition to the business owner.
- If you spend time with people who smoke, let them know that you don't want them to smoke while you're with them. If they are willing, help them to quit smoking altogether.

Follow-up Activities

1. In the library, look up state and local laws about smoking in public places. If you think that the laws are not strong enough, write to your mayor or state legislator and encourage him or her to work on getting tougher antismoking laws passed.
2. Create a poster for a business with a smoke-free environment. The poster should tell people in a creative, interesting way that smoking is off-limits.

The Costs to Society

Did You Know?

Deadly Smoke

The American Heart Association reports that nonsmokers who are married to smokers have a 20 percent higher risk of dying of heart disease than those married to nonsmokers. Passive smoking could account for as many as 40,000 deaths a year from heart disease.

Individuals who use tobacco are not the only ones who are harmed by its effects. Cigarette and cigar smoke also threaten the health of nonsmokers. In addition, the harm tobacco causes to individuals—both smokers and nonsmokers—adds up to serious costs for society.

Public Health Costs of Tobacco

Tobacco is the leading preventable cause of death in this country. Each year more than 400,000 Americans die prematurely because of cigarette smoking. One out of every five deaths in the United States is tobacco-related. About one out of every three teens who start to smoke will die of a smoking-related disease. **Figure 13.5** compares tobacco with other leading causes of death in the United States.

Smokers are not the only people placed in danger by tobacco. **Secondhand smoke,** which is *smoke that nonsmokers inhale as a result of being around smokers,* threatens the health of nonsmokers as well. *People who don't smoke but are exposed to tobacco smoke* are called **passive smokers.** They are forced to breathe two types of secondhand tobacco smoke. *Smoke that the smoker exhales* is called **mainstream smoke.** *Smoke that comes from the burning tip of a cigarette* is called **sidestream smoke.** Sidestream smoke, which has not passed through a smoker's lungs, carries twice as much tar and nicotine as mainstream smoke. According to the U.S. Department of Environmental Protection, secondhand smoke is responsible for 3,000 deaths from lung cancer each year.

Taken together, the financial costs of tobacco addiction are staggering. The Centers for Disease Control and Prevention recently estimated the annual health care costs caused by tobacco at $50 billion.

Figure 13.5

Leading Causes of Death in the United States

Smoking is almost twice as deadly as AIDS, alcohol, car crashes, and suicide combined.

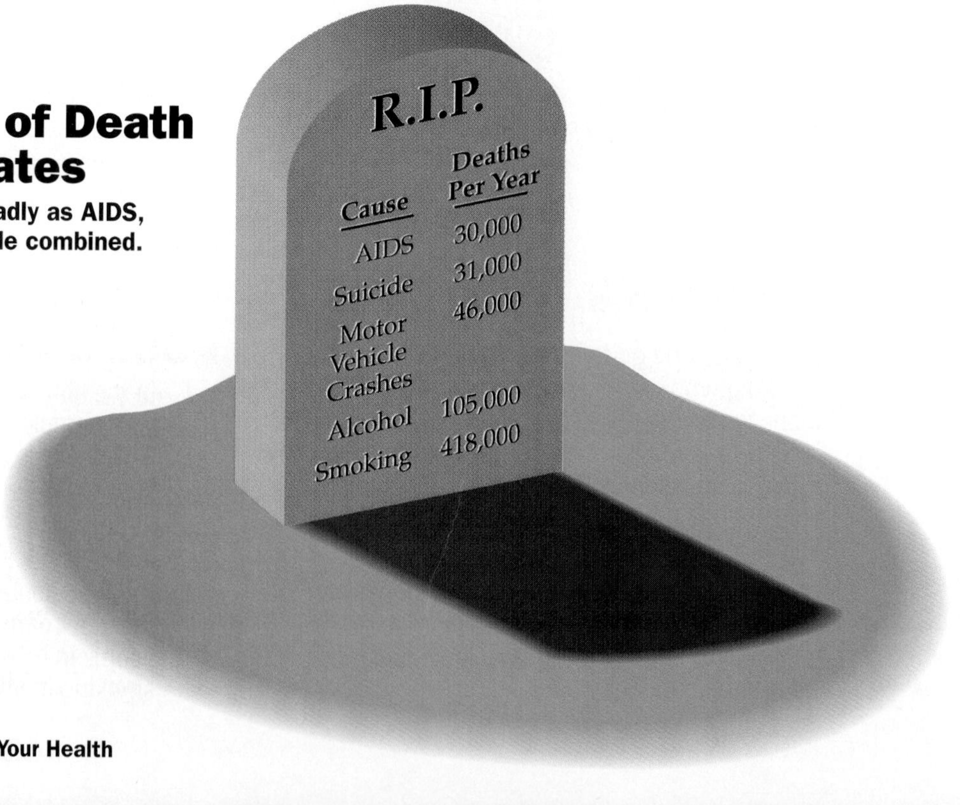

R.I.P.
Cause
Deaths Per Year
AIDS 30,000
Suicide 31,000
Motor Vehicle Crashes 46,000
Alcohol 105,000
Smoking 418,000

Tobacco's Effect on the Economy

In addition to the direct costs of health care for tobacco-related illnesses, there are also costs to the nation's economy. The United States Office of Technology Assessment, a government agency, has calculated the annual economic costs of tobacco use at $68 billion. This figure includes $6.9 billion in money lost by people who are too sick to work because of illnesses caused by tobacco use. It also includes $40.3 billion in goods and services that would have been created by people who die because of tobacco.

Illnesses are costly to society in two ways. Caring for sick people costs money. Society also suffers by losing the contributions which the sick people could have made. Preventable illnesses—including those caused by tobacco—needlessly hurt individuals and society as a whole.

Tobacco Costs Will Remain High

Each year the tobacco industry must replace 2 million lost customers—people who either quit using tobacco or die as a result of tobacco use. Most new users are children and teens. Although the percentage of adults in the United States who smoke has dropped over the past years, the rate of tobacco use among teens has remained the same. In some teen groups, the rate has actually grown. It is estimated that each day more than 3,000 young people begin to smoke. More than 3 million children and teens smoke cigarettes, and about 1 million young men use smokeless tobacco. As long as the tobacco industry can persuade young people to smoke, the costs of tobacco use—both to individuals and to society—will remain high.

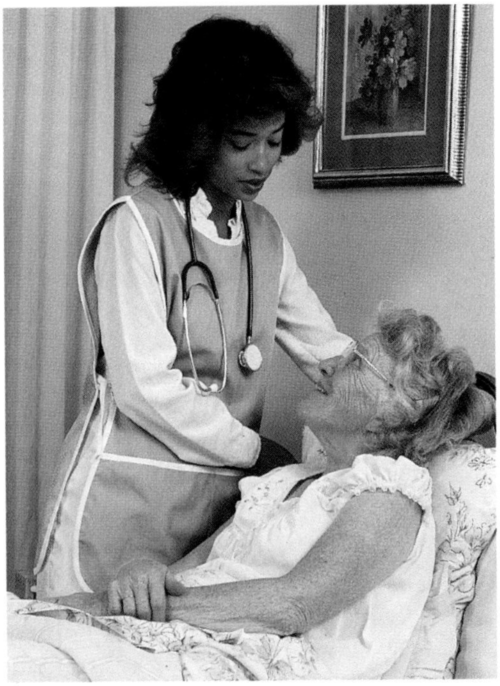

Review

Lesson 2

Using complete sentences, answer the following questions on a separate sheet of paper.

Reviewing Terms and Facts

1. **Vocabulary** Define the term *addiction.* Use it in an original sentence.
2. **Recall** Describe the different types of smoke that passive smokers inhale.

Thinking Critically

3. **Compare and Contrast** List the similarities and differences between physiological dependence and psychological dependence. Which one contributes more to withdrawal symptoms? Explain.
4. **Summarize** What are some of the personal costs of tobacco addiction? What are some of the costs to society?

Applying Health Concepts

5. **Growth and Development** Interview members of your family on how they have stayed smoke free, how they quit smoking—or why they want to. Compile your findings into a report titled "Some Reasons Why People Don't Smoke."
6. **Health of Others** Make a poster showing the effects of secondhand smoke on passive smokers. Your poster should express a point of view on the rights of nonsmokers.

TEEN HEALTH DIGEST

CON$UMER FOCU$

Cyber-Smoke

Is going on-line hazardous to your health? The Center for Media Education says that it might be. The group issued a report on Web sites that promote alcohol and tobacco. The sites have splashy, interactive designs that attract Netsurfers—including teens.

"The Web, unlike radio and television, is a much more fluid and open medium," says the group's president, Kathryn Montgomery. That openness means that people can get away with communicating messages that might not be allowed on television or radio.

Try This: *Hold a class discussion about the impact of tobacco advertising on the Internet. Do you think that it is dangerous for teens to see these ads? Why or why not?*

HEALTH UPDATE

Fresh Air at Work

The dangers of secondhand smoke have led more than 70 percent of workplaces in the United States to ban smoking. Creating a nonsmoking atmosphere has turned out to have an unexpected benefit. Besides protecting nonsmokers, workplace smoking bans also help smokers kick the habit. A recent study by the Bureau of Economic Research found that smoking rates have dropped far more steeply among people who work than among the unemployed.

The message is clear: fresh air at work works!

This is a Smoke
Free Workplace

Myths and Realities

Try This:
Find out about local programs for people who want to stop smoking. How do the programs help quitters deal with possible weight gain? Report on your findings.

Lean and Smoke Free

Everyone knows it: Stop smoking and you pack on the pounds. Like so many bits of wisdom that everyone "knows," this information is myth, not fact! A recent study in Canada found that women who quit smoking were, after two years, *less* likely than smokers to be obese.

The keys to staying trim are a sensible diet and plenty of exercise. Smoking does not fit into that equation.

Sports and Recreation

Smokeout at the Sports Stadium

Since 1971 tobacco companies have been banned from showing commercials on television. You might still see their ads, however, when you watch televised sports events. Why? Many stadiums carry billboards for tobacco. When games are shown on television, these ads show up as clear as day.

That's why many sports teams are voluntarily banning tobacco ads from their stadiums. Eighteen of the clubs in major league baseball have banned tobacco ads from their ballparks.

Teens Making a Difference

Butt Out!

Name: Marie Fleming

Hometown: Spokane, Washington

Accomplishments:

- Worked with Spokane Teens Against Tobacco (STAT) to teach more than 2,000 younger children about the dangers of smoking
- Worked with National Cancer Institute, advising the organization on effective ways to reach teens with antismoking messages
- Went undercover to catch stores selling tobacco to kids
- Led rallies against smoking at the state capitol

Quote: "Three of my relatives died from smoking-related causes. It really hit me in the heart. Smoking doesn't just hurt the primary smoker."

Lesson 3

How to Be Tobacco Free

This lesson will help you find answers to questions that teens often ask about staying tobacco free or overcoming tobacco addiction. For example:

- **Why do teens start to use tobacco?**
- **How can I stay tobacco free?**
- **How can tobacco users break the habit?**
- **How can I help others remain tobacco free?**

Words to Know

media
advertising
cold turkey

Why Teens Start to Use Tobacco

Despite the health risks, financial burden, and social limitations of tobacco use, every day thousands of teens choose to become tobacco users. Why are they willing to take on all the problems associated with smoking? There is no simple answer. They may be influenced by several factors, including friends, family, advertising, and popular culture. Some like the way the drug makes them feel. Others are attracted to the image they think tobacco use promotes.

Tobacco: A False Crutch

Some teens may choose to use tobacco as a crutch. They think that it will help them cope with stress. Some use tobacco as a way to take a break from daily chores and responsibilities. Other teens may choose to use tobacco in an attempt to control their weight.

The truth is, tobacco is not an effective way to cope with stress or control weight. Most new tobacco users never intend to become addicted, but most in fact do, and fairly quickly. They do not realize that the symptoms of withdrawal from nicotine that arise as often as every half hour will add to their daily stresses. Tobacco use also reduces a person's capacity for aerobic exercise, which is a key to healthy weight control.

Most public spaces and workplaces have banned smoking. Tobacco users stand outside in the cold and rain to indulge their habit.

Tobacco: False Independence

According to a recent report from the United States Surgeon General, the "mannerisms and processes" of smoking are appealing to many teens. These mannerisms and processes include using lighters and blowing smoke. These acts make some teens feel mature.

Other teens smoke in order to be accepted by peers or to form friendships. Teens may think of smokers as an independent group. Many teens join the group in an attempt to feel and appear adult.

Tobacco use may seem to be a sign of independence. However, it is really just the opposite. Tobacco users are slaves to a habit that damages their health and eventually threatens their lives. The habit also harms their appearance and costs them thousands of dollars over time.

Tobacco in the Media

Many teens use tobacco because of the images they see in the **media,** which are the various *methods of communicating information, such as newspapers, magazines, radio, or television.* In some movies, for instance, characters may show that they are tough and independent by smoking. In addition, tobacco companies spend billions of dollars each year on **advertising,** or *media messages intended to influence people's behavior and opinions.* Tobacco ads and promotional campaigns are designed to attract young people. They show tobacco users as athletic, fun-loving, free spirits. Studies by the United States Surgeon General show a direct link between tobacco ads and teen smoking. **Figure 13.6** shows the difference between the image of tobacco as it is often presented in the media and the reality of addiction.

in Your Journal

For one day, record in your journal every time you see tobacco used in movies or on television. Also, record every tobacco ad you encounter in magazines and newspapers on that day. Finally, note every time you see a tobacco company's name on a T-shirt, knapsack, or some other piece of merchandise.

How many times did you see references to tobacco in one day? What sorts of messages were delivered along with the tobacco image? Were the messages honest?

Figure 13.6

The "Tobacco Mask"

Smokers in advertising and the media do not show their real faces. The image of tobacco use in the media is just the opposite of the reality.

Image
Smokers are
- healthy.
- athletic.
- rebels.
- mature.
- attractive.

Reality
Smokers are
- sickly.
- constantly short of breath.
- social outcasts.
- dependent on a drug.
- prematurely aged.

How Not to Start

in your journal

The Centers for Disease Control and Prevention estimate that more than 5 million American children and young people living today will die prematurely from smoking and from exposure to secondhand smoke. In your journal, discuss your reactions to this statistic. Does it make you angry? Sad? What can you do to make sure that you and your friends will not be a part of this statistic?

The best way to lead a tobacco-free life is never to start using tobacco products. However, resisting the pressure to smoke can be difficult. It is important to develop refusal skills that will help you avoid tobacco and other harmful habits throughout your life.

One strategy that can help you avoid tobacco is to choose friends who do not use it. If you don't spend time with people who smoke, you will not be pressured to smoke yourself. You will also be able to avoid secondhand smoke, which is damaging to your health.

Suppose that you do have friends who use tobacco. If your relationship is good, you and your friends probably have many common interests other than smoking. You don't need to share a dangerous addiction in order to remain friends. True friends will respect your decision, and you will know that you are making a healthy choice.

If the smokers you know do urge you to try tobacco, you can simply say no. Often, if you refuse a cigarette when it is offered, the smoker will accept your decision and not bring the subject up again.

Did You Know?

From Bad to Worse ACTIVITY!

In 1952 one cigarette maker introduced a brand with a "Micronite" filter. The company boasted that the filter offered "the greatest health protection in cigarette history." The filter's secret ingredient? Asbestos—a substance that is now known to cause cancer when inhaled!

If the pressure continues, however, you can explain your reasons for choosing not to smoke. Here are some reasons that you can mention if you find yourself being pressured to smoke.

- "I don't like the smell (and/or taste) of cigarettes."
- "I need to keep my lungs healthy for soccer (or other sport)."
- "I don't want to give up my health for smoking."
- "I don't want yellow teeth and bad breath."

Be assertive. Stand up for yourself in firm but positive ways. Others will respect you, and you will end up feeling good about yourself. If, however, your peers continue to pressure you, leave. Friends who try to harm your health are friends you don't need.

The only sure way to a tobacco-free life is *never* to start smoking

How to Break the Tobacco Habit

One way to quit is **cold turkey,** or *simply stopping all at once, without first cutting back.* Cold turkey is thought to be more effective than trying to quit gradually. Tobacco users who need additional help to overcome their addiction may use products that contain nicotine to help them quit. These products include nicotine gum, which is sold over the counter, and nicotine patches, which are prescribed by a doctor. These products allow smokers to give up cigarettes right away while gradually cutting down on nicotine.

Whether smokers quit cold turkey or with nicotine products, they can get help from a number of groups. National groups such as the American Lung Association, the American Heart Association, and the American Cancer Society have materials and programs to help smokers quit. There are also programs run by local hospitals and health groups.

How To Help Others Remain Tobacco Free

If you know someone who is trying to break the tobacco habit, use the facts in **Figure 13.7** to remind them of the health benefits of not smoking. In dealing with friends or family members who want to give up tobacco:

- **Be positive.** Focus on the smoker's choice to quit, not on the fact that he or she is going through a difficult time.
- **Don't be judgmental.** No one wants to hear "I told you so," especially someone who is trying to beat an addiction.
- **Help them avoid temptation.** Help the quitter avoid situations in which he or she may be tempted to light up.

Did You Know?

Women and Smoking

Do you know any women who smoke? Share these facts with them.

- Smoking can increase a woman's chance of dying from breast cancer by 25 percent.
- Smoking doubles a woman's chance of getting cancer of the cervix.
- Twenty-five percent of women who are pregnant smoke. Smoking during pregnancy causes
  —14 percent of premature deliveries.
  —up to 30 percent of low birth weight babies.
  —4,600 infant deaths a year.

Figure 13.7

Tobacco-Free Benefits Over Time

Memorize these facts. Share them with people who are trying to quit using tobacco.

If You Quit Smoking Right Now . . .

- Your blood pressure and pulse rate return to normal *after 20 minutes.*
- Your blood's carbon monoxide level drops to normal, and its oxygen level raises to normal, *after 8 hours.*
- Your risk of heart attack begins to decrease *after 24 hours.*
- Your risk of heart disease drops to half that of a smoker *after 1 year.*
- The rate of death from lung cancer is the same as for nonsmokers *after 10 years.*
- Your risk of heart disease is the same as nonsmokers' *after 15 years.*

Teen Issues

Teens! Don't Smoke!

The U.S. government wants to stop all teens from using tobacco. Government proposals to reduce the appeal of tobacco to teens have included the following actions:

- Banning outdoor ads for tobacco within 1,000 feet of schools and playgrounds
- Banning color and photography from all outdoor ads for tobacco
- Banning the sale of products, such as caps or gym bags, that carry tobacco product names and logos
- Banning tobacco companies from sponsoring sports or entertainment events

Do you agree with these proposed measures? What others would you suggest?

A Tobacco-Free Community

Restricting the sale and use of tobacco can be a worthwhile community service project. By helping your community curb tobacco use, you can reduce the risk of young people picking up the habit. You will protect the rights of nonsmokers and may help current tobacco users quit.

Look up antismoking advocates in your community. Many will be affiliated with local hospitals, churches, or pubic service associations. Ask how you can get involved in helping your community become tobacco free.

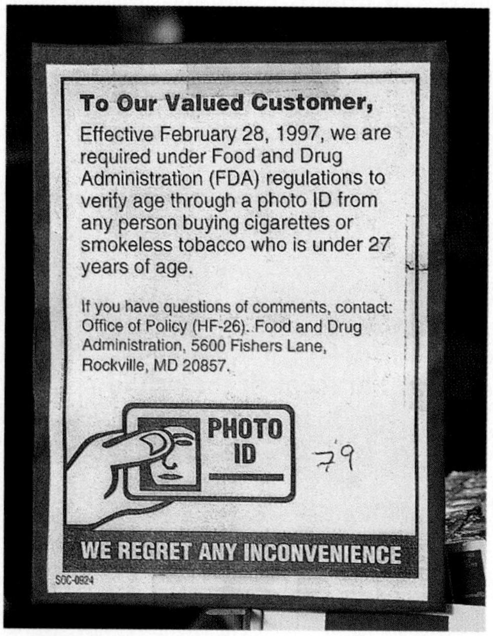

The law requires all smokers between the ages of 18 and 27 to show photo ID before buying cigarettes.

HEALTH LAB

Research the Solution

Introduction: Limiting tobacco use is a challenge that faces our entire society. To reduce the number of people using tobacco in your community, someone must determine what forms of action will be most likely to curb tobacco use.

Objective: Conduct a public opinion survey to determine which actions people think would be most effective in limiting tobacco use in your community.

Materials and Method: You will be taking an opinion poll. To guarantee useful results, it is important to get your information from the broadest possible group of people. You may want to work in teams to conduct your survey.

First, come up with a set of questions. Your questions should ask basic facts about the people responding to the survey, such as age, gender, and whether or not each person has ever used tobacco. Next, your questionnaire should ask which actions the respondents think would be most useful in preventing tobacco use. Possible actions include

- banning tobacco advertising.
- raising taxes on cigarettes.
- restricting the sale of cigarettes to special stores.
- increasing antitobacco education in schools.

You may come up with other ideas.

Review

Lesson 3

Using complete sentences, answer the following questions on a separate sheet of paper.

Reviewing Terms and Facts

1. **Restate** List the factors that may lead a teen to use tobacco.
2. **Vocabulary** Explain the meaning of the word *media.* Use the term in an original sentence.
3. **Recall** Describe the two strategies for quitting tobacco addiction.

Thinking Critically

4. **Analyze** Why do you think tobacco companies give away merchandise with their logos on it? Think of at least two ways in which this practice benefits tobacco companies.
5. **Explain** Why do you think the government wishes to help people give up tobacco? What benefits would society gain if the country were smoke free?

Applying Health Concepts

6. **Health of Others** Select one group you know well, such as elementary school students, middle school teachers, or parents. Design an antismoking advertisement for that group. Be sure to focus on issues that concern the group you have targeted with your ad.

Now conduct your survey. Present your questions to as many people as possible. Be sure to talk to smokers as well as nonsmokers. Also, talk to people who used to smoke but have quit.

Observations and Analysis: When you are done with your survey, prepare a chart that shows the results. Write a brief report summarizing your findings and presenting your recommendations for reducing tobacco use. You may wish to share the report with your local newspaper, town council, or state legislators.

Chapter 13 Review

Chapter Summary

- **Lesson 1** Dried tobacco leaves are used to make cigarettes, cigars, pipe tobacco, chewing tobacco, and snuff. Cigarette smoke contains many harmful chemicals, the most powerful of which is nicotine.
- **Lesson 2** Tobacco use can lead to both physiological and psychological addiction. Tobacco use has high personal costs to both smokers and nonsmokers and high costs to society.
- **Lesson 3** The best way to stay healthy is never to start smoking. Even so, some teens do start smoking for various reasons, such as influence by peers and advertising. There are several methods to help these teens to quit tobacco use.

Reviewing Key Terms and Concepts

Using complete sentences, answer the following questions on a separate sheet of paper.

Lesson 1

1. Define the term *cilia.*
2. Name five forms of tobacco.

Lesson 2

3. Give some examples of withdrawal symptoms.
4. Which type of secondhand smoke is more dangerous: mainstream smoke or sidestream smoke? Explain why.

Lesson 3

5. What is the meaning of the term *advertising?* Give examples of three forms of advertising.
6. How long must a former smoker remain tobacco free to have a risk of heart disease no greater than a nonsmoker's?

Thinking Critically

Using complete sentences, answer the following questions on a separate sheet of paper.

7. **Synthesize** How does tobacco affect a person's level of fitness?
8. **Hypothesize** Why do you think so many people smoke, knowing the negative short- and long-term effects tobacco can have on the body?
9. **Interpret** What are some of the reasons why smokers might want to quit?
10. **Suggest** Besides people, what else might be affected by secondhand smoke in the home?
11. **Analyze** How might the new law requiring tobacco purchasers under the age of 27 to show photo ID before buying tobacco products affect teens who smoke?

Chapter 13 Review

Your Action Plan

A smoke-free environment makes everyone healthier. Review your journal entries for this chapter. Follow the steps below to make an action plan to help you and others remain smoke free.

Step 1 Decide on a long-term goal that you want to achieve, and write it down. For example, you may want to avoid secondhand smoke.

Step 2 Set several short-term goals that will help you achieve your long-term goal. For example, you may look for smoke-free stores and restaurants.

Step 3 Make a schedule for reaching each short-term goal. If your goal is to remain smoke free, you may not be able to set a specific date to achieve each goal.

Since it may take a while—even a lifetime—to achieve certain long-term goals, reward yourself with an enjoyable smoke-free activity after reaching several short-term goals.

In Your Home and Community

1. **Health of Others** Contact the American Lung Association and the American Heart Association. Obtain pamphlets on tobacco and its effects on health, including the effects of secondhand smoke. Ask permission to display the pamphlets in the school library or nurse's office.
2. **Community Resources** Make a list of local restaurants. Check the smoking policy at each one—whether they are completely smoke free, have a separate room for smoking, or have a separate section for smoking. Make copies of the list and ask permission to post it in public places in your community.

Building Your Portfolio

1. **Tobacco Advertisements** Look through magazines aimed at adults, and cut out tobacco advertisements. Write a critique of each ad, explaining how the ad seeks to sell the product and whether its intended message about tobacco is true. Add the advertisements and summaries to your portfolio.
2. **Ways to Say No** Create a list of ten ways to say no to tobacco. Be sure to include ways of saying no to new friends, or even relatives, who may pressure you to try tobacco. Add the list to your portfolio.
3. **Personal Assessment** Look through all the activities and projects you did for this chapter. Choose one that you would like to include in your portfolio.

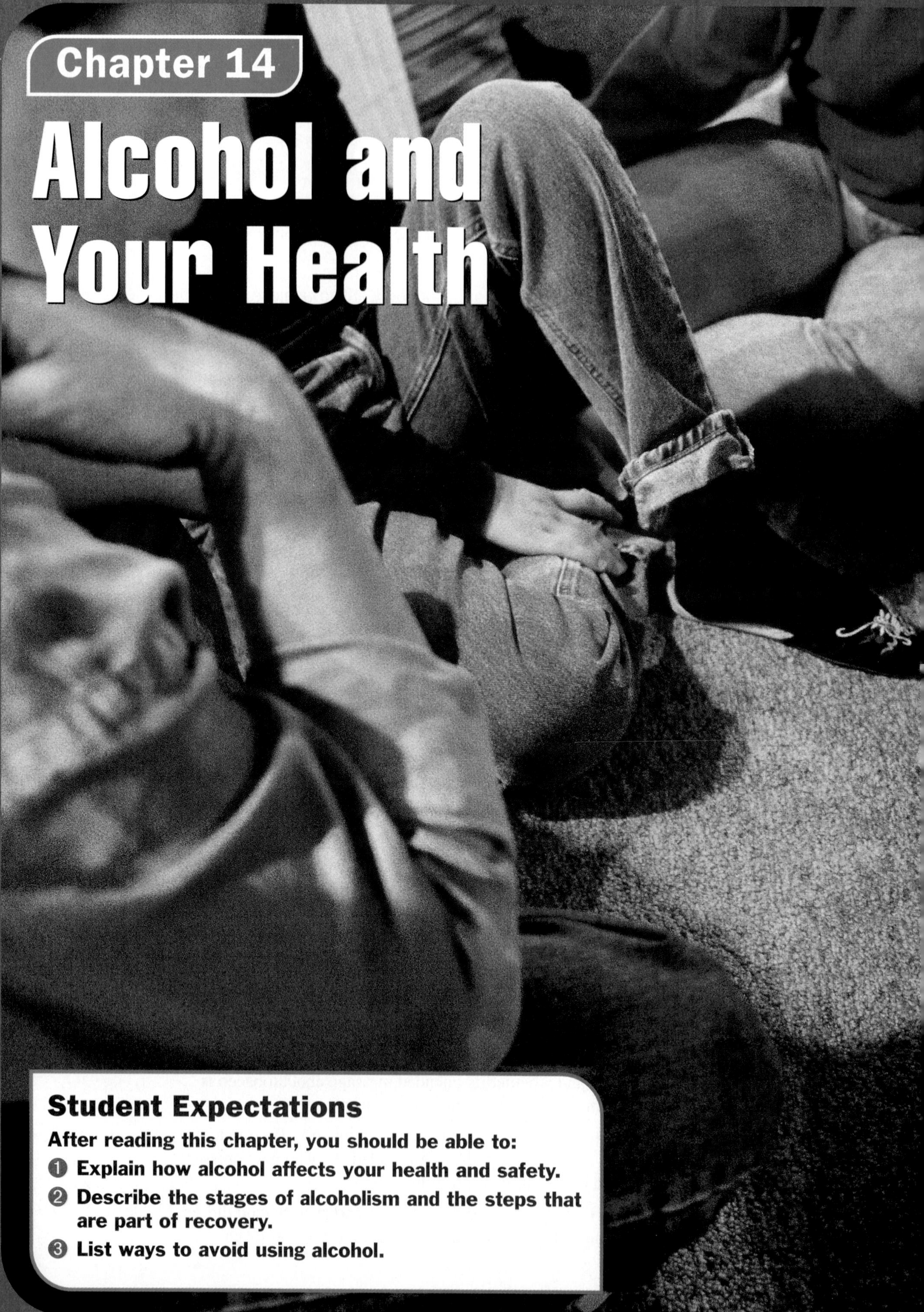

Chapter 14

Alcohol and Your Health

Student Expectations

After reading this chapter, you should be able to:

1. Explain how alcohol affects your health and safety.
2. Describe the stages of alcoholism and the steps that are part of recovery.
3. List ways to avoid using alcohol.

Teen Chat Group

Rosa: I have a problem I wanted to talk about. I just found out that some of my friends drink. I want them to like me, but I know drinking can really get you in trouble.

Michael: Are you worried that they'll try to pressure you into drinking, or are you worried about what could happen to them?

Rosa: Both, I guess.

Thomas: You're right to worry, either way. My older sister was at a college party last month, and some people were drinking. Well, the police came in and arrested everybody under 21.

Jeffrey: At least no one got hurt. Last year, my uncle's car was hit by a drunk driver. My uncle was in a cast for weeks, and the other driver was killed.

Rosa: I don't want my friends to end up like that, but I don't want to sound like I'm criticizing them, either. What can I do?

Michael: Why don't you tell them how you feel about it? If they're really your friends, they'll take you seriously.

in your journal

Read the dialogue on this page. Has alcohol ever had an effect on your life? Start your private journal entries on alcohol by answering these questions:

- **What advice would you give to Rosa about being friends with people who drink?**
- **How much do you know about alcohol's effect on the body?**
- **What would you do if someone offered you a drink?**

When you reach the end of the chapter, you will use your journal entries to make an action plan.

Lesson 1

What Alcohol Does to Your Body

This lesson will help you find answers to questions that teens often ask about alcohol's effect on the body. For example:

- **Why do people who have been drinking often act silly and have trouble walking and talking?**
- **Why do some people seem to tolerate alcohol better than other people?**
- **How much alcohol does a person need to drink before becoming drunk?**
- **Why is drinking alcohol illegal for teens but not for adults?**

Words to Know

alcohol
depressant
cirrhosis
blood alcohol concentration (BAC)
fetal alcohol syndrome (FAS)
addiction

Alcohol and American Society

Alcohol (AL·kuh·hawl) is *a drug that is produced by a chemical reaction in fruits, vegetables, and grains.* It has a powerful effect on the body. In America, decisions about using alcohol are up to each individual. To make such important decisions, people need to know how alcohol affects their bodies and their judgment. Understanding these facts can help them make decisions that are right for them and for society.

Over 17 million Americans have physical, social, and psychological problems related to alcohol use. There are over 95,000 alcohol-related deaths each year. Drinking alcohol is illegal for teens—which is a good reason to avoid it. In addition, alcohol can seriously damage your body.

Alcohol and Your Body

Alcohol is a **depressant** (di·PRE·suhnt), *a drug that slows down the working of the brain and other parts of the nervous system.* **Figure 14.1** shows the short-term effects of drinking alcohol. Chronic, excessive use of alcohol can seriously damage nearly every organ and function of the body. It can even cause death. **Figure 14.2** shows the long-term effects of alcohol use.

Staying away from alcohol helps keep you mentally and physically healthy.

Figure 14.1

Short-Term Effects of Alcohol

Alcohol has many negative effects on the drinker's body and behavior. The short-term effects are those that occur within minutes of drinking an alcoholic beverage.

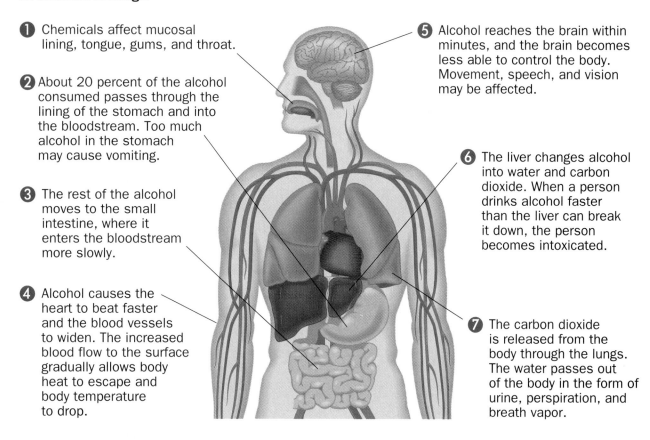

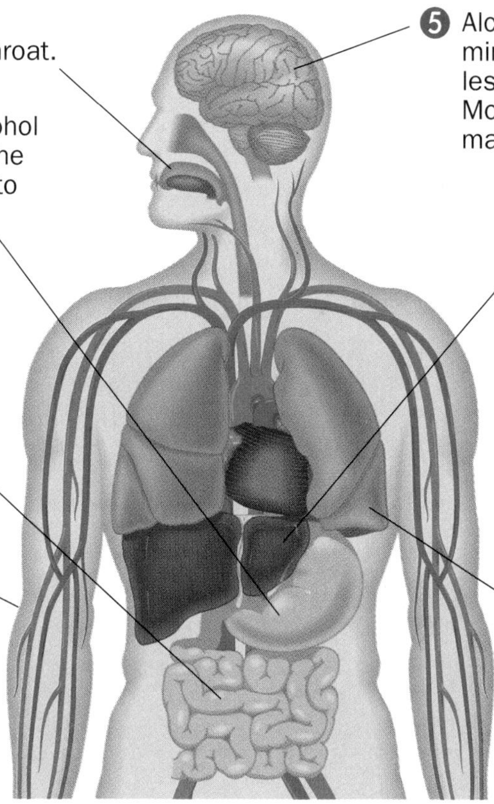

1. Chemicals affect mucosal lining, tongue, gums, and throat.
2. About 20 percent of the alcohol consumed passes through the lining of the stomach and into the bloodstream. Too much alcohol in the stomach may cause vomiting.
3. The rest of the alcohol moves to the small intestine, where it enters the bloodstream more slowly.
4. Alcohol causes the heart to beat faster and the blood vessels to widen. The increased blood flow to the surface gradually allows body heat to escape and body temperature to drop.
5. Alcohol reaches the brain within minutes, and the brain becomes less able to control the body. Movement, speech, and vision may be affected.
6. The liver changes alcohol into water and carbon dioxide. When a person drinks alcohol faster than the liver can break it down, the person becomes intoxicated.
7. The carbon dioxide is released from the body through the lungs. The water passes out of the body in the form of urine, perspiration, and breath vapor.

Figure 14.2

Long-Term Effects of Alcohol

The person who drinks excessively for a long period of time is at risk for developing serious health problems.

Brain	Liver	Heart	Stomach
Drinking alcohol for many years eventually destroys millions of brain cells. Unlike other body cells, brain cells cannot be repaired or replaced.	A person who has several alcoholic drinks a day, over a long period of time, is likely to suffer liver damage. He or she may develop **cirrhosis** (suh·ROH·sis), which is *scarring and destruction of liver tissue.* Cirrhosis can cause death.	Heavy drinking contributes to high blood pressure and may damage the heart muscle. It can even cause heart failure by putting extra strain on already damaged heart muscle.	Alcohol increases the flow of gastric juices from the stomach lining. Large amounts of alcohol cause a larger flow of these high-acid juices, irritating the stomach lining. Repeated irritation can cause open sores called ulcers.

Alcohol and the Individual

The effect that alcohol has on a person is influenced by a number of factors. They are listed here. **Figure 14.3** shows how the alcoholic content differs for some common beverages.

- **Speed.** Drinking a lot in a short period of time causes the alcohol to remain in the bloodstream longer.
- **Quantity.** The metabolism of alcohol takes place at a fairly constant rate. If consumption exceeds this rate, alcohol levels in the bloodstream will rise.
- **Food.** A person who has eaten recently has food in the stomach. This slows down the passing of the alcohol into the bloodstream.
- **Weight.** A lighter person feels the effects of alcohol sooner than a heavier person.
- **Gender.** Generally, females have more body fat and less body water than males. This means alcohol moves into the bloodstream faster in females.
- **Mood.** A drinker who starts off depressed usually finishes up more depressed.
- **Other drugs.** Mixing alcohol with other drugs increases the effects of the alcohol or of the other drug. Even aspirin makes a difference in how alcohol affects the body.

Cultural Connections

Attitudes About Alcohol

Attitudes about alcohol are influenced by a person's beliefs. For example, Muslims and members of the Church of Jesus Christ of Latter-day Saints have strong rules against the use of alcohol. The Chinese value moderation in behavior and apply this value to drinking behavior as well.

Q&A

Hangover

Q: What exactly is a hangover? Can you cure it?

A: A hangover refers to the physical symptoms that follow an episode of drinking. These include thirst, nausea, headache, diarrhea, and sensitivity to light and noise. A hangover could be considered a mild state of withdrawal as the body adjusts itself to being without alcohol. There is no cure for a hangover. As the liver breaks down the alcohol and the body metabolizes it, the symptoms will fade.

Figure 14.3

Alcoholic Content of Beverages

No alcoholic drink is a safe drink. Beer and wine contain a lower percentage of alcohol by volume than vodka or whiskey. However, a 12-ounce can of beer or a 4-ounce glass of wine contain the same amount of alcohol as 1.5 ounces of vodka or whiskey.

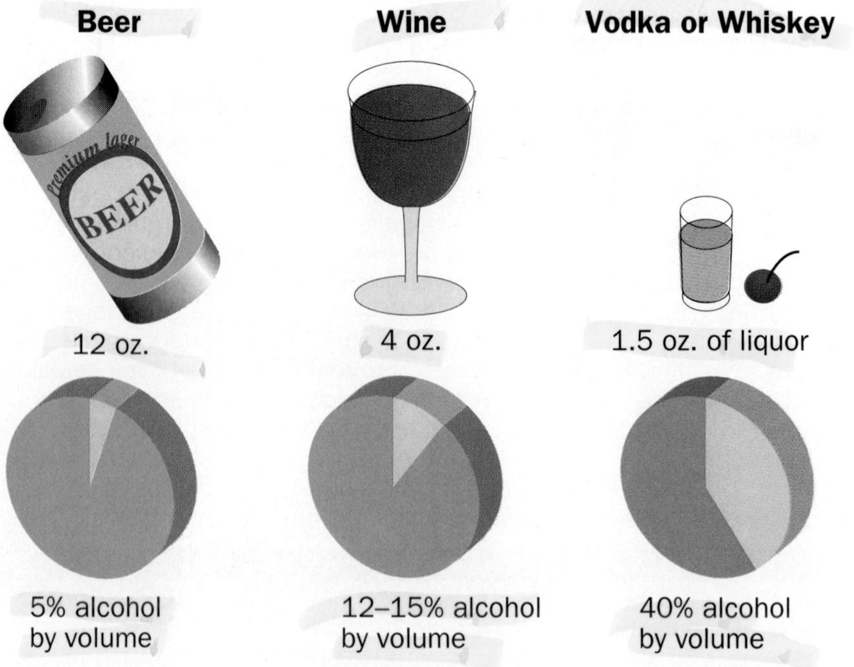

Blood Alcohol Concentration

The amount of alcohol in a person's blood is expressed by a percentage called **blood alcohol concentration (BAC).** The person's BAC depends on the amount of alcohol consumed, body weight, and the other factors discussed on the previous page.

Most states have a BAC limit of 0.10 percent (14 states have a 0.08 percent limit). At this limit, an individual is considered legally intoxicated and incapable of operating an automobile safely. A BAC of 0.1 percent means that 1/10 of 1 percent of the fluid in the blood is alcohol. **Figure 14.4** shows how blood alcohol levels affect a person.

interNET CONNECTION

Find out more about the effects of alcohol on your health, and how you can stay alcohol free.

http://www.glencoe.com/sec/health

Fetal Alcohol Syndrome

A woman who drinks alcohol when she is pregnant may cause permanent damage to her developing baby. The alcohol passes from her body into the baby's bloodstream. Because the baby's liver is not developed enough to process the alcohol, the alcohol remains in the baby's bloodstream for a long time. The baby may be born with a condition called **fetal alcohol syndrome** or **FAS.** Babies born with FAS suffer from *a group of alcohol-related birth defects that may include both physical and mental problems.* These babies may weigh less than normal at birth, be weak, and have facial deformities. They may be mentally retarded or have learning difficulties, and they may have behavior problems.

The tragedy of FAS is that the unborn baby has no control over what enters its body. The decision to drink alcohol or not is the mother's. Because even small amounts of alcohol may be harmful, the safe decision for a pregnant woman is not to drink any alcoholic beverages. FAS is entirely preventable.

Did You Know?

Fetal Alcohol Syndrome

During 1996, between 10 and 30 children per 10,000 births were affected by fetal alcohol syndrome. This is more than three times the rate reported for 1992. Fetal alcohol syndrome is the third leading cause of mental retardation due to birth defects in the United States.

Figure 14.4

Blood Alcohol Levels

Number of Drinks	Blood Alcohol Concentration	Effects
1–2	0.05%	Small decrease in reaction time; some loss of coordination, self-control
3	0.1%	Significant decrease in coordination, judgment, self-control, vision
6	0.2%	Drunk—serious loss of self-control, memory, muscle control, ability to think clearly, and depth perception
8–9	0.3%	Confusion, stupor, may pass out
12–plus	0.5%	Coma or death

Note: Calculations of BAC are based on drinks consumed by a 120-pound person in a two-hour period. Individual reactions will vary according to factors discussed earlier.

Drinking and Driving

Alcohol impairs a person's vision, reaction time, and motor coordination. When a person who has been drinking alcohol gets behind the wheel of a car, he or she is turning the car into a dangerous weapon.

Some people claim that having a drink or two does not affect them or their driving. In fact, the opposite is true. Even one drink slows reaction time and results in some loss of coordination. In 1995, drinking drivers were involved in over 40 percent of the fatal traffic accidents in the United States. Alcohol causes other accidents as well. The following facts paint a tragic picture.

in your journal

In your private journal, describe your attitude toward alcohol use. Try to analyze the role your family, friends, religious values, and the media have played in shaping your attitude.

Alcohol's Safety Record

- About one-third of all bicyclists who die in traffic accidents have been drinking.
- About 40 percent of all adult pedestrians who die in traffic accidents have been drinking.
- More than half of all people who die from drowning accidents have been drinking.
- About half of all deaths by fire involve drinking.

HEALTH LAB

The War Against Drunk Driving

Introduction: Each year alcohol-related traffic accidents cause thousands of deaths and an even greater number of injuries on highways in the United States. Drunk driving is the leading cause of death among teenagers over the age of 15. Government agencies and private citizens' groups have waged a forceful campaign against drunk driving.

Objective: To find out whether progress is being made in the campaign against drunk driving.

Materials and Method: You will need graph paper, a ruler, and a pencil. Study the following statistics from the National Highway Traffic Safety Administration. Then make a graph to illustrate the statistics. The percentages refer to the number of drivers involved in fatal traffic accidents who were legally drunk.

1984	27.0 percent	1990	25.0 percent
1985	26.0 percent	1991	24.0 percent
1986	26.0 percent	1992	21.9 percent
1987	25.0 percent	1993	21.0 percent
1988	25.0 percent	1994	19.3 percent
1989	24.5 percent	1995	19.3 percent

Alcohol and Teens

Right now, your body is going through some very important changes. Alcohol interferes with these changes. Furthermore, the use of alcohol by young people leads to some sobering statistics as shown in **Figure 14.5.**

Figure 14.5

Alcohol: A Danger for Teens

Approximately one-third of the crimes committed by youth are related to alcohol consumption. Drinking gives them "false courage" to commit crimes, and it also increases their chances of being victims of violent attacks.

Nearly 50 percent of all teen suicide victims had been drinking alcohol at the time of their death.

About 12,000 young people die in this country each year in accidents that involve alcohol.

Almost one-third of all traffic deaths involving a person under the age of 25 are related to alcohol.

Drinking alcohol is the leading factor in unplanned pregnancies and sexually transmitted diseases, because making healthy choices is difficult if a person is under the influence of alcohol.

Observation and Analysis:

After completing the graph, write a brief paragraph interpreting the statistics from the National Highway Traffic Safety Administration. Then discuss the following with a group of your classmates.

- By what overall percentage did the number of drinking drivers involved in fatal accidents change between 1984 and 1995?
- What does the graph indicate about the pattern of drunk driving in the United States?
- What do you think are the reasons for the change between 1984 and 1995?

Follow-up Activity

Research local (city or county) or state statistics on arrests for driving under the influence (DUI). Compare the figures for the number of people arrested for DUI last year and ten years ago. How have they changed? Find out what efforts are being made in your community or your state to combat drunk driving.

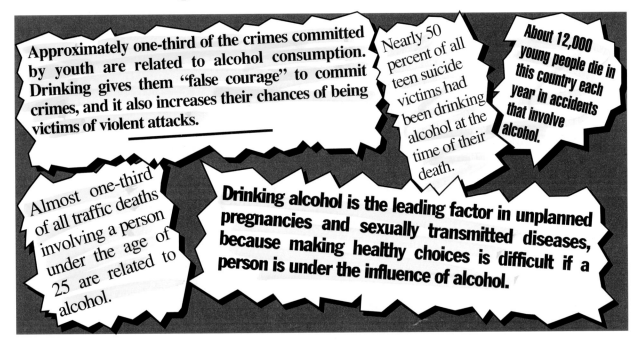

There are lots of ways to have fun without alcohol. In fact, alcohol can get in the way of having fun.

Social Studies Connection

Mothers Who Are MADD ACTIVITY!

An organization called Mothers Against Drunk Driving (MADD) is active in pushing for harsher penalties for drunk drivers. Check your school or local library to find out how MADD started. Find out what the penalties are in your community and in your state for drunk driving.

Alcohol Can Be Habit-forming

People who drink alcohol regularly need to drink more and more of it for the desired effect. After a while, this increased use causes the drinker to form an addiction to alcohol. An **addiction** (uh·DIK·shuhn) is *a physical or mental need for a drug or other substance.* Studies show that people who begin drinking at an early age have a greater chance of becoming addicted. This increases the risk of family problems, losing jobs, and poor health.

An addicted person who stops drinking alcohol will suffer withdrawal symptoms. Signs of alcohol withdrawal include sweating, inability to sleep, shakiness, and irritability. The person may experience unreasonable fears, seizures, and other disturbances of the nervous system. Withdrawal can be very painful.

Lesson 1

Review

Using complete sentences, answer the following questions on a separate sheet of paper.

Reviewing Terms and Facts

1. **Vocabulary** Define the term *alcohol.* Use it in an original sentence.
2. **Recall** List the factors that affect a person's blood alcohol concentration (BAC).

Thinking Critically

3. **Analyze** If alcohol is a depressant, why do people serve it at parties?
4. **Synthesize** Suppose a friend told you it is okay to drink, as long as you only drink beer. How might you respond?

Applying Health Concepts

5. **Personal Health** With a partner, plan a skit in which a young teen must decide whether or not to accept a ride from someone who has been drinking. Together, act out your skit for the rest of the class.

Lesson 2

What Is Alcoholism?

This lesson will help you find answers to questions that teens often ask about alcoholism. For example:

- **How can you tell whether a person is an alcoholic?**
- **Can alcoholism be cured?**
- **If someone I know has a problem with alcohol, how can I help?**

Alcoholism: Problems and Disease

Alcohol can become addictive. In some cases, this *physical and mental need for alcohol turns into a progressive and chronic disease* called **alcoholism.** People with this disease are called alcoholics. They cannot keep from drinking. They cannot stop drinking once they have started. They drink even when they know they are harming their own health. **Figure 14.6** on page 436 describes the stages of alcoholism.

Alcoholics have a physical and a psychological addiction. In psychological addiction, the mind sends the body the message that it needs more and more alcohol. In physical addiction, the body itself feels a direct need for alcohol.

Many studies have been done in an effort to find out why people become alcoholics. It has been observed that the children of alcoholics are more likely to become alcoholics than children in general. One possible explanation for this is that children inherit the susceptibility to the disease from alcoholic parents. Another theory suggests that a child's environment—growing up in a home with alcoholism—has a greater influence on a person's chances of becoming an alcoholic than heredity. Researchers agree, however, that children of alcoholic parents will not automatically become alcoholics themselves.

Words to Know

alcoholism
recovery
Alcoholics Anonymous (AA)
Al-Anon
Alateen

Teen Issues

Ideas About Alcoholism ACTIVITY!

Write down some of the ideas you have about alcoholism. For example, do you think alcoholism is a disease or a personality weakness? Are certain types of people more likely to be alcoholics than others? After reading this lesson, look back on what you wrote. Have any of those ideas changed?

Alcohol abuse harms individuals' lives as well as society. More than one-third of the young people under 18 in juvenile institutions were under the influence of alcohol when they were arrested.

Figure 14.6

Stages of Alcoholism

Experts say that alcoholism develops in three stages. These stages occur over a period of time.

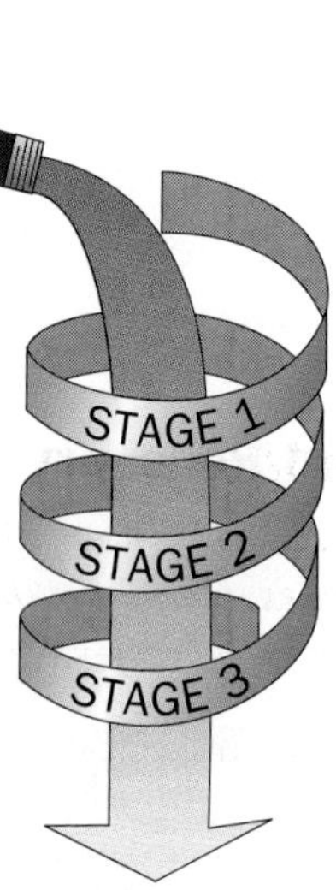

Stage 1
A person starts using alcohol to relieve stress or to relax. Soon the person needs alcohol to cope with the daily pressures of life. The drinker begins to make excuses about his or her drinking habits.

Stage 2
As the person continues to drink, the body develops a need for more and more alcohol. The drinker is often absent from school or work but continues to deny that there is a problem.

Stage 3
In the final stage of alcoholism, the problem is clear to other people. The drinker's body is strongly addicted, and the drinking is now out of control.

Help for the Dependent Person

A person who is addicted to alcohol is said to be dependent on it, but this addiction can be treated. With proper care, the majority of alcoholics who try to stop drinking succeed. After stopping, however, these people must never drink alcohol. Otherwise, they have a very high chance of becoming addicted again. Recovering from alcoholism is a difficult, lifelong struggle. It is much better not to get involved with alcohol in the first place.

MAKING HEALTHY DECISIONS

Helping a Friend Get Help

Katie and Jennifer had been best friends for years. Then, all of a sudden, Jennifer started to pull away. She told Katie that she didn't feel like going out or that she had too much homework to get together.

One Friday evening Katie decided to stop at Jennifer's house after a basketball game. She rang the doorbell three times before Jennifer finally answered. Katie thought that she looked flushed and confused. A few kids from school were in the living room. They all had beer and wine coolers.

Jennifer told Katie that she had invited a few friends over to work on a science project. When Katie asked where Jennifer's father was, she was told that he had gone to help her grandmother. Jennifer said they had to get back to work, and she would call Katie over the weekend. Katie thought she smelled alcohol on Jennifer's breath.

A few days later, Katie overheard two girls talking about what a great time they had raiding the liquor cabinet at Jennifer's on Friday. They said it was lucky that Jennifer's father had to spend so much time taking care of her grandmother.

When Katie told Jennifer what she'd heard, Jennifer got angry. She said that what she did was none of Katie's business and then stormed out of the room.

There are many programs to help the dependent person recover from alcoholism. They often involve groups of people who try to help each other learn to live without alcohol.

Treatment and Recovery

People recover from alcoholism at different rates and in different ways. *The process of becoming well again* is known as **recovery.** The recovery process generally includes the following steps.

- **Step One.** The dependent person admits to having a problem and asks for help in giving up alcohol.
- **Step Two.** The alcoholic goes through a process called detoxification to remove all alcohol from the body.
- **Step Three.** The alcoholic receives counseling on how to live without alcohol. This involves learning how to rebuild self-esteem and taking responsibility for his or her own life.

Some hospitals have medical detoxification units. There are clinics that offer treatment and counseling. Support groups play a vital role in recovery. One of the most successful *support groups for alcoholics* is **Alcoholics Anonymous** (uh·NAH·nuh·muhs), or **AA.** At AA meetings, people who are recovering from alcoholism help others who are struggling to stay sober.

Katie wants to help Jennifer, but she doesn't know what to do. She feels that she can't talk to Jennifer and get through to her. She doesn't want to talk to Jennifer's father because he might punish her for sneaking the liquor. Katie uses the step-by-step decision-making process to help her.

1. **State the situation**
2. **List the options**
3. **Weigh the possible outcomes**
4. **Consider your values**
5. **Make a decision and act**
6. **Evaluate the decision**

Follow-up Activities

1. Apply the decision-making steps to Katie's problem.
2. Along with a partner, role-play a scene in which Katie confronts Jennifer about her drinking.
3. Now role-play a scene in which Katie talks to her own parents about Jennifer's drinking.

Because alcoholism is a serious disease that cannot be cured, recovery must be an ongoing process. People need to work at staying sober one day at a time for the rest of their lives. Without recovery, alcoholism results in irreversible harm to the mind and body, and premature death.

in your journal

You don't need to be an alcoholic to benefit from a support group. Everyone needs to talk to people who have experienced similar problems and concerns. Who are the people in your support group? Write about them in your private journal.

Help for the Family

The harmful effects of alcohol do not stop with the drinker. The family members and friends of heavy drinkers suffer, too. Alcohol abuse and addiction are major factors in marital separation and divorce. The children of alcoholics frequently have problems, such as depression and anxiety. In addition, many cases of spouse and child abuse are committed by people who have been drinking.

One in four families in the United States is touched by alcoholism. This means that a growing number of young people know or are living with a person addicted to alcohol. These people often need help for themselves as well as for the problem drinkers in their lives. The first step to take is to admit that the problem exists. The second is to reach out for help.

Individual or family therapy is often recommended for people whose lives are affected by alcohol abuse. There are also many support groups available to help the family and friends of alcoholics. Two support groups are described here.

- **Al-Anon** is a *support group that helps family members and friends of alcoholics.* Al-Anon members learn how to help themselves as well as the person dependent on alcohol. The meetings are confidential and free.
- **Alateen** is *a support group that helps young people cope with having a family member or friend who is an alcoholic.* Its members share their experiences and work together to recover.

Family programs are offered at many alcohol treatment centers. They provide a way for family members to learn about the disease of alcoholism and discuss how they have been affected by it. Family members of alcoholics work toward their own recovery and support others in the family during the recovery process.

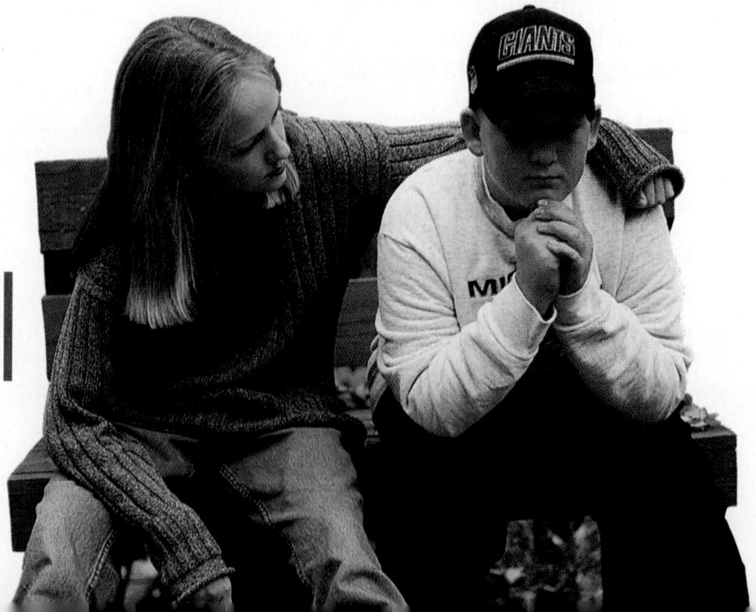

Support is available to help teens who have family members or friends who are alcoholics.

How Can You Help?

Someone who has a drinking problem needs help. If a friend or family member has a problem with alcohol, you can try to help in several ways. To be helped, the alcoholic must admit that he or she has a problem. Your most important responsibility is to yourself. If you are close to an alcoholic, make sure that the person's drinking problem does not change your own behaviors and attitudes. Keep in mind, however, that some actions—no matter how well intended—will *not* help.

What to Do

- Talk calmly with the drinker about the harm that alcohol does. Discuss this when he or she is sober.
- Tell the drinker how concerned you are and offer to help.
- Help the drinker to feel good about quitting.
- Give the drinker information about groups that can help.
- Encourage the drinker to get help.

What Not to Do

- Do not argue with the person when he or she is drunk.
- Avoid using an "I'm-better-than-you" tone of voice when talking about the person's drinking problem.
- Do not make excuses to others for the drinker's behavior.
- Do not feel that you are responsible for the drinker's actions.
- Do not be afraid to seek help for the drinker if he or she won't do it.

Cultural Connections

Talking Circles

Many programs for preventing and treating alcohol addiction among Native American children and youth are turning to Indian culture for inspiration. Traditional Indian ceremonies, rituals, and prayers help Native American youth develop a sense of belonging and self-esteem. One Indian tradition used in treatment programs is the "talking circle." Participants sit in a circle and share their feelings. Stones, feathers, or other symbolic objects are passed around the circle to absorb or release bad feelings.

Review

Lesson 2

Using complete sentences, answer the following questions on a separate sheet of paper.

Reviewing Terms and Facts

1. **Recall** Why are children of alcoholics more likely to become alcoholics than children in general?
2. **Vocabulary** What is the difference between *Alcoholics Anonymous, Al-Anon,* and *Alateen?*
3. **Review** Describe the three steps in the recovery process.

Thinking Critically

4. **Analyze** Is there a difference between a heavy drinker and an alcoholic? Explain your answer.
5. **Explain** Can alcoholism be cured? Why or why not?

Applying Health Concepts

6. **Personal Health** Read one or two magazine articles in which teens describe their problems with alcohol. Write a paragraph telling what you can learn from the experiences of these young people.

TEEN HEALTH DIGEST

Teens Making a Difference

Awesome Dawesome

Dominique Dawes, nicknamed "Awesome Dawesome" by her coach, Kelli Hill, is an Olympic gold medalist in gymnastics. Only 4 feet 11 inches tall, Dawes was named 1994 Sportsperson of the Year by U.S.A. Gymnastics at age 17. As a member of the U.S. gymnastics team, Dominique keeps busy. Not only does she attend classes at the University of Maryland, but she also participates in programs such as "Say No to Drugs" and "Stay in School."

Dawes is also involved with "Girl Power!", a public education campaign launched by the Department of Health and Human Services in 1996. The goal of the "Girl Power!" campaign is to encourage girls between the ages of nine and fourteen to make the most of their lives. "Girl Power!" provides these girls with opportunities to build their skills and self-confidence; the program also emphasizes the ills of using tobacco, alcohol, or illicit drugs for any reason. Dawes, who appears on posters for the campaign, knows that determination is the key for these girls. She knows that tobacco, alcohol, and drugs should have no place in anyone's life, and she intends to spread the message through this campaign.

Sports and Recreation

Ring In the New Year

No doubt about it, New Year's Eve is the biggest party night on the calendar. These days, people all across the United States celebrate the new year in an enjoyable, safe, and sober way with "First Night" parties.

"First Night" parties are community events designed to let everyone in town have a good time. Participants buy a badge which gains them admission to alcohol-free parties, shows, musical events, fireworks, and more. Communities that sponsor "First Night" celebrations range from big cities like New York to small suburban towns. Big or small, towns that hold "First Night" parties make New Year's Eve safe and memorable for the young and old alike.

Try This:

Find out about "First Night" celebrations in or near your town. What businesses and organizations take part? Find out from the local police how these celebrations have affected the crime rate on New Year's Eve.

CON$UMER FOCU$

Warning Labels: What Should They Say?

Since November 1989, the Surgeon General's office has required that all alcohol sold in the United States come with a warning label describing the dangers of drinking. The labels caution specifically against drinking while pregnant and when intending to drive or operate heavy machinery.

Mark Lehto, associate professor at Purdue University, studies warning labels. Lehto believes that the existing labels are not as strong as they could be, and as a result their effect has diminished. He believes that the warnings need to be updated to be effective.

What do you think? Do warning labels alone prevent people from abusing alcohol? Should they be used in combination with other efforts, such as antialcohol TV ads?

A study conducted in Florida has shown that warning posters boost knowledge of alcohol risks. The awareness of alcohol's addictiveness increased from 25 to 90 percent in a small Florida community.

Myths and Realities

Sober Up!

You may have seen the following scene in movies or on television. Someone is drunk but needs to sober up quickly. The character is shoved under a cold shower and served strong coffee. Suddenly the person appears sober.

Unfortunately, that scenario could never happen. The caffeine in coffee and the shock of cold water cannot make a drunk person sober.

There is no way to "get sober quick." To be sober at a moment's notice, you have to stay sober.

People at Work

Alcoholic Beverage Control Board Chief and Local Teens

Names: Mike Tolbert, Melissa, and Mark

Goal: To prevent clerks from making illegal sales of alcohol to minors

Mike Tolbert started an education program in 1996 to teach convenience store clerks what to look for when selling alcohol. Employees are also taught the legal aspects of selling alcohol and how to handle the situation when they catch a minor trying to buy alcohol. The program allows the officers, stores, and volunteer teens to work together to prevent illegal sales of alcohol.

Results: In a recent spot check, Melissa and Mark, teens who work undercover with Tolbert, came up empty at all 15 stores at which they tried to buy alcohol. One clerk even confiscated Mark's license.

Quote: "This program is better at preventing minors from getting alcohol" than traditional stake-out methods. "It's the better way."

Lesson

3 Choosing to Be Alcohol Free

This lesson will help you find answers to questions that teens often ask about choosing to be alcohol free. For example:

- **Why do some teens decide not to drink?**
- **How can I refuse to drink and still have friends?**
- **How can I have fun and not drink?**

Word to Know

alternative

Why Some Young People Drink

There are many reasons not to drink. In spite of them, many young people still experiment with alcohol. At present about 1.78 million youths in the United States between the ages of 12 and 20 have drinking problems. Here are some of the reasons they give for drinking:

- **"All my friends drink."** Some teens choose to go along with the crowd even if the crowd is drinking.
- **"Alcohol makes me look grown-up."** Some young people want to look and act mature. They think drinking does that.
- **"Alcohol helps me forget about my problems."** Alcohol is not an escape, though. The problems are still there when the alcohol wears off—with some additional problems.
- **"Alcohol helps me relax."** The teen years are hectic. Some young people think alcohol will help them relax. Jogging or listening to music are much better ways to relax.
- **"Alcohol helps me feel less shy around other people."** Most teens feel awkward in social situations. Some feel that alcohol puts them at ease. However, teens who rely on alcohol to boost their self-confidence may fail to develop effective social skills.

There are lots of healthy ways to have fun at a party. How many can you think of?

Some Reasons Not to Drink

Over 15 percent of people over the age of 18 in the United States have never drunk alcohol. Twenty-three percent have not drunk alcohol in the past year. Many people who used to drink have stopped. As people are becoming aware of the physical and emotional damage that drinking can cause, fewer and fewer drink.

More and more young people are choosing not to drink. Here are some of the reasons they are giving.

- **It is illegal.** Drinking is against the law in every state for anyone under age 21. Obeying the law makes your life easier and safer. It spares you expensive fines and a blot on your record.
- **It gets in the way.** As a teen, your life is full of activities. You study, take tests, play sports, and try to be your best around your friends and family. Teens who choose not to drink will be more alert to meet these challenges. Athletics are especially difficult to pursue with a hangover.
- **It is not fun.** Drinking can make people sick. It can also cause them to do something that may embarrass them. Drinking may even lead to injury or death. Many young people have decided that they can do without that kind of "fun."
- **It is not smart.** Many teens know that they do not need to drink to be popular. They know that drinking does not make a person more mature. Acting responsibly is a sign of maturity.
- **It does not solve problems.** Many teens understand that drinking does not solve problems. Instead, it creates them.
- **It disappoints others and makes the user feel guilty.** Teens who drink alcohol live a lie because they have to hide their habit. Many young people would rather not have to sneak around and be dishonest with people they care about.
- **It harms your health.** Drinking alcohol impairs development. It overworks the body system, particularly the liver. It also interferes with the absorption of nutrients from food.

in Your Journal

Read the list of reasons teens give for choosing not to drink. In your journal, write your own list of reasons for saying no to alcohol.

Drinking can bring serious legal consequences to teens that can affect the rest of their lives.

Alcohol Advertising and Teens

Every day on television, in magazines, and on billboards, teens see good-looking, healthy people drinking alcohol. Entertainers promote the idea that it's normal, smart, and sophisticated to drink. Beer advertisements associate drinking with sporting events, fast cars, popularity, and fun. It is no wonder that teens are inclined to believe what they see.

Advertisers spend billions of dollars each year promoting alcohol. Their advertisements focus on how people act while using their products rather than the products themselves. The atmosphere is usually partylike with upbeat music or set in an outdoor environment that looks like fun, such as the beach. It's important to evaluate advertisements for the facts. Will that product make you more attractive or more popular? Will your relationships be successful and problem free as a result of drinking?

Promotion gimmicks are also popular. For example, at many sports and entertainment events you can buy T-shirts and hats that feature the name of the beer company sponsoring the event. When you wear the T-shirt or the hat, you provide free advertising for the product or company.

Few advertisements focus on the negative consequences of drinking. Those that do are usually public service announcements sponsored by organizations such as SADD (Students Against Destructive Decisions) or MADD. Their advertising budgets simply cannot compete with those of major alcohol companies.

Some communities are trying to change the way alcohol companies advertise their products. They believe that promotions aimed at high school and college students, as well as sponsorship of sports and entertainment events, should be ended. They propose that billboard advertisements for alcohol should not be permitted near schools or hospitals. They know that alcohol causes problems for young people who use it.

Teen Issues

Raising Money ACTIVITY!

Along with several other teens, hold a bake sale, car wash, or rummage sale to raise money for a "no-alcohol" publicity fund. Then use the money for posters, brochures, and other effective ways of getting your message to other teens.

Advertisers promote the idea that recreation is more fun when you are drinking their product. Name some of the health risks associated with drinking alcohol.

Many community groups sponsor dances and other social events for teens that focus on fun, healthy activities. Can you name some in your community?

LIFE SKILLS

How to Say No to Alcohol

You know that drinking causes problems for you as well as friends and family members close to you. However, there will be times when you feel pressured to drink. How you handle such situations will affect your health and well-being for years to come.

There are many effective ways to avoid using alcohol. You need to find the technique that you feel comfortable using. Regardless of the technique you use, remember that no one has the right to pressure you to do something you do not want to do.

- **Choose a way that speaks the truth for you.** One teen might say, "I don't want to risk getting suspended from the team." Another might simply respond that the smell of alcohol makes her sick.
- **Avoid situations where people may be drinking.** Do not go to a party where you suspect there will be alcohol. If you attend a party and find that people are drinking, leave. Underage drinking is illegal. You could get arrested and have a record for the rest of your life.
- **Suggest alternatives.** Change the subject. You might ask if there's anything to eat, or say that you would rather dance instead.
- **Stick together with friends who support you.** You will find it easier to say no to alcohol if your friends also avoid it.

Follow-up Activities

1. Along with a partner, create a skit in which a teen is offered alcohol. Show the teen using one or more of the above techniques to refuse the alcohol. Act out your skit for the class.
2. Along with your classmates, think of more ways to avoid using alcohol. Publish your suggestions in the school newspaper, or prepare a flyer and distribute it to other students in school.

Steps for a healthy, productive life start with avoiding alcohol and other harmful substances.

Personal Inventory

HOW DO YOU FEEL ABOUT ALCOHOL?

The way you behave toward alcohol and your attitudes about drinking will affect the decisions you make throughout life. However, behavior and attitudes can be changed. Only you can decide if you need to make changes regarding alcohol.

On a separate sheet of paper, write "true" or "false" for each statement below. Your answers can help you identify and set goals to improve your behavior and attitudes toward alcohol. Total the number of true responses you have to the questions below. Then compare your score with the ranking at the end of the survey.

1. I have never had a drink containing alcohol.
2. My friends do not drink alcohol.
3. I avoid situations and places where I know there will be alcohol.
4. If I find myself in a place where others are drinking, I leave.
5. I have never ridden in a car driven by someone who had been drinking alcohol.
6. I think that alcohol is bad for the body and the mind.
7. I do not think drinking alcohol will make me more popular.
8. I do not believe the images I see in alcohol advertisements.
9. I do not believe that alcohol will make me more self-confident.
10. I believe that alcohol can ruin people's lives.

Give yourself 1 point for each true response. A score of 9–10 is very good. A score of 7–8 is good. A score of 5–6 is fair. If you score below 5 points, you need to set some goals for improving your behavior (if you answered false to the first five questions) or your attitudes (if you answered false to the last five questions) toward drinking.

Things to Do Instead of Drinking

Why do some teens simply give in when they are pressured to try alcohol? One reason is that they have not thought about alternatives. **Alternatives** (ahl·TER·nuh·tivz) are *other ways of thinking or acting*. There are plenty of alternatives to drinking. A few of them are suggested below.

- **Get good at something that requires a steady hand.** You could put together a model airplane, paint a picture, or practice calligraphy. Then remind yourself that a person whose senses are dulled by alcohol could not enjoy these activities.
- **Start a no-alcohol fund.** Every time you say no to alcohol put aside a small sum of money. At the end of a few months, treat yourself to a present with the money.
- **Join with other teens for alcohol-free fun.** You could plan an alcohol-free dance or have a basketball or volleyball game, keeping in mind that you will play better if you do not drink alcohol because you will be in control.
- **Volunteer to help others.** Teens who want to look mature can show their maturity by helping others. You could also volunteer at a hospital or nursing home helping sick or elderly people.
- **Learn a new sport or join a team.** Learn a sport you have never tried before, such as tennis or karate. You could practice your skills with a more experienced friend or relative.
- **Spread the word.** You could volunteer to teach younger children about the dangers of alcohol and the benefits of saying no. Younger children look up to teens as role models.

in your journal

Look at the alternatives to drinking shown on these pages. For each alternative, give an example of something you currently do or something you would like to do. Write your examples in your journal. What would you buy with the money you save in a no-alcohol fund?

Review Lesson 3

Using complete sentences, answer the following questions on a separate sheet of paper.

Reviewing Terms and Facts

1. **Vocabulary** Define the term *alternatives*. Use it in a sentence.
2. **Recall** List four reasons not to drink.

Thinking Critically

3. **Give Examples** How might drinking create more problems for a teen who is already troubled?
4. **Decide** You are at a party and someone offers you a drink in a glass with ice. You do not recognize the drink and suspect that it may contain alcohol. What would you do?

Applying Health Concepts

5. **Personal Health** Make a poster that shows healthy alternatives to using alcohol. Find or draw pictures that show young people taking part in worthwhile activities. At the top or bottom of your poster, write a headline that will persuade others about the importance of alternatives to drinking. Display your finished poster at school.

Chapter 14 Review

Chapter Summary

- **Lesson 1** Alcohol is a drug that slows down the working of the brain and nervous system. Excessive drinking can lead to serious health problems and, if used by a pregnant woman, can affect a developing baby. Alcohol is a major cause of traffic fatalities and other accidents. Teens who drink alcohol are more likely to become involved in unsafe behavior. Alcohol can be addictive and can increase one's risk of family- and job-related problems.
- **Lesson 2** Alcoholism is a disease in which a person has a physical and mental need for alcohol. Recovery from alcoholism is possible, but it is a slow and difficult process. Treatment programs and support groups are available to help alcoholics through the steps of recovery. Support groups are also available to help family members and friends of alcoholics.
- **Lesson 3** In spite of the many reasons not to drink, alcohol abuse is a serious problem for many American teens. The best way to avoid problems with alcohol is to avoid using it and to develop healthy alternatives to drinking.

Reviewing Key Terms and Concepts

Using complete sentences, answer the following questions on a separate sheet of paper.

Lesson 1

1. Describe alcohol's immediate effects on the brain.
2. Define the following terms and explain how each is related to alcohol: *depressant, cirrhosis, fetal alcohol syndrome,* and *addiction.*

Lesson 2

3. Define *alcoholism.*
4. Describe the stages in the development of alcoholism.

Lesson 3

5. List at least three reasons why some teens drink even though they know about the harmful effects of alcohol.
6. List four ways to say no to alcohol.

Thinking Critically

Using complete sentences, answer the following questions on a separate sheet of paper.

7. **Explain** Tom weighs more than Alfredo. If the two men consume the same amount of alcohol in the same amount of time, who will probably be more strongly affected by the alcohol? Why?
8. **Analyze** What do you think is a teen drinker's greatest risk? Why?
9. **Recommend** What should you tell a pregnant woman who continues to drink alcohol?
10. **Synthesize** What are some ways to help a person who you think has a drinking problem?
11. **Analyze** How do advertisers try to convince young people to drink?
12. **Hypothesize** How can you respond to a teen who drinks because "everyone else does"?

Chapter 14 Review

Your Action Plan

Review your private journal entries for this chapter. Decide on a long-term goal that you would like to achieve, related to alcohol and health.

Step 1 Write down the long-term goal you selected.

Step 2 Choose several short-term goals that will help you achieve your long-term goal. For example, if your goal is to remain alcohol free, one short-term goal might be to practice ways of saying no if you are ever offered alcohol.

Step 3 Identify sources of help and support. This is an important step for goals relating to alcohol use.

Step 4 Make a schedule for meeting each short-term goal.

Monitor your progress to keep yourself on track. If your goal is to remain alcohol free, your reward will be a healthier life and increased self-confidence.

In Your Home and Community

1. **Health of Others** SADD (Students Against Destructive Decisions) is an organization created by and for students to prevent drunk driving. Does your school have a SADD chapter? If so, find out how you can become a member. Collect information about their activities and achievements, and create a bulletin board for your class.
2. **Community Resources** Find out where there are treatment centers, counseling services, and support groups in your community for adults and teens who have alcohol-related problems or who live with people who do. Make a brochure that lists the names, addresses, and phone numbers of these services and display the brochure in a public place.

Building Your Portfolio

1. **Advertising Analysis** Make note of the use of alcohol in the movies and television shows that you watch for the next week. List the name of the show or movie, whether or not the characters drink alcohol, and if so, in what situations. Do any of the shows glamorize drinking? Write a paragraph or two that summarizes what you have observed. Add this project to your portfolio.
2. **Making Healthy Choices** Write a short story about a teen who has some friends who drink alcohol. Imagine that the main character is offered a drink and turns it down. What are the consequences of your character's action? Add the story to your portfolio.
3. **Personal Assessment** Look through all the activities and projects you did for this chapter. Choose one or two that you would like to include in your portfolio.

Chapter 15

Drugs and Your Health

Student Expectations

After reading this chapter, you should be able to:

1. Describe some of the uses for medicines.
2. Explain how stimulants and depressants can harm the body.
3. Describe the health risks associated with the use of marijuana, hallucinogens, and inhalants.
4. Identify ways to remain drug free.

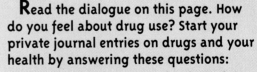

Teen Chat Group

Emilio: Hey, Coach, where's David?

Coach: Well, I guess you guys might as well know the story. The fact is, he's been kicked off the team for drug use.

Jared: You're joking! He was one of our best players! Why would he do something that would mess up the team like that?

Cody: I can't believe it. David had everything going for him. He's our star player—everyone at school likes him. Why would he start using drugs?

Coach: All I can tell you is that sometimes teens don't make the best decisions. Guys like David think that nothing can hurt them. They don't think about how the things they do now can affect their future.

Emilio: He wasn't thinking about how it would affect us, either. Now we'll have to finish the season without him.

Coach: That's true, but I'd rather work with a team of players I can trust.

in your journal

Read the dialogue on this page. How do you feel about drug use? Start your private journal entries on drugs and your health by answering these questions:

- **If you could talk to David, what advice would you give him?**
- **How do you think drugs affect the body?**
- **What can you do to avoid drugs?**
- **When you reach the end of the chapter, you will use your journal entries to make an action plan.**

Lesson 1

The Role of Medicine

This lesson will help you find answers to questions that teens often ask about medicines. For example:

- **What is the difference between drugs and medicine?**
- **How do medicines affect the body?**
- **What is the difference between prescription and over-the-counter medicines?**
- **How can I be sure I am using medicine properly?**

Words to Know

drugs
medicine
antibiotic
side effect
tolerance
prescription medicine
over-the-counter (OTC) medicine

Drugs and Health

In this century, medical discoveries and the development of more effective drugs have changed the overall health of the American people. Many drugs are now available to prevent, treat, or cure diseases, injuries, and medical problems. These drugs have helped millions of people live longer, healthier lives.

Not all of the changes brought about by modern drugs have been healthful, however. Sometimes drugs are not used the way they are supposed to be used. When that happens, drugs become dangerous. They can do great harm to people's bodies and minds, as well as to society as a whole.

Types of Drugs

Drugs are *substances other than food that change the structure or function of the body or mind.* Most of the time, people use the term *drug* when they refer to medicine. **Medicines** are *drugs that are used to treat or prevent diseases and other conditions.*

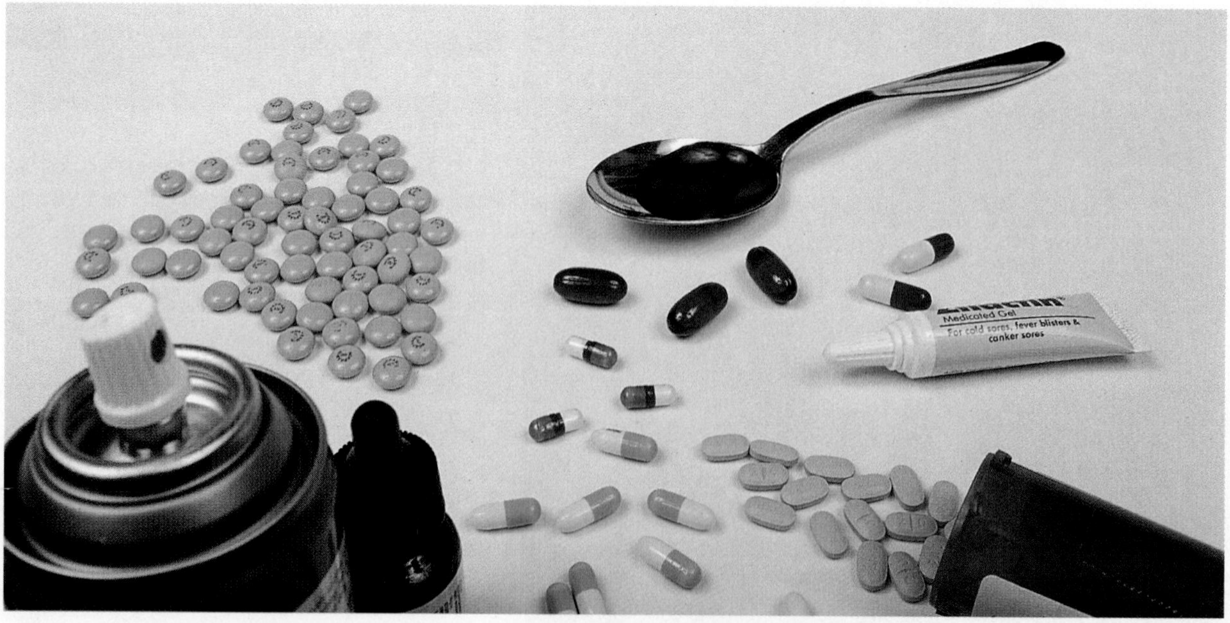

Medicines are available in a variety of forms to prevent diseases, fight infection, and provide pain relief.

Medicines are usually grouped according to their effect on the body. Some of the most commonly used types of medicines include those that prevent diseases, those that fight infection, and those that provide pain relief. Each type of medicine is briefly discussed on the following pages.

interNET CONNECTION

Visit the Glencoe Web site and get the facts about which drugs can heal you and which can harm you.

http://www.glencoe.com/sec/health

Medicines That Prevent Diseases

Vaccines are medicines that prevent diseases. Made from preparations of dead or weakened germs, vaccines cause the immune system to produce antibodies. The antibodies then fight off the germs that cause the disease. The polio vaccine is one you probably had before you started school. It provides long-lasting protection against the polio virus. Other vaccines are for diseases such as diphtheria, tetanus, whooping cough, measles, mumps, rubella, hepatitis B, and influenza.

Medicines That Fight Germs

Many germs and diseases cannot be prevented with vaccines. Instead, medicines are used to restore people to health. A medicine commonly used to fight germs is an antibiotic. **Antibiotics** (an·ti·by·AH·tiks) are *medicines that reduce or kill harmful bacteria in the body.* Many types of antibiotics are available. They are usually sold in liquid or tablet form. Physicians also may give antibiotics to patients in a shot.

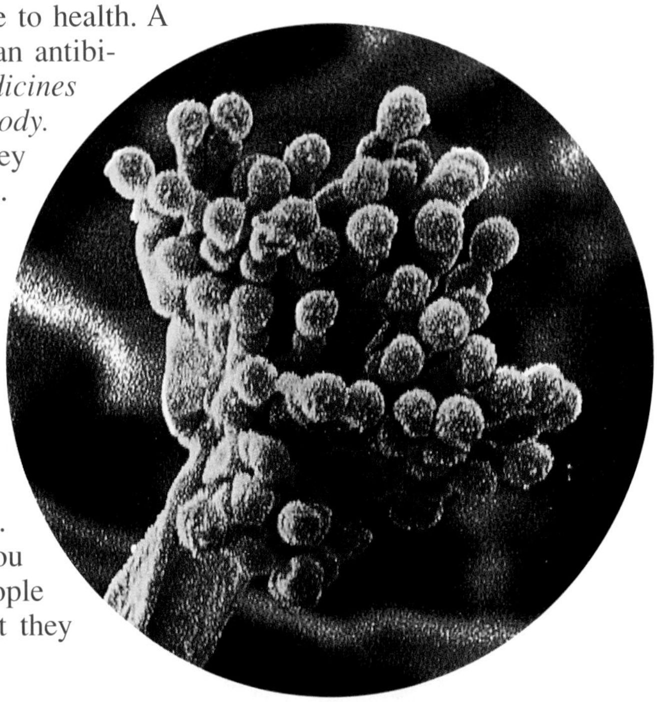

Some types of penicillin are derived from natural molds or bacteria such as this. Others, known as synthetic penicillins, are chemically processed.

Each type of antibiotic fights only certain types of bacteria. For example, *penicillin* (pen·uh·SI·luhn), one of the most commonly used antibiotics, is highly effective in killing bacteria that cause strep throat and pneumonia. Unfortunately, antibiotics do not kill infections caused by viruses. Therefore, they are not effective in helping you when you have a cold or the flu. Some people are allergic to some of these medicines, but they can use others.

Medicines That Provide Pain Relief

Many people take medicine to relieve pain. With over $1 billion in annual sales, aspirin is the most widely used pain relief medicine available without a doctor's prescription. Aspirin and its substitutes (including acetaminophen) are used for headaches, toothaches, and muscular pain. They are also used to reduce fever and inflammation.

Prescription pain relievers are also available. Doctors may prescribe these when a person is recovering from a serious illness or to help a person manage the pain that accompanies a chronic disease, such as arthritis. Narcotics, one specific type of prescription pain reliever, are so powerful that they may cause physical and psychological dependence.

Other Medicines

A variety of medicines are available to treat people with certain health problems or conditions. Specific medicines are used by people with chronic conditions. These conditions include heart and blood pressure problems, diabetes, and allergies.

Some medicines have negative effects. Yet their use is essential for the health and well-being of some people. In those cases, additional medicine may be used to offset the negative effect of the first medicine. For instance, people who take certain types of blood pressure medicine may need to take another medicine to keep from retaining fluids.

Science Connection

Drug Discoveries ACTIVITY!

At your school or local library, research one of the following scientists who discovered an important medicine: Sir Frederick Banting, Sir Alexander Fleming, or Edward Jenner. Write a one-page paper on your findings.

Medicine in the Body

The effect of a medicine in the body depends on several factors. The type and amount of medicine a person takes are two important factors. The way you take medicine—by pill or shot—also has a lot to do with the effect of the medicine. Study **Figure 15.1.** Through which method are the effects of medicine more immediate? The shot is more immediate because it bypasses the digestive system going directly into the circulatory system.

in your journal

What medicines have you used in the past three months? In your private journal, list the medicines and explain why you used them.

You are different from everyone else. Your body chemistry is different from every other person's body chemistry. As a result, medicines can affect you differently from other people. For example, some people have reactions to certain medicines. This is why it is very important for medicine to be used only as prescribed and only by the person it is prescribed for.

Reactions to Medicine

One type of reaction to medicine is a **side effect,** which is *any reaction to a medicine other than the one intended.* Side effects include upset stomach, dizziness, and drowsiness. If you have any

HEALTH LAB

Home Remedies

Introduction: Throughout history, and even today, people have used home remedies for a variety of ailments. Home remedies exist for illnesses, skin and hair care, and childbirth.

Many of these remedies have been handed down from generation to generation. Some of them may be useless, or even harmful. However, many others have been proven to work and, in fact, have real medicinal value. For example, one home remedy suggests using tea to dry up canker sores. This remedy is based on scientific evidence because the tannic acid in tea brings relief to the canker sore pain. On the other hand, the home remedy of applying butter to a burn can be harmful because there is a high risk of infection from the butter.

Objective: During the next week, identify and list home remedies that you have heard of or that you or members of your family use. Evaluate the effectiveness of the remedies.

side effects to medicine, talk to a physician, nurse, or pharmacist. Some side effects can be very serious. Both prescription and over-the-counter medicines list possible side effects on their labels.

Figure 15.1

How Drugs Enter the Body

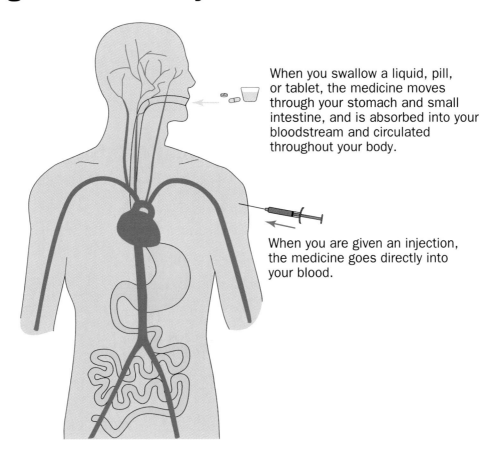

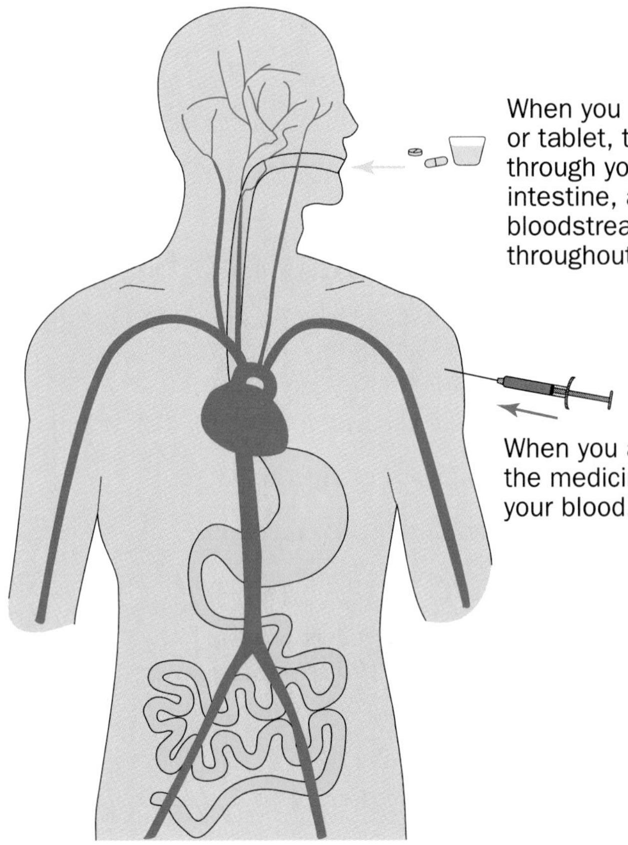

When you swallow a liquid, pill, or tablet, the medicine moves through your stomach and small intestine, and is absorbed into your bloodstream and circulated throughout your body.
When you are given an injection, the medicine goes directly into your blood.

Materials and Method: You will need a sheet of paper divided into three columns. Label the columns *Home Remedy, What It Is Used For,* and *How Effective Is It?* In the *Home Remedy* column, describe the remedy. In the *What It Is Used For* column, indicate what the particular remedy is supposed to cure or what condition it is supposed to relieve. In the *How Effective Is It?* column, evaluate the remedy's effectiveness. To get information for this column, you might need to do research at the library or interview people who have tried the remedy. If you cannot find any information on a particular remedy, write "undetermined" in this column.

Observation and Analysis: At the end of the week, share your home remedies and their effectiveness with your classmates. See how many different home remedies your class can identify. You could work with your classmates to make a bulletin board display of the most popular remedies.

Tolerance

When used over a long period of time, certain medicines can cause a person to develop a tolerance. **Tolerance** means that *a person's body becomes used to the effect of a medicine and needs greater amounts of it to be effective.*

Reactions to Mixing Medicines

When two or more medicines are taken at the same time, the effects may be dangerous. Any of the following reactions is possible.

- Each medicine may have a stronger effect than if taken alone.
- The medicines may combine to give unexpected effects.
- The medicines may cancel out each other's expected effects.

Your Total Health

Keep Alert

Are you, or is anyone in your family, allergic to a medicine routinely administered, such as penicillin? People with such allergies need to wear a medical identification tag. This tag provides important information that emergency caregivers need in case the person with the allergy has an accident that leaves him or her unconscious.

Drug Safety and the Government

In the United States, the Food and Drug Administration (FDA) is responsible for regulating the use of drugs, or medicines. To make sure that all medicines are safe, the FDA requires any company that manufactures a drug to state the following facts:

- The chemicals in the medicine
- The medical use of the medicine
- The effects of the medicine, as well as any possible side effects

Before any medicine is released for sale, it must be thoroughly tested by the FDA. **Figure 15.2** shows the process new medicines must go through. In some cases, it takes years for a medicine to be approved for use.

Figure 15.2

How the FDA Tests and Approves Medicines

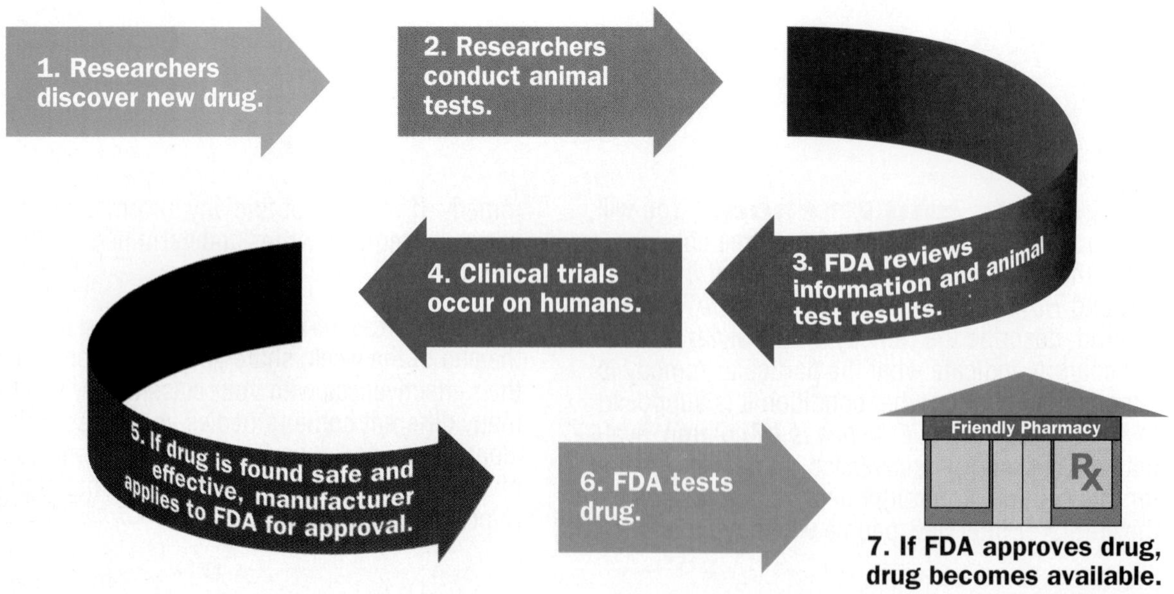
1. Researchers discover new drug.
2. Researchers conduct animal tests.
3. FDA reviews information and animal test results.
4. Clinical trials occur on humans.
5. If drug is found safe and effective, manufacturer applies to FDA for approval.
6. FDA tests drug.
Friendly Pharmacy
Rx
7. If FDA approves drug, drug becomes available.

Prescription Medicine

Because some medicines are very strong and potentially harmful, physicians must write special orders for them. These **prescription** (pri·SKRIP·shuhn) **medicines** are *medicines that can be sold only with a written order from a physician.* **Figure 15.3** shows the basic information that must appear on a prescription label.

Figure 15.3

Prescription Medicine Label

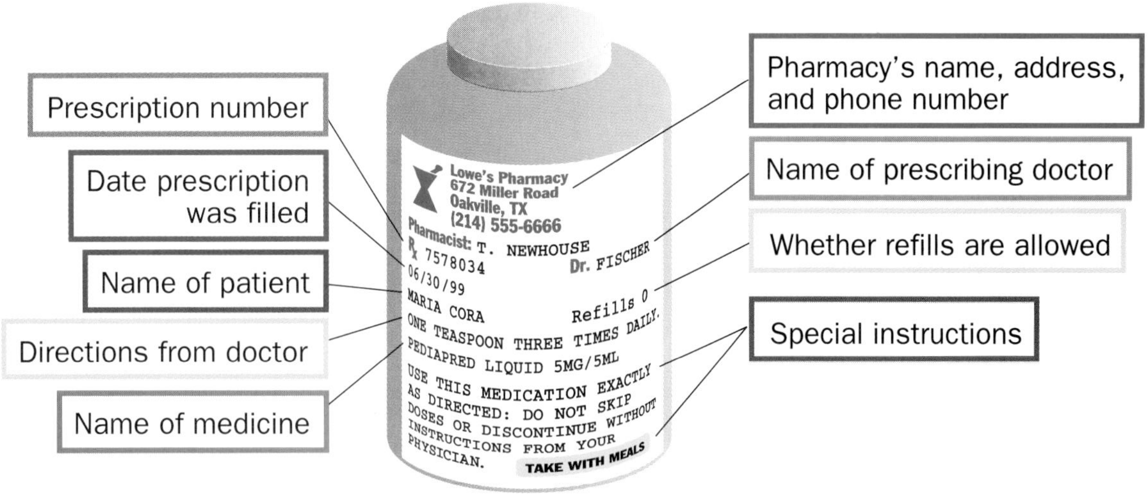

Over-the-Counter (OTC) Medicine

Some *medicines are safe enough to be taken without a written order from a physician.* They are called **over-the-counter (OTC) medicines.** Although not as strong as prescription medicines, they still may be harmful if not used as directed.

OTC medicines can be bought at any store that sells medications. Aspirin and cold pills are examples. **Figure 15.4** shows what every OTC medicine should include on its label.

Figure 15.4

Over-the-Counter Medicine Label

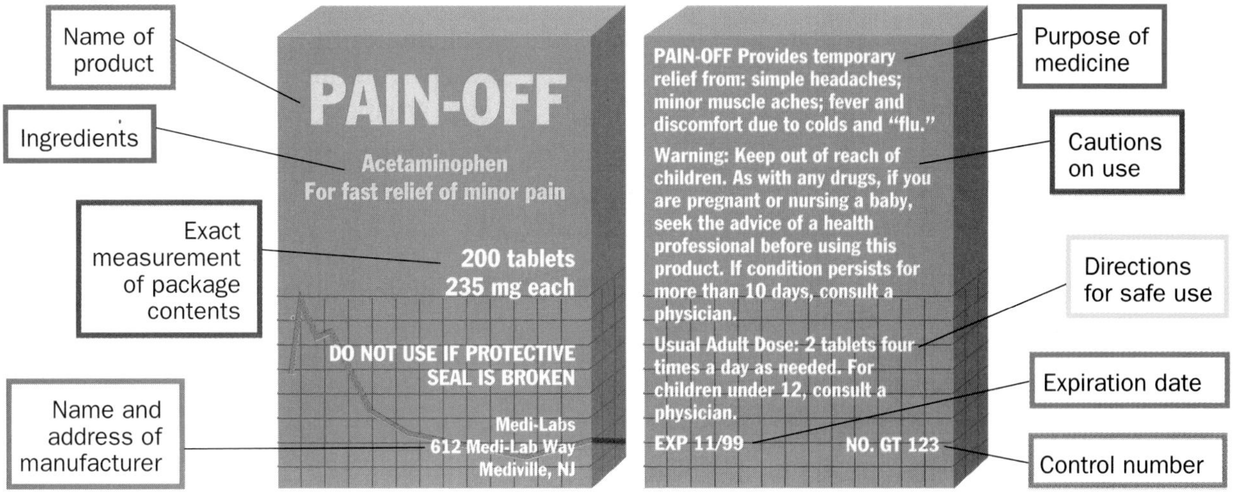

Keeping medicines high above the reach of children is an important safety measure.

Using Medicine Safely

Although consumers receive accurate information from the FDA, they still are ultimately responsible for using medicine properly. Some people use medicines in ways that are not intended. For instance, they may take four aspirins instead of two (hoping to get relief twice as fast) or use a medicine prescribed for someone else.

Misusing medicine is dangerous. Medicines have powerful effects on the body. If you are not sure how to use a medicine, ask the pharmacist or call your doctor. They can provide you with the information you need to use medicine safely.

Tips for Using Medicine

- Do not use OTC medicine for more than ten days without medical supervision. If an OTC medication does not help you, you may need something stronger. Call your physician.
- Do not share prescription medicine.
- Destroy medications that have passed their expiration date.
- Keep medicines safely sealed in childproof containers, and keep them out of the reach of children.
- Never take medication with alcohol.
- Never take two or more medicines at the same time without your doctor's approval.

Lesson 1 Review

Using complete sentences, answer the following questions on a separate sheet of paper.

Reviewing Terms and Facts

1. **Vocabulary** Which of the following is a type of medicine: *antibiotic* or *tolerance?* Describe the medicine.
2. **Give Examples** List three possible unhealthy reactions the body can have to medicine.

Thinking Critically

3. **Contrast** What is the difference between prescription and OTC medicines?
4. **Analyze** Suppose you went to your local pharmacy to buy nose spray and the lid on the tamperproof box was open on the only bottle left. Would you buy the spray? Why or why not?

Applying Health Concepts

5. **Consumer Health** Make a poster showing the three main groups of medicines. Illustrate the poster to clearly show the differences between these groups.
6. **Consumer Health** Research the Food and Drug Administration. Find out when and why it was established and the types of services it provides. Present your information in a one-page brochure.

Lesson 2

Stimulants and Depressants

This lesson will help you find answers to questions that teens often ask about drugs such as stimulants and depressants. For example:

- **Which kinds of drugs are misused or abused most often?**
- **How do stimulants affect the body?**
- **How do depressants affect the body?**

Drug Misuse and Abuse

People seriously harm their bodies by taking medicines or other drugs they should not be taking. In 1994 more than 8,000 people died as a result of misusing or abusing legal or illegal drugs.

People who harm themselves by using drugs are drug misusers or drug abusers. Drug misusers use a legal drug in an improper way. Drug abusers use substances that are against the law or are not supposed to be taken into the human body. Many of these drugs have no medical purpose and may be contaminated with lethal substances. The following are forms of drug misuse and abuse:

- Using a drug without following the directions
- Taking more or less of a drug than the doctor ordered
- Using a drug prescribed for someone else
- Giving your prescription medicine to someone else
- Using a drug for longer than a physician advises
- Combining medicines
- Using a medicine when you do not need it
- Using a drug for purposes other than medical treatment
- Taking a substance that was not meant to enter the body

Stimulants

Stimulants (STIM·yuh·luhnts) are *drugs that speed up the body's functions.* Stimulants cause the blood pressure to rise. They increase breathing and make the heart beat faster. A person using a stimulant feels alert and wakeful. Doctors may prescribe stimulants to patients who have physical or emotional problems. Other stimulants, however, are used illegally to prevent fatigue, increase alertness, and improve self-confidence.

Words to Know

stimulant
amphetamine
narcotic

Q&A

Overdosing Can Kill

Q: What does overdosing on a drug mean?

A: To overdose means to take too much. The term overdose usually refers to the abuse of illegal drugs. Only one overdose of some illegal drugs can cause death.

Effects of Stimulants on the Body

Many parts of the body are affected by stimulants. Stimulants

- speed up the central nervous system.
- cause the heart rate to increase.
- cause respiratory rates to increase.
- cause high blood pressure.

When stimulants are misused or abused, they can seriously damage the body. They are dangerous because the user cannot be sure of the purity, amount, or concentration of the drug. Furthermore, the user has no idea how the body may react. Even a first-time user could die. Another danger of stimulants is that they can become habit-forming. The more of them a person uses, the more the person needs to feel an effect. After a while, that person can develop an addiction to the drug, or a physical or mental need for it.

Some stimulants are so mild that people are unaware they are using a drug. *Caffeine* is a good example. It is found in cocoa, coffee, tea, and many soft drinks. The use of caffeine in moderate doses is a commonly accepted practice. However, other stimulants can be very dangerous. Stimulants such as amphetamines and cocaine often are abused by people who are trying to get "high."

Did You Know?

High-powered Caffeine ACTIVITY!

Caffeine is one of the main ingredients in many diet and stay-awake products. Examine some of these products to see if they contain caffeine or propanolamine. These are stimulants that cause a loss of appetite, increased energy, and increased metabolism. These products should not be taken without a doctor's supervision.

Amphetamines

Amphetamines (am·FE·tuh·meenz) are *drugs prescribed to stimulate the central nervous system.* Doctors sometimes prescribe them to treat hyperactive children and *narcolepsy,* a disease that results in an uncontrollable need to sleep. However amphetamines are highly addictive. Users may become physically and psychologically dependent. Study **Figure 15.7** on page 462. In what other ways do amphetamines affect the body?

MAKING HEALTHY DECISIONS

Helping a Friend Who Might Be Abusing Drugs

Joanna and Martina have been best friends since they were in second grade. They were both in band, and they played on the school's soccer team. Whenever possible, they took the same classes. They also spent much of their leisure time together, going to concerts and attending many of the same parties.

In the past few months, Joanna has noticed a big change in Martina. For one thing, they have been spending much less time together. When they do spend time together, Martina often seems hostile toward Joanna. Martina's grades are slipping, and she is hanging out with a different crowd. Several times in recent weeks, Joanna has seen Martina exchanging pills with them. When Joanna questioned her, Martina said she was using the pills to help her get through some bad times at home. Joanna has tried to get Martina to talk through her problems, but she has refused.

Finally, Joanna told Martina that she thought Martina was abusing drugs and that she should get help. Martina denied having a drug problem and told Joanna to leave her alone.

Cocaine

Cocaine (koh·KAYN) is a powerful, illegal stimulant. Its abuse has become a major health problem in our society. Cocaine users come from many age groups. **Figure 15.5** shows how widely cocaine is used among high school seniors.

Cocaine creates a feeling of exhilaration and a burst of energy, followed by depression as the drug wears off. When users take more of the drug to relieve depression, they become dependent on it. Cocaine also makes the user crave more of it. In its most powerful forms, cocaine is injected into the bloodstream or smoked. People also sniff the powder up their noses.

in your journal

Many teens are joining the campaign to stop using drugs. In your journal, write phrases that you might use on a poster to explain why it is healthy to avoid drugs.

Crack Cocaine

Crack cocaine is a concentrated form of cocaine that is smoked. It produces an intense high in only a few seconds, followed by an intense low that leaves the user craving more. Crack is one of the most addictive and dangerous drugs used in the United States today. Because it is smoked, crack cocaine reaches the brain within ten seconds after it is taken. However, its effects last only a few minutes (see **Figure 15.6** on the next page).

Figure 15.5

Cocaine Use Among High School Seniors

Why do you think there was a decline in cocaine use from 1987 to 1992? Why do you think it is increasing again?

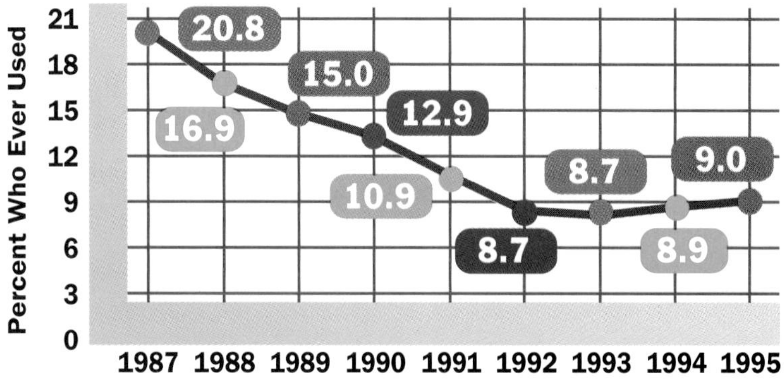

Source: *World Almanac and Book of Facts*, 1997

Joanna is torn. Should she leave Martina alone or try to get help for her? Joanna decided to use the step-by-step decision-making process to make up her mind:

1. **State the situation**
2. **List the options**
3. **Weigh the possible outcomes**
4. **Consider your values**
5. **Make a decision and act**
6. **Evaluate the decision**

Follow-up Activities

1. Apply the six steps of the decision-making process to Joanna's story.
2. With a partner, role-play a scene in which Joanna tells Martina that because she thinks Martina is abusing drugs, she doesn't want anything more to do with her.
3. Now role-play a scene in which Joanna tells Martina that she is going to find someone to help her with her drug problem. Think about suggestions Joanna can make to help Martina face her drug problem.

Figure 15.6
Crack-Craving Cycle

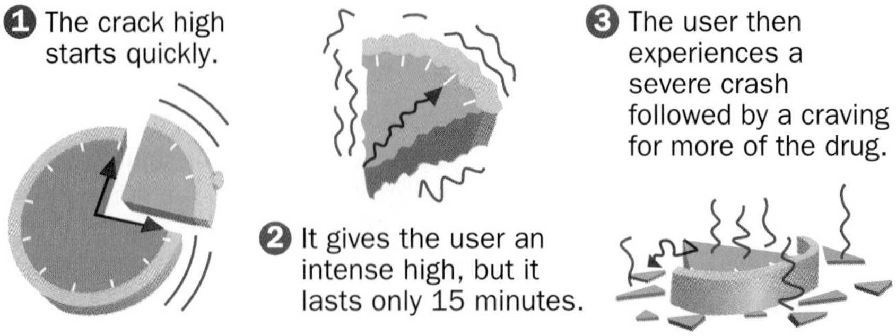

1 The crack high starts quickly.
2 It gives the user an intense high, but it lasts only 15 minutes.
3 The user then experiences a severe crash followed by a craving for more of the drug.

Smoking crack has the same effects on the body as using cocaine, only more intense (see **Figure 15.7**). Risks and side effects are also similar. In addition, users are at risk for getting emphysema from the smoke.

Figure 15.7
Stimulants

Drug	What It Is Called	How It Is Taken	What It Does
Amphetamines	Speed, crank, ice, uppers, pep pills, diet pills, ups, wake-ups, bennies, dexies, black beauties, jollies	Swallowed, by needle, inhaled, smoked	Causes uneven heart beat, rise in blood pressure, physical collapse, stroke, heart attack, and death
Cocaine	Coke, snow, toot, blow, lady	By needle, smoked, sniffed or snorted up the nose	Damages nose lining, liver, and heart; causes heart attack, seizures, stroke, and death
Crack	Rock, freebase, ready rock, teeth	Smoked	Leads to seizures, heart attack, and death

Depressants

Depressants are drugs that slow down the body's functions and reactions. Commonly called sedatives, these medications reduce blood pressure and slow down the heart rate and breathing rate. Doctors may prescribe depressants to relieve anxiety, nervousness, and sleeplessness. However, depressants are frequently abused.

Main Kinds of Depressants

- Tranquilizers (TRAN·kwuh·ly·zerz), when used as prescribed by a doctor in small amounts, can help a person relax without making him or her less alert.
- Barbiturates (bar·BI·chuh·ruhts) are powerful sedatives that are used for medical purposes.
- Hypnotics (hip·NAH·tiks) are very strong drugs that bring on sleep and reduce anxiety.

An amino acid (tryptophan) in milk, when heated, is a natural sedative. Drinking warm milk is one healthful way that a person can relieve sleeplessness.

Depressants are highly addictive. Over an extended period, they can cause physical and psychological dependence. Depressants should only be taken under a physician's supervision.

Abuse of depressants causes physical harm. When combined with alcohol, depressants are deadly. **Figure 15.8** shows some of the effects of various depressants on the body.

Figure 15.8

Depressants

Kind of Depressant	What It Is Called	How It Looks	How It Is Taken	What It Does
Tranquilizer	Valium, Librium, Xanax	Tablets or capsules	Swallowed	Reduces muscular activity, coordination, attention span, and anxiety Withdrawal can cause tremors and lead to coma or death
Barbiturate	Downers, barbs, yellow jackets, goof balls, blues	Red, yellow, blue, or red and blue capsules	Swallowed	Causes mood changes and excessive sleep Can lead to coma
Hypnotic	Quaaludes, Ludes, Sopors	Tablets	Swallowed	Impairs coordination and judgment Depresses the respiratory and circulatory systems

Narcotics

Narcotics (nar·KAH·tics) are *specific drugs that are obtainable only by prescription and are used to relieve pain.* Doctors may prescribe the narcotic *morphine,* an opiate, to treat extreme pain. *Codeine* (KOH·deen) may be prescribed to stop severe coughing. Although they are safe when taken under a physician's supervision, narcotics are so strongly addictive that their sale and use is controlled by law. In fact, pharmacists must keep records of all sales of narcotics.

Heroin

Heroin (HEHR·uh·win) is an *illegal drug that is made from morphine and is highly addictive.* Heroin users quickly develop a need for stronger and stronger doses of the drug. When users do not get the heroin they need, they feel severe pain. In addition, heroin depresses the central nervous system and can lead to coma or death.

Heroin is most commonly injected. Users of heroin and other drugs that are injected by needle run the risk of becoming infected by HIV. **Figure 15.9** shows what percentage of AIDS patients over 13 years old injected drugs.

Figure 15.9

AIDS Patients Who Inject Drugs (July 1995 to June 1996)

Drug abuse is an important risk factor in contracting HIV/AIDS and other sexually transmitted diseases. Because drug use impairs judgment, people under the influence of drugs are likely to engage in risky behaviors.

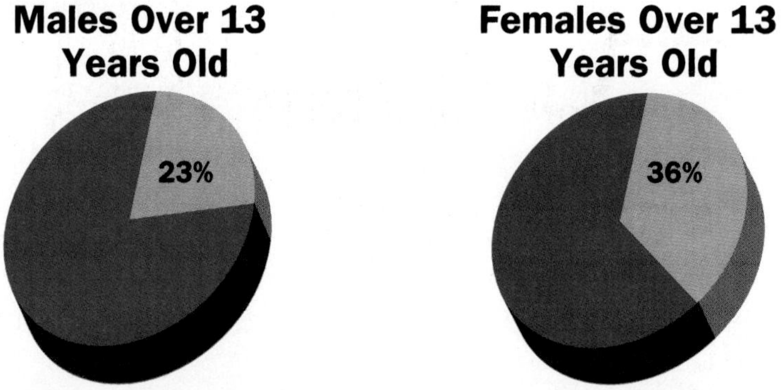

Lesson 2

Review

Using complete sentences, answer the following questions on a separate sheet of paper.

Reviewing Terms and Facts

1. **Vocabulary** Which of the following terms refer to drugs that relax you: *stimulants, amphetamines, narcotics?*
2. **Give Examples** Name an example of misuse or abuse of each of the above.

Thinking Critically

3. **Contrast** How do the effects of stimulants differ from those of depressants?
4. **Synthesize** What advice might you give a friend who said she was going to try crack cocaine?

Applying Health Concepts

5. **Consumer Health** Choose two drugs that are frequently abused. Make a poster that warns of the dangers of both drugs.
6. **Health of Others** Read about a famous person who died from a drug overdose. Find out how the person's lifestyle and habits led to his or her death. Explain what you learned from the incident. Write a report on your findings.

Lesson 3

Marijuana and Other Illegal Drugs

This lesson will help you find answers to questions that teens often ask about street drugs. For example:

- **What are the side effects and risks of using marijuana?**
- **What are hallucinogens?**
- **What are the effects of using designer drugs and inhalants?**

Words to Know

hallucinogen
designer drugs
inhalant

Street Drugs

"If drugs do so much damage," some people have asked, "why not stop making them?" The answer is that many drugs have worthwhile uses. When drugs like morphine and Valium are used carefully and under a physician's supervision, they can help people who are ill or in severe pain.

Other drugs, however, have limited—if any—medical benefits. They are commonly abused and traded on the streets. These drugs are dangerous and illegal. Anyone who uses or sells them can be fined or sent to jail for a long time.

in your journal

Imagine that you are asked to write a law that deals with users and sellers of illegal drugs. In your journal, write what the law would be and why you would write the law.

Marijuana

The most commonly used street drug today is *marijuana* (mehr·uh·WAHN·uh). Marijuana contains a number of different chemicals, including THC (tetrahydrocannabinol), its main mind-altering component. *Hashish,* a more powerful drug derived from the same plant, contains greater concentrations of THC. **Figure 15.10** provides information on marijuana.

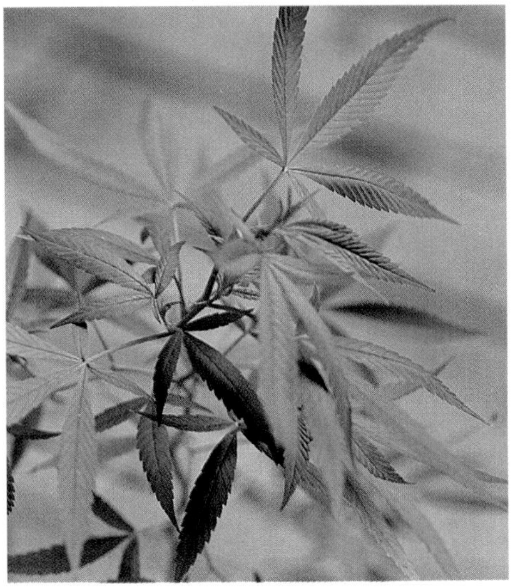

Figure 15.10
Marijuana

The common names for marijuana include pot, grass, weed, reefer, dope, joint, and mary jane.

Effects on the Body:
- Reduces memory, reaction time, and coordination
- Reduces initiative and ambition
- Increases heart rate and appetite, and lowers body temperature
- Damages heart and lungs
- Interferes with normal body development in teens by changing hormone levels
- May cause psychological dependence

Marijuana is usually smoked. Sometimes it is mixed with food and eaten. Although some people believe that smoking marijuana is safer than smoking tobacco, they are wrong. Marijuana contains as much as four to five times the amount of tar and other cancer-causing substances as tobacco.

The effects of marijuana are almost immediate, especially if a person smokes it. Most users feel mildly euphoric and relaxed, and they perceive sights and sounds more vividly. The exact effects of marijuana vary from person to person and are influenced by moods and surroundings.

Hallucinogens

Another group of street drugs is **hallucinogens** (huh·LOO·suhn·uh·jenz). These are *drugs that distort moods, thoughts, and senses.* Hallucinogens affect many parts of the body. Hallucinogens

- affect the cerebrum, the part of the brain that controls the intellect and perception.
- affect the nervous system.
- increase heart and respiratory rates.

Hallucinogens produce altered mental states that may last for several hours or several days. The effects are extremely unpredictable. Some people claim to have positive experiences, whereas others have very disturbing ones. Some people have even died while using hallucinogens because they believed they had super powers that enabled them to fly out of windows or walk on water.

PCP

Phencyclidine (fen·SI·kluh·deen), or PCP, is a powerful and dangerous hallucinogen whose effects last a long time. When the drug is used regularly, effects may come and go for as long as a year.

Many users have died from PCP. While overdoses of this synthetic drug can cause death, most deaths are a result of the strange, destructive behavior the drug produces in the user. **Figure 15.11** lists some of the dangerous effects of PCP.

- Common names are angel dust, lovely, love boat, hog, and super weed.
- Common forms are white powder, pills, capsules, and liquid.
- It may be swallowed, injected, or smoked when used with marijuana.
- It causes loss of coordination, as well as increases in heart rate, blood pressure, and body temperature.

Hallucinogens are dangerous substances that can seriously harm the body.

LSD

Another hallucinogen known by its initials is *LSD,* which is short for *lysergic* (luh·SER·jik) *acid diethylamide* (dy·e·thuh·LA·mid). LSD affects the areas of the brain that control vision and balance. This drug often distorts perceptions of sound and color. **Figure 15.11** shows how dangerous the effects of LSD are.

- Common names for LSD are acid, white lightning, sugar cubes, and microdots.
- Common forms are tablets, liquid, squares soaked on paper.
- It may be swallowed, licked, or put in with eye drops.
- It increases blood pressure and heart rate, and causes chills, nausea, tremors, and sleeplessness.

Did You Know?

A Bad Flashback ACTIVITY!

People who use hallucinogens are in danger of having flashbacks. During a flashback, the effects of the drug may recur days, months, or years after the drug was used. Write a paragraph to explain why you think this could harm someone.

Other Hallucinogens

The peyote cactus is found in northern Mexico and Texas. *Mescaline* is the hallucinogenic ingredient in peyote. Mescaline can also be synthetically produced and often comes in the form of brown disks, capsules, and tablets. The effects last 5 to 12 hours.

Psilocybin is the hallucinogenic ingredient that is found in the *Psilocybe mexicana* mushroom and a few other species of mushrooms. These mushrooms grow wild throughout the United States and other parts of the world. They are eaten in fresh or dried form, and their effects are felt for from 3 to 6 hours.

Designer Drugs

Designer drugs are *drugs that are made from chemicals that resemble illegal substances.* Street chemists make these drugs to avoid using illegal substances. *Ecstasy,* or MDMA, is one of the most popular designer drugs. The use of this drug can result in the destruction of brain cells.

Figure 15.11

Dangerous Hallucinogens

These drugs are so unpredictable that they are dangerous to try even once.

Drug	Dangerous Effects
PCP	• Convulsions, heart and lung failure, or broken blood vessels • Bizarre or violent behavior • Temporary psychosis • False feeling of having super powers
LSD	• Unpredictable behavior • Flashbacks • False feeling of having super powers

Personal Inventory

HOW DO YOU FEEL ABOUT DRUGS?

You have learned that many types of drugs are misused and abused. The harm they do to the mind and body may happen after just one use. For that reason, and because your life depends on staying drug free, it is important for you to examine your behaviors and attitudes toward drugs.

On a separate sheet of paper, write yes or no for each statement below. Your answers can help you determine if you need to change your behaviors or attitudes toward drugs. Total your number of "yes" responses. Compare your score with the ranking at the end of the survey.

1. I avoid any type of illegal drug use.
2. I never take medicine that is not prescribed for me.
3. My friends avoid illegal drugs.
4. If I find myself at a place where people are using drugs, I leave.
5. I have never gotten into a car that was driven by someone whom I knew was under the influence of drugs.
6. I believe that using illegal drugs will harm my mind and body.
7. I do not like the thought of losing control of my thoughts or senses.
8. I think that people who use drugs are not smart.
9. I do not think I would enjoy the experience of getting high.
10. I believe that using illegal drugs once could ruin my life.

Give yourself 1 point for a yes. A score of 9–10 is very good. A score of 7–8 is good. A score of 5–6 is fair. If you score below 5, you need to look seriously at changing your behaviors (numbers 1–5) or attitudes (numbers 6–10). Your life may depend on it!

Inhalants

Anyone who uses or possesses drugs faces stiff fines and penalties, as well as having a criminal record.

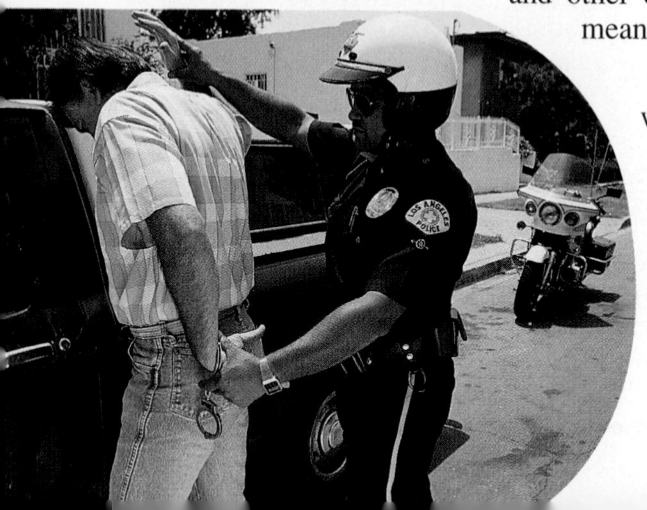

Inhalants (in·HAY·luhnts) are *substances whose fumes are sniffed and inhaled to give a hallucinogeniclike high.* Inhalants include solvents and aerosols, such as glue, spray paints, gasoline, and other equally harmful substances. These substances are not meant to be taken into the body.

Inhalants also include *nitrites* and *nitrous oxide,* which are substances that have medicinal uses. *Amyl nitrite* is a prescription drug used to control *angina* (heart pain). It is a clear yellowish liquid that comes in ampules. When used illegally, the ampules are broken, and the fumes are inhaled. Nitrous oxide, which is sometimes called laughing gas, is used by dentists as an anesthetic. It is also used by manufacturers as a propellant in canned whipped cream.

Talking to young children about the dangers of drugs is one way to work to prevent drug abuse.

When inhalants are taken into the body, their harmful fumes go directly to the brain causing mental confusion, dizziness, lack of coordination, and hallucinations. Damage to the kidneys and liver is also common. Even worse, the fumes can kill brain cells and cause permanent brain damage or death.

Drug Awareness Programs

Drug use affects almost everyone. Consider the effect drug use has on crimes, accidents, and the rising costs of treatment. Drug use is a problem that takes its toll on society as a whole.

You can be part of the solution instead of part of the problem. You can work together with adults and other teens in your community to promote drug awareness. Your program could be targeted toward teaching younger children about the dangers of drugs. Your community would be a better place as a result of your efforts.

Review Lesson 3

Using complete sentences, answer the following questions on a separate sheet of paper.

Reviewing Terms and Facts

1. **Vocabulary** Which of the following drugs distort people's senses: *hallucinogens, designer drugs, inhalants?* List some specific drugs that appear in each category.
2. **Explain** Why have designer drugs come into being?

Thinking Critically

3. **Analyze** Why is marijuana more dangerous for a teenager than it is for an adult?
4. **Synthesize** How can the feeling of having super powers make the use of PCP and LSD dangerous?

Applying Health Concepts

5. **Personal Health** Prepare a chart showing the risks marijuana poses to various body systems, such as the lungs, brain, and the immune system. Use library resources to find out what is currently known and being researched about marijuana and each body system.
6. **Health of Others** Design an advertisement for a teen magazine, warning readers about the dangers of using inhalants.

TEEN HEALTH DIGEST

Sports and Recreation

Doping = Death

The Olympics are probably the most competitive sports events in the world. Some athletes will do anything to win—including using illegal drugs such as steroids. The use of these drugs is called "doping."

The International Olympic Committee condemns doping in the strongest possible terms. Juan Samaranch, president of the committee, says that doping is "akin to death." He points out that it may cause physical death. He also says that doping results in "spiritual, emotional . . . and moral" death because cheating is harmful to a person's character.

When an Olympic competitor is found guilty of doping, he or she is banned from participating in any future Olympic Games. For example, when Ben Johnson, the 1988 gold medal winner of the 100-meter race, tested positive for steroids, he was stripped of his medal and permanently banned from the Olympics.

Try This: *Write an essay about how you think using illegal drugs may have affected the lives of Olympic and/or professional athletes. Be sure to discuss the effect the drugs could have had on each side of their health triangle.*

Myths and Realities

Hee-hee-helium?

Have you ever been at a party where someone inhaled helium from a balloon and talked in a squeaky, cartoon-character voice? At the very least, it's a silly way to get a laugh. At worst, if you're not careful, it could be a life-threatening stunt.

The Annals of Emergency Medicine tell of one 13-year-old boy who was rushed to the hospital after inhaling helium directly from a pressurized tank. The boy had suffered a stroke caused by gas bubbles in his bloodstream. He also had lung damage caused by rapid lung expansion.

"Normally, inhaling helium from a balloon doesn't cause problems," wrote one doctor. "But inhaling anything from a *pressurized tank* not meant to be used on people can be potentially lethal."

CON$UMER FOCU$

Speak Up!

An FDA study found that most people never ask questions about medicines that are prescribed for them. The American Pharmaceutical Association recommends that patients ask questions about their medicines, such as:

- What is the medication supposed to do?
- Can the medicine cause an allergic reaction?
- Should I avoid certain foods or activities while taking it?
- What should I do if I forget to take the medicine?

It is also a good idea to get your medicines from the same pharmacy every time. The pharmacy can keep track of all the medicines prescribed for one person and thus help the person avoid side effects or dangerous combinations of medicines.

Try This: *Give a copy of these questions to parents or guardians. Together, brainstorm other questions to add to the list. Suggest that they carry a copy of the questions with them on their next visit to a doctor or pharmacist.*

HEALTH UPDATE

Dopamine and Addiction

Scientists believe that they have uncovered the secret to many addictions—including alcoholism, drug abuse, and smoking. What's the key? A natural chemical in the human brain called dopamine.

Dopamine regulates the pleasure centers of the brain. Certain chemicals, like alcohol or nicotine, affect the brain's production of dopamine. An addict's brain becomes used to high levels of dopamine. As a result, addicts need to have the chemical constantly—be it nicotine, alcohol, or the active ingredient in any other drug—just to feel normal.

The bottom line: Don't "short circuit" your brain's chemistry with drugs.

People at Work

Pharmacist

Name: Miranda Ramirez

Education: Miranda is a graduate of a college of pharmacology. She completed a five-year program for a bachelor of science degree in pharmacy and a supervised one-year internship with a pharmacist. She studied chemistry, biology, and mathematics.

Job: Miranda prepares and distributes prescription medicines. She works in a pharmacy in a suburb outside a large city. Miranda fills prescriptions written by doctors and dentists, prepares the labels (including directions) for medicine containers, answers her customers' questions, and prepares some medications herself.

Quote: "My job is really rewarding. I like knowing that I am helping people to maintain their health."

Lesson 4

Choosing to Be Drug Free

This lesson will help you find answers to questions that teens often ask about ways to remain drug free. For example:

- **How can I say no when offered drugs?**
- **What are some reasons for remaining drug free?**
- **What are some places where people with drug problems can turn for help?**

Words to Know

anabolic steroids
detoxification

Avoiding Drugs

You have a responsibility to yourself to be the healthiest person you can be. With that responsibility comes the right to make choices. You have learned how dangerous drugs are and that drugs can harm your mind and body. You know that avoiding drugs is the right decision to make for your health. **Figure 15.12** illustrates drug use among high school seniors from 1979 through 1995. The decision is yours, but avoiding drugs is the only sure way to avoid becoming "hooked" on drugs.

Figure 15.12

Changes in Use of Illegal Drugs Among High School Seniors

Some young people continue to experiment out of curiosity or because they do not understand the risks they take when they use drugs.

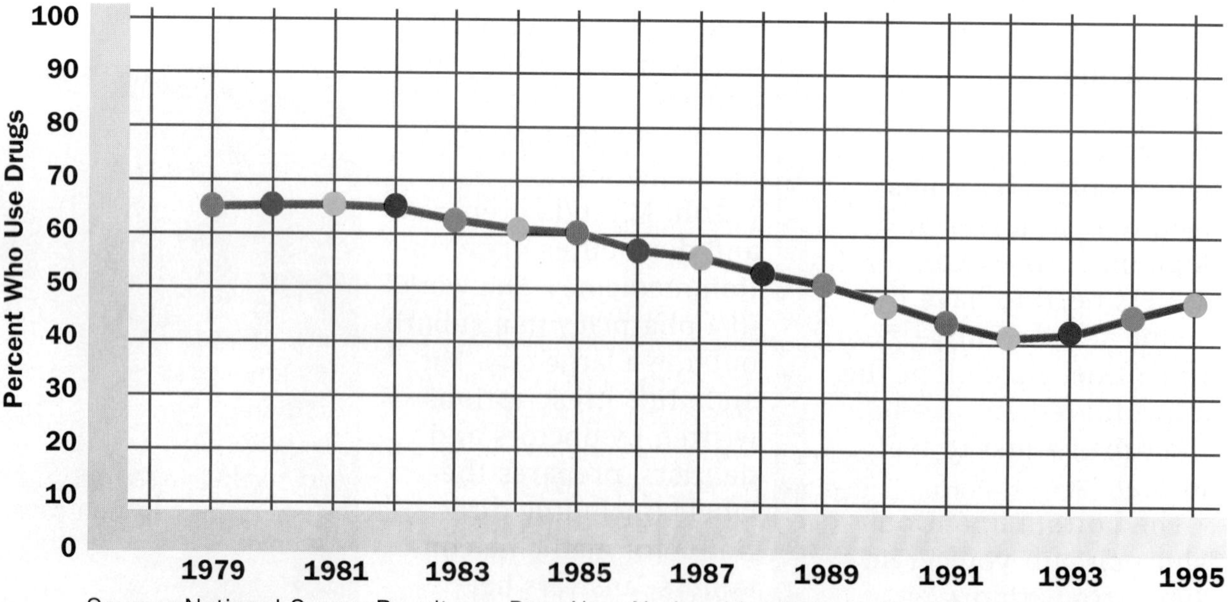

Source: National Survey Results on Drug Use, National Institute on Drug Abuse, 1996

Reasons to Be Drug Free

- You will have better concentration and memory.
- You will have more natural energy.
- You will be in control of your feelings and actions.
- You will make better decisions.
- You will not impair your judgment and do something that you will regret.
- You will not be breaking the law or causing yourself legal difficulties for years to come.
- You will be able to focus on improving your talents and enjoying your interests.
- You will not ruin your mind or body, or your future.
- You will not harm yourself or others as a result of drugs.
- You will not waste money on drugs.
- You will not be afraid of possible flashbacks for years to come.
- You respect yourself too much to take drugs.

There are many reasons to choose to be drug free.

Athletes and Drugs

Some athletes take drugs illegally because they mistakenly believe that drugs can improve their performance. Athletes may take **anabolic** (a·nuh·BAH·lik) **steroids** (STIR·oydz), *synthetic derivatives of testosterone.* They may also take amphetamines or cocaine. They use the steroids to make their muscles bigger and stronger, and the amphetamines and cocaine to give them extra energy. They believe these drugs will increase their speed and endurance. All of these drugs harm their bodies in the long run, and the costs greatly outweigh any short-term benefits.

Furthermore, these drugs—and many others—are banned by many groups that oversee athletics. Users may even sacrifice their careers. Many national and international bodies governing different sports, such as the International Olympic Committee (IOC), have established strict rules on the kinds of drugs that competitors cannot use. The National Collegiate Athletic Association (NCAA) tests athletes for these drugs. Professional sports leagues help athletes recover from drug addictions, but if the athlete cannot kick a habit, he or she may be banned from playing in the league for a long time or even permanently.

Your Total Health

Drug Abuse and Sex

A government study of young adults found that, while abusing drugs or alcohol, teens are often put in situations in which they engage in sex when they do not want to. Such behavior puts them at greater risk of pregnancy and exposure to sexually transmitted diseases, including HIV/AIDS.

Kicking the Habit

Kicking the drug habit is a lot harder than resisting pressure to start. The first step is for the drug abuser to recognize that a problem exists. From there, the road to recovery is an uphill one. If a user has become physically or psychologically addicted to a drug, then recovery involves withdrawal.

Withdrawal is usually a painful process and medications are given to ease the withdrawal symptoms. In addition to ridding one's body of the addictive substance, the recovering drug user must change his or her thinking and habits that led to the drug use. Although withdrawing from drugs is tough work, the benefits of becoming drug free are well worth the effort.

in your journal

Have you ever been in a situation in which you were pressured to take drugs? In your private journal, describe how you handled the situation. If you have never been in such a situation, imagine how you would handle pressure from a peer to try marijuana.

Getting Help

Drug abusers cannot recover from addiction on their own. They need help to recover. Most communities have a variety of treatment and support programs for drug addiction. The key is to find one that is right for the abuser. A good drug treatment program should have trained experts who provide education and support, and who help the abuser through the withdrawal period. This often requires **detoxification** (dee·tahk·si·fi·KAY·shuhn), *the physical process of freeing the body of an addictive substance.* "Detox" also involves helping the abuser overcome psychological dependence on the substance and regain health. Some programs include family members in the recovery process.

LIFE SKILLS

How to Avoid Using Drugs

Teens often say that they tried drugs because they felt pressured by friends or people they respected. You need to be ready in case you feel pressured. The way to do that is to develop ways to deal with that pressure ahead of time.

The first way to avoid drugs is through your actions. Choose friends who do not use or approve of drugs. They will support you in your decision to remain drug free.

It is important that you and your friends stay away from situations in which people might have or use drugs. For example, if you know that the party you were invited to on Saturday night will not have a parent or adult present, do not attend.

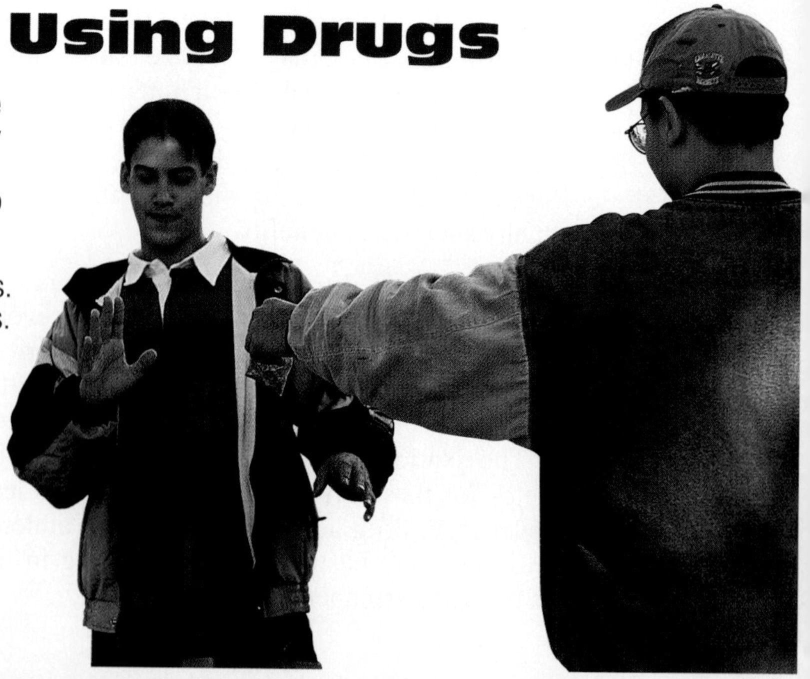

Where to Go for Help

Counseling

Young people can start to get help by speaking to a parent, teacher, school counselor, or peer counselor—someone with whom they feel comfortable talking. They also could call one of the toll-free drug and alcohol hot lines or a drug and alcohol treatment center to find a counselor.

Support Groups

A support group is a group of people who share a common problem and work together to help one another cope and recover. Support groups are the most popular form of treatment for addictions. They provide the critical support that recovering addicts need to remain drug free.

Common support groups for drug addiction are Narcotics Anonymous, Cocaine Anonymous, and Nar-Anon, which provides help for those who have been affected by someone else's drug use. Support groups are usually confidential and free. Other support groups are listed in your local telephone directory.

Support groups work together to help one another cope with and recover from their addictions.

If you are at someone's house or at a party where people begin using drugs, leave. That is the best way to avoid being pressured to take drugs. It is also a good idea to leave because people on drugs can be violent and dangerous. Also, because drug use is illegal, they may be arrested!

The second way to avoid drugs is through your words. Sometimes all you have to do is say no once. At other times, you might have to say no repeatedly.

You may find it easier to avoid drugs if you explain your reasons. For example, you might say, "Drugs are not good for me. I need all my strength to run track." You could also say, "If you were really my friend, you'd stop giving me a hard time." Do not be afraid to challenge people who are pressuring you by saying something such as "If you are really my friend, why are you trying to get me to do something that may hurt me?"

Finally, in some situations, there will be no easy way to get away from the pressure to do drugs. At those times, the best thing to say is "So long. I'll see you later."

Follow-up Activities

1. Review the suggestions for avoiding using drugs. Think of other ways and discuss them.
2. Illustrate your ideas in a brochure that you could share with younger students.

Did You Know?

Is Prohibition the Answer? ACTIVITY!

Many people believe that a more effective way to reduce the use of mind-altering drugs is to reduce the supply of these drugs. Some people believe that the United States should put pressure on foreign governments to eliminate drug-producing industries in their countries. Others believe that international drug traffickers who are captured should be turned over to the United States and tried, to ensure that they receive the maximum punishment.

Debate the following question in class: Which do you think is more effective—reducing the supply of drugs or reducing the demand for drugs through prevention and treatment efforts?

Alcohol and Drug Treatment Centers

There are a variety of centers available to help people who want to recover from drug abuse. These centers offer a wide range of services. **Figure 15.13** describes many of these services.

Figure 15.13

Specific Types of Treatment Centers

Type of Program	Description
Detox Units	These are located in hospitals and treatment centers. Alcohol and drug addicts remain under a doctor's care while being given medication to ease withdrawal symptoms.
Inpatient Treatment Centers	These are places where people stay for a month or more to fully concentrate on recovering from their drug problems.
Outpatient Treatment Centers	These are places where people get treatment for a few hours a day and then return to their homes and regular surroundings.
Continuing Programs	These are long-term support programs that are available to people who have gone through the standard short-term programs.
Halfway Houses	These are places where people who are recovering from addictions are offered housing, counseling, and support meetings. They learn the coping and living skills that they will need when they return to their regular lives.

Teen Issues

Where to Call ACTIVITY!

Check your telephone directory for toll-free hot lines that are available for people who have questions about drug abuse.

Living Drug Free

When you choose to live your life drug free, you will find that there are many exciting ways to spend your time. The alternatives to using drugs are limited only by your energy and imagination. Why don't you get started by trying some of the suggestions listed below and on the next page?

If you are lonely, depressed, or bored:

- Learn a new sport.
- Join a club.
- Start a physical fitness program.
- Volunteer to help needy people in your community.
- Exercise regularly.
- Get involved in something new that energizes you.

If you want to do something adventurous:

- Take up an exciting sport or hobby like rock climbing, fencing, or white-water rafting.
- Read about adventurous activities you would like to pursue like skydiving or parasailing.
- Learn about far-off places that sound exciting, and plan a trip for the future.

If you are looking for excitement or adventure, try a new sport, hobby, or activity instead of trying drugs.

If you need help solving personal problems:

- Talk to someone you trust and admire.
- Contact a hot line or support group.
- Read books about handling a problem such as yours.

If you are tense and anxious:

- Learn relaxation techniques.
- Get plenty of exercise.
- Do not overschedule yourself.
- Get enough rest and eat properly.

Review Lesson 4

Using complete sentences, answer the following questions on a separate sheet of paper.

Reviewing Terms and Facts

1. **Vocabulary** When does *detoxification* occur? Explain the process.
2. **Give Examples** What might you suggest to a friend who asks your advice on where to go for a drug problem that he or she has?

Thinking Critically

3. **Hypothesize** Why do you think many teens have decided to remain drug free?

Applying Health Concepts

4. **Personal Health** With a partner, role-play a situation in which you need to deal with pressure to use drugs. You might use some of the techniques discussed in this lesson.
5. **Health of Others** Find newspaper and magazine articles that deal with athletes who have problems with drugs. Choose one and write a report that tells about the athlete's problem and what was done to help him or her overcome it.

Chapter 15 Review

Chapter Summary

- **Lesson 1** Medicines are drugs that are used to treat or prevent diseases and other conditions and to relieve pain. It is important to use all medications correctly and be aware of possible side effects.
- **Lesson 2** Stimulants are drugs that speed up body functions. Depressants slow down body functions and reactions. Narcotics are specific drugs, obtainable only by prescription, that are used to relieve pain. Stimulants, depressants, and narcotics can be addictive. Some forms of these drugs are legal but should be taken only if prescribed by a doctor.
- **Lesson 3** Marijuana is the most commonly used street drug today. Other types of illegal drugs include hallucinogens, designer drugs, and inhalants.
- **Lesson 4** The choice to be drug free is important to your health. Recovering from drug addiction is a difficult process that may involve going through withdrawal. Counseling and support groups help recovering addicts stay drug free.

Reviewing Key Terms and Concepts

Using complete sentences, answer the following questions on a separate sheet of paper.

Lesson 1

1. Define the terms *drugs, medicine, side effect,* and *tolerance.*
2. List three rules for using medicine safely.

Lesson 2

3. List two ways in which drugs are misused.
4. What type of drugs stimulates the central nervous system? What type relieves pain?

Lesson 3

5. Why are hallucinogens so dangerous?
6. Define *designer drug* and *inhalant.*

Lesson 4

7. What are *anabolic steroids?* Who typically uses them, and why?
8. What is Nar-Anon? What is a halfway house?

Thinking Critically

Using complete sentences, answer the following questions on a separate sheet of paper.

9. **Suggest** Give three examples to show how reading the label of an over-the-counter medicine can help you use it safely.
10. **Predict** How might the use of heroin affect a person's life?
11. **Evaluate** Why is it dangerous to ride in a car with a driver who has been smoking marijuana?
12. **Analyze** Why does recovery from drug addiction involve more than physically withdrawing from the drug?

Chapter 15 Review

Your Action Plan

There are many reasons to remain or become drug free. Review your journal entries for this chapter about ways to avoid drugs. Then make an action plan.

Step 1 Write down a long-term goal that will help you remain drug free. One goal could be to find healthy alternatives to using drugs.

Step 2 Select and write down several short-term goals that will help you reach your long-term goal. If your long-term goal is to find alternatives to drug use, a short-term goal might be to become involved in an after-school activity.

Step 3 Plan a schedule for reaching each short-term goal. For example, you might give yourself one week to select an after-school club to join.

Step 4 Check your schedule periodically to keep yourself on track.

When you reach your long-term goal, reward yourself. You are on your way to a drug-free, more confident, healthier life.

In Your Home and Community

1. **Health of Others** What drugs are currently of concern to the police? Are these the same drugs they were concerned about five years ago? Call your local police department to obtain these facts, and make a graph that shows the changes in your community, over a five-year period, in the use of some of the drugs mentioned in the chapter.
2. **Community Resources** Look in your local phone book or ask your school health office for programs that seek to encourage students to remain drug free. Collect information about at least three programs. Present the information you gathered and your conclusions to your class.

Building Your Portfolio

1. **Drug Tests** Find out how athletes and employees of some companies are tested for drug use. Find out whether athletes in your school district are tested for drugs. Write up your findings and opinion about the issue.
2. **Personal Assessment** Look through all the activities and projects you did for this chapter. Choose one or two that you would like to include in your portfolio.

Unit 6
Safety and the Environment

Chapter 16

Safety

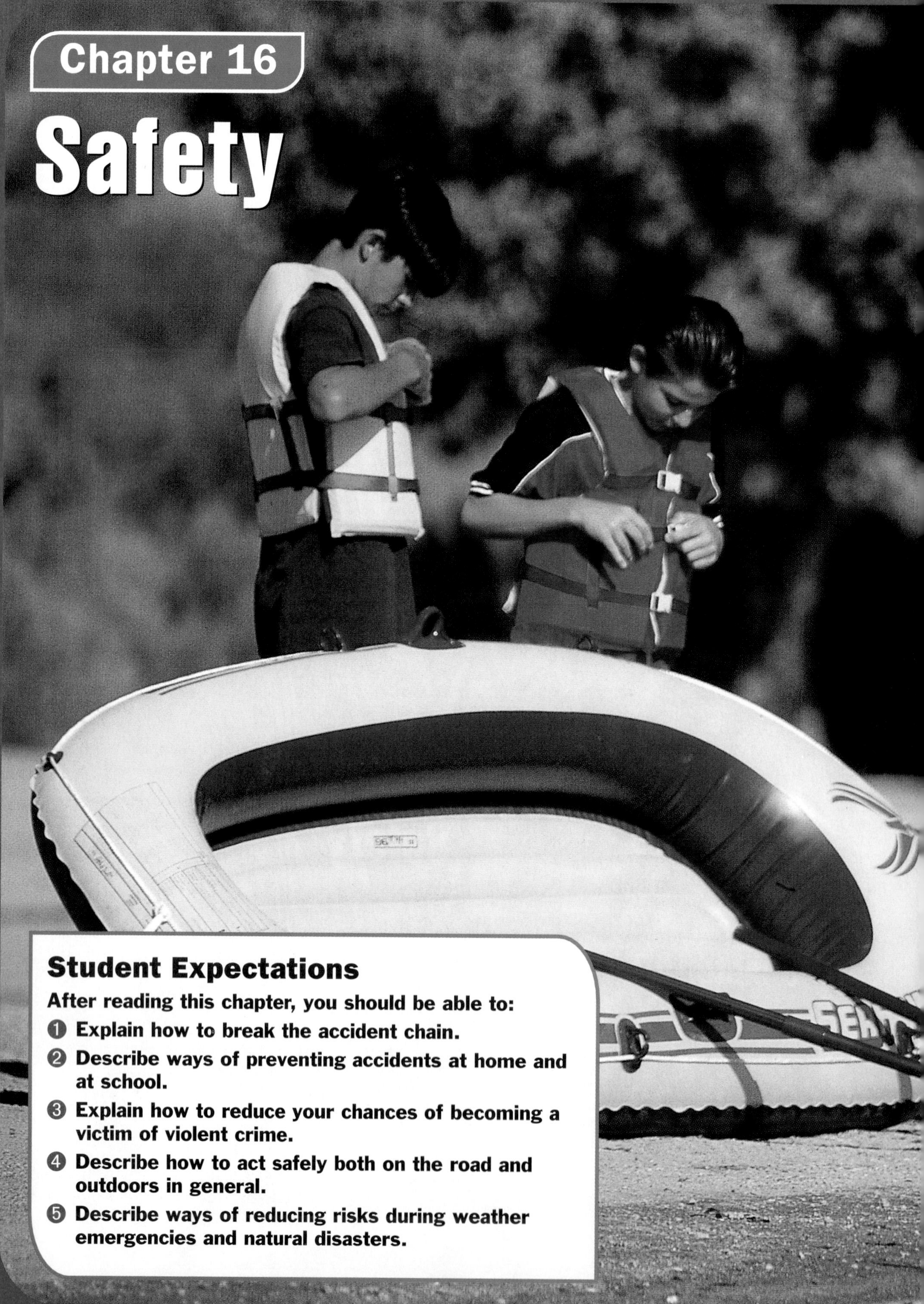

Student Expectations

After reading this chapter, you should be able to:

1. **Explain how to break the accident chain.**
2. **Describe ways of preventing accidents at home and at school.**
3. **Explain how to reduce your chances of becoming a victim of violent crime.**
4. **Describe how to act safely both on the road and outdoors in general.**
5. **Describe ways of reducing risks during weather emergencies and natural disasters.**

Teen Chat Group

Jillian: Rick, you should put on your life jacket before we get in the boat.

Rick: What's the big deal? I know how to swim.

Phillip: The instructor is right Rick. It's better to be safe. Remember what happened to my friend Nicole?

Rick: No. What happened to her?

Phillip: Her boat tipped over in the middle of the lake. Nicole wasn't wearing her life jacket, though. She thought she could swim to shore, but she started to feel really tired before she got there.

Rick: Then what happened? Did she make it?

Phillip: She was really lucky. Some people in another boat rescued her. Otherwise, she might have drowned.

Jillian: Phillip's right Rick. We don't want anything like that to happen to you. Don't forget to fasten the life jacket straps after you put it on.

in your journal

Read the dialogue on this page. Do you always observe safety rules? Start your private journal entries on safety by answering these questions:

- How would you convince Rick that he should wear his life jacket?
- What do you think are the greatest dangers to your own safety?
- What actions do you take to reduce your risk of injury from the dangers around you?

When you reach the end of the chapter, you will use your journal entries to make an action plan.

Lesson 1

Building Safe Habits

This lesson will help you find answers to questions that teens often ask about safety. For example:

- **Why do accidents happen?**
- **How can I avoid being injured?**
- **How can I have fun with my friends and still "play it safe"?**

Words to Know

safety conscious
accident chain

The Importance of Safety

No doubt you learned many safety rules when you were a small child: don't play with matches, and look both ways before you cross the street. You probably know these rules by heart. However just knowing the rules isn't enough to keep you safe. You also need to be **safety conscious,** which means *being aware that safety is important and always acting safely.*

Accidents are a major cause of death among young people as shown in **Figure 16.1.** Although many accidents that young people have are not fatal, they can cause serious problems.

In 1995 there were about 105,000 reported emergency room visits for injuries from in-line skating, one of the fastest-growing sports in the United States. These injuries range from minor scrapes and bruises to fractures, dislocated joints, concussions, skull fractures, and brain injuries.

Figure 16.1
Causes of Death Among Young People, Ages 15–24
Accidents are a major cause of death among young people. Acting safely helps prevent accidents and needless deaths.

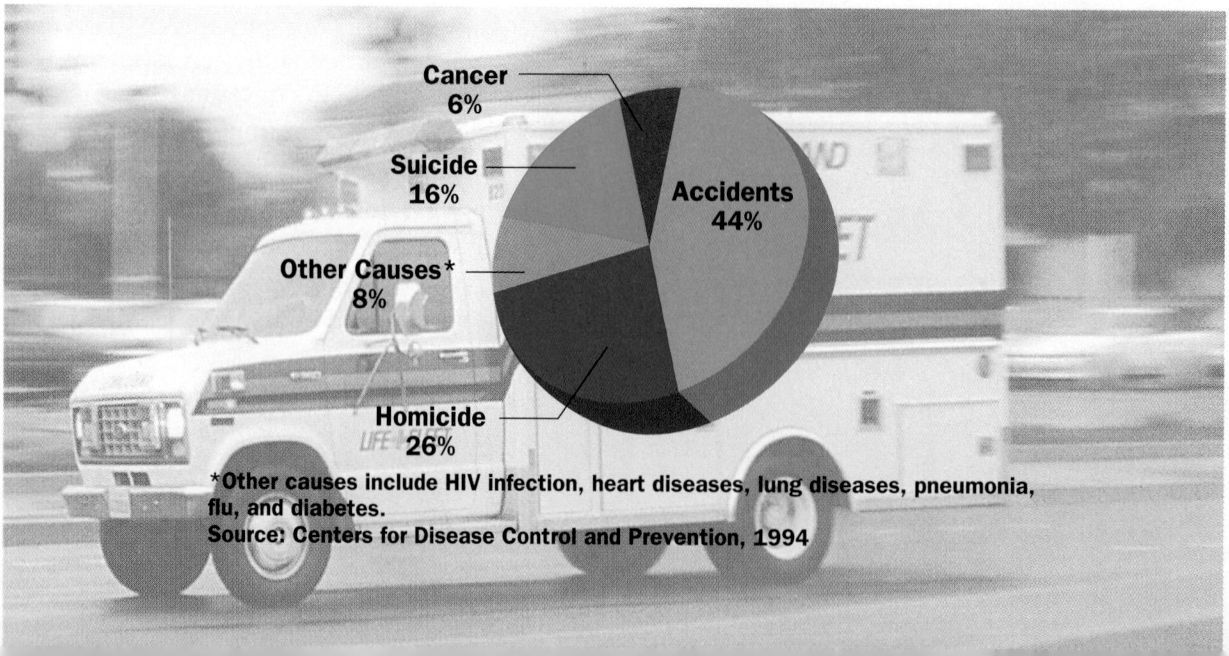

*Other causes include HIV infection, heart diseases, lung diseases, pneumonia, flu, and diabetes.
Source: Centers for Disease Control and Prevention, 1994

Acting Safely

An important part of acting safely means not taking needless risks. Risks—the chances that something harmful may occur—are all around us. When you walk in the woods, you risk touching poison ivy. When you cross a street, you risk being hit by a car. Avoiding such risks doesn't mean staying out of the woods or off the streets. It means learning to spot poison ivy and staying away from it. Avoiding risks means waiting for the light to change and looking both ways before you step off the curb. Study **Figure 16.2.** Do you follow these safety guidelines when riding a bicycle?

The greatest risk comes from being careless. To act safely, follow these guidelines. Your life may depend on it.

- **Resist peer pressure.** You may know that riding in the back of a pickup truck or diving into unknown water is dangerous, but when your friends try to talk you into taking such risks, it may be difficult to resist the pressure. Remember, resisting peer pressure takes strength and courage, too.
- **Always concentrate on what you are doing.** If you don't, you increase your chances of having an accident. Be extra careful when you are tired, excited, upset, depressed, or in a hurry. These are the times when accidents are most likely to occur.
- **Know your limits.** Don't try dangerous activities that you aren't prepared for. For example, stay off the toughest ski slope when you are just learning how to ski, and don't swim farther out in the lake than you can manage comfortably. Staying within your limits is not being cowardly—it's being smart.
- **Be prepared.** Think about the possible risks that a situation may pose *before* it's too late. If you're walking home at night, plan to use a well-lighted route. Being prepared also means using the proper safety equipment, such as a bicycle helmet, and using the equipment the way it was meant to be used.

interNET CONNECTION

Download more tips to keep you safe and help you prepare for weather emergencies.

http://www.glencoe.com/sec/health

in your journal

In your private journal, describe a real or imagined accident. Describe what led up to the injury. Then describe how the event could have been avoided by interrupting each link in the chain.

Figure 16.2

How to Act Safely

Following certain guidelines can help you be safe. How can these guidelines help you play your favorite sport safely?

A Resist peer pressure. Don't ride into oncoming traffic even if your friends do.

B Concentrate. Be aware of the traffic around you.

C Know your limits. Stay within a comfortable riding distance.

D Be prepared. Wear protective gear.

Figure 16.3
How to Break the Accident Chain
In many cases, accidents can be prevented by just being more careful.

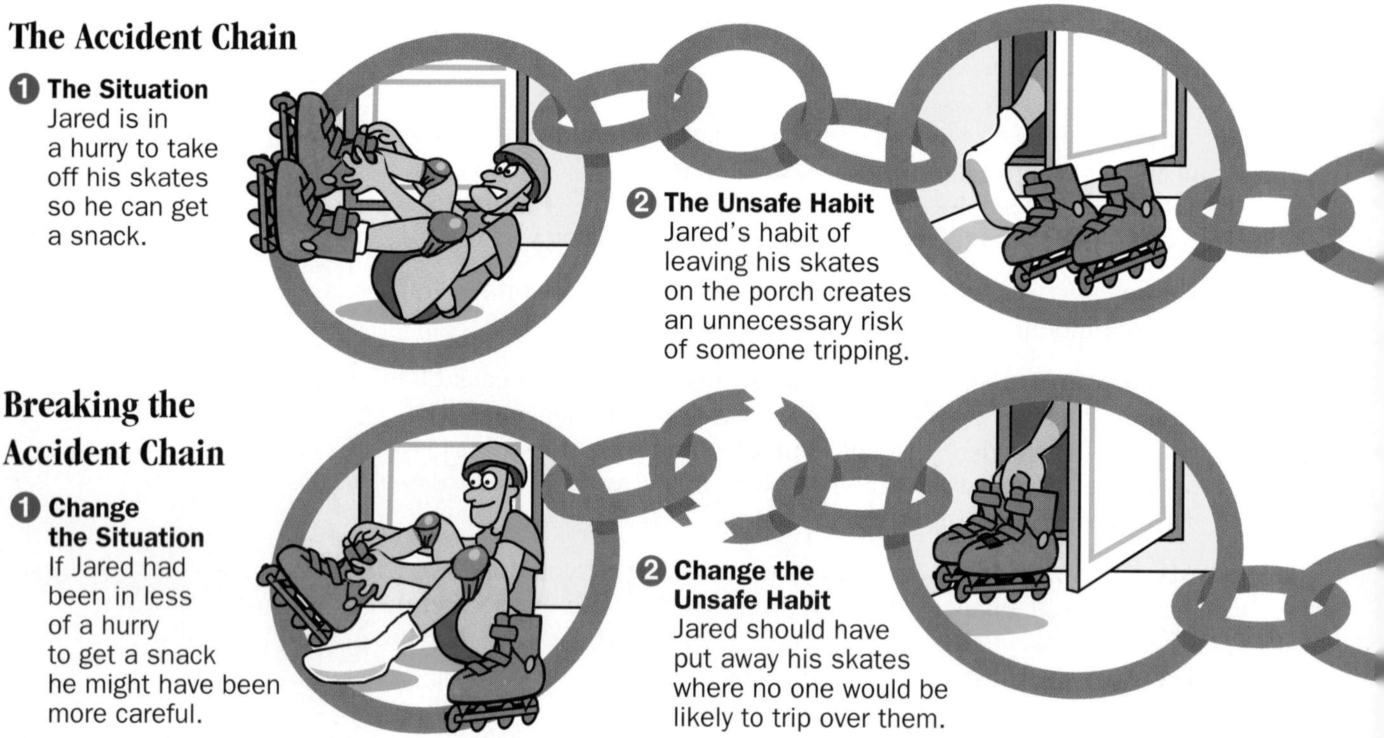

The Accident Chain
1 The Situation
Jared is in a hurry to take off his skates so he can get a snack.
2 The Unsafe Habit
Jared's habit of leaving his skates on the porch creates an unnecessary risk of someone tripping.
Breaking the Accident Chain
1 Change the Situation
If Jared had been in less of a hurry to get a snack he might have been more careful.
2 Change the Unsafe Habit
Jared should have put away his skates where no one would be likely to trip over them.

To see what can happen when you take unnecessary risks, consider the case of Jared and his nine-year-old brother, Toby. In-line skating always makes Jared hungry. When he finishes skating, he sits on the front porch, removes his skates, and goes inside for a snack. Yesterday Toby ran out the front door just after Jared came in from skating. Jared's skates were on the porch as usual, and Toby tripped over them, landing on the sidewalk and badly scraping his face and chipping a tooth.

Injuries like Toby's don't just happen. They are the result of a pattern known as an **accident chain,** *a series of events that include a situation, an unsafe habit, and an unsafe action.*

Figure 16.3 shows how the accident chain applies to the case of Jared and Toby. The accident could have been prevented by breaking the chain. In fact, any accident can be prevented by interrupting the accident chain in one of the following three ways.

- Change the situation.
- Change the unsafe habit.
- Change the unsafe action.

If Jared and Toby had done any of those three things differently, they would have broken the accident chain and avoided the accident and the injury. Remember, when you act safely, you decrease the chance of accidents and injuries.

Your Total Health

Safety Gear Smarts ACTIVITY!

In 1996, 58,000 children went to hospital emergency rooms for in-line skating injuries. Visit a sporting goods store in your community. Evaluate the ways in which the store and manufacturers provide information to consumers about the importance of safety gear for in-line skating.

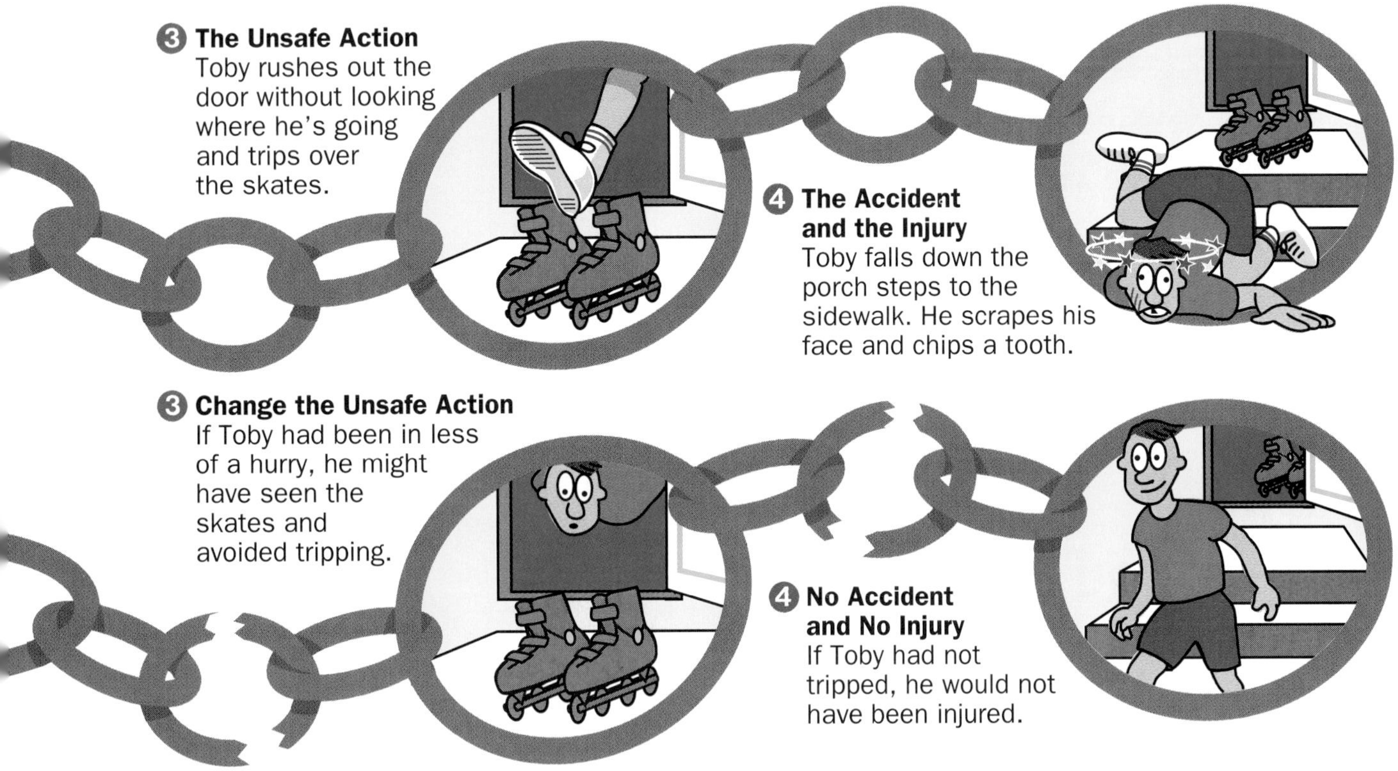

③ The Unsafe Action
Toby rushes out the door without looking where he's going and trips over the skates.
④ The Accident and the Injury
Toby falls down the porch steps to the sidewalk. He scrapes his face and chips a tooth.
③ Change the Unsafe Action
If Toby had been in less of a hurry, he might have seen the skates and avoided tripping.
④ No Accident and No Injury
If Toby had not tripped, he would not have been injured.

Review

Lesson 1

Using complete sentences, answer the following questions on a separate sheet of paper.

Reviewing Terms and Facts

1. **Vocabulary** Define *safety conscious.*
2. **List** What are the three elements of the accident chain?

Thinking Critically

3. **Explain** Why might just knowing safety rules not be enough to keep you safe?
4. **Analyze** Why do you think teens are especially likely to take unnecessary risks?
5. **Interpret** There is an old saying that states, "An ounce of prevention is worth a pound of cure." How does this relate to safety?

Applying Health Concepts

6. **Health of Others** Find a newspaper account or take notes on a television report of an accident. Break down the description of the accident into the parts of the accident chain. Show the accident chain in the form of a chart. At appropriate points in the chart, include brief descriptions of at least two ways in which the accident could have been prevented.
7. **Personal Health** Choose your favorite sport. Then make a list of the protective gear needed to participate safely in that activity. Post your list with those of your classmates as a reminder for everyone to dress properly for the activities they enjoy.

TEEN HEALTH DIGEST

Sports and Recreation

Darrell Green: Man With a Mission

They said that he was too small to succeed. Darrell Green, star defensive back of the Washington Redskins, has proved them wrong.

For more than 14 years, Green has been a star in the NFL. At the age of 37 he signed a contract with his team to play for another five years. He has also won the NFL Man of the Year Award for his accomplishments on and off the field.

Not only is Green a great athlete, but he also gives back to the community. He has formed the Darrell Green Foundation and Life Center in northwest Washington. The center provides teens with a place for safe, enjoyable, and healthy activities after school. Green also challenges students to make their parents and teachers their heroes and role models. "That's how you win the Super Bowl of your life," he says.

Personal Trainer

Caution: Concussions

A concussion occurs when the brain is slammed into the skull because of a severe blow to the head. Each year there are about 250,000 concussions suffered by football players alone. Sports doctors grade concussions on a scale of 0 to 4.

- *Grade 0–1:* A person is disoriented and has a headache.
- *Grade 2:* A person is disoriented, has blurred vision, or hears a ringing in his or her ears.
- *Grade 3:* A person is knocked unconscious for less than one minute.
- *Grade 4:* A person is knocked unconscious for one minute or more.

Concussions are serious! An athlete who has a grade 2 concussion should never return to the game or practice, and should not return to play at all until his or her symptoms have been gone for at least 24 hours. A more severe concussion requires medical treatment.

CON$UMER FOCU$

Keyboard Precautions

Do your hands, wrists, and arms ever feel sore after typing? You may be suffering from repetitive motion problems—physical problems caused by repeating the same motions over and over.

The next time you're at the keyboard, stop and do one of these exercises every half hour or so:

- *Wrist roll.* Make a fist and roll your entire hand—from the wrist —in one direction 15 times. Switch directions and do it again. Then open your hands, stretch your fingers, and roll your wrists.
- *Hand stretch.* Make a fist, then open your hand and extend your fingers as far as possible. Hold your fingers there for ten seconds, then relax. Repeat until your hands feel relaxed (five to ten times).

Myths and Realities

Always Go with the Flow

Are you with the traffic or against it? Some people who bicycle think that it is safer to ride against the flow of traffic—that is, facing the cars coming in their direction.

This is wrong! Bicyclists should always ride with the flow of traffic. If you ride into traffic, motorists can't predict what you will do, and they are more likely to collide with you.

When bicycling in traffic, remember to go with the flow and to obey the same signs, signals, and pavement markers as the motorists do.

People at Work

Water Safety Instructor

Do you like to swim? Check out your local YMCA, YWCA, or community pool. The chances are that they offer water safety instructor courses. You could turn your love of getting wet into a cool job.

Water safety instructors are trained at YMCAs and other local institutions. Most of them will also be trained as lifeguards. Instructors are taught a variety of swimming strokes as well as first-aid and lifesaving techniques.

To be a water safety instructor, you must usually be at least 17 years of age by the end of the instructor course. You must also complete certain prerequisites, such as tests of water safety and swimming skills. Some towns also offer water safety instructor aide courses. To be an aide and help out water safety instructors during swimming classes, the minimum age can be as young as 10!

Try This: *Call your local Red Cross chapter to see if water safety instructor aide courses are offered in your area. Ask what the requirements are to become an aide, and see if your skills could land you a job!*

Lesson 2

Acting Safely at Home and at School

This lesson will help you find answers to questions that teens often ask about safety at home and at school. For example:

- **What causes injuries at home and how can I avoid them?**
- **How can I keep safe at school?**

Words to Know

hazards
expiration date
smoke alarm

Safety at Home

You may think of your home as a happy and comfortable place. In reality, every home has many **hazards** (HAZ·erds), or *possible sources of harm.* Each year, hundreds of thousands of people are injured at home by such hazards as cleaning products, slippery bathtubs, and objects left on stairs. Like accidents in general, most injuries at home can be prevented.

Figure 16.4

Safety in the Home

Homes can be safe if people are careful to make them so. What are some ways of making a home safe?

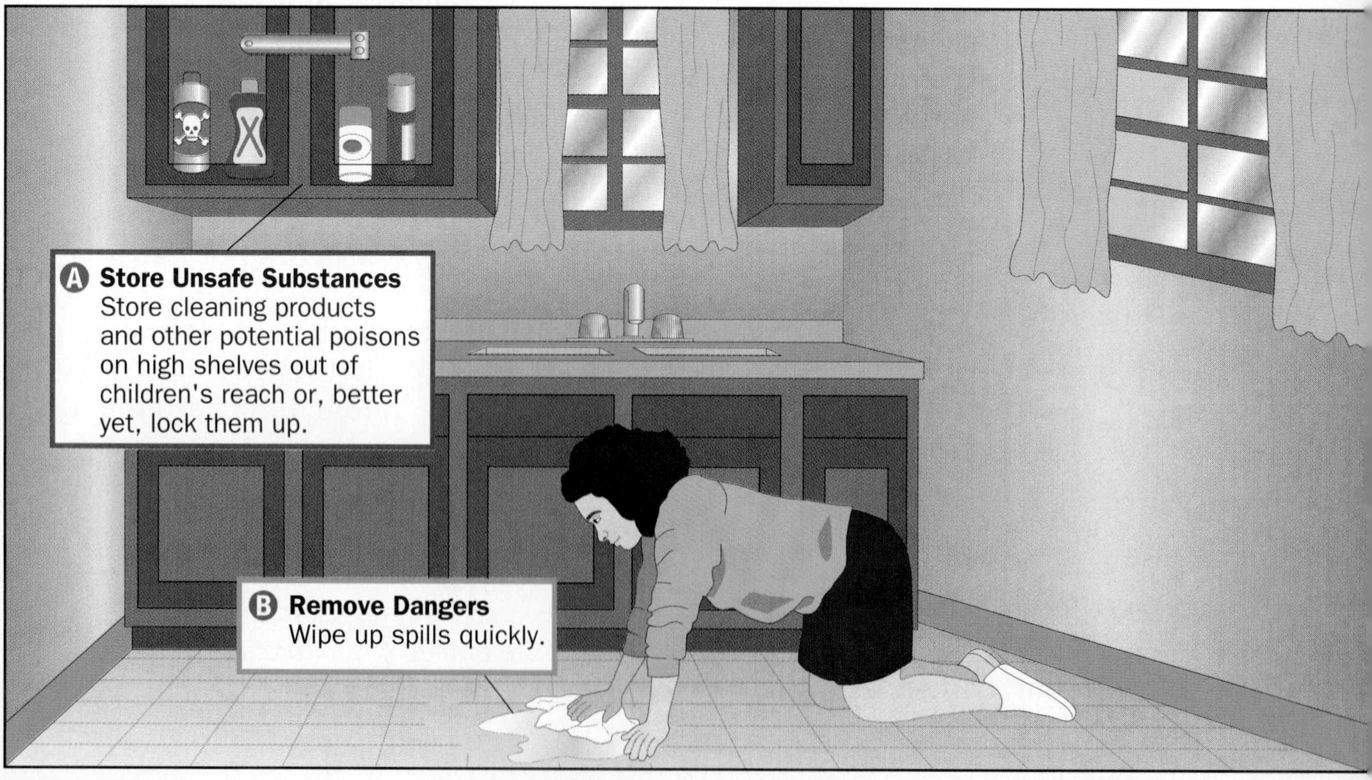

A Store Unsafe Substances
Store cleaning products and other potential poisons on high shelves out of children's reach or, better yet, lock them up.
B Remove Dangers
Wipe up spills quickly.

Preventing Falls

Falls are very common in the home and can lead to serious injuries. They occur most often in kitchens and bathrooms and on stairs. Falls account for many broken bones in older family members, whose bones may be brittle. Study **Figure 16.4.** In what two ways can falls be prevented?

Preventing Poisonings

Poisonings are a serious problem, especially for young children. Curious about everything but unable to read labels, toddlers and preschoolers may eat or drink toxic substances without knowing they are poisonous. Cleaning products and medicines are the most common causes of home poisonings. According to **Figure 16.4,** how can this type of poisoning be prevented?

Preventing Electrical Shocks

Electricity provides us with many of life's necessities, including heat and light. However, electricity can be deadly if misused. Most home electrical accidents involve problems with wires or outlets or misuse of electrical appliances. To prevent electrical shocks, never pull out a plug by its cord. Pull on the plug instead. Do not overload an outlet with too many cords. Make sure you keep electrical products away from water, and never use an electrical product when you are wet. Unplug appliances that are not working properly, and have them serviced.

in Your journal

Look through the kitchen and bathroom cabinets in your home. In your private journal, make a list of all the potentially dangerous substances you find. Are any of these stored within the reach of young children? If so, suggest better storage places for them.

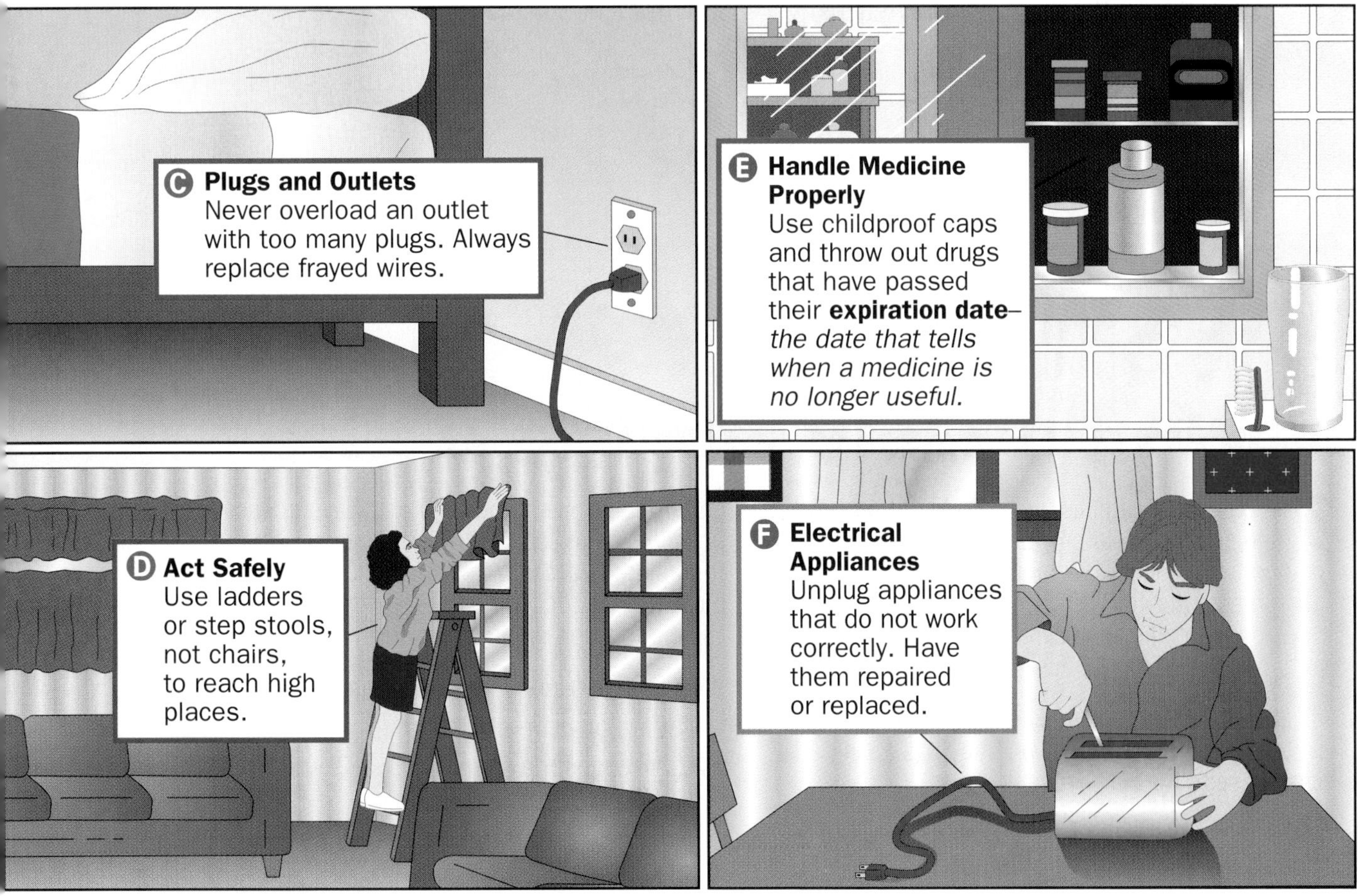

C Plugs and Outlets
Never overload an outlet with too many plugs. Always replace frayed wires.
E Handle Medicine Properly
Use childproof caps and throw out drugs that have passed their **expiration date**–*the date that tells when a medicine is no longer useful.*
D Act Safely
Use ladders or step stools, not chairs, to reach high places.
F Electrical Appliances
Unplug appliances that do not work correctly. Have them repaired or replaced.

Smoke alarms provide a warning system to alert your family in case of fire.

Fire Safety at Home

Fire needs three elements: fuel, heat, and air. Fuel can be stored rags, wood, gasoline, or paper. Heat may be a match, an electrical wire, or a cigarette. Oxygen in the air feeds the flames. These elements are found in most homes. To prevent most fires that occur at home, follow these simple rules:

- Keep stoves clean to avoid burns and grease fires when cooking.
- Make sure that electrical wires, outlets, and appliances are safe.
- Make sure that no one smokes in bed.
- Keep flammable objects at least 3 feet from a portable heater.
- Throw out old newspapers and other materials that burn easily.
- Use and store matches properly, and keep matches and cigarette lighters out of the reach of small children.

The most dangerous home fires are those that occur during the night when everyone is asleep. By installing smoke alarms in your home, your family can reduce the risk of injury from fire. A **smoke alarm,** or smoke detector, is *a device that makes a warning noise when it senses smoke.* The sound is loud enough to warn your family to move to safety, even if everyone is asleep. A smoke alarm should be installed on each level of your home, especially outside bedroom areas. Be sure to test the smoke alarm regularly and replace the battery if needed. Another important step in preparing for a fire is to plan a fire escape route and practice using it. Agree on a place where everyone will meet outside.

LIFE SKILLS

Acting Safely During a Fire

If your home catches fire, getting out quickly and safely should be your first priority. Most fatal home fires occur late at night, when it's easy to become confused. The best protection against confusion is to plan an escape route ahead of time and to practice using it often.

This exercise will help you develop a fire escape plan for your home. If your family already has a plan, use the exercise to try to improve that plan.

First, draw a floor plan of each level of your home. Include doors, hallways, and windows in your floor plan. Use arrows to point to two ways of escape, if possible, from each room in the house. Two escape routes are necessary in case one of the routes is blocked. A ladder or coil of rope is necessary for escape through upstairs windows.

Your escape plan should include these steps:

1. Turn on bedroom lights.
2. Arrange for a signal, such as a whistle, that will alert everyone to the fire.

What to Do if There Is a Fire

Even with safe practices, fire can occur. Your risk of injury from fire can be reduced if you know what to do when a fire does occur in your home. Here is what you should do.

- Leave the house quickly and call the fire department from a neighbor's house or a car phone.
- Never return to a burning house for any reason.
- Stay close to the floor so that you are below the smoke.
- Before opening a closed door, feel it to see if it is hot.
- If your clothing should catch fire, drop to the ground and roll around to put out the flames (see **Figure 16.5**).
- Leave firefighting to the experts; don't try it yourself.

Did You Know?

Kitchen Fires ACTIVITY!

Small kitchen fires are the only house fires that are safe to extinguish by yourself. Grease fires can usually be smothered by a metal lid or by baking soda. If your family has a fire extinguisher, learn how to use it.

Figure 16.5
Personal Fire Safety

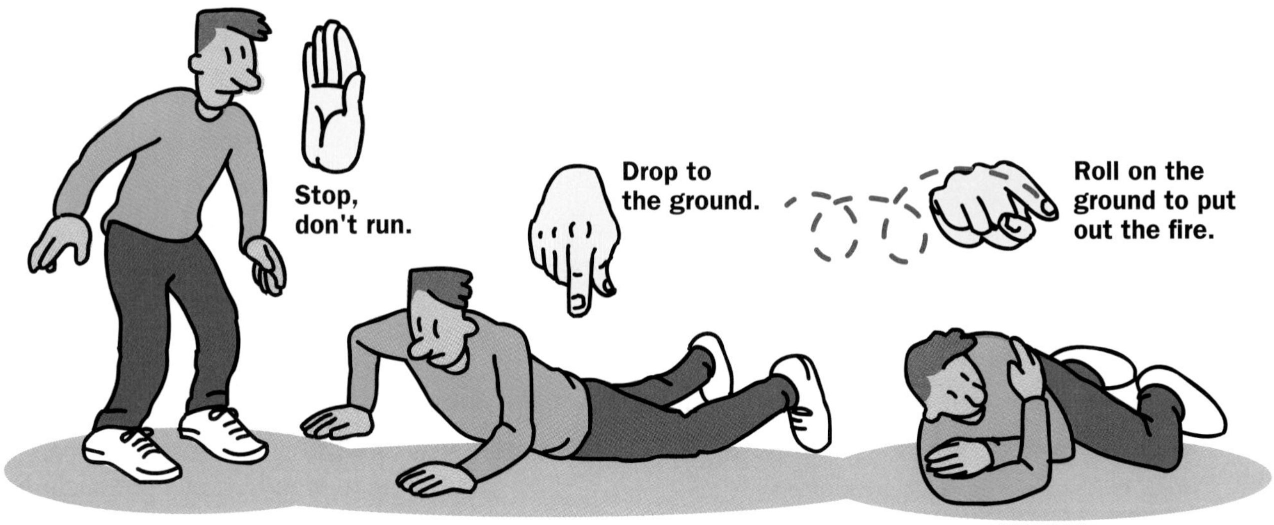
Stop, don't run.
Drop to the ground.
Roll on the ground to put out the fire.

3. Meet your family outside at a prearranged spot, and don't go back into the house.
4. Call the fire department from a neighbor's house or from a car phone.

Your plan also should include these safety tips for all the members of your family to follow:

1. When using your fire escape route, test closed doors for warmth before opening. If the doors are warm, do not open them. Use the alternate escape route.
2. Stay close to the floor in smoke-filled rooms. This will help you see better and will also help you have more oxygen for breathing.

Follow-up Activity

After making your escape plan, practice it with family members. Ask them for advice, and work together to improve the plan. Remember that the more you practice your escape plan, the greater the likelihood that you and your family will exit safely in the event of a real fire.

Safety at School

Safety is a concern in places where many people gather. Schools are such places, so they must meet certain safety standards.

Equally important for safety at school is the behavior of the students. The following list includes some of the ways in which students can help make school a safe place for themselves and others.

- **Industrial arts and family and consumer sciences classes.** Wear appropriate safety gear and follow your teacher's instructions carefully.
- **Physical education class and after-school sports.** Concentrate on what you and those around you are doing.
- **Science labs.** Use equipment and chemicals only as directed.
- **Hallway traffic.** Walk, don't run, in halls and locker rooms.

Lesson 2 Review

Using complete sentences, answer the following questions on a separate sheet of paper.

Reviewing Terms and Facts

1. **Vocabulary** Define *expiration date* and use the term in an original sentence.
2. **Give Examples** List some ways in which students can contribute to making their school a safe place.

Thinking Critically

3. **Explain** Why might cleaning products be hazardous in the home?
4. **Synthesize** How would you convince a younger brother or sister not to leave toys or other objects on the floor?
5. **Discuss** How do smoke alarms help make a house or an apartment safe?

Applying Health Concepts

6. **Health of Others** Take a survey of your home to identify potential hazards that could cause falls, poisonings, electrical shocks, or fires. Describe each hazard, the type of accident it could cause, and a plan to remove or reduce the potential danger. Share your survey with family members, and work together to put your plans into action to make your home safer.
7. **Health of Others** Ask a physical education, art, family and consumer sciences, or science teacher to identify the most important safety rule for his or her class. Then make a poster that states the rule and reminds students in the class to follow it. With the teacher's permission, display your poster in the room where the class meets.

Lesson 3

Violence Prevention

This lesson will help you find answers to questions that teens often ask about violence. For example:

- **Why is there so much violence in our country?**
- **How can I avoid becoming a victim of violent crime?**

Violence and Victims

Violence is a real problem in the United States. One murder, rape, assault, or armed robbery is committed every 18 seconds in this country. In 1995 an average of 60 murders a day were committed in the cities and towns of America.

Violence occurs in our schools as well. In 1995 almost 50,000 children brought a gun to school. In fact, nearly all crimes committed by teens are on the rise.

Several factors that contribute to the growing violence have been identified. Almost half of the violent crimes committed in this country involve drugs and alcohol. Other factors associated with violence include poverty, racial tension, possession of firearms, and the lack of economic opportunities.

Anyone can be a victim of a violent crime. For this reason, it is important to know what to do to prevent becoming a victim. Many acts of violence are not random acts. In fact, the victims of violence often know their attackers and may even have ongoing relationships with them. **Figure 16.6** shows that the most common cause of homicides, or murders, are arguments.

Figure 16.6

Factors Associated with Murders

Over 22,000 murders were committed in 1994. Arguments accounted for nearly one-third of them.

Contributing Factor	Number of Murders
Arguments	6,581
Crimes involving drug trade	1,238
Sexual assault	133
Robbery	2,076
Other felonies	618
Unknown	6,206

Source: *Statistical Abstracts*, 1997

Words to Know

- **assertive**
- **rape**
- **acquaintance rape**
- **date rape**

Math Connection

How Much Violence Is There? ACTIVITY!

During a typical day in the United States, the following numbers of violent crimes are likely to be committed: 60 murders, 288 rapes, and 2,979 assaults. At this rate, how many murders, rapes, and assaults are likely to be committed in the United States in a week, a month, and a year?

Your Total Health

Drugs and Violence

Some people are more likely to display violent behavior when they use drugs. Alcohol, PCP (angel dust), cocaine, and steroids have all been shown to produce highly aggressive behavior.

in your journal

Look at the lists of Do's and Don'ts on this page. Add to these lists other ways that people can protect themselves from crime. Write your ideas in your journal.

Protecting Yourself from Crime

The best way to protect yourself from violent crime is to avoid situations that are unsafe. Stay away from a place that you feel is dangerous. Leave a situation that makes you feel uncomfortable. If you need help, find a police officer or other adult. If you are near a telephone, dial 911 or the police. Always carry important phone numbers and change for phone calls with you. Here are some additional precautions to follow.

DO'S

- Always stay in well-lighted public places at night.
- Walk by the curb and avoid doorways.
- Lock doors and windows when you are at home alone.
- Tell police the license numbers of suspicious cars in your neighborhood.

DON'TS

- Don't walk alone at night or in wooded areas or on deserted streets.
- Don't put your money in an easy-to-grab place.
- Don't open the door to anyone you don't know.
- Don't give personal information over the telephone or by computer.

In some areas, residents work together to watch over the neighborhood and to help reduce crime.

Neighborhood Watch Programs

Many areas have Neighborhood Watch programs. In these programs, neighbors watch each other's homes to ensure safety. Police officers train program participants to look for and report suspicious actions or people who look dangerous. In this way, the neighborhood residents protect their area and help reduce crime. You may wish to participate in a program in your neighborhood.

MAKING HEALTHY DECISIONS

Dealing with Violence

Emily's 16-year old sister, Sandy, has confided to her that she is feeling uncomfortable about her relationship with her boyfriend Jake. She told Emily that sometimes Jake gets really angry with her and yells at her. He has even slapped her a couple of times. Sandy used to look forward to her dates with Jake, but lately she worries about saying or doing things that might upset him.

Jake is a popular boy in school, and Sandy feels that no one would believe that Jake could behave so badly. She doesn't want to talk to Jake about his behavior, because she is afraid that this would make him angry. She also doesn't want to tell her parents, because she's afraid that Jake might get in trouble and that he would take it out on her.

Emily suggests that Sandy use the six-step decision-making strategy she learned in school to help her decide what to do.

Self-defense Strategies

Some people have learned to defend themselves against violent crimes by using physical strength and agility to stop attacks. However, this method is not the only way to defend yourself.

Many attackers look for easy targets—victims they can overpower quickly. You are less likely to be seen as an easy target if you are assertive. Being **assertive** means *behaving confidently.* It means speaking with conviction, standing straight, and walking with a determined walk. It's important to act assertively even when you don't feel that way. Some people find it difficult to be assertive. Assertiveness training classes help people feel and act as if they are more in charge of their lives.

Rape and Rape Prevention

Rape is *forcing another person to have sexual relations.* It is an act of violence, and it is illegal. According to FBI reports, over 100,000 rapes are reported in the United States each year (since 1990). Rapes occur among all age, ethnic, racial, and social groups.

Victims of rape often know their attackers. *When the attacker is known to the victim,* the act is called **acquaintance rape.** *When the attacker is a date,* it's called **date rape.**

The best way to prevent rape is to avoid situations in which an attack is possible. Going out with a group of friends, for example, will help prevent date rape. Here are some other suggestions.

- Make it clear to your date that you're not interested in sex.
- Respect and accept your date's refusal to have sex.
- Don't drink alcohol or use other drugs or date people who do.
- Don't enter an elevator alone with a stranger.

Teen Issues

Help for Victims of Rape

Victims of rape need two kinds of help. They need immediate medical help in case of injury, infection, or pregnancy. They also need emotional support and counseling. Telling a trusted family member or friend is the first step in getting both kinds of help.

1. **State the situation**
2. **List the options**
3. **Weigh the possible outcomes**
4. **Consider your values**
5. **Make a decision and act**
6. **Evaluate the decision**

Follow-up Activities

1. Imagine that you are in Sandy's situation. Use the six steps of the decision-making process to come to a decision.
2. Along with a classmate, role-play three scenes: one in which Sandy decides to confront Jake about his behavior, one in which she talks about Jake's behavior to an adult she trusts, and one in which she breaks up with Jake.
3. Sandy writes in her diary every night. Write a diary entry that Sandy might have written in which she evaluates her decision.

Preventing Violence in Your Relationships

Family violence is a growing problem in this country. Like other types of violence, family violence often involves alcohol or other drugs. If you live in a home where violence exists, you need to find help. Remember that the violence is not your fault and that nobody deserves abuse. You can help to end the violence by reporting it.

Brothers and sisters often play roughly and tease each other. However, no matter how close you are to someone, speak up if his or her behavior threatens you. Demand a change in behavior, or leave. Take all slaps and threats seriously. Remember that insults and yelling are sometimes followed by physical violence.

Violence is never the answer to anger and frustration. Talking over the situation will leave both people feeling better.

Lesson 3 Review

Using complete sentences, answer the following questions on a separate sheet of paper.

Reviewing Terms and Facts

1. **Identify** What are some of the causes of violence in the United States?
2. **Give Examples** List some precautions you can take to avoid becoming the victim of a violent crime.
3. **Vocabulary** What is the difference between *acquaintance rape* and *date rape?*

Thinking Critically

4. **Hypothesize** Why do you think violent crimes are on the increase in some cities in the United States?
5. **Analyze** Explain how assertiveness is related to violence prevention.

Applying Health Concepts

6. **Personal Health** Take a survey of friends to find out what they do that increases or decreases their risk of becoming victims of violence. Use the lists of Do's and Don'ts in this lesson to develop your questionnaire. Compare their responses to your own. Are there any changes you should make in your behavior to reduce your risk of becoming a victim?
7. **Health of Others** Make a poster that highlights several ways to decrease one's chances of being raped. With your teacher's approval, display the poster in the cafeteria or another location where many students are likely to see it.

Lesson 4

Acting Safely on the Road and Outdoors

This lesson will help you find answers to questions that teens often ask about safety on the road and outdoors. For example:

- **What are the traffic rules for bicycle riders?**
- **How can I skateboard without getting hurt?**
- **What can I do to avoid injuries in the water and outdoors?**

Words to Know

jaywalk
defensive driving
hypothermia
frostbite

Traffic Safety

Knowing—and obeying—traffic signals, signs, and pavement markings is just as important for pedestrians and bicyclists as it is for motor vehicle drivers. The purpose of these traffic controls is to regulate the movement of all people who use the streets and highways. When you obey traffic controls, other road users can predict your actions. This helps prevent accidents from happening.

Traffic Signals

There are two types of traffic signals. One type is the *walk/don't walk* signal, which is found at crosswalks and controls pedestrian movement. The other type of traffic signal is the traffic light.

Traffic Signs

There are three types of traffic signs. *Warning signs* alert you to upcoming changes. *Guide signs* notify you of the roadway that you are on or are approaching. *Regulatory signs* control the flow of traffic. Here are some typical traffic signs.

- **Stop sign.** Stop, check traffic in all directions, and proceed through the intersection if it is clear.
- **Yield sign.** Allow traffic on the other road to pass, and then proceed through the intersection.
- **One-way sign.** Proceed only in the direction in which the arrow on the sign is pointing.
- **Do-not-enter sign.** Do not enter a one-way street incorrectly and signal other drivers who are about to.
- **Directional sign.** In a given lane of traffic, go in the direction the arrows indicate.
- **Road changes sign.** Use caution when proceeding. Be alert for changes in the road condition or direction.

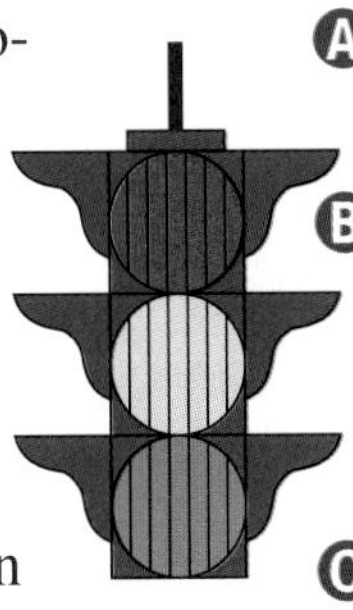

A Red Light
Stop at the intersection.

B Yellow Light
Stop at the intersection.
If you are in the intersection, continue through.

C Green Light
Proceed through the intersection if it is clear.

Pavement Markings

Various markings are painted on the pavement to control the movement of traffic. Among the most important pavement markings are the lines that separate lanes of traffic (see **Figure 16.7**).

Figure 16.7
Pavement Markings

Knowing the meaning of pavement markings is very important for drivers. Why would knowing the difference between solid white lines and solid yellow lines be important?

A Solid white lines separate lanes of traffic traveling in the same direction. Solid white lines may not be crossed.

C Solid yellow lines separate lanes of traffic traveling in opposite directions. Solid yellow lines may not be crossed.

B Broken white lines show that passing or changing lanes is allowed.

D Broken yellow lines may be crossed by a driver who is passing another vehicle if the road is clear.

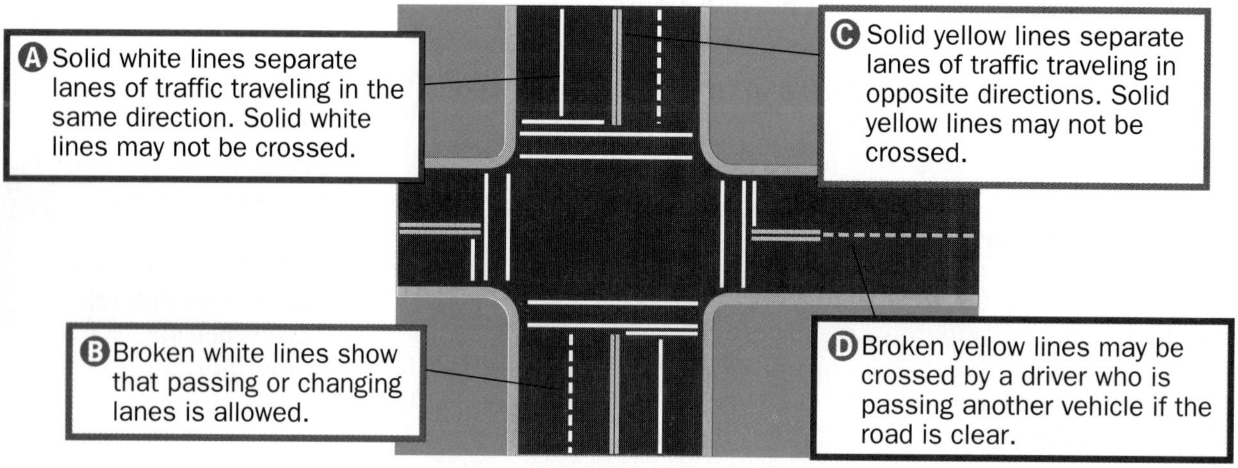

Being a Safe Car Passenger

If you are on the passenger side of the front seat, sit back in the seat, and do not lean on the dashboard. This will prevent you from being injured if the driver needs to stop suddenly. Never distract the driver, who needs to concentrate on driving safely. Most important, wear a seat belt whenever you are a passenger.

Pedestrian Safety

A pedestrian is anyone who travels on foot. Pedestrian injuries are among the most common traffic accidents involving young teens. Follow these Do's and Don'ts to lessen your chances of being struck by a vehicle.

DO'S

- Cross streets at crosswalks and obey traffic lights.

- Look both ways before crossing streets and roads.

- Wear bright clothing in daylight; wear reflective gear and carry a flashlight at night.

- Where there is no sidewalk, stay to the left, facing oncoming traffic.

DON'TS

- Don't **jaywalk,** or *cross the street in the middle of the block.*

- Don't move into the street from between parked cars.

- Don't enter the street without first looking left, right, and then left again.

- Don't assume that a driver will see you just because you can see him or her.

in Your Journal

Draw a map of a route you often walk. Mark all the areas where there is traffic danger, such as roads without sidewalks or hidden driveways. Next to each, write the traffic rule you should follow to ensure your safety at each danger spot. The next time you walk that route, take your map and follow the traffic rules.

Bicycle Safety

Bicycling is fun, good exercise, and a great way to travel. Bicyclists, like drivers, should practice **defensive driving.** This means not just obeying traffic laws but also *watching out for other road users.* Because you obey the rules yourself, you will not do things to surprise drivers or other cyclists. Surprises can be dangerous. Also, because you watch what other road users are doing, you can react safely when someone else makes a mistake.

You can also reduce the risk of bicycle accidents by making sure that your bike has the proper safety equipment. Which equipment in **Figure 16.8** do you feel is essential?

- Ride on the right side of the road with traffic, not against it.
- Obey all traffic signals, signs, and pavement markings.
- Use lights and reflective clothing when riding after dark.
- Avoid loose clothing, which could catch in the chain.
- Keep your bike in good working order.
- Avoid riding at night and in bad weather.

Even though you follow the safety rules, bike accidents do happen. A helmet can prevent serious head injuries. Head injuries are the cause of 70 to 80 percent of the fatalities from bike accidents. Wearing a helmet could save your life.

Did You Know?

Bicycle Accidents

Most fatal bicycle accidents involve cars and occur on roads with speed limits of 55 MPH or higher. However, bicycle accidents that result in injury usually do not involve cars. Most injuries are due to falls or to collisions with stationary objects, other bikes, or pedestrians. Whenever you ride your bike, be sure to watch for pedestrians, potholes, and stationary objects as well as cars.

Your Total Health

Helmets Save Lives

About three-fourths of deaths among bicyclists are from head injuries. Of the remaining injuries, many cause permanent brain damage. Helmets reduce the risk of head injuries by 85 percent and the risk of brain injuries by 88 percent. Given these facts, can you think of a convincing reason not to wear a bike helmet?

Figure 16.8

Bicycle Safety Equipment

This drawing shows bicycle safety features that are recommended. Why do you think reflectors are important?

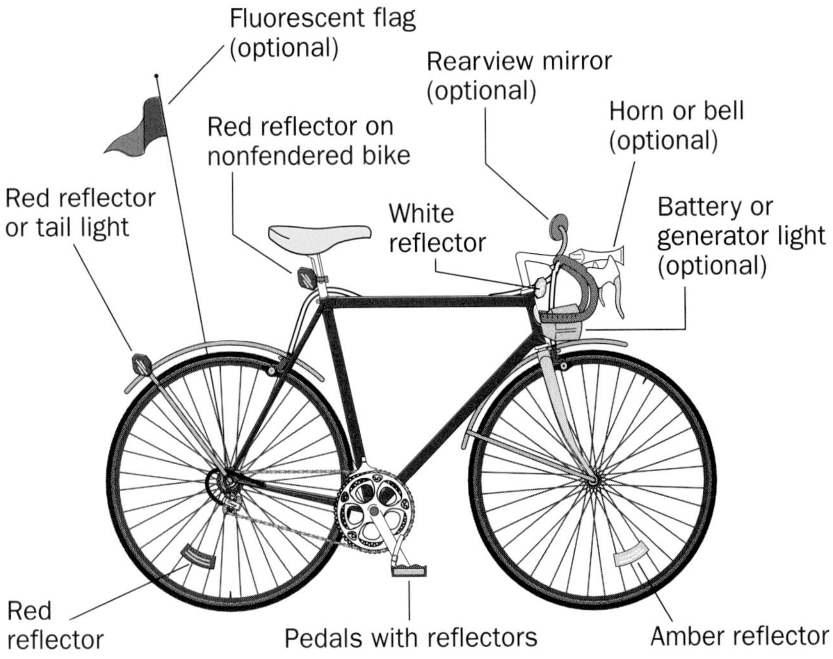

Skate and Motorbike Safety

For safe skateboarding and in-line skating, keep your speed down to a controllable level, and watch for pedestrians. Avoid parking lots, streets, and other areas with traffic. Before heading downhill, practice the correct way to fall. If you do stunts, wear protective gear, including a helmet (see **Figure 16.9**).

Like bicyclists, motorbike and moped riders must follow all traffic rules. To be safe, they, too, should practice defensive driving. They also should wear the appropriate safety gear, which includes hard-shell helmets.

Did You Know?

Deadly Two-Wheelers

A person on a motorcycle is almost ten times as likely to be killed in a crash as someone in a car. Why do you think this is the case?

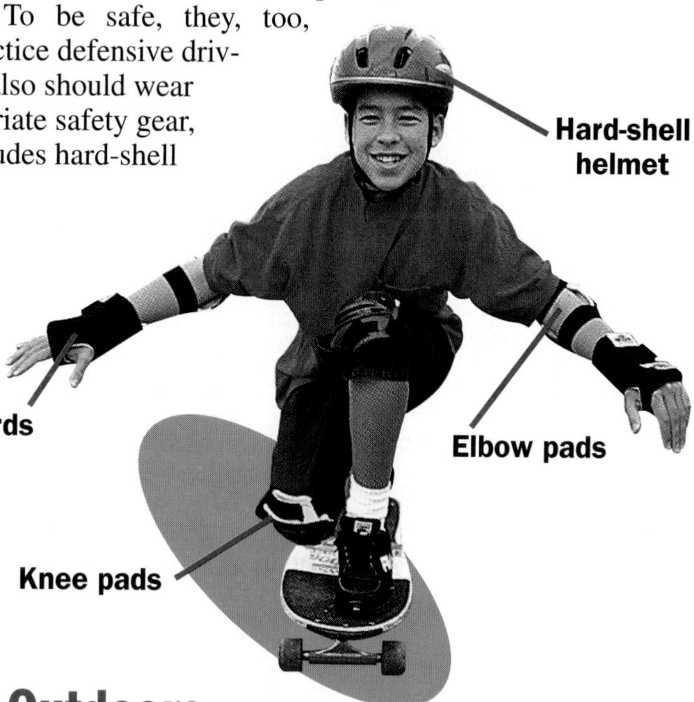

Figure 16.9
Safety Gear for Skateboarders and In-Line Skaters

Safety Outdoors

You're not at home. You're not at school. You're not on the road. You're on vacation in the great outdoors. So you can enjoy yourself and forget about safety, right? Wrong! It doesn't pay to spoil a good time by taking risks. No matter what outdoor activity you prefer, it's better to do it safely. You can do that by following safety rules and using common sense. Here are two important tips to ensure your safety outdoors.

- **Use the buddy system.** The buddy system is an agreement between two people to stay together. Always do outdoor activities with a friend—the two of you can watch out for each other's safety and help each other in case of an emergency.
- **Be aware of the weather.** Use your common sense and try to avoid electrical storms, extreme heat, and extreme cold. If you are caught outdoors in an electrical storm, try to get into a car or house. If you cannot, take shelter under a group of bushes, or squat and put your head down. Do not stand under a tall tree. Get out of and away from water. If you are outdoors on a very hot day, keep your head covered from the sun, drink plenty of water, and don't exercise too hard. When it's very cold, dress in layers, stay dry, and warm up quickly if you begin to shiver. That way you will avoid **hypothermia** (hy·poh·THER·mee·uh), *a dangerous drop in body temperature.*

in your journal

List two or more outdoor activities that you enjoy. Next to each, write all the potential dangers associated with that activity. Then list the safety gear you need and the safety rules you should follow to protect yourself from injury when you do the activity.

Safety in the Water

Whether your sport is swimming, diving, or boating, it's important to know about water safety. Over 7,000 people die from drowning in the United States each year. More than 1 million people have close calls. Drownings occur when boats overturn and when children wander off into unattended pools. They also happen if swimmers panic when they experience a cramp, swim farther out than they should, or get caught in a current. Most drownings and near-drownings are avoidable if people follow some water safety rules.

- Go in the water only if you know how to swim. Knowing how to swim not only helps keep you safe in the water, but it is also a lot of fun and great exercise.
- Always swim with a buddy and only in pools or at beaches that have trained lifeguards.
- If you ever feel yourself drowning, do not panic. Breathe slowly and tread water until help arrives. Thrashing about in the water only makes you tired and the situation worse.
- To prevent a cramp, or muscle tightening, avoid swimming when you're tired or right after eating.
- Dive only if you have had lessons from a qualified instructor. Always check the depth of the water and look for obstacles and other swimmers before diving in.
- When boating, always wear a life jacket. Don't stand up or move around in a small boat. If you're steering the boat, practice so you know how to handle it. If you plan to go boating regularly, take a course in boating safety.
- Learn the technique for drowning prevention (see **Figure 16.10**).

Your Total Health

Diving Disasters

Many diving injuries occur in rivers or lakes, where the depth of the water varies from place to place. In fact, most serious diving injuries—about 95 percent—result from dives into water less than five feet deep. Consider the places where you swim. Where is it safe to dive, and where is it unsafe?

Did You Know?

Under the Influence

Operating a boat while under the influence of alcohol is just as dangerous as driving a car after drinking.

Figure 16.10

Drowning Prevention

This drawing shows a technique called *drowning prevention.* Both swimmers and nonswimmers can use this technique to save themselves from drowning. The main points to remember are do not panic and do not thrash around. Push down with cupped hands at the same moment as the walking motion takes place, to achieve more thrust.

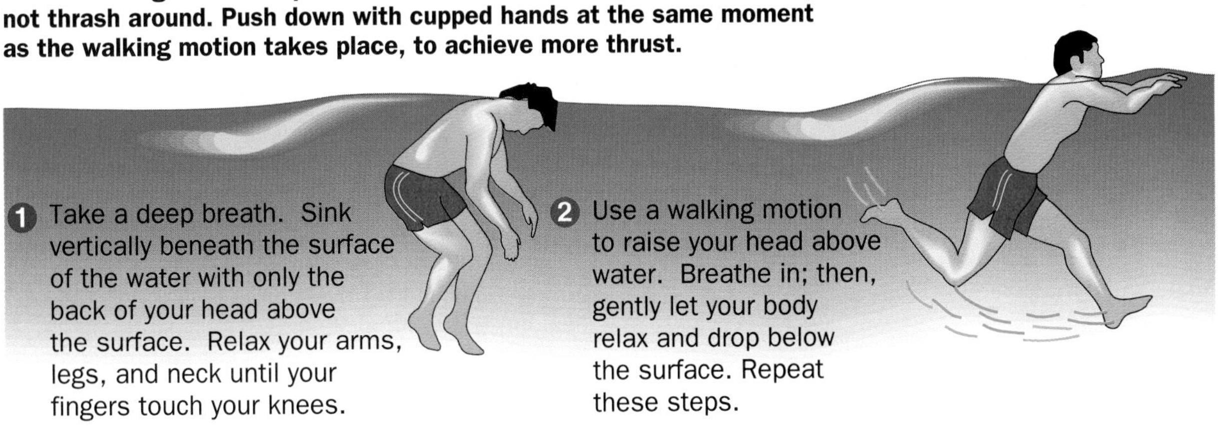

1 Take a deep breath. Sink vertically beneath the surface of the water with only the back of your head above the surface. Relax your arms, legs, and neck until your fingers touch your knees.
2 Use a walking motion to raise your head above water. Breathe in; then, gently let your body relax and drop below the surface. Repeat these steps.

Figure 16.11

Getting Equipped for Safe Camping

Safety When Hiking and Camping

Hiking and camping are popular ways to enjoy the sights and sounds of nature. Good preparation is the key to a successful hike or camping trip. Careful planning will ensure that you take the proper clothing and equipment. **Figure 16.11** shows some of the items needed for safe camping. Always tell someone where you will be and when you expect to return. Camping is more fun when you follow safety precautions. Unsafe behavior in and around campsites can lead to serious accidents. When you camp, follow these safety tips.

HEALTH LAB

Identifying Poison Ivy and Poison Oak

Introduction: Have you ever heard the saying, "Leaves of three, let it be"? It refers to poison ivy and poison oak. Both plants have leaves that are divided into three leaflets.

Poison ivy grows throughout most of the country, especially in the East and Midwest. Poison oak is less abundant, except along the Pacific coast, where it is often the most common small plant around. Both plants grow as vines, creepers, or low shrubs.

Sooner or later, almost everyone who spends time outdoors is going to come in contact with poison ivy or poison oak. About 85 percent of people are allergic to the oil in these plants, which causes a blistery, red rash that itches terribly.

Objective: Poison ivy and poison oak are toxic year round. To prevent an allergic reaction to these plants, you must avoid contact with them. In this lab, you will learn what poison ivy and poison oak plants look like. Then, when you are outdoors, you can stay clear of them.

Materials and Method: Study the photos of poison ivy and poison oak on page 505. Sketch the leaves by copying the pictures and read the descriptions of the plants below.

Poison ivy leaflets are usually shaped like arrowheads. The leaflets are a bright, shiny green. The leaves turn red in the fall, and the plant has white flowers and cream-colored berries in late summer. In the winter, the flower stems wither but still bear some berries.

Poison oak leaflets resemble oak leaves, with several lobes on each leaflet. Although most often there are three leaflets, there may be five or even more. The leaflets always have a shiny, oily appearance. They are deep green in the summer and then red or yellow in the fall. In late summer, poison oak has yellowish or whitish berries and greenish flowers that hang in loose clusters.

- **Shoes and clothes.** Dress for the weather and wear heavy shoes and socks to prevent getting blisters. Dressing in layers can ensure that you'll be ready for extremes in temperature and changes in weather. In some mountainous regions, you may be in danger of getting both sunburn during the day and **frostbite,** or *freezing of the skin,* at night. Be prepared with cold-weather, hot-weather, and wet-weather gear. Depending on where you will be, you may need to pack such items as sunscreen lotion, mittens and a ski mask, and waterproof boots.
- **Equipment and supplies.** Make sure you have a compass, a well-equipped first-aid kit, a flashlight with extra batteries, and an adequate supply of fresh water.
- **Campfires.** Drown your campfire with water, continually stirring it as you add water. If no water is available, use dirt that is free of twigs, leaves, and paper. Make sure the fire is out before leaving the area, or you could start a forest fire.
- **Poisonous plants and animals.** Learn which plants, snakes, and insects are poisonous and how to avoid them. Learn basic first-aid for treating reactions to poisonous plants, insect stings and bites, and snakebites. Don't eat berries unless you are sure they are not poisonous.

Biology Connection

Killer Bees ACTIVITY!

"Killer Bees Invade the U.S." Does this sound like a science-fiction movie? It's not. The bees are a cross between common honeybees and African honeybees. However, they are not as dangerous as their name suggests. Their venom isn't any more harmful than that of common honeybees, though they are more aggressive and more likely to sting you. Read more about this variety of bee and give a brief report to your class.

Observation and Analysis:
If poison ivy or poison oak grow in your part of the country, try to find the plants growing outdoors. Look for them alongside roads, trails, and streams; in unused clearings; and climbing up tree trunks. Be careful to avoid touching the plants or stepping on them. If you have difficulty identifying the plants, try to find someone who knows what they look like to help you find them.

You can also follow these steps to minimize an allergic reaction.

- Remove the oil from your skin immediately, within five minutes if possible, by washing with plenty of soap and water, with rubbing alcohol, or with cool water and hydrogen peroxide or bleach.
- Apply calamine lotion or hydrocortisone cream to temporarily soothe the itch.
- Take an oral antihistamine to relieve itching if hydrocortisone cream can't control it.
- See your doctor if your symptoms are severe.
- Avoid breathing smoke in a fire where poison oak or poison ivy is burning.

Poison ivy

Poison oak

Safety When Enjoying Winter Sports

Ice skating, sledding, and skiing are all healthy ways to enjoy the outdoors in the winter. All of these activities can be dangerous, however, because of the cold and the risk of falls and collisions. Wear layers of clothing, a hat, and gloves or mittens to keep your hands warm. By following the safety guidelines below, you can increase your enjoyment of these winter sports.

Winter sports are more enjoyable if you dress properly to protect yourself from the cold.

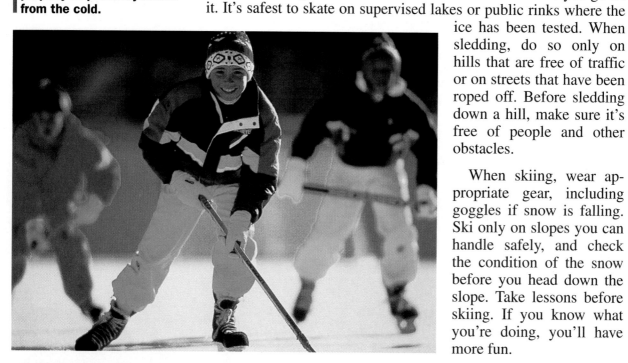

When skating, make sure the ice is frozen solid before you go on it. It's safest to skate on supervised lakes or public rinks where the ice has been tested. When sledding, do so only on hills that are free of traffic or on streets that have been roped off. Before sledding down a hill, make sure it's free of people and other obstacles.

When skiing, wear appropriate gear, including goggles if snow is falling. Ski only on slopes you can handle safely, and check the condition of the snow before you head down the slope. Take lessons before skiing. If you know what you're doing, you'll have more fun.

Lesson 4

Review

Using complete sentences, answer the following questions on a separate sheet of paper.

Reviewing Terms and Facts

1. **Vocabulary** How does *defensive driving* increase the safety of bicyclists?
2. **Recall** What are some rules for skateboard and in-line skating safety?

Thinking Critically

3. **Analyze** Why is it equally important for bicycle riders and motor vehicle drivers to follow traffic signals, signs, and pavement markings?
4. **Explain** How does using the buddy system help keep you safe outdoors?
5. **Explain** Why is it important to remain calm if you feel you're drowning?

Applying Health Concepts

6. **Growth and Development** Design a poster that advertises a swimming program in your area. Include information that would encourage teens to learn how to swim.
7. **Health of Others** Research car occupant restraints and seat belts, and make a video or brochure about them. Include information such as the number of lives seat belts save and the proper way to wear a seat belt.

Lesson 5

Acting Safely in Weather Emergencies

This lesson will help you find answers to questions that teens often ask about weather emergencies. For example:

- **What should I do to stay safe in case of a severe storm in my area?**
- **How can I protect myself during a flood or an earthquake?**

Words to Know

tornado
tornado watch
tornado warning
hurricane
blizzard
earthquake

Hazardous Weather and Natural Disasters

Hazardous weather and natural disasters can be devastating. In Oregon in 1996, severe flooding in northern sections of the state left more than 15,000 people homeless, 50 injured, and 8 dead. This "Great Flood of 1996" wiped out roads and highways, isolated communities, and displaced tens of thousands of people.

The possibility of hazardous weather and natural disasters exists at certain times of the year and in certain parts of the United States (see **Figure 16.12**). You can reduce the risk of injury from hazardous weather and natural disasters by taking certain precautions to ensure your safety.

Figure 16.12

Hazardous Weather and Natural Disasters in the United States

Tornadoes generally occur in the spring and early summer. Hurricanes usually occur between June and November, with most occurring in September.

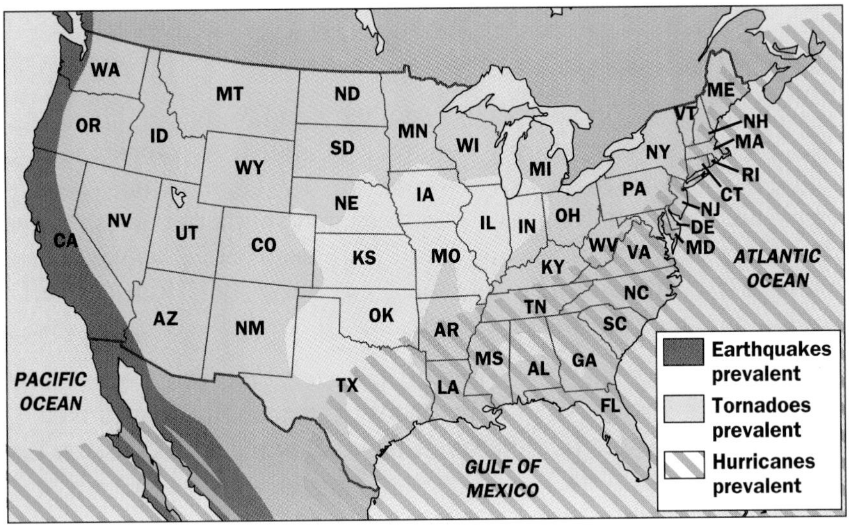

Tornadoes

A **tornado** is the most violent of all storms. It is a *whirling, funnel-shaped windstorm that drops from the sky to the ground.* The winds of a tornado—at speeds that can reach more than 200 miles an hour—are exceedingly dangerous. A tornado can destroy almost everything in its path. Although tornadoes occur mainly in the central part of the United States, they may also occur along the coasts after hurricanes. They are most frequent in the spring and summer.

Because tornadoes have such high winds and are so dangerous, the National Weather Service closely monitors the weather to see when a tornado may form. When the weather conditions indicate the possibility of a tornado, the Weather Service issues a **tornado watch,** which is *a news bulletin that tells people to stay tuned for further bulletins.* If conditions change and the tornado seems less likely to occur, the watch is removed.

When a tornado is actually approaching an area and the people living there are in danger, the Weather Service issues a **tornado warning** for that area. When that happens, people must take certain steps to protect themselves from harm. The safest action to take is to go to a cellar or basement that has no windows and to stay there until the storm passes. If you cannot do that, you should follow the steps listed below.

Your Total Health

Be Prepared ACTIVITY!

For all types of hazardous weather or natural disasters, many of the same basic survival tips apply. For example, in most emergencies, power is likely to go off. Check your family's preparedness by making sure you have a battery-powered radio, several working flashlights, and extra fresh batteries. Purchase or replace any items as needed.

What to Do When a Tornado Strikes

- **Avoid places with windows.** Take cover in a hallway or bathtub. Stay as far away from windows as possible.
- **Cover yourself.** Duck down and cover your head with a mattress, blanket, or clothing to protect yourself from flying objects.
- **Lie down.** If you are outside, lie down in a ditch or other low ground.

Hurricanes

Another kind of hazardous weather condition is a hurricane. This storm can extend over hundreds of miles. A **hurricane** is a *strong windstorm with driving rain.* In the United States, hurricanes are most common on the eastern and southern coasts, where they may produce unusually high and destructive waves. They occur most often in late summer and early fall. **Figure 16.13** shows the wind patterns in a hurricane.

A hurricane is an area of low air pressure that forms over tropical regions near the Atlantic or Pacific Oceans. Hurricanes consist of storm clouds that circle around the eye, which is a calm area in the center of the storm.

in your journal

Ask an elderly relative, family friend, or neighbor to tell you about the worst storm, flood, or earthquake he or she has experienced. Record those recollections in your journal.

Figure 16.13

Wind Patterns of a Hurricane

Hurricanes, like tornadoes, are dangerous weather storms. How are the two storms similar?

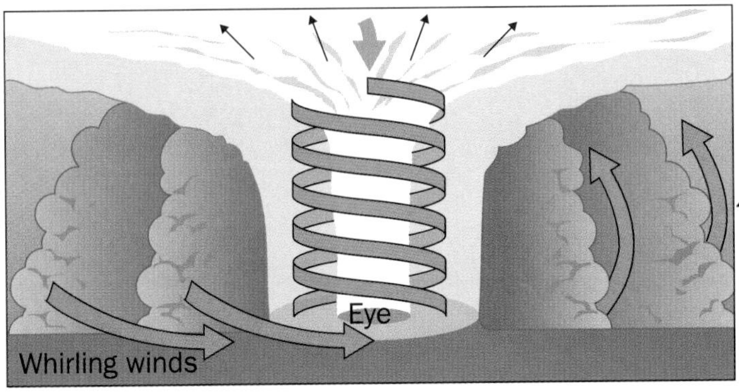

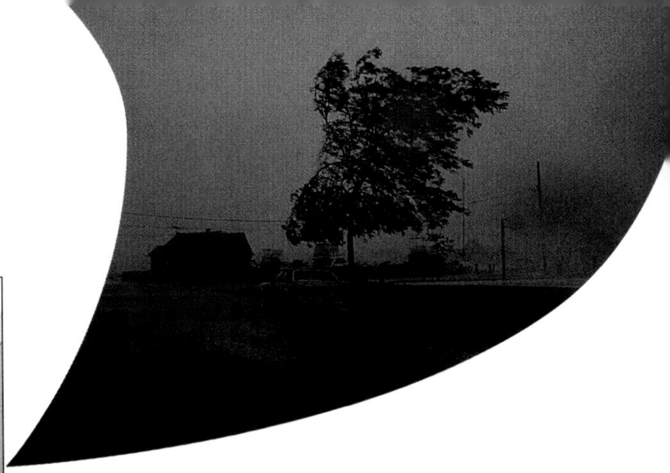

The National Weather Service also monitors hurricanes as they do tornadoes. Hurricanes are serious storms that can cause major damage. You can prepare for a hurricane by following these steps.

- **Board up the windows and doors of your house.** This will prevent high winds from blowing them in.
- **Take inside any objects that may be blown away.** This means taking in any loose objects such as toys and lawn furniture.
- **Leave the area.** If you live on the coast, go inland. The farther inland you go, the safer you will be.

Blizzards

In winter months, some parts of the United States experience severe snowstorms called blizzards. A **blizzard** is a *very heavy snowstorm with winds of between 35 and 45 miles an hour.* The combination of strong winds and heavy snowfall results in poor visibility—usually less than 500 feet. It is very easy to get lost in a blizzard. Blizzards occur when a cold air mass from the Arctic moves into the temperate zone. Blizzards often follow periods of unusually warm winter weather.

What to Do When a Blizzard Strikes

Blizzards are dangerous. Snow piles up in great drifts, stopping traffic and disrupting life for several days. You can protect yourself from blizzards by following a few simple steps.

- **Stay inside.** The safest place to be during a blizzard is indoors. If you have to go out, follow the other precautions.
- **Keep your nose and mouth covered and keep moving.** These actions can keep you from freezing.
- **Avoid getting lost.** Find a landmark to walk along.
- **Wear protective clothing.** Wear thermal underwear, extra socks, and outer clothes that keep out wind and moisture.

Did You Know?

Lightning Strikes

You can avoid the dangers of lightning by doing the following.

- Stay in a house or in an enclosed car or truck.
- Use the telephone only in emergencies.
- Do not stand under or near a tall tree or other object.
- Stay out of and away from water.

Your Total Health

First Aid for Frostbite ACTIVITY!

Frostbite needs to be treated right away to avoid permanent damage of the injured body part. Bring the person indoors and cover him or her with a blanket. Give the person a warm drink. Place the frozen part in luke-warm, not hot, water or wrap it in blankets. Do not rub the frozen part. Get medical attention as soon as possible.

Figure 16.14

What Happens During an Earthquake

This diagram shows what causes an earthquake. On which part of the earth's surface do you think an earthquake is felt most strongly?

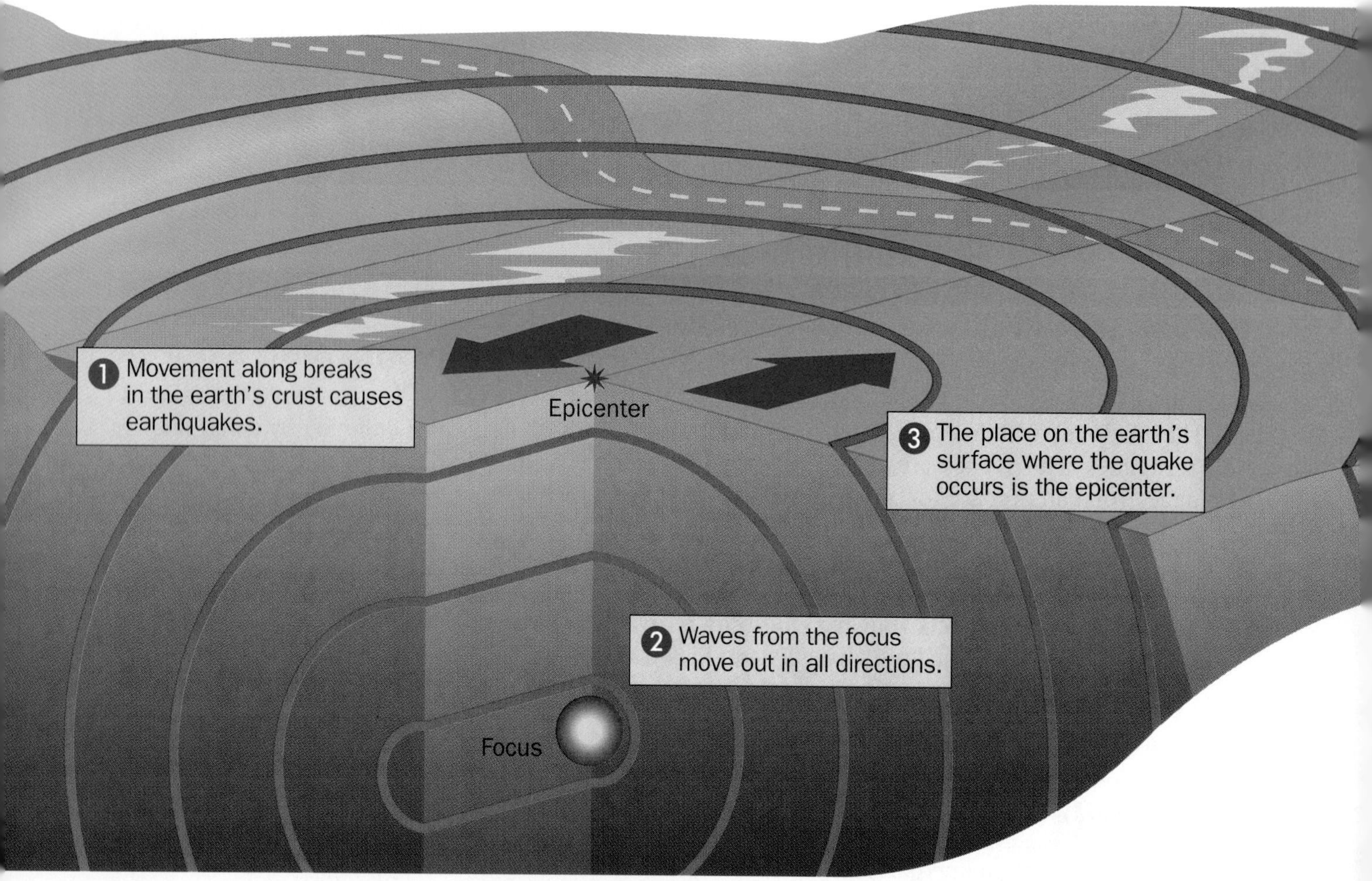

1 Movement along breaks in the earth's crust causes earthquakes.
Epicenter
3 The place on the earth's surface where the quake occurs is the epicenter.
2 Waves from the focus move out in all directions.
Focus

Teen Issues

Be Cool in an Emergency

Following these guidelines will help ensure your safety and the safety of others.

- Stay calm.
- Follow the directions of officials.
- Stay with your parents or another adult.
- Stay in your safe location until you hear official word that the danger is over.

Earthquakes

Earthquakes occur often in some parts of the United States. Alaska records over 50 percent of all earthquakes. Other western states record about 4,000 weak but noticeable earthquakes each year.

An **earthquake** is *a shaking movement of the earth's surface.* **Figure 16.14** shows what happens during an earthquake. Small earthquakes cause little, if any, damage. Severe earthquakes can topple buildings. Most earthquake injuries are caused by falling objects and collapsing buildings.

What to Do When an Earthquake Strikes

- **Stay inside.** If you are at home, remain inside. Brace yourself in an inside doorway or in a hallway, or crouch under a sturdy table. Stay away from objects that could fall or cave in and from windows or mirrors that may shatter.
- **If you are outdoors, stand in the open.** Stay away from utility poles, chimneys, trees, brick or stone fences, electric wires, and buildings. These structures can be dangerous.

Earthquakes can cause structural damage to roads, bridges, and buildings. In 1994, this California highway buckled under the pressure and took months to rebuild.

Floods

Floods are another natural disaster that have caused severe damage and destruction. Floods may occur when rain falls too fast to be absorbed by the ground. Instead it runs off and fills rivers and streams until they overflow their banks and flood the surrounding land. Emergency barriers, such as sandbag levees, may keep a river from overflowing. You should leave the area for higher ground until the flood waters subside.

Did You Know?

What Is an Epicenter?

An earthquake occurs when there is sudden rock movement inside the earth. The site of the movement is the focus. The epicenter is the point on the surface just above the focus. This is where the seismic waves are the strongest.

Lesson 5 Review

Using complete sentences, answer the following questions on a separate sheet of paper.

Reviewing Terms and Facts

1. **Vocabulary** Differentiate between a *tornado* and a *hurricane.*
2. **Recall** List three steps to take to prepare for a hurricane.

Thinking Critically

3. **Analyze** Why is it important to stay indoors during blizzards?
4. **Synthesize** Why should you stay out of damaged buildings after an earthquake?

Applying Health Concepts

5. **Health of Others** Most communities have Civil Defense shelters to be used during weather emergencies and natural disasters. Find out where the shelters are in your community. What qualifies a place to serve as a shelter? What have they been used for in the past? Summarize your findings in writing.

Chapter 16 Review

Chapter Summary

- **Lesson 1** Accidents are the leading cause of injury and death among teens. Acting safely will help you avoid accidents. An accident is the outcome of a chain of events. Changing any one link in the chain can prevent the accident.
- **Lesson 2** Every home has hazards that can cause accidents. People can prevent most home injuries by being safety conscious and by taking a few preventive actions.
- **Lesson 3** You can reduce your chances of being a victim of violence by avoiding unsafe situations and by acting assertively.
- **Lesson 4** Acting safely on the road means knowing and obeying traffic rules and riding your bicycle defensively. Being aware of dangers, following safety guidelines, and sharing activities with a buddy will help you stay safe outdoors.
- **Lesson 5** By taking proper precautions and acting safely, you can reduce your risk of injury from storms and natural disasters.

Reviewing Key Terms and Concepts

Using complete sentences, answer the following questions on a separate sheet of paper.

Lesson 1

1. List four general guidelines for acting safely.
2. Identify the three ways of breaking an accident chain.

Lesson 2

3. Define *hazard.* Identify three hazards found in most homes.
4. List three rules for preventing electrical shocks.

Lesson 3

5. What is the single best way to protect yourself from violent crime?
6. Define *rape.* List two ways to lower the risk of being raped.

Lesson 4

7. Define *jaywalk.* List four pedestrian safety rules.
8. Define *hypothermia* and *frostbite.* List a safety rule that will help prevent each one from occurring.

Lesson 5

9. Define *blizzard* and *earthquake.* List two ways to stay safe during each.
10. In which sections of the United States are tornadoes most likely to occur?

Thinking Critically

Using complete sentences, answer the following questions on a separate sheet of paper.

11. **Evaluate** How can the idea of an accident chain be used to prevent injuries?
12. **Hypothesize** Why do so many accidents in homes occur in kitchens and bathrooms?
13. **Explain** How can acting assertively reduce your risk of becoming a victim of a violent crime?
14. **Deduce** Why should bicyclists ride with traffic, not against it?

Chapter 16 Review

Your Action Plan

Review your journal entries for this chapter. What did you list as the greatest dangers to your safety? Choose an area of personal safety in which you would like to be more careful. An action plan will help you make this part of your life safer.

Step 1 Choose a long-term goal. For instance, you might want to pay more attention to safety in a sport that you play.

Step 2 Write down a series of short-term goals that will help you achieve your long-term goal. If your long-term goal is to reduce your risk of injury from bicycling, for example, a short-term goal might be to buy a headlight for riding your bike at night.

Step 3 Identify sources of help. For example, you might want to talk to someone in a bicycle shop about what safety equipment is important for bicyclists.

Step 4 Set a schedule for achieving each short-term goal. Check your schedule periodically to keep yourself on track.

When you reach your long-term goal, reward yourself.

In Your Home and Community

1. **Health of Others** Make a poster listing the six rules to follow in case of a fire emergency. Make the poster easy to read and eye-catching for younger children. Ask to hang your poster in the hall outside an elementary school classroom.
2. **Personal Health** Being prepared helps prevent accidents. Write a safety list for an activity, such as camping or skiing, that you participate in with your family. Ask for your family's help in writing the list. Use this list the next time you and your family participate in this activity.

Building Your Portfolio

1. **Media Survey** For one week, every time you watch a television show, music video, or movie, write down every act of violence that occurs. At the end of the week, add up how many occurrences of violence you observed. How does this number compare to the amount of violence you observe in your everyday life? Discuss your findings with the class. Include your survey and observations in your portfolio.
2. **Personal Assessment** Look through the activities and projects you did for this chapter. Choose one or two that you would like to include in your portfolio.

Chapter 17

Handling Emergencies

Student Expectations

After reading this chapter, you should be able to:

1. **List the steps in providing basic first aid.**
2. **Explain what to do in a life-threatening emergency.**
3. **Describe how to handle some common emergencies.**

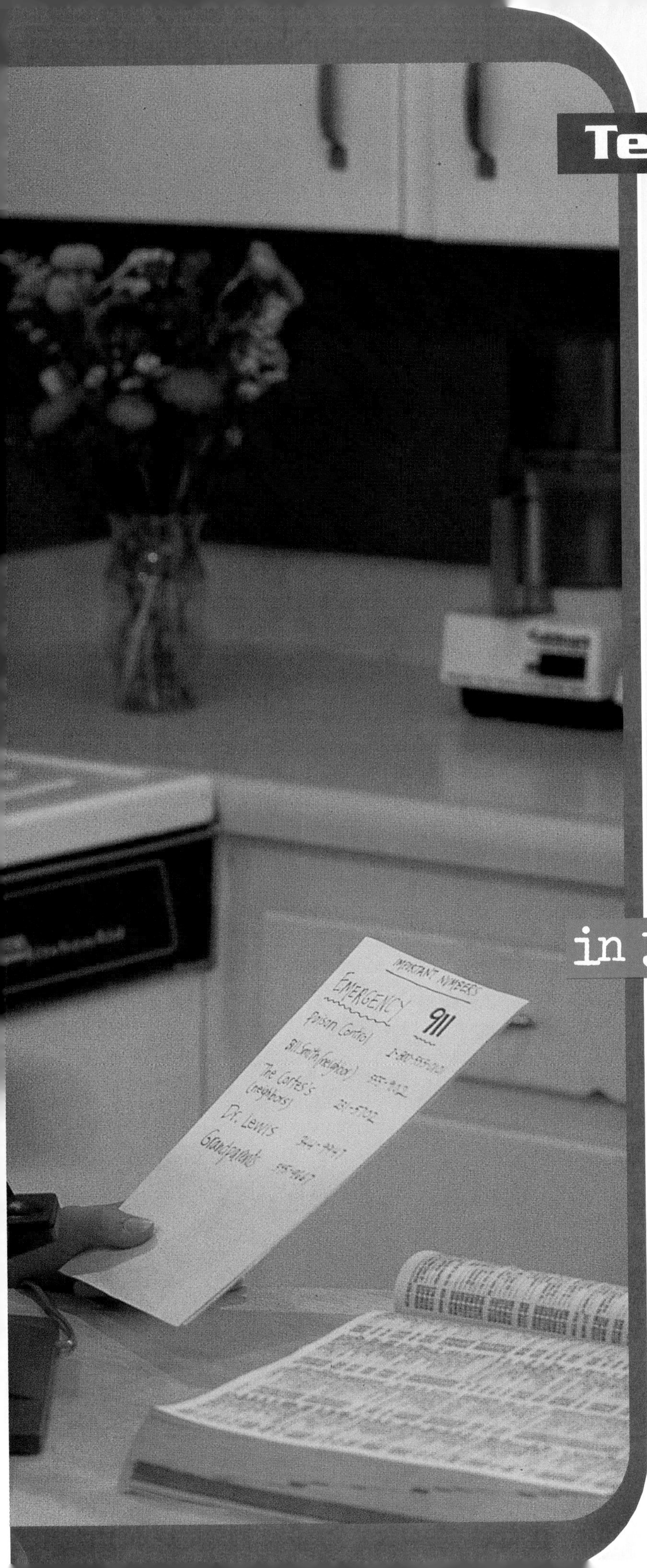

Teen Chat Group

Dylan: I heard that you went to the hospital the other day. What happened?

Jun: While I was watching my little brother, he tripped and hit his head on the coffee table. He had a big gash, and it was bleeding a lot.

Dylan: That sounds serious! What did you do?

Jun: I called 911 right away. I stayed calm, just like the operator told me. I answered all her questions about what happened. Then I followed her directions to stop the bleeding.

Dylan: Why did you go to the hospital?

Jun: When the paramedics got there, they said that my brother needed stitches.

Dylan: Did your mom get mad?

Jun: No. She was proud of me for being able to handle an emergency, and of course, she was happy that my brother was all right.

in your journal

Read the dialogue on this page. Would you know what to do in an emergency situation? Start your private journal entries on handling emergencies by answering these questions:

- **Have you ever been faced with an emergency like Jun's? If so, how did you react?**
- **Do you know how to provide basic first aid?**
- **Do you know how to handle emergencies that are a matter of life or death, such as choking?**

When you reach the end of the chapter, you will use your journal entries to make an action plan.

Lesson 1

Basic Principles of First Aid

This lesson will help you find answers to questions that teens often ask about first aid. For example:

- **What are the basic steps to follow when someone needs first aid?**
- **How would I help someone who has stopped breathing?**
- **What would I do to help control severe bleeding?**

Words to Know

rescue breathing
shock

Your Total Health

Immediate Medical Knowledge

If you are unconscious, you may be unable to give your rescuer information about medical conditions you have, such as asthma or diabetes. A worldwide service called Medic Alert can provide you with a bracelet engraved with Medic Alert's 24-hour hot line number and will record your important medical facts. Your local Red Cross office, physician, or pharmacist can provide registration information.

What Is First Aid?

First aid is the immediate care given to a person who becomes injured or ill. Knowing what kind of first aid to perform can prevent serious and sometimes permanent damage to the victim. In some cases, first aid can even prevent death.

You need to handle emergencies differently, depending on the severity of the illness or injury. A life-threatening emergency, such as occurs when someone is not breathing, requires a very fast, skillful response. A common emergency, such as a sprained ankle, usually is not as serious or as pressing. Because first aid can mean the difference between life and death, you need to know what to do in a variety of situations.

Regardless of the type of illness or injury involved, stay calm. In doing so, you will help the victim remain calm, too. Furthermore, getting scared or excited will only waste valuable time.

The First Things to Do

Figure 17.1 shows the sequence of steps to take when someone needs first aid. Each step is described in detail on the following pages. To be effective in any emergency, you must act quickly and carefully. Every second you take can make a difference. The Life Skills feature on the next page explains how you can use your senses to recognize emergencies.

Figure 17.1
First Steps in an Emergency

A Recognize that an emergency exists. → B Decide to act. → C Call the local emergency number for help. → D Provide care until help arrives.

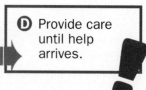

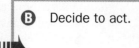

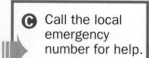

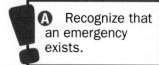

Decide to Act

Only you can decide whether you want to act. Do not be afraid to help emergency victims for fear that you will try and fail—or be sued by the victim or the victim's family. The Good Samaritan Law says that anyone who tries to help in an emergency cannot be sued unless he or she knowingly acted unsafely. If you know what you are doing and you use common sense, you cannot be sued and found financially responsible for the victim's injury.

However, do not put your own life in danger. For example, do not jump into a lake to save someone from drowning. Instead, throw the victim a life jacket or an inflated object. You will not be able to help anyone if you get hurt, too.

interNET CONNECTION

Would you know what to do in a life-threatening emergency? Prepare yourself at the Glencoe Web site.

http://www.glencoe.com/sec/health

Call for Help

If no one has called for medical assistance, you need to do so now. You should call the police department, the fire department, or Emergency Medical Services (EMS). EMS can be summoned in many areas by dialing either 911, 0, or a direct number. Remember to provide the emergency operator with all the necessary information, such as the street address, nature of the emergency, and your name. Then stay on the phone until the operator has the necessary information and tells you that you can hang up.

LIFE SKILLS

Recognizing Emergencies

Emergencies are a combination of unplanned and unexpected circumstances that require immediate action. Everyone can be taught how to respond to an emergency. In order to do so, however, you must be able to recognize the signs of an emergency. Did you realize that you carry with you, at all times, tools that help you do this? They are your senses of hearing, sight, and smell. You can use these senses to help you recognize an emergency.

- **Hearing.** Unusual, sudden, and loud noises often are signs of an emergency. You may hear human noises that attract your attention, such as screaming or calls for help. Other noises that may be associated with an emergency include shattering glass, smashing metal, screeching tires, or a machinery noise that suddenly changes.
- **Sight.** You may also see something that does not look quite right. For example, a car may be located in an odd place. Broken glass, chemical spills, downed electrical wires, smoke, fire, or a person lying motionless are often indicators of an emergency.

  Seeing a person behaving oddly may also be a sign of an emergency. For instance, you might see someone clutching her chest as if she were having a heart attack. Other unusual behaviors to investigate include slurred speech, unexplained confusion, unusual skin color, or facial expressions that show pain or discomfort.
- **Smell.** An odor that is familiar but is unusually strong may signal an emergency. For instance, you may be familiar with the smell of chlorine in a pool. If you notice that smell without being near a pool, there may have been a chlorine spill. Smelling an odor that you do not recognize can also indicate an emergency.

Follow-up Activity

Use your senses for one week to look for signs of emergencies. List all the "possible" signs that you heard, saw, or smelled. Were any of them actual emergencies? Share and discuss your lists with your classmates.

Your Total Health

Rescue Breathing Safety Tips

When you have to perform rescue breathing for an unconscious person, the American Red Cross recommends that you use a barrier to protect yourself from viruses. Although it has not been proven that HIV is transmitted this way, other viruses can be contracted from saliva. If you do not have protective equipment, use a cloth as a barrier. After you administer rescue breathing, wash your hands and mouth with hot, soapy water.

Provide Care Until Help Arrives

Providing care is a matter of learning the ABCs of first aid (see **Figure 17.2**). Move the person only if he or she is not safe. For example, move the victim if he or she is in danger from oncoming traffic or an explosion. A person should *not* be moved if he or she has a broken bone or if there seems to be damage to the head, neck, or spine. If the victim has to be moved for safety reasons, do so as gently as possible. Support the victim's spine to minimize movement.

When Rescue Breathing Is Needed

If the victim has stopped breathing but has a pulse, you can use rescue breathing. **Rescue breathing** is *a substitute for normal breathing in which someone forces air into the victim's lungs.* Rescue breathing for adults and children is different from rescue breathing for infants. **Figure 17.3** shows the steps to follow for adults and children. **Figure 17.4** shows the steps to follow for infants.

Figure 17.2

The ABCs of First Aid

A Airway
If the airway is blocked, it must be cleared. Gently roll the person on his or her back. Move the whole body at once. To open the airway, gently tilt the person's head back and at the same time lift up on the chin.

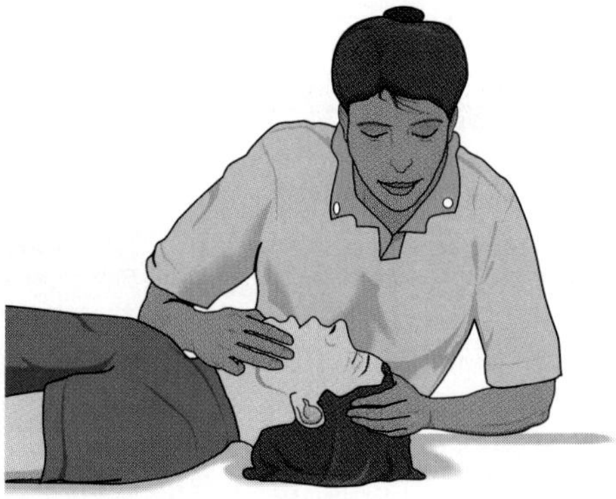

B Breathing
Check for breathing. *Look* for the rise and fall of the chest. *Listen* for air moving out of the mouth and nose. *Feel* for exhaled air on your hand or cheek. If the victim is not breathing, perform rescue breathing as shown in **Figures 17.3** and **17.4.**

C Circulation
Check the victim's *carotid pulse* on either side of the neck. If there is a pulse, you can continue doing rescue breathing until the person revives. If there is no pulse, the heart must be stimulated by someone who is trained in CPR. Call to passersby to see if someone has this skill. In the meantime, keep up the rescue breathing.

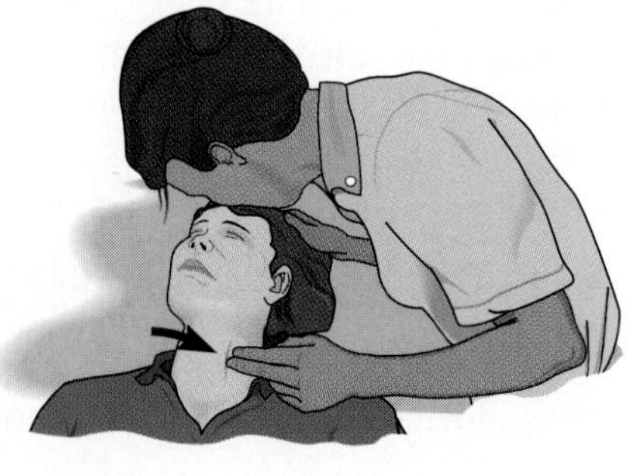

Figure 17.3
Rescue Breathing for Adults and Children

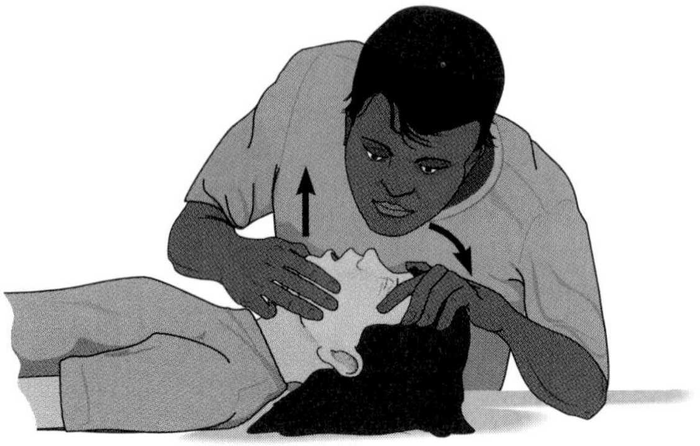

❶ Tilt the person's head back by placing one hand under the chin and lifting up while putting the other hand on the forehead and gently pressing down.

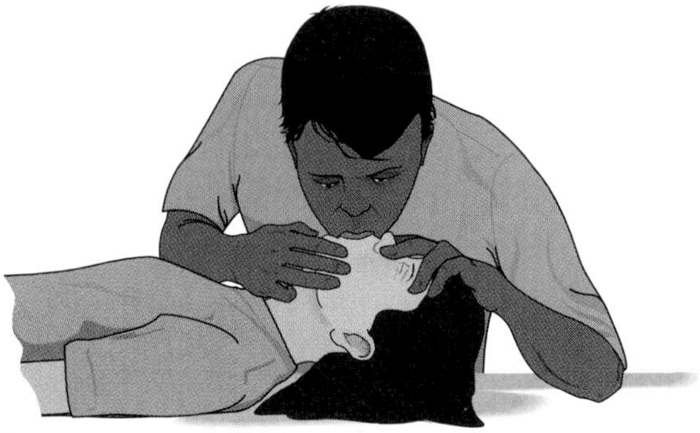

❷ Pinch the person's nostrils shut. Take a deep breath and place your mouth over the person's mouth, forming a seal. Give two slow breaths.

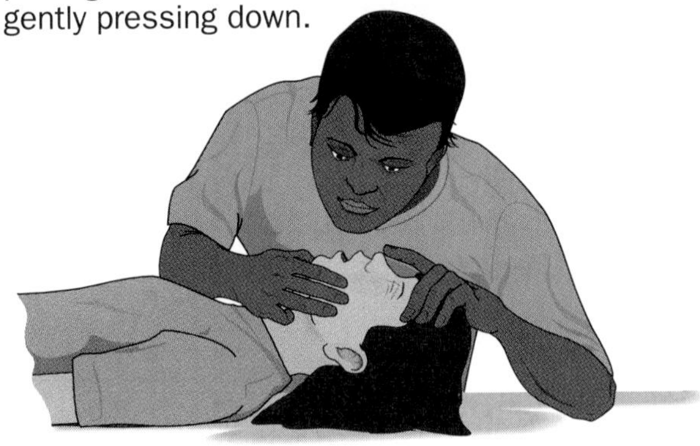

❸ For an adult or child 8 years or older, continue this procedure by giving about 12 breaths per minute or 1 breath every 5 seconds. For a child under 8 years old, give about 15 breaths per minute or 1 breath every 3 seconds. After each breath, remove your mouth to allow the victim to exhale.

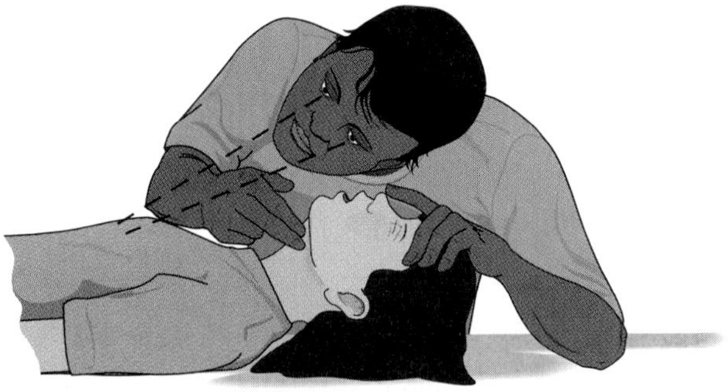

❹ Keeping the head tilted, check the victim's breathing. *Look* and *listen* for air in the lungs. Check the carotid artery for a pulse. If the victim has not started breathing or there is no pulse, repeat steps 2 and 3.

Figure 17.4
Rescue Breathing for Infants

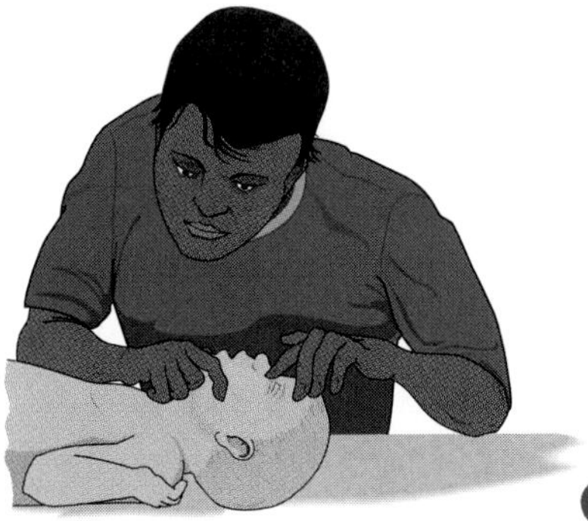

❶ Slightly tilt the head back—not as far back as you would an adult's. Gently support the infant's head.

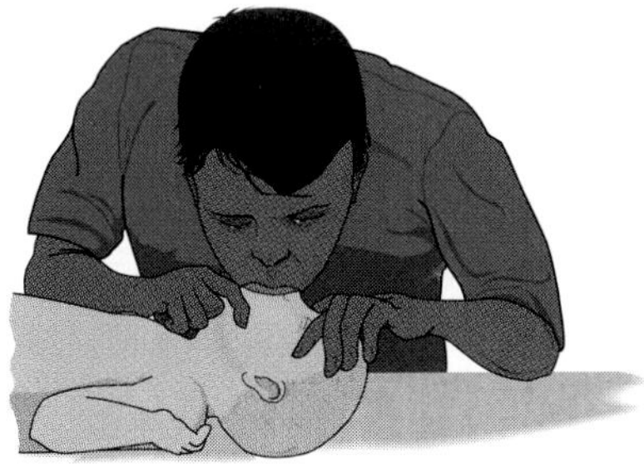

❷ Take a breath and place your mouth over the infant's nose and mouth, forming a seal. Give 1 breath and count to 3 (15 breaths per minute). The breaths should be *very* gentle.

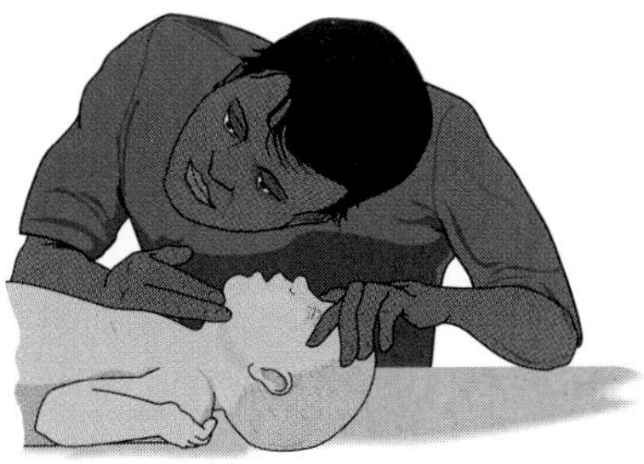

❸ After each breath, remove your mouth to allow the victim to exhale. *Look* and *listen* for air in the lungs. Recheck the pulse and breathing about every minute. If the victim has not started breathing, repeat step 2.

How to Control Severe Bleeding

The next step is to control any severe bleeding. To stop or slow the rapid loss of blood, you can use one of the three methods presented in **Figure 17.5.** Always remember to wear gloves when helping a victim who is bleeding. When you have stopped the bleeding, it is important to cover the wound to prevent infection.

Figure 17.5
Methods to Control Severe Bleeding

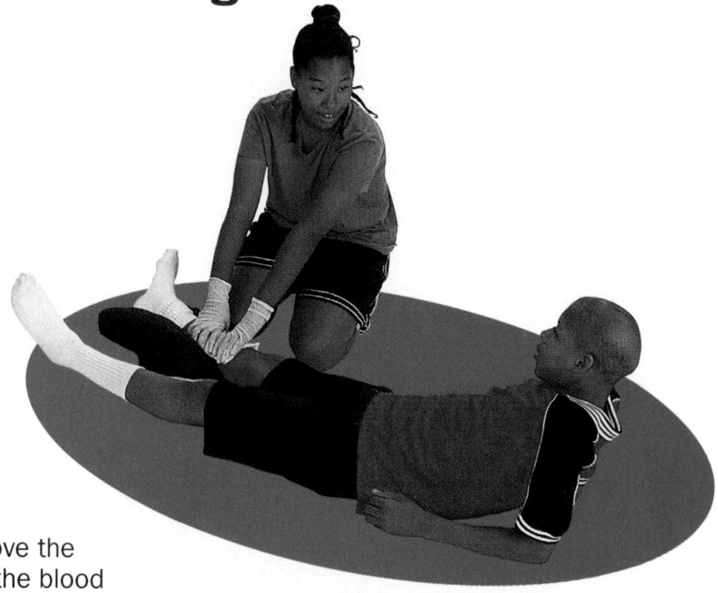

1. Apply direct and steady pressure to the wound. Place a clean cloth over the wound and press on it firmly. Add more cloth if the blood soaks through, but do not remove the first piece.

2. Combine direct pressure on the wound with pressure to a main artery leading to the wound. This is only done if you have tried method 1 several times. Push on the pressure point until you feel a bone. At the same time, apply direct pressure to the wound. (See **Figure 17.6** to locate the pressure points to the main arteries.)

3. Gently raise the bleeding body part above the level of the victim's heart. This forces the blood to travel uphill, which slows its movement. However, if the victim has a broken bone, do *not* move the body part.

Figure 17.6
Six Pressure Points

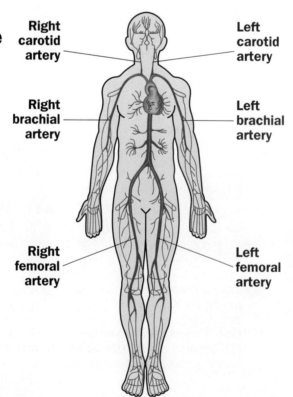

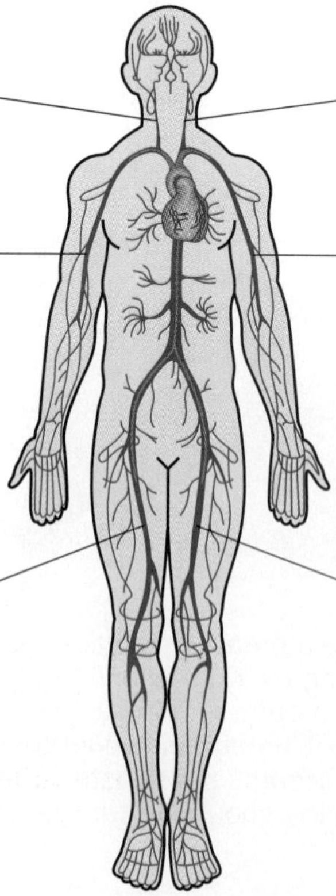

What to Do If the Victim Is in Shock

Shock can be caused by severe bleeding, heart attack, electricity, or poisoning. This is a *serious condition in which the circulatory system fails to deliver blood to all parts of the body.* Signs of shock include restlessness or irritability (after the person shows other signs of experiencing a significant problem); rapid, shallow, or uneven breathing; pale, cool, and moist skin; and rapid or weak pulse or no pulse. Cover the person with a blanket, coat, or other wrap to maintain body heat. Get help immediately.

Social Studies Connection

Natural Disaster Rescues ACTIVITY!

Use newspapers and magazines to research the rescue efforts that are required after a tornado, a hurricane, or an earthquake. Then work with a classmate to determine what steps are involved in rescuing people and saving lives after a natural disaster.

First Aid for Poisoning

Many substances in homes, such as cleaning fluids and soaps, are *poisons.* Victims of poisoning need immediate treatment.

- **Call the 24-hour poison control center or a doctor.** The center's phone number is usually listed on the inside front cover of the telephone book. Listen for and follow all instructions.
- **Call Emergency Medical Services if you are told to.**
- **Remove any extra bits of the poison from around the person's mouth with a clean, damp cloth.**
- **Save the container of the poisonous substance.** Show it to the medical team and give them any details you are aware of.

Review

Lesson 1

Using complete sentences, answer the following questions on a separate sheet of paper.

Reviewing Terms and Facts

1. **Compare and Contrast** Describe how the steps for rescue breathing for adults and older children are the same as and different from the steps for rescue breathing for infants and young children.
2. **Vocabulary** Define the term *shock.* Use it in an original sentence.

Thinking Critically

3. **Evaluate** List the four basic steps of first aid in the sequence in which they should be performed. Explain why the steps are in that order.
4. **Interpret** You are baby-sitting, and you find the child unconscious in the kitchen alongside an open can of cleanser. What has probably happened? What should you do?

Applying Health Concepts

5. **Personal Health** Use a book on health and first aid to make a list of first-aid supplies every home should have. Compare the list to supplies in your home.
6. **Health of Others** With a partner, plan a skit showing the use of basic first aid in one of these situations: you see someone fall off a bicycle and injure herself; a young child cuts himself and is severely bleeding; a friend goes into shock as a result of touching electricity. Together, act out your skit for the rest of the class.

TEEN HEALTH DIGEST

People at Work

Emergency Medical Technician

Answer each statement with "true" or "false":

1. I keep my cool in an emergency.
2. I can stand the sight of blood.
3. I am physically fit.
4. I like to help people.
5. I am interested in learning more about first aid and medicine.

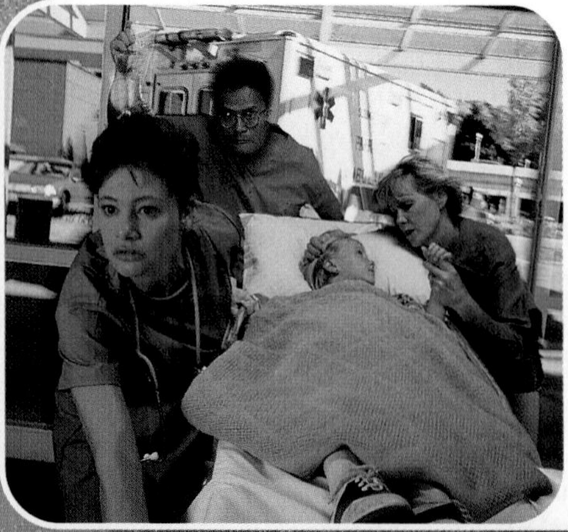

If you answered "true" to all five statements, then maybe a job as an emergency medical technician (EMT) is in your future. An EMT is often the first person at the scene of an accident or medical emergency. EMTs provide immediate medical care for people who are hurt or ill and then transport them to a hospital.

To become an EMT, you will need a high school diploma and additional training from the American Red Cross, a community college, or a local hospital.

Try This: *In your journal, write detailed responses to the five statements above. Do you still want to be an EMT? Why or why not? If so, make an action plan.*

Sports and Recreation

Beat Heatstroke

Heatstroke can occur when someone either works for a long time in heavy clothing or works out too hard and too long in very hot weather. Heatstroke caused by exposure to direct sun is called sunstroke.

The body of a heatstroke victim stops sweating and loses its ability to cool down. Therefore, the body temperature rises and remains high. Excessive body heat can lead to damage of internal organs and may even cause death.

Here are some symptoms of heatstroke:

- Red, dry, hot skin
- Rapid pulse
- Small pupils
- Fever
- Disorientation

If you come upon a heatstroke victim, remove the person from the sun and try to cool him or her down. Seek medical help immediately.

Myths and Realities

Fitness and Freezing Weather

Myth: It's important to continue with your outdoor exercise routine, no matter what the weather.

Reality: Working out in very cold weather can lead to hypothermia, which means that the body temperature drops significantly below 98.6° F. To stay warm enough, dress in layers. Be sure that the layer closest to your skin draws sweat away from your body—polyester will do this. Your outer layer should protect you from the wind—a nylon windbreaker is a good choice. Also, wear mittens or gloves and a hat. Remember, don't wait until you sweat profusely to start removing layers; you could overheat!

CON$UMER FOCU$

First-aid Kits

Do you have first-aid kits in your home and in the family car? You should, according to the American Red Cross. Here's their checklist for a well-stocked first-aid kit:

- Gauze pads and roller gauze
- Adhesive tape and bandages
- Cold pack
- Plastic bags
- Disposable gloves
- Hand cleaner
- Small flashlight and batteries
- Scissors and tweezers
- Blanket
- Triangular bandage
- Pocket mask (for rescue breathing)
- Antiseptic ointment
- Emergency phone numbers

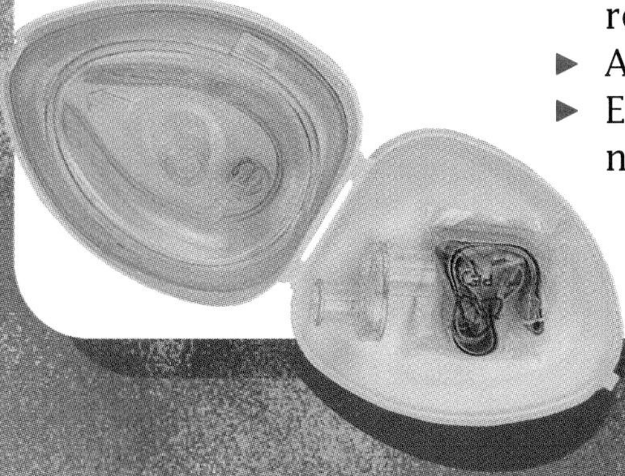

Try This: *Using the list above, create a first-aid kit for your class or family. Explain why each of the items might be necessary.*

HEALTH UPDATE

AIDS and Emergencies

You come upon a stranger in a medical emergency. You want to help, but you also want to avoid contracting HIV.

According to the American Red Cross, it is essential in medical emergencies to avoid contact with blood. Rescuers are encouraged to use barriers such as the following:

- **Pocket masks.** Use these when performing rescue breathing and CPR.
- **Latex gloves.** These should be used when you try to stop bleeding or are placing a bandage on a wound.
- **Sterile dressings or plastic.** If you don't have latex gloves or a pocket mask, use these substitutes.

Always wash your hands with hot, soapy water after treating injuries involving blood or bodily fluids.

Lesson

2 Life-threatening Emergencies

This lesson will help you find answers to questions that teens often ask about helping someone in a life-threatening emergency. For example:

- **Should I try to help someone in a life-threatening emergency?**
- **What should I do to help a choking victim?**
- **How do I know if someone needs CPR?**

Words to Know

abdominal thrust
chest thrust
CPR (cardiopulmonary resuscitation)

Life-threatening Emergencies

In life-threatening emergencies, immediate first aid is essential. Its purpose is to prevent the injury from becoming worse, to maintain vital functions, and to reassure the victim until medical assistance arrives. Learning basic first-aid procedures for choking and cardiopulmonary resuscitation (kar·dee·oh·PUHL·muh·nehr·ee ri·suh·suh·TAY·shuhn) will help you deal with medical emergencies and save lives.

As in all emergencies, perform the first steps in first aid that you learned in Lesson 1. Although you need to summon help, you should never leave a victim with a life-threatening emergency alone. Instead, call out for someone to get help. Then provide the first-aid techniques described on the following pages.

First Aid for Choking

Nearly 4,000 choking deaths occur each year in the United States. Death by choking can be prevented, however. Choking occurs when a person's airway becomes blocked by an object. If the object is not removed, air cannot reach the lungs and the victim can die. **Figure 17.7** shows the universal sign of choking.

The hand is on the throat with the finger and thumb extended.

Figure 17.7
Universal Sign of Choking
A choking person who cannot talk will grab his or her throat. Other signs of choking include problems with breathing and turning reddish, then bluish. The person may also faint.

To help a choking victim, you need to remove the object that is blocking the airway. Strong force may be needed to do this. **Figure 17.8** explains first-aid procedures for choking in adults and older children. **Figure 17.9** explains the procedure in infants and young children. Practice the steps on a large doll.

Did You Know?

Accidental Death ACTIVITY!

More than 90 percent of choking deaths involve children under five years of age. Survey your home and remove all the things that crawling babies could choke on. This method of "child-proofing" a house is recommended by pediatricians.

First Aid for Choking in Adults and Older Children

If you suspect a person is choking, ask, "Are you choking?" If you do not get an answer and other signs of choking are present, use the method known as **abdominal thrusts.** This method uses *quick, upward pulls into the diaphragm to force out the substance blocking the airway.* Use the technique shown in **Figure 17.8.**

Figure 17.8
First Aid for a Choking Adult

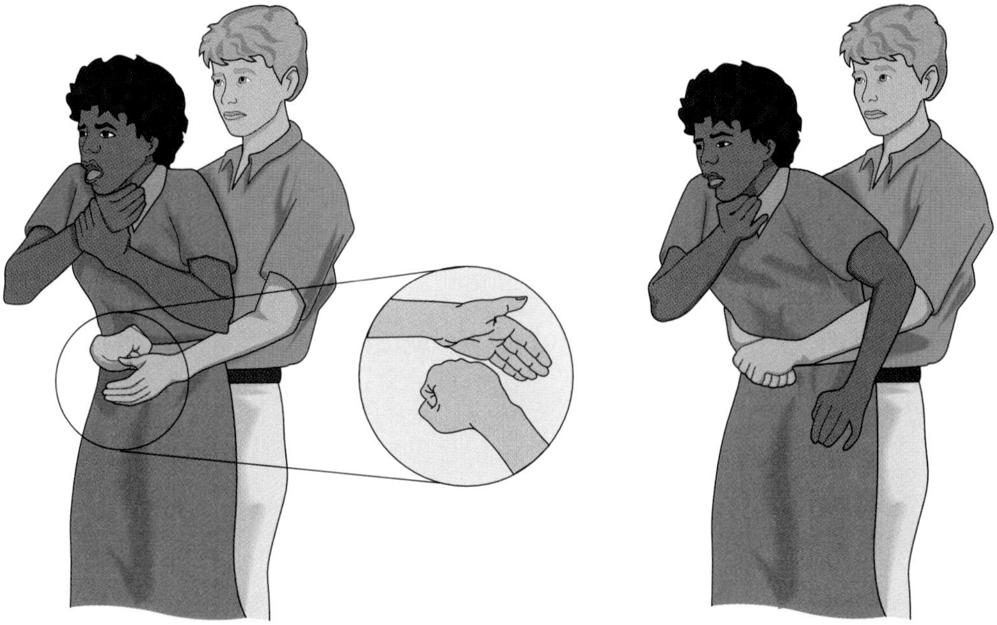

1. Stand behind the victim, sliding your arms under his or her armpits and wrapping your arms around his or her waist. Put the thumb side of your wrist against the midline of the person's abdomen, between the waist and the rib cage.
2. Grasp your fist with your other hand and apply pressure inward and up toward the person's diaphragm in one smooth movement. Deliver up to five rapid inward thrusts up toward the diaphragm. Once the object is dislodged, give rescue breathing if needed. Then monitor the victim.

First Aid for Choking in Infants and Young Children

If an infant or young child appears to be choking, use the first technique shown in **Figure 17.9** on the next page. If the blows between the victim's shoulder blades do not dislodge the object, try the second technique shown in **Figure 17.9.** This technique, which is called **chest thrusts,** uses *quick presses into the middle of an infant or child's breastbone to force out the substance blocking the airway.* Repeat both techniques if the victim does not cough up the object or start breathing on his or her own.

Figure 17.9
First Aid for Choking Infants and Young Children

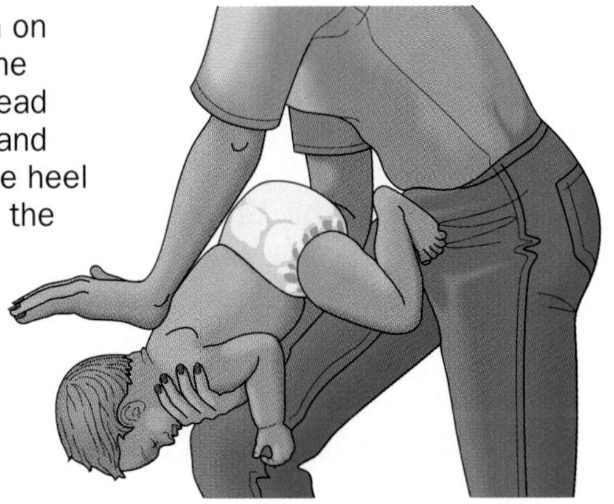

1 Hold the infant or young child face down on your forearm with the head lower than the trunk. You must support the patient's head by placing a hand around the lower jaw and chest. Give the victim four blows with the heel of your hand to the spinal area between the victim's shoulder blades.

2 Turn the victim face up on your thigh, making sure that you provide adequate support for the head. Ensure that the head is lower than the trunk. Give four slow, distinct chest thrusts by pressing two or three fingers into the middle of the victim's chest, with the index finger placed just below an imaginary line drawn directly between the nipples.

HEALTH LAB
Locating Pressure Points

Introduction: If a person is bleeding severely, it is important to know where the main pressure points are located in the body. As you have read, if direct pressure on the wound does not stop the bleeding, you need to push on the main pressure point of the artery that provides the wounded area with blood. To do this, you need to know where these pressure points are located.

If a person stops breathing, you need to take the person's pulse to know if he or she needs more than rescue breathing. The pulse indicates whether the heart has stopped beating. If it has, you need to provide rescue breathing and stimulation to the heart. Always remember that when working with a bleeding victim and/or performing rescue breathing, you need to use barriers such as latex gloves and face masks.

Objective: Learn to find pressure points and take pulses by using the following steps.

Refer to **Figure 17.6** on page 520. Use your index and middle fingers on one hand to find each of the six main pressure points shown in the illustration. Locate the pressure points by gently moving your fingers around until you feel a regular throbbing known as a pulse. The pulse in the arteries is caused by the pumping action of the heart.

Next, decide which pressure point you would push to stop bleeding in wounds located in the following places: on the right calf, on the left forearm, on the right wrist, on the left side of the chest, on the right side of the head.

The best pressure points on the body to use to take a pulse are the carotid arteries in the neck. These arteries have the strongest pulse. Find a carotid artery on your neck.

First Aid for Choking If You Are the Victim

If you are choking, alert someone around you to the emergency. Use the universal sign of choking as shown in **Figure 17.7** on page 524. If no one is around to help you, use the technique described in **Figure 17.10** to give yourself an abdominal thrust. Simply make a fist and thrust it quickly into your upper abdomen to push free the object that is choking you. Another way to give yourself an abdominal thrust is to press your abdomen into a firm object, such as the back of a chair or sofa.

Figure 17.10

First Aid If You Are Choking

Make a fist and thrust it quickly into your upper abdomen.

CPR

CPR, or **cardiopulmonary resuscitation,** is *a first-aid procedure in which another person breathes for a victim and stimulates the heart by pushing on the chest.* You cannot perform CPR unless you have successfully completed a CPR course and been certified. If CPR is done improperly, you could harm the victim by cracking a rib, puncturing a lung, or causing internal bleeding.

Using your index and middle fingers, count the number of throbs or beats in the pulse in 30 seconds. Multiply this number by 2. This gives you your pulse rate per minute. For the next two days, you will be taking your pulse rate at various times of the day. Each day, take your pulse rate when you wake up in the morning, after you exercise or play a sport, and before you go to bed.

Materials and Method: You will need a sheet of paper for each observation. Divide the sheet into two columns: *Observation* and *Analysis.* In the *Observation* column, write the facts, such as which pressure point to use for which wounds. In the *Analysis* column, write your interpretation of the activity. Answer questions such as these: Why do you think pushing on a pressure point helps stops severe bleeding? When is your pulse rate the lowest? When is it the highest? Divide another sheet of paper into three columns: *Awakening, Exercising, Retiring.* Log your pulse rate at various times of the day in the columns.

Observation and Analysis: Share your observations and analyses with a group of your classmates. Compare pulse rates.

in your journal

Now that you have read about some of the first-aid emergencies that could happen, would you consider taking a course in first aid or CPR? Why or why not?

In Lesson 1, you learned how to determine whether cardiopulmonary resuscitation is needed. Even if you are not trained in CPR, there are several ways to help.

- Gently shake the person to determine responsiveness. If there is no response, call for help.
- Make sure the person is lying down on a hard surface.
- Check for breathing.
- If the person is not breathing, deliver two breaths at one and a half to two seconds each.
- Check for a carotid pulse in the person's neck. If there is no pulse, CPR needs to be performed as quickly as possible.
- If you are not trained to perform CPR, call out, "This person needs CPR. Is anyone trained?"
- If you are alone with an injured person, you will need to phone or run for help.

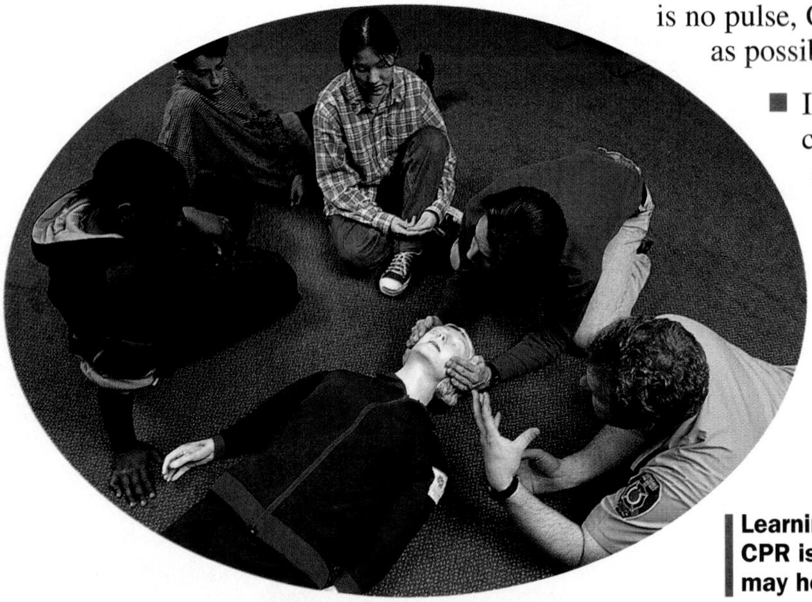

Learning how to perform CPR is a valuable skill that may help you save lives.

Lesson 2 Review

Using complete sentences, answer the following questions on a separate sheet of paper.

Reviewing Terms and Facts

1. **Vocabulary** Describe the following techniques and when they are used: *abdominal thrusts, chest thrusts.*
2. **Explain** Where is the carotid pulse located? How would you take your own carotid pulse?

Thinking Critically

3. **Compare and Contrast** How is first aid for choking in adults and older children the same as and different from first aid for choking in infants and young children?
4. **Draw Conclusions** You are at a recreational center. Suddenly an adult collapses. You think that CPR might be required, but you are not trained to perform it. What should you do?

Applying Health Concepts

5. **Consumer Health** Find out about first-aid and CPR classes taught in your community. Prepare a directory of the courses. Include the course name, a description of the course, where and when the course is held, any costs involved, and how to sign up for the course. Get permission to display the directory on a bulletin board in a public library or shopping center.

Lesson 3

First Aid for Common Emergencies

This lesson will help you find answers to questions that teens often ask about first aid for common emergencies. For example:

- **How should I help someone who has a sprain, bruise, or broken bone?**
- **How do I determine what type of burn a person has?**
- **What is the best first aid for other common emergencies, including objects in the eye, fainting, nosebleeds, and insect bites and stings?**

Words to Know

fracture
first-degree burn
second-degree burn
third-degree burn

Common Emergencies

First aid for common emergencies usually involves treating injuries such as broken bones, sprains, burns, nosebleeds, and insect bites and stings. Medical assistance may not be required, but if you are in doubt, summon help. Proper treatment is essential for injuries to heal. For that reason, you should know simple first-aid techniques for handling common emergencies, and you should always have first-aid supplies on hand.

Broken Bones

Your body contains over 200 bones, many of which protect the organs of your body. Broken bones may put vital organs in danger. Breaks commonly result from falls or playing contact sports. A **fracture,** or *a break in a bone,* is usually painful. If someone around you gets hurt and you suspect a broken bone, do not try to straighten it. Doing so might force the bone to break through the skin. Instead, follow these steps.

- Tell the person not to move the injured part.
- Put a cold pack on the injured bone.
- Summon medical assistance. If a leg is broken, have the medical help come to the victim. If an arm is broken, the victim can travel to a doctor's office or clinic. Take special care to keep the injured arm immobilized.

One way to prevent fractures is to take safety precautions, such as wearing protective gear when playing a sport.

Sprains and Bruises

A sprain results when a joint is suddenly and violently stretched. Wrists, knees, and ankles are the most frequently sprained areas. A bruise results from a blow to part of the body.

Both of these injuries are very common and usually not serious. The sprained or bruised part of the body is often painful, and it may become swollen. To relieve the pain and swelling, follow these first-aid steps.

- *Do not* use the sprained or bruised part of the body.
- Elevate the sprained or bruised part.
- Apply cold packs for the first 24 hours.
- If the pain and swelling do not stop, see a doctor.

Insect Bites and Stings

Sometimes an insect bites or stings a person, causing pain and swelling at the site of the bite or sting. Some people, however, have an allergy to insect bites or stings. If a rash develops or the person shows signs of shock, get medical help right away.

First Aid for Insect Bites
- Wash the bite.
- Apply a special lotion for bites.

First Aid for Insect Stings
- Scrape against the stinger with a credit card or fingernail to remove the stinger.
- Apply cold compresses or ice to relieve the pain.
- Watch for allergic reactions, such as a rash; difficulty breathing; swelling of the face, neck, and tongue.
- See **Figure 17.11** for instructions on removing a tick.

Insect repellents are effective against ticks and other insects. There are important rules to follow when using repellents. Do not use repellents on an open wound or irritated skin. After you go indoors to stay, wash the repellent from treated skin with soap and water and remove treated clothing. If you have a reaction to the repellent, wash your skin immediately and call your doctor.

in your journal

Find information in first-aid books on Lyme disease—a disease that infected ticks carry. Write a report in your journal on how the disease is spread, how to prevent it, and first aid for a person who is bitten by a tick.

Figure 17.11
How to Remove a Tick

❶ Drop oil or petroleum jelly on the area where the tick is in order to suffocate it.

❷ Place tweezers close to the head of the tick and pull it away. Wash the area with soap and water. If the tick's head breaks off, seek medical attention immediately to remove it.

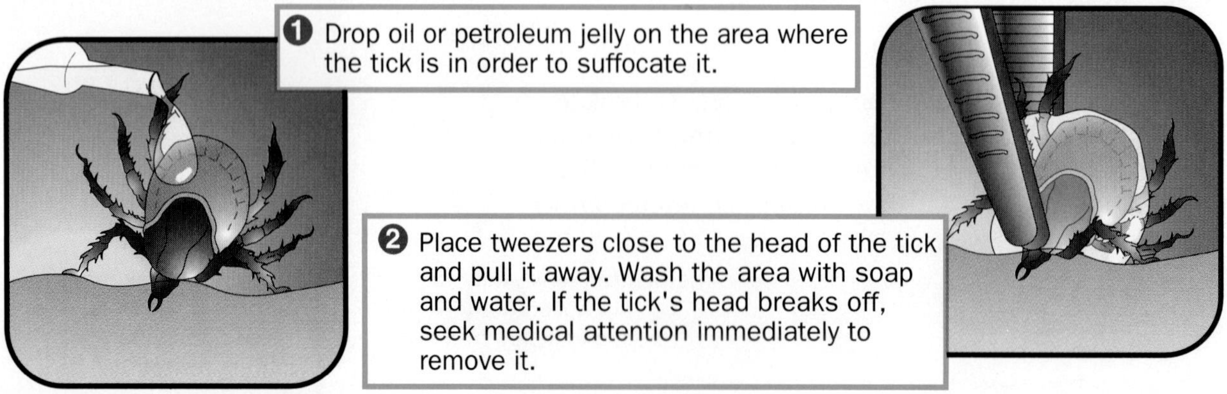

Burns

Burns vary widely in the extent of damage done to the skin and in the amount of discomfort that the victim feels. **Figure 17.12** shows how deeply the skin is damaged in each degree of burn. Burns may be caused by fire, hot objects or liquids, electricity, the sun, and chemicals. First aid for burns differs, depending on the degree of injury involved. See **Figure 17.12** for specific steps for treating each degree of burn.

A **first-degree burn** is *a burn in which only the outer layer of the skin is burned and turns red.* A first-degree burn usually heals quickly. A common type of first-degree burn is sunburn. A **second-degree burn** is *a serious burn in which the burned area blisters.* Although it may cause intense redness, pain, and swelling, this type of burn usually heals without scarring. A **third-degree burn** is *a very serious burn in which deep layers of the skin and nerve endings are damaged.* The burned areas may be white or charred, and pain may be intense.

Science Connection

Skin Banks? ACTIVITY!

To treat third-degree burns, doctors use a sheet of skin from another person. They place the skin over the burned area and remove healthy skin cells from elsewhere on the victim's body. These cells grow until there is enough to form new skin to graft to the burned area. Find out more about skin grafts for burn victims. Write a two-page report.

Figure 17.12

First Aid for the Three Degrees of Burns

A First-Degree burns
1. Submerge burned area in cold water for 10 to 30 minutes.
2. Wrap burn loosely in clean, dry dressing.

B Second-Degree burns
1. Submerge burned area in cold water. Do not pop blisters or remove loose skin.
2. Wrap burn loosely in clean, dry dressing.
3. Elevate the burned area.

C Third-Degree burns
1. Call for medical help.
2. Cover the burned area with a clean dressing.
3. Elevate the victim's feet and arms.
4. If possible, have the victim drink small amounts of fluids.

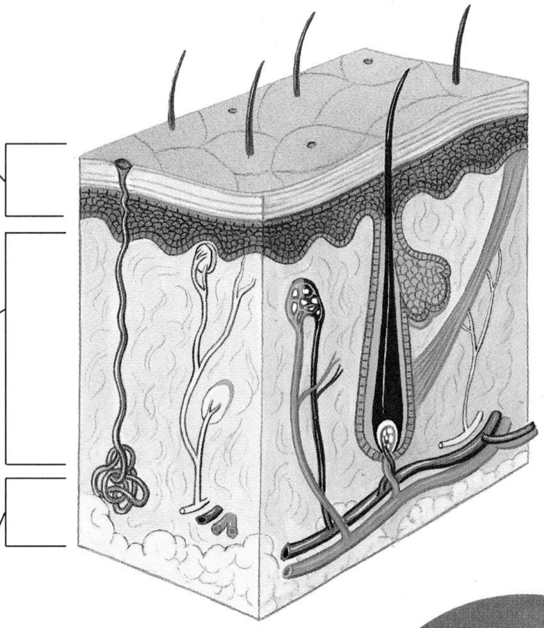

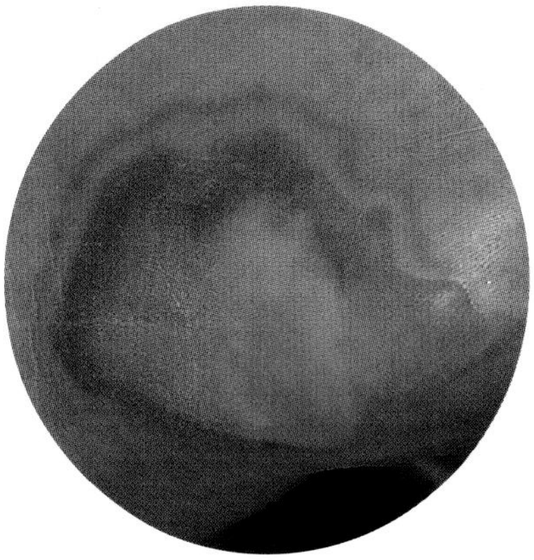

The blister shown here is characteristic of a second-degree burn.

Figure 17.13

First Aid for Someone with an Object in the Eye

Use a moist, clean corner of a handkerchief to gently remove the object. Then flood the eye with water.

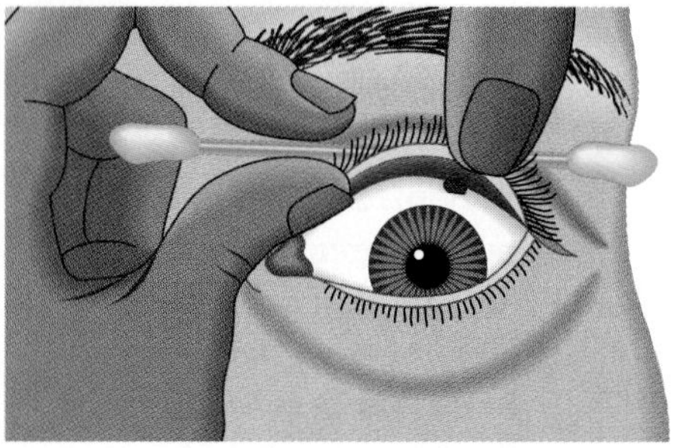

A If the object is under the upper lid, pull the lid over a cotton swab.

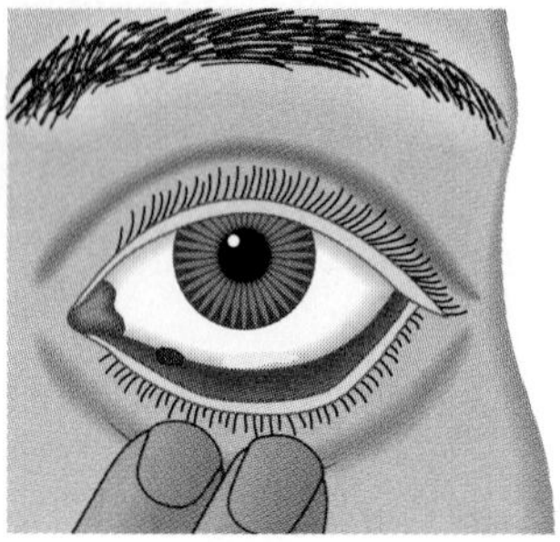

B If the object is under the lower lid, pull the lid down.

Objects in the Eye

A foreign object in the eye can cause pain and irritation. When this occurs, do not rub the eye. Doing so can cause further injury. Instead, follow the steps given in **Figure 17.13** to remove an object. If you cannot remove the object, or if the pain or irritation continues, cover the eye with a loose, dry, clean bandage and get medical help immediately.

Nosebleeds

Nosebleeds often occur without warning. They can be caused by an injury, by being in a very dry place for a long time, or even by a cold. Nosebleeds are usually not serious. Stopping a nosebleed is usually not difficult. The nosebleed victim should sit down, lean slightly forward, bow his or her head low, and firmly pinch the nose for about 5 minutes. If bleeding continues, get medical help.

MAKING HEALTHY DECISIONS

Should You Help Someone Who Is Hurt?

Bryan was taking his usual early morning bike ride. He approached his favorite part of the path—a one-way bridge over a small creek. The bridge was steep so he had to use most of the gears on his ten-speed to reach the top. Then he quickly made the descent.

As Bryan rode to the bottom of the bridge, he saw a large skid mark and some bent branches and he heard someone moaning. Bryan came to an abrupt stop. He saw a boy about his age lying to the left of the path beyond the bridge. His head was bleeding and he was motionless.

The sight of so much blood frightened Bryan. The boy was moaning softly, but Bryan could tell that he was not conscious. Although Bryan had taken a course in emergency first aid, he felt uneasy putting his knowledge into practice.

Many questions entered Bryan's mind while he was deciding what to do. I don't know this person, so why should I help him? Why don't I just go on and let someone else help him? What if he has a contagious disease? How do I know for sure what kind of injuries he has? I want to help, but what will happen to me if I do something wrong?

Fainting

Fainting occurs when the blood supply to the brain is cut off for a short amount of time. A person who faints temporarily loses consciousness. If someone faints, follow these steps.

- *Do not* lift the victim. Leave him or her lying down.
- Raise the victim's legs 8 to 12 inches.
- Loosen any tight clothing.
- Check the victim's breathing, keeping his or her airway open.
- If the victim does not regain consciousness, get medical help.
- Be aware that fainting may signal a more serious condition.

Review Lesson 3

Using complete sentences, answer the following questions on a separate sheet of paper.

Reviewing Terms and Facts

1. **Vocabulary** Describe the extent of damage to the skin for each of the following: *first-degree burns, second-degree burns, third-degree burns.*
2. **Recall** What is the procedure for stopping a nosebleed?

Thinking Critically

3. **Interpret** How do you know when to get medical help for an insect sting?

Applying Health Concepts

4. **Health of Others** Write a scenario for dealing with a common emergency. With a classmate, role-play your scenario for the class.

Bryan was confused. He decided to use the step-by-step decision-making process to make up his mind about responding to this emergency.

1. **State the situation**
2. **List the options**
3. **Weigh the possible outcomes**
4. **Consider your values**
5. **Make a decision and act**
6. **Evaluate the decision**

Follow-up Activities

1. Work in small groups and apply the six steps of the decision-making process to Bryan's situation. Have one person in each group record the members' thoughts as the group goes through each step. Have the recorder share the group's thoughts with the class.
2. With a classmate, role-play Bryan's situation, showing how Bryan decides to react to the emergency.

Chapter 17 Review

Chapter Summary

- **Lesson 1** To be helpful in an emergency situation, it is important to stay calm and to know the basic principles of first aid. Once you recognize that an emergency exists, you must decide how to act; call for help; and provide care until help arrives. Knowing how to provide rescue breathing, control severe bleeding, help a person in shock, and aid a poison victim can save a person's life.
- **Lesson 2** In life-threatening emergencies, immediate first aid is essential. The techniques used to help someone who is choking are different for adults and children. You can also help yourself if you are choking. CPR can be performed only by people who are specially trained, but there are ways to help victims who need CPR until aid arrives.
- **Lesson 3** By knowing simple first-aid techniques, you can handle common problems, such as bruises and insect bites, on your own. More serious problems, such as broken bones, require medical care. Even common problems can, in some instances, require medical attention. When in doubt, summon help.

Reviewing Key Terms and Concepts

Using complete sentences, answer the following questions on a separate sheet of paper.

Lesson 1

1. What is first aid? Why is it important to know first-aid techniques?
2. Whom should you call for help?

Lesson 2

3. Explain what you should do if you are choking.
4. What does the abbreviation *CPR* stand for? Explain what it is.

Lesson 3

5. If you fracture a bone, what does that mean? What first aid should you give a person who has fractured a bone?
6. How should you help someone who has fainted?

Thinking Critically

Using complete sentences, answer the following questions on a separate sheet of paper.

7. **Explain** How should you control bleeding if applying direct pressure to the wound does not work?
8. **Deduce** Why do you think it is important to tell a medical team the kind of poison that a victim has swallowed?
9. **Hypothesize** Why are the techniques for helping a choking victim different for adults and young children?
10. **Analyze** How do you decide if a victim needs to be given rescue breathing or CPR?
11. **Compare** What are the differences that characterize *first-, second-,* and *third-degree burns?*
12. **Evaluate** How do you determine whether you can handle a situation without medical assistance or the need to call for help?

Chapter 17 Review

Your Action Plan

Follow the steps outlined below to make an action plan that will improve the way you handle an emergency.

Step 1 Choose a long-term goal, and write it down. For instance, you might want to learn the first-aid procedures for fractures, sprains, and bruises.

Step 2 Write down a series of short-term goals that will help you achieve your long-term goal. One short-term goal might be to volunteer to assist the person who administers first aid during school sports games.

Step 3 Write out a schedule for reaching each short-term goal. Check your schedule periodically to make sure that you stay on track.

When you reach your long-term goal, reward yourself.

In Your Home and Community

1. **Health of Others** Find out what you could do to help with a community blood drive. You could encourage people to donate blood or volunteer at a blood drive. You could also help spread the word about the time and place of the blood drive.
2. **Community Resources** Find out about first-aid courses offered in your community. Collect information about where and when they are offered, how much they cost, what techniques are covered, and whether there is an age requirement. Share the information with students in your class.

Building Your Portfolio

1. **School Nurse Interview** Interview the school nurse about typical situations that occur at school that require first aid. Ask what kind of situations he or she takes care of and when a doctor needs to be called. Tape-record your interview, and add it to your portfolio.
2. **First Aid Steps** Write a first-aid pamphlet for an emergency that might occur in your home. Be sure that the first-aid steps are clear, concise, and accurate. Try to include illustrations that help explain the procedures. Distribute your booklet to class members. Include a copy in your portfolio.
3. **Personal Assessment** Look through the activities and projects you did for this chapter. Choose one that you would like to include in your portfolio.

Chapter 18

The Environment and Your Health

Student Expectations

After reading this chapter, you should be able to:

1. **State the causes of different kinds of environmental pollution.**
2. **Explain the importance of clean air and water.**
3. **Explain how conserving energy helps the environment.**
4. **Discuss the importance of finding safe ways to dispose of wastes.**

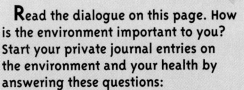

Teen Chat Group

Raoul: Hi! What are you two doing out here?

Amanda: We volunteered to plant trees for the Parks Department. Do you want to help?

Raoul: What made you decide to do that?

Katie: We use the trees, plants, soil, water, and air in our environment every day. We thought that it was time to give something back.

Amanda: If we don't take care of our planet, who will? We want to make sure that our environment stays clean and healthy for a long, long time.

Katie: Even though this is just a little tree right now, someday it will be big and strong. Over the years we can watch it grow and know that we made a difference.

Raoul: I didn't know that planting trees could be so important! How can I help?

in your journal

Read the dialogue on this page. How is the environment important to you? Start your private journal entries on the environment and your health by answering these questions:

- Have you ever done anything to improve or beautify your environment? If so, what did you do?
- How would you describe the living and nonliving parts of your environment?
- How do you interact with these parts of your environment?

When you reach the end of the chapter, you will use your journal entries to make an action plan.

Lesson 1

Earth As a System

This lesson will help you find answers to questions that teens often ask about their environment, its condition, and how their actions can affect it. For example:

- **What is the environment made of?**
- **Why is a healthy environment important to me?**
- **What is pollution?**

Words to Know

environment
ecosystem
groundwater
toxic
pollution

Health and Your Environment

In Chapter 1, the word *environment* was defined as the sum total of your surroundings. There, the focus was on your friends, your family, and your community. This chapter uses **environment** in a broader sense to refer to *all the living and nonliving elements around you.* Your environment includes the birds that fly overhead, the trees that grow along the street, the air you breathe, the water you drink, and the other people who live on this planet.

You interact with your environment in many ways. You depend upon it for the air, water, and food you need to live. You affect the environment when you plant flower seeds, cut down a tree, feed the birds, or use products that harm plants, animals, water, or air.

All life forms affect the environment, but the actions people take often have far-reaching effects. For example, for many years a chemical called DDT was used to kill insects that were considered harmful to crops. Unfortunately, DDT also killed many birds, fish, and animals. DDT is now outlawed. Understanding the effects our actions may have is an important step in protecting the environment and keeping it healthy. You should pay attention to the environment because your health depends on it.

in Your journal

List the living and nonliving factors of your classroom ecosystem. Describe how you interact with each.

Enjoying outdoor activities in a clean, unpolluted environment is one of the great pleasures of life.

Interdependence in the Environment

Different parts of the environment interact within an ecosystem. An **ecosystem** (EE·koh·sis·tuhm) is *all the living and nonliving elements in an area and the way they relate to each other.* Ecosystems can be just about any size, from a drop of water to a huge forest. In fact, the whole earth is a vast ecosystem. Each ecosystem includes everything needed for the survival of the plants and animals in it. **Figure 18.1** shows the parts of an ecosystem.

interNET CONNECTION

Check out the Glencoe Web site and discover what *you* can do to keep the environment healthy.

http://www.glencoe.com/sec/health

Figure 18.1

Elements of an Ecosystem

The living elements of an ecosystem can be divided into producers, consumers, and decomposers.

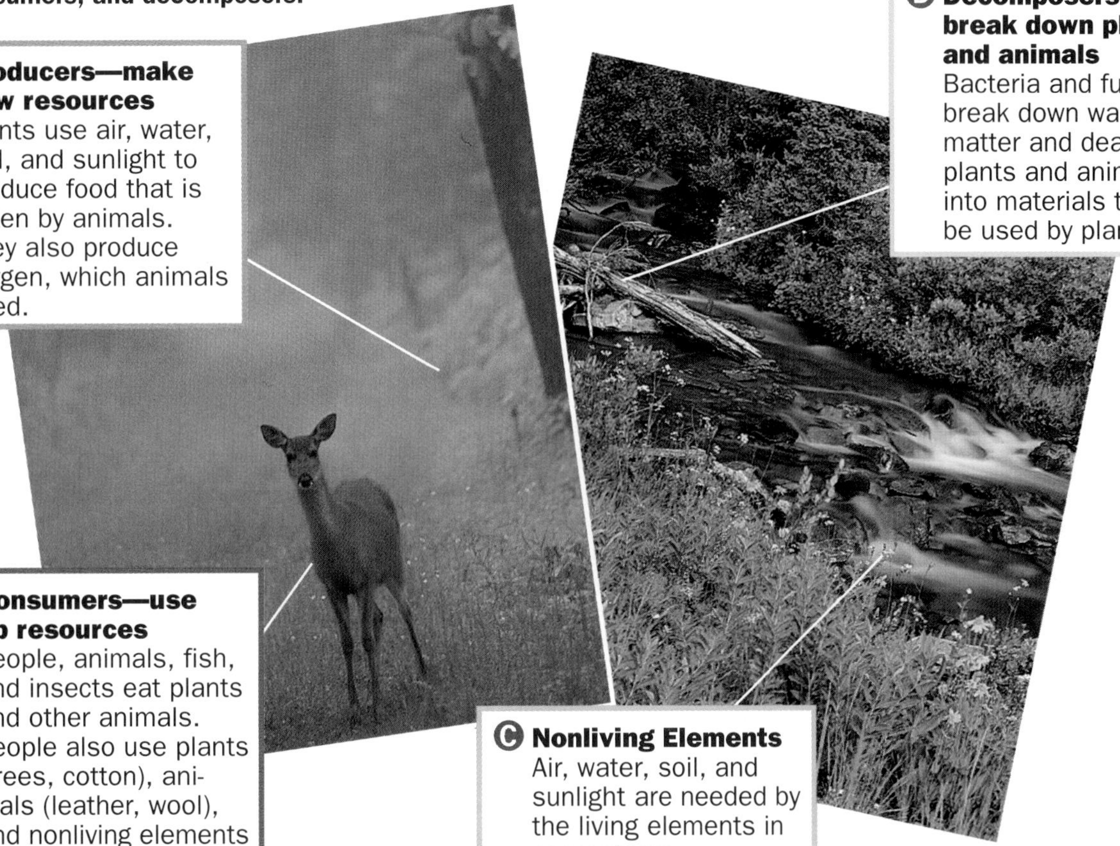

A Producers—make new resources
Plants use air, water, soil, and sunlight to produce food that is eaten by animals. They also produce oxygen, which animals need.
B Consumers—use up resources
People, animals, fish, and insects eat plants and other animals. People also use plants (trees, cotton), animals (leather, wool), and nonliving elements (iron, oil) to produce shelter, clothing, and energy.
C Nonliving Elements
Air, water, soil, and sunlight are needed by the living elements in ecosystems.
D Decomposers—break down plants and animals
Bacteria and fungi break down waste matter and dead plants and animals into materials that can be used by plants.

The health of an ecosystem depends on the well-being of its parts. If something damages one part of the ecosystem, all the other parts will be affected.

Air

Air is one of the nonliving elements in your environment. Almost all life forms need air to survive. You certainly do. When you breathe, you interact with the air around you. Your body removes oxygen from the air and releases carbon dioxide. Your body uses the oxygen to help produce energy. Plants use the carbon dioxide in air to help produce food, which you also need to live.

Science Connection

Climate and Environment ACTIVITY!

An area's climate affects its environment. Find out the climate in your area and how that affects your area's environment.

Water

Water is another important nonliving element in your environment. Like air, water is essential to all living things. Many plants and animals live in the lakes, rivers, and oceans of the world. They get the nutrients they need to survive from the water. These plants and animals in turn provide food for people.

About 70 percent of the earth's surface is covered by water. Most of this is the salty water of the oceans, but many plants and animals need clean, fresh water to survive. Streams, rivers, and lakes are the main sources of fresh water at the earth's surface. However, **groundwater,** which is *water below the earth's surface,* is a major source of fresh water in many areas.

The crops farmers grow to feed us are producers that need soil, air, water, and sun.

Soil

The solid part of the earth you live on—the soil—is a third nonliving element in your environment. Soil is the loose material on the earth's surface in which plants can grow. The plants get the nutrients and water they need from the soil. These nutrients must be replaced over a period of time by decaying plant and animal matter or the soil will wear out. Minerals in the soil, such as salt, phosphorus, and iron, have many uses.

LIFE SKILLS

Consumer Be Aware

Your health depends on the health of your environment. For this reason it is important that you do your part to keep the environment healthy. When you go shopping, use the following guidelines to help you become an environmentally conscious consumer.

- **Containers.** Many items you buy are in containers you will throw away, so avoid wasteful packaging. Whenever possible, choose products packaged in materials that break down easily, such as paper and cardboard.
- **Labels.** Read all labels carefully. Many common household products, such as oven cleaners and paint thinners, contain toxic substances. **Toxic** substances are *harmful or poisonous to humans or to plant and animal life.* If you must use a toxic material, follow label directions carefully for proper application and safe disposal of leftover material.
- **Recycling.** Select products made of materials that can be collected and used again in some way. Many materials, such as glass, paper, aluminum, and some plastics, can be processed for reuse in other products. This saves energy and reduces the amount of solid waste being added to the environment.

Environmental Problems

Some actions that people take have a harmful effect on the environment and upset the balance of ecosystems.

- **Pollution.** *Dirty or harmful substances in the environment,* called **pollution** (puh·LOO·shuhn), may affect the air, water, or soil. Most pollution is caused by burning fuels and disposing of waste materials.
- **Demand for food.** Many activities carried on to increase the food supply harm the environment. Chemical fertilizers used on crops pollute the water supply. Cutting down forests for more farmland leads to soil being blown or washed away.
- **Too many people.** The environment is also harmed by too many people living in an area. More people make more pollution and strain food and water resources. The world's population almost doubled between 1900 and 1960, and is expected to double again by the year 2000 (see **Figure 18.2**).
- **Waste disposal.** What to do with solid wastes, or garbage, becomes more of a problem every year, especially in developed countries like the United States. As populations grow, they produce even more solid wastes.

Figure 18.2
Growth of World Population

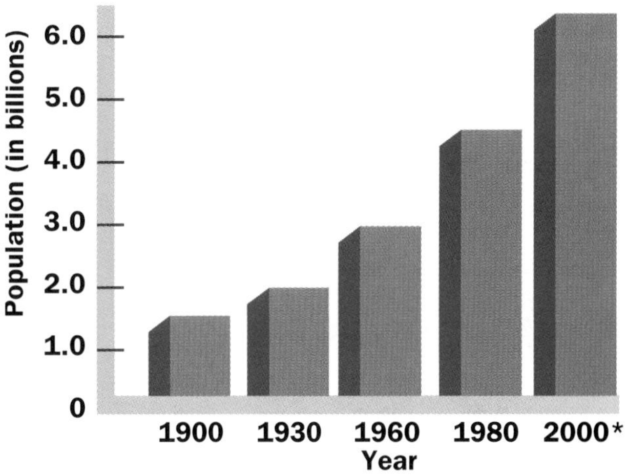

*Estimate
Source: *Statistical Abstract of the United States,* 1996

Review

Lesson 1

Using complete sentences, answer the following questions on a separate sheet of paper.

Reviewing Terms and Facts

1. **Vocabulary** Define *environment* and *ecosystem* and explain how they are related.
2. **Give Examples** Name some steps you might take to reduce the amount of material you personally throw away.

Thinking Critically

3. **Analyze** What is meant by the "health" of the nonliving elements in your environment?
4. **Synthesize** Explain why efforts to increase the food supply often result in environmental problems.

Applying Health Concepts

5. **Consumer Health** Read the labels on the cleaning products in your home. List the uses of each product and whether they contain harmful or toxic substances. Investigate substitutes for any products that are harmful. With classmates, make a poster that explains how to use these products safely and suggests replacements for unsafe products.

TEEN HEALTH DIGEST

Sports and Recreation

Kaiparowits Forever

It rises 600 feet above the red rock lowlands of southern Utah. Its 650,000 acres are covered with canyons, buttes, and precariously balanced rocks. The Kaiparowits Plateau is so rugged and remote that it was the last spot in the continental United States to be mapped.

On September 18, 1996, President Bill Clinton declared the plateau a national monument. This declaration saved the plateau from being dug up by miners. Shortly after that, a team of mountain bikers took a trip across the plateau. The bikers discovered trails had been plowed in parts of the plateau. They notified the authorities immediately.

Will all of the plateau be saved for later generations to explore? Thanks to the mountain bikers, the Kaiparowits National Monument remains safe in the southern Utah wilderness.

Personal Trainer

Walk or Ride This Way

Problem #1: Americans, on average, are out of shape.

Problem #2: The environment is damaged by pollution from car exhausts and the manufacture of gasoline and other oil products.

Could these two problems be related? Yes! Pollution and poor personal health are both linked to the excessive use of cars.

Fortunately, there's an easy way to help fix both problems—take a walk, or jump on your bike! Don't beg a ride every time you need to head to the store or the library. Walk or ride your bike unless the distance is too great. You'll improve your health as you do your part to save the planet.

Try This:

Want to help preserve the environment in your area? Contact the nearest branch of the Sierra Club, and learn about the programs they offer for teens.

HEALTH UPDATE

Get the Lead Out

Over the past 30 years, the government has banned lead in products such as gasoline and paint. The ban on lead is working. The levels of lead in the blood of Americans have dropped drastically in the past few years.

Still, many Americans are at risk of lead poisoning. One study found that almost 1 million children in the United States have high lead levels in their blood. Most of these children were found living in older homes where the paint or plumbing contained high levels of lead. The U.S. Department of Housing and Urban Development estimates that in about 4 million American homes where young children live, there are still lead-based paints.

Try This: *To learn more about lead in homes and what to do about it, write to: National Lead Information Center at 1025 Connecticut Avenue NW, Suite 1200, Washington, DC 20036. Report your findings to the class.*

CON$UMER FOCU$

"Eco-Shopping"

Every time you shop, you have the chance to harm or help the environment. Here are tips to follow if you want to be an "eco-shopper."

- *Plan!* Make a shopping list. It will help you buy only what you need.
- *Precycle.* Look for packaging that can be recycled or is made of recycled materials.
- *Bag it.* Bring your own bags to the stores. Use them over and over to cut down on waste.
- *Buy in bulk.* Look for larger packages of foods such as cereal and snacks. This cuts down on the packaging you throw away.

Teens Making a Difference

Young Angelenos Save Their River

Who: Teens from the Thomas Starr King Middle School

What: The Great Los Angeles River Cleanup

When: Every May

Where: Los Angeles, California

"We thought the Great Los Angeles River Cleanup would be boring," says Juan, a student who took part. "Once we got there and started picking up the trash, it became fun... I found a vacuum cleaner, my friend Leopoldo found three supermarket carts, and my friend Sevak found three more."

Try This: *Is there a river in your town that needs cleaning up? Work with your teachers to organize a great river cleanup of your own!*

Lesson 2

Clean Air and Clean Water

This lesson will help you find answers to questions that teens often ask about the quality of the air and water and how their activities can affect that quality. For example:

- **How clean is the air I breathe?**
- **Where does my drinking water come from and how clean is it?**
- **How can pollution affect my health?**

Words to Know

fossil fuels
ozone
particulates
pesticides
acid rain
smog
greenhouse effect
sewage
biodegradable

The Air You Breathe

Air is a mixture of many different invisible gases. As you can see in **Figure 18.3,** nitrogen and oxygen are the main ingredients of dry air. Small quantities of carbon dioxide, argon, and other gases are also present. In addition, the air near the earth's surface always contains some water vapor.

When you breathe, your body interacts with the air in your environment. You breathe so that your body can get the oxygen it needs to function properly. The rest of the gases in clean air have little or no effect on your body.

Q&A

Natural Pollution

Q: Is all pollution caused by human activities?

A: No. Natural events, such as forest fires and volcanoes, can produce materials that make the environment dirty. At certain times of the year, pollen from trees and flowers can make the air unhealthy for some people to breathe.

Figure 18.3

Composition of the Air

You take in oxygen from the air when you breathe, and exhale carbon dioxide. Carbon dioxide is also released by the burning of oil, gas, and other fuels. Scientists are concerned that the level of carbon dioxide in the atmosphere is increasing. This could upset the balance of gases in the atmosphere and lead to climate changes.

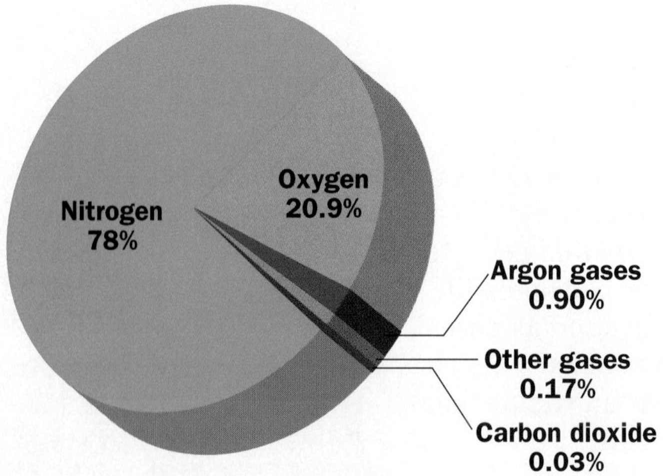

Unfortunately, the air you breathe is not completely clean. It contains all kinds of impurities (im·PYOOR·uh·tees)—things that make the air dirty. Every time you inhale, you bring these impurities into your body. They may include dust, pollen, smoke, chemical particles, and harmful gases. None of these substances are good for you. Some can be very harmful to your health.

in your journal

Make a list of all your activities that use energy produced by fossil fuels. Beside each activity, tell which fossil fuel is used and if its use contributes to air pollution.

Sources of Air Pollution

Air pollution consists of gases and particles. The major sources of air pollution are described below.

- **Burning fossil fuels.** The *oil, coal, and natural gas burned to provide energy* are called **fossil** (FAH·suhl) **fuels.** This energy is used to produce electricity, heat buildings, and run motor vehicles. However, burning these fuels releases toxic gases, such as carbon monoxide and sulfur dioxide. Another gas that comes from fossil fuels is **ozone** (OH·zohn), *a form of oxygen* that is harmful when produced by motor vehicle and industrial pollution. Burning oil or coal can also produce **particulates** (par·TIK·yuh·lits), *tiny particles that can remain in the air for a long time.* Many particulates are bits of soot or ash. Some particulates, such as lead or mercury, are poisonous.
- **Other sources of smoke.** Most kinds of fires produce smoke containing gases and particulates. Bonfires or burning leaves or trash contribute in a small way to pollution.
- **Chemicals.** Some common products found around the house contain chemicals that pollute the air. For example, many **pesticides** (PES·tuh·sydz), which are *products used to kill insects and other pests,* contain harmful chemicals. CFCs (chlorofluorocarbons), the cooling agents used in air conditioners and refrigerators, damage a layer of the atmosphere (the ozone layer) that protects the earth from dangerous solar radiation. Production of CFCs was halted in developing countries in 1996, and will be phased out in other countries by 2006, in an effort to stop this damage.

Increasing the use of electric cars will reduce air pollution from automobile exhaust fumes. California law requires that by the year 2003, 2 percent of the cars sold in the state must be powered by electricity or some other source of energy that does not contribute to air pollution.

Figure 18.4
How Acid Rain Occurs

When coal, oil, and other fossil fuels are burned, they produce sulfur dioxide and nitrogen oxides. These gases form sulphate and nitrate particles that mix with water vapor and form weak acids. The acids fall to the earth as acid rain, which is *rain (or snow) that is more acidic than normal.*

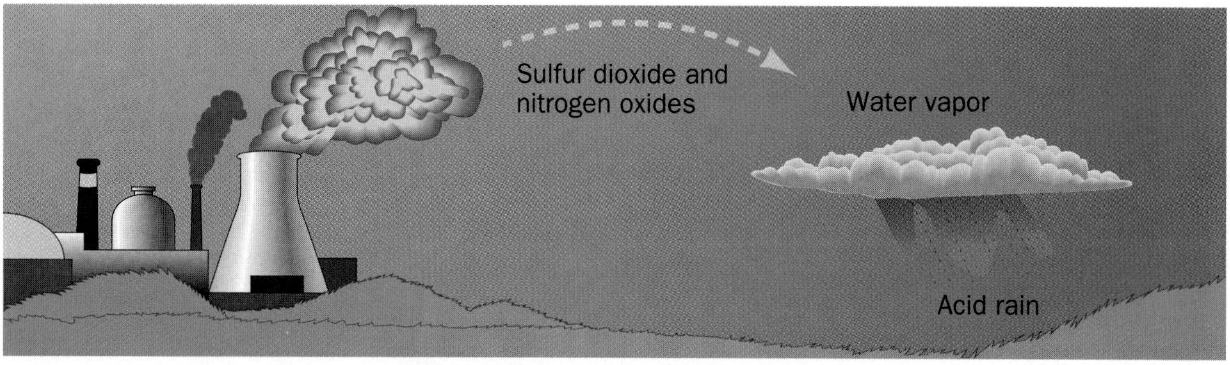

Effects of Air Pollution

Air pollution has many harmful effects on the environment. Some of the effects are described in the following paragraphs.

- **Acid rain.** Gases from burning fossil fuels may combine with moisture in the air to form acid rain (see **Figure 18.4**). Over time, acid rain can damage forests and destroy fish and plant life.
- **Smog.** In cities with heavy traffic, a special kind of **smog** often develops. It is a *yellow-brown haze that forms when sunlight reacts with impurities in car exhaust.* The smog screens out sunlight, preventing it from reaching the earth.
- **Greenhouse effect.** The burning of fossil fuels produces carbon dioxide, and this gas acts like a blanket holding heat near the earth's surface. *The trapping of heat by carbon dioxide and other gases in the air* is known as the **greenhouse effect.** Increased levels of carbon dioxide in the air may lead to a global warming, a rise in the earth's temperatures. This in turn could affect the water level of oceans and change weather patterns.
- **Ozone destruction.** Although toxic near the earth's surface, ozone high in the atmosphere forms a layer that shields living elements on earth from the sun's harmful ultraviolet (UV) radiation. However, certain kinds of air pollution, especially from CFCs, may be destroying some of the ozone layer. This thinning of the ozone layer allows excessive UV radiation to reach the earth's surface, which can harm humans.
- **Health problems.** Air pollution can cause a variety of health problems, including shortness of breath, sneezing, and itchy eyes. Air pollution can cause serious problems for people with such breathing disorders as asthma (AZ·muh) and emphysema (em·fuh·SEE·muh). (See Chapters 12 and 13 for more information on breathing disorders.)

Did You Know?

Household Pesticides ACTIVITY!

Many households in the United States use pesticides. If not used carefully, these chemicals can pollute the air you breathe at home. Use the following tips for safety.

- Use insect traps.
- Use chemical sprays sparingly and with lots of ventilation.
- Store and discard unused pesticides according to directions.

Go through your home and make a list of potentially toxic items. Talk to your parents about safer alternatives to the products on your list.

Water: A Vital Resource

Like you, all plants and animals need fresh water, a resource that is in limited supply. In fact, one out of every five people in the world do not have an adequate amount of clean, fresh water. Even though the supply of this precious resource is limited, people still use water carelessly.

Water Pollution

The earth's water is polluted by various kinds of wastes, chemicals, and other substances. **Sewage** is *water containing wastes that are washed down people's drains.* Sewage includes food, human wastes, detergents, and other products. Harmful chemicals are another major cause of water pollution. Some enter the water from factories. Pesticides and chemical fertilizers can wash out of farms to pollute water.

Much human illness and disease is caused by harmful substances in water. Typhoid (TY·foyd) fever and cholera (KAH·luh·ruh) are caused by bacteria in untreated sewage. Hepatitis (he·puh·TY·tuhs), a disease of the liver, can be caused by eating shellfish taken from polluted water. Drinking water that contains lead or mercury can result in serious damage to the brain, liver, and kidneys.

Q&A ?

Pesticides and Healthy Water

Q: How do pesticides get into our drinking water?

A: This can happen in two ways. When pesticides are sprayed into the air, some of the chemicals may be carried by the wind to reservoirs. Pesticides on land can be carried into the soil by rainwater until they reach groundwater supplies.

HEALTH LAB

The Effect of Water Pollutants

Introduction: Detergents, fertilizers, and garbage in rivers and lakes can affect the health of the water. They may, for example, cause the amount of algae in the water to change. Algae (AL·jee), the green scum you see in ponds and other bodies of fresh water, are very simple plants that use sunlight to make their own food. Some forms of pollution can cause algae to multiply rapidly and form a thick layer that blocks the sunlight. Deprived of light, the algae below the surface die and decay, consuming large amounts of oxygen in the water. Deprived of oxygen, fish and other forms of life in the water also die.

Objective: To find out what effect detergents and garbage have on algae.

Materials and Method: You will need tap water that has been left to stand uncovered for three days; fresh water from a pond or aquarium with some algae; liquid detergent; some potato or carrot scraps; three clean glass jars of the same size with lids; and labels.

Label the jars D (detergent), G (garbage), and N (no additions). Fill each one halfway with the tap water. Add enough pond water to bring the level to three-fourths. Then add a tablespoon of detergent to Jar D and some vegetable scraps to Jar G. Do not add anything to Jar N. Put the jars on a windowsill for two weeks.

Observation and Analysis: Observe the jars every other day. Compare and note the color of the water in the three jars. In which jar was there the greatest increase of algae? In which jar was there the least increase of algae?

Using your own power rather than riding in a car or bus helps you and the environment.

Working for Cleaner Air and Water

Anything you do that uses energy produced by burning fossil fuels contributes to air pollution. This includes such activities as using electric appliances, driving a car, and running a power lawn mower. Here are some ways you can help keep the air cleaner.

- Whenever practical, walk or ride a bicycle rather than having someone drive you in a car.
- Use public transportation. Buses, trains, and subways reduce air pollution by transporting many people at one time.
- Avoid outdoor burning of trash, leaves, and brush.
- Don't smoke! This advice is good for your health and good for the environment.
- Save electricity. Turn off lights and appliances when not in use. Don't overheat or overcool your house.

Here are some ways you can help keep water cleaner.

- Use detergents that are **biodegradable.** This means that they can be *easily broken down in the environment.*
- Discard all waste materials properly. Do not dump anything in the water or on the ground where it might get into groundwater.

Lesson 2 Review

Using complete sentences, answer the following questions on a separate sheet of paper.

Reviewing Terms and Facts

1. **Vocabulary** What is the *greenhouse effect?*
2. **List** Name two sources of both air and water pollution.

Thinking Critically

3. **Synthesize** Explain how fossil fuels are connected to acid rain.
4. **Compare and Contrast** How can the same gas, ozone, be both harmful and necessary to people?
5. **Apply** You and three of your friends are going to meet at the mall. Each of you is going to have someone drive you to the mall in a car. What other arrangements could you and your friends make to reduce air pollution?

Applying Health Concepts

6. **Health of Others** Make a list of actions you or members of your family take that contribute to air or water pollution. Then draw up a second list of ways you could cut down on this pollution.
7. **Consumer Health** Find out the source of the fresh water used in your community. Visit the local water department to learn what measures are used to make sure that your water supply is kept clean. Write a brief report to present to your class.
8. **Health of Others** If you are concerned about your environment, you can do something about it. Write to a local political figure expressing your concerns and what you think should be done about them. Your efforts will be even more effective if you get a number of your friends and classmates to each send his or her own letter.

Lesson 3

Reduce, Reuse, Recycle

This lesson will help you find answers to questions that teens often ask about conserving natural resources. For example:

- **What kinds of materials can be recycled?**
- **How does recycling help to save natural resources?**
- **What can I do to help conserve energy?**

Words to Know

nonrenewable resource
conservation
recycled
precycling

Conservation

You use natural resources every day. A natural resource is any material from the earth that can be used: air, water, trees from the forest, and the fish from the sea.

Many natural materials are **nonrenewable resources,** which are *substances that cannot be replaced once they are used.* Fossil fuels are one example. Once a barrel of oil is burned, it is gone forever. **Figure 18.5** explains how energy is used in one manufacturing process. It's important that people learn to use nonrenewable resources wisely. **Conservation** is *the saving of resources.* The best way to conserve a resource is to use less of it. There are many ways to save energy at home.

- Turn off lights and appliances when they are not being used.
- In winter, put on a sweater instead of turning up the heat.
- Repair all leaking faucets, especially hot-water faucets.
- Seal air leaks around any doors and windows in your home to prevent heat from escaping.

Q&A

A Self-Renewing Resource

Q: Is water a nonrenewable resource?

A: No. The earth's supply of water is constantly being renewed, or replenished, through the water cycle. However, conservation of fresh water is necessary because it is always in limited supply.

Figure 18.5
Energy Used in Making an Aluminum Can

The diagram shows the steps needed to make an aluminum can. The energy is provided by fossil fuels.

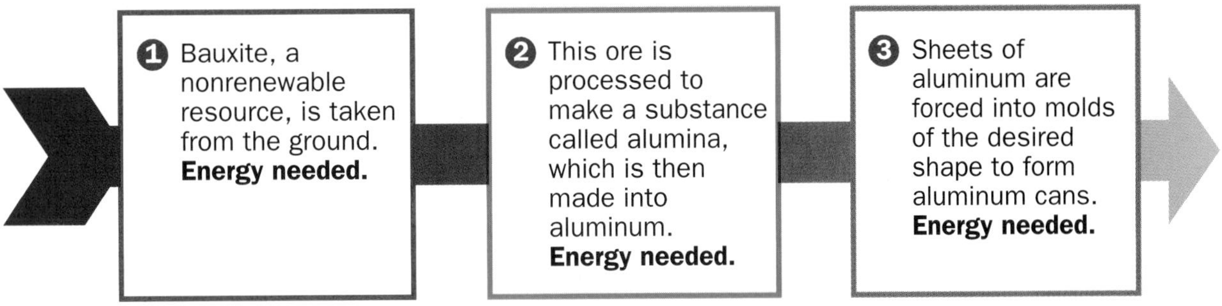

1 Bauxite, a nonrenewable resource, is taken from the ground. Energy needed.
2 This ore is processed to make a substance called alumina, which is then made into aluminum. Energy needed.
3 Sheets of aluminum are forced into molds of the desired shape to form aluminum cans. Energy needed.

Cultural Connections

In the Bag

ACTIVITY!

In many countries, people take along their own bags or baskets when they go shopping. Grocery stores and markets do not provide free bags for purchases. Many people who move to this country carry on the tradition of supplying their own shopping bags, thus helping the environment. Keep a supply of grocery bags in the trunk of your family car. Encourage family members to use them each time they shop.

Recycling

Imagine yourself in the school cafeteria. You have just finished lunch and are emptying your tray. You place a glass juice bottle in one bin and a foil sandwich wrapper in another. The banana peel goes into a third bin. In short, you have separated your trash into items to be thrown away and items that can be **recycled.** This means that they can be *changed in some way and used again.*

The symbol shown here is fast becoming a familiar sight on many kinds of products. It shows that an item can be recycled or is made of recycled materials. Recycling has become a popular means of conserving energy and natural resources. At the same time, recycling helps to reduce the quantities of solid wastes.

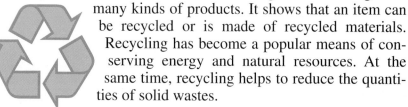

How does recycling help conserve energy and natural resources? As you saw in **Figure 18.5** on page 549, energy is needed to mine the ore that is used to make aluminum, to process the ore, and to manufacture the cans. When aluminum cans are recycled, they are changed back into sheets or blocks of aluminum. These sheets can then be used to make new cans or other aluminum products. No new ore is taken from the ground and much less energy is needed.

Not everything can be recycled. However, many of the items that people normally throw away can be recycled. The most common materials collected for recycling today are aluminum, glass, plastic, yard waste, and paper (see **Figure 18.6**).

MAKING HEALTHY DECISIONS

Deciding on Priorities

Larry belongs to a community environmental group. He believes that the group's work is very important and devotes a lot of time and energy to it. Because of his dedication, he has recently been appointed a junior member of the town's environmental commission.

The environmental group has been working on plans for a Highway Beautification Day on Saturday. A section of highway will be closed for the day, and volunteers will be cleaning up litter and planting thousands of spring bulbs, wildflower seeds, and grass seed. The day will end with a picnic.

Larry has been asked to bring his family and he would really like them to come. However, he knows that they have already planned an outing to the beach that day with some cousins. When he mentioned the problem to his father, his father suggested that Larry spend the day on his own and get a ride home with the group leader.

Larry doesn't know what to do. He loves the beach but feels he should be involved in the highway project. Should he participate in the project and miss the trip to the beach? Should he try to persuade his father and sister that the environmental project is more important than going to the beach that particular day? He uses the step-by-step decision-making process.

1. **State the situation**
2. **List the options**

Precycling

Some of the bother involved in recycling can be avoided by being a wise shopper and by **precycling,** *reducing waste before it occurs.* Here are some basic guidelines for precycling.

- Buy products in packages that can be reused or recycled.
- Buy products in glass, metal, or paper containers.
- Look for products in refillable containers.
- Bring a cloth bag to carry your purchases.

❸ **Weigh the possible outcomes**
❹ **Consider your values**
❺ **Make a decision and act**
❻ **Evaluate the decision**

Follow-up Activities

1. Apply the six steps of the decision-making process to Larry's situation.
2. With a partner, role-play a scene in which Larry tries to convince his family to participate in the Highway Beautification Day with him.
3. Now role-play a scene in which Larry explains to his environmental group that he will not be joining them. Think of suggestions he can make for finding other volunteers for the project.

Learning to repair items—large and small—is an important step in cutting down waste and protecting the environment.

in your journal

Review how your own habits and lifestyle affect the environment. Include your use of resources (such as water and energy), the items you throw out, and your efforts to reuse and recycle. Write a paragraph describing your habits and their effect on the environment.

Other Actions to Take

There are more things you can do to protect the environment.

- **Reuse.** When you buy a product, think about ways it or its container can be reused. Store such items for use later.
- **Repair.** If an item breaks or wears out, try to fix it instead of throwing it away.
- **Pass it on.** Possessions that you don't want or can't use anymore can be donated to charitable groups that will give them to people who can use them.
- **Be informed.** Get more information about environmental issues.

Lesson 3 Review

Using complete sentences, answer the following questions on a separate sheet of paper.

Reviewing Terms and Facts

1. **Name** What is a natural resource? Give three examples of natural resources that you use.
2. **Vocabulary** Give an example of a nonrenewable resource.
3. **List** Name four ways that you can conserve energy around your home.
4. **Identify** Which item that we throw away makes up the largest portion of our trash?

Thinking Critically

5. **Compare** What is the difference between recycling and precycling? Give an example of each.
6. **Apply** You have an old bicycle that you don't ride anymore. Instead of throwing it away, what can you do with it that will help the environment?

Applying Health Concepts

7. **Health of Others** Set up a recycling center in your home. Use cartons or containers to organize and collect recyclable materials.

Lesson 4

Handling Environmental Hazards

This lesson will help you find answers to questions teens often ask about solid wastes and hazardous materials in their environment. For example:

- **What happens to the trash collected at my house?**
- **What kinds of waste materials can cause illness?**
- **What is radon?**

Solid Waste: The Leftovers

Every year, Americans throw out about 200 million tons of trash. That's enough trash to fill 5 million large truck trailers! This trash is known as solid waste.

Sometimes people just throw their trash anywhere. All across the country, paper bags, plastic wrappers, newspapers, cans, and bottles can be found cluttering roadsides and public parks. This waste is called litter. Litter is a type of environmental pollution. While it may not pose a health threat, it is wasteful and unpleasant to look at, and cleaning it up can be expensive.

Disposing of Solid Waste

Most solid waste is produced by businesses and households. Trucks haul it off to a **landfill,** a *place where wastes are dumped and buried.* At one time, everything and anything could be dumped in a landfill. As a result, these sites were dirty and unhealthy. Because some landfills had harmful waste, they were even dangerous.

Today, most landfills are strictly regulated, and only certain wastes can be dumped in them. The wastes are spread in layers and covered with layers of soil. However, no matter how hard landfill operators may try, landfills are unpleasant and unsightly places.

Words to Know

landfill
hazardous waste
nuclear waste
radon

Math Connection

Getting Rid of Trash ACTIVITY!

About 17 percent of the solid waste produced in the United States is recycled and reused. About 16 percent is burned. Most of the rest goes to landfills. Calculate the percentage of solid waste that goes into landfills.

Americans throw out about 200 million tons of trash a year. That comes to about 4.3 pounds of garbage per person per day.

Another problem with landfills is that they take up tremendous amounts of space. As the human population increases, more land is needed for homes, schools, shops, and businesses. At the same time, more solid waste is produced. In some areas the problem is so great that wastes are being transported hundreds of miles to places far away that still have landfill space available.

One possible way to reduce the amount of solid waste dumped in landfills is to burn as much of our trash as possible. The energy produced by burning wastes in special furnaces, called *incinerators* (in·SIN·uh·ray·terz), can be used to heat homes or generate electricity. This cuts down on the use of fossil fuels.

There are disadvantages to burning wastes. Incinerators are very expensive to build and operate, and only certain waste materials can be burned safely. Many people argue that the smoke and ashes produced by burning solid waste are harmful to the environment. These people believe that recycling and reusing materials is a better and safer method of dealing with the problem of solid waste.

Did You Know?

Batteries

Ordinary batteries—used for flashlights, toys, and portable radios and tape players—make up a sizeable portion of the hazardous household wastes in this country. Many types of batteries contain harmful chemicals that leak out and get into the soil and water supplies.

Personal Inventory

DO YOU PROTECT YOUR ENVIRONMENT?

You play an important role in the environment. For this reason, it is important for you to know how the products you use and the actions you take affect your environment. Many of the products found in your home are hazardous or contain hazardous materials. Some of these products can be found on the list below.

batteries	**nail polish remover**
bleach	**oven cleaner**
drain cleaner	**paint, paint thinner**
insecticides	**rubber cement**
motor oil, antifreeze	**spot remover**

Look over the list and pick out the items that you use. Write these down on a sheet of paper. Add to your list any other items you use that you think may be hazardous. Then answer the following questions for each item on your list.

1. What do you use it for?
2. Do you read the directions for the use of these products and follow those directions carefully?
3. Why or how is it hazardous?
4. What do you do with the remains of the product when you have finished with it?

When you have answered the questions, think about what you can do to help protect the environment from the hazards of these products.

Hazardous Wastes

Over the past 50 years or so, advances in science and technology have led to many changes. New industries have developed and thousands of new products have been introduced. These changes have led to a new problem—*waste products that may cause illness.* Such wastes are called **hazardous** (HAZ·er·duhs) **wastes.**

Hazardous wastes are dangerous in a number of different ways. Some are explosive. Some easily catch fire and can produce poisonous smoke. Some, called *toxic wastes*, are poisonous. When hazardous wastes enter and pollute the soil, water, or air, they can cause injury, illness, and even death (see **Figure 18.7**).

Hazardous wastes cannot be disposed of like other wastes. They need special handling. The government has a strict set of rules about how to get rid of hazardous wastes. The Environmental Protection Agency (EPA) has the job of enforcing the rules.

Many places in this country have been identified as toxic waste sites where hazardous wastes were dumped in the past. Millions of dollars are being spent to clean up these sites.

in your journal

Make a list of all the products in your house that may be hazardous or contain hazardous chemicals. Tell how each is used, stored, and disposed of. Make note of any unsafe practices and tell how those practices can be changed and made safer.

Chemicals

As the number of types of industries has grown over the years, the use of different kinds of chemicals has increased dramatically. Chemicals are used in the manufacture of hundreds of different products and materials. Many products, such as medicines, paints, fertilizers, and pesticides, can be dangerous if they are not used, stored, and disposed of properly.

Industrial by-products are chemicals left over from the manufacturing process. Careless disposal of these by-products in the past has produced many of the world's most dangerous toxic waste sites.

Figure 18.7
The Effects of Hazardous Wastes

Substance	Uses	Effects
Asbestos	Insulation, filler	Scars lungs, causes cancer
Benzene	Fabrics, detergents	May cause cancer
Carbon tetrachloride	Refrigeration, solvents	Can cause death or illness if inhaled
DDT	Pesticides	Kills fish, birds; toxic to humans
Lead	Paints, batteries	Causes brain, liver, kidney damage
PCBs	Plastics	Birth defects, liver damage, cancer
Vinyl chloride	Plastics	Causes cancer

Love Canal

Love Canal, a community in New York State, is a good example of the dangers of improper disposal of hazardous wastes. Love Canal was built on the site of an old chemical dump. After some years, it was noticed that many cases of birth defects, nervous disorders, and cancer occurred in the community. It was then discovered that buried chemicals had leaked from their containers and poisoned the soil and the water supplies. Nearly a thousand families had to be relocated. The site was closed to residents for more than ten years while it was being cleaned up. Since then, about 140 families have moved into renovated homes in Love Canal, where the environment continues to be monitored for their safety.

Love Canal was the first hazardous waste site to gain nationwide recognition. Enormous public awareness of the dangers of toxic wastes led the federal government to take serious measures, such as the creation of the landmark Superfund Trust. The Superfund closely monitors toxic waste cleanup and encourages businesses to use and produce environmentally safe products.

Science Connection

Nuclear Energy

Nuclear energy is so named because the energy comes from the nuclei of radioactive elements. When the nucleus of an atom breaks down, energy is released in the form of radiation.

Did You Know?

Industrial Wastes

In 1994 alone, industries reported releasing over 2 billion pounds of toxic chemicals into the environment. About half of this amount is released into the air.

Nuclear Wastes

Some industries use materials that are radioactive. These materials give off radiation, a form of energy that can be harmful to living things. Radiation has been linked to cancer in humans. Radioactive materials are used as fuel in atomic power plants. They are also used in weapons research and production and in medical research and treatment. The *harmful by-products of industries that use radioactive materials* are called **nuclear** (NOO·klee·er) **wastes.**

Nuclear wastes continue to give off radiation for hundreds or thousands of years. Therefore, the safe disposal of these wastes presents a very difficult problem. Scientists are working on it but still have not come up with a satisfactory solution.

Radon

In recent years, scientists have discovered a natural source of radioactive pollution. **Radon** (RAY·dahn) is *a colorless, odorless, radioactive gas.* It forms when radium (RAY·dee·uhm) breaks down. Radium is a radioactive element present in some rocks. Radon becomes a problem when it leaks from the ground and collects in the interiors of homes. Long-term exposure to high levels of radon can cause lung cancer.

Checking the radon level in your home is easy and inexpensive to do.

Dealing with Hazardous Wastes

Industry and government must find solutions to the major problems associated with hazardous wastes. Every individual can also help to reduce the problem and protect the environment.

Proper disposal of hazardous waste ensures a healthier environment for us and for future generations.

- Use hazardous materials properly. Follow directions carefully when using materials such as pesticides, paint thinners, and oven cleaners.
- Follow the proper procedures in your community for disposal of materials such as motor oil, paints, batteries, and pesticides.
- Whenever possible, buy environmentally safe household chemicals.
- Form community action groups to clean up areas around local rivers and lakes.
- Support groups that work to get environmental laws passed and enforced.

Review

Lesson 4

Using complete sentences, answer the following questions on a separate sheet of paper.

Reviewing Terms and Facts

1. **Vocabulary** What is meant by the term *hazardous wastes?*
2. **Recall** Name two methods of waste disposal and describe how each one works.
3. **Give Examples** List at least three products that can be hazardous to the environment.
4. **Identify** Explain what radon is and where it is found.
5. **Outline** List four steps you can take to reduce pollution from hazardous wastes.

Thinking Critically

6. **Explain** Why is the disposal of hazardous wastes more of a problem than the disposal of other solid wastes?
7. **Evaluate** When you go to the store to buy a product for a cleanup job, you are offered two products. Product A is strong and will do the job quickly. However, it gives off dangerous fumes and you need to wear rubber gloves when you use it. Product B is safe to use but costs twice as much and will take longer to do the job. Which product would you use? Explain your reasoning.

Applying Health Concepts

8. **Health of Others** Check with state or local health agencies to learn if radon gas is a potential problem where you live. Find out how you can check the radon level in your home and what can be done if levels are high.
9. **Health of Others** Research alternative energy sources, such as solar power and wind power. Report on the advantages and disadvantages of each energy source.

Chapter 18 Review

Chapter Summary

- **Lesson 1** The environment is all living and nonliving elements around you. Air, water, and soil are the major nonliving elements in your environment. The actions of people affect the health of the environment. The health of all living things depends on a healthy environment.
- **Lesson 2** Burning fossil fuels is a major cause of air pollution. Sewage and chemicals are major sources of water pollution.
- **Lesson 3** Conservation is an important way to keep the environment clean and to reduce the use of nonrenewable resources. Recycling, precycling, and reusing are important methods of conserving resources and energy.
- **Lesson 4** Americans produce a tremendous amount of solid waste, which is usually either brought to a landfill or incinerated. Hazardous wastes are dangerous and must be disposed of in special ways. Hazardous wastes include chemicals and nuclear wastes.

Reviewing Key Terms and Concepts

Using complete sentences, answer the following questions on a separate sheet of paper.

Lesson 1

1. Define *groundwater.* Why is it important that groundwater be clean?
2. Define the terms *toxic* and *pollution.* What are the two major causes of pollution?

Lesson 2

3. Define the following terms, and explain how each is related to air pollution: *pesticides, acid rain, smog.*
4. Define *sewage* and *biodegradable.*

Lesson 3

5. Define *nonrenewable resource* and *conservation.*
6. What are some ways in which you can precycle when you shop?

Lesson 4

7. What are two problems with using landfills to dispose of solid waste? What are two problems with using incinerators to dispose of solid waste?
8. Define *nuclear waste.* Why are nuclear wastes so dangerous?

Thinking Critically

Using complete sentences, answer the following questions on a separate sheet of paper.

9. **Relate** Explain how cutting down forests in another part of the world can affect the environment where you live.
10. **Apply** How can conserving energy help to keep the environment clean?
11. **Apply** Explain why precycling conserves more energy than recycling.
12. **Synthesize** Describe several ways in which the increasing world population affects the environment.

Chapter 18 Review

Your Action Plan

Your actions affect the health of the environment in which you live. Review your journal entries for this chapter. Then create an action plan, as outlined below, to help you improve the way you interact with your environment.

Step 1 Write down a long-term goal. For example, you might want to find more ways to recycle, precycle, and reuse.

Step 2 Write down a series of short-term goals that will help you reach your long-term goal. A short-term goal might be to form the habit of throwing beverage cans, paper, and plastic into recycling bins.

Step 3 Establish a schedule to meet each short-term goal.

Step 4 Check your schedule periodically to keep yourself on track.

Reward yourself when you reach your long-term goal.

In Your Home and Community

1. **Community Resources** Find out about groups in your community that work on environmental issues. Find out what kind of projects they sponsor and how they try to improve the health of the environment. Share your findings with your class.
2. **Health of Others** Survey your school to find out if resources are wasted or mishandled. You might prepare a checklist with questions such as: Are recycling bins for paper available in every class? Present your findings to the school principal along with an action plan for improving the school's commitment to a healthy environment.

Building Your Portfolio

1. **Ecosystem at Work** Take photographs of a local park or other green space. Include pictures of producers, composers, nonliving elements, and decomposers. Arrange the photographs in a folder. Explain the part each picture plays in the ecosystem of the area you photographed. Add this folder to your portfolio.
2. **Business Conservation** Interview the manager of a local factory, power plant, or large business (such as a grocery store). Find out what methods they use to conserve energy and reduce environmental pollution. Find out if the business uses any recycled products, and if so, what kind. Ask them to explain the recycling process they use. Tape-record your interview. Include a summary statement, and add the tape to your portfolio.
3. **Personal Assessment** Look through all the activities and projects you did for this chapter. Choose one or two that you would like to include in your portfolio.

Nutritive Value of Selected Foods

Nutrients in Indicated Quantity

Foods	Food energy (Calories)	Protein (Grams)	Fat (Grams)	Carbohydrate (Grams)	Calcium (Milligrams)	Iron (Milligrams)	Sodium (Milligrams)	Vitamin A value (IU) (International units)	Thiamin (Milligrams)	Riboflavin (Milligrams)	Niacin (Milligrams)	Ascorbic acid (Milligrams)
Dairy Products												
Cheese:												
Cheddar1 oz	115	7	9	Tr	204	0.2	176	300	0.01	0.11	Tr	0
Cottage, lowfat1 cup	205	31	4	8	155	0.4	918	160	0.05	0.42	0.3	Tr
Feta1 oz	75	4	6	1	140	0.2	316	130	0.04	0.24	0.3	0
Mozzarella1 oz	80	6	6	1	147	0.1	106	220	Tr	0.07	Tr	0
Pasteurized process (American) ...1 oz	105	6	9	Tr	174	0.1	406	340	0.01	0.10	Tr	0
Milk:												
Whole1 cup	150	8	8	11	291	0.1	120	310	0.09	0.40	0.2	2
Lowfat (2%)1 cup	120	8	5	12	297	0.1	122	500	0.10	0.40	0.2	2
Nonfat (skim)1 cup	85	8	Tr	12	302	0.1	126	500	0.09	0.34	0.2	2
Chocolate milk (commercial) ..1 cup	210	8	8	26	280	0.6	149	300	0.09	0.41	0.3	2
Ice cream, vanilla:												
Regular1 cup	270	5	14	32	176	0.1	116	540	0.05	0.33	0.1	1
Soft serve (frozen custard) ...1 cup	375	7	23	38	236	0.4	153	790	0.08	0.45	0.2	1
Yogurt (made with lowfat milk):												
Fruit-flavored8 oz	230	10	2	43	345	0.2	133	100	0.08	0.40	0.2	1
Eggs												
Eggs, fried in margarine ...1 egg	90	6	7	1	25	0.7	162	390	0.03	0.24	Tr	0
Eggs, scrambled1 egg	100	7	7	1	44	0.7	171	420	0.03	0.27	Tr	0
Fats and Oils												
Butter1 pat	35	Tr	4	Tr	1	Tr	41	150	Tr	Tr	Tr	0
Margarine1 tbsp	100	Tr	11	Tr	4	0.0	151	460	Tr	Tr	Tr	Tr
Oils, corn1 tbsp	125	0	14	0	0	0.0	0	0	0.00	0.00	0.00	0
Salad dressings (commercial)												
French:												
Regular1 tbsp	85	Tr	9	1	2	Tr	188	Tr	Tr	Tr	Tr	Tr
Low calorie1 tbsp	25	Tr	2	2	6	Tr	306	Tr	Tr	Tr	Tr	Tr
Mayonnaise:												
Regular1 tbsp	100	Tr	11	Tr	3	0.1	80	40	0.00	0.00	Tr	0
Salad dressing (home recipe)												
Vinegar and oil1 tbsp	70	0	8	Tr	0	0.0	Tr	0	0.00	0.00	0.0	0
Fish and Shellfish												
Fish sticks1 stick ...	70	6	3	4	11	0.3	53	20	0.03	0.05	0.6	0
Haddock, breaded, fried ...3 oz	175	17	9	7	34	1.0	123	70	0.06	0.10	2.9	0
Shrimp, fried3 oz	200	16	10	11	61	2.0	384	90	0.06	0.09	2.8	0

Foods		Food energy	Protein	Fat	Carbohydrate	Calcium	Iron	Sodium	Vitamin A value (IU)	Thiamin	Riboflavin	Niacin	Ascorbic acid
		Calories	Grams	Grams	Grams	Milligrams	Milligrams	Milligrams	International units	Milligrams	Milligrams	Milligrams	Milligrams
Tuna, canned, drained solids:													
Oil pack, chunk light	3 oz	165	24	7	0	7	1.6	303	70	0.04	0.09	10.1	0
Water pack, solid white	3 oz	135	30	1	0	17	0.6	468	110	0.03	0.10	13.4	0
Fruits and Fruit Juices													
Apples, raw unpeeled	1 apple	80	Tr	Tr	21	10	0.2	Tr	70	0.02	0.02	0.1	8
Apple juice	1 cup	115	Tr	Tr	29	17	0.9	7	Tr	0.05	0.04	0.2	2
Applesauce:													
Sweetened	1 cup	195	Tr	Tr	51	10	0.9	8	30	0.03	0.07	0.5	4
Unsweetened	1 cup	105	Tr	Tr	28	7	0.3	5	70	0.03	0.06	0.5	3
Bananas	1 banana	105	1	1	27	7	0.4	1	90	0.05	0.11	0.6	10
Cranberry juice cocktail	1 cup	145	Tr	Tr	38	8	0.4	10	10	0.01	0.04	0.1	108
Grapefruit	½ grapefruit	40	1	Tr	10	14	0.1	Tr	10	0.04	0.02	0.3	41
Grapes, green seedless	10 grapes	35	Tr	Tr	9	6	0.1	1	40	0.05	0.03	0.2	5
Lemonade (from concentrate)	6 oz	80	Tr	Tr	21	2	0.1	1	10	0.01	0.02	0.2	13
Oranges	1 orange	60	1	Tr	15	52	0.1	Tr	270	0.11	0.05	0.4	70
Orange juice (from concentrate)	1 cup	110	2	Tr	27	22	0.2	2	190	0.20	0.04	0.5	97
Peaches:													
Fresh	1 peach	35	1	Tr	10	4	0.1	Tr	470	0.01	0.04	0.9	6
Canned, in syrup	1 cup	190	1	Tr	51	8	0.7	15	850	0.03	0.06	1.6	7
Pears:													
Fresh	1 pear	100	1	1	25	18	0.4	Tr	30	0.03	0.07	0.2	7
Canned, in syrup	1 cup	190	1	Tr	49	13	0.6	13	10	0.03	0.06	0.6	3
Raisins, snack pack		40	Tr	Tr	11	7	0.3	2.0	Tr	0.02	0.01	0.10	Tr
Strawberries:													
Raw, whole	1 cup	45	1	1	10	21	0.6	1	40	0.03	0.10	0.3	84
Frozen, sweetened, sliced	1 cup	245	1	Tr	66	28	1.5	8	60	0.04	0.13	1.0	106
Grain Products													
Bagels	1 bagel	200	7	2	38	29	1.8	245	0	0.26	0.20	2.4	0
Biscuits, from mix	1 biscuit	95	2	3	14	58	0.7	262	20	0.12	0.11	0.8	Tr
Breads:													
Pita bread, 6½ in diam	1 pita	165	6	1	33	49	1.4	339	0	0.27	0.12	2.2	0
Rye bread	1 slice	65	2	1	12	20	0.7	175	0	0.10	0.08	0.8	0
White bread	1 slice	65	2	1	12	32	0.7	129	Tr	0.12	0.08	0.9	Tr
Whole-wheat bread	1 slice	70	3	1	13	20	1.0	180	Tr	0.10	0.06	1.1	Tr

Notes: *Tr* indicates presence of nutrients in trace amounts. All fruits and vegetables are fresh unless noted. Vegetables are fresh cooked unless noted.

Nutritive Value of Selected Foods (continued)

Foods	Quantity	Food energy (Calories)	Protein (Grams)	Fat (Grams)	Carbohydrate (Grams)	Calcium (Milligrams)	Iron (Milligrams)	Sodium (Milligrams)	Vitamin A value (IU) (International units)	Thiamin (Milligrams)	Riboflavin (Milligrams)	Niacin (Milligrams)	Ascorbic acid (Milligrams)
Breakfast cereals:													
Oatmeal	1 cup	145	6	2	25	19	1.6	2	40	0.26	0.05	0.3	0
Cornflakes	1¼ cups	110	2	Tr	24	1	1.8	351	1,250	0.37	0.43	5.0	15
Crackers, snack-type	1 cracker	15	Tr	1	2	3	0.1	30	Tr	0.01	0.01	0.1	0
French toast (home recipe)	1 slice	155	6	7	17	72	1.3	257	110	0.12	0.16	1.0	Tr
Macaroni	1 cup	190	7	1	39	14	2.1	1	0	0.23	0.13	1.8	0
Pancakes, 4-in diam.	1 pancake	60	2	2	8	36	0.7	160	30	0.09	0.12	0.8	Tr
Popcorn:													
Air-popped, unsalted	1 cup	30	1	Tr	6	1	0.2	Tr	10	0.03	0.01	0.2	0
Popped in vegetable oil, salted	1 cup	55	1	3	6	3	0.3	86	20	0.01	0.02	0.1	0
Rice, white, cooked	1 cup	225	4	Tr	50	21	1.8	0	0	0.23	0.02	2.1	0
Tortillas, corn	1 tortilla	65	2	1	13	42	0.6	1	80	0.05	0.03	0.4	0
Legumes, Nuts, and Seeds													
Beans, dry:													
Cooked, drained, black	1 cup	225	15	1	41	47	2.9	1	Tr	0.43	0.05	0.9	0
Peanuts, roasted and salted	1 oz	165	8	14	5	24	0.5	122	0	0.08	0.03	4.2	0
Peanut butter	1 tbsp	95	5	8	3	5	0.3	75	0	0.02	0.02	2.2	0
Refried beans, canned	1 cup	295	18	3	51	141	5.1	1,228	0	0.14	0.16	1.4	17
Soy products:													
Miso	1 cup	470	29	13	65	188	4.7	8,142	110	0.17	0.28	0.8	0
Tofu (2½ by 2¾ by 1 in.)	1 piece	85	9	5	3	108	2.3	8	0	0.07	0.04	0.1	0
Sunflower seeds	1 oz	160	6	14	5	33	1.9	1	10	0.65	0.07	1.3	Tr
Meat and Meat Products													
Bacon	3 slices	110	6	9	Tr	2	0.3	303	0	0.13	0.05	1.4	6
Frankfurter, cooked	1 frankfurter	145	5	13	1	5	0.5	504	0	0.09	0.05	1.2	12
Ground beef, broiled	3 oz	245	20	18	0	9	2.1	70	Tr	0.03	0.16	4.9	0
Ham, cooked	2 slices	105	10	6	2	4	0.6	751	0	0.49	0.14	3.0	16
Poultry and Poultry Products													
Chicken:													
Fried	3.5 oz	220	31	9	2	16	1.2	74	50	0.08	0.13	13.5	0
Roasted	3.0 oz	140	27	3	0	13	0.9	64	20	0.06	0.10	11.8	0
Vegetables													
Broccoli, cooked	1 spear	50	5	1	10	82	2.1	20	2,540	0.15	0.37	1.4	113
Carrots:													
Raw	1 carrot	30	1	Tr	7	19	0.4	25	20,250	0.07	0.04	0.7	7

Foods		Food energy	Protein	Fat	Carbo-hydrate	Calcium	Iron	Sodium	Vitamin A value (IU)	Thiamin	Riboflavin	Niacin	Ascorbic acid
		Calories	Grams	Grams	Grams	Milli-grams	Milli-grams	Milli-grams	Interna-tional units	Milli-grams	Milli-grams	Milli-grams	Milli-grams
Cooked, sliced, drained	1 cup	70	2	Tr	16	48	1.0	103	38,300	0.05	0.09	0.8	4
Celery, raw	1 stalk	5	Tr	Tr	1	14	0.2	35	50	0.01	0.01	0.1	3
Collards, cooked, drained	1 cup	25	2	Tr	5	148	0.8	36	4,220	0.03	0.08	0.4	19
Corn, sweet:													
Cooked	1 ear	85	3	1	19	2	0.5	13	170	0.17	0.06	1.2	5
Canned (cream style)	1 cup	185	4	1	46	8	1.0	730	250	0.06	0.14	2.5	12
Lettuce, raw:													
Iceberg, pieces	1 cup	5	1	Tr	1	10	0.3	5	180	0.03	0.02	0.1	2
Leaf, pieces	1 cup	10	1	Tr	2	38	0.8	5	1,060	0.03	0.04	0.2	10
Onions, cooked, drained	1 cup	60	2	Tr	13	57	0.4	17	0	0.09	0.02	0.2	12
Peas, edible pod, cooked, drained	1 cup	65	5	Tr	11	67	3.2	6	210	0.20	0.12	0.9	77
Potatoes, baked	1 potato	220	5	Tr	51	20	2.7	16	0	0.22	0.07	3.3	26
Spinach, cooked, drained	1 cup	40	5	Tr	7	245	6.4	126	14,740	0.17	0.42	0.9	18
Tomatoes:													
Raw	1 tomato	25	1	Tr	5	9	0.6	10	1,390	0.07	0.06	0.7	22
Canned, solids and liquid	1 cup	50	2	1	10	62	1.5	391	1,450	0.11	0.07	1.8	36
Other													
Cookies:													
Brownies (home recipe)	1 brownie	95	1	6	11	9	0.4	51	20	0.05	0.05	0.3	Tr
Chocolate chip	4 cookies	180	2	9	28	13	0.8	140	50	0.10	0.23	1.0	Tr
Sandwich type	4 cookies	195	2	8	29	12	1.4	189	0	0.09	0.07	0.8	0
Corn chips	1 oz	155	2	9	16	35	0.5	233	110	0.04	0.05	0.4	1
Doughnuts, cake type	1 doughnut	210	3	12	24	22	1.0	192	20	0.12	0.12	1.1	Tr
French fries	10 pieces	110	2	4	17	5	0.7	16	0	0.06	0.02	1.2	5
Gelatin dessert	½ cup	70	2	0	17	2	Tr	55	0	0.00	0.00	0.0	0
Jam and preserves	1 tbsp	55	Tr	Tr	14	4	0.2	2	Tr	Tr	0.01	Tr	Tr
Pizza, cheese	1 slice	290	15	9	39	220	1.6	699	750	0.34	0.29	4.2	2
Potato chips	10 chips	105	1	7	10	5	0.2	94	0	0.03	Tr	0.8	8
Puddings:													
Chocolate, canned	5 oz can	205	3	11	30	74	1.2	285	100	0.04	0.17	0.6	Tr
Chocolate, dry mix	½ cup	155	4	4	27	130	0.3	440	130	0.04	0.18	0.1	1
Syrup, maple	2 tbsp	122	0	0	32	1	Tr	19	0	0.00	0.00	0.0	0
Taco	1 taco	195	9	11	15	109	1.2	456	420	0.09	0.07	1.4	1

Notes: *Tr* indicates presence of nutrients in trace amounts. All fruits and vegetables are fresh unless noted. Vegetables are fresh cooked unless noted.

Glossary

The Glossary contains all the important terms used throughout the text. It includes the **boldfaced** terms listed in the "Words to Know" lists at the beginning of each lesson and that appear in text, captions, and features.

The Glossary lists the term, the pronunciation (in the case of difficult terms), the definition, and the page on which the term is defined. The pronunciations here and in the text follow the system outlined below. The column headed "Symbol" shows the spelling used in this book to represent the appropriate method.

Pronunciation Key

Sound	As in	Symbol	Example
ă	hat, map	a	abscess (AB·sess)
ā	age, face	ay	atrium (AY·tree·uhm)
a	care, their	ehr	capillaries (KAP·uh·lehr·eez)
ä, ŏ	father, hot	ah	biopsy (BY·ahp·see)
ar	far	ar	cardiac (KAR·dee·ak)
ch	child, much	ch	barbiturate (bar·BI·chuh·ruht)
ĕ	let, best	e	vessel (VE·suhl)
ē	beat, see, city	ee	acne (AK·nee)
er	term, stir, purr	er	nuclear (NOO·klee·er)
g	grow	g	malignant (muh·LIG·nuhnt)
ĭ	it, hymn	i	bacteria (bak·TIR·ee·uh)
ī	ice, five	y	benign (bi·NYN)
		eye	iris (EYE·ris)
j	page, fungi	j	cartilage (KAR·tuhl·ij)
k	coat, look, chorus	k	defect (DEE·fekt)
ō	open, coat, grow	oh	aerobic (e·ROH·bik)
ô	order	or	organ (OR·guhn)
ȯ	flaw, all	aw	palsy (PAWL·zee)
oi	voice	oy	goiter (GOY·ter)
ou	out	ow	fountain (FOWN·tuhn)
s	say, rice	s	dermis (DER·mis)
sh	she, attention	sh	conservation (kahn·ser·VAY·shuhn)
ŭ	cup, flood	uh	bunion (BUHN·yuhn)
u	put, wood, could	u	pulmonary (PUL·muh·nehr·ee)
ü	rule, move, you	oo	attitudes (AT·i·toodz)
w	win	w	warranty (WAWR·uhn·tee)
y	your	yu	urethritis (yur·i·THRY·tuhs)
z	says	z	hormones (HOR·mohnz)
zh	pleasure	zh	transfusion (trans·FYOO·zhuhn)
ə	about, collide	uh	asthma (AZ·muh)

Abdominal thrusts Quick, upward pulls into the diaphragm to force out a blockage of the airway when someone is choking. (page 525)

Abscess (AB·sess) A painful tooth condition in which pus collects in the bone sockets around a tooth. (page 41)

Abstinence (AB·stuh·nuhns) Avoiding high-risk behavior, such as the use of tobacco, acohol, drugs, or engaging in sex. (page 73)

Abuse (uh·BYOOS) Physical or mental mistreatment of another person. (page 152)

Accident chain The combination of a situation, an unsafe habit, and an unsafe act leading to an injury. (page 486)

Acid rain Rain that is more acidic than normal. (page 546)

Acquaintance rape A situation in which a person is forced to have sexual intercourse with someone he or she knows. (page 497)

Acquired immunodeficiency syndrome (AIDS) A deadly disease that destroys the body's ability to fight infection. (page 363)

Active listening Receiving someone's message by hearing it, thinking about it, and responding to it. (page 107)

Addiction (uh·DIK·shuhn) A physical or mental need for a drug or other substance. (pages 204, 411, 434)

Adolescence (a·duhl·E·suhns) The time of life between childhood and adulthood. (page 208)

Adrenaline (uh·DRE·nuhl·in) A hormone that increases the level of sugar in the blood, which gives the body extra energy in response to emergencies. (page 77)

Advertising Creating and sending messages that are designed to interest consumers in buying certain goods and services; also called *ads*. (page 170)

Aerobic (e·ROH·bik) **exercise** Vigorous, rhythmic activity that aids the heart and increases the body's capacity to take in and use oxygen. (page 234)

Al-Anon A support group that helps anyone affected by close contact with an alcoholic. (page 438)

Alateen A support group that helps the children of an alcoholic parent. (page 438)

Alcohol (AL·kuh·hawl) A drug that is produced by a chemical reaction in some foods and that has powerful effects on the body. (page 428)

Alcoholics Anonymous (uh·NAH·nuh·muhs) **(AA)** A support group that helps alcoholics recover from their addiction. (page 437)

Alcoholism An illness caused by a physical and mental need for alcohol. (page 435)

Allergen (AL·er·juhn) Substance that causes allergic reactions in some individuals. (page 390)

Allergy An extreme sensitivity to a substance. (page 390)

Alternatives (ahl·TER·nuh·tivz) Other ways of thinking or acting. (page 442)

Alveoli (al·vee·OH·ly) Microscopic air sacs in the lungs in which the exchange of gases occurs. (page 306)

Alzheimer's (AHLTS·hy·merz) **disease** A disease that causes impaired thinking, memory, and behavior. (page 219)

Amino acids Chains of building blocks that make up proteins. (page 262)

Amphetamines (am·FE·tuh·meenz) Highly addictive stimulant drugs; may be prescribed to treat attention disorders in children or obesity. (page 460)

Anabolic steroids (a·nuh·BAH·lik STIR·oydz) Drugs that some athletes take illegally because they believe the drugs will build stronger muscles. (page 473)

Anaerobic (an·e·ROH·bik) **exercise** Intense physical activity that lasts a short time and involves great bursts of energy in which the muscles work hard to produce energy. (page 234)

Anorexia nervosa (a·nuh·REK·see·uh ner·VOH·suh) An eating disorder that is characterized by an intense fear of weight gain and that often leads to extreme weight loss from self-starvation. (page 282)

Antibiotic (an·ti·by·AH·tik) A drug that inhibits or kills microorganisms that cause disease. (page 453)

Antibodies Proteins in the blood that react to foreign bodies and destroy or neutralize them. (page 346)

Antihistamines Drugs that relieve the symptoms of allergic reactions. (page 391)

Anus (AY·nuhs) Excretory opening through which feces pass out of the body. (page 321)

Anxiety disorder The condition of feeling abnormally uneasy or worried about what may happen. (page 82)

Arteries (AR·tuh·reez) The largest blood vessels, which take blood from the heart to all parts of the body. (page 302)

Arteriosclerosis (ar·tir·ee·oh·skluh·ROH·sis) A condition in which the arterial walls thicken and harden. (page 378)

Arthritis (ar·THRY·tuhs) A disease of the joints characterized by painful swelling and stiffness. (page 394)

Artificial respiration (art·uh·FISH·uhl res·puh·RAY·shuhn) See *Rescue breathing.*

Assertive (uh·SER·tiv) Behaving with confidence. (page 497)

Asthma (AZ·muh) A chronic respiratory disease in which the bronchi swell and become blocked, causing the person to have difficulty breathing. (page 392)

Astigmatism (uh·STIG·muh·tiz·uhm) An eye condition in which images are distorted. (page 51)

Atherosclerosis (a·thuh·roh·skluh·ROH·sis) A condition in which fatty deposits build up on artery walls. (page 378)

Athlete's foot A problem caused by fungi growing in warm, damp areas of the foot. (page 57)

Atrium (AY·tree·uhm) Each of the two upper chambers of the heart. (page 299)

Attitudes (AT·i·toodz) Feelings and beliefs. (page 12)

Auditory (AW·di·tor·ee) **nerve** The network of nerves in the cochlea that carries messages to the brain. (page 53)

Autonomic (aw·tuh·NAH·mik) **system** The part of the peripheral nervous system that deals with involuntary body actions. (page 296)

Bacteria (bak·TIR·ee·uh) Tiny microscopic organisms that live everywhere. (page 341)

Barbiturates (bar·BI·chuh·ruhts) A type of depressant drug that is a powerful sedative; often prescribed as a sleeping aid. (page 463)

Battery The unlawful beating of another person. (page 153)

B-cells Lymphocytes that produce antibodies. (page 346)

Behavior The way a person acts in many different situations. (page 11)

Benign (bi·NYN) **tumor** A mass of cells that is not cancerous. (page 383)

Biodegradable A substance that is easily broken down by bacteria and other organisms. (page 548)

Biological (by·uh·LAH·ji·kuhl) **age** Age that is measured by how well various body parts are working. (page 218)

Biopsy The surgical removal of cells or tissue from the living body for purposes of examination and diagnosis. (page 385)

Birth defects (DEE·fekts) Abnormalities in a developing or newborn baby. (pages 203, 374)

Blended family A type of family that consists of a remarried parent, a stepparent, and their children. (page 112)

Blister A small, fluid-filled swelling on the skin, often caused by burns or rubbing. (page 57)

Blizzard A heavy snowstorm with high winds. (page 509)

Blood alcohol concentration (BAC) The percentage of alcohol in the bloodstream. (page 431)

Blood pressure The force of the blood against the walls of the blood vessels. (page 379)

Blood vessels Tubes that carry blood throughout the body. (page 302)

Body composition The amount of body fat compared to lean tissue. (page 238)

Body language Messages transmitted through body movements and gestures rather than words. (page 108)

Brain An organ of the nervous system composed of neurons that control your actions, thoughts, and emotions. (page 294)

Brain death The result of oxygen being cut off from the brain. (page 221)

Bronchi (BRAHN·ky) The two passages through which air enters the lungs. (page 304)

Bronchodilators (brahn·ko·dy·LAY·terz) Medications that relax the muscles around the bronchial air passages. (page 393)

Bulimia (boo·LEE·mee·uh) An eating disorder characterized by extreme overeating followed by purging. Also called bulimia nervosa. (page 283)

Bunion (BUHN·yuhn) A painful swelling at the base of the big toe. (page 57)

Bypass surgery A surgical procedure to create a new path for blood to flow around a blocked artery. (page 380)

Caffeine (ka·FEEN) A substance found in coffee, tea, and some soft drinks that stimulates the heart and nervous system. (page 273)

Callus A hardened, thickened part of the skin. (page 57)

Calorie A unit of heat that measures the energy available in different foods or used up during exercise. (page 278)

Cancer A disease characterized by the rapid and uncontrolled growth of abnormal cells. (page 383)

Capillaries (KAP·uh·lehr·eez) The smallest blood vessels in the body. (page 302)

Carbohydrates Nutrients, such as sugar and starches, that are the main source of energy to the body. (page 262)

Carbon monoxide (KAR·buhn muh·NAHK·syd) A colorless, odorless, poisonous gas produced when a substance burns. (page 405)

Carcinogens (kar·SIN·uh·juhnz) Substances in the environment that cause cancer. (page 385)

Cardiac muscle The muscle of the heart. (page 314)

Cardiopulmonary resuscitation (kar·dee·oh·PUHL·muh·nehr·ee·ri·suh·suh·TA·shuhn) **(CPR)** A first-aid procedure to restore breathing and circulation. (page 527)

Cardiovascular (KAR·dee·oh·VAS·kyoo·ler) **system** The circulatory system. (page 298)

Carrier A person who has a virus and can pass it on to other people, but who may not show the symptoms of the disease. (page 363)

Cartilage (KAHR·tuhl·ij) Tough, flexible tissue that covers the ends of bones and supports soft tissue. (page 308)

Cell The basic unit, or building block, of life. (page 196)

Cementum (se·MEN·tuhm) Material that covers the root of a tooth. (page 40)

Central nervous system (CNS) The part of the nervous system made up of the brain and spinal cord. (page 293)

Cerebellum (ser·uh·BE·luhm) The part of the brain that controls balance, posture, and coordination. (page 294)

Cerebrum (suh·REE·bruhm) The largest part of the brain, which controls the senses, muscles, thought, and speech. (page 294)

Cervix (SER·viks) The neck, or opening, of the uterus. (pages 200, 330)

Chemotherapy (kee·moh·THEHR·uh·pee) The use of chemicals to kill cancer cells. (page 386)

Chest thrust A technique used on an infant or child to dislodge a blockage in the airway. (page 525)

Chlamydia (kluh·MI·dee·uh) An STD that does great damage to the reproductive system. (page 359)

Cholera (KAH·luh·ruh) A disease caused by bacteria in untreated sewage and characterized by cramps, vomiting, and diarrhea. (page 547)

Cholesterol (kuh·LES·tuh·rawl) A waxy, fat-like substance found in the cells of all animals. (page 271)

Chromosomes (KROH·muh·sohmz) Threadlike structures in the nucleus of a cell that carry the codes for inherited characteristics. (page 202)

Chronic (KRAH·nik) **diseases** Illnesses that last a long time or that recur frequently. (page 373)

Chronological (krah·nuh·LAH·ji·kuhl) **age** A person's age measured in years. (page 218)

Cilia (SIH·lee·uh) Tiny hairlike projections. (page 407)

Circulatory (SER·kyuh·luh·tohr·ee) **system** The group of organs that transports blood throughout the body to deliver essential materials to body cells and to remove waste materials from the cells. (page 298)

Cirrhosis (suh·ROH·sis) Condition in which liver tissue is scarred and damaged. (page 429)

Clinical (KLI·ni·kuhl) **death** The result of the shutdown of a person's body systems. (page 221)

Cocaine (koh·KAYN) An illegal stimulant. (page 462)

Cochlea (KOK·lee·uh) A bony structure of the inner ear that is essential to the sense of hearing. (page 53)

Codeine (KOH·deen) A narcotic drug used in cough medicine. (page 463)

Cold turkey The process of quitting a habit all at once, such as smoking. (page 421)

Colon (KOH·luhn) The large intestine. (page 321)

Commitment (kuh·MIT·muhnt) A pledge or promise. (page 130)

Communicable (kuh·MYOO·ni·kuh·buhl) **diseases** Illnesses that can be transmitted from one person to another. (page 340)

Communication The exchange of thoughts, ideas, and beliefs between two or more people. (page 102)

Comparison (kum·PEHR·i·suhn) **shopping** Judging the merits of different goods and services. (page 167)

Compromise (KAHM·pruh·myz) To settle differences by a mutual agreement. (page 102)

Confidentiality (KAHN·fuh·den·shee·A·luh·tee) Maintaining the secrecy of something that has been said in private, such as during a mediation. (page 146)

Conflict A disagreement, struggle, or difference of opinion between opposing viewpoints. (page 138)

Conservation The saving of resources. (page 549)

Consumer (kuhn·SOO·mer) A person who purchases goods and services. (page 162)

Consumer advocates (AD·voh·kets) People or groups who help consumers with problems. (page 184)

Contagious (kuhn·TAY·juhs) **period** The period of time during which some diseases can be passed to another person. (page 343)

Contract To tighten or become shorter. (page 312)

Contraction (kuhn·TRAK·shuhn) A sudden tightening in the muscles of the uterus as part of the birth process. (page 200)

Cool-down A slow winding down of an activity, such as exercise. (page 249)

Cooperation Working together to achieve a common goal. (page 103)

Coping strategy A way of dealing with a sense of loss when someone close dies. (page 224)

Corn A hardened, thickened growth of skin on a toe. (page 57)

Cornea (KOR·nee·uh) The clear outer layer of the eyeball. (page 48)

Coronary (KAWR·uh·nehr·ee) **arteries** Large blood vessels that carry blood away from the heart. (page 378)

Coupon (KOO·pahn) A piece of paper that offers savings on certain brands of goods. (page 169)

Crown The part of a tooth that is visible to the eye. (page 40)

Cuticle (KYOO·ti·kuhl) Nonliving band of epidermis around the fingernails and toenails. (page 37)

Dandruff (DAN·druhf) Whitish scales of dead skin that flake off the scalp. (page 37)

Date rape A situation in which a person is forced to have sexual intercourse with someone on a date. (page 497)

Decision making A six-step process for making up one's mind or resolving a problem. (page 20)

Defense mechanism (duh·FENS·MEK·uh·nizm) Temporary way of dealing with stress. (page 78)

Defensive driving Obeying traffic laws and watching out for other road users. (page 501)

Degenerative (di·JE·ne·ruh·tiv) **disease** A noncommunicable disease characterized by the breakdown of body tissues. (page 372)

Dehydration (dee·hy·DRAY·shuhn) A serious loss in the body's water content. (page 283)

Dentin (DEN·tin) The hard, bony material surrounding the pulp of the tooth. (page 40)

Depressant (di·PRE·suhnt) A drug that slows down body functions, including breathing and brain activity. (page 428)

Depression An emotional state characterized by extreme sadness, inability to eat or sleep, and a loss of interest in life. (page 83)

Dermatologist (DER·muh·TAHL·uh·jist) A doctor who treats skin diseases. (page 34)

Dermis (DER·mis) The sensitive inner layer of the skin. (page 33)

Designer drugs Substances that are designed to be chemically similar to various controlled substances. (page 467)

Desired weight The weight that is right for a person based on his or her gender, height, and body frame. (page 276)

Detoxification (dee·tahk·si·fi·KAY·shuhn) The removal of harmful substances, such as drugs or alcohol, from the body. (page 474)

Developmental (di·vel·uhp·MEN·tuhl) **task** Something that must be accomplished in order for a person to continue growing toward a healthy, mature adulthood. (page 211)

Diabetes (dy·uh·BEE·teez) A disease in which the body cannot properly convert food into energy. (page 396)

Diaphragm (DY·uh·fram) The large muscle that separates the chest from the abdomen. (page 304)

Diet The combination of what one eats and drinks regularly. (page 261)

Digestion (dy·JES·chuhn) The process of changing food into substances that can be absorbed into the bloodstream. (page 318)

Digestive (dy·JES·tiv) **system** The organs that change food into nutrients for the cells to use. (page 318)

Discount store A store that carries regular merchandise at reduced prices. (page 169)

Disease An illness that affects the body or mind. (page 340)

Distress Negative stress that can prevent a person from doing something. (page 76)

Drug A substance other than food that changes the structure or function of the mind or body. (page 452)

Earthquake A shaking or vibration of the earth's surface due to an underground shift. (page 510)

Eating disorder Extreme and dangerous eating behavior that can result in serious illness or death. (page 282)

Ecosystem (EE·koh·sis·tuhm) The various organisms and plants that make up a particular community or environment. (page 539)

Egg cell The female reproductive cell that joins with the sperm cell to make a new life. (page 197)

Embryo A developing organism in the period of its growth between fertilization and when its organs are developed enough to sustain life. (page 198)

Emotional need A need that affects a person's feelings and sense of well-being. (page 72)

Emotions Feelings, such as love, anger, or fear. (page 70)

Emphysema (em·fuh·SEE·muh) A lung disease in which the alveoli are damaged or destroyed. (page 307)

Enamel (ee·NA·muhl) The hard outer layer of the tooth. (page 40)

Endocrine (EN·duh·krin) **system** The glands that produce the hormones to regulate body activities. (page 324)

Environment (en·VY·ruhn·ment) All the conditions that surround a person and affect his or her development. (pages 11, 203, 538)

Epidermis (e·puh·DER·mis) The outermost layer of skin. (page 33)

Epiglottis (e·puh·GLAH·tis) A small flap of tissue that covers the trachea when a person swallows, keeping food out of the windpipe. (page 304)

Eustachian (you·STAY·shun) **tube** The tube from the nose to the inner ear that equalizes the air pressure on both sides of the eardrum. (page 53)

Excretion (ek·SKREE·shuhn) The act of removing wastes from the body. (page 321)

Exercise frequency The number of times a person exercises in a specified period of time. (page 248)

Exercise intensity The amount of energy a person uses when he or she exercises. (page 248)

Exercise time The amount of time spent exercising during one session. (page 248)

Expiration date The date stamped on a package that tells when the contents are no longer useful. (page 491)

Extend To move muscles so they lengthen or stretch out. (page 312)

Extended family A nuclear family and other relatives living together. (page 112)

Eye contact The ability to look directly at the person to whom one is speaking. (page 108)

Fallen arches A foot condition characterized by flatness of the bottom of one's feet. (page 57)

Family The basic unit of society; a group of related people. (page 111)

Fatigue Extreme tiredness. (page 77)

Fats Nutrients that are a source of energy to the body. (page 263)

Fertilization (fer·til·i·ZAY·shuhn) The process of joining a male sperm cell and a female egg cell, which is necessary to produce a new life. (page 197)

Fetal (FEE·tuhl) **alcohol syndrome (FAS)** A group of alcohol-related birth defects. (pages 204, 431)

Fetus An embryo during the later stages of development in the mother's uterus. (page 198)

Fiber The part of fruits, vegetables, and grains that cannot be digested. Also called Dietary fiber. (page 270)

First-degree burn A mild burn that affects only the epidermis and is characterized by reddening of the skin. (page 531)

Flexibility The ability to move body joints in certain ways. (page 237)

Follicle (FAHL·i·kuhl) A small opening or sac in the dermis, the deepest layer of the skin in which hair grows. (page 36)

Food Guide Pyramid A guideline to help people choose what and how much to eat from each food group in order to get the needed nutrients. (page 266)

Fossil (FAH·suhl) **fuels** Fuels taken from the earth, such as coal, oil, and natural gas. (page 545)

Fracture A break or crack in a bone. (page 529)

Frostbite Freezing of the skin. (page 505)

Fungi (FUHN·jy) Simple life forms that cannot make their own food and which can cause disease. (page 341)

Gallbladder A small organ beneath the liver that stores excess bile. (page 320)

Gang A group of people interacting together. (page 156)

Generic (juh·NEHR·ik) **product** A product sold in a plain package and at a lower price than a comparable brand name product. (page 169)

Genes Basic units of heredity; carry codes for individual traits. (page 202)

Genetic (juh·NE·tik) **disorder** A disease or disorder caused by a problem with the genes. (pages 202, 373)

Genital herpes (HER·peez) An STD that is caused by the herpes simplex II virus and is characterized by blisters in the genital area. (page 360)

Genital warts An STD characterized by warts in the genital area that multiply quickly if not treated. (page 359)

Germs Microscopic organisms that cause disease. (page 340)

Gingivitis (jin·juh·VY·tis) A gum disease caused by plaque or decaying food between the teeth. (page 44)

Gland A part of the body that produces a chemical substance. (page 324)

Goal Something to aim for. (page 23)

Gonorrhea (gah·nuh·REE·uh) A common STD caused by a bacteria, and, if untreated, results in damage to reproductive organs. (page 359)

Goods Products made for sale. (page 162)

Greenhouse effect An atmospheric condition caused by pollutants and characterized by warming climate trends. (page 546)

Grief Deep and painful sorrow related to the death of a loved one. (page 223)

Ground water Water that collects in the ground and supplies wells and springs. (page 540)

Group dating Going out with a group of male and female friends. (page 125)

Hallucinogen (huh·LOO·suhn·uh·jen) A drug that creates imaginary images or distorts real ones in the mind of the user. (page 466)

Hate crime Crime committed against a person or group because of racial, religious, or cultural differences. (page 157)

Hazard (HAZ·erd) A danger. (page 490)

Hazardous (HAZ·er·duhs) **waste** A waste product that can cause illness if not disposed of properly. (page 555)

Head lice Tiny insects that live in the hair. (page 37)

Health A combination of physical, mental, and social well-being. (page 5)

Health care facility A place where people can receive health care. (page 174)

Health care system The way in which people receive and pay for their health care. (page 172)

Health education Providing health information in a way that influences people to take positive actions regarding their health. (page 14)

Health insurance (in·SHUR·uhns) A program in which a person pays an annual fee to a company that agrees to pay certain health care costs. (page 174)

Health maintenance (MAYN·te·nuhns) **organization (HMO)** A group of many different types of doctors who provide health care for members. (page 176)

Heart and lung endurance How well the heart and lungs get oxygen to the body during exercise and how quickly they return to normal. (page 238)

Heart attack A serious condition in which heart muscle is damaged by a stoppage in the flow of blood to the heart. (pages 303, 379)

Hepatitis (he·puh·TY·tis) An inflammatory disease of the liver. (page 352)

Heredity (huh·RED·i·tee) The passing-on of characteristics from parents to their children through genes. (pages 10, 202)

Histamine (HIS·tuh·meen) A substance that causes the symptoms of allergic reactions. (page 391)

Hives A skin condition caused by an allergy and characterized by itching and raised, red patches. (page 391)

Homicide (HAH·muh·syd) The killing of one human being by another. (page 156)

Hormones (HOR·mohnz) Chemicals that are produced in the glands to regulate various body functions. (pages 70, 208)

Hospice A facility that cares for people who are terminally ill. (page 222)

Human immunodeficiency (im·yoo·noh·di·FI·shuhn·see) **virus (HIV)** The virus that causes AIDS. (page 363)

Hurricane A storm with heavy rains and high winds that usually begins in the tropical regions. (page 508)

Hypertension (hy·per·TEN·shuhn) High blood pressure. (page 379)

Hypothermia (hy·poh·THER·mee·uh) A sudden drop in body temperature. (page 502)

Immunity (i·MYOO·nuh·tee) The body's resistance to germs and other harmful substances that may be produced by those germs. (page 345)

Individual sports Sports people enjoy on their own or with a friend. (page 252)

Infancy (IN·fuhn·see) The first year after birth. (page 207)

Infection (in·FEK·shuhn) A condition that occurs when germs enter body cells and multiply. (page 340)

Influenza (in·floo·EN·zuh) A serious and contagious respiratory disease caused by viruses. (page 352)

Inhalant (in·HAY·luhnt) A substance that is inhaled to give a hallucinogenic high. (page 468)

Insulin (IN·suh·lin) A hormone produced in the pancreas that regulates the level of sugar in the blood. (page 396)

Interferon Substance produced by cells that stops a virus from reproducing and thus helps control infection. (page 346)

Iris (EYE·ris) The colored part of the eye that surrounds the pupil. (page 48)

Jaywalk To cross the street without paying attention to traffic rules. (page 500)

Joint A place in the body where bones are joined. (page 310)

Keratin (KEHR·uh·tin) A substance that makes nails hard. (page 38)

Kidneys The two bean-shaped organs that remove the body's water-soluble wastes. (page 321)

Landfill A place where garbage and other waste are dumped and covered with dirt in order to build up low-lying or wet land. (page 553)

Larynx (LA·ringks) The upper part of the respiratory tract that contains the vocal cords. (page 304)

Laxative (LAK·suh·tiv) A medicine that speeds foods through the digestive system with little time to release their nutrients. (page 283)

Lens (LENZ) The structure behind the pupil that focuses light. (page 48)

License Legal permission to do something. (page 185)

Lifestyle disease A disease that is caused by a person's health habits. (pages 14, 374)

Lifestyle factor A life-related habit. (page 13)

Lifetime sport A physical activity that can be enjoyed throughout life. (page 255)

Ligament (LI·guh·ment) A type of firm, strong tissue that connects bones at joints. (page 310)

Liver A gland with many digestive functions, including the breakdown of fats. (page 320)

Love Great affection for another person. (page 129)

Lymphatic (lim·FA·tik) **system** A secondary circulatory system that carries lymph. (page 346)

Lymph nodes Clusters of cells along the lymphatic vessels that filter out harmful matter from the lymph. (page 346)

Lymphocytes (LIM·fuh·syts) White blood cells that are the body's primary means of fighting germs. (page 346)

Mainstream smoke The smoke that the smoker exhales. (page 414)

Malignant (muh·LIG·nuhnt) **tumor** A mass of cancer cells. (page 383)

Malnutrition A condition in which the body does not receive the nutrients it needs to grow and function well. (page 283)

Malocclusion A condition in which the teeth fail to line up properly. (page 44)

Malpractice (mal·PRAK·tis) A failure to provide an acceptable degree of quality health care. (page 185)

Media Methods of communicating information, such as television, radio, newspaper, or magazines. (page 419)

Mediation (mee·dee·AY·shuhn) The process of resolving conflicts with the help of a neutral third person. (page 146)

Medicaid (MED·i·kayd) A government health insurance program that pays the medical care costs for poor people. (page 175)

Medicare (MED·i·kehr) A government health insurance program for people 65 years old and older. (page 175)

Medicine A drug that cures or prevents diseases or other health-related conditions. (page 452)

Melanin (MEL·uh·nin) The substance that gives skin most of its color. (page 33)

Menstrual (MEN·struhl) **cycle** The time between the beginning of one menstruation to the beginning of the next one; the process of menstruation. (page 331)

Menstruation (men·struh·WAY·shuhn) The process of discharging blood and tissue from the uterus. (page 330)

Mental and emotional health The ability to accept oneself and adapt to and cope with emotions. (page 64)

Metastasis (muh·TAS·tuh·sis) The spread of cancer cells from a tumor to other parts of the body. (page 384)

Minerals A class of nutrients that are needed in small amounts by the body. (page 262)

Mood disorder When a person experiences extreme or prolonged emotions or mood changes that he or she cannot control. (page 83)

Mononucleosis (MAH·noh·noo·klee·OH·sis) A viral disease that is common among young people and is characterized by an abnormal increase of white blood cells. (page 352)

Mucus (MYOO·kuhs) A fluid that moistens and protects the mucous membranes. (page 345)

Muscle endurance (en·DER·uhns) How well a muscle group can perform over a given time without becoming overly tired. (page 236)

Muscle strength The most work muscles can do at any given time. (page 236)

Muscular (MUHS·kyuh·ler) **system** The group of tough tissues that enables body parts to move. (page 312)

Narcotic (nar·KAH·tik) An addictive depressant drug that is used to relieve pain and can be obtained legally only with a doctor's prescription. (page 463)

Neck The part of the tooth between the crown and the root. (page 40)

Negotiation (ni·goh·shee·AY·shuhn) Process of reaching a solution by discussing problems face-to-face. (page 146)

Neuron (NOO·rahn) A nerve cell. (page 292)

Neutrality (noo·TRA·luh·tee) Not taking sides in an argument. (page 146)

Nicotine (NI·kuh·teen) An addictive stimulant drug in tobacco that speeds up the heartbeat. (page 405)

Noncommunicable diseases Diseases that are caused by how people live, by conditions they are born with, or by hazards in the environment. (page 372)

Nonrenewable resource A resource from the earth that cannot be replaced once it has been used up. (page 549)

Nuclear (NOO·klee·er) **family** A family that consists of a mother, a father, and their children living in the same household. (page 112)

Nuclear waste Harmful by-products of atomic reactions. (page 556)

Nutrient (NOO·tree·ent) One of six types of substances in food that the body needs to grow and function properly. (page 262)

Nutrient density The nutrients in foods compared with the calories they provide. (page 278)

Nutrition (noo·TRI·shuhn) The process of taking in and using nutrients. (page 261)

Obesity A condition in which a person's weight is 20 percent or more above his or her desired weight. (page 277)

Obstetrician (ahb·stuh·TRI·shuhn) A doctor who specializes in the care of a pregnant woman and her developing baby. (page 203)

Opportunistic infection Any disease that attacks a person with a weakened immune system. (page 364)

Optic (AHP·tik) **nerve** A bundle of nerve fibers that carries messages from the eye to the brain. (page 48)

Organ A part of a living organism that is composed of tissue organized to perform a certain function. (page 197)

Osteoarthritis (ahs·tee·oh·ahr·THRY·tuhs) A chronic bone disease, common in the elderly, in which joints deteriorate. (page 395)

Ovaries (OH·vuh·reez) The two female reproductive organs that store egg cells. (page 330)

Over-the-counter (OTC) medicine Any medication that can be purchased without a doctor's prescription. (page 457)

Overweight Having more than the desired weight for a person's size, gender, and body frame. (page 277)

Ovulation (ahv·yuh·LAY·shuhn) The process of releasing an egg cell from an ovary. (page 330)

Ozone A form of oxygen present in the air, especially after a thunderstorm. (page 545)

Pacemaker (PAYS·may·ker) A small electrical device that sends pulses to the heart to make it beat regularly. (page 381)

Pancreas (PAN·kree·uhs) The organ that produces insulin and releases enzymes to digest carbohydrates, proteins, and fats. (page 320)

Parenting The raising of children. (page 130)

Particulates (pahr·TIK·yuh·lits) Tiny pollutants, such as dust and soot, found in the air. (page 545)

Passive smoking Inhaling the smoke of nearby people who are smoking. (page 414)

Peer A person of the same age. (page 119)

Peer pressure The pressure to go along with the beliefs and actions of your friends and classmates. (page 119)

Periodontium (pehr·ee·oh·DAHN·shee·um) The supporting structures of the teeth, including the jawbone, gums, and ligaments. (page 40)

Peripheral (puh·RIF·uh·ruhl) **nervous system (PNS)** The system made up of nerves that connects the central nervous system to all parts of the body. (page 293)

Personality The qualities and characteristics that make a person different from everybody else. (page 65)

Pesticide (PES·tuh·syd) A chemical used to kill or control animals and insects. (page 545)

Phagocytes (FAG·uh·syts) Special white blood cells that destroy germs. (page 346)

Phagocytosis (fag·uh·suh·TOH·suhs) The process of white blood cells destroying germs. (page 346)

Phobia A fear so great it interferes with reasonable action. (page 82)

Physical fatigue Extreme tiredness of the body. (page 77)

Physically fit A state of being in which the body is able to handle the demands placed on it. (page 230)

Physiological (fi·zee·uh·LAH·ji·kuhl) **dependence** A type of addiction in which the body feels a need for a drug. (page 412)

Pituitary (pi·TOO·i·tehr·ee) **gland** The gland at the base of the brain that controls other glands. (page 325)

Placebo (pluh·SEE·boh) **effect** Health improvement as a result of using a pill or preparation that contains no active ingredients. (page 181)

Placenta (pluh·SEN·tuh) The tissue that lines the walls of the uterus and that nourishes the developing baby. (page 199)

Plaque (PLAK) **1.** A thin film that forms on teeth. (page 41) **2.** Fatty deposits that build up on arterial walls. (page 378)

Pollen A powdery substance released by certain plants and grasses that causes allergic reactions in some people. (page 390)

Pollution Anything that dirties the environment or makes it unhealthy. (page 541)

Pores Tiny openings in the skin. (page 33)

Precaution Care taken beforehand to ensure good results or avoid bad ones. (page 19)

Precycling The process of reducing waste before it occurs. (page 551)

Preferred provider A physician approved by a particular health plan. (page 174)

Prejudice (PRE·juh·duhs) A negative and unjustly formed opinion, usually against people of a different racial, religious, or cultural group. (page 142)

Prenatal (pree·NAY·tuhl) **care** Steps taken to provide for the health of a pregnant woman and her unborn baby. (page 203)

Prescription (pri·SKRIP·shuhn) **medicine** Medication that may be purchased only with a doctor's written order. (page 457)

Primary care provider A doctor who provides general health care to patients. (page 173)

Proteins (PROH·teenz) Nutrients that are essential for growth and repair of body cells. (page 262)

Protozoa (proh·tuh·ZOH·uh) Single-celled organisms that sometimes cause diseases. (page 341)

Psychiatrist (sy·KY·uh·trist) A medical doctor who treats serious mental health problems. (page 92)

Psychological (sy·kuh·LAH·ji·kuhl) **dependence** A type of addiction in which the mind feels a need for a drug. (page 412)

Psychological fatigue Extreme mental tiredness. (page 77)

Psychologist (sy·KAH·luh·jist) A mental health professional with a master's or doctoral degree who is licensed to counsel. (page 92)

Puberty (PYOO·ber·tee) The period of adolescence when a person begins to develop certain traits of his or her sex. (page 209)

Public health Maintaining and improving community health, especially as a function of government. (page 186)

Pulp The soft, sensitive inner part of the tooth that contains blood vessels and nerves. (page 40)

Pupil (PYOO·puhl) The dark opening in the center of the iris that regulates the amount of light entering the eye. (page 48)

Quackery (KWAK·uh·ree) A fraud or scam. (page 180)

Radiation (ray·dee·AY·shuhn) A treatment used for some types of cancer. (page 386)

Radon (RAY·dahn) A radioactive gas formed by the decay of radium. (page 556)

Rape A crime in which one person forces another person to have sexual relations. (page 497)

Recommended Dietary Allowances (RDA) Guidelines for the amount of each nutrient you should get from the food you eat. (page 264)

Recovery Returning to a normal state of being, usually after illness or addiction. (page 437)

Recycling The process of changing various materials so they can be reused. (page 550)

Refusal skills Effective ways of saying no. (pages 73, 109)

Relationship (ri·LAY·shuhn·ship) The connection one has with another person or group. (page 101)

Reliable Dependable and trustworthy. (page 118)

Reproductive (ree·pruh·DUHK·tiv) **system** The group of organs involved in the production of offspring. (page 328)

Rescue breathing A way of restoring normal breathing by forcing air into the victim's lungs. (page 518)

Resource A thing that has use value, such as goods, services, time, property, or money. (page 139)

Respiratory system The group of organs that delivers oxygen to the body and removes carbon dioxide from the body. (page 304)

Responsibility An obligation. (page 130)

Responsible dating Being trustworthy, respectful, and careful about the other person in a dating situation. (page 126)

Retina (RE·tin·uh) The light-sensing part of the inner eye. (page 48)

Rheumatoid (ROO·muh·toyd) **arthritis** A chronic disease characterized by pain, inflammation, swelling, and stiffness of the joints. (page 394)

Rickettsias (ri·KET·see·uhs) Tiny, disease-causing organisms that are spread by fleas, ticks, and lice. (page 341)

Risk behavior Acting in a manner that increases one's chances of being harmed. (page 19)

Risk factor A trait or habit that raises a person's chances of getting a particular disease. (page 374)

Root The part of the tooth that is beneath the gum. (page 40)

Rubella (roo·BE·luh) A contagious disease; also known as German measles. (page 205)

Safety conscious Having an awareness of the importance of safety. (page 484)

Saliva (suh·LY·vuh) The substance produced by the salivary glands; contains enzymes that start the digestion of foods. (page 318)

Sanitation (san·i·TAY·shuhn) The disposal of sewage and wastes to protect public health. (page 188)

Saturated fats Fats found in meats and some dairy products. (page 263)

Schizophrenia (skit·zoh·FREE·nee·uh) A serious mental disorder in which one loses touch with reality. (page 84)

Sclera (SKLEHR·uh) The tough outer layer of the eye. (page 48)

Sebum (SEE·buhm) An oily secretion associated with acne. (page 34)

Second-degree burn A burn that destroys the first layer of skin and damages the second layer, causing redness and blisters. (page 531)

Secondhand smoke Smoke nonsmokers inhale as a result of being around smokers. (page 414)

Second opinion After consulting one's regular physician, seeing another doctor to confirm the first diagnosis or recommend another course of treatment. (page 185)

Self-concept The view a person has of himself or herself. (page 65)

Self-esteem Confidence in one's own ability. (page 23)

Semicircular (SEM·i·SER·kyuh·ler) **canals** Three interconnecting, partially fluid-filled canals of the inner ear that are responsible for balance. (page 53)

Services Useful activities that are sold to others. (page 162)

Sewage (SOO·ij) Food, human waste, detergents, and other products carried away in sewers and drains. (page 547)

Sexual harassment (SEK·shuh·wuhl·huh·RAS·muhnt) Sexual comments, behavior, or contact that are not desired by the recipient and are abusive. (page 155)

Shock A serious condition in which body functions are slowed down. (page 521)

Side effect A related condition that results from a treatment or medication. (pages 92, 454)

Sidestream smoke The smoke from the burning tip of a cigarette. (page 414)

Skeletal muscles Muscles that work with bones to facilitate movement. (page 314)

Skeletal system The bones of the body. (page 308)

Small-claims court A state court that handles civil cases involving small amounts of money. (page 184)

Small intestine The long, tubelike organ in which most digestion occurs. (page 319)

Smog An unhealthy mixture of pollutants and fog in the air, usually over cities. (page 546)

Smoke alarm A device that makes a loud noise when it senses smoke. (page 492)

Smooth muscles The involuntary muscles in the digestive system and circulatory system. (page 314)

Social age Age measured by a person's lifestyle. (page 218)

Social health One's ability to get along with the people around him or her. (page 100)

Socializing Being with and enjoying being with other people. (page 124)

Somatic (soh·MA·tik) **system** The part of the peripheral nervous system that involves voluntary actions. (page 296)

Specialist (SPE·she·list) A physician who is trained to handle particular kinds of patients or diseases. (page 173)

Sperm cell The male reproductive cell that joins with the egg cell to make a new life. (page 197)

Sphygmomanometer (sfig·mo·muh·NAH·muh·ter) The instrument used to measure blood pressure. (page 302)

Spinal cord A long bundle of neurons that relays messages to and from the brain and all parts of the body. (page 294)

Stepparent Someone who marries a child's mother or father. (page 112)

Stimulant (STIM·yuh·luhnt) A drug that speeds up body functions. (page 459)

Stomach A muscular organ in which some digestion occurs. (page 319)

Stress The body's response to changes. (page 76)

Stressor A trigger of stress. (page 77)

Stroke A serious condition that occurs when the blood supply to the brain is cut off, usually due to a blockage in the artery that goes to the brain. (page 378)

Subcutaneous (suhb·kyoo·TAY·nee·uhs) **layer** Fatty tissue under the skin. (page 33)

Suicide The taking of one's own life. (page 84)

Sympathetic (sim·puh·THE·tik) Having and showing kind feelings toward another person. (page 118)

Syphilis (SI·fuh·lis) An STD that progresses through several stages and can cause death. (page 360)

Tar The dark, sticky substance that forms when tobacco burns. (page 405)

Tartar (TAR·ter) Hardened plaque on the teeth. (page 41)

T-cells Lymphocytes that fight germs. (page 346)

Team sports Organized activities with a group of people playing on the same side. (page 253)

Tendon Tough tissue that connects muscles to bones. (page 310)

Testes (TES·teez) The glands of the male reproductive system that produce sperm. (page 329)

Third-degree burn A severe burn that damages all layers of the skin and the nerve endings. (page 531)

Tissue A mass of similar cells that performs a specific function. (pages 40, 196)

Tolerance (TAHL·er·ens) **1.** Accepting and respecting other people's beliefs and customs. (page 103) **2.** A condition that occurs when a person's body becomes used to a drug's effect. (page 456)

Tornado A whirling, funnel-shaped windstorm that drops from the sky to the ground. (page 508)

Tornado warning A news bulletin announcing that a tornado is approaching. (page 508)

Tornado watch A news bulletin indicating that a tornado may be forming. (page 508)

Totally fit Physically, mentally, and socially ready to handle whatever comes along from day to day. (page 230)

Toxic Poisonous or harmful. (page 540)

Trachea (TRAY·kee·uh) The windpipe. (page 304)

Tradition (truh·DI·shun) The usual way of doing things. (page 170)

Tumor A swelling or abnormal growth of cells. (page 383)

Umbilical (uhm·BIL·i·kuhl) **cord** The tube that connects the fetus and the mother's placenta and through which the developing baby receives nourishment. (page 199)

Unsaturated fats The liquid fats that are generally found in vegetable oils. (page 263)

Uterus (YOO·tuh·ruhs) A pear-shaped female organ in which a fetus grows and develops until it is ready to be born. (page 198)

Vaccine (vak·SEEN) A preparation of dead or weak germs put into the body to cause the immune system to produce antibodies to certain diseases. (page 348)

Values Beliefs or ideals that guide one's actions. (pages 21, 65)

Veins (VAYNZ) Blood vessels that carry blood from various parts of the body to the heart. (page 302)

Verbal communication The exchange of ideas, opinions, and feelings through words. (page 105)

Vestibule (VES·ti·byool) The central cavity of the inner ear. (page 53)

Victim A person who has been physically or emotionally hurt or abused. (page 152)

Virus (VY·ruhs) Disease-producing agents. (page 341)

Vitamins Nutrients that the body needs in small amounts for proper functioning. (page 262)

Warm-up Body movements that stretch the muscles and prepare the body for physical activity. (page 246)

Warranty The manufacturer's written promise to repair a product during a specified period of time. (page 167)

Weight control Reaching and maintaining one's desired weight. (page 276)

Wellness Actively making choices and decisions that promote good health. (page 7)

Withdrawal A series of painful physical and mental symptoms associated with recovery from addiction to alcohol or other drugs. (page 412)

Glosario

Abdominal thrusts/presiones abdominales Presiones rápidas y hacia arriba que se hacen sobre el diafragma para forzar la salida de algo que esté bloqueando la tráquea de una persona ahogada.

Abscess/absceso Condición dolorosa de un diente, debido a la acumulación de pus en el alvéolo o hueso donde está implantado el diente.

Abstinence/abstinencia Evitar conducta arriesgada, como el uso de tabaco, alcohol, drogas y el sexo.

Abuse/abuso Maltrato físico o mental que se da a una persona.

Accident chain/cadena de accidentes La combinación de una situación, un hábito peligroso, y un acto peligroso que pueden provocar un daño.

Acid rain/lluvia ácida Lluvia que está contaminada.

Acquaintance rape/violación por un conocido Situación en la cual una persona es forzada por alguien conocido a tener relaciones sexuales.

Acquired immunodeficiency syndrome (AIDS)/síndrome de inmunodeficiencia adquirida (SIDA) Enfermedad mortal que destruye la capacidad del cuerpo para combatir infecciones.

Active listening/audición activa El procesamiento de un mensaje el cual es escuchado, analizado, y respondido.

Addiction/adicción Necesidad física o mental de drogas u otras substancias.

Adolescence/adolescencia Periodo de la vida entre la niñez y la edad adulta.

Adrenaline/adrenalina Hormona que aumenta el nivel del azúcar en la sangre, y que da energía extra al cuerpo para responder a emergencias.

Advertising/propaganda La creación y envío de mensajes o anuncios diseñados para captar el interés de los consumidores con el fin de que compren determinados bienes y servicios.

Aerobic exercise/ejercicio aeróbico Actividad vigorosa y rítmica que ayuda al corazón y que aumenta la capacidad del cuerpo para inhalar y usar oxígeno.

Alcohol/alcohol Droga que es producida a través de una reacción química en algunos alimentos y que tiene efectos poderosos en el cuerpo.

Alcoholics Anonymous (AA)/Alcohólicos Anónimos Organización que actúa como grupo de apoyo, para ayudar a los alcohólicos a recuperarse de su adicción al alcohol.

Alcoholism/alcoholismo Enfermedad causada por la necesidad física y mental de consumir alcohol.

Allergen/alergeno Sustancia que causa reacciones alérgicas a algunas personas.

Allergy/alergia Sensibilidad extrema a una sustancia.

Alternative/alternativa Diferentes maneras de pensar o actuar.

Alveoli/alvéolo Sacos microscópicos de aire ubicados en los pulmones en donde ocurren intercambios de gases.

Alzheimer's disease/enfermedad de Alzheimer Enfermedad que causa deterioro en el pensamiento, la memoria y la conducta.

Amino acids/aminoácidos Bloques de sustancias que forman las proteínas.

Amphetamines/anfetaminas Drogas estimulantes altamente adictivas; estas drogas pueden ser prescritas para tratar trastornos de la atención en los niños y para la obesidad.

Anabolic steroids/esteroides anabólicos Drogas tomadas ilegalmente por algunos atletas debido a la creencia de que producen músculos más fuertes.

Anaerobic exercise/ejercicio anaeróbico Intensa actividad física de corta duración, que demanda gran consumo de energía y en la cual los músculos trabajan duramente, para producir esa energía.

Anorexia nervosa/anorexia nerviosa Trastorno caracterizado por un miedo irracional de ganar peso y que frecuentemente conlleva pérdida extrema de peso debida a autoinanición.

Antibiotic/antibiótico Drogas que inhiben o matan microorganismos causantes de enfermedades.

Antibodies/anticuerpos Proteínas de la sangre que destruyen o neutralizan los cuerpos extraños que invaden el organismo.

Antihistamines/antihistamínicos Drogas que alivian los síntomas de las reacciones alérgicas.

Anus/ano Abertura del intestino, a través de la cual las heces salen fuera del cuerpo.

Anxiety disorder/trastorno de ansiedad Condición en la que se siente excesiva preocupación por las cosas que pasan.

Arteries/arterias Los vasos sanguíneos más largos, que llevan la sangre del corazón a todas las partes del cuerpo.

Arteriosclerosis/arterioesclerosis Condición en la cual las paredes de las arterias se engruesan y endurecen.

Arthritis/artritis Enfermedad causada por la inflamación y endurecimiento de las articulaciones.

Artificial respiration/respiración artificial Vea *Rescue breathing.*

Assertive/resuelto(a) Comportarse con seguridad en sí mismo.

Asthma/asma Enfermedad respiratoria crónica en la cual los bronquios se inflaman y bloquean, causando una dificultad en la respiración de la persona.

Astigmatism/astigmatismo Condición del ojo en la que las imágenes se presentan distorsionadas.

Atheroesclerosis/ateroesclerosis Condición en la cual materias grasas se depositan en las paredes arteriales.

Athlete's foot/pie de atleta Problema infeccioso causado por el crecimiento de hongos en áreas húmedas del pie.

Atrium/aurícula Cada una de las dos cámaras superiores del corazón.

Attitudes/actitudes Sentimientos y creencias.

Auditory nerve/nervio auditivo Grupo de nervios de la coclea del oído que llevan los mensajes al cerebro.

Autonomic system/sistema autónomo Parte del sistema nervioso periférico, que se ocupa de los movimientos corporales involuntarios.

Bacteria/bacteria Organismos microscópicos que viven en todas partes.

Barbiturates/barbitúricos Tipo de droga depresora, la cual es un poderoso sedativo y que, frecuentemente, se receta como una ayuda para dormir.

Battery/agresión Golpear a una persona, ilegalmente.

B-cells/células B Linfocitos que producen anticuerpos.

Behavior/conducta La forma en que una persona actúa en ocasiones diferentes.

Benign tumor/tumor benigno Masa de células no cancerosas.

Biodegradable/biodegradable Sustancias que pueden ser descompuestas fácilmente por bacterias y otros organismos.

Biological age/edad biológica Medida de la edad, por medio de la determinación del buen funcionamiento de varias partes del cuerpo.

Biopsy/biopsia La remoción quirúrgica de células o tejidos del cuerpo con el fin de examinarlos y obtener un diagnóstico.

Birth defects/defectos de nacimiento Anormalidades en un feto o en un bebé recién nacido.

Blended family/familia incorporada Tipo de familia en donde uno o ambos de los padres es casado por segunda vez, hay un padrastro o madrastra, y hay hijos.

Blister/ampolla Pequeña inflamación acuosa de la piel, frecuentemente causada por quemadura o fricción.

Blizzard/tormenta Fuerte tormenta de nieve con grandes vientos.

Blood alcohol concentration (BAC)/ concentración de alcohol en la sangre Porcentaje de alcohol contenido en la sangre.

Blood pressure/presión sanguínea La fuerza de la sangre contra las paredes de los vasos sanguíneos.

Blood vessels/vasos sanguíneos Tubos que transportan la sangre a través del cuerpo.

Body composition/composición del organismo La cantidad de grasa del cuerpo comparada con la cantidad de tejidos magros.

Body language/lenguage corporal Mensajes transmitidos a través de movimientos corporales y gestos, más que con palabras.

Brain/cerebro Organo del sistema nervioso compuesto de neuronas, las cuales controlan las acciones, los pensamientos y las emociones.

Brain death/muerte cerebral La que resulta debido al paro total de suministro de oxígeno al cerebro.

Bronchi/bronquios Los dos pasajes a través de los cuales entra el aire en los pulmones.

Bronchodilators/broncodilatadores Medicamentos que relajan los músculos ubicados alrededor de los pasajes de aire bronquiales.

Bulimia/bulimia Un trastorno alimenticio caracterizado por el consumo exagerado de comida seguido de purgantes. También se llama bulimia nervosa.

Bunion/juanete Inflamación dolorosa en la base del dedo gordo del pie.

Bypass surgery/cirugía de bypass Procedimiento quirúrgico que crea un nuevo camino para que circule la sangre alrededor de una arteria bloqueada.

Caffeine/cafeína Sustancia que se encuentra en el café, el té, y algunos refrescos y la cual estimula el corazón y el sistema nervioso.

Calorie/caloría Unidad de energía que mide la energía contenida en diferentes alimentos, o la energía usada después de hacer ejercicio.

Callus/callo Dureza que se forma en un lugar de la piel.

Cancer/cáncer Enfermedad que se caracteriza por el crecimiento rápido e incontrolable de células anormales.

Capillaries/capilares Los vasos sanguíneos más pequeños del cuerpo.

Carbohydrates/carbohidratos Nutrientes, como el azúcar y las harinas, que son la fuente principal de energía para el cuerpo.

Carbon monoxide/monóxido de carbono Gas venenoso, inodoro, e incoloro, que se produce cuando una sustancia se quema.

Carcinogens/carcinógenos Sustancias del medio ambiente que producen cáncer.

Cardiac muscle/músculo cardiaco El músculo del corazón.

Cardiopulmonary resuscitation/ resucitación cardiopulmonar Ayuda de emergencia para restaurar la respiración y la circulación.

Cardiovascular system/sistema cardiovascular El sistema circulatorio.

Carrier/portador Persona que tiene un virus y puede contaminar a otra persona, en algunos casos sin que los síntomas de la enfermedad se hayan manifestado.

Cartilage/cartílago Tejido fuerte y flexible que cubre las terminaciones de los huesos y soporta los tejidos suaves.

Cell/célula La unidad básica de la vida, que conforma la estructura de los seres vivientes.

Cementum/cemento Material que cubre la raíz del diente.

Central nervous system/sistema nervioso central La parte del sistema nervioso formada por el cerebro y la espina dorsal.

Cerebellum/cerebelo La parte del cerebro que controla el balance, la postura, y la coordinación.

Cerebrum/cerebro La parte más grande del encéfalo, que controla los músculos, sentidos, pensamientos y lenguaje.

Cervix/cervix El cuello o abertura del útero.

Chemotherapy/quimioterapia El uso de químicos para matar células cancerosas.

Chest thrust/presión toráxica Técnica usada en niños para desalojar algún objeto que esté bloqueando el paso del aire.

Chlamydia/clamidia Enfermedad transmitida sexualmente y que causa graves daños al sistema reproductivo.

Cholera/cólera Enfermedad causada por bacterias en aguas no tratadas y caracterizada por calambres, vómitos, y diarrea.

Cholesterol/colesterol Sustancia semejante a la grasa y que se encuentra en todos los animales.

Chromosomes/cromosomas Estructuras filiformes contenidas en el núcleo de las células y que contienen los códigos genéticos de las características hereditarias.

Chronic diseases/enfermedades crónicas Las enfermedades que duran largos períodos de tiempo o que reaparecen con frecuencia.

Chronological age/edad cronológica La edad de una persona medida en años.

Cilia/filamentos Pequeñísimas estructuras parecidas al cabello.

Circulatory system/sistema circulatorio El grupo de órganos que transporta la sangre a través del cuerpo, con el fin de proporcionar materias esenciales a las células y remover materiales desechables de las células.

Cirrhosis/cirrosis Condición en la cual el tejido del hígado presenta cicatrices y está dañado.

Clinical death/muerte clínica El resultado del paro completo de todos los sistemas del cuerpo de una persona.

Cocaine/cocaína Un estimulante ilegal.

Cochlea/cóclea Estructura ósea del oído interno y la cual es esencial para la audición.

Codeine/codeína Droga narcótica usada en medicinas para la tos.

Cold turkey/parar en seco El proceso de abandonar de una vez un hábito como el fumar.

Colon/colon El intestino grueso.

Commitment/compromiso Una promesa u obligación.

Communicable diseases/enfermedades contagiosas Enfermedades que pueden ser transmitidas de una persona a otra.

Communication/comunicación El intercambio de pensamientos, ideas y creencias entre dos o más personas.

Comparison shopping/compras comparadas Las que se efectúan basándose en las ventajas de los diferentes bienes y servicios.

Compromise/transigir Solución de diferencias a través de un mutuo acuerdo.

Confidentiality/confidencialidad Mantener en secreto algo que se ha comunicado en privado, por ejemplo durante la mediación.

Conflict/conflicto Un desacuerdo, lucha o diferencia de opinión entre puntos de vista opuestos.

Conservation/conservación El ahorro de recursos.

Consumer/consumidor La persona que adquiere bienes y servicios.

Consumer advocates/defensores del consumidor Personas que defienden a consumidores con problemas.

Contagious period/período de contagio El lapso de tiempo durante el cual algunas enfermedades pueden ser transmitidas.

Contract/contraer El movimiento de los músculos cuando se contraen o se hacen más cortos.

Contraction/contracción Encogimiento fuerte y repentino de los músculos del útero, que ocurre durante el proceso de dar a luz.

Cool down/enfriamiento Disminución progresiva de una actividad, como el ejercicio.

Cooperation/cooperación Trabajar en conjunto para lograr un objetivo común.

Coping strategy/estrategia de adaptación Forma de manejar el sentimiento de pérdida que se experimenta cuando alguien allegado muere.

Corn/callo Crecimiento y endurecimiento de un área de la piel, en algún dedo del pie.

Cornea/córnea La membrana transparente de la parte anterior del globo del ojo.

Coronary arteries/arterias coronarias Los vasos sanguíneos que transportan sangre fuera del corazón.

Coupon/cupón Papel que ofrece descuento en determinada marca de productos.

Crown/corona La parte del diente que es visible al ojo.

Cuticle/cutícula Piel muerta alrededor de las uñas de los pies y manos.

Dandruff/caspa Escamas de piel muerta que se forman en el cuero cabelludo.

Date rape/violación durante una cita Situación en la cual una persona es forzada, por otra persona con la que ha salido en una cita, a tener relaciones sexuales.

Decision making/toma de decisiones Procedimiento de seis pasos a seguirse para tomar decisiones o resolver problemas.

Defense mechanism/mecanismo de defensa Forma temporal de manejar el estrés.

Defensive driving/manejo defensivo El que ocurre cuando se obedecen las leyes de tránsito y se observa cuidadosamente a los demás conductores.

Degenerative disease/enfermedad degenerativa Enfermedad no transmisible en la cual los tejidos del cuerpo se destruyen.

Dehydration/deshidratación Pérdida del agua contenida en el cuerpo.

Dentin/dentina El material óseo que rodea la pulpa del diente.

Depressant/depresor Tipo droga de que disminuye las funciones del cuerpo, incluida la actividad del cerebro y de la respiración.

Depression/depresión Estado emocional caracterizado por extrema tristeza, incapacidad de comer o dormir, y pérdida del interés por la vida.

Dermatologist/dermatólogo Un médico que trata enfermedades de la piel.

Dermis/dermis La capa más profunda de la piel.

Designer drugs/drogas sintéticas Sustancias que están diseñadas para ser químicamente similares a otras sustancias controladas.

Desired weight/peso deseado El peso apropiado para una persona, basado en su sexo, altura, y estructura del cuerpo.

Detoxification/desintoxicación La eliminación de sustancias dañinas, como las drugas y el alcohol, ya existentes en el cuerpo.

Developmental task/tarea requerida para el desarrollo Algo que se debe de hacer, para que una persona pueda convertirse en un adulto saludable y maduro.

Diabetes/diabetes Enfermedad en la cual el cuerpo no puede convertir los alimentos en energía.

Diaphragm/diafragma El músculo que separa el pecho de la cavidad abdominal.

Diet/dieta La combinación de comidas y bebidas que una persona consume con regularidad.

Digestion/digestión El proceso de convertir los alimentos en substancias que puedan ser absorbidas por la corriente sanguínea.

Digestive system/sistema digestivo Los órganos que convierten los alimentos en nutrientes, para que sean usados por las células.

Discount store/tienda de descuento La que tiene surtido de mercancías regulares a precios reducidos.

Disease/enfermedad Todas los trastornos que afectan el cuerpo y la mente.

Distress/angustia Angustia negativa que impide a una persona ejecutar determinadas actividades.

Drug/droga Sustancias diferentes a la comida, que cambian la estructura del funcionamiento de la mente o del cuerpo.

Earthquake/terremoto Temblor o vibración de la superficie terrestre debido a cambios subterráneos.

Eating disorder/trastorno alimenticio Conducta en el comer, extremada y peligrosa, y que puede causar graves enfermedades o la muerte.

Ecosystem/ecosistema Los organismos y plantas que forman parte de una determinada comunidad o medio ambiente.

Egg cell/óvulo La célula femenina que unida a la célula espermatozoide forma una nueva vida.

Embryo/embrión Organismo en desarrollo, durante el período que comienza con la fertilización, hasta el momento en que los órganos están desarrollados para sostener una vida.

Emotional need/necesidad emocional Una necesidad que afecta el sentimiento de bienestar de una persona.

Emotions/emociones Sentimientos como el amor, la ira o el miedo.

Emphysema/enfisema Enfermedad de los pulmones en la que los alvéolos se dañan o destruyen.

Enamel/esmalte El material que cubre la parte externa o corona del diente.

Endocrine system/sistema endocrino Las glándulas que producen las hormonas que regulan las actividades del cuerpo.

Environment/medio ambiente Todas las condiciones que rodean a una persona y que afectan su desarrollo.

Epidermis/epidermis La capa exterior de la piel.

Epiglottis/epiglotis Cartílago que cubre la tráquea cuando una persona traga, con el fin de evitar que los alimentos entren a los tubos respiratorios.

Eustachian tube/trompa de Eustaquio Conducto que va de la nariz al oído interno y que equilibra la presión del aire en ambos lados del oído medio.

Excretion/excreción El acto de eliminar los desperdicios del cuerpo.

Exercise frequency/frecuencia del ejercicio El número de veces, durante un lapso de tiempo determinado, en que una persona hace ejercicio.

Exercise intensity/intensidad del ejercicio La cantidad de energía que una persona consume cuando hace ejercicio.

Exercise time/tiempo de ejercicio La cantidad de tiempo que una persona gasta en una sesión de ejercicios.

Expiration date/fecha de vencimiento La fecha estampada en paquetes, que indica cuando ya no sirve su contenido.

Extend/extender El movimiento de los músculos cuando se estiran.

Extended family/familia extendida La familia nuclear y otros parientes que conviven bajo el mismo techo.

Eye contact/contacto con los ojos La habilidad de mirar directamente a los ojos de la persona con la que se habla.

Fallen arches/arcos caídos Condición del pie plano, que no tiene arco.

Family/familia La unidad básica de la sociedad; un grupo de personas relacionadas.

Fatigue/fatiga Cansancio extremo.

Fats/grasas Nutrientes que son fuente de energía para el cuerpo.

Fertilization/fertilización El proceso de juntar el espermatozoide masculino con el óvulo femenino, con el fin de producir una nueva vida.

Fetal alcohol syndrome/síndrome de alcoholismo fetal Grupo de defectos de nacimiento causados por alcoholismo.

Fetus/feto El embrión en sus últimas etapas de desarrollo en el útero de la madre.

Fiber/fibra La parta de las frutas, vegetales y granos que no se puede digerir. También se llama fibra dietética.

First-degree burn/quemadura de primer grado Quemadura leve que afecta solo la epidermis y que se caracteriza por el enrojecimiento de la piel.

Flexibility/flexibilidad La habilidad de mover de cierta manera las articulaciones del cuerpo.

Follicle/folículo La pequeña abertura o saco en la dermis, o capa más profunda de la piel, en donde crece el pelo.

Food Guide Pyramid/pirámide de alimentos Una guía para ayudar a la gente a elegir sus alimentos y a decidir cuanto comer de cada grupo de alimentos, con el fin de obtener los nutrientes necesarios.

Fossil fuels/combustibles fósiles Combustibles tomados de la tierra, como el carbón, el aceite y el gas natural.

Fracture/fractura Una ruptura o fisura en el hueso.

Frostbite/congelación Congelamiento de la piel.

Fungi/hongos Organismo viviente que no puede alimentarse a sí mismo y que puede causar enfermedad.

Gallbladder/vesícula biliar Pequeño órgano situado debajo del hígado y que almacena el exceso de bilis.

Gang/pandilla Un grupo de personas que se tratan.

Generic product/producto genérico Producto que se vende en paquete sin marca y que a menudo cuesta mucho menos que los productos similares con marca.

Genes/genes Unidad básica que contiene los códigos de los caracteres hereditarios de cada individuo.

Genetic disorder/trastorno genético Enfermedad o trastorno causado por problemas en los genes.

Genital herpes/herpes genital Enfermedad transmitida sexualmente causada por el virus herpes simplex II y que se caracteriza por ampollas en el área genital.

Genital warts/verrugas genitales Enfermedad transmitida sexualmente, caracterizada por verrugas en el área genital y que se extiende rápidamente si no se trata.

Germs/gérmenes Organismos microscópicos causantes de enfermedades.

Gingivitis/gingivitis Enfermedad de las encías causada por placas o alimentos en descomposición, localizados en medio de los dientes.

Gland/glándula Parte del cuerpo que produce sustancias químicas.

Goal/meta Objetivo a ser obtenido.

Gonorrhea/gonorrea Enfermedad transmitida sexualmente, causada por una bacteria y que puede causar daños al área genital, si no es tratada médicamente.

Goods/mercancías Productos hechos para la venta.

Greenhouse effect/efecto de invernadero Condición de la atmósfera, causada por contaminación y que se caracteriza por una tendencia al calentamiento de la temperatura.

Grief/pesar Sentimiento de pesar, profundo y doloroso, relacionado con la muerte de un ser querido.

Ground water/aguas subterráneas Agua acumulada debajo de la superficie terrestre y que suple a pozos y manantiales.

Group dating/salidas en grupo Salir en grupo, con amigos o amigas.

Hallucinogen/alucinógeno Droga que crea imágenes imaginarias o que distorsiona las imágenes reales en el individuo que la usa.

Hate crime/crimen por odio Es el crimen cometido por una persona o grupo debido a diferencias raciales, religiosas o culturales.

Hazard/peligro Posibilidad de daño.

Hazardous waste/desperdicios peligrosos Desperdicios que pueden causar enfermedad, si no son eliminados en forma apropiada.

Head lice/piojos Insectos muy pequeños que viven en el pelo.

Health/salud La combinación de bienestar físico, mental y social.

Health care facility/servicios de salud Lugar donde una persona recibe cuidados de salud.

Health care system/sistema de salud La forma como una persona recibe y paga por sus cuidados de salud.

Health education/educación sobre salud Información sobre salud proporcionada de tal manera, que estimule a las personas a actuar positivamente en relación a su salud.

Health insurance/seguro de salud Programa mediante el cual una persona se compromete a pagar una suma anual a cambio del pago de ciertos gastos médicos por una compañía.

Health maintenance organization (HMO)/organización para el mantenimiento de la salud Grupo de diferentes clases de médicos que proporcionan cuidados médicos a los miembros.

Heart and lung endurance/resistencia del corazón y los pulmones La capacidad del corazón y los pulmones de proporcionar oxígeno al cuerpo, durante el ejercicio, y el tiempo que se toman para volver a la normalidad.

Heart attack/ataque al corazón Condición seria en la cual el músculo cardiaco es dañado, debido al paro del flujo de sangre que va al corazón.

Hepatitis/hepatitis Enfermedad inflamatoria del hígado.

Heredity/herencia La transferencia de características de padres a hijos a través de los genes.

Histamine/histamina Substancia que causa los síntomas de reacciones alérgicas.

Hives/urticaria Condición de la piel causada por una alergia y que se caracteriza por picazón y erupciones enrojecidas.

Homicide/homicidio La muerte de una persona causada por otra persona.

Hormones/hormonas Los químicos producidos por las glándulas y que regulan varias funciones del cuerpo.

Hospice/hospicio Lugar donde se cuida a las personas con enfermedades incurables.

Human immunodeficiency virus (HIV)/virus de inmunodeficiencia humana (VIH) El virus que causa el SIDA.

Hurricane/huracán Tormenta con fuertes lluvias y ráfagas de vientos y que con frecuencia comienza en zonas tropicales.

Hypertension/hipertensión Elevación de la presión arterial.

Hypothermia/hipotermia Disminución repentina de la temperatura del cuerpo, por debajo de lo normal.

Immunity/inmunidad La resistencia del cuerpo a los gérmenes y a las sustancias dañinas que puedan ser producidas por esos gérmenes.

Individual sports/deportes individuales Los deportes que la gente disfruta individualmente o con un amigo(a).

Infancy/infancia El primer año después del nacimiento.

Infection/infección Condición que ocurre cuando los gérmenes invaden las células del cuerpo y luego se multiplican.

Influenza/influenza Una enfermedad respiratoria seria y contagiosa, causada por un virus.

Inhalant/inhalante Sustancia que al aspirarse produce un estado de alucinación.

Insulin/insulina Hormona producida en el páncreas y que regula el nivel de azúcar en la sangre.

Interferon/interferón Sustancia producida por las células que impide que un virus se reproduzca y que, por lo tanto, ayuda a controlar infecciones.

Iris/iris La parte coloreada del ojo que rodea la pupila.

Jaywalk/caminar descuidado Cruzar la calle sin prestar atención a las reglas del tráfico.

Joint/articulación El lugar del cuerpo en donde se unen los huesos.

Keratin/queratina La substancia que endurece las uñas.

Kidneys/riñones Los dos órganos que remueven las aguas solubles desechables del cuerpo.

Landfill/rellenos sanitarios Lugar donde la basura y otros desperdicios son enterrados, con el fin de rellenar terrenos bajoso húmedos.

Larynx/laringe La parte superior del tracto respiratorio, que contiene las cuerdas vocales.

Laxative/laxante Medicinas que hacen pasar rápidamente los alimentos a través del sistema digestivo, sin que éstos tengan tiempo de liberar sus nutrientes.

Lens/cristalino La estructura debajo de la pupila que enfoca la luz.

License/licencia Permiso legal para hacer algo.

Lifestyle disease/enfermedad debida al estilo de vida Es la enfermedad causada por los malos hábitos de salud de una persona.

Lifestyle factor/factor del estilo de vida Hábito relacionado con el modo de vivir de una persona.

Lifetime sport/deporte vitalicio Actividad que se puede disfrutar durante toda una vida.

Ligament/ligamento El tejido firme y fuerte que conecta los huesos en las articulaciones.

Liver/hígado Una glándula corporal que tiene varias funciones digestivas, incluida la disolución de las grasas.

Love/amor Gran afecto por una persona.

Lymphatic system/sistema linfático Sistema circulatorio secundario que transporta la linfa.

Lymph nodes/nódulos linfáticos Grupos de células del sistema linfático, que filtran las sustancias dañinas del sistema linfático.

Lymphocytes/linfocitos Los glóbulos blancos, los cuales son las principales células responsables de defender el cuerpo de gérmenes.

Mainstream smoke/humo directo El humo que exhala el fumador.

Malignant tumor/tumor maligno Masa de células cancerosas.

Malnutrition/malnutrición Condición en la cual el cuerpo no recibe los nutrientes que necesita, para crecer y funcionar bien.

Malocclusion/maloclusión Condición en la cual los dientes no están alineados en la forma debida.

Malpractice/negligencia médica Cuando no se proporcionan cuidados de salud con un grado aceptable de calidad.

Media/medios de comunicación Métodos de comunicar información, como la televisión, radio, periodicos o revistas.

Mediation/mediación El proceso de resolver conflictos, con la ayuda neutral de una tercera persona.

Medicaid/Medicaid Programa de seguro médico del gobierno y que paga gastos médicos a la gente pobre.

Medicare/Medicare Programa de seguro médico del gobierno y que paga gastos médicos a las personas mayores de 65 años.

Medicine/medicina Droga que cura o previene enfermedades u otras condiciones relacionadas con la salud.

Melanin/melanina La sustancia que proporciona la mayor parte del color a la piel.

Menstrual cycle/ciclo menstrual El lapso del tiempo entre una menstruación y el comienzo de la siguiente; el proceso de la menstruación.

Menstruation/menstruación El proceso de eliminación de sangre y tejidos del útero.

Mental and emotional health/salud mental y emocional La habilidad de aceptarse a sí mismo y de adaptarse y hacer frente a las emociones.

Metastasis/metástasis El proceso de propagación de las células cancerosas de un tumor a otras partes del cuerpo.

Minerals/minerales Una clase de nutrientes que el cuerpo necesita en pequeñas cantidades.

Mood Disorder/trastorno del estado de ánimo Cuando una persona experimenta emociones extremas o prolongadas o cambios de humor que no puede controlar.

Mononucleosis/mononucleosis Enfermedad viral, común entre la gente joven y que se caracteriza por el aumento anormal del número de glóbulos blancos.

Mucus/moco Fluido que humedece y protege las membranas mucosas.

Muscle endurance/resistencia muscular La cantidad de tiempo durante el cual un grupo de músculos puede funcionar, sin cansarse demasiado.

Muscle strength/resistencia muscular El máximo de trabajo que pueden enfectuar los músculos, en un momento determinado.

Muscular system/sistema muscular El grupo de tejidos fuertes que le permite al cuerpo moverse.

Narcotic/narcótico Depresor adictivo usado para suprimir el dolor y el cual se puede obtener legalmente, únicamente con una receta médica.

Neck/cuello La parte del diente entre la corona y la raíz.

Negotiation/negociación El proceso de llegar a una solución mediante la discusión de problemas, cara a cara.

Neuron/neurona Célula nerviosa.

Neutrality/neutralidad El no tomar posición frente a un argumento.

Nicotine/nicotina Estimulante adictivo contenido en el tabaco y que acelera los latidos del corazón.

Noncommunicable diseases/enfermedades no contagiosas Las enfermedades que son causadas por la forma en que vive la gente, por las condiciones con las que nacen, o por peligros en el medio ambiente.

Nonrenewable resource/recurso no renovable Un recurso de la tierra que no puede ser sustituido una vez que se gasta.

Nuclear family/familia nuclear La familia que consiste en el padre, la madre y los hijos que conviven bajo un mismo techo.

Nuclear waste/desecho nuclear Materias dañinas producidas por reacciones nucleares.

Nutrient/nutriente Una de las seis sustancias en la comida y que el cuerpo necesita para crecer y funcionar bien.

Nutrient density/densidad de los nutrientes Los nutrientes en los alimentos, comparados con las calorías que proporcionan.

Nutrition/nutrición El proceso de tomar y usar nutrientes.

Obesity/obesidad Condición en la cual el peso de una persona está en un 20 por ciento o más por encima de su peso deseado.

Obstetrician/obstetra El médico que se especializa en el cuidado de la mujer embarazada y de su futuro hijo.

Opportunistic infection/infección oportunista Cualquier enfermedad que ataque a una persona que tenga su sistema de defensas debilitado.

Optic nerve/nervio óptico Grupo de fibras nerviosas que transportan mensajes del ojo al cerebro.

Organ/órgano Parte de un organismo viviente que está compuesta de tejido y que ejecuta una función determinada.

Osteoarthritis/osteoartritis Una enfermedad crónica de los huesos, común entre la gente mayor, en que las articulaciones se deterioran.

Ovaries/ovarios Los dos órganos reproductivos femeninos que producen los óvulos.

Over-the-counter medicine/medicamento sin receta Medicamento que puede ser comprado sin una prescripción médica.

Overweight/sobrepeso El peso que es mayor al deseado para una persona, de acuerdo a su tamaño, sexo y estructura corporal.

Ovulation/ovulación El proceso mediante el cual se libera un óvulo del ovario.

Ozone/ozono Forma de oxígeno presente en el aire, especialmente después de una tormenta.

Pacemaker/marcapasos Pequeño aparato eléctrico que envia pulsaciones al corazón, para que los latidos sean regulares.

Pancreas/páncreas El órgano que produce insulina y libera enzimas para la digestión de carbohidratos, proteinas y grasas.

Parenting/crianza de hijos El cuidado y la educación los niños por los padres.

Particulates/partículas Pequeñísimas partículas contaminantes que se encuentran en el aire, tales como el polvo y el hollín.

Passive smoking/fumar pasivamente Cuando se inhala el humo del cigarrillo fumado por personas que están cerca.

Peer/contemporáneo Una persona de la misma edad.

Peer pressure/presión de contemporáneos La presión ejercida a través de las creencias y acciones de amigos y compañeros.

Periodontium/periodoncia Las estructuras que soportan los dientes, incluida la quijada, las encías y los ligamentos.

Peripheral nervous system/sistema nervioso periférico El sistema formado por los nervios que conectan el sistema nervioso central, con todas las demás partes del cuerpo.

Personality/personalidad Las cualidades y características que hacen a una persona diferente de todas las demás.

Pesticide/pesticida Químico que se usa para matar o controlar animales o insectos.

Phagocytes/fagocitos Las células blancas de la sangre, que destruyen gérmenes.

Phagocytosis/fagocitosis El proceso de los glóbulos blancos que destruyen gérmenes.

Phobia/fobia Un miedo de tal magnitud que interfiere con cualquier acción razonable.

Physical fatigue/fatiga física Cansancio extremo del cuerpo.

Physically fit/físicamente capaz Estado en el que el cuerpo es capaz de manejar las situaciones que se le presenten.

Physiological dependence/dependencia fisiológica Tipo de adicción en la cual el cuerpo siente la necesidad de una droga.

Pituitary gland/glándula pituitaria La glándula situada en la base del cerebro, que controla otras glándulas.

Placebo effect/efecto placebo Mejora en la salud, como resultado del uso de una píldora o preparación que no contiene ingredientes activos.

Placenta/placenta El tejido que cubre las paredes del útero y que alimenta al feto.

Plaque/placa La película delgada de sarro que se forma en el diente. Los depósitos grasos que se forman en las paredes arteriales.

Pollen/polen Sustancia en forma de polvo que es liberada por ciertas plantas y hierbas y que causan reacciones alérgicas a algunas personas.

Pollution/polución Cualquier cosa que ensucie el medio ambiente o que lo haga insalubre.

Pores/poros Aberturas pequeñísimas en la piel.

Precaution/precaución Cuidado que se toma con anticipación, con el fin de asegurarse buenos resultados o evitarse resultados negativos.

Precycling/preciclaje El proceso de reducción de la producción de desperdicios, antes de que los mismos se produzcan.

Preferred provider/médico preseleccionado Un médico aprobado por un plan de salud particular.

Prejudice/prejuicio Una opinión negativa formada sin justificación y que, generalmente, es contra gente de un grupo racial, religioso, o cultural diferente.

Prenatal care/cuidado prenatal Pasos que se toman para cuidar la salud de una mujer embarazada y su futuro bebé.

Prescription medicine/medicamento con receta Medicina que solo puede ser comprada con una receta médica.

Primary care provider/médico de cabecera Médico que proporciona a sus pacientes cuidados de salud generales.

Proteins/proteínas Nutrientes que son esenciales para el crecimiento y reparación de las células del cuerpo.

Protozoa/protozoos Organismos unicelulares que, algunas veces, causan enfermedades.

Psychiatrist/psiquiatra Un doctor en medicina que trata problemas graves de la salud mental.

Psychological dependence/dependencia psicológica Cualquier tipo de adicción en la cual la mente siente la necesidad de una droga.

Psychological fatigue/fatiga psicológica Extremo cansancio mental.

Psychologist/psicólogo Un profesional de la salud mental con título de maestro o doctor y licensia para aconsejar.

Puberty/pubertad El período de la adolescencia cuando una persona comienza a desarrollar ciertas características propias de su sexo.

Pulp/pulpa La parte interna y sensitiva del diente, que contiene vasos sanguíneos y nervios.

Public health/salud pública Mantenimiento y mejora de la salud de la comunidad, especialmente, como una función gubernamental.

Pupil/pupila La abertura oscura en el centro del iris que regula el monto de luz que entra en el ojo.

Quackery/curanderismo Charlatanería, fraude.

Radiation/radiación Tratamiento usado para algunos tipos de cáncer.

Radon/radón Un gas radioactivo formado por la decadencia del radio.

Rape/violación Crimen en el cual una persona fuerza a otra a tener relaciones sexuales.

Recommended Dietary Allowances/ Raciones Dietéticas Recomendadas Guía de la cantidad de cada nutriente que uno debe obtener de los alimentos que come.

Recovery/recuperación Regreso del cuerpo a un estado normal, generalmente, después de una enfermedad o adicción.

Recycling/reciclaje El proceso de tratamiento de materiales para que puedan ser usados nuevamente.

Refusal skills/habilidad de rehusar Maneras efectivas de decir no.

Relationship/relación La conexión que una persona tiene con otra persona o grupo.

Reliable/confiable Digno de confianza.

Reproductive system/sistema reproductivo Grupo de órganos involucrados en la reproducción de la descendencia.

Rescue breathing/respiración de rescate Forma de restaurar la respiración normal, a través del refuerzo de aire que se dé a los pulmones de la víctima.

Resource/recurso Una cosa con valor, como bienes, servicios, propiedad o dinero.

Respiratory system/sistema respiratorio Grupo de órganos que llevan oxígeno al cuerpo y que remuevan el dióxido de carbono del cuerpo.

Responsible dating/citas responsables Ser digno de confianza, respetuoso, y cuidadoso con la persona con quien se sale en una cita.

Responsibility/responsabilidad Una obligación.

Retina/retina La parte interna del ojo que es sensora de la luz.

Rheumatoid arthritis/artritis reumática Enfermedad crónica que se caracteriza por dolor, inflamación, y endurecimiento de las articulaciones.

Rickettsias/rickettsia Pequeñísimos organismos causantes de enfermedades y que son propagados por pulgas, piojos, y garrapatas.

Risk behavior/conducta riesgosa Manera de actuar que aumenta los riesgos de daño.

Risk factor/factor de riesgo Característica o hábito que aumenta los riesgos de una persona, de sufrir una determinada enfermedad.

Root/raíz Parte del diente que está dentro de la encía.

Rubella/rubéola Enfermedad contagiosa.

Safety conscious/conciencia de la seguridad Estar consciente de la importancia de la seguridad personal.

Saliva/saliva La sustancia producida por las glándulas salivales y que contiene las enzimas que dan comienzo a la digestión de los alimentos.

Sanitation/aseo público La eliminación de aguas residuales y desechos, con el fin de proteger la salud pública.

Saturated fats/grasas saturadas Las grasas que se encuentran en las carnes y algunos productos lácteos.

Schizophrenia/esquizofrenia Enfermedad mental seria, en la que la persona pierde su contacto con la realidad.

Sclera/esclerótica La membrana dura que está ubicada en la parte exterior del ojo.

Sebum/sebo Secreción aceitosa relacionada con el acné.

Second-degree burn/quemadura de segundo grado Quemadura que destruye la capa externa de la piel y que daña la segunda capa, causando enrojecimiento y ampollas.

Secondhand smoke/humo indirecto El humo que no fumadores inhalan de los fumadores que estén cerca.

Second opinion/segunda opinión Consulta que se hace a un segundo médico, después de la visita al médico regular de la persona, con el fin de confirmar el primer diagnóstico o de solicitar la recomendación de un tratamiento diferente.

Self-concept/autoimagen La imagen que una persona tiene de sí misma.

Self-esteem/autoestima La confianza que una persona tiene en sus propias habilidades.

Semicircular canals/canales semi-circulares Los tres canales interconectados del oído interno, parcialmente llenos de líquido, y que son responsables del equilibrio del cuerpo.

Services/servicios Actividades útiles que se ponen a la venta.

Sewage/aguas residuales Comida, desechos humanos, detergentes y otros productos, arrastrados por cloacas y desagües.

Sexual harassment/acoso sexual Conducta, contacto o comentarios sexuales que son indeseados por el que los recibe y abusivos.

Shock/choque Condición seria en la que las funciones del cuerpo se vuelven lentas.

Skeletal muscles/músculos del esqueleto Los músculos que trabajan con los huesos, para facilitar el movimiento.

Skeletal system/sistema óseo Todos los huesos del cuerpo.

Side effect/efecto secundario Condición que se produce como consecuencia de un tratamiento o medicación.

Sidestream smoke/humo secundario El humo producido por la colilla prendida de un cigarrillo.

Small claims court/tribunal de demandas menores Corte estatal que atiende los casos civiles relacionados con reclamaciones de pequeñas sumas de dinero.

Small intestine/intestino delgado El órgano semejante a un largo tubo, en donde ocurre la mayor parte de la disgestión.

Smog/niebla Mezcla insalubre de contaminantes y neblina en el aire, generalmente localizada sobre ciudades.

Smoke alarm/alarma de humo Aparato que emite un sonido agudo cuando detecta humo.

Smooth muscles/músculos lisos Los músculos involuntarios en los sistemas digestivo y circulatorio.

Social age/edad social La edad calculada de acuerdo al estilo de vida de una persona.

Social health/salud social La habilidad de una persona de relacionarse bien con la gente a su alrededor.

Socializing/socialización El disfrute de la compañía de la gente.

Somatic system/sistema somático La parte del sistema nervioso periférico relacionada con las acciones voluntarias.

Specialist/especialista El médico que está entrenado para tratar determinada clase de pacientes o enfermedades.

Sperm cell/espermatozoide La célula masculina reproductiva, que al unirse con el óvulo produce una nueva vida.

Sphygmomanometer/esfigmomanómetro Instrumento que mide la tensión sanguínea.

Spinal cord/médula expinal Una larga estructura formada de neuronas que lleva mensajes al cerebro y desde el cerebro a todas las partes del cuerpo.

Stepparent/padrastro o madrastra La persona que se casa con la madre o el padre de un niño.

Stimulant/estimulante Droga que acelera las funciones del cuerpo.

Stomach/estómago El órgano muscular en donde ocurre parte de la digestión.

Stress/estrés La respuesta que da el cuerpo ante algún cambio.

Stressor/estresante Un causante de estrés.

Stroke/embolia cerebral Condición seria que ocurre cuando se paraliza el flujo de sangre al cerebro, generalmente, debido al bloqueo de la arteria que va al cerebro.

Subcutaneous layer/capa subcutánea Tejido grasoso localizado debajo de la piel.

Suicide/suicidio El quitarse la propia vida.

Sympathetic/compasivo La persona que tiene y demuestra sentimientos de compasión por otra persona.

Syphilis/sífilis Enfermedad transmitida sexualmente, que progresa a través de varias etapas y que puede causar la muerte.

Tar/alquitrán La substancia oscura y pegajosa que se forma cuando se quema tabaco.

Tartar/sarro Placa endurecida que se forma en el diente.

T-cells/células T Linfocitos que combaten los gérmenes.

Team sports/deportes en equipo Actividades organizadas en donde un grupo de gente juega para un equipo.

Tendon/tendón Tejido fuerte que conecta los músculos con los huesos.

Testes/testículos Las glándulas del sistema reproductor masculino, que producen la esperma.

Third-degree burn/quemadura de tercer grado Quemadura severa que daña todas las capas de la piel y las terminaciones de los nervios.

Tissue/tejido Masa de células similares que desempeña una función específica.

Tolerance/tolerancia 1. La aceptación y respeto de las creencias y costumbres de otras personas. 2. Condición que ocurre cuando el cuerpo de una persona se acostumbra a los efectos de una droga.

Tornado/tornado Tormenta de fuertes vientos, en forma de torbellino, que gira en grandes círculos y que cae del cielo a la tierra.

Tornado warning/alerta de tornado Boletín de noticias que anuncia que un huracán se está acercando a una zona.

Tornado watch/aviso de tornado Boletín de noticias que indica que un huracán se puede estar formando.

Totally fit/completa buena forma El estar física, mental y socialmente listo(a), para manejar cualquier situación de la vida diaria.

Toxic/tóxico Algo venenoso o dañino.

Trachea/tráquea El conducto del aire del cuerpo.

Tradition/tradición La manera usual de hacer las cosas.

Tumor/tumor La inflamación o crecimiento anormal de células.

Umbilical cord/cordón umbilical El tubo que conecta el feto a la placenta de la madre y a través del cual se alimenta el feto.

Unsaturated fats/grasas no saturadas Las grasas líquidas que, generalmente, se encuentran en los aceites vegetales.

Uterus/útero El órgano femenino en el cual crece y se desarrolla el feto, hasta que está listo para nacer.

Vaccine/vacuna Una preparación de gérmenes débiles o muertos que se coloca dentro del organismo, con el fin de hacer que el sistema de defensas produzca anticuerpos contra ciertas enfermedades.

Values/valores Creencias o ideas que guían las acciones de una persona.

Veins/venas Vasos sanguíneos que llevan la sangre desde varias partes del cuerpo hasta el corazón.

Verbal communication/comunicación verbal El intercambio de ideas, opiniones y sentimientos, a través de palabras.

Vestibule/vestíbulo La cavidad central del oído interno.

Victim/víctima Una persona que ha sido herida o abusada física o emocionalmente.

Virus/virus Agentes productores de enfermedades.

Vitamins/vitaminas Nutrientes que el cuerpo necesita en pequeñas cantidades, para funcionar de forma apropiada.

Warm-up/calentamiento Los movimientos del cuerpo que estiran los músculos y los preparan para actividades físicas.

Warranty/garantía La promesa escrita de un fabricante, de reparar un producto, durante un lapso específico de tiempo.

Weight control/control de peso La obtención y mantenimiento del peso deseado.

Wellness/bienestar Decisiones y selecciones que promueven la buena salud y que son hechas de forma activa.

Withdrawal/retirada Una serie de síntomas mentales y físicos, asociados con la recuperación de una adicción al alcohol o a otras drogas.

Index

Note: Page numbers in *italics* refer to art and marginal features.

Credits

PHOTOGRAPHS

Cover photo:Elaine Sulle/Image Bank and Myrleen Cate/Tony Stone Images

Allsport: Scott Halleran, pages xv, 488; Mike Powell, page 440.

Julie Bidwell Photography: page 354.

CMCD Library: page 215 (left).

Comstock: pages 194-95, 388.

David Crow: pages ii–iii, 150, 211, 265, 269 (all), 276, 281, 282, 340, 343 (both), 353, 362, 365, 444.

Custom Medical Stock Photo: page 403 (right); Delilah R. Cohn, pages 198 (right), 199 (both); Sylvia Miller, page 408 (left).

DRK Photo: Tom Bean, page 542.

© FPG International: C. Jose Luis Banus-March, page 166; Ron Chapple, page 145 (middle); Ken Chernus pages 30-31; Spencer Grant, page 222; Guy Marche, page 404; Stephen Simpson, pages 370-71; C. Jeffrey Sylvester, page 509; Telegraph Colour Library, page 224; Arthur Tilley, page 86.

Tim Fuller Photography: pages xi (top), 2-3, 17, 47, 62-63, 71 (1 & 3), 74, 75 (both), 108 (both), 126, 127, 128, 136-37, 149 (both), 160-61, 169 (left), 178, 186, 219, 228-29, 236 (bottom), 242, 258-59, 272, 274, 290-91, 338-39, 389, 393, 395, 402-03, 409, 413 (bottom), 416, 418, 441, 450-51, 470, 482-83, 489, 514-15, 520, 536-37, 543, 553.

Ann Garvin: page 322.

General Motors: page 545.

H. Armstrong Roberts: Valbuena Chimps, page 207 (left); J. Nettis, page 200; M. Roessler, page 206 (right).

Richard Hutchings: pages ix (bottom), 84, 114, 230–31, 232, 234 (right), 236 (top), 237 (all), 238, 241, 243, 246 (both), 247 (all), 249, 250, 251, 252, 253 (left), 255, 435, 480–81.

The Image Bank: Murray Alcosser, page 79; Barros & Barros, page 522; M. David de Lossy, page 46; Mel Di Giacomo, page 23; John P. Kelly, page 506; Romilly Lockyer, page 185.

International Stock: Caroline Wood, page 523 (top).

Ken Lax: pages x (bottom), xii (bottom), 130, 375, 376, 381, 391, 397, 524, 527, 528, 529, 538, 547, 548, 551 (bottom), 552, 556, 557.

Leo de Wys: David Lissy, pages 67, 316.

Jay Maisel: pages 98-99.

William M. McLoed: page 214.

Medical Images, Inc.: Michael English, page 531; Frederick C. Skvara, pages 359 (bottom), 383 (both); Howard Sochurek, page 359 (top).

Medichrome: page 415.

Cliff Moore: pages 208 (all), 209 (bottom), 215.

Peerless Photography: page 268.

© Photo Researchers, Inc.: CNRI/Science Photo Library, page 202, 328 (right), 394, 453; Motta & Familiari/Anatomy Dept./University “La Sapienza,” Rome/Science Photo Library, page 328 (left); Will and Deni McIntyre, page 367; A. Sieveking/Petit Format, page 206 (left); Jim Steinberg, page 539 (right); Norm Thomas, page 540.

PhotoEdit: Billy E. Barnes, pages xi (bottom), 412, 421, 458; Leslye Borden, pages 129, 223 (right); Robert Brenner, pages 25, 551 (top); Michelle Bridwell, pages 5 (right), 10, 24, 207 (right), 212; Jose Carillo, page 11 (bottom); Myrleen Ferguson Cate: page 217 (right), 218 (bottom); Paul Conklin, page 505 (left); Deborah Davis, page 103; Mary Kate Denny,